Choice

AMERICAN CRIMINOLOGY

AMERICAN CRIMINOLOGY: New Directions

Walter C. Reckless
The Ohio State University

New York
APPLETON-CENTURY-CROFTS
Educational Division
MEREDITH CORPORATION

73 74 75 76 77/10 9 8 7 6 5 4 3 2 1

Library of Congress Card Number: 72-12049

PRINTED IN THE UNITED STATES OF AMERICA

C-390-72924-8

Preface

There is no question about the fact that the direction of thinking and research in the field of criminology needs to find new pathways that can give realistic insights into human behavior and, at the same time, provide important leads for effective measures for the control, treatment, and prevention of crime and delinquency. The major contributions to the new pathways will undoubtedly come from the social and behavioral sciences, but important ideas will also come from legally trained experts and from research in the biophysical sciences.

The focus of attention in the following pages will be placed upon two major areas of growing concern: understanding the involvement of individuals in delinquent and criminal behavior and understanding the operation of the criminal justice system.

The first-mentioned concern, namely the study of involvement, has two aspects: (1) the study of the "doer" and (2) the study of the objects of the doer's behavior, including the human victim. The second-mentioned concern deals (1) with the input of persons into the criminal justice system at all points from complaint to arrest, to court action, to probation, to institutionalization, and to parole; and (2) with the output or product of the criminal justice system at its several points of exodus.

The emphasis on new directions or new pathways of study and research as set forth in this monograph is not intended to close the door upon advances in research and study of the standard topics that comprise the general coverage of textbooks in criminology. Certainly, it is still important to shed light upon the relation of crime and deviance to law and social values; the regional and area variations in reported delinquent and criminal occurrences; the demographic characteristics of arrested persons; the patterns of criminal careers, organized crime, and white-collar crime; the revision of theories explaining criminal and delinquent behavior; the history and trends in punishment, etc. Rather, the focus on new directions as presented herein is intended to help cultivate promising leads which are coming to the fore in the development of American criminology.

If the author had audiences in mind, they would embrace students at the university (advanced undergraduates and graduates) who are interested in a second course in criminology, following the introductory course; students in schools of law who have been exposed to lectures and textbooks on criminal law and procedure; advanced students in political science and public administration who are interested in systems analysis; the staff in state and federal attorney general's offices; the personnel in large prosecutor's offices; the policy controllers and statistical specialists of large city police departments and of large county sheriffs' offices; and the central office staff of departments of corrections. Hopefully, some interested laymen and legislators might thumb through the contents to discover clues for possible action and improvement.

Attention is called to the numerous research efforts which are attempting to obtain insight into the several phases of criminal involvement and of the operation of the criminal justice system. In most instances, these contributions will take the form of special data-collecting instruments or summarized reports and will appear in the appendices of the several chapters. They are the major exhibits of the new pathways and directions in the development of American criminology. They are the basic documents and need to be consulted and reconsulted in terms of the context in the text.

Contents

PART II

The study of the operation of the criminal justice system

PART I

THE STUDY OF INVOLVEMENT IN CRIME AND DELINQUENCY

Chapter 1

The how factor in doer involvement

The "doer" aspect of involvement should concentrate on three factors: (a) how people get involved in delinquent and criminal behavior, (b) the extent of involvement, and (c) who gets involved. For sake of brevity, the three factors will be called the "how" factor, the "extent" factor, and the "who" factor.

The study of how individuals become involved in deviant behavior is very close to the study of the causes of crime and delinquency. But the former has greater possibilities of focusing on the more immediate and more direct propulsions and processes of behavior than the latter. Likewise, fewer assumptions have to be made in studying the "how" than in studying the causes of involvement.

Norm erosion

There is a strong suspicion that a large part of ordinary criminal and delinquent behavior consists of a sort of "slippage"—an erosion of accepted norms of conduct. Shoham and the author identified this process and called it "norm erosion."[1] The norms of honesty slip; they become less important; they lose their reinforcement. The person slides over to dishonesty, with appropriate blackout of conscience.

Norm erosion applies to the more general patterns of contramorality such as immorality, cheating, lying, falsifying, stealing, desertion, and

[1] Walter C. Reckless and Shlomo Shoham, "Norm Containment Theory as Applied to Delinquency and Crime," *Excerpta Criminologica,* 3:6 (November-December 1963), pp. 637–644.

short-changing, as well as to nonconformity in general, rather than to specific current models of criminal behavior such as vandalism, auto theft, robbery, and the like.

The assumption is that the overwhelming majority of individuals in most societies, even among the most disadvantaged segments of urban populations, internalizes existing norms of morality and develops a reinforcing conscience. It appears to be true also that the overwhelming majority of people in a fluid society violates the moral and ethical norms, some more and some less. But the same overwhelming majority manages to hold on to most of its norms in spite of slips and lapses. This is part of the process of norm retention.

Norm erosion and its counterpart, norm retention, represent the complementary aspects of norm containment. There is also a phase of retention, which is becoming more and more noticeable in adults of modern society. This phase can be identified as compliance. A person ostensibly follows the norm, but he really does not believe in it. It is less risky to comply than not to comply because of the visibility of nonconformity.

There is no doubt that norm erosion is closely connected with the "extent factor," which will be discussed subsequently. The amount of erosion is probably an index of the extent of violation and vice versa. Likewise, norm erosion is related closely to the "who" factor in involvement. Undoubtedly, those individuals who are not able to hold the line demanded by their internalized norms are the ones who slip into deviant behavior, while the actual slippage in turn helps the individual to abandon his norms. Who are the ones that slip more than others? Who are the ones that slip further than others? Who, beside the saints and the holy men, hold the line completely? Nonetheless, norm erosion is a "how" factor—the slippage toward nonconforming, deviant, and criminal behavior.

Although it appears that norm erosion is the way in which most individuals become involved in nonconforming, deviant, and criminal behavior, the process of norm erosion, apart from any exaggerated mental components, is not readily subject to systematic research. One possible approach is to develop a list of concrete nonconforming, deviant, and criminal behaviors and submit it to an appropriate sample of adults via the interview method of opinion poll surveys. The idea would be to get a public rating on the seriousness of each item. Behavioral items could then be selected from this poll, at several points along a continuum from least to most in terms of seriousness ratings.

A second survey could then be made to indicate the amount of self-reported "give" of the sampled respondents on the various rated behaviors. Naturally, class, race, sex, age, and religious differentials in self-reported involvement in nonconforming, deviant, and criminal actions could be indicated.

Several years ago, Paul Crissman developed a Moral Judgments scale that has been found to gauge the "slippage" in norm erosion in a modern country such as the United States. More specifically, the scale measures the degree to which an individual or sample of individuals embrace the rightness or the wrongness of specific behaviors, very few of which are actually contained in the criminal code but all of which represent slippage in moral and ethical norms. See Appendix 1-A for Crissman's Moral Judgment scale of 50 items.[2]

Another possible measure of the degree of norm erosion might be the administration of scales to gauge the extent to which individuals cling to or reject their religious beliefs and ethics. If, in various class, race, religious, sex, and age samples, self-reported involvement in nonconforming, deviant, and criminal behavior were found to correlate with disectional scores on religious and ethical slippage, then such an instrument also could act as an index of norm erosion—a substitute indicator, as in the instance of the moral judgments index, for actual as well as potential involvement in ordinary violational behavior. One should consult some of the instruments measuring religious attitudes and religious commitment as presented by a publication of the Survey Research Center of the Institute for Social Research at the University of Michigan.[3]

Very close to norm erosion are the "techniques of neutralization," which consist of rationalizations that justify delinquent behavior. Such rationalizations certainly facilitate the recurring involvement in delinquency. Certainly, they facilitate norm erosion.

Sykes and Matza identified five techniques of neutralization.[4]

1. Denial of responsibility. [The delinquent deflects blame from himself in his own eyes by rationalizing that he was not responsible for what he did.]

2. Denial of injury. [The delinquent finds a way of claiming to himself and others that what he did really did not hurt anybody; thus, the person who lost by the act could well afford it, stealing an auto is only borrowing, vandalism is just boyish mischief.]

3. Denial of the victim. [Here the thinking is that while the act may have caused harm or injury, the victim really had it coming to him—really deserved the injury. The doer by his rationalization becomes a sort of moral avenger.]

[2]Paul Crissman, "Temporal Changes and Sexual Differences in Moral Judgments," *Journal of Social Psychology*, 16 (1942), 29-38. Also consult Solomon Rettig, "Relation of Social Systems to Intergenerational Changes in Moral Attitudes," *Journal of Personality and Social Psychology*, 4 (1966), pp. 409-414.

[3]John P. Robinson and Philip R. Shaver, *Measures of Social Psychological Attitudes*, (Ann Arbor, Mich: University of Michigan Press, 1969), chap. 9. In particular, one should consult the instrument developed by Glock and Stark to measure "Dimensions of Religious Commitment" (*supra*, pp. 556-563) and the "Religious Attitude Scale" developed by Poppleton and Pilkington (*supra*, pp. 607-610).

[4]Gresham M. Sykes and David Matza, "Techniques of Neutralization: A Theory of Delinquency," *American Sociological Review*, 22 (December 1957), pp. 667-669. [Summary statements mine.]

4. Condemnation of the condemners. [The delinquent shifts blame from himself by focusing on the motives and shortcomings of those who sit in authority or judgment over him—such as the arresting officer, the adjudicating judge, the preacher, the school principal, etc. By exposing their short-comings—really attacking them in his inner forum—he silences the qualms of his own deviance.]

5. Appeal to higher loyalties. [Here the act is viewed as something which was necessary to do because of close ties to companions, to family, to important primary groups. The loyalty to a friend or close relative takes precedence over conformity to the laws and norms of the larger society.]

Richard A. Ball attempted to operationalize the general idea of neutralization as applied to a sample of committed delinquent boys and a sample of public-school boys in an inner-city high school. See Appendix 1-B. He developed a scale to measure the degree to which respondents neutralize their behavior. In general, Ball found that the institutionalized delinquent boys had higher neutralization scores than did the inner-city school boys; that neutralization scores increased from the high school boys reporting no appearances in juvenile court, to those reporting some appearances in juvenile court, to the institutionalized delinquents reporting few juvenile court appearances, to the institutionalized delinquents reporting several appearances in juvenile court; and that neutralization scores tended to be higher for boys in both samples (public school and institutionalized state school) who reported several involvements on a self-reporting schedule than for boys who reported few involvements.[5]

Impact of two or more persons

It is generally conceded that the overwhelming majority of delinquent and criminal acts is committed by two or more persons, especially in the instance of males. Companionship in the deed has been accepted as one of the principal causes of violational behavior, although a famous team of researchers discounted the primacy of the companionship factor in their first-hand findings.[6] The propelling element in companionship undoubtedly

[5] Richard Allen Ball, "Neutralization as a Self Factor in Delinquency Risk," Ph.D. dissertation (The Ohio State University, 1965), pp. 168–169.

[6] Although the Gluecks found very strong evidence of the presence of a gang and companionship factor operating in the cases of delinquent rather than nondelinquent boys, they concluded that such a factor appears after the onset of delinquency and not before and that, therefore, such a factor could not be considered as a causative factor. See Sheldon and Eleanor Glueck, *Unravelling Juvenile Delinquency*, The Commonwealth Fund, (Cambridge, Mass: Harvard University Press, 1950). The Gluecks make a definite statement in regard to denial of the operation of the gang in onset of delinquency in still another publication which compared the same sample of cases of 500 delinquent and 500 matched nondelinquent boys from Boston. See *Physique and Delinquency* (New York: Harper & Row, 1956), p. 41.

is the escalation of interaction between the persons involved in any episode. Although research has not been able to get close to the generating scene, the strong likelihood is that the culminating deed is the result of a sort of interactional explosion. It could very well be that the inner controls of individuals give way under interaction.

Sociologists might claim that the interaction of close friends (primary contacts) is likely to generate more deviant behavior than is the interaction of acquaintances and strangers (secondary contacts), because there is less social distance between the participators. Nevertheless, one should expect acquaintances and strangers to generate a large share of delinquent and criminal behavior. The statement by Simon Dinitz, as presented in Appendix 1-C, attempts to uncover some of the seldom recognized aspects of interaction between two or more persons as they apply to the generation of deviant or criminal behavior.

Interpersonal conflict

One of the more obvious results of interaction between two or more persons is a fast escalation of tension and conflict, which sometimes generates fighting and violence. Behavioral scientists have really not observed the quick rising, short-span, person-to-person conflict in a systematic way. They do not know under what circumstances and between what kinds of persons do tension and conflict lead to violent behavior as the terminal result. They do not know how person-to-person conflict takes other directions or even breaks off or the extent to which it does. They do not know what kinds of persons get involved in escalation and avoid it, or the effect of situations. Research models that can give insight into person-to-person conflict, its escalation, and its termination need to be developed.

It looks as if, in the majority of instances, murder and aggravated assault are the terminal results of interpersonal conflict, at several levels of human contact: between strangers, acquaintances, friends, relatives, married couples, etc. Likewise, it is apparent that conflict, leading to assault and murder, is more easily generated between persons, particularly males, who live in areas of the world with a tradition or a subculture of violence.

The behavioral scientist as researcher or observer will find himself on the borderline of true excalating interpersonal conflict when he comes across instances of persons who harbor a grudge and who initiate combat when the appropriate person-object is encountered. Still further removed from spontaneous escalation are cases of persons who seek out a figure upon whom to vent their ideological hatred.

Pattern following and take-over

In addition to escalation (explosion or culmination) and generation of conflict, the interaction between two or more persons may also lead to actual following or taking over of new patterns of behavior, thereby adding to the individual's repertoire, but more frequently it merely leads to the activation of an already existing repertoire of behavior.

Sociological criminologists from Tarde to Sutherland have assumed that if a behavior pattern is in circulation, it will be taken over. Tarde called the take-over process imitation. But imitation does not reveal the ingredients of the take-over process. It has been assumed that if the carrier of a behavior pattern has prestige in the eyes of the respondent, take-over is facilitated. Likewise, identification of the respondent with the carrier is also supposed to facilitate the following of the presented models.

When and how often are new patterns of crime invented? There is a suspicion that individuals sometimes stumble upon or develop new modes and techniques of crime, but we do not know the extent to which such patterns are actually invented or "re-invented" in the modern world of communication. Certainly, the invention of criminal patterns and techniques is much less frequent than of scientific or medical inventions. Nevertheless, it should be possible to study the appearance of a new pattern of crime and to plot its dissemination in space and in time. Comparisons might be made in such instances with the spread of contemporaneous non-criminal patterns, to discover something about differential facilitation.

There is no doubt that taking over or following a pattern of behavior, in its close-range aspects, is a consequence of interaction or of contact between companions, acquaintances, and strangers. The interaction leads to the following of an available model. To use an analogy, the two-some, three-some, or group interaction instead of generating a shout, results in the singing of a tune (following a pattern).

Sutherland's theory of differential association hypothesized that patterns of behavior were "learned" (taken over) in close-range contacts. Four important attempts to throw light on the operation of differential association or of companionship in delinquency are summarized in Appendix 1-D-i. James F. Short's research indicates that the amount of self-reported involvement is related to factors of differential association that Sutherland identified as frequency, duration, priority, and intensity of contact.

From a consecutive sample of white boys admitted during 1958 to the state school for committed delinquent boys (Boys Industrial School, Lancaster, Ohio), Thomas G. Eynon found that 75 percent of the boys were with someone (a companion) at the time they committed the deed that brought them for the first time to the attention of the juvenile court. He found, contrary to the contention of the Gluecks, that the committed delinquents were "likely to have companions (in the deed) regardless of when they began their delinquency. Thus, boys starting early were no more likely to have companions (in the deed) than boys starting later."[7]

Using a self-reporting schedule similar to that used by Short as mentioned above, Eynon selected out of his data bank the earliest self-reported act of delinquency and discovered that 71.7 percent of the sample admitted that they had been with someone at the time they had committed the deed.[8] The amount of self-reported companionship in the self-reported first act of delinquency was fairly close for the early starters and the later starters, say under and over 12 years of age. "No matter when the boys commit the earliest act, they are likely to have companions." Hence, Eynon's findings from self-reported data confirm his findings from officially recorded "case-folder" data. See Appendix 1-D-ii for the pertinent instruments Eynon used in his research. It should be noted that the companionship factor in Eynon's research was just one of three dimensions he attempted to relate to onset of the first official act and onset of the first admitted (self-reported) act.

Appendix 1-D-iii presents a summary of a study by Reiss. One notes that he attempted to shed some light on the actual adopting or following of similar patterns of delinquency by best friends in three-some (triad) combinations. The variable of primary contacts is thereby established (best or closest friends). But even in these triadic relationships some variation in behavioral involvement was discovered, although about two-thirds of the members of the triad reported they committed a deed if one member indicated he had done so. Reiss might be said to conclude *inter alia* that selection of close friends has much to do with the kind of behavior they are known to display.

Erickson and Empey investigated still another dimension related to the companionship factor, namely commitment or identification with one's peers.[9] They concluded that associates and commitment to associates are more related to delinquent and nondelinquent behavior—and more predictive of this—than social-class status. Their data was obtained from personal interviews, in which the individual interviewee was able to answer questions relating to the extent and type of delinquency involvement as well as to participating with associates and identification with peers. See Appendix 1-D-iv for a summary of Erickson and Empey's conclusions.

Studies are certainly needed to throw light on the "take-over" of patterns of behavior, including attitudes and perceptions, involved in the interaction between two or more persons, which "take-over" adds to the

[7] Thomas G. Eynon, "Factors Related to Onset of Delinquency" (Ph.D. dissertation, The Ohio State University, 1959), p. 24.

[8] *Ibid.*, p. 29.

[9] Maynard L. Erickson and LaMar T. Empey, "Class Position, Peers and Delinquency," *Sociology and Social Research*, 49:3 (April 1965), pp. 268–282.

participants repertoires and which in turn can be evoked in future interactional episodes. Unfortunately, very little is known about models following behavior after "take-over," as a sort of "feed-back" repertoire in interpersonal interaction. Criminologists at present do not know enough to conjecture whether "take-over" and "feed-back" are due primarily to the length and closeness of association as well as to the prestige of the associates or to the receptivity and retention of the recipients.

Mass media

There is no doubt that mass media facilitate the spreading and adopting of new patterns of behavior, although one does not know exactly the differential impact of television, radio, newspapers, and magazines upon individuals. Undoubtedly, the greatest contemporary impact that mass media in a democratic society have on the public lies in the generating of take-over of fashions, especially through advertising. The adoption of new opinions, attitudes, and beliefs is not so readily facilitated, although propaganda can be very effective.

Apparently, deviant and criminal patterns of behavior are not taken over from mass media as readily as are modes of dress and of language. However, research has not established any realistic base lines for making this judgment. The probability is that greater resistance is thrown up by a particular segment of the American public to the use of switch-blade knives than to the adoption of a new male hair style.

No matter whether the model of behavior presented by mass media falls within the area of fashion, opinion, or crime, there is a differential receptivity, or readiness to accept, on the part of the individuals who are reached. For many different reasons, individuals vary considerably in their resistance to presented models, even in spite of "slick" techniques of presentation and dissemination. These are questions for research in social psychology and mass communication to shed light upon.

Consequently, at this juncture, criminologists should accept the implication that much more deviance is imparted and generated in two-some and three-some interactions than is imparted by mass media. It is dubious even in the mass eruptions in the large cities and universities of the United States during recent years whether the mass media generated very much participation in these collective expressions. It seems easier for the mass media to facilitate the spread of "hippyism" than of riots. (Note should be made of the fact that the above comments and observations assume the existence in the United States of a "free" press, "free" television, and "free" radio.)

The effects of mass media on the behavior of the American audience have been explored by a special task force of experts for the National

Commission on the Causes and Prevention of Violence (the so-called Eisenhower Commission). Their conclusions are reprinted in Appendix 1–E. They concentrated largely on the impact of television, because television was found to have more effect on the audience's attitude to violence than other forms of mass media. In studying the summary of findings in Appendix 1–E, one will note that mass media, especially television, apparently extend the "boundaries of violence beyond legal and social norms espoused by a majority of Americans", that audiences learn how to perform violent acts; that "persons will behave in accordance with the norms, attitudes, and values for violence contained in media presentations." But, unfortunately, it is still not known whether the "take-over" and "feed back" in the field of collective violence is as extensive as it is in the areas of fashion and fads, opinion change, voting behavior, and propaganda.

Peer-group contacts

Besides ordinary contacts between two or more persons, the participation of individuals in various kinds of "peer" groups also engenders interaction which sometimes—although we do not know how often—culminates in delinquent and criminal behavior. The "peer" group in the present context is used to include play groups, clubs, and gangs, as well as groups that "hang out" in pool halls, cigar stores, cafes, saloons, etc. Such meeting places enable two or more participants to generate interactional explosions. resulting in aggression toward property and in violence toward persons. But sometimes, as in the instance of so-called fighting gangs, the entire group becomes involved, especially when the gang is conscious of an enemy gang. In such instances, the fighting gang generates behavior that is close to what a mob generates, namely violence.

In his first-hand observations of over 1,300 boys' gangs in the Chicago of the early twenties, Thrasher found that they were a "protean manifestation"—no two of them were alike.[10] They represented the "spontaneous effect of boys to create a society for themselves where none adequate to their needs exists." The interstimulation among the participants, according to Thrasher, leads to motor (playful) activity, "talk fest," "smut session," rehearsal of adventure, loafing, gambling, drinking, smoking, and sex. He recognized that the gang could become inflamed, in which instance it acted like a mob.[11] The boys' gang, as Thrasher observed it, was certainly a medium in which two or more members could generate delinquent behavior. Very seldom did the gang as a whole become involved, unless it was attacked by or went on the offensive against a near-by gang.

[10] Frederic M. Thrasher, *The Gang: A Study of 1,313 Gangs in Chicago* (Chicago: University of Chicago Press, 1926), p. 5.

[11] *Ibid.*, pp. 37, 50, 53.

A generation later Albert Cohen claimed that boys' gangs in American cities developed a "delinquent subculture," consisting of a particular set of values and attitudes as well as of a repertoire of delinquent practices.[12] Cohen and his colleague, James F. Short, identified five types of boys' gangs in the urban areas of the United States: the parent-male subculture, the conflict-oriented subculture, the drug-addict subculture, the semi-professional subculture, and the middle-class deliquent subculture.[13]

Cloward and Ohlin described the process by which a boy gravitated to the gang in terms of the withdrawal of legitimacy from the values and goals of conventional (middle-class American) society and the attribution of legitimacy to the illegal means to ends.[14] Cloward and Ohlin also accepted the contention that boys' gangs develop or manifest a delinquent subculture that is a sort of collective solution for blocked opportunity. They, however, identified only three types of delinquent subcultures: the criminal pattern focused on crimes for gain, the conflict pattern focused on obtaining status through violence, and the retreatist pattern consisting mainly of drug use that enables members to develop euphoria in alienation from society.[15]

If the delinquent subculture hypothesis is established as paramount in gang composition, then any deviant, delinquent, or criminal behavior of gang members would represent a take-over of behavior patterns of the group rather than the spontaneous generation of behavior from inter-reaction between two or three members who congregate at the gang's meeting place. It is the contention of the author that the latter alternative is more likely to be the realistic one. If this were not so, then the boys' gang would have to operate like an isolated primitive tribe or an isolated peasant village, where everyone is engulfed in a particular way of life.

If the contention is correct, namely that a boys' gang provides a setting where two or more individuals can generate action and follow one or more available patterns of behavior, then the boys' gang is merely providing a place of contact and, consequently, is functioning in basically the same way as any other gathering point for individuals which gives them the chance to generate consequent behavior. Certainly, "hangouts" of various kinds, no matter whether they are clubs, saloons, or street corners, provide the locus, and interaction escalates from this point on.

Mass eruptions

Conflict in one form or another sets the stage for mass confrontations and disturbances. But apart from wars, rebellions, and revolutions, our modern

[12] Albert K. Cohen, *Delinquent Boys: The Culture of the Gang* (New York: Free Press, 1955).

[13] Albert K. Cohen and James F. Short, Jr., "Research in Delinquent Subcultures," *The Journal of Social Issues*, XIV:3 (1958), pp. 24–28.

[14] Richard A. Cloward and Lloyd E. Ohlin, *Delinquency and Opportunity: A Theory of Delinquent Gangs* (New York: Free Press, 1960), pp. 16–20.

[15] *Ibid.*, pp. 20–27.

world has seen protests and strikes of labor groups. Still more recently, it has witnessed demonstrations of university students and widespread eruptions of black peoples in the urban ghettos of the United States.

Violence against persons and property usually follows in the wake of mass explosions. But criminal lawyers and criminologists are not quite clear as to whether violence committed in a mass eruption is really a crime, although destruction of property, looting of stores, occupancy of buildings, and killing of persons would unquestionably be considered criminal under nonexplosive conditions. Although appropriate research has not been done on the subject, it appears doubtful that those who participate in riots perceive their looting, damage to property, and injury to persons as crimes.

Apparently, the mass disorders of recent years in the United States display a sequence. 1. The mass eruptions generate from a fermenting unrest—probably an acute dissatisfaction with the social, economic, and political order. 2. There always seems to be an event that triggers the eruption. 3. The eruption spreads through an immediate local territory, undoubtedly through the mechanism of suggestion that operates in those individuals who have a readiness to become involved. 4. The collective action reaches a maximum parameter and a maximum intensity; then it subsides.

The President's Commission on Law Enforcement and Administration of Justice was able to summarize the data and observations collected on the five-day riot in Watts (Los Angeles) that began August 11, 1965. The summary, duplicated in Appendix 1–F, amounts to a case study of a riot. One notices the spark or ignition, the spread, the culmination, and the winding-down. The summarized report gives clues also as to the participators and contrasts them with the nonparticipators.

From more recently published reports of various commissions in the United States, it is evident that mass disorders or eruptions are not easy to observe and study. The Walker Report on the disorders that occurred in Chicago at the time of the Democratic Convention (August 1968) made an attempt to recapture the sequence of events prior to, during, and after the Convention.[16] But, although they had a close view of the events, its members were largely limited to a news-reporting type of coverage, which is not able to penetrate the behavioral dimensions of a mass disorder.

The Kerner Report (The National Advisory Commission on Civil Disorders), which studied primarily the uprisings of black people in American ghettos during 1967, chartered the sequence of events in several cities, attempted to study the background causes of the unrest, and tried to discover the kinds of individuals who became involved. Appendix 1–G

[16] *Rights in Conflict; the Violent Confrontation of Demonstrators and Police in the Parks and Streets of Chicago during the Week of the Democratic National Convention of 1968*, Report submitted by Daniel Walker, Director of the Chicago Study Team, to the National Commission on the Causes and Prevention of Violence (New York: Bantam Books, 1968).

contains selective excerpts from the observations and findings of the Commission.

The Commission on the Causes and Prevention of Violence was able to take a much larger perspective on disorders and mass eruptions in the United States. However, its efforts resulted mainly in a scholarly interpretation, yielding insight into the generation of mass behavior as well as into its political focus. The Commission's Report can give the criminologist and the behavioral scientist a fine background orientation, but it does not bring the researcher in the field of criminal and delinquent behavior very near the target of discovering how mass behavior actually operates; who gets involved and who does not; who of the involved destroy property, loot, fight, shoot; who get arrested, etc. New techniques for photographing and recording riot behavior need to be developed since ex post facto research is not sufficient. See the selected excerpts from the reports of the so-called Eisenhower Commission on Violence, which are presented in Appendix 1-H.

Mental propulsion

Some individuals are propelled toward deviant and criminal behavior via the operation of sociopathy, compulsive neuroses, or schizophrenia. The antisocial sociopath, whether through a defect or lesion in the sympathetic nervous system or through faulty character formation in early childhood, gravitates toward uncontrollable behavior. It is not known why the sociopath does not erupt continuously, although evidently he displays enough uncontrollable eruption to make him a rather difficult and dangerous person. Cleckley has developed a checklist instrument that enables psychiatrists and psychologists to spot the more obvious levels of sociopathy in adults. (See Appendix 1–I.) Likewise, Lykken has developed a pencil and paper test that also has shown considerable validity in diagnosing antisocial sociopaths. (See Appendix 1–J.) Notations as to score levels which designate serious sociopathy are given in both appendixes.

The how factor at the back of sociopathic behavior is evidently the inability to sense or to recognize the meaning or outcome of behavior, amounting to a lack of control in delicate, sensitive, or dangerous situations. It is thought that between 1 and 3 percent of the adult population are sociopathic, and that as many as 15 to 20 percent of the adult prison population are sociopathic. A recent study by Harry E. Allen presents the background and behavioral facts about two types of sociopathic prisoners. (See Appendix 1–K). Certainly the life experiences of these subjects indicate a propulsion which is virtually uncontrollable.

Another type of mental propulsion takes the form of a compulsive neurosis. The one that is most frequently encountered in the study of crime and delinquency is that of compulsive theft or compulsive shoplifting. Just how extensive this form of propulsion is is not known, although it is usually agreed that such a neurosis is based in the unconscious, unfolding under mechanisms that are not recognizable by the person nor readily controllable. To what extent a neurosis of this sort is amenable to psychotherapy and how far interview therapy or even hypnosis can dissolve this particular collection of drives in the unconscious mind is not known, nor is the exact method whereby the neurosis develops a fixation on certain objects. Whether the type of objects "lifted" has particular symbolic significance to the person is likewise conjectural.

Fetishism is also a propellant that emerges out of the residues of early life experiences that have been relegated to the unconscious mind. In this instance, the object touched, fondled, coveted, taken, or possessed has definite symbolic significance, as for example a locket of hair belonging to the mother of the person in question. The objects contain an unusual amount of libidinal gratification, and fondling of these objects sometimes acts as substitute for actual physical gratification. It is suspected that the preponderant expressions of fetishism do not involve the person in criminal behavior, but there are some expressions of fetishism that do, such as breaking into a house and taking only a silver slipper from the many objects on the "what-not" table, or clipping a lock of hair from a young girl looking in a shop window, and then running off. Fetishism has not really been explored by systematic research by criminologists for the reason that, as is true with so many other mental propellants, it is difficult to set up appropriate research projects. Is it just accidental that the fetishistic focus of persons crosses over into criminal involvement? What are the differences between those whose fetishistic behavior does not cross the path of crime and those whose propulsion gravitates to criminal expression?

There are other mental disorders that act as propellants of rather specific deviant behavior, voyeurism (peeping) and exhibitionism (display of self to girls and women). Both of these propulsions apparently emerge out of a faulty psychosexual development in early childhood. Although they cause no physical harm to their victims, research needs to investigate voyeurs and exhibitionists. Should their behavior still be legally defined as criminal? What is the effect on the so-called victims? Why do these two propulsions generally apply to males rather than to females? Do voyeurs and exhibitionists gravitate to other forms of criminal behavior? Is there any kind of effective therapy for such persons?

A very extensive sexual propellant is male and female homosexuality. While medical and psychiatric experts in Europe are apt to explain the phenomenon in terms of biological inheritance and/or hormonal inbalance, the American and English experts tend to relate homosexuality to faulty psychosexual development in early childhood. In most European countries, homosexual relationships between consenting adults are not considered crimes, legally or socially. In the United States, however, they are. In most countries, homosexual aggressions invested upon children and upon unconsenting adults, and homosexual displays in public, are usually considered criminal and covered by criminal law. Systematic research that can yield insights into which homosexuals become aggressive and which fixate upon young objects will certainly be most welcome to the field of criminology.

To what extent the sociological factor of "labeling" and alienating the homosexual increases his problems of adjustment is not fully known. It is known that homosexuals develop a life apart from heterosexuals, even to the point of frequenting or patronizing certain bars and night clubs. How much ordinary crime the homosexual becomes involved in as compared with the heterosexual is likewise unknown. Is there any difference in criminal involvement between the homosexual who develops the passive role and the one who develops the active role?

In the area of mental disorders it is recognized that some psychotics, especially schizophrenics, are propelled to exhibit bizarre and sometimes criminal behavior; but research on criminal involvement of the mentally disturbed persons has never been systematic, so very little of the real linkage is known. There are the obvious instances of slayings of well-known men of state (such as kings, presidents, and other important figures) by mentally disturbed persons who had developed an ideological fixation on important figures.

The problem of the linkage between psychotic propulsions and criminal behavior has been rendered doubly difficult by court procedure in the United States, where the claims and counterclaims of the defendant's insane state at the time of the deed are aired. At the same time, in the overwhelming majority of cases where there might be reasonable linkage between insanity and the criminal act, the cases pass through the criminal justice system unnoticed.

Some form of psychiatric and criminological research needs to be found that can assess the way in which psychotic propulsions are connected with crime. How is it that most psychotic persons do not come to the attention of police and courts and probably do not commit criminal acts? Is it that closely supervising relatives cover up for them? Is it the short-lived or recurring episodes in the on-going flow of mental disturbances that are directly connected to crime?

While this survey on mental propulsions is not by any means complete, some of the more obvious aspects have been mentioned. The most pressing need is for the development of models of research that can indicate how the propulsions propel.

Alcohol and drugs

There seems to be no doubt that alcoholic intoxication has a very direct connection with crime. As an intoxicant, alcohol depresses the system of inner self-control, certainly up to the point where the person is anesthetized. It is during intoxication short of anesthetization, that the person can act in many humorous, strange, deviant, bizarre, and dangerous ways resulting from this loss of control. Research has not revealed systematically how it is that some individuals become "playful" under the influence of alcohol while others become aggressive. Nevertheless, the connection between intoxication and crime is very close.

It would not be far from reality to say that of all the propellants that push people into crime, alcoholic intoxication is by far the greatest. This close connection seems to hold true not only for crimes against the person but also for crimes against property. It is strongly suspected that the majority of the murderers as well as victims are intoxicated at the time of killings, as was demonstrated in Wolfgang's study of homicides in Philadelphia.[17] The parole adminstrators of the United States know from experience that if a parolee seeks out a bar as soon as he is released, he has a good chance of getting involved in crime within the first few hours of his release and of being returned as a violator who has committed a new offense.

The abuse of alcohol is not only closely connected with crime but also with unemployment, vagrancy, family desertion, and family break-up, as well as with all major social problems. However, no well-modeled research has been developed to indicate systematically the various connections that the use of alcohol and the condition of intoxication have with behavior. Such models will have to be designed by pharmacologists, neurophysiologists, psychologists, and sociologists as interdisciplinary research.

The nonmedical abuse of drugs—of opiate derivatives as well as of non-addictive drugs—apparently has very little propellant connection with criminal behavior. The individual under the influence of opiates wants to float on "Cloud Nine"—he wants euphoria. The main propellant to crime in narcotic use is the need to find the money to buy the daily dosages, so as to maintain euphoria and avoid the agony of withdrawal symptoms.

The drugs that act as mild stimulants (nonaddictive amphetamines) apparently do not have a high propellant potential. Here again, the major connection of these drugs with crime lies in the use of theft to procure the money for obtaining supplies. The same can be said of the hallucinogens such as LSD and peyote as well as hashish.

Probably the one drug (nonaddictive) that has a terrific propellant potential is cocaine. Almost any kind of bizarre, dangerous, and aggressive behavior can be induced by it. Usually the users of cocaine also take morphine or heroin in order to calm themselves down. However, in recent years there has been very little use of cocaine in the United States.

In view of what is known of the effect of addictive narcotics, stimulants, barbiturates, and hallucinogens, criminologists should not look upon the

[17] Marvin E. Wolfgang, *Patterns in Criminal Homicide* (Philadelphia: University of Pennsylvania Press, 1958), p. 136.

use of these drugs as having a direct propelling influence. The "how" factor in drug use operates through the illegal means of procuring dosages.

Biophysical determinants

Apart from norm erosion, interactional propellants, pattern take-over and mental propulsions, criminology must be prepared to explore and accept possible chromosonal as well as biophysical determinants of deviant and criminal behavior. By way of illustration, attention will be called first to the so-called XYY chromosomal aberration and second to a suspected defect in the autonomic nervous system that is responsible for the gravitation of certain sociopaths toward criminal behavior. (It should be noted that there is a type of sociopathy explained by faulty personality development that was described in the preceding section under mental propulsions.)

In both instances, and undoubtedly in several more, one is not certain whether this sort of biophysical research is primarily uncovering a how factor or a who factor. Nevertheless, for present purposes it was decided to include the two types of research as illustrative of the search for the how factor in behavior involvement.

Ashley Montagu makes a very vivid presentation of pertinent findings relative to the operation of the XYY syndrome, which is not an inherited pattern but is rather the result of a "nondisjunction" that occurs at the second meiotic division. Another way of stating the matter is to say that XYY arises from the nondisjunction of sex chromosomes in normal parents and is not directly inherited.

The XYY chromosomal aberration naturally applies to males only. Spectacularly dramatic cases have been identified or strongly suspected, as in the instance of Richard Speck, who killed the eight nurses in Chicago (1966). Speck had had 40 previous arrests. He was also tall, low in I.Q. level, and had acne on the face—all of which are presumed to be related to the XYY syndrome.

According to Montagu, the first systematic study of the XYY aberration was made by Dr. Patricia A. Jacobs (et al.) at the Western General Hospital in Edinburgh (December, 1965). Out of 197 abnormal inmates, all of whom were dangerous, violent, and had criminal propensities, 7 cases had an XYY chromosomal constitution.

Montagu's report indicates that XYY males constitute 1.3 percent of the general population but 3.5 of the prison population. The extra Y in the chromosomal constitution apparently causes extreme and uncontrollable aggressiveness in some of the XYY males as well as tallness, facial acne, low I.Q. (80 to 85), and a high incidence of abnormal internal and external genitalia.

"It would be an error," says Montagu, "to identify the XYY constitution as predisposed to aggressive behavior," because the XYY phenotype acutally varies from normal to abnormal. But nevertheless, the YY is the demon in some XYY cases (males) and when it is, aggressive behavior starts in early childhood and persists through adulthood.[18]

Undoubtedly further evidence on the connection between XYY and criminal behavior is necessary. Caution was clearly indicated by a recent conference of experts called together by the National Institute of Mental Health.[19]

> Twelve specialists from the fields of genetics, psychiatry, psychology, sociology, and law, attending a conference at NIMH on the XYY syndrome, concluded that at the present time a link between the XYY syndrome and criminal behavior is not clearly demonstrated.
>
> The panel stated that it felt recent press reports linking the XYY chromosome to criminal behavior are misleading, since avilable research evidence is not adequate to support the assertion of a relationship between the chromosome and deviant, criminal, or violent behavior.
>
> A major focus of the conference was on the development of guidelines for research procedures in studies designed to ascertain the true prevalence and frequency of the XYY chromosome in the general population. Most previous studies on this question have been conducted among various criminal populations.

A symposium on *Chromosome Abnormality and Criminal Responsibility*, held at the Hebrew University (Jerusalem, 1969), also cast some doubt on the efficacy of the XYY factor as a propellant of violence and crimes.[20] There were, however, some overtones expressed in the symposium that the "moral blameworthiness of such an offender was—or would be if an association between chromosome deviation and criminal tendencies could be convincingly proved—in some degree reduced."[21]

After a tremendous scholarly review of the available information and opinions on the XYY syndrome, Baker arrived at the conclusion that it should be admitted as evidence in criminal trials. "Will the legal system hide from the present biological revolution and the information thus revealed? It cannot and still retain its integrity."[22]

In regard to the second area of biological research, namely the attempt

[18] Ashley Montagu, "Chromosomes and Crime," *Psychology Today*, 2:5 (October 1968), pp. 42–49.

[19] Memo from the Director, National Institute of Mental Health, Chevy Chase, Maryland, (November 1969), p. 7.

[20] Publication of the Institute of Criminology, No. 16 (The Faculty of Law, The Hebrew University of Jerusalem, 1969).

[21] *Ibid.*, p. VII.

[22] Brian C. Baker, "Chromosome Syndrome and the Law," *Criminologica; An Interdisciplinary Journal of Criminology*, VII:4 (February 1970), p. 30. The bibliography in this article is very extensive and should be consulted. *See* pp. 30–35.

to discover what is at the back of the deviant behavior of sociopaths, the neurophysiologists strongly suspect that there is a defect, caused possibly by lesions somewhere in the sympathetic nervous system, which feeds impulses into the organs of the body as well as into the central nervous system. Hence, the sociopath has less sensory input into the nervous system, and as a consequence the organs of the body develop a greater craving for stimulation, which thrusts the person toward the emotional excitement of deviant and criminal behavior.

If the above line of neurophysiological reasoning is correct, then an injection of epinephrine (adrenalin) should momentarily increase the heart rate and blood pressure of sociopaths more than it affects that of nonsociopaths (normals).

Funkenstein *et al* (c. 1949) were the first research team to inject epinephrine (adrenalin) into the bloodstream of 13 male and 2 female subjects who had been diagnosed as antisocial sociopaths and who had committed crimes of violence.[23] The subjects showed an increase in heart rate as well as an increase in blood pressure.

Schacter and Latane hypothesized that anxiety could be induced in sociopaths by the activation of the sympathetic nervous system via an injection of epinephrine. They had the clinical staff of a prison indicate which newly-admitted prisoners showed visible signs of sociopathy. The staff based their appraisal on the showing of prisoners on the so-called Cleckley criteria (duplicated in Appendix 1-I), the Lykken anxiety questionnaire (see Appendix 1-J), the number of officially recorded offenses, and the proportion of the prisoner's life since the age of nine spent in correctional institutions and prisons. The researchers asked the clinical staff to eliminate prisoners who showed visible emotionality or upset at admission as well as those who had an I.Q. of under 100.

Half of the small number of "sociopathic" subjects was given a placebo injection and half an injection of epinephrine. The sociopathic subjects who received the epinephrine showed increased heart activation, while the sociopaths who received the placebo did not. The sociopaths receiving the epinephrine injection were more activated than were the normal subjects (nonsociopaths) who also received the shot.[24] There is good reason to believe that the difference was largely due to the elimination of so many cases from the final reckoning, especially those that fell between the extremes of designated sociopath and designated nonsociopath.

Allen prepared a report of an interdisciplinary research team of The Ohio State University which among other things also subjected (c. 1967) a

[23]D. H. Funkenstein, M. Greenblatt, and H. C. Solomon, "Psychophysiological Study of Mentally Ill Patients," Part I, *American Journal of Psychiatry*, 106 (1949), pp. 16-28.

[24]S. Schacter and B. Latane, "Crime, Cognition, and the Autonomic System," *Nebraska Symposium on Motivation*, ed. by M. R. Jones (Lincoln, Nebraska: University of Nebraska Press, 1964), pp. 221-275.

small sample of male prisoners identified as sociopaths, mixed, and nonsociopaths (i.e. normals) to epinephrine, as part of a "double blind" experiment, in which neither the subjects nor the technicians (only the supervising research associate) knew who received which injection (epinephrine or placebo).[25] One week after admission, the screened 43 experimental subjects who had agreed to go through the experiment were brought to the special room of the prison that contained the necessary equipment. The experimental subjects consisted of 19 sociopaths, 10 mixed, and 14 nonsociopaths (normals). Half of each group was given the placebo and half the epinephrine injection (in the left upper arm near the shoulder). One week later, the 43 subjects were returned to the experimental room and the reverse halves of each group were given the placebo or the epinephrine injection.

Epinephrine raised the heart rate and skin resistance somewhat more in the sociopathic cases than in the nonsociopathic subjects, but not to the point of statistical significance. (It should be remembered that, with samples of size 19, compared with samples of 10 and 14, differences must be relatively very large to gain statistical significance.)

The Ohio State University research team decided that the group of 19 sociopaths was not homogeneous and further investigation revealed that 11 of the sociopathic subjects were different from the other 8. These 11 registered lower than the 8 on the Lykken scale that measures the respondent's desire for or avoidance of anxiety-laden situations. They less frequently chose anxiety-provoking situations than the 8, but much more so than the so-called mixed (10 cases) and the so-called nonsociopaths (14 cases). The 11 were given the label of "simple" sociopaths; the 8, of "hostile" sociopaths. It was discovered that the heart rate of the 11 "simples" increased more under the injection of epinephrine than that of the 8 "hostiles." The research team found evidence that these two groups of so-called sociopaths differed in their performance in real life. The "simples" were more criminally involved, tending toward property crimes; the "hostiles" were less involved than the "simples" but tended to concentrate more in assaultive offenses against the person. Further details on the differences between the hostile and simple sociopaths are presented in Appendix 1-K.

Whether further experimental research will corroborate the existence of different types of sociopaths, the future will have to decide. But at this point, the research team projected a plausible theory that might account for the development and behavior of the so-called simple sociopath. It might be hypothecated at this juncture that he displays a "diminished function

[25]Harry E. Allen, "Bio-social Correlates of Two Types of Anti-social Sociopaths" (Ph.D. dissertation, The Ohio State University, 1969). *Also see* Harry E. Allen, Lewis Lindner, Harold Goldman, and Simon Dinitz, "Hostile and Simple Sociopaths: An Empirical Typology," *Criminology, An Interdisciplinary Journal*, VIII (March 1971).

(partial or total) of the catecholamine-secreting nerve endings, including those involved with sensory receptors." Hence, a sort of denervation of the sympathetic or autonomic nervous system sets up a denervation of the entire nervous system. In consequence, the "simple" sociopath will seek stimulation to optimize his input, and he apparently needs intense emotional stimulation to overcome the denervation.

The research team mentioned the possibility of two other neurophysiologic defects beside that in nerve terminals: defective ganglionic or possibly preganglionic and extraneuronal, such as the malfunctioning of the liver.[26]

[26] L. A. Lindner, H. Goldman, S. Dinitz, and H. E. Allen, "An Antisocial Personality Type with Cardiac Lability," *Archives of General Psychiatry*, 23 (September 1970), pp. 260–267.

Appendix 1–A

CRISSMAN'S MORAL JUDGMENT QUESTIONNAIRE

Note: Respondents are asked to rate each of the following 50 items in terms of its "rightness" or "wrongness" in their eyes on a scale ranging from 1 to 10. They do this by circling the response that expresses their feelings of rightness or wrongness, whether this be 1 or 2 or 5 or 9 or 10. The respondents are told in the directions that a circled value of 1 is the least wrong or not wrong at all in their book of moral judgments and that a circled value of 10 is the most wrong or the "wrongest" possible in their book of moral judgments.

---

1. Killing a person in defense of one's own life. 1 2 3 4 5 6 7 8 9 10
2. Kidnapping and holding a child for ransom. 1 2 3 4 5 6 7 8 9 10
3. Having sex relations while unmarried. 1 2 3 4 5 6 7 8 9 10
4. Forging a check. 1 2 3 4 5 6 7 8 9 10
5. Habitually failing to keep promises. 1 2 3 4 5 6 7 8 9 10
6. Girls smoking cigarettes. 1 2 3 4 5 6 7 8 9 10
7. An industry maintaining working conditions for its workers known to be detrimental to their health. 1 2 3 4 5 6 7 8 9 10
8. A doctor allowing a badly deformed baby to die when he could save its life but not cure its deformity. 1 2 3 4 5 6 7 8 9 10
9. A legislator, for a financial consideration, using his influence to secure the passage of a law known to be contrary to public interest. 1 2 3 4 5 6 7 8 9 10
10. Testifying falsely in court when under oath. 1 2 3 4 5 6 7 8 9 10
11. Betting on horse races. 1 2 3 4 5 6 7 8 9 10
12. A nation dealing unjustly with a weaker nation over which it has power 1 2 3 4 5 6 7 8 9 10
13. A jury freeing a father who has killed a man for rape against his young daughter. 1 2 3 4 5 6 7 8 9 10

Paul Crissman, "Temporal Change and Sexual Difference in Moral Judgments," *Journal of Social Psychology*, 16 (1942), pp. 29–31. Reprinted by permission.

14. Living beyond one's means in order to possess luxuries enjoyed by friends and associates. 1 2 3 4 5 6 7 8 9 10
15. Bootlegging under prohibition law. 1 2 3 4 5 6 7 8 9 10
16. Having illicit sex relations after marriage. 1 2 3 4 5 6 7 8 9 10
17. Driving an automobile while drunk but without accident. 1 2 3 4 5 6 7 8 9 10
18. A prosperous industry paying workers less than a living wage. 1 2 3 4 5 6 7 8 9 10
19. Holding up and robbing a person. 1 2 3 4 5 6 7 8 9 10
20. Not giving to charity when able. 1 2 3 4 5 6 7 8 9 10
21. Not taking the trouble to vote at primaries and elections. 1 2 3 4 5 6 7 8 9 10
22. A strong commercial concern selling below cost to crowd out a weaker competitor. 1 2 3 4 5 6 7 8 9 10
23. Falsifying about a child's age to secure reduced fare. 1 2 3 4 5 6 7 8 9 10
24. A student who is allowed to grade his own paper reporting a higher grade than the one earned. 1 2 3 4 5 6 7 8 9 10
25. Not giving to support religion when able. 1 2 3 4 5 6 7 8 9 10
26. Keeping over-change given by a clerk in mistake. 1 2 3 4 5 6 7 8 9 10
27. Copying from another's paper in a school examination. 1 2 3 4 5 6 7 8 9 10
28. Speeding away after one's car knocks down a pedestrian. 1 2 3 4 5 6 7 8 9 10
29. Charging interest above a fair rate when lending money. 1 2 3 4 5 6 7 8 9 10
30. Falsifying a federal income tax return. 1 2 3 4 5 6 7 8 9 10
31. Buying bootleg liquor under prohibition law. 1 2 3 4 5 6 7 8 9 10
32. Married persons using birth-control devices. 1 2 3 4 5 6 7 8 9 10
33. Seeking divorce because of incompatibility when both parties agree to separate (assuming no children). 1 2 3 4 5 6 7 8 9 10
34. Depositing more than one ballot in an election in order to aid a favorite candidate. 1 2 3 4 5 6 7 8 9 10
35. Living on inherited wealth without attempting to render service to others. 1 2 3 4 5 6 7 8 9 10
36. Taking one's own life (assuming no near relatives or dependents). 1 2 3 4 5 6 7 8 9 10
37. Using profane or blasphemous speech. 1 2 3 4 5 6 7 8 9 10
38. Being habitually cross or disagreeable to members of one's own family. 1 2 3 4 5 6 7 8 9 10
39. Seeking amusement on Sunday instead of going to church. 1 2 3 4 5 6 7 8 9 10
40. Refusing to bear arms in a war one believes to be unjust. 1 2 3 4 5 6 7 8 9 10

41. Advertising a medicine to cure a disease known to be incurable by such a remedy. 1 2 3 4 5 6 7 8 9 10
42. Misrepresenting the value of an investment in order to induce credulous persons to invest. 1 2 3 4 5 6 7 8 9 10
43. Taking money for one's vote in an election. 1 2 3 4 5 6 7 8 9 10
44. Newspapers treating crime news so as to make hoodlums and gangsters appear heroic. 1 2 3 4 5 6 7 8 9 10
45. A man having a vacant building he cannot rent sets it on fire to collect insurance. 1 2 3 4 5 6 7 8 9 10
46. Nations at war using poison gas on the homes and cities of its enemy behind the lines. 1 2 3 4 5 6 7 8 9 10
47. Slipping out secretly and going among people when one's home is under quarantine for a contagious disease. 1 2 3 4 5 6 7 8 9 10
48. A man deserting a girl whom he has got into trouble without himself taking responsibility 1 2 3 4 5 6 7 8 9 10
49. Disbelieving in God. 1 2 3 4 5 6 7 8 9 10
50. A man not marrying a girl he loves because she is markedly his inferior socially and in education. 1 2 3 4 5 6 7 8 9 10

Appendix 1–B

BALL'S NEUTRALIZATION SCALE

Note: The total schedule that was administered to fifteen- to eighteen-year-old youths at a state school for committed delinquents in Ohio and at an inner-city high school included several other scales besides the neutralization scale, in order to test directionality. Most of both samples concentrated on years sixteen and seventeen. The neutralization scale that is duplicated below consists of 10 different sets of realistic excuses to 4 behavioral situations: gang fight, shiplifting, robbery at point of knife, gang attack with weapons. The response to each excuse among the different sets of excuses under each situation is on a five-point scale: strongly agree (SA), agree (A), undecided (U), disagree (D), and strongly disagree (SD). SA is scored 5; A, 4; U, 3; D, 2; and SD, 1, which scoring system is in the direction of greater to lesser neutralization. High scores on the individual excuses, on any set of 10 excuses, or on the total 40 excuses (10 sets of excuses for 4 situations) are therefore in the unfavorable direction—that is, towards neutralization—while low scores are in the favorable direction—away from neutralizing oneself out of the moral bind.

No.________

THE WAY A GUY LOOKS AT THINGS

Grown-ups make a lot of statements about guys that get into trouble and guys that stay out of trouble, but we think it is best to let guys speak for themselves. We want to find out how you look at things. We don't want your name, just how you look at things.

DON'T SIGN YOUR NAME.

Name of School________________________________

Age:__________years and__________months

Grade__________

Place of Birth:____________________city____________________state__________

DON'T SIGN YOUR NAME

Richard Allen Ball, "Neutralization as a Self Factor in Delinquency Risk," Ph.D. dissertation (The Ohio State University, 1965), pp. 283–298.

A sixteen-year-old boy, named Jack, gets into trouble. Read each situation carefully and see how you feel about the various excuses given. If you strongly agree *with the statement*, circle *SA* (Strongly Agree). If you agree with the statement, circle *A* (Agree). Circle *U* (Undecided) if you are undecided. If you disagree with the statement, circle *D* (Disagree). Circle *SD* (Strongly Disagree) if you strongly disagree with the statement.

REMEMBER! This is not a test.
There are no right or wrong answers. The right answer for you is *how you feel about the various excuses*. Try to answer for one excuse at a time without thinking about any of the others.

SITUATION # 1

Jack gets a club and goes with his friends to look for another group of boys. They find them in a park, and a fight starts. During the fight Jack hits another boy with the club, and almost kills him.

SA A U D SD 1. People should not blame Jack this time *if he was trying to protect himself.*

SA A U D SD 2. People should not blame Jack this time *if the other boys were trying to take over his part of town.*

SA A U D SD 3. People should not blame Jack this time *if he just "went crazy" with anger for a second.*

SA A U D SD 4. People should not blame Jack this time *if he had been drinking.*

SA A U D SD 5. People should not blame Jack this time *if he was swinging the club just to scare the boy.*

SA A U D SD 6. People should not blame Jack this time *if all the boys were using clubs.*

SA A U D SD 7. People should not blame Jack this time *if the other boy had been trying to hit him.*

SA A U D SD 8. People should not blame Jack this time *if the boy was an outsider who came to cause trouble.*

SA A U D SD 9. People should not blame Jack this time *if the other boy had once made him look like a coward.*

SA A U D SD 10. People should not blame Jack this time *if the other boy was beating one of Jack's friends.*

DO NOT TURN THE PAGE YET

REMEMBER! Circle the answer . . . which best fits the way you feel about each excuse.

SA = Strongly Agree
A = Agree
U = Undecided
D = Disagree
SD = Strongly Disagree

SITUATION # 2

While loafing around in a store, Jack takes some things without paying for them.

SA A U D SD 11. People should not blame Jack *if this was the normal thing to do where Jack lived.*

SA A U D SD 12. People should not blame Jack *if the owner had fired his father without any reason.*

SA A U D SD 13. People should not blame Jack *if the store has more of the things than it can ever sell.*

SA A U D SD 14. People should not blame Jack *if the owner is rich and won't miss it.*

SA A U D SD 15. People should not blame Jack *if the things were old and could not be sold anyway.*

SA A U D SD 16. People should not blame Jack *if everybody knows the owner sells things that are against the law.*

SA A U D SD 17. People should not blame Jack *if the owner himself had stolen a lot of money and left town.*

SA A U D SD 18. People should not blame Jack *if he was getting even with the owner for cheating him.*

SA A U D SD 19. People should not blame Jack *if everyone knows that the owner is very crooked.*

SA A U D SD 20. People should not blame Jack *if the owner cheats poor people out of everything.*

DO NOT TURN THE PAGE YET

REMEMBER! Circle the answer . . . which best fits the way you feel about each excuse.

SA = Strongly Agree
A = Agree
U = Undecided
D = Disagree
SD = Strongly Disagree

SITUATION # 3

Jack stops a man on a dark street one night when nobody else is around. He pulls a knife and makes the man hand over his money.

SA A U D SD 21. People should not blame Jack *if the man had stolen money from Jack.*

SA A U D SD 22. People should not blame Jack *if the man is a big crook himself.*

SA A U D SD 23. People should not blame Jack *if the man had dared anybody to try to rob him.*

SA A U D SD 24. People should not blame Jack *if the man had got this money by cheating poor people.*

SA A U D SD 25. People should not blame Jack *if he had to prove to his friends he could do it.*

SA A U D SD 26. People should not blame Jack *if all the boys had promised to try it.*

SA A U D SD 27. People should not blame Jack *if someone said he was too afraid to try it.*

SA A U D SD 28. People should not blame Jack *if he did it to prove his courage to everybody.*

SA A U D SD 29. People should not blame Jack *if his mother needed some money bad.*

SA A U D SD 30. People should not blame Jack *if he was doing it just to help a friend.*

DO NOT TURN THE PAGE YET

REMEMBER! Circle the answer . . . which best fits the way you feel about each excuse.

SA = Strongly Agree
A = Agree
U = Undecided
D = Disagree
SD = Strongly Disagree

SITUATION # 4

Jack goes along with his gang. All the boys carry knives and guns. They attack another gang, and Jack shoots a boy. The boy is badly hurt, but he lives.

SA A U D SD 31. People should not blame Jack *if the other gang had been getting ready to attack.*

SA A U D SD 32. People should not blame Jack *if the other gang had asked for the fight.*

SA A U D SD 33. People should not blame Jack *if the other boy jumped him.*

SA A U D SD 34. People should not blame Jack *if the other boy said he would kill him.*

SA A U D SD 35. People should not blame Jack *if the other boy was trying to shoot him.*

SA A U D SD 36. People should not blame Jack *if the other boy came at him with a knife.*

SA A U D SD 37. People should not blame Jack *if the other boy was always looking for trouble.*

SA A U D SD 38. People should not blame Jack *if he was only trying to prove he was a man.*

SA A U D SD 39. People should not blame Jack *if he had to go along to show he was a real friend.*

SA A U D SD 40. People should not blame Jack *if it was either fight or leave his friends alone.*

DO NOT TURN THE PAGE YET

Here are some other things. If the statement is true about you, put a circle around *T* (True). If the statement is *not* true about you, put a circle around *F* (False).

REMEMBER! This is not a test. The right answer is whether the statement does or does not apply to you.

T F 41. At times I have very much wanted to leave home.

T F 42. When someone does me a wrong I feel I should pay him back if I can, just for the principle of the thing.

T F 43. During one period when I was a youngster I engaged in petty thievery.

T F 44. As a youngster I was suspended from school one or more times for cutting up.

T F 45. I believe women ought to have as much sexual freedom as men.

T F 46. In school I was sometimes sent to the principal for cutting up.

T F 47. Most people will use somewhat unfair means to gain profit or an advantage rather than to lose it.

T F 48. I do not worry about catching diseases.

T F 49. When I was a child, I belonged to a crowd or gang that tried to stick together through thick and thin.

T F 50. I have the wanderlust and am never happy unless I am roaming or traveling about.

T F 51. I am afraid when I look down from a high place.

T F 52. I liked school.

T F 53. I like to flirt.

T F 54. I very much like hunting.

T F 55. My parents have often objected to the kind of people I went around with.

GO ON TO NEXT PAGE

T F 56. I don't blame anyone for trying to grab everything he can get in this world.

T F 57. I am entirely self-confident.

T F 58. When in a group of people I have trouble thinking of the right things to talk about.

T F 59. I can easily make other people afraid of me, and sometimes do for the fun of it.

T F 60. At times I have been so entertained by the cleverness of a crook that I have hoped he would get by with it.

T F 61. I have never been in trouble with the law.

T F 62. If several people find themselves in trouble, the best thing for them to do is to agree upon a story and stick to it.

T F 63. At times I have very much wanted to leave home.

T F 64. I have had very peculiar and strange experiences.

T F 65. I am often said to be hotheaded.

T F 66. I played hooky from school quite often as a youngster.

T F 67. I am attracted by members of the opposite sex.

T F 68. I would like to be an auto racer.

T F 69. It is all right to get around the law if you don't actually break it.

T F 70. If I were in trouble with several friends who were equally to blame, I would rather take the whole blame than to give them away.

T F 71. I do not worry about catching diseases.

DO NOT TURN THE PAGE YET

Here are some more questions about the way you look at things. If you feel that the statement applies to you, circle *Y* for *Yes*. If the statement does *not* apply to you, circle *N* for *No*.

REMEMBER! This is not a test. The right answer is whether or not the statement applies to you.

Y N 72. Are things difficult for you because your folks are usually short of money?

Y N 73. Are you troubled because your folks differ from you regarding the things you like?

Y N 74. Do you often wish your father (mother or guardian) had a better job in the community?

Y N 75. Do some of those at home seem to feel that they are better than you?

Y N 76. Do folks seem to think well of your family's social standing?

Y N 77. Do your folks appear to doubt whether you will be successful?

Y N 78. Do you often wish your father was a more important man in the community?

Y N 79. Do you avoid inviting others to your home because it is not as nice as theirs?

Y N 80. Do your folks seem to think that you are going to amount to something?

Y N 81. Are you considered a failure in many of the things you do?

Y N 82. Do your friends and acquaintances seem to have a better time at home than you do?

Y N 83. Do you usually like to be somewhere else than at home?

Y N 84. Are you often discouraged because people fail to recognize your worth?

Y N 85. Have you often wished you had different parents than you have?

Y N 86. Do folks seem to think well of your family's social standing?

DO NOT TURN THE PAGE YET

Here are some opinions about the ways things are in the world around you. If you strongly agree with the statement, circle *SA* (Strongly Agree). If you agree, circle *A* (Agree). Circle *U* (Undecided) if you are undecided. If you disagree, circle *D* (Disagree). Circle *SD* (Strongly Disagree) if you strongly disagree.

SA A U D SD 87. In spite of what some people say, the lot of the average man is getting worse.

SA A U D SD 88. I wouldn't take a promotion, no matter how big an improvement it was for me, if it meant endangering my health.

SA A U D SD 89. I'd probably turn down a substantial advancement if it involved being away from the family a great deal.

SA A U D SD 90. It's hardly fair for adults to bring children into the world the way things look for the future.

SA A U D SD 91. Nowadays a person has to live pretty much for today and let tomorrow take care of itself.

SA A U D SD 92. I'd be all in favor of staying with a job that might never get me much prestige as a "big shot" but was a good bet as far as peace of mind is concerned.

SA A U D SD 93. These days a person doesn't really know whom he can count on.

SA A U D SD 94. There's little use for anybody to complain to public officials because often they aren't really interested in the problems of the average man.

DO NOT TURN THE PAGE YET

Everyone, young and old, breaks some rules and regulations during his lifetime. Some of us break them frequently, others less often. Here are some frequently broken. Put an X in front of the statement which gives the number of times for you.

HAVE YOU EVER:

95. Driven a car without a driver's license or permit (do not include driver training courses)?
    __________Very Often
    __________Several Times
    __________Once or Twice
    __________Never

96. Taken some little things (worth less than $2) that did not belong to you?
    __________Very Often
    __________Several Times
    __________Once or Twice
    __________Never

97. Bought or drunk beer, wine, or liquor (include drinking at home)?
    __________Very Often
    __________Several Times
    __________Once or Twice
    __________Never

98. Purposely damaged or destroyed public or private property that did not belong to you?
    __________Very Often
    __________Several Times
    __________Once or Twice
    __________Never

99. Skipped school without a legitimate excuse?
    __________Very Often
    __________Several Times
    __________Once or Twice
    __________Never

100. Defied your parents' authority (to their face)?
    __________Three Times
    __________Twice
    __________Once
    __________Never

DO NOT TURN THE PAGE YET

It will help us to know a little bit about you. Fill in the right answer for you. *Don't sign your name*.

101. How old are you?

 ______years and______months

102., What grade have you reached in school?

 ______grade

103. Place of birth:

 ______city______state

104. Are you:

 ______white boy
 ______colored boy

105. Are you:

 ______Protestant
 ______Catholic
 ______Other

106. Check where you came from

 ______Cleveland (including Cuyahoga county)
 ______Cincinnati, Columbus, Toledo, Youngstown, Canton, Dayton, or Akron (including Hamilton, Franklin, Lucas, Mahoning, Stark, Montgomery, and Summit counties)
 ______Other places

107. How many times have you been taken before the juvenile court for committing an offense?

 ______times

108. What does your father (stepfather or guardian) do for a living? Try to explain in detail.

THANK YOU FOR TELLING US HOW YOU LOOK AT THINGS.
DON'T SIGN YOUR NAME

Appendix 1–C

INTERACTIONAL AND SMALL-GROUP COMPONENTS IN DEVIANT AND CRIMINAL BEHAVIOR

Although delinquency and crime in the United States, and in most other nations which report and record official data, is a companionate activity, little or no criminological research has been devoted to the interactional process promoting and precipitating such behavior. Except for homicide and, to a lesser extent aggravated assault, most other Part I crimes, including forcible rape, are usually committed by groups of two or three adolescent or young adult males frequently acting in what appears to be a spontaneous and random manner.

It is a criminological cliché that only the most seriously disturbed or isolated individuals commit offenses alone; the "loner" in crime—the individual delinquent or criminal—is almost by definition seen in a psychopathological framework. Healy, Wertham, Burt, Karpman, Alexander and Staub, Abrahamsen, and other psychologically and psychiatrically oriented observers have always focused on such offenders in their etiological schemes. The very uniqueness of the "loner" in crime has also led to special sociological interest in the naive check forger, the embezzler, the shoplifter, and the tax evader. In short, the "loner" in crime is a deviant; legal violations are best viewed in the context of the small group.

Yet, despite our understanding of criminality as a small group phenomenon and despite the twin traditions and perspectives of symbolic interactionism and small group research, almost nothing significant has been done in this area of criminology. It is, of course, true that Simmel and von Wiese were interested in the nature of interaction in groups resulting in the emergence of norms, roles, and expectancies. More relevant still were the insights of that noted French jurist and sociologist, Gabriel Tarde. Tarde dwelled on the role of imitation and suggestion—one conscious and the other not—in the acting out of unlawful conduct and the internalization of delinquent norms. He emphasized the social transmission of unlawful behavior through contact with deviant patterns of behavior, the "filtering down" from the upper to lower class of new kinds of violations, and the differential responsitivity to what Williams has since called "normative evasions" and deviant norms. Sutherland's understanding of Tarde shifted the

Statement prepared by Simon Dinitz, Department of Sociology, The Ohio State University, September, 1970.

original position from the interactional encounter to differential association, i.e., selective involvement with carriers of criminal values, rationalizations, and techniques. Even this tradition, however, no longer is central in the field.

The criminological perspective has shifted even more dramatically to sociocultural, rather than interactional and interpersonal inputs. Thus, in its most extreme statement, the concern is not even with the illegal or deviant behavior as such, but rather with the societal reaction to the non-conformist. Since the etiology of the unlawful conduct has defied specific explanation, some criminologists have shifted the problem to a different level of analysis—the process of labeling, stigmatization, and disculturation, and the emergence of deviant collectivities.

1. *Unorganized small groups*

Despite the increasing, and now overwhelming, emphasis on societal reaction and its consequences rather than the nature and imperatives for unlawful and deviant behavior, criminologists have not completely neglected their intellectual antecedents. Thrasher, for example, argued that a gang is, and must, of necessity, be restricted to a small enough group to make face-to-face interaction possible. The larger the gang, the greater the number of small interaction groups—the "splintering" phenomenon. Whyte in *Street Corner Society* examined two small groups: one oriented to the street corner and the other, to persons, norms, and institutions of middle-class society. In both groups, the role of the self-appointed leader, duly legitimated in interaction, was the critical "other" in suggesting and sustaining activities. Yablonsky, after examining a violent gang in New York City, concluded that the notion of a cohesive entity called a gang is a myth; the gang is a "near group" with a very small number of interacting "hard core" members and larger numbers of participants who move in and out and are largely marginal. More recently, Yablonsky in his *Hippie Trip* has shown the same pattern of small interactional networks within the larger constellation of communes and related arrangements. Again, the role of a leader in organizing and sustaining each small group was absolutely critical. Each successful leader had all the qualities subsumed under the term charisma—a much abused but nonetheless useful concept. Indeed, the Charles Manson "family," allegedly involved in the multiple murders of actress Sharon Tate and her friends as well as an elderly couple, can hardly be comprehended in other than these terms.

The interactional framework is even more pertinent, if such is possible, in looking at other than "gang" forms of delinquent and criminal behavior. For example, the process through which two or three boys, with time on their hands, are transformed into vandals, school window smashers, auto thiefs and joyriders, burglars, armed or unarmed robbers, or even multiple offender rapists remains something of a mystery. In Bales' terms, who initiates the criminal act in these small groups, who agrees, who questions, who is antagonistic, who reacts negatively to the suggestion, how is consensus formed? Once-decided upon, how is the behavior implemented, whether breaking and entering, beating an innocent victim, or snatching a purse, etc? How is the victim chosen? How is the guilt neutralized? In short, what actually occurs in the unfolding of the episode? More importantly, how is this interaction to be described and interpreted?

Neither interactionist theory nor small group research provides the needed answers. The former focuses on the definitions of the situation of the actors and their responsitivity to "significant others." The latter tries to simulate the reality—from the justly famous Sherif experiment on the autokinetic effect and the influence of group norms, the Bennington experiment in attitude change, the Roethlisberger and Dickson bank wiring and related experiments, the task organization studies, interpersonal choice behavior, all the way to the impressively terrifying recent experiment of Milgram on the ease of inducing perfectly rational and otherwise humane persons to systematically inflict pain on others. Yet, despite the ingenuity and variety of these experiments, the delinquent and criminal decision-making process remains enigmatic, precisely because it fits no laboratory model.

Cohen identifies the characteristics of the behavior which arises out of this twosome and threesome delinquent interaction as non-utilitarian, malicious, negativistic, inversions of middle-class norms, and as implying group autonomy. Few will question the explosiveness and impulsiveness of the window breaking, vandalism, fighting, or thievery and their relation to the barely conscious attempts to subvert middle-class values, particularly the long range future orientation, to focus on excitement and "kicks," to express one's maleness or femaleness in the sexual chase and conquest, to establish one's identity as tough, smart, and a risk taker, and above all to embellish one's concept of self.

Apart from this subcultural baggage, the interactional process of twosomes and threesomes also involves diverse personality factors. Unlike most small groups, the twosome and threesome adolescent and young-adult delinquent groups are not harnessed to a task. In the absence of a task, which normally functions to submerge personalities and to unify the group under an instrumental leader (e.g., gang fight), personality attributes are much more significant. Considerable research on apprehended delinquents suggests that apart from the hostile and aggressive few, most adjudicated delinquents tend to be "field dependent" or peculiarly vulnerable to peer influence. Devoid of socially prescribed expectations, and without inner controls sufficient to steer them away from trouble, these vulnerables can be pushed or shoved into violative acts in the small group situation. At the same time, they are self selected to the point of seeking such friendship groupings. Fortunately, as they approach twenty-five years of age and become older, there is a drop off in such friendship-circle involvement and a decreasing focus on "machismo" while the previously unfocused criminality often is transformed into behavior of public nuisance such as drunkenness, disorderly conduct, and disturbing the peace.

2. *Deviant small groups*

Thus far, the unorganized twosome and threesome patterns have been explored. There is a second level of involvement in which the goal is clear and the interaction patterns much better understood. Indeed, there is an extensive amount of literature on the subject. For example, Becker has discussed in some detail how, through interaction, one learns to become a marijuana user. Since the initial sensation is generally unpleasant and the possession illegal, group support is required in the induction and schooling of the novice. Recently, with the explosion of available classes of drugs and drug usage, there is a new interest in the role of interaction in transmitting drug practices and inducting non-users. Fischer, perhaps the most authoritative source on the experimental effects of hallucinogens on humans, has said that he has never observed a "bad trip" on psycilocybin in good company or a "good trip" when alone. In other words, the setting, more than the drug, determines the effect—a powerful argument for the need of small group research to study the milieu, mind, and mood-altering effects of drugs.

In other areas, Paul Cressey's earlier work on the taxi-dance hall girl—her origins, induction, training, and history in the "life"—has been supplemented by more recent research. Greenwald did a psychoanalytic study of the "call girl" which focused on her induction and interaction with other girls, clients, and keeper or pimp. Bryan looked at the socialization and apprenticeship of the prostitute. Most recently, McCaghy and Skipper have studied the process of becoming and remaining a "stripper," with special emphasis on the group support in this occupation. Finally, Weinberg and others have looked at nudism and who, how, and why one becomes involved in "sunshine" activities.

Interactional research on homosexuality is also receiving increasing attention. Cory, Gagnon and Simon, Ward and Kassebaum, Stearn, Martin, Weinberg, Leznoff and Westley, and numerous others, have dissected every phase of homosexuality from the "coming out" to the agonies of aging. Different types of involvement have been studied, such as the overt, covert, class, prison, race, and sex aspects. The diversity of groups and styles have been found to be enormous. Within specific contexts, some of the relationship networks have been exhaustively researched shattering thereby some age old illusions about the problem.

An even larger body of research exists with regard to drinking and alcoholism. Everything from interaction in the tavern to appropriate behavior in the "bottle gang" and the collectivities on skid row and in AA, has been examined in depth. Bacon, Rubington, Trice, Clinard and many others have contributed to this phase of interactional deviance.

3. *Criminal small groups*

For the record, and to round out the general picture, it is necessary to mention certain insights into those criminal activities wherein the task is of over-riding concern. Here, the nature of the interaction is wholly goal oriented, and it appears as if unstable and compulsive personality types are shunned in criminal activity of an occupational variety.

Perhaps the best illustrations of small group involvement in well-defined criminal tasks can be found in the work of Maurer on the confidence gang and on the "whiz mob" (pickpockets), of Chic Conwell on the professional thief, and of Polsky on "the pool hustler." The interaction in these small groups appears to be similar to that in comparable legitimate occupational teams. Group cohesiveness is based on success, while individual personality in professional crime is a largely irrelevant consideration. All the actors are skilled, their roles are differentiated but interrelated, they share a common set of values and orientations. Interaction may occur, and usually does, apart from the work relationships, but it is not central to the maintenance of the group or to its instrumental functioning.

CONFORMITY AND INTERACTION

While group pressures to deviant and violational conduct are hard to demonstrate empirically, the effect of the small group in producing conformity can be more easily shown. Generally speaking the more deviant the member, in terms of group norms, the greater the change in his behavior toward conformity under group pressure. Groups, however small, seek to achieve solidarity. Without it, the group ceases to exist. Hence, in observing the interactional processes leading to conformity, one can infer the nature of the interaction which induces deviance and violational conduct. The following principles, derived from Hare's review in his *Handbook of Small Group Research*, are clearly applicable.

1. *The more ambiguous the standard or norms* (object in laboratory research), *the greater the influence of the group*. Translated into field terms one would expect that Hutterite, Amish or Mormon children with their very unambiguous behavioral standards are hard to push or move by external groups. Conversely, their violational "potential" is further reduced as they interact with others who share the same unambiguous values.

2. Whichever the group, the task, the pressures, the dissonance or other variables, small group interaction research has shown that *persons who conform in one situation will most likely conform in other situations*. Such will be the result particularly if those persons also lack self-confidence and have a high need for approval. Self-sufficient, competent, neurotic, and high-anxiety people are likely to be more difficult to persuade and to convert to personally unacceptable modes of conduct.

3. Most important, *conformity to violational patterns is more difficult to achieve when the subject's behavior is "anchored" in another reference group or value system*. Simply stated, "good" boys rarely go bad; "bad" boys, unfortunately, rarely become good. It is this "anchoring" which leads to stability and consistency in behavior. Self selection for interaction is, of course, one obvious outcome. Thus, group formation is facilitated by personal similarities in ideological characteristics and is hampered by ideological divergencies.

4. *The higher the social status of the members of a small group, the greater the likelihood of conformity to its standards*. In a world of perceived scarcity, getting selected into a high-status group is a considerable accomplishment and will exact conformity, particularly if the initiation is severe and highly ceremonial. In the terms of discourse in delinquency, the younger boy is more likely to engage in vandalism or some other criminal act if his companions have a "rep" of sorts and if they allowed him to "tag" along with them.

5. Finally, where the norms of the small group (e.g., a group of delinquent boys) conflict with those of a secondary group or a widely-accepted institution, the interaction in the smaller group will be more predictive of behavior than that in the larger group. Pressure from the latter will serve to unify the former and will solidify the deviant standards and/or deviant modes of behavior of the small group.

Appendix 1–D

FOUR STUDIES OF DIFFERENTIAL ASSOCIATION AND COMPANIONSHIP

i

James F. Short tried to implement Sutherland's theoretical contention that a person becomes criminal through his criminal associates and that associations (the how, in this instance) vary in frequency, duration, priority, and intensity of contact. (Actually Short was of the opinion that variation in these four factors was the main, if not the only, aspect of Sutherland's theory that was testable.)

He administered a self-reporting instrument to a sample of delinquent boys in a school for delinquents in the state of Washington, to a small sample of delinquent girls also in the school for delinquent girls in the state of Washington, and to samples of boys and girls in a high school in a suburban community, a small town, and a rural-urban fringe community, also in the state of Washington. As will be seen below, the 11 self-reporting items deal with deviant behavior. The response format for each item is in terms of the frequency of having behaved in the way indicated: never, once or twice, three or four times.

The schedule also included 9 items dealing with differential association. Answer formats to these items were also in terms of frequency or amount: most were, several were, very few were, none were; or very well, fairly well, not very well, only knew their names, didn't even know their names.

1. Driving a car without a driver's license or permit.
2. Buying or drinking beer, wine, or liqor (including drinking at home).
3. Skipping school without a legitimate excuse.
4. Taking little things (worth less than $2) that did not belong to you.
5. Purposely damaging or destroying public or private property.
6. Sex relations with a person of the opposite sex.
7. Taking things of medium value (worth $2 to $50).
8. "Running Away" from home.

9. Taking things of large value (worth more than $50).
10. Defying parents' authority to their face.
11. Narcotics violations.[1]

x x x x x x

1. Think of the friends you have been associated with *most often*. Were (or are) any of them juvenile delinquents?
2. Think of the friends you have known *for the longest time*. Were (or are) any of them juvenile delinquents?
3. Think back to the *first* friends you can remember. Were any of them juvenile delinquents at the time you first knew them?
4. Have any of your *best* friends been juvenile delinquents while they were your best friends?
5. Was there much crime or delinquency committed by young people (in their teens or below) in the community in which you grew up?
6. Have any of your friends been juvenile delinquents?
7. Are any of your present friends juvenile delinquents?
8. Do you know any adult criminals?
9. How well have you known criminals?[2]

One notices that the first 4 items in the second list attempt to implement specifically the 4 elements in differential association (frequency, duration, priority, and intensity of contact). One notices also that the 11 self-reporting items give a measure of the amount of involvement in deviant behavior—how good a measure, we do not know.

Short was able to correlate the self-reported involvement with the self-reported indications of differential association. In general, the higher the frequency of involvement, the greater the differential association—more for boys than for girls, however. While this initial study demonstrated that the factors of differential association were connected with amount of involvement, it did not indicate how the factors worked to produce the involvement, whether by interactional escalation or by take-over from carriers.

ii

The model for Eynon's research into the onset of delinquency, in which the companionship factor was studied, is presented in diagram 1–D–1. Note should be taken of the fact that Eynon analyzed his sample of committed white boys according to factors

[1] James F. Short, "Differential Association and Delinquency," *Social Problems*, 4:3 (1957), pp. 233–239.

[2] James F. Short, "Differential Association with Delinquent Friends and Delinquent Behavior," *Pacific Sociological Review*, 1:1 (1958), pp. 21–22.

DIAGRAM 1–D–1. ANALYTICAL CATEGORIES IN EYNON'S STUDY[3]

Early Onset							
Companions				No Companions			
Serious		Less Serious		Serious		Less Serious	
Poor Self-Concept	Good Self-Concept	Poor Self-Concept	Good Self-Concept	Poor Self-Concept	Good Self-Concept	Poor Self-Concept	Good Self-Concept

Late Onset							
Companions				No Companions			
Serious		Less Serious		Serious		Less Serious	
Poor Self-Concept	Good Self-Concept	Poor Self-Concept	Good Self-Concept	Poor Self-Concept	Good Self-Concept	Poor Self-Concept	Good Self-Concept

[3] Thomas G. Eynon, "Factors Related to Onset of Delinquency," Ph.D. dissertation (The Ohio State University, 1959), p. 10.

associated with the first official act of delinquency (for which they were taken to the juvenile court) and with the first self-reported act of delinquency. In addition to age of occurrence of both involvements (official and unofficial), Eynon related the "onset" of delinquency in terms of admitted companions or no companions in the deed, of serious or less serious delinquency direction as measured by the Harrison Gough DE (Delinquency Scale), which is now called the Socialization Scale, and good or poor self-concept toward law and order.

The part of Eynon's schedule that is of interest at this point is the part dealing with self-reported delinquency. He used 24 such items in his total schedule and analyzed the responses of the boys to just 12 of the 24 items that he found to be the most frequently reported. The 12 items are indicated by an asterisk.

The first listing is to obtain responses of frequency of having committed the various acts. The second listing of the 24 self-reporting items is to get the reported age at the time. The third listing is to obtain the involvement with others in the deed.

EYNON'S SELF-REPORTING ITEMS[4]

Everyone of us, young and old, breaks some laws, rules and regulations during his lifetime. Some break them frequently, others less often. Here are some frequently broken. *Put an X* in front of those that you have broken and *give the right answer for you.*

1. Drive a car
   ______very often
   ______several times
   ______once or twice
   ______never

*2. Drive a car without permission
   ______very often
   ______several times
   ______once or twice
   ______never

*3. Play hookey
   ______very often
   ______several times
   ______once or twice
   ______never

*4. Run away from home
   ______very often
   ______several times
   ______once or twice
   ______never

5. Have a fist fight
   ______very often
   ______several times
   ______once or twice
   ______never

6. Get on school probation or be expelled
   ______often
   ______several times
   ______once or twice
   ______never

[4] *Ibid.*, pp. 186–188.

7. Defy parents' authority to their face
   ________very often
   ________several times
   ________once or twice
   ________never

8. Drive too fast or recklessly in an automobile
   ________very often
   ________several times
   ________once or twice
   ________never

*9. Take some little thing (worth less than $2) that did not belong to you
   ________very often
   ________several times
   ________once or twice
   ________never

10. Take something of medium value (between $2 and $50)
   ________very often
   ________several times
   ________once or twice
   ________never

11. Take something of large value (over $50)
   ________very often
   ________several times
   ________once or twice
   ________never

12. Take something you really didn't want
   ________very often
   ________several times
   ________once or twice
   ________never

*13. Use force to get money from another person
   ________very often
   ________several times
   ________once or twice
   ________never

*14. Take part in gang fights
   ________very often
   ________several times
   ________once or twice
   ________never

*15. Beat up on kids who hadn't done anything to you
   ________very often
   ________several times
   ________once or twice
   ________never

16. Drink beer, wine, or liquor in your own home
   ________very often
   ________several times
   ________once or twice
   ________never

*17. Buy or drink beer, wine or liquor outside your home)
   ________very often
   ________several times
   ________once or twice
   ________never

*18. Hurt someone else just for the fun of it
   ________very often
   ________several times
   ________once or twice
   ________never

*19. Purposely damage or destroy public or private property
_____very often
_____several times
_____once or twice
_____never

*20. Use or sell narcotic drugs
_____very often
_____several times
_____once or twice
_____never

*21. Have sex relations with another person of the same sex
_____very often
_____several times
_____once or twice
_____never

22. Have sex relations with another person of the opposite sex
_____very often
_____several times
_____once or twice
_____never

23. Go hunting or fishing without a license or violate any other game law
_____very often
_____several times
_____once or twice
_____never

24. Get complained on to the police or school for fighting
_____very often
_____several times
_____once or twice
_____never

NOW: *HOW OLD WERE YOU WHEN YOU FIRST DID THESE THINGS:* If you never did these things put an N in the blank.

25. _____Drive a car

26. _____Drive a car without permission

27. _____Play hookey

28. _____Run away from home

29. _____Have a fist fight

30. _____Get on school probation or be expelled

31. _____Defy parent's authority to their face

32. _____Drive too fast or recklessly in an automobile

33. _____Take some little thing (worth less than $2) that did not belong to you

34. _____Take something of medium value (between $2 and $50)

35. _____Take something of large value (over $50)

36. _____Take something you really didn't want

37. _____Use force to get money from another person

38. _____Take part in gang fights

39. ______Beat up on kids who hadn't done anything to you

40. ______Drink beer, wine, or liquor in your own home

41. ______Buy or drink beer, wine or liquor outside your home

42. ______Hurt someone else just for the fun of it

43. ______Purposely damage or destroy public or private property

44. ______Use or sell narcotics

45. ______Have sex relations with another person of the same sex

46. ______Have sex relations with another person of the opposite sex

47. ______Go hunting or fishing without a license or violate any other game law

48. ______Get complained on to the police or school for fighting

NOW: *HOW MANY PEOPLE WERE WITH YOU WHEN YOU FIRST DID THESE THINGS:* If you were *by yourself put a zero* (0) in the blank; and if you *never did* these things *put an N* in the blank.

49. ______Drive a car

50. ______Drive a car without permission

51. ______Play hookey

52. ______Run away from home

53. ______Have a fist fight

54. ______Get on school probation or be expelled

55. ______Defy parents' authority to their face

56. ______Drive too fast or recklessly in a car

57. ______Take some little thing (worth less than $2) that did not belong to you

58. ______Take something of medium value (between $2 and $50)

59. ______Take something of large value (over $50)

60. ______Take something you really didn't want

61. ______Use force to get money from another person

62. ______Take part in gang fights

63. ______Beat up on kids who hadn't done anything to you

64. ______Drink beer, wine, or liquor in your own home

65. ______Buy or drink beer, wine or liquor outside your home

66. ______Hurt someone else just for the fun of it

67. ______Purposely damage or destroy public or private property

68. ______Use or sell narcotic drugs

69. ______Have sex relations with another person of the same sex

70. ______Have sex relations with another person of the opposite sex

71. ______Go hunting or fishing without a license or violate any other game law

72. ______Get complained on to the police or school for fighting

---

iii

Albert J. Reiss also attempted to implement Sutherland's differential association hypothesis in a study of "triad" combinations (three best friends) in a sample of 299 white schoolboys in Nashville, Tennessee. In so doing, he also made a contribution to the study of the "how" factor in delinquency involvement. The boys were asked to indicate their two closest friends. A self-reporting instrument, similar to that used by Short, was administered. In particular, Reiss attempted to find answers to three questions:

1. Does the probability of an individual committing kinds of delinquent acts depend upon his close friends committing these acts?
2. Is there variation in dependence upon friends committing a delinquent act among different kinds of delinquent behavior?
3. Is the probability of committing a delinquent act less dependent upon one's friends committing the act in some kinds of conforming or delinquent groups than in others.

One notices that the questions deal with the "how" factor in self-reported involvement.

The following statements represent a partial list of Reiss' findings.[5]

---

1. Boys generally choose boys as close friends whose law-abiding or delinquent behavior is similar to their own.
2. For each kind of delinquent behavior, the probability of an individual's committing a specific delinquent act depends upon the commission of the act by other members of the friendship triad.
3. Confidence in the finding that the probability for a boy committing a delin-

[5]Albert J. Reiss, Jr., and A. Lewis Rhodes, "An Empirical Test of Differential Association Theory," *The Journal of Research in Crime and Delinquency*," 1:1 (January 1964), pp. 9-13.

quent act is not independent of the behavior of his closest friends is increased with the observation that fewer of the triads than expected have only one boy reporting he engaged in the delinquent activity.

4. For each kind of act, significantly more of the original sociometric subjects (the index member's choices of best friends) who reported the offense, than those who did not, have friends who also committed the act.
5. Although (by way of caution), in the aggregate, commission of a kind of delinquent act by other members of a close friendship triad, the correlation varies with the kind of delinquent behavior and is far from perfect for any kind.
6. There is a substantial number of triads where only one or two members of the triad committed the same kind of delinquent act, thereby calling into question any postulate about the homogeneity of law-violative behavior in triads through differential association.
7. In two-thirds or more of the triads, for each kind of delinquent offense, all members report they committed the act, i.e., if more than one member did it, it was probably three. There remained nonetheless a substantial minority of triads in which only two members committed the same act of delinquency. The more serious offenses are least likely to show triadic uniformity.
8. Selection of close friends who commit a specific kind of act within a given type of conforming-delinquent group is largely a function of the rate of that kind of delinquency within each group.

One notices that Reiss developed evidence to indicate that following the same pattern of behavior or committing the same act of delinquency was not by any means universal in the various triads. This finding suggests that even long-term interaction between "best friends" may not always generate the escalation or acting-out of similar forms of behavior.

iv

The excerpts that follow are taken from a report by Erickson and Empey, that studied, among other variables, the involvement of various samples of boys with delinquent associates as well as their commitment or identification with their peers. The sample was primarily drawn from white boys in a fairly large county in Utah (110,000), but it also included boys throughout the state who had been incarcerated in an institution for delinquent boys. Information was obtained by interviews, in which questions were asked about their involvement in different types of delinquent behavior as well as their participation with delinquent or nondelinquent peers.[6]

---

[6] Maynard L. Erickson and LaMar T. Empey, "Class Position, Peers and Delinquency," *Sociology and Social Research*, 49:3 (April 1965), pp. 268–282. Reprinted by permission.

In order to provide some assessment of these variables, each boy was asked to list his 5 best friends, how long he had known each of them and the number of times each week he associated with them. The names of these friends were then checked through court records to determine their official delinquent-nondelinquent standing.

Once this information was known, an index of delinquent-nondelinquent associations was constructed. A high score on the index indicates extensive and regular association with delinquents while a low score indicates the opposite. One primary weakness with the instrument is its reliance upon official data. This makes it subject to many of the limitations mentioned earlier. It is difficult, therefore, to determine whether delinquent, but not officially designated, peers are any more important to one than another.

The low- and middle-class groups were similar in their tendencies to associate with known delinquents but both differed significantly from the upper-class group. In fact, the extent of difference was greater between the middle- and upper-class groups ($P<.001$) than it was between the low- and upper-class groups ($P<.01$).

Coupled with the previous findings, a pattern begins to emerge. So far it indicates that those respondents who had been most delinquent were also those who were most inclined to have delinquent associates. But it does not indicate that such a pattern is primarily a low-class phenomenon. Rather it includes middle- as well as low-class respondents and excludes only the upper-class.

Because mere association with delinquents or nondelinquents alone may not connote identification with them, it was thought important to determine the extent to which each respondent identifies with, or was committed in an ideological way to, the expectations of his peers. Would he be inclined to do what the group asked of him? Would he go along with them? Would he protect them?

These findings contributed to the emerging pattern. On the nondelinquent peer scale, low- and middle-class respondents did not differ significantly from each other but both differed, and to the same extent ($P<.01$), from upper-class respondents. Both were significantly more committed to the expectations of peers, even though in this case the expectations were nondelinquent.

On the delinquent peer scale the pattern was generally the same except that it was the middle- rather than the low-class group which displayed the greatest commitment to delinquent expectations. Whereas the level of significance between the low and upper-class groups on this scale was only .05, it was at the .001 level for the middle- and upper-class groups.

On the "fink" scale (would the boy "rat" on his friends), there were no significant differences, either within or between classes. The implication was clear that, whether delinquent or nondelinquent, lower or upper class, these adolescents were ideologically opposed to informing on a peer. This finding was at variance with the emerging pattern in the sense this scale made no distinctions and would not be useful in predicting delinquency.

The pattern thus far has not conformed closely to theoretical expectation. It has suggested that delinquency is concentrated toward, but not primarily at, the bottom of the class ladder. Middle-class respondents report having been about as delinquent as low-class respondents. Only the upper-class group differs.

Similarly, the tendency has been greater among low- and middle-class boys to associate with, and be committed to, delinquent peers than upper-class boys. The question that is significant, therefore, is whether peer relationships are themselves a more, or less, efficient predictor of delinquency than social class. Hypothetically, they might be a key, intervening variable.

The pattern was confirmed even more in the analysis of respondent commitment to peer expectations. Upper-class respondents were significantly less committed than others to the expectations of their peers, delinquent or nondelinquent. But, in addition, there was some suggestion that it was the middle- rather than the low-class group which had the greatest commitment of all.

The data would definitely not support the notion that peer standards have more importance for the low- than the middle-class juvenile. In fact, these findings might lead one to hypothesize that, because they are departing perhaps even further from the expectations of their parents than low-class children, middle-class offenders have greater need for peer support than low-class offenders.

Delinquent associates and peer commitment variables proved to be far more predictive of delinquent behavior than did social class. As a part of an overall pattern, it strongly implied the need to examine more carefully the role of peers, as contrasted to class, in attempting to understand delinquency.

The need for qualification is always present. There are two ways in which this need is apparent here. In the first place, the sample was drawn in a Western State and from relatively small communities. Therefore, the fact that delinquency and commitment to peers showed up so strongly among the middle-class group might come as some surprise.

Appendix 1–E

EFFECTS OF MASS MEDIA PORTRAYALS OF VIOLENCE

1. GENERAL CONCLUSIONS

1. The weight of social science stands in opposition to the conclusion that mass media portrayals of violence have no effect upon individuals, groups, and society.
2. To the extent that mass media portrayals of violence have effects upon individuals, groups, and society, it is a variety that most persons would deem costly and harmful to individuals and society.
3. The direction of effects of mass media portrayals of violence is to extend the behaviorial and attitudinal boundaries of acceptable violence beyond legal and social norms currently espoused by a majority of Americans.

a. *Short-run effects*

1. Exposure to mass media portrayals of violence stimulates violent behavior when—
   - (a) Subjects are either calm or anxious prior to exposure, but more so when they are not frustrated, insulted, or otherwise angered.
   - (b) Aggressive or violent cues are presented (e.g., weapons of violence).
   - (c) Subjects are exposed either to justified or unjustified violence, but more so when justified violence is portrayed.
2. The weight of relevant research evidence throws doubt on the tenability of the "catharsis" hypothesis.
3. Audiences exposed to mass media portrayals of violence learn how to perform violent acts.
4. Audiences who have learned violent behavior from the mass media are likely to exhibit that learning (i.e., engage in acts of violence) if they encounter a situation similar to the portrayal situation, expect to be rewarded for violent behavior, or do not observe disapproving reactions to the portrayed aggression from another person in the viewing situation.

These are the conclusions from the staff report: Robert H. Baker and Sandra J. Ball, *Violence and the Media*, 9, National Commission on the Causes and Prevention of Violence (November 1969), pp. 375–379.

b. *Long-run effects*

The following statements contain hypotheses which are clearly consistent with and suggested by established research findings and by the most informed social science thinking about the long-run effects of exposure to mass media portrayals of violence.

1. Exposure to mass media portrayals of violence over a long period of time socializes audiences into the norms, attitudes, and values for violence contained in those portrayals. The probability of socialization increases as —
   (a) The duration of exposure increases;
   (b) The intensity of exposure increases (e.g., number of hours per day);
   (c) The age of the viewer decreases;
   (d) The number of other sources of socialization into violence decreases;
   (e) The number of senses stimulated by the medium increases (e.g., sight or sound);
   (f) The primacy of the part played by violence in media presentations increases.
2. Persons who have been effectively socialized by mass media portrayals of violence will under a broad set of precipitating conditions behave in accordance with the norms, attitudes, and values for violence contained in media presentations. Persons who have been effectively socialized into the norms for violence contained in the television world of violence would behave in the following manner:
   (a) They would probably resolve conflict by the use of violence.
   (b) They would probably use violence as a means to obtain desired ends.
   (c) They would probably passively observe violence between others.
   (d) They would not be likely to sanction or punish others' use of violence.
   (e) They would probably use a weapon when engaging in violence.
   (f) If they were policemen, they would be likely to meet violence with violence, often escalating its level.
3. Persons exposed to mass media portrayals of violence over a long period of time are influenced by their exposure, especially when:
   (a) The mass media are the sole or major sources of information about violence.
   (b) There is ambiguity in the communities' norms for violence.
   (c) There is ambiguity in audience members' minds about the violent or relatively non-violent character of groups which are portrayed.
4. Persons influenced by the television world of violence would be influenced in at least the following ways:
   (a) Development of more positive attitudes toward violence as a means to fulfillment of individual ends.
   (b) Support and extension of the attitude that young men can enhance their masculinity by displaying proficiency in the use of violence.
   (c) Lowering the value of non-violent means of problem-solving.
   (d) Development of the attitude that it is not the responsibility of individual citizens to help each other out of violent situations.

(e) Development of and support for the belief that policemen are as violent as criminals.

(f) Development of and support for the attitude that successful people may not break the law as they please.

5. Distinctions between fantasy and reality presentations of media violence are not consistently perceived by child audiences.
6. Appearance in the media confers status upon those appearing, regardless of their portrayed behavior.
7. Long-term exposure to mass media portrayals of violence may make audience members insensitive or emotionally neutral in response to real acts of violence.
8. Long-term exposure to mass media portrayals of violence in which the physical, psychological, and social effects of violence are not realistically shown can lower inhibitions against the use of violence.
9. The effects of long-term exposure to goreless, unrealistic portrayals of violence and gory realistic presentations are probably both conducive to lowering emotional reactions to violence, making the audience more likely to use violence and to passively tolerate violence by others. There is some reason to suggest that periodic presentations of gory, realistic, violence would have more salutory effects than either completely unrealistic and goreless or realistic and gory portrayals.
10. The extent and intensity of mass media portrayals of violence, especially in the case of television, probably have the effect of creating and/or supporting a view of the world as totally violent. Such a world view tends to promote widespread toleration of violence, a feeling that it is hopeless to try to control violence, and the belief that individuals must be violent in order to survive in a violent world.
11. The high value placed upon action, immediacy, and simple resolution of problems in the mass media works against the idea that one should react to problems and conflict by deliberation and communication.
12. To the extent that mass media portrayals of violence contain rigid "good-guy"–"bad-guy," right–wrong, and other either–or distinctions, young audiences are likely to develop and maintain psychological rigidity characteristic of adolescence.
13. Inaccurate portrayals of class, ethnic, racial, and occupational groups in mass media presentations retard productive communication between groups. To the extent that certain groups are portrayed as violent, members of those groups may emulate their portrayal, while non-members may react with fear, hatred, and other emotions conducive to intergroup conflict and violence. The effects of these portrayals are especially potent when members of those groups have no direct personal contact with one another.

2. TELEVISION AND VIOLENCE

1. Of all the mass media, television portrayals of violence have the greatest potential for short and long term effects upon audiences.

(a) The combined properties of audiovisual stimulation and the home-viewing environment make television the most authentic appearing of the mass media.

(b) Commercial television is the most frequently used mass medium for entertainment.

(c) Television plays a more central and pervasive role in the total comunication of modern society than any other mass medium.

(d) Television more than any other mass medium, is re-shaping the traditional definitional and socializing activities of political, economic, educational, recreational, and religious institutions.

2. The television world of violence:[1]

(a) Is not an accurate reflection of the real world of violence as experienced by adult and teenage Americans;

(b) Is not what the majority of adult and teenage Americans want;

(c) Is the primary source of exposure to severe acts of violence for the majority of Americans;

(d) Constitutes the vast majority of network entertainment (eighty-one percent of all programs analyzed for 1967, and eighty-two percent of all programs analyzed for 1968 contain violence), the majority of every type of programming (e.g. cartoon comedy), and has not significantly changed from 1967 to 1968;

(e) Is dominated by norms for violence which are inconsistent with those espoused by a mjaority of adult and teenage Americans;

(f) Explicitly and implicitly portrays norms for violence which are most similar to a minority of adult and teenage Americans who—

i. Have the experience with violence as victims, assailants, and observers;

ii. Have the strongest preference for violence in mass media presentations;

iii. Use commercial television more than any other mass medium entertainment;

iv. Are the most similar in age and sex to violent characters in the television world of violence (young to middle-aged males).

A representative sample of adult Americans was asked whether or not television violence has a series of effects. The series contains an equal number of "positive" and "negative" effects, and these six represent the best-known hypotheses concerning the effects of mass media.

The responses given by adult Americans are presented in table 1–E–1.

[1]The Television World of Violence consists of all programs containing violence which were broadcast during the week of October 1–7, in 1967 and 1968 during prime-time viewing hours. This week of programming has been shown to be typical of all weeks of programming in both 1967 and 1968. (See Michael Eleey, "Variations in Generalizability resulting from Sampling Characteristics of Content Analysis Data: A Case Study," unpublished master's thesis, Annenberg School of Communications, University of Pennsylvania, 1964.)

Table 1–E–1. Adult American judgments on the effect of TV violence

	In Percent		
	Likely or possible	Unlikely	Not sure
1. Plays a part in making America a violent society	75	20	5
2. Triggers violent acts from people who are maladjusted and mentally unstable	86	8	6
3. Makes people insensitive to real acts of violence that they hear about or see	60	31	9
4. Allows viewers to blow off steam by watching violence, thus decreasing the likelihood of their being violent	44	45	11
5. Provides entertainment and relaxation without harmful or bad effects	62	32	6
6. Supports and strengthens traditional American values	34	52	14

The judgments of a majority of adult Americans are in substantial agreement with the conclusions drawn by the Mass Media and Violence Task Force concerning the effects of mass media portrayals of violence. These judgments do not validate or add any scientific support to the findings and conclusions presented, but they do demonstrate the widespread concern that adults express about the effects of television violence.

Appendix 1–F

THE WATTS RIOT

The 5-day riot that began on Wednesday, August 11, 1965, in the South Central Los Angeles ghetto (the area of which the Watts neighborhood is a small part) has probably been more carefully examined than any riot that has ever occurred. The McCone Commission, appointed by the Governor of California to make a general report on the riot, held 60 formal hearings during which it received sworn testimony from 80 witnesses; it interviewed 90 of those arrested during the riot; and it opened an office in the riot area so that members of its staff could interview local residents. The Bureau of Criminal Statistics of the California Department of Justice made a detailed statistical study of the 3,927 people arrested during the riot.

The Watts riot was, of course, different from the other riots of the last three summers in several ways; no two riots are exactly alike. The most striking difference was its extreme violence and destructiveness. Thirty-four people were killed and 1,032 injured. Two hundred buildings were burned to the ground and 720 more looted or damaged; the total property loss was estimated at $40 million. The resources of the Los Angeles Police Department, the Los Angeles Fire Department, the Los Angeles County Sheriff's Department, and the California Highway Patrol were so overtaxed that 13,400 troops of the California National Guard were finally committed to controlling the riot.

South Central Los Angeles does not look any more like Harlem than the Sunset Strip looks like Times Square, but in that the conditions of life there compare unfavorably in all essential respects with those in the rest of the city, it is a typical ghetto. The density of population is greater. The unemployment rate is higher. The average income is lower. The housing is in worse repair. The average educational achievement is less. The crime rate is higher. The hostility toward the police is greater. And, perhaps the crux of the matter, those residents who have the means and the desire to move to better neighborhoods have only limited opportunities to do so, a fact of which they must be acutely aware; in 1964 the voters of California overwhelmingly repealed by referendum a State fair housing law. It is not too fanciful to compare a district like South Central Los Angeles to a heap of inflammable material that has been carelessly left, out

The President's Commission on Law Enforcement and Administration of Justice, *Task Force Report: Crime and its Impact—An Assessment* (Washington, D.C.: U.S. Government Printing Office, 1967), pp. 118–122.

of sight and mind, in an obscure corner of a cellar or an attic; the feeblest, most random spark can ignite it and sometimes does.

Certainly the spark that ignited Watts was feeble and random. At about 7 p.m. on August 11, a day on which the temperature reached 94°, a Negro driving a pickup truck in a portion of South Central Los Angeles that is outside the city limits called the attention of a white California highway patrolman to the reckless way in which an old gray Buick was being driven north (toward the city limits) on Avalon Boulevard. The patrolman followed the Buick on his motorcycle and determined that it was going 50 miles an hour in a 35-mile-an-hour zone. He turned on his red light and siren pulled alongside the car and ordered the driver to the curb. The driver, a 21-year-old Negro named Marquette Frye, obeyed at once and without demur. He was evidently drunk and he did not have a driver's license. The patrolman told him he was under arrest and radioed for his backup officer and a transport car to come and help him place Frye in custody. Both arrived promptly. Meanwhile 20 or 30 passersby and residents of nearby buildings had gathered to watch the scene, apparently purely for entertainment. There was no sign of trouble. The patrolman was friendly and polite. Frye was good humored, even jocular.

Suddenly the situation changed. Vociferously and belligerently Frye refused to get into the transport car. The officers attempted to handcuff him. He resisted. The spectators became sullen and hostile. The officers radioed for more help. Frye's stepbrother, who had been riding in the car, and his mother, who owned the car and who had hastened to the scene when a neighbor told her what was happening, came to Frye's assistance. More highway patrolmen and members of the Los Angeles Police Department arrived. The size of the crowd increased. Frye was forcibly subdued, and put in the car. The spectators who by then numbered several hundred, hurled abuse at the police, who by then numbered about 50. Finally the police, with the three Fryes as prisoners, managed to disengage themselves from the crowd and leave the scene, under a shower of rocks and bricks and bottles. In the course of doing so they made another arrest, of a young woman who, according to the police, was spitting and cursing at them and, according to herself, was doing nothing more than talking and giggling. She was a barber and was wearing her professional smock, which gave rise to an impression that the police had manhandled a pregnant woman; a report of this instance of "police brutality" spread through the ghetto area, and as it spread it became a rumor that the police had beaten and kicked Frye's pregnant mother. The crowd did not disperse after the police left. On the contrary, it stayed on Avalon Boulevard, which is a main thoroughfare through South Central Los Angeles, and bombarded passing motorists with whatever missiles were avilable. Meanwhile angry groups began assembling in other parts of the ghetto. The riot was on.

What is most suggestive—and alarming—about the events that began the Watts riot is the chain of accident and chance. The highway patrolman, responding to a complaint by a Negro citizen, had more than sufficient cause to arrest Frye, and he went about his business with efficiency and propriety. The act for which Frye was arrested, driving drunkenly and recklessly on a main city thoroughfare, could not possibly be interpreted as either a harmless lapse or as a gesture of protest, conscious or unconscious, against white oppression. Frye was not an agitator or a militant; there is not even reason to believe that he was an especially aggrieved young man. The people who first gathered to watch the scene were not looking for trouble, but for amusement. The particular police force against which there was the most antagonism in South Central Los Angeles was not the California Highway Patrol but the Los Angeles Police Department. If the highway patrolmen doing what they did could precipitate a catastrophe like Watts, it is surely safe to say that almost anything might have precipitated it. Central Los Angeles was ready and willing—and perhaps even eager—to run amok.

That the Watts riot was a general outbreak in which all kinds of people took part—not just agitators or adolescents or criminals or new arrivals in town or the unemployed or "riff-raff"—is indicated by all the available information about the participants. The California Department of Justice's statistical analysis of those arrested in connection with the riot makes this case strongly. Of the 3,927 people arrested by the Los Angeles Police Department, the Los Angeles Sheriff's Office, the Compton and Long Beach Police Departments, and the California Highway Patrol the large majority, of course, were Negro men and boys; 3,609 were Negroes and 3,409 were males. But beyond these unsurprising figures there are some surprises. The rioters, to the extent that those arrested were a cross section of those who rioted, were not mostly adolescents or young adults. Only 556 were legally juveniles (under 18), while 2,111 were over 25; 602 were over 40. They were not predominantly people with serious criminal histories; 1,113 had no arrest records at all, and of the adults, 965 of those who had been arrested previously had not been convicted. At the other end of the spectrum, 363 adults had served prison terms on criminal convictions, and 52 juveniles had a record of institutional commitment. Considering the fact that a Negro male who grows up in a slum has something like a 75-percent chance of being arrested during his lifetime, these figures suggest that the Watts rioters were drawn from all parts of the community.

The results of the UCLA survey point in the same direction. They indicate that roughly 20 percent of the Negroes in the area actually did participate more or less actively in the riot, and that the general impression in the area was that many more people than that took part; more than 50 percent, by consensus. A more detailed breakdown of the circumstances of those who reported to interviewers that they were active fail to show significant differences between them and those who were inactive, in respect to place of origin, length of residence in Los Angeles, degree of education, importance of religion in childhood, or self-classified social class. For example, 28.6 percent of those who said they were lower class were active; 20.4 percent of those who said they were working class; 23.5 percent of those who said they were middle class; and 15.7 percent of those who said they were upper class. Findings of this sort are not conclusive, of course. For one thing they are based on information volunteered after the riot and not on direct observation at the time of the riot, for another, precise questions about kinds of riot activity could not be asked because the interviewers could not guarantee the interviewees immunity from prosecution. They do not *prove* that the rioters were a faily representative cross section of the males in the community, but they do suggest it.

A final indication that the riot was not the work of a tiny extremist or criminal minority is the reaction to the riot that the UCLA interviewers found among the Negroes in the area. More than half, 57.9 percent, said that its long-run effects would be favorable; 83.9 percent said that whites were now more aware of Negro problems; 64.4 percent said the victims of the riot deserved being attacked; 61.9 percent said the riot was a Negro protest; 9.9 percent even said that "everyone" in the area supported the riot. In sum, the riot was looked upon favorably by many people from every section of the community, an attitude that again suggests that participation in it was probably representative.

In summary, the Watts riot appears to have been caused by no one set of people or conditions or grievances. It was a manifestation of a general sense of deep outrage, outrage at every aspect of the lives Negroes are forced to live, outrage at every element of the white community for forcing (or permitting) Negroes to live such lives. According to 56.1 percent of the Negroes interviewed in the course of the UCLA survey, the riot had a "purpose." This purpose, according to more than half of those who said there was one, was to express (in the survey's words) "hostility, resentment, revenge." As has already been noted almost two-thirds of the Negroes interviewed said the victims had deserved the attacks upon them. If the quality of life for so many Americans in Los Angeles, and undoubtedly in other cities as well, is such that they are filled with hostility, resentment, and a desire for revenge, there may be more cause for surprise over how few riots there have been than over how many. And in any case it is surely intolerable for hundreds of thousands, or millions, of Americans to have cause to feel that way, whether or not they riot.

Appendix 1–G

SELECTIVE FINDINGS ON CIVIL DISORDERS IN THE UNITED STATES DURING 1967

We found a common social process operating in all 24 disorders in certain critical respects. These events developed similarly, over a period of time and out of an accumulation of grievances and increasing tension in the Negro community. Almost invariably, they exploded in ways related to the local community and its particular problems and conflicts. But once violence erupted, there began a complex interaction of many elements—rioters, official control forces, counterrioters—in which the differences between various disorders were more pronounced than the similarities. [p. 67.]

Our examination of the background of the surveyed disorders revealed a typical pattern of deeply held grievances which were widely shared by many members of the Negro community. The specific content of the expressed grievances varied somewhat from city to city. But in general, grievances among Negroes in all the cities related to prejudice, discrimination, severely disadvantaged living conditions, and a general sense of frustration about their inability to change those conditions.

Specific events or incidents exemplified and reinforced the shared sense of grievance. News of such incidents spread quickly throughout the community and added to the reservoir. Grievances about police practices, unemployment and underemployment, housing, and other objective conditions in the ghetto were aggravated in the minds of many Negroes by the inaction of municipal authorities.

Out of this reservoir of grievance and frustration, the riot process began in the cities which we surveyed. [p. 68.]

In virtually every case a single "triggering" or "precipitating" incident can be identified as having immediately preceded—within a few hours and in generally the same location—the outbreak of disorder. But this incident was usually a relatively minor, even trivial one, by itself substantially disproportionate to the scale of violence that followed. Often it was an incident of a type which had occurred frequently in the same community in the past without provoking violence.

We found that violence was generated by an increasingly disturbed social atmosphere, in which typically not one, but a series of incidents occurred over a period of weeks or months prior to the outbreak of disorder. Most cities had three or more such

Report of the National Advisory Commission on Civil Disorders (Washington, D.C · U.S. Government Printing Office, March 1, 1968), pp. 67, 68, 71, 73–74, 77, and 89.

incidents; Houston had 10 over a 5-month period. These earlier or prior incidents were linked in the minds of many Negroes to the preexisting reservoir of underlying grievances. With each such incident, frustration and tension grew until at some point a final incident, often similar to the incidents preceding it, occurred and was followed almost immediately by violence.

As we see it, the prior incidents and the reservoir of underlying grievances contributed to a cumulative process of mounting tension that spilled over into violence when the final incident occurred. In this sense the entire chain—the grievances, the series of prior tension-heightening incidents, and the final incident—was the "precipitant" of disorder. [p. 68.]

In all 24 disturbances, including the three university-related disorders, the initial disturbance area consisted of streets with relatively high concentrations of pedestrian and automobile traffic at the time. In all but two cases—Detroit and Milwaukee—violence started between 7 p.m. and 12:30 a.m., when the largest numbers of pedestrians could be expected. Ten of the 24 disorders erupted on Friday night, Saturday, or Sunday.

In most instances, the temperature during the day on which violence first erupted was quite high. This contributed to the size of the crowds on the street, particularly in areas of congested housing.

Major violence occurred in all 24 disorders during the evening and night hours, between 6 p.m. and 6 a.m., and in most cases between 9 p.m. and 3 a.m. In only a few disorders, including Detroit and Newark, did substantial violence occur or continue during the daytime. Generally, the night-day cycles continued in daily succession through the early period of the disorder.

At the beginning of disorder, violence generally flared almost immediately after the final precipitating incident. It then escalated quickly to its peak level, in the case of 1-night disorders, and to the first night peak in the case of continuing disorders. . . .

Nineteen of the surveyed disorders lasted more than 1 night. In 10 of these, violence peaked on the first night, and the level of activity on subsequent nights was the same or less. In the other nine disorders, however, the peak was reached on a subsequent night.

Disorder generally began with less serious violence against property, such as rock- and bottle-throwing and window-breaking. These were usually the materials and the targets closest to hand at the place of the initial outbreak.

Once store windows were broken, looting usually followed. Whether fires were set only after looting occurred is unclear. Reported instances of fire-bombing and Molotov cocktails in the 24 disorders appeared to occur as frequently during one cycle of violence as during another in disorders which continued through more than one cycle. However, fires seemed to break out more frequently during the middle cycles of riots lasting several days. Gunfire and sniping were also reported more frequently during the middle cycles. [p. 71.]

Only partial information is available on the total numbers of participants. In the Detroit survey, approximately 11 percent of the sampled residents over the age of 15 in the two disturbance areas admittedly participated in rioting; another 20 to 25 percent admitted to having been bystanders but claimed that they had not participated; approximately 16 percent claimed they had engaged in counterriot activity; and the largest proportion (48 to 53 percent) claimed they were at home or elsewhere and did not participate. However, a large proportion of the Negro community apparently believed that more was gained than lost through rioting, according to the Newark and Detroit surveys. [p. 73.]

The typical rioter in the summer of 1967 was a Negro, unmarried male between the ages of 15 and 24. He was in many ways very different from the stereotype. He was not a migrant. He was born in the state and was a lifelong resident of the city in which the riot took place. Economically his position was about the same as his Negro neighbors who did not actively participate in the riot.

Although he had not, usually, graduated from high school, he was somewhat better educated than the average inner-city Negro, having at least attended high school for a time.

Nevertheless, he was more likely to be working in a menial or low status job as an unskilled laborer. If he was employed, he was not working full time and his employment was frequently interrupted by periods of unemployment.

He feels strongly that he deserves a better job and that he is barred from achieving it, not because of lack of training, ability, or ambition, but because of discrimination by employers.

He rejects the white bigot's stereotype of the Negro as ignorant and shiftless. He takes great pride in his race and believes that in some respects Negroes are superior to whites. He is extremely hostile to whites, but his hostility is more apt to be a product of social and economic class than of race; he is almost equally hostile toward middle-class Negroes.

He is substantially better informed about politics than Negroes who were not involved in the riots. He is more likely to be actively engaged in civil rights efforts, but is extremely distrustful of the political system and of political leaders. [pp. 73–74.]

The typical counterrioter, who risked injury and arrest to walk the streets urging rioters to "cool it," was an active supporter of existing social institutions. He was, for example, far more likely than either the rioter or the noninvolved to feel that this country is worth defending in a major war. His actions and his attitudes reflected his substantially greater stake in the social system; he was considerably better educated and more affluent than either the rioter or the noninvolved. He was somewhat more likely than the rioter, but less likely than the noninvolved, to have been a migrant. In all other respects he was identical to the noninvolved. [p. 74.]

In the riot cities we surveyed, we found that Negroes were severely disadvantaged, especially as compared with whites; that local government is often unresponsive to this fact; that Federal programs have not yet reached a significantly large proportion of those in need; and that these facts create a reservoir of unredressed grievances and frustration in the ghetto. [p. 77.]

On the basis of all the information collected, the Commission concludes that the urban disorders of the summer of 1967 were not caused by, nor were they the consequence of, any organized plan or "conspiracy." Specifically, the Commission has found no evidence that all or any of the disorders or the incidents that led to them were planned or directed by any organization or group—international, national, or local.

Militant organizations, local and national, and individual agitators, who repeatedly forecast and called for violence, were active in the spring and summer of 1967. We believe that they deliberately sought to encourage violence, and that they did have an effect in creating an atmosphere that contributed to the outbreak of disorder.

Appendix 1–H

HISTORICAL AND POLITICAL PERSPECTIVES ON COLLECTIVE VIOLENCE

Over the long run, the processes most regularly producing collective violence are those by which groups acquire or lose membership in the political community. The form and locus of collective violence therefore vary greatly depending on whether the major ongoing political change is a group's acquisition of the prerequisites of membership, its loss of those prerequisites, or a shift in the organization of the entire political system. [Vol. 1, p. 10.]

Primitive varieties of collective violence include the feud, the brawl among members of rival guilds or communes, and the mutual attacks of hostile religious groups. (Banditry, as E. J. Hobsbawm has said, stands at the edge of this category by virtue of its frequent direction against the existing distribution of power and wealth, and its frequent origin in the state's creation of outlaws as part of the attempt to extend legal authority to formerly ungoverned areas.) Primitive forms of collective violence share several features: small-scale, local scope, participation by members of communal groups as such, inexplicit and unpolitical objectives. [Vol. 1, p. 12.]

The modern varieties of political disturbance (to use another tendentious term) involve specialized associations with relatively well-defined objectives, organized for political or economic action. Such disturbances can easily reach a large scale. Even more clearly than in the case of reactionary collective violence, they have a tendency to develop from collective actions that offer a show of force but are not intrinsically violent. The demonstration and the violent strike are the two clearest examples, but the coup and most forms of guerrilla also qualify. These forms deserve to be called "modern" not only because of their organizational complexity but also because the participants commonly regard themselves as striking for rights due them, but not yet enjoyed. They are, that is, forward looking. [Vol. 1, p. 19.]

A cursory glance at the histories of Western Europe and the United States during

Excerpts from two staff reports of the National Commission on the Causes and Prevention of Violence. The first set of excerpts have been taken from: Hugh Davis Graham and Ted Robert Gurr, *Violence in America: Historical and Comparative Perspectives*, 1 and 2 (Washington, D.C.: U.S. Government Printing Office, June 1969). The second set of excerpts have been taken from Jerome Skolnick, *The Politics of Protest: Violent Aspects of Protest and Confrontation*, 3 (Washington, D.C.: U.S. Government Printing Office, 1969).

the past two centuries suggests that working-class demands for resolution of economic and related political grievances have been the most common and persistent source of turmoil, if not of revolution or civil war. [Vol. 1, p. 193.]

The United States has had the bloodiest and most violent labor history of any industrial nation in the world. Labor violence was not confined to certain industries, geographic areas, or specific groups in the labor force, although it has been more frequent in some industries than in others. There have been few sections and scarcely any industries in which violence has not erupted at some time, and even more serious confrontations have on occasion followed. Native and foreign workers, whites and blacks have at times sought to prevent strike replacements from taking their jobs, and at other times have themselves been the object of attack. With few exceptions, labor violence in the United States arose in specific situations, usually during a labor dispute. The precipitating causes have been attempts by pickets and sympathizers to prevent a plant on strike from being reopened with strikebreakers, or attempts of company guards, police, or even by National Guardsmen to prevent such interference. [Vol. 1, p. 221.]

Racial violence in the 20th century has undergone a fundamental transformation. Innterracial riots in the early years of the century were essentially pogroms in which the Negroes were victims of white aggression. In the 1960's the Negroes have been the aggressors; however, in contrast to the earlier riots, deaths have been few, the attacks being concentrated on property rather than persons. Deaths have occurred primarily as the result of conflict between police and Negro civilians, rather than between Negro and white civilians, as had been the case in the early-20th century. . . . First, 50 years ago, the typical race riot in American cities was an interracial clash on the boundaries of expanding black neighborhoods, one in which whites more often than Negroes took offensive action. Second, during World War II, these communal clashes began to give way to large-scale riots, wholly within the black community. Often triggered by a police incident, the outbursts resulted in a clash between the local population and officers and agents of the larger society, with implied overtones of political protest. Because the outbursts resulted in widespread looting, they can be described as commodity riots. Third, by the summer of 1968, however, this form of racial violence appeared to be in decline, being replaced by a new form: a more selective, terroristic use of force against whites by small, organized groups of blacks with crude ideological motives. [Vol. 2, pp. 304–305.]

One can identify perhaps two major factors responsible for this contrast between the old-style and the new-style riot. One is the relatively marked shift in the climate of race relations in this country over the past generation. On the one hand, whites have become, on the whole, more sensitive to the Negro's plight, more receptive toward Negro demands, and less punitive in their response to Negro aggression. The black masses, on the other hand, have raised their expectations markedly and, disillusioned by the relatively slow pace of social change which has left the underprivileged urban Negro of the North scarcely, if at all, better off than he was 10 or 15 years ago, have become more restless and militant than before. [Vol. 2, pp. 311–312.]

During World War II, the pattern of rioting underwent a transformation which took full form with outbreaks in Harlem and Brooklyn in 1964, in Watts in 1965, and in Newark and Detroit in 1967. For lack of a better term, there has been a metamorphosis from "communal" riots to "commodity" riots. . . . Most important, it was a riot that started within the Negro community, not at the periphery. It did not involve a confrontation between white and Negro civilians. It was an outburst against property and retail establishments, plus looting—therefore the notion of the commodity riot in the Negro community. These establishments were mainly owned by outside white proprietors. The deaths and casualities resulted mainly from the use of force against the Negro population by police and National Guard units. Some direct and active participation by white civilians may take place in such a riot, as was the case in Detroit in 1967, but this is a minor element. [Vol. 2, p. 321.]

Although there are numerous statistical and methodological weaknesses in the various analyses of the arrest data and sample surveys, the findings are relevant for describing the social characteristics of the rioters. All sources agree that women were a significant minority of the activists in the commodity riots, reflecting a broadening of the base of involvement as contrasted with the communal riots, which were mainly a men's affair. Interestingly enough, the police tended to arrest few women, either because their infractions of the law were minor or because they believed that women were not at the core of the riot.

As expected, the bulk of the rioters were young males between the ages of 15 and 34 whose skill levels were low. . . . Clearly, these data indicate that the activists were not a tiny minority of chronic law offenders nor highly unrepresentative in terms of selected social background characteristics. The full personal and social dynamics will probably never be adequately described, for involvement relates not merely to the demographic and social characteristics but to the patterns of primary and informal group structures of the ghetto community, as well as social personality and attitude. Some clues can be drawn from the observation of various surveys that the participants over-represented single men, who frequently lived outside of family units. These were persons who were less subject to the informal group structure linked to family life and more to informal street and community life. [Vol. 2, p. 326.]

Escalated rioting and the rioting of commodity looting appeared in 1967 to be giving way to more specific, more premeditated, and more regularized uses of force. It was as if the rioters learned the lesson emphasized in the mass media, that mass destruction achieves too few tangible benefits. New outbursts appeared to be more goal directed. . . . The participants were likely to be persons who have taken part in previous outbursts. There was an element of organization, at least to the extent that activists are concerned with personal survival and avoidance of the police. There was an element of organization to the extent that the target seems to be selected, and the patterns repeated for a specific purpose. The local school was a particular target. The form of violence can be the harassment of a group of white schoolteachers active in union work, an assault on teacher picket lines during a strike, or a small-scale outburst at the neighborhood schoolyard and on occasion sniper fire against police. Housing projects, especially integrated housing projects, were repeatedly subject to rifle fire and fire bombing. These incidents are created for the purpose of developing solidarity in local gangs and in paramilitary groups. . . . Dramatic manifestations of the third phase of political violence, or conspiratorial violence, were the shootouts which occurred with police personnel during the summer of 1968 in New York City, Cleveland, Pittsburgh, Oakland, Los Angeles, and elsewhere. [Vol. 2, pp. 331–332.]

Probably the most important cause of major increases in group violence is the widespread frustration of socially deprived expectations about the goods and conditions of life men believe theirs by right. These frustratable expectations relate not only to material well-being but to more intangible conditions such as security, status, freedom to manage one's own affairs, and satisfying personal relations with others. [Vol. 2, p. 631.]

Mass protest is an essentially political phenomenon engaged in by normal people; that demonstrations are increasingly being employed by a variety of groups, ranging from students and blacks to middle-class professionals, public employees, and policemen; that violence, when it occurs, is usually not planned, but arises out of an interaction between protesters and responding authorities; that violence has frequently accompanied the efforts of deprived groups to achieve status in American society; and that recommendations concerning the prevention of violence which do not address the issue of fundamental social and political change are fated to be largely irrelevant and frequently self-defeating. [Vol. 3, p. xxi.]

Rather, the results of our research suggest that mass protest is an outgrowth of social, economic and political conditions; that such violence as occurs is usually not planned, but arises out of an *interaction* between protesters and the reaction of authorities; and that recommendations concerning the prevention of violence which do not address the issue of fundamental social, economic and political change are fated to be largely irrelevant and frequently self-defeating. [Vol. 3, p. 3]

Almost uniformerly, the participants in mass protest today see their grievances as rooted in the existing arrangements of power and authority in contemporary society, and they view their own activity as political action—on a direct or symbolic level—aimed at altering those arrangements. A common theme, from the ghetto to the university, is the rejection of dependency and external control, a staking of new boundaries, and a demand for significant control over events within those boundaries. [Vol. 3, pp. 5–6.]

The number of participants in demonstrative protest seems to be increasing and includes an ever larger proportion of the members of society. Antiwar demonstrations in the United States, for example, are estimated to have grown almost continuously from the spring of 1965 to the spring of 1968. The student population, castigated in the 1950's as the "silent generation," produced at least 221 demonstrations in 101 colleges between January 1 and June 15, 1968, involving 38,911 participants, according to a study conducted by the National Student Association. [Vol. 3, pp. 14–15.]

The student movements in Latin America and Asia continue to function as part of a relatively long tradition of student activism; on the other hand, new student movements in the West have emerged in response to rather different problems and issues. Despite the differences among student movements in developed and underdeveloped countries, however, it is clear that a process of mutual influence is at work among them. For example, the white student movement in America received inspiration in its early stages from dramatic student uprisings in Japan, Turkey and South Korea. More recently, American activists have been influenced by street tactics learned from Japanese students and by ideological expressions emanating from France and West Germany. [Vol. 3, p. 67.]

Until recently, riots were regarded as the work of either outsiders or criminals. The "riff-raf" theory, as it is known, has three assumptions—that a small minority of the black population engages in riot activity, that this minority is composed of the unattached, uprooted, and unskilled, and that the overwhelming majority of the black population deplores riots. . . . Official investigations generally publicize the fact that normal, ordinary, and law-abiding persons do not instigate riots. According to the FBI, riots are typically instigated by a "demagogue or professional agitator" or by "impulsive individuals who are the first in the mob to take violent action or to keep it going when it wanes." Thus, "hoodlums" were responsible for the 1943 riot in Detroit, "marauding bands" of criminals in Watts, "a small fraction of the city's black population" in Chicago in 1968, and "self-appointed leaders, opportunists, and other types of activists" in Pittsburgh. . . . The "riff-raff" theory has been challenged by various studies. . . . The most convincing attack on this theory came from Fogelson's and Hill's study of participation in the 1967 riots which was published at the end of the Kerner Commission's supplemental studies. The authors found that (1) a substantial minority, ranging from 10 to 20 percent, participated in the riots, (2) one-half to three-quarters of the arrestees were employed in semi-skilled or skilled occupations, three-fourths were employed, and three-tenths to six-tenths were born outside the South, and (3) individuals between the ages of 15 and 34 and expecially those between the ages of 15 and 24 are most likely to participate in riots. [Vol. 3, pp. 110–111.]

Although it is far too early for certainty, limited evidence suggests that the massive ghetto riot—typified by the uprisings in Watts, Newark, and Detroit—may be a thing of the past. None of the disorders of 1968 matches these in scope. The specific explanation for this is far from clear. It lies somewhere in the interaction between more massive and immediate "riot control" efforts by authorities and the apparent perception by many blacks that the "spontaneous riot," as a form of political protest, is too costly in terms of black lives. It is clear that some militant ghetto organizations, such as the Blackstone Rangers in Chicago and the Black Panther Party in Oakland, have made direct and markedly successful efforts to "cool" their communities, especially in the wake of the King assassination. [Vol. 3, p. 128.]

In a study done under a grant from the Office of Law Enforcement Assistance of the United States Department of Justice, and submitted to the President's Commission on Law Enforcement and the Administration of Criminal Justice in 1966, Donald J. Black and Albert J. Reiss, Jr. found overwhelming evidence of widespread, virulent prejudice by police against Negroes. [Vol. 3, p. 184.]

It seems clear that police prejudice impairs the capacity of the police to engage in impartial crowd control. If anything, the behavior which typifies day-to-day policing is magnified in riot situations. [Vol. 3, p. 185.]

On the basis of our interviews with police and a systematic study of police publications, we have found that a significant underpinning is what can best be described as a "rotten apple" theory of human nature. . . . Under this doctrine, crime and disorder are attributable mainly to the intentions of evil individuals; human behavior transcends past experience, culture, society, and other external forces and should be understood in terms of wrong choices, deliberately made. Significantly—and contrary to the teachings of all the behavioral sciences—social factors such as poverty, discrimination, inadequate housing, and the like are excluded from the analysis. . . . The "rotten apple" view of human nature puts the policeman at odds with the goals and aspirations of many of the groups he is called upon to police. For example, police often relegate social reforms to the category of "coddling criminals," or, in the case of recent ghetto programs, to "selling out" to trouble-makers. [Vol. 3, p. 195.]

Police militancy is hostile to the aspirations of other dissident groups in our society. Police view students, the anti-war protesters, and blacks as a danger to our political system, and racial prejudice pervades the police attitudes and actions. No government institution appears so deficient in its understanding of the constructive role of dissent in a constitutional democracy as the police. [Vol. 3, p. 215.]

We find conventional theories of riots open to challenge on the following counts:

1. They tend to focus on the destructive behavior of disaffected groups while accepting the behavior of authorities as normal, instrumental and rational. Yet established, thoroughly institutionalized behavior may be equally destructive, or considerably more so, than are riots. No riot, for example, matches the destructiveness of military solutions to disputed political issues. Further, available evidence suggests both that (a) armed officials often demonstrate a greater propensity to violence against persons than unarmed civilians: and (b) these actions often escalate the intensity of the disorder and comprise a good part of the "destructiveness" of riots, especially in terms of human deaths and injuries. . . .

2. They tend to describe collective behavior as irrational, formless, and immoderate. . . . A measure of irrationality, then, is not a defining characteristic of collective behavior generally or of riots in particular; rather, it is an element of many routine social processes and institutions *and* forms of collective behavior. The more significant difference may be that established institutions are usually in a more advantageous position from which to define "rationality." . . .

3. Finally, it is insufficient to analyze riots in terms of "tension" and "frustration." It is not that this perspective is wrong, but that it tells at once too little and too much. Too little, because the idea of "tension" or "strain" does not encompass the subjective meaning of objective impact of subordinate caste position or political domination. Too much, because it may mean almost anything; it is a catch-all phrase that can easily obscure the specificity of political grievances. [Vol. 3, pp. 255–256.]

Appendix 1–I

CLECKLEY'S CRITERIA FOR DIAGNOSING SOCIOPATHS

Note: The following 16 items represent a sort of checklist that physicians and clinicians might use in diagnosing sociopathic cases as distinct from clinical characteristics of psychotic and neurotic patients. The list is duplicated here merely to give the student of criminology some concrete indication of the direction of sociopathic behavior and to supplement the standard definition of sociopathy—as published by the American Psychiatric Association Diagnostic Manual (OO-X61)—that refers to "chronically antisocial individuals who are always in trouble, profiting neither from experience nor punishment, and maintaining no real loyalties to any persons, group, or code. They are frequently callous and hedonistic, showing marked emotional immaturity, with lack of sense of responsibility, lack of judgment and an ability to rationalize their behavior so that it appears warranted, reasonable, and justified."

---

1. Superficial charm and good "intelligence."
2. Absence of delusions and other signs of irrational thinking.
3. Absence of "nervousness" or psychoneurotic manifestations.
4. Unreliability.
5. Untruthfulness and insincerity.
6. Lack of remorse or shame.
7. Inadequately motivated antisocial behavior.
8. Poor judgment and failure to learn by experience.
9. Pathologic egocentricity and incapacity for love.
10. General poverty in major affective reactions.
11. Specific loss of insight.
12. Unresponsiveness in general interpersonal relations.
13. Fantastic and uninviting behavior with drink and sometimes without.
14. Suicide rarely carried out.
15. Sex life impersonal, trivial and poorly integrated.
16. Failure to follow any life plan.

Hervey M. Cleckley, *The Mask of Sanity*, 4th ed. (St. Louis, Mo.: Mosby, 1964), pp. 362–363.

Appendix 1–J

LYKKEN'S ANXIETY QUESTIONNAIRE

Note: This scale consists of 33 alternatives. The selection of the (a) alternative represents the choice of the lesser; of the (b), the greater frightening, embarrassing, or unpleasant happening. The scale is scored by counting the number of (b) responses. Scores of over 12 have been found to indicate a direction toward a "low" anxiety level and toward the sociopathic direction. Scores under 12 are in the direction of high anxiety and away from the sociopathic direction (i.e. greater sensitivity toward frightening, embarrassing, or unpleasant happenstances).

Directions: In each item below, there are two activities or occurrences listed. Many of them are more or less unpleasant. Imagine that, under normal circumstances, you were forced to do one or the other of each pair. Which one would you choose? Choose the one of each pair that you would rather do or have happen and write its letter (a or b) in the parentheses beside that item.

Example:

(_____) 0. (a) Hitting your thumb with a hammer; (b) Being run over by a train.

(_____) 1. (a) Having a gabby old woman sit down next to you on the bus; (b) Going out to dinner with someone for the first time.

(_____) 2. (a) Cleaning up a spilled bottle of syrup; (b) Knocking over a glass in a restaurant.

(_____) 3. (a) Having to cancel your vacation; (b) Standing on a ledge of the 25th floor of a building.

(_____) 4. (a) Having to "go out" with a visiting relative; (b) Having to introduce someone whose name you've forgotten.

(_____) 5. (a) Getting up to go to work in the morning; (b) Getting a Christmas present from someone you didn't give one to.

David T. Lykken, "A Study of Anxiety in the Sociopathic Personality," Ph.D. dissertation, University of Minnesota, 1955, pp. 124–125.

(______) 6. (a) Spending a week in solitary on bread and water; (b) Being broke and having to beg money on the street for a meal.

(______) 7. (a) Spending an evening with some boring people; (b) Being seen naked by a neighbor.

(______) 8. (a) Reading a dull book for a school report; (b) Getting a threatening letter.

(______) 9. (a) Losing some money through a hole in your pocket; (b) Being bawled out by a teacher.

(______) 10. (a) Whitewashing a long board fence; (b) Being called on in school.

(______) 11. (a) Putting 1000 names in alphabetical order; (b) Getting caught at something.

(______) 12. (a) Cleaning out a cesspool; (b) Having an accident with a borrowed car.

(______) 13. (a) Having to stay home every night for two weeks with a sick relative; (b) Falling down and breaking your arm.

(______) 14. (a) Being bossed around by someone for a full day; (b) Being in an air raid.

(______) 15. (a) Getting up to answer the phone and finding it's a wrong number; (b) Having to ask where the bathroom is at a party.

(______) 16. (a) Getting stuck in traffic when you're in a hurry; (b) Finding you've lost your bus-fare when it's time to pay and get off.

(______) 17. (a) Washing the dinner dishes; (b) Walking alone late at night.

(______) 18. (a) Just sitting around with nothing to do on Sunday afternoon; (b) Being introduced to some new people.

(______) 19. (a) Working all day when it's 90 in the shade; (b) Asking someone to pay you money that he owes you.

(______) 20. (a) Having to walk five miles for gas; (b) Having a tooth pulled by the dentist.

(______) 21. (a) Waiting for an overdue bus; (b) Having to complain to the neighbors about being too noisy.

(______) 22. (a) Carrying a ton of coal from the backyard into the basement; (b) Finding a dead body in an alley.

(______) 23. (a) Having a sick headache; (b) Having your name in the papers for drunken driving.

(______) 24. (a) Sewing on a button; (b) Being interviewed for a job.

(______) 25. (a) Memorizing something for a test in school; (b) Being sent to the principal's office when you were in school.

(______) 26. (a) Banging your head on a cabinet door; (b) Going to work or to school with a black eye.

(______) 27. (a) Changing a baby's diaper; (b) Going to a doctor for a physical.

(______) 28. (a) Digging a big rubbish pit; (b) Making a parachute jump.

(______) 29. (a) Having a friendly dog jump up on you with wet and muddy feet; (b) Bringing home a bad report card.

(______) 30. (a) Run a steam pressor in a laundry for a week; (b) Breaking a lamp at someone else's home.

(______) 31. (a) Walking a mile when it's 15 degrees below zero; (b) Swimming where sharks have been reported.

(______) 32. (a) Having the phone ring when you're taking a bath; (b) Having a barking dog run after you while you are walking along the street.

(______) 33. (a) Wanting to go out some night and not having any money; (b) Telling a lie to somebody.

Appendix 1–K

CHARACTERISTICS OF HOSTILE AND SIMPLE SOCIOPATHS

1. Heart Rate and Skin Resistance.

Physiologically, the two sociopath groups—the eight hostile (more aggressive) and the 11 simple (less aggressive)—differed significantly in heart rate under epinephrine. (It should be remembered that the two groups were identical on the other five criteria necessary for inclusion in the original sociopath group.) The low-Lykken or simple sociopath showed far greater reactivity to epinephrine than did the hostile sociopaths. The 11 simple (less aggressive) sociopaths experienced an increased heart rate of 12.3 beats per minute, as measured by the difference of the heart rate rise following epinephrine injection, minus that following saline injection. The other three groups of subjects—the eight hostile sociopaths, the 10 mixed, and the 14 non-sociopaths—only increased an average of about 6 beats per minute. The difference between the simple and the hostile sociopaths, despite the large standard deviations, falls at the .10 level ($t = 1.54$).[1]

On the other hand, no significant intergroup differences could be demonstrated in the mean palmar skin resistance under epinephrine, between any groups. This lack of difference is probably due to the instrumentation which provided a less precise measurement of skin response. Perhaps, this is why we failed to replicate Lykken's skin resistance findings.[2]

Harvey E. Allen, "Bio-Social Correlates of Two Types of Anti-social Psychopaths," Ph.D. dissertation, The Ohio State University, 1969, pp. 46–76.

[1]There are those who would argue for a stringent level of significance. The issue of level of significance still continues, but an extremely helpful series of suggestions as to choice of significance level is found in Sanford Labovitz, "Criteria For Selecting a Significance Level: A Note on the Sacredness of the .05," *The American Sociologist*, 3:3 (August 1968), pp. 220–222. This paper follows Labovitz's suggestions urging the use of larger error rates with small sample size and crude measurements. He is willing to accept the less serious consequence of making a Type II error (false positive).

[2]In this connection, it should be noted that much more sophisticated instruments are being used at the Ohio Reformatory for Women, and that even further refinement is anticipated in studies to follow.

2. Demographic Data.

That the simple and hostile sociopath subjects indeed represent different groups is also evident in their social background characteristics. The eight hostile sociopaths are two years younger on the average than the 11 simple sociopaths. There is very little difference between the groups of sociopaths in terms of race or rural-urban background. The hostile sociopaths, however, are very different in marital status, most being divorced or never married.

More often, too, the hostile sociopaths come from smaller families of procreation that do the simple sociopaths. The hostile sociopaths come from families with an average of 4.4 children while the average for the simple is 5.3. Hostile sociopaths marry on the average of less than half as frequently as the simple sociopaths; the average is .63 to 1.46, respectively. Furthermore, they have fewer children on the average. These latter two differences may be spurious because of the over two years average age difference. Even more important, the hostile sociopaths come from non-intact families as contrasted with simple sociopaths. Using intact to signify being reared by two parents until at least age 10, only 25 percent of the hostiles as compared to 73 percent of the simples were so reared. Both of these latter variables suggest that family configuration and familial variables might be etiologically significant.

Educationally, there is almost no difference at all between the two groups of sociopaths. Both averaged less than a 10th grade education. In terms of socio-economic status as measured by Reiss' occupational criteria,[3] the hostiles are somewhat lower in social class standing. Looking at their occupational histories, the hostiles, although much younger, held an average of 4.3 jobs since age 18, in contrast to 3.6 for the simples.

3. Military History.

In general, hostile sociopaths were more often than simple sociopaths, accepted by the armed forces. Those who were inducted, however, without exception, received less than honorable discharges. In this respect, they do not differ from the simple sociopaths, but are somewhat different from the mixed and markedly different from the non-sociopaths. Interestingly enough, the simple sociopaths, when they do serve, tend to be cashiered more quickly. This suggests that their anti-social behavior is either more frequent, more visible, or less tolerable. The hostile sociopaths, on the other hand, when accepted by the military, serve for an appreciably longer period of time. If the crimes for which they are generally convicted is an indicator, they perform the more aggressive acts leading to their dismissal from the military service.

4. Criminal Histories.

The criminal histories of the hostile and simple sociopaths are also different. The hostile sociopaths differ from the simple sociopaths on type of offense, especially on rape and

[3]Albert J. Reiss, Jr., *Occupation and Social Status* (New York: Free Press of Glencoe, 1964), p. 263.

larceny. Of the hostile sociopaths, 12.5 percent had been convicted for rape, while no simple sociopath had been so convicted. On the other hand, no hostile had been convicted of larceny, whereas 36.4 percent of the simples had been.

Hostile sociopaths experienced an average of more than five arrests each; simple sociopaths were arrested more than six times each. In contrast, non-sociopaths were arrested only an average of 2.9 times each. Not only are the two types of sociopath different in number of arrests, they are markedly different in number of times they have been incarcerated. The hostiles have averaged 2.8 incarcerations each, while the simple sociopaths have averaged 4.1 incarcerations.

Simple sociopaths have a somewhat higher frequency of counts on convictions (crimes for which they have been convicted and for which they are sentenced) than do hostile sociopaths. When, however, these rates are corrected for discrepancies in age, hostile sociopaths are convicted on more counts than are simple sociopaths. Furthermore, hostile sociopaths are convicted on relatively more counts of crime against the person than are simple sociopaths. It is for this reason that the high-Lykken Scale scorers are referred to as hostile sociopaths.

In addition, the hostile sociopaths averaged 55 months and the simple sociopaths 81 months in all incarcerations, both juvenile and adult. In terms of the average number of months incarcerated since age 18, the hostile sociopaths spent 50 months in prison and the simple sociopaths, 70 months. Controlling for age discrepancies does not alter these relationships. The simple sociopaths still averaged proportionately more time in prison.

As for parole violations, these too follow the same pattern. The hostiles have averaged 0.6 violations, while the simple sociopaths averaged over twice as many violations (1.36).

Despite their generally more lengthy criminal histories, the simple sociopaths were recommended for about the same level of custody and supervision as the hostile sociopaths, by the Classification Officers at the Ohio Penitentiary. As for their official diagnosis at intake, and surely most startling in view of their life histories, only three of the eight hostiles (37.5 percent) and three of the 11 simples (27.3 percent) were officially classified by the Psychological Services staff either as sociopaths or as exhibiting dyssocial reactions.

Finally, an examination of their escape attempts reveals that only one hostile subject was successful in escaping, and he did so on four different occasions. In contrast, two of the 11 simples were credited with one escape each.

5. *I.Q., Cleckley Checklist, and the Taylor Manifest Anxiety Scale.*

I.Q. was one of the screening criteria. Only inmates with an I.Q. of 100 or higher on the OPCT were accepted into the study. As a result, there was no difference in average I.Q. score of the hostiles and simples. Their means were 122 and 120, respectively. On the Cleckley Checklist, also one of the initial screening criteria, the two groups were largely indistinguishable. The Taylor Manifest Anxiety Scale scores for the two groups were significantly different. The hostile sociopaths averaged only 5.8, while the simple sociopaths averaged 10.2 on the scale. The scores corroborate the Lykken scores, since the Lykken purports to measure the propensity of subjects to choose anxiety or non-anxiety provoking activities. The high-Lykken subjects (hostile sociopaths) presumably select anxiety producing choices, because their level of anxiety is extremely low—an observation or interpretation observed on the Taylor Manifest Anxiety Scale.

6. MMPI Subscale Scores.

The corrected MMPI subscale scores were obtained from the Psychological Services case folders. The MMPI is one instrument which has been administered routinely by the administration staff to all new admissions with at least a sixth grade education. Following Schachter and Latané, who used the psychopathic deviation (Pd) minus the psychasthenia (Pt) subscale scores as one of their screening criteria, the same criterion was used in this study. In addition, however, all of the other subscales were examined and two in particular—the hypomania (Ma) and the social introversion (Si)—proved highly discriminating. Parenthetically, the Pt did not differentiate as expected. On all of the other subscales, no differentiation between the hostiles and the simples could be found.

The Pd subscale has been thought to be especially useful in prison and deliquent populations, who generally show marked elevation in scores as compared with non-criminal subjects:[4]

> "The scale was developed to reflect the concept of 'psychopathic deviancy,' which refers to people who are unable to form satisfactory emotional relationships or to appreciate the feelings of others and who cannot anticipate the consequences of their own behavior."

Research tends to confirm this latter point. On the scale, both sociopath groups showed considerable elevation, with the hostile showing by far the highest peak.

The hypomania (Ma) subscale, when taken in conjunction with the psychopathic deviate (Pd) subscale, is considered to be highly indicative of sociopathy. An examination of our results shows that this subscale differentiated the hostiles from the simples better than any other measure, except the Lykken Scale. The hostiles peaked some seven points higher than the simples.

The psychasthenia (Pt) subscale, ostensibly a measure of neurotic characteristics, unfortunately failed to differentiate the two groups. However, all 19 sociopaths were clearly differentiated from the non-sociopath subjects. This of course indicates some face validity to the subscale, but not enough sensitivity to differentiate between these two groups of sociopaths.

Finally, the social introversion (Si) subscale, purportedly measuring introversion-extroversion, and social adeptness, clearly distinguished the two sociopath categories. The hostile sociopaths peaked much lower, indicating greater facility and adequacy in interpersonal relations than the simples, whose scores were elevated.

[4] R. I. Lanyon, *A Handbook of MMPI Group Profiles* (Minneapolis: University of Minnesota Press, 1968), p. 7.

Based on this experience, future research ought to use a more complex combination of subscales. An MMPI expert has suggested that the hypomania (Ma) and psychopathic deviate (Pd) subscales (in t-scores) be utilized to separate the two types of sociopaths. Also recommended was the inclusion of the depression (D) subscale.

7. Correlation Matrix of Psychological Indicators of Sociopathy.

An analysis of the intercorrelations within each of the two groups of sociopaths of the Cleckley Checklist, psychopathic deviate (Pd), psychasthenia (Pt), and Lykken Scale (sociopathy) scores revealed marked differences in the size and directions of the intercorrelations. In the hostiles, the Cleckley Checklist was significantly negatively correlated with the Pd subscale. In the same group, the Pd and the Pt were significantly and positively correlated. The Lykken Scale was seemingly measuring something other than that which the other scales were measuring, based on its low intercorrelation values.

In the simple sociopaths, only the Pd subscale was significantly and positively intercorrelated with any of the other scales—in this instance, the psychasthenia (Pt) and the Lykken Scale.

In concluding this chapter, it should be stressed that although the whole emphasis has been on differentiating the sub-groups of sociopaths from one another, the two groups combined are even more different from the non-sociopaths in this study, and even from the mixed group, than they are from each other.

RESULTS: CONSECUTIVE ADMISSIONS

In the preceeding [statement], detailed examination was presented of the two groups of sociopaths who had been isolated from each other on a variety of psychological, clinical, criminal history, demographic and especially physiological bases. The concern [at this point] is with determining whether these same groups can be isolated in a much larger sample. Reference here is to the 277 consecutive admissions to the Ohio Penitentiary, on whom all but the experimental test data were obtained. These 277 subjects, unlike the 43, were not eliminated on the bases of age and I.Q., and hence reflect the universe of inmates at the Ohio Penitentiary.

To recapitulate rather briefly, these 277 consecutive admissions were tested by the Psychological Services staff. They were also administered the Lykken and Anomie Scales, and the Criminality Level Index. Criminal histories and MMPI subscale scores were obtained, from their folders, as were socio-economic status, familial, and related background data.

The same classificatory weights were utilized with these 277 consecutive admissions cases as with the 43 experimentals. Specifically, the number of previous arrests, the percentage of time incarcerated since age 18, and the Lykken Scale score, each were weighted 25 percent, while the Cleckley Checklist score, a record of successful escapes, and the psychopathic deviate (Pd) minus the psychasthenia (Pt) subscale scores of the MMPI were each weighted around eight percent. As before, to be classified as a sociopath, it was necessary that one be above the median on at least two of the three major variables and also on two of the three minor criteria. It was also possible to be so classified by meeting all three of the major criteria.

The application of these criteria initially yielded three groups of subjects—70 sociopaths, 66 mixed, and 141 non-sociopaths. Again, following earlier precedent, the Lykken Scale scores were used to differentiate the hostile from the simple sociopath. The former (hostile) included 47 and the latter (simple) included 23 subjects. The emphasis as before was on differentiating these two groups from each other and, much less importantly, both together from the others.

1. Demographic Variables.

The 47 hostile sociopaths averaged 30.8 years of age as compared with the much older simple sociopaths, whose mean age was 39.7. Both groups were at least two-thirds white, of urban background, and undistinguishable in terms of religious affiliation. At the time of imprisonment, nearly three-quarters of the hostiles and 64 percent of the simples were either single, divorced, or separated. The former had been wed an average of 0.8 times, as contrasted with 1.2 marriages for the simples. The hostiles, in line with their less frequent marriages, had fathered an average of only 0.8 children, while the simples showed a mean of 1.2 children. Looking backwards, many fewer of the hostile than of the simple sociopaths came from intact family situations, in which they had been reared by two parents until age 10. Along the same lines, the hostiles came from families with slightly fewer children than did the simple sociopath subjects (5.1 versus 5.4). The socio-economic status level as measured by Reiss' occupational criteria showed the hostile group to be of slightly higher status than the simples. Finally, the average grade school attainment level was 9.7 for the hostile and 8.1 for the simple sociopath subjects.

On nearly every one of these measures, with the exception only of last grade completed in school and socio-economic status (mentioned above), the direction of the results is identical to that obtained when the eight hostile and 11 simple sociopaths were contrasted. It appears, therefore, that the application of the Lykken criterion reliably differentiates the same sub-groups on these demographic characteristics. Whatever it may be that the Lykken Scale is tapping seems to distinguish these sub-categories from each other. By the same token, the weighted criteria differentiate both sociopathic groups from the mixed and the non-sociopaths.

2. Military History.

The three variables concerning military history which were presented in the analysis of the 43 experimental subjects were percent ever serving in armed forces, termination of military service, and average months in military service. Comparable data were obtained on the 47 hostile and the 23 simple sociopaths on all three variables. While the proportions of subjects who ever served in the military is approximately the same, only 44.7 percent of the hostiles and 52.2 percent of the simples ever served in the military. Of the total groups, 14.9 percent and 26.1 percent of the hostile and simple sociopaths respectively received honorable discharges, while about 30 and 26 percent, respectively, received other than honorable discharges. Interestingly enough, none of the experimental sociopath subjects, whether hostile or simple, received honorable discharges. Despite this minor discrepancy, the direction of difference in both cohorts—experimental and consecutive admissions—was the same.

Another reversal occurred on the variable, number of months in military service. In this instance, the hostile group averaged 9 months of service while the simple sociopaths were somewhat higher at 11.4 months in the military.

Neither of these discrepancies seems to offset the preponderant weight of the evidence that the simple sociopaths are likely to engage in more frequent but less aggressive anti-social behavior. This is attested to by a considerable number of criminal history variables.

3. *Criminal History.*

To begin, the distribution of offenses for which committed indicates that hostile sociopaths committed more than twice the rate of crimes against the person (criminal homicide, rape, and assault) than did the simple sociopaths—19 percent to 8.6 percent, respectively. The simple sociopath subjects averaged 5.3 officially recorded arrests as opposed to 4.6 for the hostile sociopaths. The latter had 3.4 previous incarcerations while the simple averaged 3.7 previous prison sentences. The hostile sociopaths had spent some five years (66 months) in correctional institutions, which was much less than the mean of nearly 12 years (140 months) spent by the simple sociopaths in institutions. The picture is much the same when one looks at the record of incarceration since age 18—62.0 months for the hostile and 134.0 months for the simple sociopaths. Perhaps an even better way of showing the same thing while at the same time controlling for the nine year age difference is the percentage of time incarcerated since age 18. The hostiles had spent about 44.5 percent of their adult lives behind bars and the simple sociopaths 49.4 percent.

In addition, judgements of the intake staff regarding the prognosis on the present commitment, custody recommendations, and supervision showed no differences between the groups.

As far as escapes are concerned, the hostiles averaged 0.19 and the simple sociopaths .78 escapes. Finally, the hostile sociopaths showed far fewer parole violations (0.79) than the simple group, which averaged 1.26.

With regard to all these variables but one, it is fair to say that the direction of difference in means or percentages were of the same order and in the same direction as those obtained in the comparisons of the nine hostile versus 11 simple experimentals on these variables. The single reversal concerned escapes in which, as already noted, the simples had succeeded more often than the hostile sociopaths.

4. *I.Q. and Cleckley Checklist.*

In selecting the experimental subjects, an I.Q. minimum of 100 on the OPCT was used as a screening criterion. Hence all subjects were above this level of I.Q. It will be recalled that the two sociopath groups averaged 120 or over while the average for all 43 subjects was 114. With regard to the 277 (for whom I.Q. was not used as a screening variable), the mean I.Q. on the OPCT was 101.5. Both sociopath groups, though nearly identical to one another, were above this mean, at approximately 104.

As before, the Cleckley Checklist failed to differentiate the two groups of sociopaths from each other and from the non-sociopaths. The mean score on the Cleckley Checklist for the entire group of 277 was 9.1, and it was 10.3 for the hostiles and 10.0 for the simple sociopaths.

5. *MMPI Subscale Scores.*

Although the peaks vary slightly between the two cohorts—experimental and consecutive admissions—taken as a whole, the 8 experimental hostile and the 47 consecutive admission hostile sociopaths are not appreciably different. The same holds for the two sets of simple sociopath subjects.[5]

As before, the subscales which seemed to differentiate most effectively were the Pd and Ma subscales. There were also some differences in the averages on the K, Pt, Sc and Si subscales. On the Pd the respective means for the hostile and simple sociopaths were 31.6 and 29.5; on the Ma, 22.7 and 20.6; on the K, 18.2 and 16.6; on the Pt, 28.0 and 26.2 (something of a reversal); on the Sc, 28.5 and 25.4; and on the Si, 20.9 and 23.3. It should be noted that with the exception of the Pt, the direction of these differences parallels those obtained between the hostile and simple experimental sociopathic subjects.

With regard to the MMPI subscale scores and profiles, it is again necessary to emphasize that the two groups of sociopaths combined differed from the mixed and non-sociopath groups among the consecutive admissions in very much the same manner and to approximately the same degree as did the 19 experimental sociopaths from the 24 experimental non-sociopaths.

[5]The minimum educational requirement for taking the MMPI is a sixth grade education. On the 277 consecutive admissions, 58 did not meet this requirement; the MMPI profiles and the mean subscale scores that follow are based on the 219 cases who successfully completed the test.

Chapter 2

The extent factor in doer involvement

There is no doubt that in the past academic criminologists have given primacy among their various concerns to the operation of the "how" factors. They accordingly made theoretical contributions to the study of the causes of crime and delinquency. At present, there is a growing concern about the so-called increase in the amount of crime and delinquency in modern countries, and this concern is focused on the ways and means of indicating the extent of the problem. Not only the academic criminologists, but also those in the fields of sociology, psychology, psychiatry, law, as well as the operators of the criminal justice system, the police, the prosecutors, the judges, and the correctional administrators have also expressed concern for understanding and regulating the growing volume of cases coming to their attention. The press and the caretakers of government likewise have become increasingly sensitive to the "reported" increase in the extent of crime and delinquency, and they struggle with one another over solutions and remedies.

Unfortunately, the techniques for measuring extent of involvement in crime and delinquency are in their infancy, but nevertheless they are making some gains in efficacy. At present, there are three principal methods whereby data on and insights into extent of involvement can be obtained: (a) through the collection of police statistics, (b) by making surveys or taking polls, and (c) by the administration of self-reporting instruments.

Collection of police statistics

Recorded statistics that process complaints on crime and delinquency coming to the attention of the police are perhaps the major source for indicating volume of crime. The details on how this is done are presented in Chapter 7, which deals with the input of cases into the various way stations of the criminal justice system. Suffice it to say here that the Federal Bureau of Investigation has for years undertaken to get police departments to collect statistics in a uniform way, especially the statistics dealing with the reported "occurrences" of the so-called "index crimes" and the reports on arrests.

As indicated in Chapter 7, in the late twenties, experts in the field of police statistics devised a system of reporting seven major offenses coming to the attention of the police. The experts contended, and rightly so, that these offenses had more chance of coming to the attention of the police than all other kinds of offenses. The major seven so-called "index crimes" are as follows: homicide, forcible rape, robbery, aggravated assault, burglary, theft (particularly of over $50), and auto theft.

Several important insights into volume can be gleaned from the yearly F.B.I. reports on the "index crimes" or the "crimes known to the police." In the first place, the index crimes can be used to indicate trends in crime from year to year, and they can be compared with the estimates of the yearly population. Over a period of time, trends in volume can be discerned quite easily. For example, during the 1960s the yearly increase in the number of reported index crimes has greatly outstripped the increase in population of the United States.

Such a disproportional increase in volume of crime has raised several important criminological questions. Is this trend a real increase? Is the increase due to greater facility and willingness to report criminal events to the police? If at least part of the disproportional increase in index crimes is due to a real increase, is this due to the mobility and fluidity of life in the United States; to the growing amount of alienation of persons from families, groups, and organizations; to the breakdown of social controls; to the emancipation of youth; to the impact of an affluent society, etc.? Here is a cluster of sociological "how" factors that are not easily or readily investigated by obtaining first-hand data.

In the second place, the index crimes, as collected annually by the F.B.I. from police departments all over the country, can give indications of the differential extent of reported involvement by type of offense. In the F.B.I. report for the year 1968, the order of estimated frequencies from highest to lowest, for the major seven offenses, were as follows: burglary, 1,828,900; larceny $50 and over, 1,271,100; auto theft, 777,800; aggravated assault, 282,400; robbery, 261,730; forcible rape, 31,060; murder, 13,650.[1] One notices that crimes against property are the most numerous in the index crimes, while crimes against the person are quite infrequent, with the exception of robbery which usually uses force and/or threat of violence. Do the

[1] *Crime in the United States; Uniform Crime Reports—1968*, Federal Bureau of Investigation, U.S. Department of Justice (Washington, D.C.: U.S. Government Printing Office, August 13, 1969), p. 5.

above differentials in reported extent reflect for the most part the impact of society on the doer? Or do they reflect psychological variables in the behavior of the doer? Criminology can surmise at this point, but it cannot give answers from findings of "hard data."

In the third place, the reported index crimes can indicate extent of variation by regions of the country, by states, by size of cities, and by rural areas. Here, again, area and regional variations in extent rates for the various index crimes force the sociological criminologists to make "good guesses" as to why these variations exist. They can be assisted in this matter of interpretation by correlating or associating variations in other socio-economic data with the variations in reported crime. But there is a tendency for sociologists who are concerned with area and regional variations in reported crime to project explanations without taking into account the concommitant variations in associated variables, such as the use of assumed cultural differences in regions of the United States, the use of an assumed homogenity or heterogenity of an area's population, the prevalence of industrialization, the presence of minority groups, etc.

Volume or extent of crime can also be indicated by the arrest statistics kept by local police agencies and also reported to the F.B.I., becoming a major part of its annual Uniform Crime Reports. The technical aspects of recording and reporting arrests are presented in Chapter 7. At this point, suffice it to say that arrest statistics cover not only the major seven offenses discussed above under "index crimes" but also 22 additional offense categories, and these embrace in one way or another the violations of all the criminal codes of the various states and local ordinances, as well as of the federal government.

Arrest statistics may be considered by some criminological experts as having some overlap in coverage. After investigation by the police, a doer might be held and charged with two or more offenses or all the doers in any event, if the police get their hands on them, can be so charged. In the seven index crimes, only one event is tabulated, no matter how many doers were involved and how many different acts took place in this reported event. For example, for purposes of the index crime report, a case of three men who had broken into a house, one had forcibly raped the wife of the household, while all three took available money and valuables, would be recorded as one event, namely the most serious in the line from seven to one, from auto theft to homicide. In this instance, the report in the index crimes would be recorded as ONE FORCIBLE RAPE. For purposes of the arrest statistics, if the police were to get their hands on two of the doers, they would book two men on breaking and entry and two men on theft of over $50—provided they did not get their hands on the rapist.

As will be realized, arrest statistics are limited to the cases the police take into custody after investigation, whereas index crime statistics include reported events, even if the police do not arrest any of the doers. But arrest statistics have certain advantages over index crime reports as a measure of volume. In the first place, they cover the multiple offenses taking place in the same event. In the second place—and many think this is the most significant point of all—they record age, sex, race, occupation, marital status, address, place of the crime, etc.

Although the arrest statistics published by the F.B.I. only give the breakdown on age, sex, and race, it is possible to explore the differential extent of arrests by those three demographic variables, which push these data toward the "who" factor in doer involvement, since demographic trends over the years can be deduced from the age, race, and sex indications of persons arrested. Are more young people getting involved, are fewer black persons getting arrested, are female arrestees staying in the same ratio to male over the years?

Police arrest statistics can also be used to make area and regional comparisons, between sections of the country, states, cities, small towns, and rural areas. They can also be used to study the ecological distribution of "doers" in cities since the police have the addresses of the doers, or the ecological distribution of the recorded place of the crime. Arrest statistics giving location of the place of the deed and the address of the doer can be associated with the economic and population variables of the different census tracts of cities in the United States, yielding insights into the ecological aspects of urban crime distribution.

A description of the crime situation in one police district of Chicago—an inner-city district but not the worst of such districts—is presented in Appendix 2-A, taken from the published report of the President's Crime Commission. Of particular interest is the account of the police "calls" on one weekday in October 1966. From this vivid description, one gets a picture of the "acted upon" events that eventually go through the sieve and become index crime reports and arrest reports.

Finally, it should be noted that arrest statistics undoubtedly are influenced to a large extent by the decisions of the police to take persons into custody and to book them on one or more offenses. In other words, they must be expected to reflect a discrepancy—how much, we do not know—between the actual behavior of doers and the "booked" behavior. Arrests represent a screening or a processing of events; how far they would vary from a Tel-Star recording, no one knows. Undoubtedly, the disparity is considerable. Nevertheless, criminologists must live with the system of recording arrests as the major indicator of doer involvement.

Surveys and polls

During the past generation, very extensive use has been made of survey research and opinion polls, in an attempt to spot the extent or trend of the public's reaction to a wide range of situations and problems. Several nationwide survey or polling agencies have come into existence, making their service available to business, government, and organizations. Over the years, technical skills have been developed, not only in the preparation, of efficacious schedules for the purposes at hand, but also in the method of approach to the interviewees, and in the development of "stratified samples." The public generally has developed considerable confidence in the methods, procedure, and findings of surveys and polls.

However, the great majority of topics surveyed have dealt with questions of the moment, such as political leanings or endorsement of a certain candidate or program, the acceptance of a newly marketed product, etc. Very rarely has the accumulated expertise of the survey agencies been directed toward the problem of gauging the extent of crime and delinquency.

Almost a generation ago, Wallerstein and Wyle made a survey of professed violations of the criminal code in Metropolitan New York city. Certainly this study is a pioneer effort to obtain information on the extent of crime involvement *via* the survey method. Ninety-nine percent of the respondents reported that they had *in their adult life—(over 16 years of age)* —committed one or more of a list of 49 offenses taken from the criminal code of New York state. The average numbers of professed violations was 18 for the male respondents, 11 for the women respondents; 64 percent of the male and 29 percent of the female respondents admitted that they had committed a felony.[2] (The list of 49 offenses included 14 felonies.)

There is no doubt that this early pioneer effort displayed several basic limitations and shortcomings, especially with respect to sampling procedure and schedule format. Nevertheless it gives indications that, even among the cooperative respondents, involvement in crime appeared to be very much more extensive that it ever appears on the police records or the records of recidivists in prison. The moral of the Wallerstein-Wyle findings is that the amount of reported crime or crime coming to the attention of police apparently is very much smaller than that of actual involvement in crime. In the language of Wallerstein and Wyle, two important conclusions on the "extent" factor emerged: "the number of acts legally constituting crime is far in excess of those officially reported" and "unlawful behavior, far from being an abnormal social or psychological manifestation, is in truth a very common phenomenon."[3]

Such a conclusion is born out by some recently administered surveys carried out for the President's Crime Commission in 1966, which represent the application of advanced techniques in survey research to the crime problem. One important innovation introduced by these surveys was the attempt to obtain information from stratified samples of interviewed house-

[2]James S. Wallerstein and Clement J. Wyle, "Our Law-Abiding Law Breakers," *Probation* (April 1947), pp. 107–112. Published by the National Probation and Parole Association, New York; now called the National Council on Crime and Delinquency.

[3]*Ibid.*, p. 111.

holders who were asked to indicate the number and kinds of offenses committed against any member of their household in the past year. This information included not only the number and type of offenses but also the reasons for not having reported these offenses to the police. See Appendix 2-B for a summary of information on the extent of crime as collected by modern survey methods for the President's Crime Commission.

The number of criminal events so reported is much larger than the number of events known to the police of the surveyed police precincts. However, while the extent of events discoverable by a survey of householders is larger than that coming to the attention of the police, the amount of involvement does not appear to be anywhere near as large as that obtained by the "returned questionnaire" method used by Wallerstein and Wyle (although comparisons cannot be made).

Self-reporting

Realizing that official statistics did not really indicate the actual extent of involvement in delinquency and crime, sociologists, American sociologists in particular, have attempted, during the last generation, to obtain insights from the administration of self-reporting schedules to voluntary samples of respondents. Actually, the basic difference between household surveys and self-reporting investigations is not altogether methodologically clear, and it may be that in the future the two may fuse together. At any rate, there have been such a wide variety of self-reporting studies that it is necessary to give condensed descriptions of their methods and findings. At this juncture it is important to realize that nearly all of the self-reporting contributions to criminological insight into the extent of deviant behavior have been made by sociologists and have focused on juvenile or youthful subjects. Adult respondents have been practically left out of the reckoning.

The pioneer study of Porterfield

Austin L. Porterfield made the pioneer attempt to gauge the extent of delinquent and deviant behavior in the pre-college years of a sample of 200 male and 137 female college students attending Texas Christian University in Fort Worth, Texas during 1940–41 and 1942–43. In each group 100 percent of the respondents reported having committed one or more of 55 listed forms of deviant and criminal behavior. The average number of admitted involvements (offenses committed) in their pre-college life for the males was 17.6; for the females, 4.7. When the 1941–42 sample of 100 college men was asked to indicate the extent to which they committed the 55 behavioral items during their college years, they reported an average of 11.2 violations.[4]

The Porterfield study of self-reporting by college students also indicated that the percentage of respondents, both male and female, who admitted having committed one or more of the 55 listed violations varied greatly according to type of behavior. By way of illustration, note should be taken particularly of those behaviors in the Porterfield self-responding schedule that high and low percentages of the respondents admitted to having committed (*see* Table 2–1). One can merely hazard the guess that behaviors

Table 2–1. Percentage of male and female college students reporting selected offenses committed during their pre-college period of life[5]

Offense	*Percentage*	
	male	*female*
Fireworks in public buildings	49.5	8.8
Spitwads at others' displeasure	77.0	29.9
Drunken driving	22.0	0.0
Reckless driving	51.5	22.6
Speeding	67.5	46.0
Setting fires in buildings	13.0	1.5
Breaking windows	36.5	2.2
Breaking street lights	47.0	8.7
Trespassing	57.5	16.7
Slipping into theater	62.5	10.2
Ordinary fighting	61.5	5.8
Abusive language	79.0	36.5
Runaway, wandering	14.5	4.3
Truancy	42.5	34.3
Buying (liquor) as a minor	38.0	2.2
Auto theft	0.5	0.0
Burglary	7.5	0.0
Shoplifting	10.0	1.5
Miscellaneous, petty (theft)	23.0	8.8
Stealing melons, fruit	69.0	16.0
Possessing stolen goods	20.0	3.6
Passing slugs, bad coins	24.0	0.0
Gambling	58.5	17.4
Attempt to rape	5.5	0.0
Indecent exposure	24.5	2.2
Extramarital coitus	58.5	0.7
Carrying concealed weapons	14.0	0.0
Homicide, murder	0.5	0.0
Homicide, negligent	0.5	0.0

[4] Austin L. Porterfield, *Youth in Trouble* (Fort Worth: The Leo Potishman Foundation, 1946), p. 38.

[5] *Ibid.*, pp. 40–41.

with high percentages of admitted involvement do not have the internalized taboos that the behaviors with low percentages display—according to American standards of moral values.

Among other dimensions, the early attempt of Porterfield to gauge the extent of violational behavior indicates that multiple involvement in deviance, whether in childhood, adolescence, or young adulthood, is the mode, even for a favored sample of college students.

The Nye-Short study

Several years after Porterfield's pioneer effort to gauge the amount of involvement in deviance on the part of college students, Nye and Short developed a methodologically sophisticated self-reporting instrument for testing the extent of involvement of youths (boys and girls) in deviant and criminal behavior.[6] Their samples consisted of high school pupils in the ninth through the twelfth grades and of youths committed to a state correctional institution for committed delinquents. The self-reporting instrument consisted of a checklist of 21 items, to which the subjects replied in terms of four forced choices: (1) very often . . ., (2) several times . . ., (3) once or twice . . ., (4) no . . ., or in reverse order (1) no, (2) once or twice, (3) several times, and (4) very often, for purposes of standardizing the responses made by the respondents. The respondents were asked to check the number of times since the beginning of grade school they had broken the rules or regulations involved in the 21 items.

Nye and Short found that 7 (* items) of the 21 items were effective for testing the involvement of sixteen- and seventeen-year-old high school boys as well as fourteen- and fifteen-year old high school boys; 4 additional items (** items) out of the 21 were used in gauging involvement of boys committed to the state training school, and these consisted of somewhat more serious delinquencies than those of the seven above. In most instances, the scoring system on the 21 items—including the 7* plus 4**—was 0 for no, 1 for once or twice, and 2 for several times and very often.[7] The listing of the 11 significant items in the Nye-Short delinquency scale consisted of the following:[8] (How many times since grade school have you:)

*1. Driven a car without a driver's license or permit? (Do not include driver training courses.)
*2. Taken little things (worth less than $2) that did not belong to you?
*3. Bought or drank beer, wine, or liquor? (Include drinking at home.)
*4. Skipped school without a legitimate excuse?

[6] F. Ivan Nye and James F. Short, Jr., "Scaling Delinquent Behavior," *American Sociological Review*, 22 (June 1957), pp. 326–331.

[7] *Ibid.*, pp. 328–329; also footnote to their Table 2, p. 330, duplicated in Appendix 2-C.

[8] *Ibid.*, p. 330, footnote to Table 2.

*5. Purposely damaged or destroyed public or private property that did not belong to you?
*6. Had sex relations with a person of the opposite sex?
**7. Taken things of medium value (between $2 and $50)?
**8. Taken things of large value (worth more than $50)?
**9. "Run away" from home?
*10. Defied your parents' authority (to their face)?
**11. Used or sold narcotic drugs?

Nye and Short's findings on the extent of self-reported delinquency involved in the 11 behaviors listed above are presented in Appendix 2–C. In this instance, the researchers are reporting on the responses of a sample of 570 sixteen- and seventeen-year-old boys in small-town high schools and 170 boys of similar ages at a state training school for committed delinquents. Interestingly enough, the high school sample of 570 reported an overwhelming concentration of their involvement since entering grade school in the first eight behaviors of the above list. In particular, 128 of the 570 (22.5%) reported having driven a car without a driver's license or permit once or twice; 133 (23.3%), having driven a car without a license or permit, having taken things worth less than $2, having bought or drunk beer, wine or liquor, and having skipped school without excuse, once or twice; 97 (17%), having driven a car without license or permit several times and very often, plus taken little things worth less than $2 once or twice, bought or drunk beer, wine, or liquor several times and very often, skipped school once or twice, purposely damaged or destroyed property of others once or twice, and had sex relations with a member of the opposite sex once or twice.

On the other hand, the sample of 170 committed delinquents reported much greater involvement in all 11 behaviors. Almost 62 percent of the delinquents indicated involvement in 7 to 11 of the 11 behaviors. See Appendix 2–C. Inspection of the distribution in Appendix 2–C also indicates that the delinquents reported more frequent involvements in the various behaviors than the high school boys, as indicated by the prevalence of 2's over 1's in their responses to the checklist (2 = several times and very often, whereas 1 = once or twice).

Eynon's report on committed delinquents

Reference to Appendix 1–Dii will show that Eynon developed a checklist of 24 items for self-reporting of delinquent behavior by committed delinquent white boys, many of which items correspond to those used by Nye and Short in their original checklist. However, his schedule asked the newly admitted delinquents to indicate the frequency with which they had "done these things" in their lifetime. It will be noted that Eynon used 12 of the most frequently indicated behaviors as the basis for his analysis, six of which duplicate behaviors that are found in Nye and Short's 11 items presented above.[9] The percentage of his sample of 363 committed white delinquent boys from the Boys Industrial School, Ohio who admitted having "done these things" one or more times during their lifetime is presented in Table 2-2. Playing "hookey," taking "some small thing," and drinking outside the

Table 2-2. Number and percent of 363 white boys committed to the Boys Industrial School, Ohio, admitting having committed twelve delinquent behaviors.[10]

Behavior	*Number of boys*	*Percent*
Play hookey	299	82.4
Take some little thing	287	79.1
Drink outside home	259	71.3
Steal a car	214	59.0
Destroy property	193	53.2
Run away from home	189	52.1
Gang fights	161	44.4
Beat up on kids	85	23.4
Hurt someone for fun	82	22.6
Use force to get money	66	18.2
Homosexual activities	33	9.1
Use or sell narcotics	21	5.8

home were the most numerous reported deeds (roughly 70 to 80 percent), while using or selling narcotics and homosexual activities were reported very infrequently. (The former might increase considerably if similar studies were made today.)

The Clark-Tifft polygraph re-test

While there have been several self-reporting studies since the pioneer effort of Porterfield and the technically more sophisticated approach of Nye and Short, there have been very few attempts to validate the accuracy of such reports. Indeed, it is not at all clear that any approximation of absolute accuracy in self-reporting can ever be devised. However, Clark and Tifft developed a method of re-test for accuracy under personal interview conditions and a second re-test under conditions of polygraph control. The subjects were 45 male students at a midwestern university who volunteered to go through the second and third steps. The details of the procedure are presented in Appendix 2-D. The time period for self-reporting started from the time the subject entered high school.[11]

[9] Thomas G. Eynon, "Factors Related to Onset of Delinquency" (Ph.D. dissertation, The Ohio State University, 1959), pp. 186-189.

[10] *Ibid.*, p. 76, Table 72.

[11] John P. Clark and Larry L. Tifft, "Polygraph and Interview Validation of Self-Reported Deviant Behavior," *American Sociological Review*, 31:4 (August 1966), pp. 516-523.

A list of 35 items covering deviant and criminal behavior had been developed by Clark and Tifft from two preliminary pre-tests, in which students had been asked first to "suggest behaviors which other students might tend to under- or over-report having done" and then asked second "to estimate the amount of 'normative pressure' on persons of their age and sex to respond in either direction" to the questions on involvement in deviant behavior.[12] As one will notice from Appendix 2-D, several of the original Nye-Short items survived this preliminary two-step pretesting.

The experimental subjects were administered the final checklist of 35 items and asked to indicate the frequency of having committed each listed behavior—this was a collective (group) administration. Then each student was contacted and asked to appear for a personal interview under cooperation-eliciting conditions, at which time he was asked to review in private his responses and make corrections for accuracy in view of the fact that he should later attest to their accuracy by submitting to the polygraph. Then when the subject had been attached to the polygraph, the examiner went through the subject's responses once again and recorded any changes in the responses since the initial collective administration.

Clark and Tifft found that 58 percent of the changes of responses were made at the time of the "personal interview" (i.e. the second step) and 42 percent at the time of the polygraph examination. Interestingly enough, three-fourths of the changed responses actually increased the frequency of admitted deviant behavior, while only 25 percent decreased the frequency. The overall validity of the first set of responses on frequency of involvement as tested against those given in the third step of the process (the responses under polygraph conditions) was found to be 81.5 percent, with a range from 47 to 97 percent. Further details are given in Appendix 2-D. Consequently, Clark and Tifft concluded that "there is substantial empirical evidence" for considering the involvement responses "valid" for the population sampled and the conditions of administration.[13]

The Erickson-Empey interview method

Erickson and Empey tried the use of initial interviews to obtain self-reporting data on the type and extent of involvement in juvenile delinquency. They were of the opinion that the interview method of eliciting information on involvement was superior to group administration of a schedule, in view of the fact that there are so many poor readers among youth of disadvantaged classes and youth already delinquent.[14] Three skilled interviewers spoke

[12] *Ibid.*, p. 517.

[13] *Ibid.*, p. 521.

[14] Maynard L. Erickson and LaMar Empey, "Court Records, Undetected Delinquency and Decision-Making," *Journal of Criminal Law, Criminology and Police Science*, 54:4 (December 1963), p. 459.

with a sample of 50 lads who had never been sent to the juvenile court; 30 who had been referred to the court once; 50 who were repeaters and were on probation; and 50 who were incarcerated. The age range of the subjects was from fifteen to seventeen years of age, and all the subjects were males and white (no Negroes or Mexicans). The first three sets of subjects came from a county in Utah with a population of 110,000; the last set, from an insitution to which they had been committed for delinquency.

A list of 22 items covering delinquent behavior was developed for use in the interview. The subjects were asked whether they had committed (during their lifetime) each of the 22 acts and if so, how many times. They were also asked whether they had ever been caught, arrested, or taken to court for each of the 22 acts and if so, how many times.

The admitted extent of violations of the type covered by the 22 items in the Erickson-Empey Study was simply staggering. One should consult Appendix Tables 2–E–1 and 2–E–2. In general, the non-delinquents and the one-time delinquents admitted to a very much lower number of offenses committed during their lifetime than did the repeated delinquents on probation (in the community) and the incarcerated delinquents. The delinquents in the community, however, outdistanced those incarcerated on the number of admitted theft offenses but appeared to be lower in admitted involvement than the incarcerated delinquents in all the other offenses in the list of 22 behaviors.

Apart from the actual number of times the boys in the sample said they had committed each of the 22 offenses, the percentage of the subsamples who admitted committing the various offenses in the listing also varied considerably. With some glaring, and probably unaccountable, exceptions, the incarcerated delinquents had a higher percentage of reported involvement in the total list than did the delinquents on probation, who reported higher involvement than the one-time delinquents, who in turn reported higher involvement than the non-delinquents.

Incidentally, all four subsamples indicated in their individual interviews that their violational behavior went almost completely undetected as well as unacted upon by the police and courts. Most of the reported information on this matter revealed the percentages of the various offenses remaining undetected and unacted upon as hovering in the high nineties and in many instances as being 100 percent. And it appeared that no variation in absence of detection and official notice between the four subsamples was evident.

Hence, the Erickson-Empey research on extent of self-reported violations indicates wide variations in total admitted involvement according to subsample and to type of behavior; it also indicates the almost total absence of notice and action by the caretakers of society. (The author wishes to indicate that the above conclusions are primarily slanted toward the purposes at hand and do not necessarily correspond to the emphasis that Erickson and Empey present in their summary of findings.)

Hardt's study of junior high school boys

In 1963 Hardt collected self-reporting schedules from a sample of boys (age range: twelve to fifteen years) in the seventh, eighth, and ninth grades of four sections of a city of 250,000 population in New York State. Actually, the samples were obtained from schools in one low-income, predominantly Negro area; two low-income, predominantly white areas; and one middle-income, white area. The first three areas were selected on the basis of having high official rates of delinquency and high rates of dropouts from the schools. The fourth area was selected because of low delinquency and low dropout rates.

A self-reporting schedule of 19 items was administered to the respondents, of which 11 were used for a delinquency involvement score, referred to as the "omnibus" score. Although Hardt's self-reporting schedule (see Appendix 2–F) actually asked the subjects to check each item "the *last time* this happened," whether in the last seven days, in the last 12 months, over a year ago, or never, the responses were scored 0 for never and 1 for any of the other three periods.[15] Accordingly, it was found that high "violators" scored 6 and above on the 11 items selected for scoring; medium violators, 3–5; low violators, 2 and below. The project also cleared the subjects through a central registry of juvenile police contacts.

While most of the subjects who were recorded on the police files came out as high violators on the self-report, most of the high violators (omnibus score of 6 or more on 11 items) were not recorded in the police files.[16]

In the total sample of boys, the "suspect" rate (boys recorded in the police files) was only 19.8 percent. For the high violator boys alone, the percentage was 22.6 percent. These rates were found to vary according to area of the city. They were highest for the section of low-income, predominantly Negro population and lowest for the middle-class, predominantly white area. The rates of self-reported involvement and registration in the police files were lower for the younger boys than the older boys in the sample (twelve- to thirteen- versus fourteen- to fifteen-year-old boys). See Appendix 2–F for details as well as for the self-reporting schedule.

On the basis of overall findings, Hardt concludes that "accurate inferences about the relative incidence of boys involved in extensive delinquency behaviors in low and middle status neighborhoods cannot be made from official records."[17]

[15] Robert H. Hardt, *Delinquency and Social Class: Studies of Juvenile Deviations or Police Dispositions,* mimeographed, (Syracuse, New York: Youth Development Center, Syracuse University, December 15, 1964), pp. 2–3. *See also* Robert H. Hardt and Sandra J. Peterson, "Arrests of Self and Friends as Indicators of Delinquency Involvement," *Journal of Research in Crime and Delinquency*, 5:1 (January 1968), pp. 44–51.

[16] *Ibid.*, p. 4.

[17] *Ibid.*, p. 7.

The Syracuse conference on self-reporting

A few years ago (1965) a special conference at Syracuse University consisting of several researchers—mostly sociologists—who had been actively engaged in the administration and analysis of self-reporting schedules among various samples of youth came to grips with the many problems of self-reporting research. Some of the highlights from the research experience of the conferees regarding the efficacy of self-reporting are listed as follows:[18]

1. The present evidence suggests that there may be little difference in responses made to signed and unsigned questionnaires.
2. There appears to be a high correlation between self-reported behavior and respondent's admission of a police record.
3. Associations have been found between delinquent behavior and sex behavior, and between sex standards and sex behavior.
4. Many studies have failed to demonstrate any association between the socio-economic status of juveniles and the incidence of delinquent behavior.
5. Some evidence has been presented which indicates the similarity in the patterning of delinquent behaviors in various sections of the country.
6. Single omnibus delinquency scales may be inappropriate for many uses since they tend to mask subgroup differences. There is some indication that white and Negro samples display different kinds of delinquent behavior.

Ivan Nye, the father of self-reporting as it is used today, indicated at the Syracuse conference that the validity of the method needs to be improved to overcome "lying" and the "halo effect." In addition, he indicated that tests need to be run more systematically on the difference in responses when the respondents are asked to answer the questions on unsigned as opposed to signed questionnaires. He also indicated that self-reporting schedules are quite likely to include only goal-oriented items and omit items that are directed toward "acting-out, compulsive behavior."[19]

The need for standardization of self-reporting

There is no doubt that the major part of delinquency and crime remains hidden from the criminal justice system. While self-reporting represents an attempt, principally by American sociologists, to penetrate the "dark figures" of criminal and delinquent behavior, all that can be said at present is that very few violations come to official attention. The extent of the hidden

[18] Robert H. Hardt and George E. Bodine, *Development of Self-Report Instruments in Delinquency Research* (Syracuse, New York: Youth Development Center, Syracuse University, 1965), p. 13.

[19] *Ibid.*, pp. 13–14.

violations cannot as yet be accurately measured by self-reporting, and it will take years to develop valid and standardized gauges of these.

While the emphasis so far has been on indications of juvenile involvement, in the future it must be extended equally to adult involvement as well. Therefore, instruments that apply to adult and juvenile behavior alike must be developed. The items used in self-reporting should be closer to the main line of violations of the criminal code rather than to juvenile deviant behavior that might or might not even be delinquency in the strictest sense. Hence, much attention must be given, if the self-reporting movement continues, to standard items of coverage that apply to juveniles and adults alike, and these items must correspond to the terms under which the onlooker or the victim understand, the violation gets reported to the police, and the police make their decisions to investigate, to arrest, to book, and to hold for court. It is not feasible to have one set of behavioral items that apply to self-reporting respondents and another set that apply to the initial way stations of the criminal justice system.

It will also be necessary to standardize the time period of coverage in self-reported investigations; "during one's lifetime" or "since grade school" or "since sixteen years of age" are much too nebulous. "During the past year" appears to be a more sensible extent indicator for standardized research in self-reporting, as a year's time period has possibilities for checking indications of involvement against police records.

Undoubtedly also, age limits of self-reporting samples will need to be established since the whole range of ages from childhood to old age is not feasible. Much more feasible is the age range at the upper and lower limits that embraces the largest and most important segment of involvement in crime, namely from sixteen to twenty-five years of age. Sociologists who are interested in deviant behavior of adolescents could still sample groups under sixteen years of age, and for such samples, certainly, schedules dealing with the wayward types of deviance would obviously be valuable. However, to give self-reporting a more realistic use in gauging the extent of involvement, it would be much more feasible to use items dealing with the most frequent violations of the criminal code, such as burglery, theft, auto theft, robbery, and aggravated assault and to sample the age range between sixteen and twenty-five years.

As the reader may have noted, most of the self-reporting investigations have covered male samples. How to get a schedule of self-reported items that is valid for females aged sixteen to twenty-five years is not entirely obvious at this point of knowledge and experience. Certainly the robbery, burglary, and auto theft items could well be left out of the female schedule. It is difficult at this point to justify useful and reliable female self-reporting on any item with the exception of theft.

There will be less difficulty about selecting proper samples of juveniles and adults for self-reporting indications of involvement than about selecting the items in the instrument. Sociologists, psychologists, and political scientists currently have a good grasp of sampling procedures and can readily focus upon the proper age, sex, race, and class input.

However, for the immediate future it would appear that more feasible insights into the extent of involvement could come from surveys of stratified samples of adult householders and shopkeepers than from self-reporting. Their indications of offenses that they know, from personal knowledge, as having taken place during the last year can be gathered in a more standardized way than can the self-reported indications. Their indications as to time and place can also be checked against police files to measure the gap between official and observed knowledge of criminal events.

Reports by persons in close contact

A unique method of obtaining information on the extent of involvement of delinquent youths was developed in the early forties by a research team in collaboration with the Cambridge-Sommerville delinquency prevention project in these two suburban cities of Boston. The team prepared a checklist of 50 offenses and asked the case workers to indicate the extent to which their clients had committed any of the listed offenses: rarely, occasionally, or frequently (and presumably not at all to their knowledge). The case workers in this project had very small case loads, maintained very close contact with their youthful clients, and kept very detailed case-history records.[20]

The research team called all the case workers together in one session to explain the project and obtain any suggestions for implementing it. Following this, each case worker was contacted individually by the first member of the team (FJM) and together they reviewed each page of the case record on each boy in the sample; from this, the checklist sheet was filled in. The sample consisted of 114 delinquency-oriented youths who had received intensive case-worker service for a span of five years, that is from the time they were eleven until they were sixteen years of age.[21]

According to the close-contact knowledge of the case workers, 13 of the lads had never committed an act that could have brought them to the attention of the juvenile court for delinquency; 61 of the 114 cases were known to have committed offenses for which they could have been referred to the juvenile court although somehow they had managed to avoid referral or detection; the remaining 40 cases of the 114 had been complained upon to the juvenile court.

The research team devised an arbitrary weighting system, in which a

[20] Fred J. Murphy, Mary M. Shirley, and Helen L. Witmer, "The Incidence of Hidden Delinquency," *American Journal of Orthopsychiatry*, 16 (October 1946), pp. 686–687.

[21] *Ibid.*, pp. 687–688.

case worker's report of "rarely" on any of the 50 listed offenses counted 1; occasionally, 4; and frequently, 10. The violations of the 101 boys (114 minus 13) as reported by the case worker and weighted according to the above systems were as shown in Table 2-3:[22]

Table 2-3.

Violation	*Unofficial delinquents N61*	*Official delinquents N40*	*Both N101*
City Ordinance	739	655	1394
Minor Offenses	1913	2493	4406
Serious Offenses	174	442	616
TOTAL	2826	3590	6416

One notices that the weighted delinquency score for the 61 unofficial delinquents was proportionally very much less than that for the 40 official delinquents (2826 ÷ 61 versus 3590 ÷ 40). Of the 6416 weighted score for the infractions of the 101 cases only 95—27 representing minor offenses and 68 serious offenses—came to the attention of the juvenile court.[23]

Certainly this study of the case worker's intimate knowledge of the violational behavior of boys under their close supervision corroborates the fact that a very large part of delinquency is "hidden" and does not come to official attention, a fact that was just beginning to be perceived at the time of the study.

Dr. Witmer, one of the co-workers on this research project, made the following observations:[24]

> It has long been said that statistics of juvenile delinquency are unreliable indices of the amount of delinquent misconduct or of variations in it from year to year, and it has been suspected that delinquency records are not a satisfactory means of judging the social adjustment of individual children.
>
> The figures presented here show that court statistics are wholly inadequate as a measure of the amount of youthful illegal behavior in the community.

There is no doubt that certain persons in close contact with others have some knowledge—though certainly not complete—of the involvement of juveniles and adults in delinquency and crime; but undoubtedly this source of reporting is very limited. A "best friend" is in a good position to know of involvement, but it is very unlikely that he would report this even under the most favorable circumstances, nor would a brother of similar age. Parents might not have the range of knowledge that a best friend would have and would also be reluctant to report. Neighborhood recreation workers might

[22] *Ibid.*, p. 688.
[23] *Ibid.*, pp. 688–689.
[24] *Ibid.*, p. 696.

have a limited range of knowledge about the extent of involvement of young people in their territory. Even household respondents would be unlikely to reveal to survey interviewers what they know about family members regarding involvement in delinquency and crime, although they seem to be quite cooperative in indicating what crimes took place against members of the household in the last year.

For these reasons, in spite of the pioneer attempt of Murphy, *et al* to elicit information on the extent of involvement from case workers, it appears that persons in close contact are not a feasible source for obtaining information on the extent of crime and delinquency.

Appendix 2–A

CRIME IN TOWN HALL, CHICAGO

Town Hall is a district where there is considerably less crime than in the city's most impoverished sections and considerably more than in its most affluent ones. There are 21 police districts in Chicago, and in 1966 Town Hall accounted for roughly one-twentieth of Chicago's reported crimes, 12,725 out of 255,974; this was an increase over 1965 of 7.9 percent as compared with a citywide increase of 7.2 percent. By contrast, the Wabash Police District, an all-Negro low-income district with a population some 50,000 smaller than Town Hall, accounted for 18,947 crimes, an increase of 8.3 percent over 1965, and the Chicago Lawn Police District, an all-white relatively high-income district spread out over 23½ square miles with some 30,000 more people in it than Town Hall, accounted for only 9,201 crimes, an increase of only 1.3 percent over 1965.

These contrasts among districts are even more striking when specific kinds of crime are considered. Town Hall had a relatively small number of nonnegligent homcides in 1966, 10 out of 512; Wabash had 65 and Chicago Lawn had one. Town Hall was relatively low on forcible rapes, 32 out of 1,222; Wabash had 152 and Chicago Lawn 19. Town Hall was exceptionally low on robberies, 360 out of 16,720; Wabash had 2,866 and Chicago Lawn 219. And Town Hall was rather low on serious assaults, 314 out of 11,330; Wabash had 1,684 and Chicago Lawn 130. When crimes against property are considered, the picture changes drastically. Town Hall was extraordinarily high on burglaries, 1,880 out of 29,484; Wabash had 1,762 and Chicago Lawn 994. The percentage increase in burglaries in Town Hall for 1966 was 11.3 as contrasted with Wabash's 2.9, Chicago Lawn's 9 percent decrease and a decrease of 1.2 percent for the city as a whole. Town Hall's thefts of over $50, 1,193 out of 17,455, increased even more sharply, 17.6 percent; there were 712 such thefts in Wabash, a 5.6 percent decrease, and 528 such thefts in Chicago Lawn, a 30.2 percent decrease, and a 1 percent increase in the city. Finally with auto thefts, the picture changes again. Town Hall had 1,459 out of 30,946, a decrease of 3.3 percent; Wabash had 1,771, an increase of 10.2 percent; Chicago Lawn had 1,313, a decrease of 1.3 percent; auto thefts in Chicago as a whole increased by 7.6 percent. The most plausible inferences about crime in Town Hall to be drawn from these figures is that the cheek-by-jowl situation of its richest and poorest

The President's Commission on Law Enforcement and Administration of Justice, *Task Force Report: Crime and its Impact—An Assessment* (Washington, D.C.: U.S. Government Printing Office, 1967), pp. 6–9.

neighborhoods is what produces its relatively high rate of property crimes, and that its predominantly lower middle class character is what keeps its rate of crimes against the person somewhat lower than the city's as a whole, though not nearly so low as that in upper middle class neighborhoods.

According to an opinion survey that the Commission made during the summer of 1966 in four police precincts, two in Chicago and two in Boston, the residents of Town Hall are relatively content with the district. For example, only 9 percent of them, compared with an average of 18 percent for all four districts, said that the prevalence of crime and criminals gave the neighborhood a bad name. Six percent said that the best thing about the neighborhood was that it was safe, which does not seem to be much of a figure until it is compared to the 2 percent average for the four districts. When asked to compare their neighborhood with others for safety, 21 percent described it as safer, 68 percent as about average, and 11 percent as less safe; the overall percentages were 20, 53, and 19. Eleven percent, as compared with 20, said there was so much trouble in the neighborhood that they would like to move away, 86 percent as compared with 77 said they would not. In respect to the precautionary measures they have taken to protect themselves against crime, and the ways in which they have changed their habits because of crime, Town Hall residents were much like the residents of the three other districts. In general, the survey shows that the people in Town Hall are well aware that there is a good deal of crime around them and are worried about it, but not quite as worried as the people in the other precincts surveyed.

The first call the police answered on Thursday, October 27, 1966, was a product of worry. It came at five past one in the morning from a woman who lived alone in an apartment house near Lake Shore Drive. She told a confusing story about burglary. Shortly before midnight, while having a snack at a downtown restaurant with a friend who lived in the same building, she had fainted. A fire department ambulance had taken her to a nearby hospital; her friend accompanied her. She had revived quickly and then discovered her purse was missing. She made immediate inquiries by telephone of the restaurant and the fire department, with no results. She returned home with her friend. Outside her apartment door she encountered a tall Negro in a blue topcoat and blue hat whom the friend remembered seeing outside the restaurant. He said he had picked the purse up on the sidewalk and was returning it. The woman gave him a $10 reward and he left. She did not ask his name. She then entered her apartment and it seemed to her that her belongings were disarranged. She called the police, and they immediately sent out an alarm for the man. The woman then canvassed the contents of the apartment and found that nothing was missing, although various valuables, including money, were lying about in plain view. The police canceled the alarm.

While this episode was occurring, another officer was in the seventh floor apartment, three or four blocks away, of a young woman who complained of having been slapped in the face on a street corner half an hour earlier by the husband of a friend of hers. The friend, it appeared, had left her husband and was staying with the complainant. The two women were together when the slapping occurred. The officer advised the complainant to obtain a warrant for the husband's arrest. The following day a detective telephoned the complainant to ascertain the status of the case. The complainant said she had changed her mind and no longer wanted to prosecute.

The third call that morning came at 1:30 from the proprietor of a restaurant on Diversey Parkway. He reported that a thoroughly intoxicated man, bleeding at the mouth and with a stab wound in the right side of his abdomen, had just come in off the street. The man refused to discuss with the police what had happened; he muttered that he would handle the matter himself. He refused to be treated at the Illinois Masonic Hospital, which is in the district, so the police took him to the Cook County Hospital, which is not. The following afternoon the detective assigned to the case looked for him at the hospital and found that he had not been admitted; inquiry at the man's home was equally fruitless. The detective finally found him on November 19, more than 3 weeks later. The man explained that when he had seen how many people were waiting emergency treatment at Cook County Hospital, he had simply left and gone to another hospital, where he had remained until November 12. His account of the attack upon him was that he had been walking (or perhaps staggering) along Diversey Parkway that night when two young white men in dark tight pants and dark jackets had jumped him from behind. One of the assailants confronted him with a knife while the other attempted to lift the wallet from his hip pocket. He resisted and as a result was stabbed by one and punched in the mouth by the other. However, the assailants fled without the wallet. The victim said that in view of the condition he had been in, he would not be able to identify the assailants.

At 2:10 in the morning of October 27th the burglar alarm in a fur store on Irving Park Boulevard, in one of the quiestest sections of the district, went off. A policeman arrived at the scene 2 minutes later and discovered the store's show window had been smashed. He called for a dog team to search the premises; no one was found inside. An evidence technician ascertained that the window had been broken with a Seven-Up bottle, pieces of which he found inside the window. A salesman for the firm was called to the scene; he thought some furs might have been taken, but was not sure. A thorough check the next day disclosed that nothing was missing.

At 2:45 the police received an anonymous complaint that a tavern on Racine Street, just south of Diversey Parkway, was open after hours. The officer who checked the tavern found the doors locked, the lights out, and no sign of anyone inside.

At 3:15 the same officer who had first responded to the stabbing report was sent to an apartment in the northeast corner of the district where a marital dispute was in progress. The wife, who had sent for the police, told the officer that her husband had come home drunk a few minutes before. A fight started, he hit her and said he was going to get his shotgun and shoot her. The officer asked the husband about the shotgun. The husband went to a closet, produced a Winchester shotgun with a 28-inch barrel and threatened the officer with it. The officer disarmed him after a short struggle, and took him to the stationhouse. There is no record of any criminal disposition of the case, so presumably the man was sent back home after he cooled off.

At 3:30 a 35-year-old accountant who lived on Lake Shore Drive walked into district headquarters to report that he had received a threatening telegram the previous evening. In the police view there was no threat expressed in the telegram, and subsequent investigation disclosed that the accountant had made similar complaints in the past to the police and the FBI, and had besides a record of psychiatric commitment. The case was classified unfounded.

At 7:30 a man reported that his $\frac{1}{2}$-ton 1966 General Motors pickup truck with Tennessee plates was missing from the parking lot of a supermarket where he had left it, with the door and ignition locked, on Monday evening. The truck was put on the "hot list." The next morning at about the same time, the man reported that he had located his truck on the street, around the corner from where he lived. He said some friends had moved it as a prank. The truck was undamaged. It was returned to the owner and taken off the hot list.

At 9 o'clock an elderly man called to tell the police that an 11-year-old neighborhood boy had been kicking the front door of a building the man owned on Lincoln Avenue. No damage was done to the door. A week later a detective telephoned the man to go over his story again. The man said that he had called the police because he feared that his property might be damaged in the future and wanted the police to be forewarned.

At 9:20 an 11-year-old girl reported that her mother had left home the previous evening to meet her husband, with whom she was having domestic difficulties, and had not yet returned. While the patrol officer was interviewing her, the mother telephoned and said she would be home right away. It appeared that she often spent the night with friends, leaving her daughter in the care of a full-time housekeeper.

At quarter of eleven a middle-aged man walked into district headquarters and told this story: 3 days before on the corner of Clark Street and Deming Place, around the corner from where he lived, an unknown man approached him and offered him a 1964 Ford station wagon for \$300 and the victim's 1955 Chevrolet four-door sedan. The victim gave him \$150 in cash and the Chevrolet, and promised to pay the other \$150 later. The next day he was arrested for being in possession of the station wagon, which had been stolen. He gave the police the name and address to which he was supposed to deliver the other \$150. The police found that the man who answered to that name had moved away from that address on the day the theft occurred. The next day the victim received a note in the mail telling him that his Chevrolet was parked on a street in another part of town. He recovered the car undamaged. On November 7, detectives found the suspected swindler and arrested him. Final disposition of the case is not recorded in the files.

At 12:10 an officer answering a recovered-stolen-property call discovered that a burglary had taken place an hour or so earlier in a house on Diversey Parkway. Three 18-year-old neighborhood youths in an alley back of the burglarized premises saw three younger boys they did not know walking down the alley carrying boxes. The younger boys started running and the older boys chased them. The younger boys escaped but in the process of doing so one of them dropped a record player he was carrying. Inquiries in the neighborhood turned up a woman who noticed that the basement door of the house next to hers was wide open. She telephoned the occupant of the basement, an acquaintance of hers, but there was no answer. Ringing the doorbell produced the same result. The basement's occupant was summoned from work, and identified the record player as hers. Sho also discovered that various pieces of costume jewelery, a wristwatch, an electric shaver, a small camera, a tape recorder, and a transistor radio were missing. An evidence technician found no fingerprints in the house, and gave the opinion that the door had probably been forced open with a shoulder. When the occupant of the house's two top floors returned from work later in the day, he found that a wristwatch, an electric drill, and a cigar box containing a dollar's worth of pennies were missing. The older boys said that they had not been able to get a good enough look at the younger boys to identify them.

At 12:20 a man reported that his 1959 Mercedes was missing from where he had parked it, on Lakeview Avenue, 2 days before. The next day he was notified by the pound that his car had been towed there from a location a couple of miles from where he had left it as a traffic hazard. One side of the car was dented and scratched.

At 12:35 a woman reported that her nephew's 1959 Buick, which she was using while he was in the Navy, was missing from where she had parked it overnight. Six days later an officer spotted it parked on the side of an expressway, damaged on all sides, and had it towed to the pound.

Also at 12:35 the owner of a tavern on Broadway near Belmont Avenue reported that shortly after she had opened the tavern at noon to accept a beer delivery, she discovered that the previous night's receipts, $172, were missing from a cigar box where the night bartender had left them. She was at first inclined to blame the man who delivered the beer, but after being interrogated at some length by a detective 2 days later, she admitted that the bartender himself was the only likely suspect. She said that the bartender was a personal friend and that therefore she did not wish to pursue the matter further.

At 2:15 a woman living in a 15th floor apartment on Lake Shore Drive reported that she had received a lewd telephone call. She had no clue to the identity of the caller, who had first asked to speak to her daughter whose engagement had recently been announced in the papers. The officer told her how to avoid such incidents in the future.

At quarter of three the grandmother of a 19-year-old schoolgirl reported that as her granddaughter was walking to school early that morning in the western part of the district, a man had walked up to her, exposed himself and said, "Look what I've got." She had continued walking and the man had not bothered her further. The next day a detective showed the girl photographs of known sex offenders, and she identified one. This man was no longer living at his last known address, and the probation department reported that it had already issued a warrant for him for failing to report to his probation officer. The detective followed various leads to the man's whereabouts until December 1, when he had exhausted all of them. The man is still on the wanted list.

At 3:30 a construction and remodeling contractor reported that 10 days before, a man who had helped him move furniture to a new home had stolen 15 blank checks from his office. Apparently what prompted this belated report was that four of the checks had turned up at the contractor's bank, where his balance was insufficient to meet them. The contractor was able to give the police the name and description of the suspected thief, but not his address. The police were unable to find him.

At 6 o'clock a woman living alone in a ground-floor apartment reported that when she had returned home from work she discovered that someone had entered her apartment by breaking a pane of glass in the back door and had stolen a table radio and $10 in cash. There were no clues.

At 6:30 a watchman at Graceland Cemetery reported that some headstones had been pushed over. The police toured the cemetery with no results. The headstones were not damaged.

At 7:20 the police were called to a discount store on Clark Street where a 16-year-old Indian girl had been caught in the act of stealing two sweaters. She was taken to district headquarters and turned over to a youth officer.

At 7:25 a woman in the western part of the district reported that her ex-husband had confronted her in the hallway of her apartment house, had grabbed her by the neck and had threatened to kill her if he saw her on the street. The officer advised her to procure a warrant. She said she did not want to prosecute but simply wanted her ex-husband to stay away from her.

At 7:40 a student at Southern Illinois University reported that his 1956 Ford, on which there were no plates, was missing from the street near the lake where he had left it 10 days earlier when he had gone to school. The car never was found.

At 8:15 the manager of a discount store on Clark Street reported that he had been punched in the mouth by a tall man in his thirties whom the manager had caught shoplifting. The officer drove the victim around the area looking for the suspect, but he could not be found.

At 8:30 a citizen who refused to give his name stopped a patrol car toward the west end of Belmont Avenue and told the patrolman that teenagers were drinking in a nearby candy store. The officer found four 18- and 19-year-old boys drinking beer in the store, which at the time was being tended by a 15-year-old girl. He arrested the boys and confiscated 5 cans of beer. Apparently the case was adjusted informally at the district station by youth officers.

The last call of the day came at 11:15 from a woman living alone in an apartment near the lake. She reported that at some time between her departure for work at 9 in the morning and her return home at 11 in the evening, her apartment had been entered and property she valued at more than $700 had been stolen. The property included a portable television set, an AM-FM radio, a slide projector, a camera, a sewing machine, an iron, an electric clock, two empty purses, and a quantity of costume jewelry. There were no signs of forcible entry; apparently the latch had been forced back with a piece of plastic. There were no clues. That same day a Negro driving a car in another part of town was arrested for a traffic violation, and when the arresting officers discovered a quantity of property in the car they held it so that they could investigate whether it had been stolen. The suspect appeared in traffic court the following day and was released on $25 bond. The police kept the property for a week without learning where it came from, then returned it to the suspect. A week or so later they learned that it corresponded to the property stolen from the woman on October 27. On December 15 the same officers who had made the traffic arrest spotted the suspect walking along the street and arrested him. On February 2 he pleaded guilty to a reduced charge of theft and was sentenced to a year in prison. The property was not recovered.

Appendix 2–B

EXTENT OF UNREPORTED CRIME ACCORDING TO SURVEYS OF THE PRESIDENT'S COMMISSION ON LAW ENFORCEMENT AND ADMINISTRATION OF JUSTICE

Although the police statistics indicate a lot of crime today, they do not begin to indicate the full amount. Crimes reported directly to prosecutors usually do not show up in the police statistics. Citizens often do not report crimes to the police. Some crimes reported to the police never get into the statistical system. Since better crime prevention and control programs depend upon a full and accurate knowledge about the amount and kinds of crime, the Commission initiated the first national survey ever made of crime victimization. The National Opinion Research Center of the University of Chicago surveyed 10,000 households, asking whether the person questioned or any member of his or her household, had been a victim of crime during the past year, whether the crime had been reported, and, if not, the reasons for not reporting.

More detailed surveys were undertaken in a number of high and medium crime rate precincts of Washington, Chicago, and Boston by the Bureau of Social Science Research of Washington, D.C., and the Survey Research Center of the University of Michigan. All of the surveys dealt primarily with households or individuals, although some data were obtained for certain kinds of businesses and other organizations.

These surveys show that the actual amount of crime in the United States today is several times that reported in the UCR. As shown in the following table [Table 2–B–1], the amount of personal injury crime reported to NORC is almost twice the UCR rate and the amount of property crime more than twice as much as the UCR rate for individuals. Forcible rapes were more than 3½ times the reported rate, burglaries three times, aggravated assaults and larcenies of $50 and over more than double, and robbery 50 percent greater than the reported rate. Only vehicle theft was lower and then by a small amount. (The single homicide reported is too small a number to be statistically useful.)

Even these rates probably understate the actual amounts of crime. The national survey was a survey of the victim experience of every member of a household based on interviews of one member. If the results are tabulated only for the family member who was interviewed, the amount of unreported victimization for some offenses is con-

Task Force Report: *Crime and its Impact—An Assessment* (Washington, D.C.: U.S. Government Printing Office, 1967), pp. 17–19.

Table 2–B–1. Comparison of survey and UCR rates

[Per 100,000 population]

Index crimes	*NORC survey 1965–66*	*UCR rate for individuals 1965*[1]	*UCR rate for individuals and organizations 1965*[1]
Willful homicide	3.0	5.1	5.1
Forcible rape	42.5	11.6	11.6
Robbery	94.0	61.4	61.4
Aggravated assault	218.3	106.6	106.6
Burglary	949.1	299.6	605.3
Larceny ($50 and over)	606.5	267.4	393.3
Motor vehicle theft	206.2	226.0	251.0
Total violence	357.8	184.7	184.7
Total property	1,761.8	793.0	1,249.6

[1] "Uniform Crime Reports," 1965, p. 51. The UCR national totals do not distinguish crimes committed against individuals or households from those committed against businesses or other organizations. The UCR rate for individuals is the published national rate adjusted to eliminate burglaries, larcenies, and vehicle thefts not committed against individuals or households. No adjustment was made for robbery.

siderably higher. Apparently, the person interviewed remembered more of his own victimization than that of other members of his family.

The Washington, Boston, and Chicago surveys, based solely on victimization of the person interviewed, show even more clearly the disparity between reported and unreported amounts of crime. The clearest case is that of the survey in three Washington precincts, where, for the purpose of comparing survey results with crimes reported to the police, previous special studies made it possible to eliminate from police statistics crimes involving business and transient victims. As the following figure [Figure 2–B–1] indicates, for certain specific offenses against individuals the number of offenses reported to the survey per thousand residents 18 years or over ranged, depending on the offense, from 3 to 10 times more than the number contained in police statistics.

The survey in Boston and in one of the Chicago precincts indicated about three times as many index crimes as the police statistics, in the other Chicago precinct about 1½ times as many. These survey rates are not fully comparable with the Washington results because adequate information did not exist for eliminating business and transient victims from the police statistics. If this computation could have been made, the Boston and Chicago figures would undoubtedly have shown a closer similarity to the Washington findings.

In the national survey of households those victims saying that they had not notified the police of their victimization were asked why. The reason most frequently given for all offenses was that the police could not do anything. This reason was given by 68 percent of those not reporting malicious mischief, and by 60 or more percent of those not reporting burglaries, larcenies of $50 and over, and auto thefts. It is not clear whether these responses are accurate assessments of the victims' inability to help the

Figure 2-B-1. Estimated rates of offense[1] comparison of police[2] and BSSR survey data

3 WASHINGTON, D.C. PRECINCTS Rates per 1000 Residents 18 Years or Over

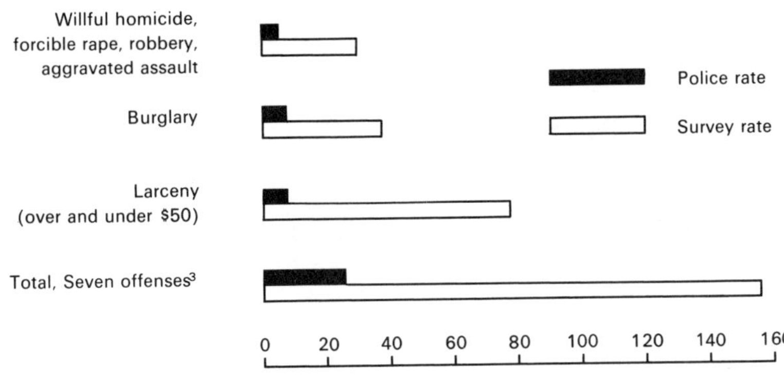

[1] Incidents involving more than one victim adjusted to count as only one offense. A victimization rate would count the incidence for each individual.

[2] Police statistics adjusted to eliminate nonresident and commercial victims and victims under 18 years of age.

[3] Willful homicide, forcible rape, robbery, aggravated assault, burglary, larceny (over and under $50), and motor vehicle theft.

police or merely rationalizations of their failure to report. The next most frequent reason was that the offense was a private matter or that the victim did not want to harm the offender. It was given by 50 percent or more of those who did not notify the police for aggravated and simple assaults, family crimes, and consumer frauds. Fear of reprisal, though least often cited, was strongest in the case of assaults and family crimes. The extent of failure to report to the police was highest for consumer fraud (90 percent) and lowest for auto theft (11 percent).

The survey technique, as applied to criminal victimization, is still new and beset with a number of methodological problems. However, the Commission has found the information provided by the surveys of considerable value, and believes that the survey technique has a great untapped potential as a method for providing additional information about the nature and extent of our crime problem and the relative effectiveness of different programs to control crime.

Appendix 2–C

NYE-SHORT'S SELF-REPORTING STUDY

Table 2–C–1. Distribution of delinquency scale types for boys, ages sixteen and seventeen*

Scale type	Offense number†											Public school		Training school	
	1	2	3	4	5	6	7	8	9	10	11	*Number*	*Cumulative percent*	*Number*	*Cumulative percent*
00	0	0	0	0	0	0	0	0	0	0	0‡	0	0	0	0
01	1	0	0	0	0	0	0	0	0	0	0	128	22.5	0	0
02	1	1	0	0	0	0	0	0	0	0	0	53	31.8	0	0
03	1	1	1	0	0	0	0	0	0	0	0	32	37.4	0	0
04	1	1	1	1	0	0	0	0	0	0	0	133	60.7	3	2.4
05	2	1	1	1	0	0	0	0	0	0	0	15	63.3	2	4.0
06	2	1	1	1	1	0	0	0	0	0	0	4	64.0	0	4.0
07	2	1	1	1	1	1	0	0	0	0	0	46	72.1	3	6.4
08	2	1	2	1	1	1	0	0	0	0	0	97	89.1	20	22.4
09	2	1	2	2	1	1	0	0	0	0	0	2	89.5	0	22.4
10	2	1	2	2	1	1	1	0	0	0	0	34	95.4	20	38.4
11	2	1	2	2	1	1	1	1	0	0	0	1	95.6	0	38.4
12	2	2	2	2	1	1	1	1	0	0	0	2	96.0	0	38.4
13	2	2	2	2	1	1	1	1	1	0	0	4	96.7	3	40.8
14	2	2	2	2	1	1	2	1	1	0	0	4	97.4	1	41.6
15	2	2	2	2	2	1	2	1	1	0	0	2	97.7	8	48.0
16	2	2	2	2	2	2	2	1	1	0	0	9	99.3	26	68.8
17	2	2	2	2	2	2	2	1	1	1	1	1	99.5	5	72.8
18	2	2	2	2	2	2	2	1	2	1	1	3	100.0	34	100.0
Total §												570		125	

*The coefficient of reproducibility of this scale is .975.

†Offense numbers refer to the following delinquent acts: (1) Driving a car without a driver's license or permit. (2) Taking little things (worth less than $2) that did not belong to you. (3) Buying or drinking beer, wine, or liquor (include drinking at home). (4) Skipping school without a legitimate excuse. (5) Purposely damaging or destroying public or private property. (6) Sex relations with a person of the opposite sex. (7)

F. Ivan Nye and James F. Short, Jr., "Scaling Delinquent Behavior," *American Sociological Review*, 22 (June 1957), p. 330. Reprinted by permission.

Taking things of medium value ($2 to $50). (8) Taking things of large value (worth more than $50). (9) "Running away" from home. (10) Defying parents' authority to their faces. (11) Narcotics violations.

‡In all cases "0" indicates that the offense has not been committed by boys in this scale type. In the case of all trichotomized items except heterosexual relations the score "1" indicates commission of the offense once or twice and a score of "2" indicates commission of the offense more than once or twice. A score of "1" for heterosexual relations indicates commissions of the offense from one to four times, while a score of "2" indicates commission more than four times. In the case of dichotomized items a score of "1" indicates commission of the offense one or more times.

§Eight public school boys and one training school boy were lost to the scale due to excessive non-responses to the delinquency questions. The procedure followed in handling non-responses was to assign them to the modal category, 0, 1, or 2. This was done, however, only when at least six of the eleven delinquency items had been answered.

Appendix 2–D

THE CLARK-TIFFT POLYGRAPH VALIDATION

THE STUDY

The study reported here was designed to test experimentally the accuracy of anonymous questionnaire responses by utilizing data obtained via a polygraph examination as external validity criteria. In the first of two preliminary studies, university students were asked to suggest behaviors which other students might tend to under- or over-report having done. In the second study, they were asked to estimate the amount of "normative pressure" on persons of their age and sex to respond in either direction on these items and items from other research of undetected delinquency. A final questionnaire was then constructed consisting of five seven-item groups reflecting consensus on their potential under- or over-reportability. (The items were presented to the respondents in five seven-item groups—one group per page in the following order:

Group 1—35, 23, 25, 8, 22, 31, 1
Group 2—34, 24, 16, 26, 17, 33, 9
Group 3—21, 29, 3, 10, 11, 18, 2
Group 4—14, 12, 15, 20, 13, 4, 5
Group 5—30, 28, 6, 32, 7, 19, 27

	Reporting error (percent)			
Deviant behavior items	*accurate*	*over-reported*	*under-reported*	*percent admitting behavior*
1. Run away from home	100.0	0.0	0.0	12.5
2. Attacked someone with the idea of taking his (her) life	100.0	0.0	0.0	0.0
3. Attempted to take my own life	100.0	0.0	0.0	2.5
4. Used force to get money or valuables from another person	95.0	2.5	2.5	2.5

John P. Clark and Larry L. Tifft, "Polygraph and Interview Validation of Self-Reported Deviant Behavior," *American Sociological Review*, 31:4 (August 1966), pp. 516–523. Reprinted by permission.

Deviant behavior items	accurate	*Reporting error (percent)* over-reported	under-reported	percent admitting behavior
5. Gotten a female other than my wife pregnant	95.0	2.5	2.5	7.5
6. Bribed or attempted to bribe a police officer or another type of official	95.0	5.0	0.0	7.5
7. Visited a house of prostitution	95.0	2.5	2.5	17.5
8. Carried a razor, switchblade, or gun as weapon	92.5	7.5	0.0	12.5
9. Taken part in gang fights	92.5	5.0	2.5	10.0
10. Used or sold narcotic drugs	92.5	0.0	5.0	10.0
11. Taken things of large value (worth more than $50) that did not belong to me	92.5	5.0	2.5	5.0
12. Broken into and entered a home, store, or building	92.5	2.5	5.0	20.0
13. Struck my girl friend or wife	92.5	2.5	5.0	15.0
14. Had a steady girlfriend	90.0	2.5	7.5	90.0
15. "Beaten up" on someone who hadn't done anything to me	90.0	5.0	5.0	10.0
16. Defied my parents' authority to their face	85.0	7.5	7.5	57.5
17. Taken a car for a ride without the owner's knowledge	85.0	2.5	7.5	17.5
18. Attempted to force or forced a female to have sexual intercourse with me	85.0	2.5	7.5	15.0
19. Driven a motor vehicle in an unauthorized drag race	80.0	5.0	15.0	45.0
20. Witnessed a crime and neither reported it nor made sure someone else had	80.0	7.5	7.5	17.5
21. Had sex relations with a person of the same sex	80.0	5.0	15.0	22.5
22. Started a fist fight	80.0	17.5	2.5	22.5

Deviant behavior items	Reporting error (percent) accurate	over-reported	under-reported	percent admitting behavior
23. Purposely damaged or destroyed public or private property that did not belong to me	77.5	10.0	12.5	55.0
24. Driven a car without a driver's license or permit (Do not include driver's training courses)	77.5	2.5	17.5	62.5
25. Falsified information while filling out an application form or report	75.0	0.0	25.0	57.5
26. Taken things from someone else's desk or locker at school without permission	72.5	2.5	25.0	47.5
27. Gambled for money or something else with persons other than my family members	67.5	7.5	25.0	80.0
28. Had sex relations with a person of the opposite sex (other than my wife)	67.5	15.0	17.5	55.0
29. Masturbated	65.0	5.0	30.0	95.0
30. Bought or drunk beer, wine or liquor illegally	65.0	2.5	32.5	95.0
31. Taken things of medium value (worth between $2 and $50) that didn't belong to me	65.0	2.5	32.5	45.0
32. Driven a motor vehicle at extreme speeds	52.5	2.5	40.0	85.0
33. Had in my possession pictures, books, or other materials which were obviously obscene and prepared to arouse someone sexually	50.0	7.5	12.5	50.0
34. Skipped school without a legitimate excuse	40.0	2.5	55.0	85.0
35. Taken little things (worth less than $2) that didn't belong to me	32.5	5.0	62.5	87.5

Individual item accuracy ranged from 33 to 100 percent. Items 19, 21, 24, 25, 27, 29, 30, 32, 34, and 35 were rather consistently under-reported; item 22 was frequently over-reported; and items 23 and 28 were both under- and over-reported. The reader will quickly recognize many of these items as parts of the Nye-Short seven-item general delinquency scale and the Dentler-Monroe five-item adolescent theft scale.

The data demonstrate that while there is a significant difference between original and final scale scores on both the Dentler-Monroe[1] and Nye-Short scales, there is a high rank correlation between the ordering of subjects on the original questionnaire and the final ordering of subjects: Dentler-Montoe r = 0.81 and Nye-Short r = 0.80.

Assuming that deviant behavior may be in conflict with norms to which individuals generally subscribe, we would expect persons in threatening situations to make errors in the direction of the norms. Such was the case in this study. Respondents were questioned on their feelings about the acceptability of the behavior described in each of the items. In 53 of 80 instances (66 percent) in which respondents did not initially admit an act but later did, they stated the act was "never permissible" according to their own feelings. Further, in 20 of the 26 instances (77 percent) in which respondents initially admitted acts in spite of their not having committed them, respondents reported the behavior was personally "permissible in a few circumstances" or "in many circumtances."

Based upon the voluminous literature which suggests that commitment to group norms helps determine public behavior, we first assumed that responding to questionnaires did not represent total escape from the respondent's meaningful group attachments, and then hypothesized that errors would fall in the direction of perceived group norms. Our data tend to support this hypothesis.

In 29 of the 80 instances (36 percent) in which respondents did not initially admit an act but later did, they stated that the act was "never permissible" according to the perceived standards of their reference group. (Reference group was operationally defined here as "the group of guys you have generally done things with.") The direct relevance of these data to the explanation of under-reporting errors is difficult to assess because every instance of group support coincided with a case of normative personal support. However, in 23 of the 26 instances (89 percent) in which respondents initially admitted acts in spite of their not having committed them, respondents perceived group support for such acts. There is strong evidence that errors on questionnaires are directly associated with perceived discrepancies between individual acts and personal and group norms. The errors represent an attempt to make reported behavior compatible with perceived norms.

A positive relationship between the amount of misconduct ultimately admitted and reporting errors was expected and obtained. However, this relationship was thought to be spurious because the greater the number of items which applied to a person, the greater his opportunity to make errors in the under-reported direction. Because of this, the sample was divided into "high changers" and "low changers" on the basis of an error rate—the number of errors divided by number of items admitted. (The number of errors is the sum of the number of items changed between initial and

[1] Robert A. Dentler and Lawrence J. Monroe, "Early Adolescent Theft," *American Sociological Review*, 26 (October 1961), pp. 733–744.

final responses minus the over-reporting errors which were resolved to the zero category. The number of items admitted is based on final responses.) Average delinquency scores, indicate no significant relationship between error rate and amount of admitted misconduct. We must conclude from this comparison that there is no relationship between questionnaire validity (accuracy) and extent of involvement in deviant behavior.

Appendix 2–E

Table 2–E–1. Erickson and Empey's data on extent of self-reported violations of Utah white boys.[1]

Classified offenses	Subsamples: non-delinquents	one-time offenders	delinquents on probation	delinquents incarcerated
Theft				
Articles less than \$2	966	1,738	7,886	4,585
Articles worth \$2 to \$50	60	80	4,671	2,585
Articles more than \$50	1	2	90	201
Auto theft	4	0	169	649
Forgery	0	0	60	452
Others				
Gambling	1,185	2,400	1,186	2,800
Smoking (habitually)	1	3	39	43
Traffic Offenses				
Driving without License	1,845	512	2,386	7,053
Traffic Viol. (not lic.)	2,040	2,142	3,068	4,900
Retreatist Activities				
Running away from Home	19	19	103	437
Skipping School	377	698	3,478	4,822
Property Violations				
Breaking and Entering	67	102	527	926
Destroying Property	477	800	4,927	4,441
Setting Fires (Arson)	2	2.	0	7
Alcohol and Narcotics				
Buying Beer or Liquor	18	57	1,453	7,362
Drinking Beer or Liquor	219	270	4,173	8,146
Selling Narcotics	0	0	0	1
Using Marcotics	0	0	3	71
Offenses Against Person				
Armed Robbery	0	0	22	24
Fighting, Assault	354	103	2.207	6,316
Open Defiance of Authority				
Defying Parents	138	128	4,804	3,072
Defying Others	124	170	1,478	4,725

[1] *Taken from* Maynard L. Erickson and LaMar T. Empey, "Court Records, Undetected Delinquency and Decision-Making," *Journal of Criminal Law, Criminology and Police Science* (December 1963), pp. 460–461. Rearranged. Reprinted by special permission of The Journal of Criminal Law, Criminology and Police Science (Northwestern University School of Law), Copyright © 1963, Vol. 54 No. 4.

Table 2–E–2. Erickson and Empey's data on proportion of white Utah boys who reported having committed offenses.[2]

Offense	*Subsamples (percent)* non-delinquents	one-time offenders	delinquents on probation	delinquents incarcerated
Theft				
Less than $2	92	98	96	86
Worth $2 to $50	22	36	78	90
More than $50	2	2	46	54
Auto Theft	2	2	54	60
Forgery	0	0	16	34
Others				
Gambling	90	100	56	72
Smoking (habitually)	2	4	76	86
Traffic Offenses				
Driving Without License	72	78	94	92
Traffic Viol. (not lic.)	84	84	72	66
Retreatist Activities				
Running Away from Home	22	24	46	60
Skipping School	66	68	96	100
Property Violations				
Breaking and Entering	32	46	74	84
Destroying Property	66	84	86	84
Setting Fires (Arson)	2	2	0	8
Alcohol and Narcotics				
Buying Beer or Liquor	4	8	46	58
Drinking Beer or Liquor	52	66	84	94
Selling Narcotics	0	0	0	2
Using Narcotics	0	0	2	12
Offenses Against Person				
Armed Robbery	0	0	4	14
Fighting, Assault	52	60	82	86
Open Defiance of Authority				
Defying Parents	40	44	64	64
Defying Others	52	54	72	78

[2] *Ibid.*, p. 463.

Appendix 2–F

HARDT'S STUDY OF SELF-REPORTED DELINQUENCY INVOLVEMENT

During June 1963, questionnaires were administered to seventh, eighth, and ninth grade pupils attending one parochial and four public junior high schools located in the study areas. A special team of test monitors provided the pupils with standard explanations and instructions. Pupils were given assurance about the confidentiality of their answers and were asked not to sign their names. Students were allotted approximately 100 minutes (two classroom periods) to complete the questionnaire. In addition to the section on reported behavior, the questionnaire sought to obtain information on a variety of other topics such as pupil's educational and occupational aspirations and perceptions of schools, neighborhoods, police and agencies.

An omnibus violation scale score has been used to define violator status. Boys with scores of six and above are considered "high violators," those with scores of two and below as "low violators," and those with intermediate scores as "medium violators." High violators are not only more extensive violators; a refined analysis reveals that they are much more likely to admit recent involvement—which suggests that they are more likely to be frequent violators. The information used to classify the juvenile population as "suspects" or "alleged delinquents" was obtained from the Central Registry of Juvenile Police Contacts. The registry provides a centralized confidential registration of juveniles alleged to be delinquent by any of the nineteen police units which operate in the country.

A moderately high correlation exists between the self-report violation scores and official suspect status, gamma = – .55. However, a more detailed analysis reveals that while most suspects tend to be high violators, most high violators are not suspects, i.e., officially recorded delinquents. Thus, despite the high correlation between the two measures, a possibility exists that independent variables may show substantially different relationships with the two delinquency variables.

Data are presented on the number of police contacts registered for boys living in the three neighborhoods. Findings are presented separately for the 12–13 and 14–15 year age groups, since age increases the risk of delinquent involvement and the age distributions in the areas differ somewhat. In each age group, Area A boys have the highest rate of suspects and Area 0 boys the lowest rate. In Area A, one-third of younger

Robert H. Hardt, *Delinquency and Social Class: Studies of Juvenile Deviations or Police Dispositions?* Youth Development Center, Syracuse University, December 15, 1964, pp. 2–12.

boys and over one-half of older boys have had at least one police contact. In Area O only one out of sixteen younger boys, and only one out of eight older boys are listed as suspects. The degree of association between neighborhood rank and number of contacts is high and similar for each age group (gamma = −.59 for 12–13 year olds and gamma = −.60 for 14–15 year olds).

Among the younger age groups, there is no significant relationship between the social rank of an area and the incidence of self-reported delinquent activity (gamma = −.07, $P > .10$). Violation status is significantly related to area variation among older boys (gamma = −.20, $P < .01$). For this age group, there is a particularly marked upward progression of high violator rates from Area O to Area B to Area A.

The discrepancy between the incidence of suspects and violators in certain categories may be demonstrated by another procedure. In the total sample, the suspect rate is 19.8 percent and the high violator rate is 22.6 percent. The suspect rate is .86 of the high violator rate. If suspect rates for different categories merely reflected violator rates, we would expect the suspect (arrest) rates to be .86 of the high violator rates. If the ratio were higher, it would reflect an over-representation of arrests, and if it were lower, it would be an under-representation. In order to make numerical comparisons simpler, the "expected ratio" of suspects to high violators has been adjusted from .86 to 1.00. Thus for any given category of boys, the index of representativeness (I.R.) equals the suspect rate for that category divided by the high violator rate for that category—with the ratio divided by .86.

$$\text{I.R.} = \frac{\text{Suspect Rate}}{\text{High Violator Rate}} \times \frac{1}{.86}$$

The index values depart considerably from the expected value of 1.00. For the older age group, Area O has a suspect rate only about half that expected, while Area A has a suspect rate over one-third of that expected. Among the younger boys, both Areas A and B have suspect rates nearly double that expected while Area O has a rate less than half of that expected. Thus, these findings suggest that accurate inferences about the relative incidence of boys involved in extensive delinquency behaviors in low and middle status neighborhoods cannot be made from official records.

Only in Area A are there a sufficient number of whites and non-whites to permit the computation of suspect and violation rates by race. The findings indicate that there is a highly significant difference in the number of police contacts received by white and non-white youth (gamma = −.63, $P < .01$). The two racial groups are quite similar, however, in their self reports of delinquency activity. The pair of I.R. values reflect a marked under-representation of police contacts among whites (.56) and a heavy over-representation of suspects among non-whites (1.81).

Finally, an examination was made of two facets of the household context in which the boys lived. First, households were divided into those headed by a father and those in which a father was not present. Households headed by a father were then subdivided on an occupational basis into white-collar and blue-collar fathers.

In the total sample, approximately twenty-three percent of the boys lived in households headed by white-collar males, and a similar percentage lived in female-based households. The majority of boys had blue-collar fathers. However, the areas differed substantially in the distribution of types of households. Since it has already been shown that area variations in arrest rates are considerable, it was decided to examine the impact of household context within each area.

Some of the general findings may be summarized as follows:

1. In all three areas, boys from female-based households have the highest suspect and violation rates; the I.R. values indicated that boys from these households are most likely to be over-represented in the suspect rates.

2. In the two low income areas, boys with blue-collar fathers have higher suspect and violation rates than sons of white-collar fathers; the I.R. values indicate that some over-representation of blue-collar sons may take place.

3. In general, it appears that differences in selectivity (I.R. values) are greater among neighborhoods than among household contexts.

What accounts for these neighborhood variations in I.R. values? At what stage of the detection and referral process do these discrepancies begin to emerge? One possibility is that delinquents from middle income neighborhoods are less likely to be detected, or at least, less likely to be referred to or apprehended by the police. There is accumulating evidence, however, that a powerful source of the selectivity of official records occurs as a result of the discretionary authority of the police officer.

On the basis of observations and interviews with 90 policemen in four Pennsylvania communities, Goldman discovered that "parents holding responsible positions in business, industry, or in politics were usually spared the official registration of their children's delinquencies." In a large-scale survey of police opinions, a majority of police agreed to the statement that "in most cases involving lower-class, underprivileged, slum type juveniles, strong police and court action are necessary because the families of these offenders are incapable of exercising proper control." In addition, one-third agreed that "most middle or upper-class juveniles come from families of responsible people who are able to take the necessary corrective action, thus making strong police and court action less necessary." In an observational study of police officers' contacts with juveniles, Piliavin and Briar found that in deciding about disposition police employed such cues as "the youth's group affiliations age, race, grooming, dress, and demeanor."

Some supplementary data collected on the self-report scale provide some further evidence about the impact of differential disposition. On item 10, boys were asked to indicate whether they had been warned or questioned by the police, and on item 17 they were asked to report police ticketing or arrests.

The percentages of boys who admit having received a warning differ little among the three neighborhoods. Such contact is reported by 54 percent of Area O boys, 59 percent of Area A boys, and 62 percent of Area B boys. In contrast, substantial area differences are found in the rates of ticketing, ranging from a low of 13 percent in Area O to a high of 40 percent in Area A. In Area A, two out of every three questioned boys have received tickets. At the other extreme, in Area O, only one out of four questioned boys received a ticket.

In each area, boys with greater involvement in delinquency activity are more likely to report that they have been questioned by the police. Police questioning is admitted by nearly nine out of ten high violators, two out of three medium violators, and one out of three low violators. Such rates differ only slightly in the three neighborhoods.

The ticketing rate is also highly related to violation status, but within each category of violators, the risk of ticketing shows a strong linkage to the boy's area of residence. For example, among high violators, the rate of ticketing is 69 percent in Area A, 52 percent in Area B, and 36 percent in Area O.

Among high violators who have been questioned by the police, 83 percent have been ticketed in Area A compared to only 40 percent in Area O. Among low violators who have been questioned, 47 percent in Area A have been ticketed, but only 9 percent in Area O. In Area A, low violators who are questioned have a greater chance of receiving a ticket than Area O high violators who have been questioned.

It appears that *one of the prime factors which accounts for area variations in official delinquency rates is the differential disposition of juvenile cases which are made by the police. Police questioning or warning boys from low-income areas is much more likely to be followed by the issuing of a ticket than in the case of boys from middle income neighborhoods.*

In summary, both suspect rates and violator rates tend to be somewhat higher in the lowest socio-economic neighborhood. However, the magnitude of area variations is much greater for suspect rates than violator rates. Race differences in suspect rates are large, but in violation status, race differences are not significant. Boys living in female-based households tend to have higher suspect rates than other boys living in the same neighborhood. Again, much greater variation between household types is shown by the suspect rates.

The percentage of boys who report police questioning shows little variation among neighborhoods. Marked area variations are shown in the percentage of ticketed boys and in the percentage of questioned boys who are ticketed, i.e., boys from low-income areas who are questioned are much more likely to be ticketed. These findings tend to reinforce the reminder furnished by Piliavin and Briar that "the official delinquent, as distinguished from the juvenile who commits a delinquent act, is the product of a social judgment, in this case, a judgment made by the police." Nearly ten years ago, Merton cautioned a group of delinquency researchers "to acknowledge the brutal hard fact with which we must cope—that often the data which are at hand on a large scale happen not to be the data which are needed."

The results of the present study suggest that official statistics cannot be counted upon to reflect variations in the incidence of delinquent youth. Delinquency theories, prevention programs, or evaluation studies which place heavy reliance on such official data are open to serious challenge.

THE SCHEDULE*

Young people do lots of things that are good—BUT ONCE IN A WHILE THEY BREAK SOME RULES. SOME OF OUR MOST FAMOUS PEOPLE SAID THEY BROKE QUITE A FEW RULES WHEN THEY WERE GROWING UP.

WE WANT TO GET A CLEAR PICTURE OF THE THINGS YOUNG PEOPLE DO. THE WAY YOU CAN HELP IS BY GIVING A TRUE PICTURE OF HOW YOUNG PEOPLE ACT,

DON'T WORRY ABOUT LOOKING GOOD—OR LOOKING BAD

WHEN WAS THE LAST TIME THAT YOU DID EACH OF THE FOLLOWING THINGS?

CHECK ONLY THE *LAST TIME* THIS HAPPENED

1(W). I SMOKED A CIGARETTE.

_______IN THE LAST 7 DAYS
_______IN THE LAST 12 MONTHS
_______OVER A YEAR AGO
_______NEVER

2(V). I BROKE STREET LIGHTS OR WINDOWS IN A BUILDING.

3. I WAS SENT TO COURT.

4(T). I TOOK SOMETHING WORTH MORE THAN 50¢ FROM A STORE.

5. I HELPED MY PARENTS AROUND THE HOUSE.

6(V). I DAMAGED OR MESSED UP SOMETHING IN A SCHOOL OR SOME OTHER BUILDING.

7(W). I STAYED OUT ALL NIGHT AND DIDN'T TELL MY PARENTS WHERE I WAS.

8(T). I BROKE INTO A PARKING METER

*NOTE: Letters in parentheses which follow the item numbers indicate the subscale to which the item was assigned. Items designated by asterisks were not included in the final scales.

F—Fighting
T—Theft
W—Wayward Acts
V—Vandalism

9(W). I DRANK SOME BEER, WINE, OR LIQUOR WITHOUT MY PARENTS KNOWING ABOUT IT.

10. I WAS WARNED OR QUESTIONED BY A POLICEMAN.

11(F). I TOOK PART IN A FIGHT WHERE OUR GROUP OF KIDS FOUGHT A DIFFERENT GROUP.

12(F). I HELPED TO JUMP SOMEBODY AND BEAT THEM UP.

*13(W). I TRIED TO GET KICKS FROM SMOKING REEFER CIGARETTES, TAKING PEP PILLS OR SNIFFING GLUE.

*14(W). I RAN AROUND WITH SOME KIDS WHO HAD A BAD REPUTATION.

*15(T). I TOOK SOMETHING WHICH DIDN'T BELONG TO ME WHICH WAS WORTH MORE THAN $2.

16(F). I TOOK PART IN A FIGHT WHERE KNIVES OR OTHER WEAPONS WERE USED.

17. I WAS GIVEN A TICKET OR WAS ARRESTED BY THE POLICE.

18(T). I WENT FOR A RIDE IN A CAR TAKEN WITHOUT THE OWNER'S PERMISSION.

19. I LET A FRIEND BORROW A LITTLE OF MY OWN MONEY.

Chapter 3

The who factor in doer involvement

Undoubtedly, better coverage on the "how" and the "extent" factors will give insights into the "who" factor, but there is a large segment of the "who" factor that needs to have special and somewhat separate consideration. The "who" factor addresses itself to the discovery of the kinds of persons that get involved in crime, if this is ultimately possible. Reference is usually made to the broad and ill-defined categories of delinquent and nondelinquent and/or criminal and noncriminal persons and groups, although it is not always clear what is the actual criterion for separation into these two sociolegal or sociobehavioral poles. Whatever the criterion, the distinction between the polar groups is not likely to be definite such as heads or tails, north and south, black and white, but is more likely to be a matter of degree: more involved versus less involved individuals as opposed to all versus none, except in a few very extreme cases.

Indications from arrest statistics

It has already been mentioned in Chapter 2 and will be further discussed in Chapter 7 that police agencies keep records that include personal information on persons they take into custody. The Federal Bureau of Investigation gathers age, sex, and race information on arrests for their annual publication on *Crime in the United States*. Although the local police records have much more information than this on cases of arrest, one does not know how accurate the additional items are.

Nevertheless, the records on age, sex, and race as compiled from police agencies in the United States give some indication of who gets involved in crime. The tables in Appendix 3–A present the age, race, and sex variables for arrests in 1969. They show that males are arrested much more often than females; persons under twenty-five years of age are more often arrested than are older persons; blacks are arrested disproportionately more often than whites. Consequently, these three categories present a differential risk for "acted upon" involvement in crime.

The question that is still not readily answerable is the extent to which arrest variations by age, sex, and race indicate a differential in actual involvement and to what extent they merely reflect arrest policy by police officers, and even willingness or unwillingness on the part of victims and observers to complain on violators. It is left to future American criminologists to find the answer to this question.

One should also be reminded of the fact that the best set of personal data on offenders is kept by juvenile and adult correctional institutions—that is not to say that their case records cannot be improved or that they are all equal in quality. Many correctional institutions have procedures that obtain validating personal information from sources other than from the incoming offender himself; however, statistics on admissions to prisons and institutions for juvenile delinquents cover such a small percentage of persons entering the criminal justice system that, in spite of their better quality and better coverage than statistics at the arrest level, they are not a very realistic indicator of the extent of involvement or of the kinds of persons that get involved in crime and delinquency. Still more unfortunately, the published annual reports, local as well as national, give very little coverage on the personal composition of newly admitted cases.

Many American criminologists have not been content with the indications from arrest statistics of who gets involved in crime and delinquency, and therefore they have tried to get behind the limited coverage of official statistics. Most of the attempts to obtain further insight into the "who" factor of involvement have concentrated on juveniles and youths. Some of the most revealing contributions that have sought to penetrate the "who" factor in involvement will be discussed in the remainder of this chapter.

The Cambridge-Sommerville method

One of the first systematic attempts to ferret out potential involvement in delinquency or its lack developed as a means to implement a delinquency prevention program called the Cambridge-Sommerville Youth Project (c. 1935–1939). The project represented an attempt to prevent delinquency in so-called predelinquent boys under twelve years of age, *via* individual guidance from counsellors. With respect to the nomination and selection of subjects for the "treatment" group and the "control" group (followed up but not treated), the following excerpts from the final report on the project give insights into how the staff distinguished between the boys heading for delinquency and those not heading toward delinquency.[1]

The study was seeking potential delinquents not yet known to the authorities.

The school presumably was in an advantageous position to select boys who seemed most likely to be well on the road toward a delinquent career, and yet teachers could not be expected to make infallible judgments.

The principals and the teachers from the kindergartens and the first, second, and third grades were asked to nominate boys below the age of ten who showed some of the following traits or habits to the extent that they might be considered difficult boys (e.g., persistent truancy, aggressiveness, persistent breaking of rules, etc.) (c. 1935–1936 school year).

During the following school year an important change was made in the experimental design of the Study: non-difficult boys were now to be included. . . . Non-difficult boys, for convenience, were called average boys, who showed no present signs of future delinquency.

(Basic information was collected from several sources such as home visiting, teacher interviews, psychological tests, physical examination, social service agency clearances, delinquency rating of neighborhood of residence, etc. and reviewed by the Selection Committee of the project.) This information was sufficient to warrant classification by the Selection Committee; to permit the matching of one boy with another in setting up a treatment and a control group; to serve as a basis for a prediction study, and to afford a counselor adequate material for initiating a treatment plan.

Gluecks' prediction of delinquency involvement

Using a special processing of data on 500 committed delinquent boys and a sample of 500 nondelinquent boys, all from Boston, closely matched for age, background, neighborhood (mostly underprivileged), I.Q., etc., which they themselves had collected (c. 1940) Sheldon and Eleanor Glueck singled out three sets of items that they found to distinquish very significantly the one group of youths from the other. One of the sets consisted of five character traits revealed by analysis of the Rorschach test: social assertion, defiance, suspicion, destructiveness, and emotional lability (impulsiveness). A second set of distinguishing items was composed of personality traits or the dynamics of temperament as discerned in psychiatric interviews with each individual boy: adventurousness, extroversion in action, suggestibility, stubborness, and emotional stability. A third set of items was selected from family factors that separated the delinquent from the nondelinquent. The five chosen

[1] Edwin Powers and Helen Witmer, *Prevention of Delinquency; The Cambridge-Sommerville Youth Study* (New York: Columbia University Press, 1951), pp. 29–30, 30–31, 50.

family factors are listed in Table 3-1 with appropriate degrees under each factor.

Table 3-1 Family Factors Used for Prediction in Gluecks' Study[2]

Factor	*Percentage failure**	*Rank order†*
1. Discipline of boy by father		10
Overstrict or erratic	71.8	
Lax	59.8	
Firm but kindly	9.3	
2. Supervision of boy by mother		5
Unsuitable	83.2	
Fair	57.5	
Suitable	9.9	
3. Affection of father for boy		22
Indifferent or hostile	75.9	
Warm (including overprotective)	33.8	
4. Affection of mother for boy		34
Indifferent or hostile	86.2	
Warm (including overprotective)	43.1	
5. Cohesiveness of family		11
Unintegrated	96.9	
Some elements of cohesion	61.3	
Cohesive	20.6	

*The Gluecks call this the weighted failure score, but it is just a percentage of failure broken down by delinquent and nondelinquent (obtained by subtracting from 100) for each subcategory within the factor.

†Refers to the rank order of the factor in the total list of factors found to be significant by the chi square method as worked out by the author in *The Crime Problem*, 2nd ed., Appleton-Century-Crofts, New York, 1955, pp. 74-76.

Regardless of the particular method of prognostication, the real validity of attempting to determine who will and who will not become involved in behavior that leads to police and court action comes from the actual facts of official involvement. The Gluecks, *via* a long, painstaking follow-up study, were able to collect the facts that enabled them to gauge the differential involvement of their original sample of 500 white committed delinquents and 500 white nondelinquents from the city of Boston

The delinquents and the nondelinquents were compared at the age of twenty-five and again at age thirty-one on several points of social adjustment such as home life, employment history, and military experience but mainly on criminal involvement after the age of seventeen. Out of the original 500 in each sample, the Gluecks presented follow-up information on 438 delinquents and 442 nondelinquents.

[2]Sheldon and Eleanor Glueck, *Unravelling Juvenile Delinquency* (Cambridge, Massachusetts: Harvard University Press, 1950), p. 261.

The assembled data on the two groups of 500 each at the point of original contact indicated that the delinquent emerged from a more unfavorable home atmosphere, represented a more "uninhibited, untamed, unreflective child and, on the basis of his behavior in school and in the neighborhood, displayed more difficulties than his matched nondelinquent peers." Of the nondelinquents, 62 were found to have become involved in officially recorded offenses after age seventeen: 46 percent during their age span from seventeen to twenty-five, and 16 percent during the age span from twenty-five to thirty-one years of age. Only 3 of the original sample of nondelinquents became involved in serious crimes.[3]

The frequency of arrest of 438 "followed-up" original delinquents is indicated by the following percentages for the time span from seventeen to twenty-five years of age: none, 19.2; one arrest during the entire period, 12.1; one in each 6 months in the community (not counting time in a penal institution), 16.5; one in each 12 months, 17.3; one in each 24 months, 16.9; one in each period of more than 24 months, 18.0. The frequency of arrest involvement for 433 of the original 500 delinquent youths during the age span of twenty-five to thirty-one was as follows (for the same frequency time categories as above): 39.3, 19.4, 9.7, 10.6, 9.9, and 11.1.[4]

The difference between the involvement of the originally designated nondelinquents and delinquents is very great indeed. Researchers in crime and delinquency should, on the basis of the Glueck data, be very much encouraged in pursuing efficacious methods of prognosticating the "who" factor in adolescent and adult involvement as well as noninvolvement in serious offenses. One very interesting trend was found within the Gluecks' delinquent sample, namely that a "slowdown" occurred in the age period between twenty-five and thirty-one. Furthermore, the Gluecks found that the delinquents displayed decreasing involvement in the more serious offenses and a gravitation toward "lesser" offenses such as drunkenness, vagrancy, simple assault, nonsupport, and desertion. This trend was interpreted by the Gluecks as representing the operation of a factor called "delayed maturation," although they recognized that some offenders "never achieve adequate maturity" and never are able to "settle down."[5]

Eleanor Glueck has explored the applicability of their originally determined prediction items to the prognostication of delinquent and nondelinquent behavior at the school entrance level (five and one-half to six years of age) as well as at a still earlier childhood level, namely two to three years of age. She has generated evidence from the Gluecks' original sample of delinquent and nondelinquent boys plus evidence from other application

[3]Sheldon and Eleanor Glueck, *Delinquents and Nondelinquents in Perspective* (1968), pp. 142–143.

[4]*Ibid.*, p. 143.

[5]*Ibid.*, pp. 151–152.

studies (such as in New York and Washington, D.C.), to indicate that the following three "family" factors and two psychophysical factors will undoubtedly indicate at an early age directionality toward or away from delinquent behavior:[6]

1. Supervision of Boy by Mother
   - suitable
   - fair
   - unsuitable
2. Discipline of Boy by Mother
   - firm but kindly
   - erratic
   - overstrict
   - lax
3. Cohesiveness of Family
   - marked
   - some
   - none
4. Nonsubmissiveness of Child to Parental Authority
   - absent
   - present
5. Destructiveness of Child
   - no evidence
   - evidence present

It should be noticed that the first three of these predictive factors appeared among the five family factors in the original prediction study and that they appeared also as the significant indicators of delinquency and nondelinquency in the application study done by the New York City Youth Board.

Furthermore, Eleanor Glueck found that the following set of five factors also discriminated potential delinquents from nondelinquents at two to three years of age:[7]

1. Pathology of Parents
   - absent
   - present
2. Attachment of Parents to Child
   - both attached
   - one or both indifferent or hostile

[6]Eleanor J. Glueck, "A More Discriminate Instrument for the Identification of Potential Delinquents at School Entrance," *Journal of Criminal Law, Criminology and Police Science*, 57:1 (1966), p. 28.

[7]Eleanor J. Glueck, "Identification of Potential Delinquents at 2–3 Years of Age," *The International Journal of Social Psychiatry*, XII:1 (1966), p. 11.

3. Extreme Restlessness in Childhood
   - absent
   - present
4. Nonsubmissiveness of Child to Parental Authority
   - absent
   - present
5. Destructiveness of Child
   - no evidence
   - evidence present.

It should be noted that the original five family factors, plus the family pathology factor in the last listing, plus the two psychophysical factors represent prognostications based upon data obtained from home interviews with the mother of the child by a trained social worker.

Prognostication of elementary schoolteachers

While family members, particularly the mother, can give predictive insights into the direction of development of a child who has lived with them for several years, it is also possible to obtain prognostic ratings from elementary teachers, who are in a position to sense trends in behavioral development of their classroom subjects. The author and his colleague, Dr. Simon Dinitz, asked the sixth-grade teachers of elementary schools in the areas of high delinquency in Columbus, Ohio to indicate the boys in their classrooms who were quite likely to get into trouble with the law, those they were not sure about, and those unlikely to get involved. There is no way to tell, without long-term research, whether such a simple one-dimensional rating is less accurate, more accurate, or of equal accuracy as the more elaborate check-list for prognostication, which climaxes in an overall directional score.

The author and his colleague at the time (c. 1955–56) were interested in exploring why only some boys in high delinquency areas became involved in "reported" delinquency. Their initial effort concentrated on white boys who were selected by their sixth-grade teachers as unlikely to get involved —the "good" boys. The following year the researchers asked the sixth-grade teachers in the same schools to indicate the boys they felt were quite likely to get into trouble with the law—the "bad" boys. Two research assistants then made home calls. Whilst one interviewed the nominated boy in the kitchen, the other interviewed the boy's mother in a different room of the house.

The findings of this initial probing indicated that the nominated "good" boy looked upon himself as not getting involved in delinquency, upon his friends as unlikely to become involved, upon his family—although slum— as a "good" family, and he predicted that he would finish school (graduate from high school). The so-called "bad" boy looked upon himself as likely to get into trouble, upon his friends as likely to get involved, upon his family as a "bad" family, and he predicted that he would drop out of school at sixteen. The interview with the mother covered many of the same items that were used in interviewing the boy at home, and there was considerable agreement between the mother and the boy, separately interviewed, as to the boy's present and future direction. There was also considerable agreement between the teacher's overall directional prognostication and the boys' view of themselves.

Four years later, when the boys had gone past their sixteenth birthday, a large percentage of the nominated "bad" boys had dropped out of school, while most of the nominated "good" boys were still at school. Almost 40 percent of the "bad" boys had been known to the juvenile court (an average of three times in the four year period). The "good" boys showed only two major contacts with the juvenile court. Perhaps a "self-fulfilling prophesy" was at work, but the researchers contended that results were due to the action of a "good" and/or "poor" self concept.[8]

Self-concept items as a "who" indicator

The items used in the original interview with the sixth-grade slum boys were improved in later studies. For example, Ernest P. Donald used an improved self-concept schedule on a large sample of sixth-grade children (girls as well as boys) in selected schools of the low as well as high delinquency areas of Columbus, Ohio. Teachers' nomination (prognosis) was also obtained on each child.[9] Each subject responded to a selected set of 46 items taken from the Socialization Scale of the California Psychological Inventory (then called the De Scale, because it measured a direction toward or away from delinquency).

Appendix 3-B gives an analysis of the findings in the instance of the

[8](1) Walter C. Reckless, Simon Dinitz, and Ellen Murray, "Self Concept as an Insulation against Delinquency," *American Sociological Review*, 21 (December 1956), pp. 744–746; (2) Walter C. Reckless, Simon Dinitz, and Barbara Kay, "The Self Component in Potential Delinquency," *American Sociological Review*, 22: (October 1957), pp. 566–570; (3) Walter C. Reckless, Simon Dinitz, and Ellen Murray, "The 'Good' Boy in a High Delinquency Area," *Journal of Criminal Law, Criminology and Police Science*, 48 (June 1957), pp. 18–25; (4) Simon Dinitz, Walter C. Reckless, and Barbara Kay, "A Self Gradient among Potential Delinquents," *Journal of Criminal Law, Criminology and Police Science*, 49 (September–October 1958), pp. 230–233; (5) Jon E. Simpson, Simon Dinitz, Barbara Kay, and Walter C. Reckless, "Delinquency Potential in High Delinquency Areas," *British Journal of Delinquency*, 10 (January 1960), pp. 211–215; (6) Frank Scarpitti, Ellen Murray, Simon Dinitz, and Walter C. Reckless, "The 'Good' Boy in a High Delinquency Area: Four Years Later," *American Sociological Review*, 25 (August 1960), pp. 555–558; (7) Simon Dinitz, Frank R. Scarpitti, and Walter C. Reckless, "Delinquency Vulnerability: A Cross Group and Longitudinal Analysis," *American Sociological Review*, 27 (August 1962), pp. 315–317.

[9]Ernest P. Donald, *Self Concept in Sixth Grade Boys: A Study of Delinquency Proneness* (Ph.D. dissertation, The Ohio State University, 1963).

boys in the original sample (354 in number). One notices that when the boys were dichotomized according to teacher's nomination, 16 out of 56 self-concept items in the administered schedule were found to be highly significant. Of these 16 self-concept items, 15 were found to be statistically significant when the sample was dichotomized into boys with high De scores (gravitating toward delinquency) and with low De scores (away from delinquency).

The self concept of boys can certainly be looked upon as a directional indicator of involvement, just as can the teacher's prognosis of the boy or the boy's performance on the Socialization Scale of the California Psychological Inventory.

Edwin Lowe Lively attempted to measure the stability of self concept and the direction of socialization in a sample of sixth, seventh, eighth, and ninth-grade boys and girls in Akron, Ohio, a middle-size industrial city.[10] He contended that it was unrealistic to predict future delinquency involvement at the age of six. He claimed that it was much more realistic to prognosticate at twelve years of age (teacher's prognosis), since it is later childhood and early adolescence that represents the real threshold for involvement. His attempt to find types of behavioral involvement among the thirteen-, fourteen-, and fifteen-year-old children that were consistent with the behavior of children at age twelve represented his main source of proof for his claim. Stability of an image of self and direction of socialization, as measured by the Socialization Scale, among children nominated by teachers as headed for trouble or not headed for trouble, was found to exist in the three subsequent adolescent years (seventh, eighth, and ninth-grades) as in the sixth grade. See Appendix 3–C for details.

A more sophisticated instrument to measure self concept than the one developed by the author and his colleague, Dr. Simon Dinitz, is the one invented by Dr. William H. Fitts. The directions for taking the Fitts' self-concept scale are duplicated in Appendix 3–D, along with 12 illustrative items from among the total of 100 items in the test. The 100 items in the Fitts scale can be separated into the respondent's perceptions of his *physical self, moral–ethical self, personal self, family self, social self,* plus items dealing with *self criticism*. In addition, it is possible to break down Fitts' self-concept items into those that indicate *identity (what he is), self satisfaction (how he accepts himself)*, and *behavior (how he acts)*.

Kvaraceus Delinquency Proneness Scale and Proneness Check List

Some years ago William C. Kvaraceus developed two instruments to prognosticate during both early and later adolescent years which children ("who")

[10]Edwin Lowe Lively, *A Study of Teen-age Socialization and Delinquency Insulation by Grade Levels* (Ph.D. dissertation, The Ohio State University, 1959).

were gravitating toward delinquency and which were not. One instrument was called the K D Proneness Scale, which was administered to the youthful subjects while the other instrument, the K D Proneness Check List, was filled in by the teacher and represented her/his observations on individual children. The scale and the checklist are duplicated in Appendix 3-E.

There are 75 items in the proneness scale although several of the items are not scored, since they were used merely as filler items to allay suspicion. The response format consists of four multiple choice responses. The particular response out of the four which represents the "proneness" direction is scored +1, while that which represents the non-delinquent direction is scored −1. Total scores are obtained by adding the plus and minus scores (+26 + −40 = −14; +38 + −24 = +14). In the several instances in which the K D Proneness Scale has been administered, the youths (boys or girls) who had already had contact with the police, juvenile courts, or correctional institutions showed average scores ranging from the low pluses (such as +5) to the low minuses (such as −8), whereas the samples of youth specified as "nondelinquent" or not delinquency prone have shown higher minus scores on average.

The checklist, as will be seen in Appendix 3-E, consists of 70 items, grouped under personal factors, home and family factors, and school factors. The items marked with an asterisk were considered by Kvaraceus to have more bearing on determining delinquency proneness than were the unmarked items. The youths' score on the checklist represents the sum of the items that have been checked by the rater (usually the teacher) in the "yes" column. These "yes" ratings indicate unfavorable elements that are conducive to delinquency in the life of the youth. In the manual of directions developed for administrators of the checklist, Kvaraceus notes that a score of 30 or more "yes" checks "warrants high priority for study" (meaning high delinquency potential), a score of 10–30 "yes" checks "merits attention" (meaning some proneness), and a score of 1–10 "evidences slight susceptibility" (meaning very little potential for delinquency).

Undoubtedly the K D Proneness Scale could be "sharpened up" and reduced in size, through extended item-analysis testings. And the instrument could be developed and modified not only to indicate the proneness of youths but also the proneness of adults toward criminal involvement.

In its original form, it certainly was capable of specifying which samples of youth ("who") were gravitating toward or away from involvement, although it probably was not efficient in indicating by test score which particular individual was actually going to become involved. Nevertheless, indication of involvement or noninvolvement for certain score levels of youths is most important, and hopefully instruments of this sort will be able to focus their validity eventually on the individual case.

Likewise, the K D Check List could also be reduced in size and "sharpened up" for prognostic ratings of pre-delinquent youths by teachers or other adult persons in close contact with the subject being rated. But a similar checklist to gauge potentiality of adults for involvement in adult deviant behavior would be more difficult to develop and to administer. What persons in what agencies or offices might be in a position to know an adult individual well enough to make a prognostication?

Assessment of proneness

In the past generation several psychological inventories with a fair potential for indicating proneness for becoming involved in delinquency and crime have been developed. One such instrument, useful for prognostication of both juvenile and adult involvement, is the Socialization Scale, which is part of a larger instrument, called the California Psychological Inventory. Appendix 3-F should be consulted for a statement on the Socialization Scale. As a directionality indicator, the Socialization Scale is certainly attempting to assess involvement proneness, whether official or unofficial violation.

One of the most searching attempts to study delinquency proneness was made by Hathaway and Monachesi in the late forties, continuing until the late fifties. As a model for research procedure to ascertain delinquency proneness and to gauge the accuracy of the original assessment (school pupils in the ninth grade) with subsequent findings (in the twelfth grade), the Hathaway-Monachesi study is outstandingly commendable. The entire inventory of the Minnesota Multiphasic Personality Inventory was administered to ninth-grade schoolchildren in Minneapolis and throughout Minnesota, while teachers' predictions of delinquency involvement as well as other pertinent school data were obtained on each subject at the same time. Two to four years later the pupils were re-tested with the MMPI. Their cases were cleared through police and juvenile court records for delinquency occurrence while adjustment and conduct ratings on each subject were made by trained fieldworkers as part of the follow-up investigation.[11]

It is interesting to note that at the point of follow-up contact, the "occurrence data" on the pupil's involvement with the police and juvenile court were rated on a scale of seriousness from 0 (no recorded occurrences) to 4 (the most serious level and amount of involvement). Likewise, the follow-up reports on conduct and adjustment as obtained by the fieldworkers with teachers and others who knew the youth were also rated on a scale of 0 to 4 (from the most favorable to the poorest showing).

Of the ten subscales of the MMPI, the so-called Pd scale (Psychopathic deviation, indicating at its high scores rebelliousness, cynicism, disregard of

[11]Starke R. Hathaway and Elio D. Monachesi, *Adolescent Personality and Behavior* (Minneapolis: The University of Minnesota Press, 1963).

rules, aggressiveness, and selfishness) appeared to be related to the most serious involvement level, namely the cases rated 4 on police and court clearances.[12] Hathaway and Monachesi's findings indicated that scores on the various subscales of the MMPI were not very stable for the pupils tested at the ninth-grade and again at the twelfth-grade level. Hence, predictions of directions of personality development as well as of deliquency involvement were rather poor.[13]

The researchers found that teachers' rating of the pupils at the time of initial data collection (in the ninth grade), in terms of whether the individual pupil "was likely to get into trouble with the law or to develop emotional problems, or both," represented somewhat more accurate predictions of outcome (two to four years later) than the original showing of the pupils on the MMPI scales. This was not only true for the Pd scale mentioned above, but also true for a special cluster of 30 MMPI items that Hathaway and Monachesi found to have a slightly better predictive potential than the standard scales of the MMPI, even the Pd scale. The 30 items of the special Deliquency Proneness Scale, developed by Hathaway and Monachesi from MMPI items, is duplicated in Appendix 3-G. In spite of the fact that the scale does not predict quite as well as teachers do, the scale certainly has a fair potential for predicting involvement—high score in the direction of proneness and low score in the direction of absence of proneness.

Hathaway and Monachesi came to the overall conclusion that "we could not find a single dimension, measurable with available items, which could be effectively used as a delinquency proneness scale."[14] In a real sense, this is somewhat of an overstatement since Hathaway and Monachesi developed plenty of evidence to predict boys and girls who stay away from problems of adjustment, emotional as well as violational. They also supplied important leads to program administrators as well as to parents, both of whom must contend with the directionality of growth in children and in youth.[15] They do not imply that it is impossible for behavioral scientists to develop an adequate instrument for the prediction of proneness.

Critique of prediction and early identification

As a result of a very complete review of all the major attempts at prediction of potential delinquents, Gordon Rose makes the following critique of the research efforts in this direction to date.[16]

[12] *Ibid.*, pp. 70, 155.

[13] *Ibid.*, p. 71.

[14] *Ibid.*, p. 90.

[15] *Ibid.*, p. 104.

[16] Gordon Rose, "Early Identification of Delinquents," *British Journal of Criminology*, 7:1 (1967), p. 25.

There are really three main problems: first, can we identify with any degree of efficiency? secondly, if we do identify potential offenders can we give them early treatment which is likely to be successful? and thirdly, if early identification is worth while at all, under what conditions is this so? And underlying these questions are others concerning what it is we want to identify, that is to say, what we are prepared to define as abnormal to the extent of indicating a delinquent future.

Rose is of the opinion that the chances of efficient prediction are quite doubtful. He calls attention to the fact that workers in the field are all the time faced with the need to make decisions as to how to handle individual cases. Yet he admits that workers need systematic data to help them make proper judgments. Especially needed is a predictive device to help workers make justifiable decisions in the middle range of cases rather than at the more visible extremes. Quite realistically, the agencies involved with the handling and routing of children and youth need to know the differential characteristics of those cases that become involved in first appearance with police and courts and those that have subsequent appearances.[17]

An earlier critique by Jackson Toby indicated that "identification of potential delinquents is possible in a crude way right now" but that more accurate prediction will depend upon a scientific understanding of the causes of various forms of delinquent behavior. In view of this limitation, so-called early identification of potential delinquents is not "a practical approach to delinquency control." In fact, Toby contends that delinquency control programs are not dependent upon prediction or early identification. He almost implies that such programs, which are not based on dichotomies of nondelinquents and potential delinquents, have certain advantages.[18] (The author is here making a liberal interpretation of Toby's critique.)

Quite recently, Robert D. Wirt has indicated that "none of the predictive procedures available meets the requirements of a well validated, practical, and useful predictive system."[19] He is of the opinion that only an instrument that has been cross-validated and uses a longitudinal follow-up approach can really "claim to be predictive of future behavior." The study that actually meets this criterion in his estimation is the one done by Hathaway and Monachesi (1963), already described above and in Appendix 3-G.

Wirt reports that Dr. Anna C. Hampton has developed a Delinquency Prediction Scale out of his Personality Inventory for Children. The PIC is composed of 600 true/false items, covering several different areas of behavior, to be answered by mothers of children between six and sixteen years of age. The difference between this instrument (PIC) and the MMPI is that

[17] *Ibid.*, pp. 25–30.

[18] Jackson Toby, "Early Identification and Intensive Treatment of Predelinquents: A Negative View," *Social Work*, 6:3 (July 1961), p. 13.

[19] Robert D. Wirt, "The Psychometric Prediction of Delinquency" (paper presented before the American Correctional Association, Minneapolis, August 17, 1969).

the subject, child or adult, responds to the latter, while the mother of the subject (child) responds to the former.

Evidently, the sifting out of items (their validation) that were found to be significantly related to later outcome was a sort of backward/forward approach, which overcomes many of the difficulties in ordinary prediction studies. A sample of boys, ten to twelve years of age, was gathered in Minneapolis in 1960–1962. The cases were cleared through police records in 1968, at which time the subjects were for the most part eighteen years of age. Using the police clearances, it was possible to compare the officially delinquent cases with the officially nondelinquent cases, according to the responses the mother had made on the PIC six to eight years earlier, and it was possible to spot the items in the PIC instrument that significantly distinguished the official delinquents from the official nondelinquents. These items then can be justifiably used for prediction of the delinquency outcome of boys in early adolescence.[20]

A retrospective approach

Practically all of the attempts at prediction of delinquency and the identification of children and youths who are likely and not likely to get involved in delinquent behavior emphasize a projective approach—a forecast of direction toward or away from delinquency. There has been one outstanding attempt to obtain insight into involvement by interviewing adult persons about their deviant behavior in childhood and adolescence. This idea was generated by Dr. Sophia M. Robison and her project was officially labeled *Career Patterns Project* but, in essense, it is a study of "The Youthful Delinquent Behavior of Men who are today Respectable Members of Society."

A sample of 259 respondents residing in Glen Cove, Long Island, a self-contained residential community, was obtained and a sample of 91 residents from the North End of Boston was also used. The respondents were between thirty and sixty years of age and all had resided in the United States as adolescents. Information was collected by skilled male interviewers from a personal interview with each respondent who volunteered to cooperate with the study.[21]

The interview schedule began with questions about the respondent's work history, the family in which he grew up, his physical characteristics, and his leisure-time outlets. It continued with probing questions relative to the respondent's attitudes toward social institutions such as the family, school, church, official agencies, etc. Questions were also asked about

[20] *Ibid.*

[21] Sophia M. Robison, "Hidden Delinquency: A Challenge to Social Work Concepts and Programs" (speech delivered at the National Conference on Social Welfare, Atlantic City, New Jersey, May 27, 1965). Taken from an unpublished report.

persons, adults or peers, who had played a significant role in the life of the respondent. About halfway through the interview schedule came questions relative to the respondent's "recollection of possible misdeeds" and whether he usually acted "on his own or with a group of youths." Questions were also directed toward obtaining what the respondent considered to be "his most serious misbehavior, how he felt about it at the time, what action followed and when and why he decided to give up his disapproved behavior." Other questions were directed toward obtaining the respondent's current set of ethical values, his attitudes toward recently publicized scandals, and his judgments about today's youth.

While 75 percent of the Glen Cove and 50 percent of the (North End) Boston respondents "recalled some behavior which might have been officially recorded as delinquent," 50 percent of the Glen Cove and 25 percent of the Boston interviewees admitted more than one offense; 5 percent of the former and 9 percent of the latter recalled no deviations that might be considered "juvenile status behavior," such as truancy, running away from home, etc.; 20 percent in both samples recalled no definitely delinquent acts. On the basis of numerically scored recalled non-serious and serious acts as a youth, 31 percent of the Boston and 41 percent of the Glen Cove respondents displayed scores above the median (average) for each sample. (High scores indicate higher amounts of reported involvement.) Some of the pertinent findings that shed retrospective insights on who becomes involved in serious delinquency as a youth are presented in Appendix 3-H.

Implementing a "who" aspect of Cohen's theory and Cloward-Ohlin's theory

Some of the widely circulating theories of delinquent and criminal behavior have contained intimations or specifications as to "who" gets involved and "who" does not get involved, but there have been very few attempts to operationalize the leads given by these theories. Mention will be made of some recent efforts to implement leads in certain major theories of delinquent behavior in the United States.

In his overall reflections on the development of boys' gangs in American cities, Albert K. Cohen contended, among other formulations, that the gangs develop a delinquent subculture, which gives their members a chance to "belong," to develop their masculinity, to amount to something (status), and to fight middle-class society. The delinquent gang, according to Cohen, attracts working-class boys in American cities who repudiate middle-class standards.[22] Such a formulation invites implementation by research, to see

[22]Albert K. Cohen, Delinquent Boys: *The Culture of the Gang*, (Glencoe, Illinois: The Free Press, 1955).

whether rejection of middle-class values by boys in American cities differentiates delinquent from nondelinquent samples.

Cloward and Ohlin more recently proposed an "opportunity" theory to account for the gravitation toward or away from delinquency in American cities. Their theory encompassed differential availability of two opportunity systems (legitimate and illegitimate); blocked aspirations within the available legitimate system, leading to "position" discontent; the generation of a delinquency subculture by lower-class youth as a way of overcoming blocked aspirations; and the withdrawal of legitimacy from conventional and the attribution of legitimacy to illegal means to ends.[23] Such theory invites attempts to measure who gets involved and who does not get involved in delinquency.

Landis and Scarpitti attempted to implement one ingredient of Cohen's theory and one ingredient of Cloward and Ohlin's theory. They developed a special scale to measure "acceptance or rejection" of middle-class values and a special scale to measure "awareness" of limited opportunity on the part of youths. They administered their scales to the inmates of a state school for committed delinquent boys and to samples of the boys in the sixth to ninth grades of selected public schools in Columbus, Ohio. Beside the legal determination of delinquency by the fact of commitment to a state school for delinquents, Landis[24] and Scarpitti[25] also used the Socialization Scale of the California Psychological Inventory, which has demonstrated its ability to indicate a direction toward good socialization (away from delinquency) and toward poor socialization (toward delinquency). In general, the study confirmed the contention of Cohen and also that of Cloward and Ohlin. The "who" factor in the Landis and Scarpitti study represented greater or lesser rejection of middle-class values, a greater or lesser awareness of limited opportunity, and a direction toward good or poor socialization. See Appendix 3-I.

Implementing one aspect of containment theory

An attempt was made to operationalize a certain aspect of the so-called Containment Theory, proposed several years ago by the author.[26] The theory represents an attempt to explain the risk of involvement in delin-

[23] Richard A. Cloward and Lloyd E. Ohlin, *Delinquency and Opportunity*, (Glencoe, Illinois: The Free Press, 1960).

[24] Judson R. Landis, "Differentials in Self, Value, and Opportunity Orientation as Related to Delinquency Potential" (Ph.D. dissertation, The Ohio State University, 1962).

[25] Frank R. Scarpitti, Differential Socialization: The Delinquent versus the Nondelinquent (Ph.D. dissertation, The Ohio State University, 1962).

[26] Walter C. Reckless, *The Crime Problem*, 4th ed. (New York: Appleton-Century-Crofts, 1967), pp. 469–483.

quency or crime, according to a combination of outer- and inner-containing factors. The former consists of the ability of groups and organizations to hold the person within limits; the latter, of the strength or weakness of self factors, such as self concept, which are capable of steering a person away from involvement.

Gordon B. Waldo[27] tried to implement one aspect of the theory. He assumed that a large part of outer containment functions through the internalized perceptions that adolescent boys hold regarding instrumental figures in their social milieu. He developed an instrument to measure six dimensions of "perceived" outer containment: these are demonstrated in the last six (unnumbered) items in the schedule included in Appendix 3-J and shown again in a different context in items 19-24.

In addition to the six items on perceived outer containment, Waldo used 65 items (see items 46 to 111 in the schedule duplicated in Appendix 3-L and 1-B, which deal with attitudes toward important aspects of the law enforcement system, such as police, juvenile courts, and probation officers. Actually, Waldo's schedule, with the exception of the last six items, is a duplicate of one used by the Youth Development Project in nine junior high schools of the inner-city of Columbus, Ohio, to measure attitude change of seventh-grade boys on a before-and-after (pre- and post-test) basis, i.e., at the beginning of the school year (September) and at the close of the school year (May).

Sixth-grade teachers of 44 elementary schools of Columbus that were located in the areas of high delinquency and were the feeder schools to the 9 junior high schools of the inner-city were asked at the end of the school year (May 1965) to nominate the boys in their classrooms who were quite *unlikely* to become involved in law-violating activity, those about whom they were unsure, and those who were quite *likely* to become involved in such behavior. In addition, Waldo used a fourth category, namely the boys of the Youth Development Project, who were already known to the Juvenile Bureau of the Columbus Police Department for reported delinquency.

Consequently, the "who" factor in Waldo's study impinges upon seventh-grade boys (in May 1966) living in high delinquency areas, approximately thirteen to fourteen years of age, who had been nominated a year earlier (May 1965) by their sixth-grade teachers as unlikely, not sure, or likely to become involved in delinquency plus a police clearance for delinquency involvement (at the end of the seventh grade, May 1966). The data for Waldo's study are taken from the "post-test" administration of the Youth Development Project schedule, namely in May 1966 at the end of the seventh grade, to a sample of 626 boys.

Cooperation with the school authorities was excellent as were con-

[27] Gordon P. Waldo, "Boys' Perceptions of Outer Containment and Delinquency Potential" (Ph.D. dissertation, The Ohio State University, 1967).

ditions of administration to the "nominated" boys, in groups of 25 to 100. Notice should be taken of the instructions at the beginning of the schedule in Appendix 3-I, which elicit cooperation and allay suspicion. Mention should be made also of the fact that the administrator of the schedule read aloud the so-called instructions and then each item of the schedule, indicating by timely repetition what the format of response to the various items was.

It is frequently desirable in most pieces of well-designed research to develop a general hypothesis and a set of specific hypotheses that can be tested by the analysis of data obtained from the responses to the items in a schedule. The overall hypothesis of the Waldo study on perceived external containment is given in Appendix 3-J in the section following the presentation of the schedule. After the general hypothesis is a list of 16 specific hypotheses.

Implementing the neutralization theory of Sykes and Matza

As a possible "self factor" that might explain why some youths gravitate toward delinquency and others do not—in other words, who gets involved—Sykes and Matza identified the operation of the so-called neutralization process, whereby internalized norms, morals, and values could be put aside by subscribing to rationalizations that release the person from the "moral bind." Sykes and Matza recognized five major types of neutralization: denial of responsibility, denial of injury, denial of the victim (he had it coming to him), condemnation of the condemners (those who complain about the boy, those who arrest, those who sit in judgment, etc.), and appeal to higher loyalties (loyalty to a close friend takes precedence over conformity to norms and laws).[28]

Richard A. Ball made an attempt to operationalize the basic contentions of neutralization and to discover whether delinquent boys really neutralize their behavior more than nondelinquent boys[29] and found that this was so. The details of the study are supplied in Appendix 3-K, along with a copy of the instrument that was developed to make the test.

The three hypotheses formulated in order to test the neutralization contention were stated as follows:

Hypothesis #1 states that there will be a significant difference between the neutralization scores of high school boys and institutionalized delinquents. Hypothesis #2 states that neutralization scores will tend to form a gradient from high school boys reporting no juvenile court appearances, to high school boys reporting juvenile court

[28]Gresham M. Sykes and David Matza, "Techniques of Neutralization: A Theory of Delinquency," *American Sociological Review*, 22 (December 1957), pp. 666-667.

[29]Richard A. Ball, "Neutralization as a Self Factor in Delinquency Risk" (Ph.D. dissertation, The Ohio State University, 1965).

appearances, to institutionalized delinquents reporting few juvenile court appearances, to institutionalized delinquents reporting many juvenile court appearances. Hypothesis #3 states that there will be a significant difference between the neutralization scores of seriously delinquent boys (many self-reported violations) and less seriously delinquent boys (few self-reported violations).

Differential perceptions of deviant behavior

It is possible that some part of the difference between those who get involved and those who do not get involved in delinquency may be found in the differential perceptions that children and adolescents have of delinquent behavior; in other words, how they view behavior. The differential perceptions may reflect the internalized values, the "labeling" process, concepts of self, etc.

John F. Davies undertook to make a preliminary sounding of whether perceptions of delinquent behavior differentiated segments of an almost complete sample of ninth-grade boys (approximately fifteen years of age) in a highly industrialized small city.[30]

A list of 45 specific "misbehaviors" was developed from a larger list and submitted to a panel of seven "external caretakers," such as a juvenile police officer, a juvenile court probation officer, a lawyer specializing in delinquency cases, a member of a state youth commission dealing with the treatment of committed delinquents, etc. The "caretakers," each of whom was very close to the problem of delinquency, checked the original list of misbehaviors and indicated the items that they considered to be definitely delinquent and those they considered to be nondelinquent. If six out of the seven "experts" or "caretakers" checked an item *as delinquent* or *as non-delinquent*, this item was accepted as such. If only five or fewer of the experts agreed on whether an item was delinquent or nondelinquent, the item was classified as "not sure."

Fifteen agreed-upon delinquency items, 15 agreed-upon nondelinquency items, and 15 "not sure" items were selected and scattered through a 45-item inventory, which asked the ninth-grade boy respondents to circle whether they looked upon each particular behavior as definitely delinquent, definitely nondelinquent, or not sure. See the first 45 items in the schedule of Appendix 3-K. A disparity score was developed to indicate whether the delinquent boys in the ninth-grade sample disagreed less with the experts' ratings than the nondelinquent boys in the sample. The respondents were also asked to rate the 45 items for seriousness, in order to detect moral value differences between the delinquent and nondelinquent segments of the ninth-grade sample.

[30]John F. Davies, "Differential Perceptions of Delinquent Behavior" (Ph.D. dissertation, The Ohio State University, 1969).

The Davies study (see the schedule in Appendix 3-L) also developed several measures of delinquency: those who came to the attention of the police, those who came to the attention of the school authorities for truancy and misconduct, those referred to the juvenile court, plus three self-reporting items. Davies also used 46 items from the Socialization Scale of the California Psychological Inventory, to indicate direction toward or away from good socialization—or toward or away from delinquency. He also included certain items to measure supplemental projections or views of delinquent behavior.

The findings indicate only very slight differences in perception in the expected directions between the segments of the sample, variously defined as delinquent and nondelinquent. The delinquent segment (variously defined) agreed slightly less (had a greater disparity score) than the non-delinquent segment with the definitions of the "external caretakers" and also showed a slightly smaller "seriousness" score than the nondelinquent segment. The Negro boys and the boys from the lower-class areas indicated a still smaller difference in perceptions of behavior and perceptions of seriousness than did the white boys and the boys from the better neighborhoods. The items attempting to measure certain supplementary perceptions of delinquent behavior barely distinguished the delinquent from the non-delinquent segments of the ninth-grade boy sample.

The Davies study certainly needs to be replicated once a more discriminating instrument for measuring differential perceptions of behavior has been developed. Moreover, the improved instrument should be administered to samples of youth not only in a small city but also in a small town and a large city. And the improved schedule should also be administered to various age levels, say to twelve-, fifteen-, and eighteen-year-old youths.

The particular reason for mentioning age-level replication is that Davies' findings indicated a surprisingly high ("unexpected") difference between the ratings of the "external caretakers" and the ratings of the ninth-grade boys (delinquent as well as nondelinquents). On the 15 delinquency items, the ninth-grade youths showed an almost 50 percent disparity score in their perceptions as to whether the items were delinquent or not. Is there as much disparity in the perception of delinquent behavior in the instance of a twelve-year-old sample as in this particular fifteen-year-old sample? Is there more or less disparity between the perceptions of the caretakers and those of eighteen-year-old youths?

Such an age-level study might give insights into a differential "generation gap" that in turn might affect readiness to become involved or not involved in delinquency.

Appendix 3–A

REPORTED ARRESTS BY AGE, SEX, AND RACE, 1969

Table 3-A-1. Total Arrests of Persons Under 15, Under 18, Under 21, and Under 25 Years of Age, 1969

[4,759 agencies; 1969 estimated population 143,815,000]

Offense charged	Grand total all ages	Number of persons arrested				Percentage			
		Under 15	Under 18	Under 21	Under 25	Under 15	Under 18	Under 21	Under 25
TOTAL............	**5,862,246**	**566,406**	**1,500,215**	**2,282,596**	**3,014,523**	**9.7**	**25.6**	**38.9**	**51.4**
Criminal homicide:									
(*a*) Murder and nonnegligent manslaughter	**11,509**	157	1,083	2,753	4,850	1.4	9.4	23.9	42.1
(*b*) Manslaughter by negligence	**3,197**	29	241	793	1,428	.9	7.5	24.8	44.7
Forcible rape............	**14,428**	541	2,902	6,067	9,391	3.7	20.1	42.1	65.1
Robbery.................	**75,533**	9,022	25,599	43,026	58,774	11.8	33.4	56.2	76.8
Aggravated assault	**113,724**	6,019	18,612	33,890	53,466	5.3	16.4	29.8	47.0
Burglary— breaking or entering	**255,937**	64,723	137,558	182,212	213,618	25.3	53.7	71.2	83.5
Larceny—theft	**510,660**	141,426	271,094	346,396	397,590	27.7	53.1	67.8	77.9
Auto theft...............	**125,686**	19,970	72,843	96,445	110,259	15.9	58.0	76.7	87.7
Violent crime.........	**216,194**	15,739	48,196	85,736	126,481	7.3	22.3	39.7	58.5
Property crime	**892,283**	226,119	481,495	625,053	721,467	25.3	54.0	70.1	80.9
Subtotal for above offenses	**1,111,674**	241,887	529,932	711,582	849,376	21.8	47.7	64.0	76.4

Crime in the United States, *Uniform Crime Reports—1969*, Federal Bureau of Investigation, U.S. Department of Justice, Washington D.C., August 13, 1970. The table on the age distribution is an exact duplication of Table 28, p. 115 of the report. The table on the sex distribution is an exact duplication of Table 29, p. 116 of the report. However, the table on the racial distribution is a duplication of only the first half of Table 31, p. 118 of the report.

Table 3–A–1. *(continued*

Offense charged	Number of persons arrested					Percentage			
	Grand total all ages	Under 15	Under 18	Under 21	Under 25	Under 15.	Under 18	Under 21	Under 25
TOTAL............	**5,862,246**	**566,406**	**1,500,215**	**2,282,596**	**3,014,523**	**9.7**	**25.6**	**38.9**	**51.4**
Other assaults...........	**259,825**	18,147	45,728	77,676	120,117	7.0	17.6	29.9	46.2
Arson.....................	**8,691**	3,770	5,398	6,206	6,871	43.4	62.1	71.4	79.1
Forgery and counterfeiting.........	**36,727**	850	4,146	10,718	19,265	2.3	11.3	29.2	52.5
Fraud.....................	**63,445**	923	2.997	9,310	21,669	1.5	4.7	14.7	34.2
Embezzlement...........	**6,309**	44	247	879	2,215	.7	3.9	13.9	35.1
Stolen property; buying, receiving, possessing	**46,176**	4,792	14,598	23,912	31,619	10.4	31.6	51.8	68.5
Vandalism................	**106,892**	51,426	78,519	88,120	94,282	48.1	73.5	82.4	88.2
Weapons; carrying, possessing, etc.........	**88,973**	3,989	15,211	28,895	44,401	4.5	17.1	32.5	49.9
Prostitution and commercialized vice.	**46,410**	88	948	8,227	27,129	.2	2.0	17.7	58.5
Sex offenses (except forcible rape and prostitution).....	**50,143**	4,313	10,927	17,047	25,548	8.6	21.8	34.0	51.0
Narcotic drug laws......	**232,690**	8,109	57,475	127,573	179,681	3.5	24.7	54.8	77.2
Gambling................	**78,020**	272	1,700	5.023	11,459	.3	2.2	6.4	14.7
Offenses against family and children..	**50,312**	173	807	6,276	15,480	.3	1.6	12.5	30.8
Driving under the influence...........	**349,326**	77	3,891	24,419	68,885	([1])	1.1	7.0	19.7
Liquor laws	**212,660**	6,084	71,159	158,211	173,778	2.9	33.5	74.4	81.7
Drunkenness............	**1,420,161**	5,123	42,903	121,671	244,213	.4	3.0	8.6	17.2
Disorderly conduct	**573,502**	41,069	117,245	209,955	300,317	7.2	20.4	36.6	52.4
Vagrancy.................	**106,269**	1.951	11,056	29,314	46,553	1.8	10.4	27.6	43.8
All other offenses (except traffic)	**664,634**	78,793	203,395	314,464	411,832	11.9	30.6	47.3	62.0
Suspicion	**88,265**	5,279	20,791	41,976	58,691	6.0	23.6	47.6	66.5
Curfew and loitering law violations.........	**101,674**	26,147	101,674	101,674	101,674	25.7	100.0	100.0	100.0
Runaways	**159,468**	63,100	159,468	159,468	159,468	39.6	100.0	100.0	100.0

[1] Less than one-tenth of one percent.

Violent crime is offenses of murder, forcible rape, robbery and aggravated assault.
Property crime is offenses of burglary, larceny $50 and over and auto theft.

Table 3-A-2. Total Arrests, Distribution by Sex, 1969

[4,759 agencies; 1969 estimated population 143,815, 000]

Offense charged	Number of persons arrested total	male	female	Percent Male	Percent Female	Percent of total[1] total	male	female
TOTAL	**5,862,246**	**5,058,200**	**804,046**	**86.3**	**13.7**	**100.0**	**100.0**	**100.0**
Criminal homicide:								
(*a*) Murder and nonnegligent manslaughter	**11,509**	9,763	1,746	84.8	15.2	.2	.2	.2
(*b*) Manslaughter by negligence	**3,197**	2,871	326	89.8	10.2	.1	.1	([2])
Forcible rape	**14,428**	14,428	—	100.0	—	.2	.3	—
Robbery	**76,533**	71,757	4,776	93.8	6.2	1.3	1.4	.6
Aggravated assault	**113,724**	99,402	14,322	87.4	12.6	1.9	2.0	1.8
Burglary—breaking or entering	**255,937**	244,786	11,151	95.6	4.4	4.4	4.8	1.4
Larceny—theft	**510,660**	375,530	135,130	73.5	26.5	8.7	7.4	16.8
Auto theft	**125,686**	119,058	6,628	94.7	5.3	2.1	2.4	.8
Violent crime	**216,194**	195,350	20,844	90.4	9.6	3.7	3.9	2.6
Property crime	**892,283**	739,374	152,909	82.9	17.1	15.2	14.6	19.0
Subtotal for above offenses	**1,111,674**	937,595	174,079	84.3	15.7	19.0	18.5	21.7
Other assaults	**259,825**	228,330	31,495	87.9	12.1	4.4	4.5	3.9
Arson	**8,691**	7,901	790	90.9	9.1	.1	.2	.1
Forgery and counterfeiting	**36,727**	28,383	8,344	77.3	22.7	.6	.6	1.0
Fraud	**63,445**	46,813	16.632	73.8	26.2	1.1	.9	2.1
Embezzlement	**6,309**	4,997	1,312	79.2	20.8	.1	.1	.2
Stolen property; buying, receiving, possessing	**46,176**	42,249	3,927	91.5	8.5	.8	.8	.5
Vandalism	**106,892**	99,142	7,750	92.7	7.3	1.8	2.0	1.0
Weapons; carrying, possessing, etc	**88,973**	83,172	5,801	93.5	6.5	1.5	1.6	.7
Prostitution and commercialized vice	**46,410**	9,448	36,962	20.4	79.6	.8	.2	4.6
Sex offenses (except forcible rape and prostitution)	**50,143**	43,551	6,592	86.9	13.1	.9	.9	.8
Narcotic drug laws	**232,690**	196,538	36,152	84.5	15.5	4.0	3.9	4.5
Gambling	**78,020**	71,965	6,055	92.2	7.8	1.3	1.4	.8
Offenses against family and children	**50,312**	45,675	4,637	90.8	9.2	.9	.9	.6
Driving under the influence	**349,326**	327,198	22,128	93.7	6.3	6.0	6.5	2.8
Liquor laws	**212,660**	185,485	27,175	87.2	12.8	3.6	3.7	3.4
Drunkenness	**1,420,161**	1,319,275	100,886	92.9	7.1	24.2	26.1	12.5
Disorderly conduct	**573,502**	491,065	82,437	85.6	14.4	9.8	9.7	10.3
Vagrancy	**106,269**	94,137	12,132	88.6	11.4	1.8	1.9	1.5
All other offenses (except traffic)	**664,634**	561,338	103,296	84.5	15.5	11.3	11.1	12.8
Suspicion	**88,265**	75,140	13,125	85.1	14.9	1.5	1.5	1.6
Curfew and loitering law violations	**101,674**	81,204	20,470	79.9	20.1	1.7	1.6	2.5
Runaways	**159,468**	77,599	81,869	48.7	51.3	2.7	1.5	10.2

[1] Because of rounding, the percentages may not add to total.

[2] Less than one-tenth of one percent.

Violent crime is offenses of murder, forcible rape, robbery and aggravated assault.

Property crime is offenses of burglary, larceny $50 and over and auto theft.

Table 3–A–3. Total Arrests by Race, 1969

[4,627 agencies; 1969 estimated population 133,028,000]

Offense charged	Total arrests						
	Total	White	Negro	Indian	Chinese	Japanese	All others (includes race unknown)
TOTAL	**5,576,705**	**3,842,895**	**1,558,740**	**115,645**	**1,426**	**3,613**	**54,386**
Criminal homicide:							
(*a*) Murder and nonnegligent manslaughter	**10,412**	3,743	6,444	63	3	5	154
(*b*) Manslaughter by negligence	**3,073**	2,192	805	21	—	8	47
Forcible rape	**13,398**	6,407	6,726	75	3	8	179
Robbery	**65,278**	21,127	42,980	438	9	20	704
Aggravated assault	**100,969**	49,443	49,631	819	21	33	1,022
Burglary—breaking or entering	**240,833**	153,496	82,938	1,612	53	185	2,549
Larceny—theft	**482,355**	316,592	156,111	3,579	338	674	5,061
Auto theft	**117,197**	71,210	42,809	1,021	45	141	1,971
Violent crime	**190,057**	80,720	105,781	1,395	36	66	2,059
Property crime	**840,385**	541,298	281,858	6,212	436	1,000	9,581
Subtotal for above offenses	**1,033,515**	624,210	388,444	7,628	472	1,074	11,687
Other assaults	**242,773**	143,700	94,402	1,730	39	106	2,796
Arson	**7,942**	5,553	2,287	38	2	8	54
Forgery and counterfeiting	**33,016**	22,567	10,073	191	7	19	159
Fraud	**61,339**	45,848	14,977	272	9	13	220
Embezzlement	**5,754**	4,426	1,296	17	1	4	10
Stolen property; buying, receiving, possessing	**35,998**	21,635	13,861	136	14	7	345
Vandalism	**100,512**	77,462	21,631	440	20	30	929
Weapons; carrying, possessing, etc	**82,806**	38,492	42,987	324	9	46	948
Prostitution and commercialized vice	**37,947**	12,484	25,107	109	21	15	211
Sex offenses (except forcible rape and prostitution	**46,697**	34,991	10,695	236	26	43	706
Narcotic drug laws	**193,743**	148,556	42,397	469	74	258	1,989
Gambling	**63,228**	18,482	42,078	27	86	438	2,117
Offenses against family and children	**49,437**	33,458	15,329	372	2	3	273
Driving under the influence	**341,828**	274,982	60,102	4,316	82	254	2,092
Liquor laws	**209,130**	179,338	24,960	3,778	23	51	980
Drunkenness	**1,405,757**	1,021,817	296,577	77.268	190	277	9,628
Disorderly conduct	**551,458**	343,688	190,404	8,026	63	85	9,192
Vagrancy	**84,646**	62,765	19,918	1,137	22	54	750
All other offenses (except traffic)	**643,187**	471,865	158,814	6,049	166	434	5,859
Suspicion	**87,457**	47,955	38,773	503	—	10	216
Curfew and loiter law violations	**100,571**	77,402	20,761	1,030	29	234	1,115
Runaways	**157,964**	131,219	22,867	1,549	69	150	2,110

Table 3-A-3. *(continued)*

Offense charged	Percent distribution					
	White	Negro	Indian	Chinese	Japanese	All others (includes race unknown)
TOTAL	**68.9**	**28.0**	**2.1**	—	**0.1**	**1.0**
Criminal homicide:						
(*a*) Murder and nonnegligent manslaughter	35.9	61.9	.6	—	—	1.5
(*b*) Manslaughter by negligence	71.3	26.2	.7	—	.3	1.5
Forcible rape	47.8	50.2	.6	—	.1	1.3
Robbery	32.4	65.8	.7	—	—	1.1
Aggravated assault	49.0	49.2	.8	—	—	1.0
Burglary—breaking or entering	63.7	34.4	.7	—	.1	1.1
Larceny—theft	65.6	32.4	.7	0.1	.1	1.0
Auto theft	60.8	36.5	.9	—	.1	1.7
Violent crime	42.5	55.7	.7	—	—	1.1
Property crime	64.4	33.5	.7	.1	.1	1.1
Subtotal for above offenses	60.4	37.6	.7	—	.1	1.1
Other assaults	59.2	38.9	.7	—	—	1.2
Arson	69.9	28.8	.5	—	.1	.7
Forgery and counterfeiting	68.4	30.5	.6	—	.1	.5
Fraud	74.7	24.4	.4	—	—	.4
Embezzlement	76.9	22.5	.3	—	.1	.2
Stolen property; buying, receiving, possessing	60.1	38.5	.4	—	—	1.0
Vandalism	77.1	21.5	.4	—	—	.9
Weapons; carrying, possessing, etc	46.5	51.9	.4	—	.1	1.1
Prostitution and commercialized vice	32.9	66.2	.3	.1	—	.6
Sex offenses (except forcible rape and prostitution)	74.9	22.9	.5	.1	.1	1.5
Narcotic drug laws	76.7	21.9	.2	—	.1	1.0
Gambling	29.2	66.5	—	.1	.7	3.3
Offenses against family and children	67.7	31.0	.8	—	—	.6
Driving under the influence	80.4	17.6	1.3	—	.1	.6
Liquor laws	85.8	11.9	1.8	—	—	.5
Drunkenness	72.7	21.1	5.5	—	—	.7
Disorderly conduct	62.3	34.5	1.5	—	—	1.7
Vagrancy	74.1	23.5	1.3	—	.1	.9
All other offenses (except traffic)	73.4	24.7	.9	—	.1	.9
Suspicion	54.8	44.3	.6	—	—	.2
Curfew and loitering law violations	77.0	20.6	1.0	—	.2	1.1
Runaways	83.1	14.5	1.0	—	.1	1.3

Appendix 3–B

ERNEST DONALD'S STUDY OF SELF-CONCEPT OF SIXTH GRADE BOYS

The present paper reports, first of all, on an item analysis of 56 self-concept items from the schedules of 354 sixth-grade boys within the total sample of 717 schedules collected in 1957 (the remainder of the 717 being girls). The 354 schedules included white and colored boys, from the sixth-grade classes of elementary schools in high and low delinquency areas of Columbus, Ohio. The various subgroups of the sample are indicated in Table 1

Table 3–B–1. The Sample of Sixth-Grade Boys by Subgroups, Columbus, Ohio, 1957

Subgroup	*Number*
Teacher's nomination	
Not headed for trouble (good)	222
Headed for trouble* (bad)	132
Race	
White	234
Negro	120
Area	
Low delinquency (good)	125
High delinquency (bad)	229
Nomination by race	
Good white	155
Good Negro	67
Bad white	79
Bad Negro	53

Ernest P. Donald and Simon Dinitz, "Self Concept and Delinquency Proneness," *Interdisciplinary Problems in Criminology: Papers of the American Society of Criminology, 1964*, ed. by Walter C. Reckless and Charles L. Newman (Columbus, Ohio, The Ohio State University Publication Service, 1965), pp. 50–55. Based upon findings in Ernest P. Donald, *Self Concept of Sixth Grade Boys: a Study of Delinquency Proneness* (Ph.D. dissertation, The Ohio State University, 1963).

Nomination by race by area	
Good white (good)	86
Good white (poor)	69
Good Negro (poor)	67
Bad white (good)	39
Bad white (bad)	40
Bad Negro (bad)	53

*Including the teacher's evaluation of "not sure." The teacher rated each boy in terms of whether she thought he was headed for trouble with the law, not sure, or not headed for trouble with the law.

THE ITEM ANALYSIS

The 56 self-concept items in the 1957 schedule consisted of questions which were structured for Yes or No replies. The replies were directionally scored, all in the unfavorable direction or toward delinquency, no matter how the question was asked. Two examples of the item questions with their directional scoring are listed below:

Y (N) 12. Do you think you'll stay out of trouble in the future?
(Y) N 21. If you could get permission to work at 14 would you quit school?

The 354 boys were dichotomized according to teacher's evaluation: headed for trouble with law, including doubtful; not headed for trouble with the law. The replies were also dichotomized according to unfavorable and favorable responses, Chi-square test of association (2 × 2) was run on the dichotomized responses to each of the 56 self-concept items and the dichotomized teacher's evaluation.

Table 3–B–2. Significant self-concept items according to teacher nomination, associated with high and low scores on the De Scale of the California Psychological Inventory

Original schedule no.	*Self-concept items*	X^2	*P*	*P (De Scale)*
1	Will you probably be taken to juvenile court sometime?	29.03	.001	.001
2	Will you probably have to go to jail sometime?	18.38	.001	.001
6	If you found that a friend was leading you into trouble would you continue to run around with him or her?	11.94	.001	.05
11	Do you plan to finish high school?	6.56	.02	.001

12	Do you think you'll stay out of trouble in the future?	9.36	.01	.001
17	Are grown-ups usually against you?	4.23	.05	.001
21	If you could get permission to work at 14 would you quit school?	15.44	.001	.001
23	Are you a big shot with your pals?	12.55	.001	.001
24	Do you think your teacher thinks you will ever get into trouble with the law?	32.92	.001	.001
25	Do you think your mother thinks you will ever get into trouble with the law?	17.12	.001	.001
26	Do you think if you were to get into trouble with the law, it would be bad for you in the future?	4.21	.05	N.S.
27	Have you ever been told that you were headed for trouble with the law?	34.03	.001	.001
39	Have most of your friends been in trouble with the law?	16.36	.001	.001
42	Do you confide in your father?	5.01	.05	.01
46	Do your parents punish you?	6.78	.01	.001
50	Do you think you are quiet.............. average..............active..............?	9.73	.01	.01

Sixteen significant self-concept items emerged from this analysis and they are listed in Table 2 with their Chi-square values and probabilities at one degree of freedom.

Nine of the 16 significant concept items have to do with the sixth-grader's perception of involvement in future difficulty with the law; 7, with more general items. When the responses to the 16 self-concept questions were directionally scored, it was possible to correlate the total score on the 9 delinquency perception items with the 7 general items. Corrected for attentuation the r was +.645. The scoring system was as follows: 1 for the favorable reply, 2 for no answer, 3 for the unfavorable reply.

Testing for consistency, the 16 self-concept items were divided into 8 odd and 8 even items in the listed sequence of Table 1 (not by original schedule item number).

Total scores on the 8 odd and the 8 even items were correlated. When corrected for attentuation, the coefficient of correlation was found to be r = +.82.

ADDITIONAL ITEM ANALYSIS

Five of the 16 self-concept items discriminated by race of the sixth-graders. Using the original schedule item number given in Table 1, the five items discriminating by race were 2, 12, 23, 39, and 52. Seven of the 16 self-concept items distinguished the sixth-grade boys by type of neighborhood (which in this study was based on high and low delinquency rates). The 7 area discriminating items were 1, 2, 12, 25, 26, 27, and 39. Six self-concept items discriminated the boys by their I.Q. level (94 and above, 93 and below): 2, 17, 23, 30, and 42. One self-concept item discriminated by scores on reading achievement, namely, item 17, while 7 of the 16 self-concept items discriminated the sixth-grade boys according to their scores on arithmetic achievement, namely, items 1, 2, 11, 12, 24, 26, and 39.

VALIDATION

The De scale of the California Psychological Inventory (now called the socialization scale) has been used as a measure of delinquency proneness—a veering toward or away from delinquency, or toward poor socialization or good socialization. As an indicator of direction of socialization, the De scale (now Soc scale) has done a good job of identifying the directionality of known criterion groups, such as the "good citizens" in high school, court martial cases in the army, delinquents, prisoners, etc.

Each of the 16 self-concept items which discriminated the sixth-grade Columbus boys by teacher evaluation was associated with the score on the De scale. If the self-concept item is measuring gravitation toward or away from delinquency, it should be significantly associated with high or low De scores (toward and away from delinquency). The last column of Table 1 indicates the probability of the Chi-square at one degree of freedom, when a dichotomous association was made between unfavorable-favorable responses on the self-concept items and the high-low scores on the De scale (unfavorable-favorable direction). Most of the P's are at the .001 of .01 level. There is only one of the 16 self-concept items which is not validated by this test of association with the De score and that is item 26, "Do you think if you were to get into trouble with the law, it would be bad for you in the future?" (See Table 1.)

DIFFERENTIALS BY RACE AND AREA

When the scores on the 16 self-concept items were totaled for each of the 354 boys and mean total score computed for various subgroupings of the sixth-graders, the difference in the mean total self-concept score (high score unfavorable) between the white and colored boys was rather slight, the P of the difference being only .02. The mean score difference by type of neighborhood yielded a P of .002. However, when the mean self-concept score for the white boys in the high and low delinquency neighborhoods was compared, the difference was not significant (P = .07). The P of the mean score difference was .003 for white boys in the good neighborhoods and Negro boys in bad neighborhoods. Finally, the difference in mean self-concept score for the white and Negro sixth-graders, both in the high delinquency neighborhoods, was not significant (P = .32). For the sake of comparison, the difference in the mean self-concept scores by high (unfavorable) and low (favorable) scores on the De scale (which measures direction of socialization) yielded a P of .00001.

COMMENT

Although we obtained a P of .02 and .002 for the mean score differences on race and neighborhood, the actual difference in the mean scores was not very great. The difference between the white boys by type of area is negligible and this holds even more true for the white and colored boys in the high delinquency neighborhoods. Once again, while the P was .003 the actual difference in the mean scores on the 16 self-concept items between the white boys in good areas and Negro boys in poor areas is very small.

One is almost ready to hazard the guess that race and type of neighborhood, whatever they may signify in the accumulated socialization of 12-year-old boys, are relatively unimportant in determining self-concepts. On the other hand, a large mean score difference on the self-concept items is found when the sixth-grade boys are divided by favorable and unfavorable direction of socialization as measured by the scores on the De scale. Evidently the big thing which determines the boy's self-concept orientation is something other than race and neighborhood. Might we say that it is the quality of family interaction and impact, apart from class and race, plus the impact of other supplementary relationships found within the child's world?

APPLICATION TO DELINQUENCY

The differential socialization clue which the self-concept orientation suggests has important application for the study of delinquency. A favorable self-concept at 12 years of age probably acts as a buffer against delinquency deflection, while a poor self-concept represents vulnerability to confrontation by patterns of delinquency and delinquent companions. While this statement might appear as an *ex post facto* rationale at this point, one of the reasons for making the series studies, from which the importance of the self-concept orientation emerged, was to discover a basic difference between boys who were insulated against delinquency in the same areas, at the threshold age of 12 years. Nevertheless, the boys with a favorable self-concept overwhelmingly held the line against delinquency during a four-year follow-up period in high delinquency areas of Columbus, Ohio, while 39 percent of the boys with an unfavorable self-concept became involved in delinquency on an average of three times during a similar period in similar areas.

It could also be that the sixth-grade Columbus boys from the high delinquency areas, who were identified as having a favorable self-concept, might also correspond in part to the working-class boy who, in Kvaraceus and Miller's formulation, avoid delinquency by possessing a favorable aspiration level. And it might very well be that the working-class boy, the corner boy, who in Cohen's observation, rejects middle-class values and gravitates to the gang, has no defense against lower-class concerns and corresponds to the boy who has an unfavorable concept of self and is prone to veer toward delinquency.

The important difference, social psychologically speaking, would be that the boy who gravitates to delinquency lacks a defense of a good self-concept or some other controlling component of self. He has this proneness before he reaches the street corner. He is selected to gravitate toward the street corner or delinquency, because he has no inner defense. The boy in the high delinquency area who manages to stay away from delinquency and bad companions has an inner direction, an inner control, an inner containment.

The same criticism can be lodged against Cloward and Ohlin's theory of limited access to legitimate opportunity and the availability of illegitimate means. It is quite possible that the boys in high delinquency areas who have the awareness of being denied legitimate opportunity and seek the ready-at-hand illegitimate means are also in large part boys with proneness toward delinquency; in other words, those who have no insulation against it and have a weaker inner containment.

Dimensions of inner direction or inner containment, which are components of the self, must be measured in order to tell who veers toward norm violation and delinquency and who conforms to expectations and stays away from delinquency. In a recent paper in *Excerpta Criminologica*, Reckless and Shoham have identified a dimension of self which they call the degree of "norm retention." Individuals who have moved past the compliance stage of conformity into a stage of erosion of originally internalized norms, are the ones who veer toward delinquency and crime in the large middle-range of cases. A high degree of norm retention represents a defense against deviation or violation of norms.

As in the case of the self-concept orientation, the strength or weakness in norm retention answers the question as to "who" responds to delinquency confrontation and "who" does not. Differential association does not identify "who" responds and "who" does not respond to carriers of criminal patterns. Neither does differential identification, delinquency subculture theory, or differential opportunity theory. But the direction of self-concept as well as other inner containing self dimensions can indicate "who" will respond to delinquency confrontation and "who" will not respond. The dimensions of self which control direction of behavior have the important predictive power. They indicate "who."

Appendix 3–C

LIVELY'S STUDY OF SELF-CONCEPT AS A PREDICTOR OF JUVENILE DELINQUENCY

One of the crucial issues in the fields of criminology and juvenile delinquency is the question of why some persons are receptive to anti-social norms and others reject them. A recent approach to this problem is that of Walter Reckless and Simon Dinitz of the Sociology Department of The Ohio State University. In a series of studies, they investigated the relationships between socialization, self-concepts, and insulation against or vulnerability toward delinquency. Based on responses from twelve-year-olds (sixth graders) who represent the threshold age of delinquency, the Reckless-Dinitz studies indicated that differential socialization has produced differential self-concepts for a number of subgroups at the sixth grade level, and that these differentiated response patterns result in varying degrees of insulation against delinquent behavior.

This dissertation reports on research designed to measure the impact of advancing age on socialization and self concepts of the various subgroups at the sixth, seventh, eighth, and ninth grade levels. Three general hypotheses postulate no significant changes in the mean scores of the subgroups with advancing age. A fourth hypothesis postulates that the subgroups with more favorable mean scores in previous studies would continue to show more favorable mean scores at all age levels.

To test these hypotheses, a sample of one thousand teenagers was drawn from the seventh, eighth, and ninth grades in six junior high schools, and two hundred sixth graders from six grade schools, in the public schools of Akron, Ohio. The schedule developed and utilized by Reckless and Dinitz in earlier studies was administered to these twelve hundred students in March and April, 1959. From the schedule data, scores on the Gough Socialization scale, a Concept of the Father scale, a Concept of Home and Parents scale, a Concept of Law and Order scale, and the Short-Nye delinquency scale, were obtained for each respondent. Each child was evaluated by a qualified member of the school staff as to the child's delinquency probabilities. All these data were analyzed by grade for four dichotomized subgroups: race (Negro-white), sex (male-female), teacher nomination (good-bad), area of residence (good-bad), and by extreme combinations of these subgroups (white female-Negro male, white female good nominee-Negro male bad nominee, white female good area-Negro male bad area).

Edwin Lowe Lively, "A Study of Teen-age Socialization and Delinquency Insulation by Grade Levels" (Ph.D. dissertation, The Ohio State University, 1959), pp. 1–3, 49–55. See also Edwin L. Lively, Simon Dinitz, and Walter C. Reckless. "Self Concept as a Predictor of Juvenile Delinquency," *The American Journal of Orthopsychiatry*, 32:1 (January 1962), pp. 159–158.

The findings indicate that the mean scores of children on the socialization and self concept measures do not change with advancing age, the mean scores of the dichotomized subgroups and combinations of subgroup extremes do not change with age, and the mean scores of girls, whites, children nominated as good, children from good areas, and the extreme combinations are higher than those of their respective opposite subgroups.

In summary, the findings of this study support the basic hypothesis of Reckless and Dinitz, namely, that the concepts of self and other are well established by the time children reach the age of twelve (sixth grade level), and that these concepts can be measured at this level. The findings further indicate that self concepts are sufficiently retained by subgroups through advancing age so as to make the sixth grade mean scores fairly reliable indicators of delinquency insulation or vulnerability of the subgroups in the seventh, eighth, and ninth grades, or up to the age of sixteen.

THE TEENAGER

My name is ____________________ School________________
last (print) first middle (print)

The Teenage Youth is in many ways the most important person in our society. We are trying to find out what the young people of your age think and feel about things. We are members of a youth-study team at The Ohio State University, Columbus, Ohio. Your answer sheets will be taken back there and counted along with several hundred other youth in other large cities of the country. The right answer is your honest opinion or the way you look at things. This is not a test. The way you feel about things is the right way to answer the questions. But first of all,

SOME FACTS ABOUT ME

1. My birthday is:
   (month________________(day)________ (year)________
2. Check whether you are:
   (1) a boy________________(2) a girl ____________
3. Where were you born?
   (1) state ________________or, (2) country ____________
4. Check which one you are:
   the oldest child in your family ________
   the youngest child ________
   in between ________
   the only child ________
5. Up to now I have been living at home: yes______no______
6. Both my parents are living: yes______no______

7. Both of my parents are living at home: yes______ no______

8. My father is dead: yes______ no______

9. My mother is dead: yes______ no______

10. I have a stepfather: yes______ no______

11. I have a stepmother: yes______ no______

12. How tall are you:________________inches

13. How much do you weigh:____________pounds

14. As well as you can remember, how many different times has your family moved its home in your lifetime:____________

THE WAY I LOOK AT THINGS

Remember this is not a test. There are no right or wrong answers. The right answer for you is the way you look at things.

Circle "T" for *True* and "F" for *False*.

T F 1. I think Lincoln was greater than Washington.

T F 2. Life usually hands me a pretty raw deal.

T F 3. A person is better off if he doesn't trust anyone.

T F 4. Sometimes I used to feel that I would like to leave home.

T F 5. If the pay was right, I would like to travel with a circus or carnival.

T F 6. I would do almost anything on a dare.

T F 7. As a youngster in school, I used to give the teachers lots of trouble.

T F 8. Even when I have gotten into trouble, I was usually trying to do the right thing.

T F 9. My parents never really understood me.

T F 10. My home as a child was less peaceful and quiet than those of most other people.

T F 11. I think that I am stricter about right and wrong than most people.

T F 12. Even the idea of giving a talk in public makes me afraid.

T F 13. It is very important to me to have enough friends and social life.

T F 14. I never worry about my looks.

T F 15. I hardly ever get excited or thrilled.

T F 16. My parents have often disapproved of my friends.

T F 17. My home life was always happy.

T F 18. I often act on the spur of the moment without stopping to think.

T F 19. I seem to do things that I regret more often than other people do.

T F 20. I would rather go without something than ask for a favor.

T F 21. I have had more than my share of things to worry about.

T F 22. I go out of my way to meet trouble rather than try to escape it.

T F 23. When I meet a stranger, I often think that he is better than I am.

T F 24. It is pretty easy for people to win arguments with me.

T F 25. Before I do something, I try to consider how my friends will react to it.

T F 26. I have never been in trouble with the law.

T F 27. In school, I was sometimes sent to the principal for cutting up.

T F 28. I keep out of trouble at all costs

T F 29. I often think about how I look and what impression I am making upon others.

T F 30. I find it easy to "drop" or "break with" a friend.

T F 31. It is hard for me to act natural when I am with new people.

T F 32. I have often gone against my parents' wishes.

T F 33. Most of the time, I feel happy.

T F 34. My table manners are not quite as good at home as when I am out in company.

T F 35. I know who is responsible for most of my troubles.

T F 36. When I was going to school, I played hookey quite often.

T F 37. People often talk about me behind my back.

T F 38. I often feel as though I have done something wrong or wicked.

T F 39. I don't think I'm as happy as others seem to be.

T F 40. I used to steal sometimes when I was a youngster.

T F 41. I am somewhat afraid of the dark.

T F 42. I never cared much for school.

T F 43. The members of my family were always close to each other.

T F 44. I sometimes wanted to run away from home.

T F 45. My parents have generally let me make my own decisions.

T F 46. My home life was always very pleasant.

SOME MORE ABOUT ME, SCHOOL, AND HOME

Remember this is not a test. The right answer is the way you look at things. Circle "Y" for *Yes* and "N" for *No*.

Y N 47. Up till now, do you think things have gone your way?

Y N 48. Do you feel that grown ups are usually against you?

Y N 49. Do you expect to get an even break from people in the future?

Y N 50. Have you ever been told you were a problem child?

Y N 51. Do you get along pretty well with your teachers and other school officials?

Y N 52. Do you expect to get much out of school from now on?

Y N 53. I plan to finish high school.

Y N 54. Have most of your friends been in trouble with the law?

Y N 55. If you found that a friend of yours was leading you into trouble, would you still run around with him (or her)?

Y N 56. Do you think there is much fighting at home?

Y N 57. Do you feel that your parents tease or nag you at home too much?

Y N 58. Do your parents punish you when you don't deserve it?

Y N 59. Do you think your father or stepfather is too strict with you?

Y N 60. Do you tell your parents where you are going?

Y N 61. Do your parents know who your friends are?

Y N 62. Do you feel free to bring your friends home?

Y N 63. Are your parents away from the house too much, when they don't have to be?

Y N 64. Do you talk things over with your father or stepfather when you get into some kind of trouble?

Y N 65. In general, do you feel that you get a "square deal" from your father or stepfather?

Y N 66. Are you interested in what your father or stepfather thinks of you?

Y N 67. I think my father or stepfather has my best interest at heart.

Y N 68. I think my father or stepfather shows more interest in my brothers and sisters than he shows in me.

Y N 69. My father or stepfather praises me when I do my work well.

Y N 70. My father or stepfather says and does things that make me feel that I am not trusted.

ABOUT ME, THE LAW, AND RULES

Here again, this is not a test. The right answer is the way you look at things and the way things have happened to you.

Circle "Y" for *Yes* and "N" for *No*.

Y N 71. Do you think you will stay out of trouble with the law?

Y N 72. I have a good opinion of policemen.

Y N 73. I have a good opinion of the juvenile court.

Y N 74. I believe that any real trouble people have with the law can be fixed for them by the right people.

Y N 75. Do you know any adult criminals personally?

Y N 76. Have you ever been told that you are headed for trouble with the law?

Y N 77. Do you think your mother or stepmother thinks you are headed for trouble with the law?

Y N 78. Do you think your teacher thinks you are headed for trouble with the law?

Y N 79. Will you probably be taken to the juvenile court sometime?

Y N 80. Will you probably have to go to jail sometime?

Everyone of us, young and old, breaks some laws, rules, and regulations during his lifetime. Some of us break them regularly, others less often. Below are some often broken. Check those that you have broken since beginning grade school and put an "X" after the right answer for you.

81. Have you skipped school without a good excuse?

no ______
once or twice ______
several times ______
very often ______

82. Have you "run away" from home?

no	______
once	______
twice	______
3 times	______
4 times	______
5 times	______
over 5 times	______

83. Have you defied your parents' authority (to their face)?

no	______
once or twice	______
several times	______
very often	______

84. Have you taken little things (worth less than $2) that did not belong to you?

no	______
once or twice	______
several times	______
very often	______

85. Have you taken things of medium value (between $2 and $50)?

very often	______
several times	______
once or twice	______
no	______

86. Have you bought or drank beer, wine, or liquor without parent consent?

no	______
once or twice	______
several times	______
very often	______

87. Have you on purpose damaged or destroyed public or private property that did not belong to you?

very often	______
several times	______
once or twice	______
no	______

A COUPLE OF THINGS WE FORGOT

88. Does your mother or stepmother work outside the home for pay?

    yes ______
    no ______
    have no mother or stepmother ______

89. If yes, tell what she does. (For example; works in a factory, sales lady at a department store, cashier in a drugstore, etc.)

    ____

    ____

90. Does your father or stepfather have a regular job?

    yes ______
    no ______
    have no father or stepfather ______

91. What does he usually work at? (For example: filling station attendant, truck driver, owns small store, etc.)

    ____

    ____

92. How long have you lived in Akron?

    less than 1 year ______ 5-10 years ______
    1-2 years ______ 10 or more years ______
    2-5 years ______ all my life ______

Appendix 3–D

THE FORMAT OF FITTS' SELF-CONCEPT SCALE

INSTRUCTIONS

On the top line of the separate answer sheet, fill in your name and the other information except for the time information in the last three boxes. You will fill these boxes in later. Write only on the answer sheet. Do not put any marks in this booklet.

The statements in this booklet are to help you describe yourself as you see yourself. Please respond to them as if you were describing yourself *to yourself*. *Do not omit any item*! Read each statement carefully; then select one of the five responses listed below. On your answer sheet, put a *circle* around the response you chose. If you want to change an answer after you have circled it, do not erase it but put an *X* mark through the response and then circle the response you want.

When you are ready to start, find the box on your answer sheet marked *time started* and record the time. When you are finished, record the time finished in the box on your answer sheet marked *time finished*.

As you start, be sure that your answer sheet and this booklet are lined up evenly so that the item numbers match each other.

Remember, put a *circle* around the response number you have chosen for each statement.

	Completely false	Mostly false	Partly false and partly true	Mostly true	Completely true
Responses–	1	2	3	4	5

TWELVE ILLUSTRATIVE ITEMS OUT OF 100 ITEMS IN THE SCALE

19. I am a decent sort of person.

30. I shouldn't tell so many lies.

Tennessee Self Concept Scale by William H. Fitts, published by Counselor Recordings and Tests, Box 6184, Acklen Station, Nashville, Tennessee 37212, copyrighted by William H. Fitts, 1964.

33. I try to change when I know I'm doing things that are wrong.

36. I have trouble doing the things that are right.

38. I have a lot of self-control.

43. I am satisfied to be just what I am.

53. I do things without thinking about them first.

60. I feel that my family doesn't trust me.

64. I should trust my family more.

72. I do not act like my family thinks I should.

84. I ought to get along better with other people.

91. I do not always tell the truth.

Appendix 3–E

K D PRONENESS SCALE

By WILLIAM C. KVARACEUS, Professor of Education, Boston University

---

Name.. Boy.............. Girl..............

School (or Group).. Grade..............

Age Last Birthday..............Years Date.............. 19.....

DIRECTIONS

THE questions in this booklet ask how you feel about certain things. This is not a test. There are no right or wrong answers. Read each question and the four answers that follow it. Select the answer that best describes how you really feel about the question. Do not skip any questions. Answer every question as you come to it. Remember, there are no right or wrong answers. Be sure to choose the answer that best tells how you feel about the question.

Here is a sample question to show you how to mark the answers.

Sample A. Of the following, the color I like best is:—
1 **red** 2 **brown** 3 **blue** 4 **green**.................... 1 2 3 4

By William C. Kvaraceus.

Decide which of these colors you like best and draw a line under your answer. Now look at the number beside the color which you picked. Put a heavy black mark in the answer space at the right which is under the number of the answer which you have picked. For example, if you like "blue" best, you will draw a line under the word "blue." Since "blue" is number 3, you will put a heavy black line in the answer space under the number 3.

When you are told to start, read each question and decide upon your answer, then record the answer in the same manner as you have done for the sample. You will be given time enough to finish all the questions.

Do not open your booklet until you are told to do so.

ANSWER SHEET

Plus Score ____

Minus Score ____

Total Scale Score ____

Page 6

Row				
61	41	42	43	44
62	45	46	47	48
63	49	50	51	52
64	53	54	55	56
65	57	58	59	60
66	61	62	63	64
67	65	66	67	68
68	69	70	71	72
69	73	74	75	76
70	77	78	79	80
71	81	82	83	84
72	85	86	87	88
73	89	90	91	92
74	93	94	95	96
75	97	98	99	100

Page 5

Row				
41	61	62	63	64
42	65	66	67	68
43	69	70	71	72
44	73	74	75	76
45	77	78	79	80
46	81	82	83	84
47	85	86	87	88
48	89	90	91	92
49	93	94	95	96
50	97	98	99	100
51	1	2	3	4
52	5	6	7	8
53	9	10	11	12
54	13	14	15	16
55	17	18	19	20
56	21	22	23	24
57	25	26	27	28
58	29	30	31	32
59	33	34	35	36
60	37	38	39	40

Page 4

Row				
21	81	82	83	84
22	85	86	87	88
23	89	90	91	92
24	93	94	95	96
25	97	98	99	100
26	1	2	3	4
27	5	6	7	8
28	9	10	11	12
29	13	14	15	16
30	17	18	19	20
31	21	22	23	24
32	25	26	27	28
33	29	30	31	32
34	33	34	35	36
35	37	38	39	40
36	41	42	43	44
37	45	46	47	48
38	49	50	51	52
39	53	54	55	56
40	57	58	59	60

Page 3

Row				
1	1	2	3	4
2	5	6	7	8
3	9	10	11	12
4	13	14	15	16
5	17	18	19	20
6	21	22	23	24
7	25	26	27	28
8	29	30	31	32
9	33	34	35	36
10	37	38	39	40
11	41	42	43	44
12	45	46	47	48
13	49	50	51	52
14	53	54	55	56
15	57	58	59	60
16	61	62	63	64
17	65	66	67	68
18	69	70	71	72
19	73	74	75	76
20	77	78	79	80

NOTE. *This answer sheet is not intended for machine scoring*

1. Of the following, the drink I like best is:—
   1 **soda pop** 2 **milk** 3 **water** 4 **coffee**.......................... 1

2. Of the following subjects, the one I like to study best is:—
   5 **English** 6 **science**
   7 **art or drawing** 8 **manual training or home economics**................ 2

3. Those who get the best jobs are usually the ones who:—
   9 **know the right person** 10 **are the best trained**
   11 **are the luckiest** 12 **work the hardest**.................................... 3

4. Going to high school is:—
   13 **a waste of time**
   14 **all right for some people but not for me**
   15 **all right if you can take the course you want**
   16 **necessary for success**.. 4

5. If a person called me a dirty name, I would:—
   17 **fight the person** 18 **tell him where to get off**
   19 **say and do nothing** 20 **laugh it off**....................................... 5

6. Of the following sports, the one I like best to watch is a:—
   21 **baseball game** 22 **prize fight**
   23 **horse race** 24 **basketball game**... 6

7. When I do my schoolwork I get my reward:—
   25 **always** 26 **sometimes** 27 **seldom** 28 **never**................. 7

8. Parents usually understand their children:—
   29 **very well** 30 **quite well**
   31 **not very well** 32 **not at all**.. 8

9. If I want to be popular I have to do what the crowd does:—
   33 **all of the time** 34 **most of the time**
   35 **some of the time** 36 **seldom or never**.................................... 9

10. Failure is usually due to:—
    37 **bad habits** 38 **bad companions**
    39 **lack of ability** 40 **lack of hard work**..................................... 10

11. The pupils who have the best attendance records are almost always:—
    41 **honor students** 42 **good students**
    43 **poor students** 44 **sissies**.. 11

(Go right on to the next page.)

12. During the summer I would like best to stay:—
    45 **around the house** 46 **at a summer camp away from home**
    47 **at a YMCA (YWCA) day camp**
    48 **at the playground near home**...12

13. Of the following, I would *least* like to be a:—
    49 **teacher** 50 **minister** 51 **doctor** 52 **crooner**................13

14. You have lots more fun if you live in a family with:—
    53 **no brothers or sisters** 54 **only one brother or sistor**
    55 **two or three brothers or sisters**
    56 **four or more brothers or sisters**...14

15. Most boys stay in school because they:—
    57 **are required by law to do so**
    58 **have to learn to make a living**
    59 **want to go to college** 60 **like school**.......................................15

16. Most teachers are:—
    61 **very fair** 62 **fair most of the time**
    63 **seldom fair** 64 **never fair**...16

→

17. Smoking is a habit that:—
    65 **does not hurt anyone** 66 **hurts everyone a little**
    67 **hurts some people but not others**
    68 **hurts most people a great deal**...17

18. The scret of success is:—
    69 **just luck** 70 **hard work** 71 **ability** 72 **money**.............18

19. Of the following, I would like most to be a famous:—
    73 **movie actor (actress)** 74 **athlete**
    75 **scientist** 76 **writer**...19

20. Most people who do something wrong do not think that they:—
    77 **will be caught** 78 **will be punished**
    79 **are really doing wrong** 80 **are hurting others**..........................20

21. Which of the following drinks do you like best?
    81 **ginger ale** 82 **coke** 83 **root beer** 84 **milk shake**.........21

(Go right on to the next page.)

22. If I am asked to do something which I think is not reasonable, I:—
    85 **refuse to do it** 86 **argue first and then do just enough to get by**
    87 **do what I'm told and then argue later**
    88 **do what I'm told and say nothing**........22

23. The schoolwork that the teacher gives me is usually:—
    89 **very hard** 90 **fairly hard**
    91 **fairly easy** 92 **very easy**........23

→

24. I have the most fun when I play:—
    93 **in my own house** 94 **in my own yard**
    95 **on my street** 96 **on the playground near my house**........24

25. Being successful usually means having:—
    97 **a big fortune** 98 **many friends**
    99 **your name in the paper** 100 **the respect of many people**........25

26. The best teachers are the ones who are:—
    1 **very easy** 2 **fairly easy** 3 **fairly hard** 4 **very hard**........26

27. Most policemen try to:—
    5 **help you** 6 **scare you**
    7 **boss you** 8 **get something on you**........27

28. I would like to attend the movies:—
    9 **once a week** 10 **twice a week**
    11 **three or four times a week** 12 **every day**........28

29. Cheating in school is usually done by:—
    13 **only a few bad pupils** 14 **none of the pupils**
    15 **most of the pupils** 16 **all of the pupils**........29

30. Whenever I get into serious trouble, other people are to blame:—
    17 **always** 18 **almost always**
    19 **sometimes** 20 **seldom or never**........30

31. Teachers know what they are talking about:—
    21 **always** 22 **most of the time**
    23 **some of the time** 24 **seldom or never**........31

→

32. Older people understand younger people:—
    25 **very well** 26 **rather well** 27 **only a little** 28 **not at all**...32

(Go right on to the next page.)

33. Of the following subjects, which do you *dislike* the most?

29 **history or social studies** 30 **mathematics**
31 **English** 32 **shop**..........33

34. A boy or girl should be allowed to be his own boss when he is:—

33 **14 years old** 34 **16 years old**
35 **18 years old** 36 **21 years old**..........34

35. People who live in fine houses usually are:—

37 **the best people in town**
38 **smarter and more educated than most people**
39 **just lucky** 40 **crooked in business**..........35

36. In a family it is best to be:—

41 **the oldest child** 42 **the youngest child**
43 **the only child** 44 **one of a large family**..........36

37. In schools the good marks are usually given to those who:—

45 **do the best work** 46 **work the hardest**
47 **only make believe they are working** 48 **are teachers' pets**..........37

38. When I leave school or graduate, I shall:—

49 **take any job that comes along** 50 **find a good job**
51 **take it easy for a while** 52 **go to another school or college**..........38

39. Happiness is impossible without:—

53 **love** 54 **friends** 55 **a home** 56 **money**..........39

40. Of the following, the color I like best is:—

57 **red** 58 **black** 59 **yellow** 60 **blue**..........40

41. I usually have the best time when I do things:—

61 **all by myself** 62 **with one friend**
63 **with two or three friends** 64 **with a big gang**..........41

42. For the most serious trouble I have ever been in:—

65 **others were to blame more than I was**
66 **others were to blame as much as I was**
67 **I was mostly to blame** 68 **I was wholly to blame**..........42

43. I would like to stay in bed late in the morning:—

69 **every day** 70 **Saturdays and Sundays**
71 **Sundays** 72 **seldom or never**..........43

(Go right on to the next page.)

44. Of the following, the sport I like best is:—

73 **fishing or hunting** 74 **overnight hiking**

75 **football or baseball** 76 **wrestling**.. 44

45. Of the following, the vegetable I like best is:—

77 **squash** 78 **potato** 79 **spinach** 80 **carrot**.................... 45

➡

46. In the schools, teachers can usually be depended upon to do:—

81 **nothing to help me** 82 **a little to help me**

83 **much to help me** 84 **all they can to help me**.......................... 46

47. In school, my friends:—

85 **always get me into trouble** 86 **almost always get me into trouble**

87 **sometimes get me into trouble** 88 **never get me into trouble**.......... 47

48. Of the teachers I have known, I have liked:—

89 **all of them** 90 **most of them**

91 **some of them** 92 **only one of them**.. 48

49. During the past month I have worried about my family:—

93 **all the time** 94 **most of the time**

95 **some of the time** 96 **not at all**.. 49

50. I think about what I'll do when I get out of school:—

97 **all the time** 98 **most of the time**

99 **some of the time** 100 **not at all**.. 50

51. Going to school causes me to be worried and upset:—

1 **all the time** 2 **most of the time**

3 **some of the time** 4 **never**.. 51

➡

52. I have been:—

5 **extremely lucky** 6 **lucky**

7 **extremely unlucky** 8 **unlucky**.. 52

53. Taking part in school clubs is:—

9 **very important** 10 **quite important**

11 **not very important** 12 **very unimportant**.................................. 53

54. The most popular boys are the ones who:—

13 **almost always get into mischief** 14 **sometimes get into mischief**

15 **seldom get into mischief** 16 **almost never get into mischief**............ 54

(Go right on to the next page.)

55. When not in school, I can have the most fun:—
    17 **in the mornings** 18 **in the afternoons**
    19 **around noon** 20 **around midnight**..........55

56. The pupils who skip school are usually the ones who get:—
    21 **the best marks** 22 **good marks**
    23 **fair marks** 24 **the poorest marks**..........56

➡

57. Going to college is:—
    25 **necessary for success** 26 **all right if you can afford it**
    27 **all right if you have the ability** 28 **just a waste of time and money**...57

58. Most teachers act like other human beings:—
    29 **always** 30 **most of the time**
    31 **some of the time** 32 **seldom or never**..........58

59. The time when I shall leave home I look forward to:—
    33 **not at all** 34 **sometimes** 35 **often** 36 **very often**..........59

60. Going to school right now is doing me:—
    37 **a great deal of good** 38 **some good**
    39 **more harm than good** 40 **a great deal of harm**..........60

61. During the past month I have been worrying about my health:—
    41 **all the time** 42 **most of the time**
    43 **some of the time** 44 **none of the time**..........61

62. Teachers and principals usually treat pupils like:—
    45 **slaves and work animals** 46 **someone beneath them**
    47 **little children** 48 **their equals**..........62

63. The police:—
    49 **are usually very fair** 50 **make some mistakes**
    51 **favor the rich** 52 **are usually unfair**..........63

➡

64. Failing marks on your report card usually mean:—
    53 **you didn't do your work** 54 **you are dumb**
    55 **your teacher doesn't like you** 56 **you have been absent a lot**..........64

65. The best time of the year is:—
    57 **Christmas** 58 **Easter** 59 **summer** 60 **Thanksgiving**......65

(Go right on to the next page.)

66. Of the following, the dessert I like best is:—
61 **jello** 62 **bread pudding** 63 **custard** 64 **pie**.................66

67. On my report card I usually get:—
65 **all honor marks** 66 **mostly good marks**
67 **fair marks** 68 **some failure marks**.......................................67

68. Of the following, the game I like best is:—
69 **checkers** 70 **bingo** 71 **marbles** 72 **authors**.................68

69. School rules and regulations have good reasons behind them:—
73 **always** 74 **almost always**
75 **some of the time** 76 **seldom or never**.......................................69

70. When I am with someone else and we want something to drink, I like to:—
77 **buy my own drink** 78 **match to see who will pay**
79 **fix it so the other person usually pays** 80 **pay for all the drinks**....70

71. If I had the money, I would like best to go to a:—
81 **dance** 82 **movie** 83 **concert** 84 **bowling alley**.............71

➡

72. People who wear fine clothes usually are:—
85 **just lucky** 86 **smarter than other people**
87 **better educated than others** 88 **the best people in town**................72

73. It is the most fun to have:—
89 **no girl friends** 90 **one girl friend**
91 **a few girl friends** 92 **lots of girl friends**...................................73

➡

74. It is the most fun to have:—
93 **no boy friends** 94 **one boy friend**
95 **a few boy friends** 96 **lots of boy friends**...................................74

75. I have learned that I can trust:—
97 **most people** 98 **some people**
99 **a few people** 100 **no one**...75

K D PRONENESS CHECK LIST (REVISED)

By WILLIAM C. KVARACEUS, Professor of Education, Boston University

Name of Subject.......................... Boy......... Girl......... Date.................

Age Last Birthday......... Years. School (or Group)......... Checker(s)...........

DIRECTIONS

Before using this Check List study the Manual of Directions carefully, particularly that section pertaining to the use of the Check List.

For each item place a check in the appropriate "Yes," "No," "?" column. Count the number of check marks in each column and enter these numbers in the spaces provided at the end of the Check List. A large number of checks in the "Yes" column will indicate a child who is vulnerable to the establishment of delinquent patterns of behavior. Those characteristics which have the greatest bearing on potential delinquent behavior are marked with an asterisk.

The sources from which information is obtained should be entered in the proper spaces at the end of the Check List. For example, such entries as "Cumulative Records," "Child-serving Agency," and "Parents" will be made.

Yes	No	?	**I. Personal Factors**
			1. Is between 10 and 16 (if boy); 12 and 16 (if girl)
			*2. Is below average in academic apititude
			3. Is in poor health
			4. Has physical defect
			*5. Reacts to situations in overly aggressive manner
			*6. Attends movies at least twice a week
			*7. Never belonged to a club or organization
			*8. Shows lack of success in out-of-school activities
			9. Avoids positions and activities involving responsibilities
			*10. Has previous record of delinquent behavior
			*11. Evidences a philosophy of "good" or "bad" luck
			12. Is satisfied with self
			*13. Associates with others who are or have been delinquent
			14. Declares he is afraid of nothing
			*15. "Runs" with a "gang"
			16. Is the middle child in a large (five or more) family
			17. Has three or more sisters
			18. Is slovenly and unkempt in appearance
			19. Seldom attends church or Sunday school

By William C. Kvaraceus.

Yes	No	?	**II. Environmental Factors—Home and Family**
			20. Birth unplanned or accidental
			*21. Family broken by divorce, desertion, or death
			*22. Relationships in family life unwholesome
			*23. Emotional conflicts between parents
			*24. Emotional conflicts between siblings
			**25. Emotional conflicts between parents and siblings
			*26. Poor home discipline (very lax, extremely rigid, or very erratic)
			*27. Overindulgence exhibited toward child
			*28. Feels disliked or unwanted
			*29. Drunkenness in family
			30. Much nagging among family members
			*31. Evidence of neglect
			32. Is overprotected by family
			33. Intense rivalry among siblings
			34. Dislikes home
			35. Extreme parental domination
			*36. Cultural conflicts between parents and siblings
			*37. Delinquent brothers and/or sisters
			*38. Parents have court records
			39. Family is large (five or more)
			*40. Family belongs to marginal group (Negro, foreign-born, etc.)
			*41. Lives in other than natural home
			*42. Family income inadequate for comfortable living
			43. Record of family contacts with welfare agencies
			44. Father is unskilled or slightly skilled worker
			*45. Mother is employed outside the home
			*46. Inadequate living quarters
			47. Lives in multi-family dwelling
			*48. Overcrowding (more than 1.5 persons per room) prevails
			49. Inadequate furnishings in home
			50. Family without automobile
			51. Home unsanitary
			*52. Family is mobile or migratory
			53. Lives in underprivileged neighborhood
			*54. Lives in high delinquency-rate area
			55. Has few facilities for play (home, yard, neighborhood)
			56. Lives over business establishment
			57. Family rents home and pays less than prevailing average
			58. Lives in racially mixed neighborhood

Yes	No	?	III. School Factors
			*59. Has below average verbal ability
			*60. Has little interest in schoolwork
			*61. Is unsuccessful in schoolwork
			*62. Has repeated one or more grades
			63. Grade placement too high for mental ability
			*64. Is in a special class
			*65. Is indifferent to or dislikes school
			*66. Transfers frequently from school to school
			*67. Is truant from school frequently
			*68. Intends to leave school as soon as the law will allow
			*69. Feels that he does not belong to the class group
			*70. Takes little or no part in extracurricular or club activities of school

TOTAL NUMBER OF ITEMS CHECKED

Yes	No	?

Sources of Information:

1. ....
2. ....
3. ....
4. ....
5. ....

Summary and Interpretation

....

....

....

Appendix 3–F

THE SOCIALIZATION SCALE OF THE CALIFORNIA PSYCHOLOGICAL INVENTORY

The Socialization Scale is composed of 54 items in a total of 480 items which comprise the California Psychological Inventory. The items in the total inventory, including those which comprise the socialization cluster, are answered True or False. The favorable response to any item, whether yes or no, counts 1, and the total score on any cluster of items, such as the Socialization Scale, which are answered in the favorable direction are totalled. The total score is then compared with norms giving the directionality of the individual's answers.

Originally, the items in the Socialization Scale were labelled a DE scale, meaning delinquency scale and the interpretation of scores according to available norms at the time was made in the direction of tending toward or away from delinquency. Subsequently, it was found that the items in the so-called DE scale were really measuring directionally toward good or poor socialization. However, the more recent scale description of the Socialization Scale says that it indicates "the degree of social maturity, probity, and rectitude which the individual has attained. HIGH SCORERS: honest, industrious, obliging, sincere, modest, steady, conscientious, and responsible; self-denying and conforming. LOW SCORERS: defensive, demanding, opinionated, resentful, headstrong, rebellious, and undependable; guileful and deceitful; given to excess, ostentation, and exhibition in behavior."

While the scale description is certainly a more comprehensive behavioral science statement, the writer, who has used the scale in many studies and several samples of youths and adults, still feels that the scale is an efficient measure of directionality towards or away from delinquency and crime, undoubtedly resulting from poor or good socialization.

The Socialization Scale's 54 items contains 8 items which primarily apply to adults. In the total of the 480 items of the California Psychological Inventory, these 8 items

The Socialization Scale constitutes a subscale of the California Psychological Inventory, which was developed by Dr. Harrison G. Gough. The Inventory may be procured from the Consulting Psychologists Press, Inc., Palo Alto, California. See Harrison G. Gough, "Theory and Measurement of Socialization," *Journal of Consulting Psychology*, Vol. 24, No. 1, February 1960, pp. 23–30.

comprise items number 12, 94, 323, 334, 339, 389, 393, 409. For example, item 12 reads: I often feel I made a wrong choice in my occupation; item 323 reads: I have never done any heavy drinking; item 389 reads: I get pretty discouraged with the law when a smart lawyer gets a criminal free. The writer, in using the Socialization Scale on sample groups under 18 years of age, eliminated these 8 items from the scale and used a corrected score by adding approximately one seventh to the total score of a youthful subject, so as to make the scores comparable with the statistical norms of the test.

The following are representative items from the 54 items of the Socialization Scale:

When I was going to school I played hookey quite often.

I would do almost anything on a dare.

My parents have often disapproved of my friends.

My home life was always happy.

I have never been in trouble with the law.

I keep out of trouble at all costs.

Appendix 3–G

HATHAWAY AND MONACHESI'S DELINQUENCY PRONENESS SCALE

	Item	*Delinquent Response*
1.	At times I have very much wanted to leave home.	True
2.	When someone does me a wrong I feel I should pay him back if I can, just for the principle of the thing.	True
3.	During one period when I was a youngster I engaged in petty thievery.	True
4.	As a youngster I was suspended from school one or more times for cutting up.	True
5.	I believe women ought to have as much sexual freedom as men.	True
6.	In school I was sometimes sent to the principal for cutting up.	True
7.	Most people will use somewhat unfair means to gain profit or an advantage rather than to lose it.	True
8.	I do not worry about catching diseases.	True
9.	When I was a child, I belonged to a crowd or gang that tried to stick together through thick and thin.	True
10.	I have the wanderlust and am never happy unless I am roaming or traveling about.	True
11.	I am afraid when I look down from a high place.	False
12.	I liked school.	False
13.	I like to flirt.	True
14.	I very much like hunting.	True
15.	My parents have often objected to the kind of people I went around with.	True
16.	I don't blame anyone for trying to grab everything he can get in this world.	True
17.	I am entirely self-confident.	True

Starke R. Hathaway, and Elio D. Monachesi, *Adolescent Personality and Behavior*, University of Minnesota Press, Minneapolis, University of Minnesota, copyright 1963, p. 89.

18. When in a group of people I have trouble thinking of the right things to talk about. False
19. I can easily make other people afraid of me, and sometimes do for the fun of it. True
20. At times I have been so entertained by the cleverness of a crook that I have hoped he would get by with it. True
21. I have never been in trouble with the law. False
22. If several people find themselves in trouble, the best thing for them to do is to agree upon a story and stick to it. True
23. At times I have very much wanted to leave home. True
24. I have had very peculiar and strange experiences. True
25. I am often said to be hotheaded. True
26. I played hookey from school quite often as a youngster. True
27. I am attracted by members of the opposite sex. True
28. I would like to be an auto racer. True
29. It is all right to get around the law if you don't actually break it. True
30. If I were in trouble with several friends who were equally to blame, I would rather take the whole blame than to give them away. True

Appendix 3–H

ROBISON'S STUDY OF REPORTED INVOLVEMENT IN DELINQUENCY AS YOUTHS BY ADULT MALES

The data confirm the hypothesis that the more active and gregarious the respondent the more likely he was to be involved in behavior which might have been labeled delinquent. For the Glen Cove respondents who said they were active, 45 percent had SDB scores (serious delinquent behavior), in comparison with 38 percent for those who said they were not. In the Boston sample, the comparable figures are 38 percent vs. 22 percent. More than 50% in both samples who said their usual "delinquent" activity was with companions, had high SDB scores, in contrast to about 25 percent who said that they engaged in their disapproved behavior alone.

A high percent of SDB (serious delinquent behavior) scores appears at this stage of the analysis to be associated with two family characteristics, i.e., (1) those families in which the father was *not* in the home—the comparable figures for Glen Cove are 47 vs. 38 when the father was in the home—in Boston 42 contrasts with 25 in the two parent households. (2) Families in which there was a male sibling within two years of age of the respondent. Comparable percents of high scores in Glen Cove are 43 for families with male sibling vs. 31 without male siblings. In Boston, the contrast is 31 vs. 23.

Glen Cove respondents who recalled good relations with the father, 37 percent in contrast to 50, and in Boston 28 percent vs. 43. When they said their relations with *both* parents were good, the percent of high SDB scores was 24 percent in both samples in contrast to 48 in Glen Cove and 34 in Boston, when it was remembered or reported as good with *only one* parent.

The high percent of SDB scores for respondents whose families used physical punishment was 43 percent in Glen Cove and 31 in Boston versus 39 and 26 when methods other than strict physical punishment were used for control.

One of the major hypotheses of the study is that men who say they had little interest in school would be more apt to engage in activities which might have brought them under the jurisdiction of the juvenile court, especially if their parents were not concerned with their progress in school.

The data show that the respondent's continuing in school is associated with the encouragement of parents. When *neither* parent was recalled concerned with the Glen

Sophia M. Robison, "Hidden Delinquency: A Challenge to Social Work Concepts and Programs" (speech delivered at the National Conference on Social Welfare, Atlantic City, New Jersey, May 27, 1965). Taken from unpublished report.

Cove respondent's progress, the high percent of SDB scores was 47 versus 33 when *both* parents "kept after him." While comparable figures for Boston are in the same direction, they are less definitive probably because fewer of the Boston respondents went beyond the 8th grade.

When the parents are mentioned as role models the percent of high SDB scores is 36 for Glen Cove and 26 for Boston. When parents were not mentioned, however, 53 percent in Glen Cove and 32 percent in Boston had SDB scores.

Respondents who mentioned *teachers* as role models also had lower SDB scores. The contrasting figures are 33 percent SDB scores in Glen Cove for those who *did* mention teachers and 44 for those who *did not*.

When *both* parents and teachers were mentioned the percent of high SDB scores is 32 and when *neither* parents nor teachers were mentioned, it is 54.

The tabulation of the data on income obscures comparisons for respondents who grew up in poverty (a) because unfortunately there was no inquiry for incomes under $3000 and (b) obviously the adequacy of income depends upon the purchasing power at the particular time.

The data on working mothers, however, and SDB scores, do not confirm the Gluecks' generalization that respondents whose mothers worked are likely to be more delinquent than those whose mothers do not work outside the home. The percents of high SDB scores for the two categories in our samples are 41 and 40 percent respectively.

Although almost 40 percent in each sample replied that they were caught by the police, official action by the police, however, was quite different in the two samples. Twenty-two percent of the Boston respondents in comparison with 11 percent of the Glen Cove respondents said that they were arrested more than once in comparison with one percent in Glen Cove.

The outcome in the court was likewise different. The actions for almost two-thirds (63%) of the Glen Cove, but only one-third of the Boston respondents, was dismissal. Probation was ordered for 33 percent of the Boston respondents in contrast to 8 percent of the Glen Cove respondents. Obviously the "cross currents" of different distributions should be simultaneously considered with the parameters of the four components in the analytic equation.

Appendix 3–I

DELINQUENT AND NON-DELINQUENT VALUE ORIENTATION AND OPPORTUNITY AWARENESS

Two scales were built in order to test a major tenet of the Cohen theory and of the Cloward-Ohlin theory. The first of these scales attempts to measure acceptance or rejection of middle class values; the second, an awareness of limited access to opportunity. These two instruments were inserted in a larger schedule containing two additional inventories: one dealing with socialization and the other dealing with self-concept.

This schedule of four instruments was administered to 1,030 middle- and lower-class sixth and ninth grade white and Negro boys and girls in Columbus, Ohio, and to 515 white and Negro boys between the ages of 13 and 18 who were inmates of the Fairfield School for Boys in Lancaster, Ohio. The social class status of the Columbus sample was determined by an ecological analysis based on 1960 census data, and by a North-Hatt ranking of the respondent's father's occupation. The sample of school children in Columbus enables us to test the Cohen and Cloward-Ohlin theories in a smaller, more homogeneous city not characterized by great class and ethnic differences such as seen in New York and Chicago. The Fairfield School respondents come mainly from lower-class high delinquency areas in major Ohio cities similar to Columbus—cities not comparable in size or complexity with metropolitan areas like New York.

Table 3–I–1. Mean scores for four scales for public schools and Fairfield school respondents

	Criterion group	*N*	*Value*	*ALO*	*SO*	*Self*
a.	9th MC white girls	68	21.76	23.81	38.48	...
b.	6th MC white girls	101	24.26	25.71	38.67	...
c.	9th MC white boys	68	28.00	26.18	33.74	...
d.	6th MC white boys	100	28.97	27.20	34.92	...

Judson R. Landis and Frank R. Scarpitti, "Delinquent and Non-delinquent Orientation and Opportunity Awareness," *Interdisciplinary Problems in Criminology: Papers of the American Society of Criminology*, 1964, ed. by Walter C. Reckless and Charles L. Newman (Columbus, Ohio: The Ohio State University, 1965), pp. 62–69.

Table 3-I-1. *(continued)*

	Criterion group	*N*	*Value*	*ALO*	*SO*	*Self*
e.	9th LC white boys	61	31.43	32.28	32.16	...
f.	9th LC white girls	78	32.23	32.18	34.90	...
g.	6th LC white girls	145	34.48	32.50	34.32	17.81
h.	6th LC white boys	145	35.92	32.34	30.86	16.50
i.	6th LC Negro girls	146	37.25	32.31	34.40	17.51
j.	6th LC Negro boys	118	39.36	34.08	31.17	16.42
k.	Total public-school girls	538	31.38	30.03	35.77	17.66
l.	Total public-school boys	492	33.68	30.85	32.32	16.46
m.	Total public-school	1030	32.23	30.42	34.12	17.10
n.	White Fairfield School boys	281	37.29	37.17	24.24	14.62
o.	15 yr. old white Fairfield School boys	82	37.52	36.87	24.75	...
p.	16 or over Fairfield School boys	319	37.79	36.82	21.55	14.54
q.	15 yr. old Fairfield School boys	140	39.86	36.73	25.41	14.74
r.	Negro Fairfield School boys	206	40.15	36.89	22.55	14.58
s.	Total Fairfield School boys	515	38.80	37.06	25.15	14.60

Code: Value = Value Orientation Scale
ALO = Awareness of Limited Opportunity Scale
SO = Socialization Scale
Self = Self-Concept Scale
6th = Sixth-grade public school
9th = Ninth-grade public school
MC = Middle Class
LC = Lower Class
... = Not administered

VALIDATION FINDINGS

Mean scores on the four inventories for the groups sampled are shown in Table 1. Low scores on the value orientation and awareness of limited opportunity instruments are in the favorable direction; that is, low scores indicate acceptance of middle-class values and absence of feelings of limited opportunity. High scores on the socialization (SO) and self-concept scales are in the favorable direction; that is, high scores indicate a veering toward good socialization (*i.e.*, away from delinquency) and a favorable self-concept regarding absence of future contact with the law.

The degree of significance of the difference between means for selected groups is shown in Table 2. The basic criterion of difference for each pair of groups is in italics. Data obtained from public school children were used mainly as proof or disproof of certain hypotheses concerning the anticipated performance of the scales we had built. These had to do with the expected variations of mean scores according to race, age, sex, and social class. Some of these findings will be briefly mentioned.

Distinct social class differences were obtained in the value orientation and awareness of limited opportunity scales (1–4, Table 2). This is not surprising, since the items for the two scales were selected on the basis of discriminating by class of the children.

Some age differences appeared on value orientation, primarily at the lower-class level (5–8, Table 2). Awareness of limited opportunity scores show relatively little change with age for the most part. Value orientation differences are also noted between Negro and white lower-class children (9–10, Table 2).

Significant sex differences in value orientation appeared at the middle-class level (11–15, Table 2).

PUBLIC SCHOOL AND INDUSTRIAL SCHOOL COMPARISON

The second major purpose of this study was to test the Cohen and the Cloward-Ohlin theories with a sampler from smaller, more homogeneous communities. A comparison between the scores of Fairfield School boys and Columbus public school boys would seem to provide this test, assuming that our scales measure aspects of the Cohen and Cloward-Ohlin theories. Distinct differences are noted between the scores of the Fairfield School boys and public school boys on both value orientation and awareness of limited opportunity (16, Table 2). The groups were purified somewhat on the basis of age, race, and social class and again compared, and again distinct differences significant at the .001 level were observed on both scales (17, Table 2).

Table 3–I–2. Significance of difference between means for selected groups computed by critical ratio

	Value	*ALO*	*SO*	*Self*
1. 9th *MC* white PS boys/9th *LC* white PS boys	.02	.001	ns	...
2. 9th *MC* white PS girls/9th *LC* white PS girls	.001	.001	.001	...
3. 6th *MC* white PS boys/6th *LC* white PS boys	.001	.001	.001	...
4. 6th *MC* white PS girls/6th *LC* white PS girls	.001	.001	.001	...
5. *6th* MC white PS boys/*9th* MC white PS boys	ns	ns	ns	...
6. *6th* MC white PS girls/*9th* MC white PS girls	.01	.05	ns	...
7. *6th* LC white PS boys/*9th* LC white PS boys	.01	ns	ns	...
8. *6th* LC white PS girls/*9th* LC white PS girls	.001	ns	ns	...
9. 6th LC *white* PS boys/6th LC *Negro* PS boys	.01	ns	ns	ns
10. 6th LC *white* PS girls/6th LC *Negro* PS girls	.01	ns	ns	ns
11. 6th MC white PS *boys*/6th MC white PS *girls*	.001	ns	.001	...
12. 6th LC white PS *boys*/6th LC white PS *girls*	ns	ns	.001	.001
13. 6th LC Negro PS *boys*/6th LC Negro PS *girls*	ns	ns	.001	.001
14. 9th MC white PS *boys*/9th MC white PS *girls*	.001	.02	.001	...
15. 9th LC white PS boys/9th LC white PS girls	ns	ns	.05	...
16. *Fairfield School* boys/*Public School* boys	.001	.001	.001	.001
17. 9th LC white *PS* boys/15 yr. old white *Fairfield School* boys	.001	.001	.001	...
18. *White Fairfield School* boys/*Negro Fairfield School* boys	.01	ns	.001	ns
19. 15 yr. old Fairfield School boys/16 and over Fairfield School boys	.05	ns	.001	ns

Code: Value = Value Orientation Scale
ALO = Awareness of Limited Opportunity Scale
SO = Socialization Scale
Self = Self-Concept Scale
6th = Sixth-grade
9th = Ninth-grade
MC = Middle Class
LC = Lower Class
PS = Public School
... = Not administered

Cohen's theory appears to be modestly substantiated in that Fairfield respondents (committed delinquents) show a somewhat higher level of rejection of middle-class values than non-delinquent public school children of the same age. Cloward and Ohlin's theory is upheld to the extent that Fairfield respondents show also somewhat greater feelings of limited opportunity than public-school children. An important question, whether these two factors are causative or merely manifestations of institutionalization, remains to be answered.

Some pertinent evidence on this point can be presented, however, when the scores on the socialization (SO) and the self-concept scales are examined. Referring to Table 1, the expected variation in mean scores among the public school boys and the Fairfield boys is to be found for all four instruments of the schedule. Compare the scores for group 1 and with group n and group e with group o. The public-school boys (groups 1 and e) have lower mean scores (more favorable) on the value and awareness instruments than the Fairfield boys (groups n and o); while the former also have higher scores on the socialization and self-concept instruments (more favorable direction) than the latter. For all the various groups of public school cases, relatively high scores on value and awareness instruments are associated with relatively low scores on the socialization and self-concept inventories, and conversely.

This relationship is made somewhat clearer by examining Table 3, where intercorrelation coefficients for public school children's responses for the four scales are shown. The data indicate significant associations between the measures in all cases. These findings would tend to further substantiate Cohen's and Cloward-Ohlin's theories, and additionally, to indicate that the relationship between value orientation, awareness of limited opportunity, and delinquency exists prior to, and is not a mere manifestation of, institutionalization.

VALUE ORIENTATION AND AWARENESS OF LIMITED OPPORTUNITY AS SOCIALIZATION AND SELF MEASURES

Another way of looking at value orientation and awareness of limited opportunity would be to consider them as self perceptions or self components. The self can be viewed as an integrated set of perceptions, attitudes, and values—*residua* of the socialization process—which has potential for resisting or succumbing to delinquency.

It would seem that a generally favorable direction in the development of self acts as an internal buffer against delinquency. Reasonably accurate measurement of any one of these self components should give a good indication of the degree of extent insulation against or proneness toward delinquency.

SUMMARY

This paper has reported the findings of a study designed to implement and test one tenet each of the Cohen and of the Cloward-Ohlin theories of delinquency, namely, rejection of middle-class values and awareness of limited opportunity. It appears that the class-oriented perceptions, though difficult to measure empirically, are modestly related to antisocial behavior in adolescent years. Such a relationship appears to hold true for urban areas other than those suggested by the original theorists; that is, for smaller, more homogeneous communities which do not have great social class or minority group differences. Finally, it may be helpful to treat value orientation and awareness of limited opportunity as socialization and self variables, the direction of which are related to insulation against or proneness toward delinquency in adolescence.

Table 3. Intercorrelation coefficients for four scales for the public school sample (N = 1030)

	SO	*Self*	*Value*
Socialization (SO)			
Self-Concept (Self)	.50*		
Value Orientation (Value)	−.52	−.47	
Awareness of Limited Opportunity	−.49	−.31	.59

*All coefficients are significant at beyond the .01 level.

CHOICE OF ITEMS FOR SCALES

Since scores on the various items in the value orientation and awareness of limited opportunity instruments varied from group to group, it was necessary to choose the significant items which distinguished between normative groups by class. Lower- and middle-class sixth-grade girls were chosen as the normative group for the final selection of significant value orientation items. It was assumed that value orientation is primarily a function of socialization within the family. Sixth-graders are less affected by extra-familial influences than ninth-graders and girls less than boys—hence, sixth-grade girls. Lower- and middle-class ninth-grade boys were chosen as the normative group for the final selection of significant items measuring awareness of limited opportunity. Perceptions of limited access to legitimate opportunity are most likely to be developed at 15 years of age than at 12 years of age and more likley to be developed by boys than girls.

Thirteen value orientation items distinguished lower- from middle-class sixth-grade girls, while 14 awareness of limited opportunity items discriminated between lower- and middle-class ninth-grade boys. These two sets of items are listed below. A five-point response pattern from strongly agree to strongly disagree was utilized.

VALUE ORIENTATION ITEMS

1. People should only keep promises when it is to their benefit.
2. Good manners are for sissies.
3. The law is always against the ordinary guy.
4. Only creeps go out for after-school activities.
5. It's mostly luck if one succeeds or fails.
6. Don't let anybody your size get by with anything.
7. Only squares take part in school clubs and school programs.
8. Money is meant to be spent.
9. It makes no difference whether you work or go on relief just so you get along.
10. Most police are crooked.
11. I should work hard only if I am paid enough for it.
12. The only thing I ought to be responsible for is myself.
13. It doesn't make much difference what a person tries to do; some folks are just lucky, others are not.

AWARENESS OF LIMITED ACCESS TO OPPORTUNITY ITEMS

1. I probably won't be able to do the kind of work that I want to do because I won't have enough education.
2. A guy like me has a pretty good chance of going to college.
3. Most people are better off than I am.
4. I'll never have as much opportunity to succeed as guys from other neighborhoods.
5. I am as well off as most people.
6. The world is usually good to guys like me.
7. Unless my family can afford to move out of our neighborhood, I won't get ahead very fast.
8. I won't be able to finish high school because my family will want me to get a job.
9. There is a good chance that some of my friends will have a lot of money.
10. My family can't give me the opportunities that most kids have.
11. I'll never have enough money to go to college.
12. There isn't much chance that a kid from my neighborhood will ever get ahead.
13. If a kid like me worked hard he can get ahead.
14. Most successful men probably used illegal means to become successful.

In order to put these two sets of items (which by now were in scale form) to practical test, a final administration was conducted. The 13 discriminating value items were interspersed among 19 filler items (not scored) to prevent detection of any answer pattern among the 13 scored items. The 14 awareness items were also interspersed among filler items, to compose a 40-item instrument.

These two instruments, with the hidden scales of 13 and 14 items, were inserted into a large schedule consisting of other scales dealing with socialization and delinquency proneness. A section of this schedule consisted of 46 items from the SO (socialization) scale of the California Personality Inventory. This scale measures a veering toward good socialization (away from delinquency) or toward poor socialization (toward delinquency) and was titled in the schedule: "How I Feel about Things." Another section of the schedule, entitled "About Me, Law, and Rules," consisted of 10 self-concept items developed by Reckless and Dinitz. These self-concept items have been used to measure one's perceptions regarding involvement in delinquency. Also included in the schedule were the two scales discussed above: 32 value items, entitled "The Way I Look at Things," of which 13 are scored in the direction of rejecting middle-class values (high scores rejecting, low scores accepting); and 40 awareness items called "How the Future Looks to Me," of which 14 are scored in the direction of awareness of limited opportunity (high scores indicate high awareness, low scores indicate low awareness).

Appendix 3–J

BOYS' PERCEPTIONS OF OUTER CONTAINMENT AND DELINQUENCY POTENTIAL

Although inner and outer containment are sometimes treated as separate and distinct entities, they are in actuality very much interrelated. The basic component of inner containment, at least from a sociological perspective, is the individual's self-concept. Simply stated, the manner in which the individual views himself determines his behavior. The basic components of outer containment are the various institutions with which the individual comes into contact. These act as restraints or buffers which tend to guide (both pull and push) the individual into more legitimate and socially accepted behavior.

The present study is primarily concerned with components of outer containment. What is important is the manner in which an individual perceives a certain set of conditions rather than what the set of conditions really is.

Taking the "definition of the situation" as a starting point, it would appear that the institutionalized components of outer containment become important as they are perceived and interpreted by the individual. The individual's perception of certain institutional controls is the important element in explaining his behavior rather than the concrete existence of structures in the environment. From this perspective it seems clear that we are in actuality most concerned with the middle ground between inner and outer containment. We are interested in the influence of certain institutions (outer containment) but only as the individual's attitudes and perceptions toward these institutions are incorporated into the individual's attitudes toward self (inner containment). In other words, an individual's self-concept is in part made up of his perceptions of the environment and institutional structures therein.

The instruments utilized in this study are as follows: There are six items used as indicators measuring different dimensions of outer containment. These dimensions are the peer group, ministers and priests, parents, teachers and principals, police, and relatives. These separate indicators are combined into one Guttman scale measuring boys' perceptions of outer containment.

There are nine different Guttman scales developed to measure various dimensions of boys' attitudes toward the legal institution: (1) Policemen-Relationship with Kids—this scale measures perceptions of interpersonal relationships between policemen and

Gordon P. Waldo, "Boys' Perceptions of Outer Containment and Delinquency Potential" Ph.D. dissertation, The Ohio State University, 1967.

adolescent boys; (2) Policemen-Legitimacy—this scale measures the extent to which boys perceive the role and function of policemen as being legitimate and necessary; (3) Policemen-Characteristics—this scale measures the personal characteristics which boys attribute to policemen; (4) Probation Officers-Relationship with Kids—this scale measures perceptions of interpersonal relationships between probation officers and adolescent boys; (5) Probation Officers-Legitimacy—this scale measures the extent to which boys perceive the role and function of probation officers as being legitimate; (6) Courts-Relationship with Kids—this scale measures perceptions of interpersonal relationships between personnel of the juvenile court at an abstract level and adolescent boys; (7) Courts-Legitimacy—this scale measures the extent to which boys perceive the function of the juvenile court as being legitimate and having authority over them; (8) Laws-Relationship with Kids—this scale measures perceptions of the law at an abstract level and how it relates to boys; (9) Laws-Legitimacy—this scale measures the extent to which boys perceive of the law at an abstract level as being right and proper.

The general hypothesis is as follows:

> Boys with favorable perceptions toward any dimension of outer containment will be greatly overrepresented in the low delinquency potential category, proportionately represented in the moderate delinquency potential category, and greatly underrepresented in the known delinquent category; while those with unfavorable perceptions will be greatly underrepresented in the low delinquency potential category, proportionately represented in the moderate delinquency potential category, slightly overrepresented in the high delinquency potential category, and greatly overrepresented in the known delinquent category.

A general overview of the findings indicates that in the tables containing the original associations for the total sample, most of the percentage distributions are going in the expected direction. An inspection of the gamma values obtained for the original tables shows that all of the values are positive, indicating that all of the associations are in the appropriate direction. However, none of the associations obtained is very high. There is enough association present to warrant further research, in order to further specify and explain the relationships involved.

MEDIAN SCORES OF BOYS' PERCEPTIONS OF OUTER CONTAINMENT IN FOUR DELINQUENCY PRONENESS GRADIENTS

Item or scale	*Low delinquency potential*	*Moderate delinquency potential*	*High delinquency potential*	*Known delin-quent*
Friends as Deterrent	2.69	2.77	3.02	3.36
Minister or Priest as Deterrent	2.88	2.91	2.97	3.43
Parents as Deterrent	2.07	2.26	2.38	2.33
Teachers and Principals as Deterrent	2.90	3.01	3.07	3.39

Item or scale	*Low delinquency potential*	*Moderate delinquency potential*	*High delinquency potential*	*Known delinquent*
Police as Deterrent	2.64	2.70	2.72	3.00
Relatives as Deterrent	2.67	2.67	2.64	2.98
Combined Outer containment	3.64	3.87	4.19	4.67
Policemen's Relationship with Kids	4.36	4.83	5.12	5.72
Legitimacy of Policemen	3.68	3.93	4.67	4.55
Characteristics of Policemen	3.74	4.09	4.19	4.07
Probation Officers' Relationship with Kids	5.34	5.53	5.61	5.77
Legitimacy of Probation Officers	4.35	4.57	4.65	4.83
Juvenile Court's Relationship with Kids	4.83	5.21	5.46	5.39
Legitimacy of the Juvenile Court	2.63	2.92	3.25	3.33
Laws' Relationship with Kids	4.04	4.15	4.47	4.42
Legitimacy of Laws	4.80	5.27	5.72	6.04

THE SCHEDULE

This is not a test. There are no right or wrong answers. The reason for asking these questions is to find out how boys like you *really* feel about things. We want your honest answers to these questions.

Read each statement very carefully and circle the single answer that best tells how you feel about the statement. Circle STRONGLY AGREE, AGREE, UNDECIDED, DISAGREE, STRONGLY DISAGREE, whichever you feel is the closest to your feeling about the statement. (Only selected items will be used to illustrate the coverage of the schedule.)

2. Most teachers never really give a kid a break.

   STRONGLY AGREE AGREE UNDECIDED DISAGREE STRONGLY DISAGREE

6. I am proud of my school.

   STRONGLY AGREE AGREE UNDECIDED DISAGREE STRONGLY DISAGREE

9. Grown-ups don't really think school does any good.

   STRONGLY AGREE AGREE UNDECIDED DISAGREE STRONGLY DISAGREE

23. Most teachers have trouble making school work interesting.

STRONGLY AGREE AGREE UNDECIDED DISAGREE STRONGLY DISAGREE

34. I would like to tell most of my teachers what I really think of them.

STRONGLY AGREE AGREE UNDECIDED DISAGREE STRONGLY DISAGREE

49. Most policemen don't care what happens to kids.

STRONGLY AGREE AGREE UNDECIDED DISAGREE STRONGLY DISAGREE

50. Policemen have no right to tell kids what to do.

STRONGLY AGREE AGREE UNDECIDED DISAGREE STRONGLY DISAGREE

52. Most probation officers don't care what happens to the kids with whom they work.

STRONGLY AGREE AGREE UNDECIDED DISAGREE STRONGLY DISAGREE

53. Kids would be better off if there were fewer probation officers.

STRONGLY AGREE AGREE UNDECIDED DISAGREE STRONGLY DISAGREE

55. We would be better off if we didn't have any juvenile courts.

STRONGLY AGREE AGREE UNDECIDED DISAGREE STRONGLY DISAGREE

56. Laws protect the rights of kids.

STRONGLY AGREE AGREE UNDECIDED DISAGREE STRONGLY DISAGREE

59. Life would be better if there were not as many policemen.

STRONGLY AGREE AGREE UNDECIDED DISAGREE STRONGLY DISAGREE

63. Juvenile courts are only interested in convicting a lot of kids.

STRONGLY AGREE AGREE UNDECIDED DISAGREE STRONGLY DISAGREE

68. Policemen have too much authority.

STRONGLY AGREE AGREE UNDECIDED DISAGREE STRONGLY DISAGREE

70. Most probation officers want to help kids.

STRONGLY AGREE AGREE UNDECIDED DISAGREE STRONGLY DISAGREE

71. Probation is a waste of time.

STRONGLY AGREE AGREE UNDECIDED DISAGREE STRONGLY DISAGREE

72. Juvenile courts are interested in doing what is best for a kid.

STRONGLY AGREE AGREE UNDECIDED DISAGREE STRONGLY DISAGREE

87. Most policemen are honest.

STRONGLY AGREE AGREE UNDECIDED DISAGREE STRONGLY DISAGREE

89. I would like to be a probation officer.

STRONGLY AGREE AGREE UNDECIDED DISAGREE STRONGLY DISAGREE

91. "Who you know" is what counts in the juvenile court.

STRONGLY AGREE AGREE UNDECIDED DISAGREE STRONGLY DISAGREE

92. Laws are harder on kids than on adults.

STRONGLY AGREE AGREE UNDECIDED DISAGREE STRONGLY DISAGREE

98. Poor kids don't have a chance in juvenile court.

STRONGLY AGREE AGREE UNDECIDED DISAGREE STRONGLY DISAGREE

How do you look at these things? Remember, the right answer for you is the way you see things.

1. A teenage boy should always tiptoe around the house.

STRONGLY AGREE AGREE UNDECIDED DISAGREE STRONGLY DISAGREE

5. Good manners are for sissies.

STRONGLY AGREE AGREE UNDECIDED DISAGREE STRONGLY DISAGREE

6. Finders keepers; if a person loses something, it belongs to the guy who finds it.

STRONGLY AGREE AGREE UNDECIDED DISAGREE STRONGLY DISAGREE

7. It's mostly luck if one succeeds or fails.

STRONGLY AGREE AGREE UNDECIDED DISAGREE STRONGLY DISAGREE

9. Don't let anybody your size get by with anything.

STRONGLY AGREE AGREE UNDECIDED DISAGREE STRONGLY DISAGREE

10. It's worth practicing to get good at something.

STRONGLY AGREE AGREE UNDECIDED DISAGREE STRONGLY DISAGREE

15. I should work hard only if I am paid enough for it.

STRONGLY AGREE AGREE UNDECIDED DISAGREE STRONGLY DISAGREE

17. The only person I ought to be responsible for is myself.

STRONGLY AGREE AGREE UNDECIDED DISAGREE STRONGLY DISAGREE

19. When I think about doing something against the law (such as stealing or shop lifting), I stop because I know it would make my friends turn their backs on me.

STRONGLY AGREE AGREE UNDECIDED DISAGREE STRONGLY DISAGREE

20. When I think about doing something against the law (such as stealing or shop-lifting), I stop because it would make my minister or priest unhappy.

STRONGLY AGREE AGREE UNDECIDED DISAGREE STRONGLY DISAGREE

21. When I think about doing somethin~ against the law (such as stealing or shop-lifting), I stop because I know it would upset my parents.

STRONGLY AGREE AGREE UNDECIDED DISAGREE STRONGLY DISAGREE

22. When I think about doing something against the law (such as stealing or shop-lifting), I stop because my teachers and principal would hold it against me.

STRONGLY AGREE AGREE UNDECIDED DISAGREE STRONGLY DISAGREE

23. When I think about doing something against the law (such as stealing or shoplifting), I stop because I'm afraid the police would catch me.

STRONGLY AGREE AGREE UNDECIDED DISAGREE STRONGLY DISAGREE

24. When I think about doing something against the law (such as stealing or shoplifting), I stop because it would get me in bad with my relatives.

STRONGLY AGREE AGREE UNDECIDED DISAGREE STRONGLY DISAGREE

If you were to think about doing something against the law (such as stealing or shoplifting), which of the following things would be *most likely* to stop you from doing this. Place a "1" by the one *most likely* to stop you, a "2" by the one *next most likely* to stop you, a "3" by the one *next most likely* to stop you, etc, all the way to a "6" by the one that is *least likely* to stop you. Use each number, 1 through 6, only once, giving a different number to each statement.

______It would make my friends turn their backs on me.
______It would make my minister or priest unhappy.
______It would upset my parents.
______My teachers and principal would hold it against me.
______I would be too afraid the police would catch me.
______It would get me in bad with my relatives.

Appendix 3–K

IMPLEMENTATION OF NEUTRALIZATION THEORY

This study was designed to explore Sykes and Matza's techniques of neutralization as one possible form of norm erosion contributing to delinquency. The study attempted to (a) develop an inventory to measure norm neutralization and (b) employ this instrument in investigating several hypotheses. It must be emphasized, however, that the present research permits no complete test of neutralization theory. The theory asserts that (a) delinquents accept the techniques of neutralization and that (b) these techniques facilitate violations by neutralizing the norms in advance of behavior. This study has explored the first assertion. Assessment of the second requires a longitudinal analysis.

Considerable effort was directed to the preparation of an inventory which could serve as an operational measure of neutralization and which could be used in a variety of circumstances where some form of norm erosion is hypothesized. Four situations were finally selected. Each situation was represented by 10 items with the highest validity ratings for that situation according to the consensus of the judges. The completed inventory included both personal and property offenses, and the offenses (situations) were selected which spaced at different points along the continuum of severity, as identified from students' perceived mothers' rankings. Some modifications were made as a result of intensive pretesting with 5 boys from the Juvenile Center, Columbus, Ohio.

The neutralization inventory was combined with four additional inventories, and a background information section, in a 108-item schedule. Three of the additional inventories were used as independent criteria to test the directionality of the neutralization inventory itself and to provide supplementary evidence regarding its validity. The three additional inventories included 28 items from the *M.M.P.I.* which have been found related to delinquency, an *Index of Incipient Alienation*, and the Srole scale (anomia). An abridged form of a "Nye-Short Scale" was also included, as a measure of self-reported delinquency.

A Report to the *Ohio Youth Commission and Columbus Public Schools*, prepared by Richard A. Ball, based on his dissertation, entitled "Neutralization as a Self Factor in Delinquency Risk" (Ph.D. dissertation, The Ohio State University, 1965).

This 108-item schedule was administered to two separate samples of adolescent boys. Sample "A" consisted of 197 high school boys from the Central High School, Columbus, Ohio. Sample "B" consisted of 200 institutionalized delinquents from the Fairfield School for Boys, Lancaster, Ohio. These two samples were comparable in age and socioeconomic status. Only working class boys were included. The two samples were similar in a number of characteristics, including the fact that the 200 institutionalized delinquents were themselves a selected group who were enrolled in academic training in the institution. Subsequent to the administration with the high school boys, but prior to administration with the institutionalized delinquents, it was discovered that another attempt was being made to devise an index of neutralization. Upon its completion, this so-called "alternate neutralization inventory" was attached to the 108-item schedule, and the entire schedule was administered to the sample of institutionalized delinquents.

The reliability of the neutralization inventory was assessed by computation of Kuder-Richardson reliability coefficients. Reliability coefficients were computed for the total neutralization inventory (4 situations with the 40 items) and for each one of the 4 subscales (individual situations and their sets of 10 items respectively). These coefficients indicated a high reliability for the entire inventory and for each respective subscale.

The fact that neutralization is theoretically associated with certain other variables implies that scores on the neutralization inventory should be expected to correlate positively with scores on inventories designed to measure these other variables. To investigate the directionality and validity of the neutralization inventory, a correlation matrix was prepared for high school boys' scores on the neutralization inventory (and each of the 4 subscales separately), the *M.M.P.I.* items, the *Index of Incipient Alienation*, and the Srole scale. For the institutionalized delinquents, the matrix also included the "alternate neutralization inventory." These correlation cofficients tend to support the claim that the neutralization inventory is measuring a variable related to but different from those measured by the *M.M.P.I.* Items and the Srole scale. There was less relationship than expected between the neutralization inventory and the *Index of Incipient Alienation*. The correlation between the neutralization inventory and the "alternate neutralization inventory" was the highest of those obtained. Given the fact that the two inventories were quite different in format, the results tend to reinforce the claims made for the validity of the neutralization inventory.

Since the *M.M.P.I.* items, the Srole scale, and the *Index of Incipient Alienation* were each theoretically associated with delinquency, additional analyses were conducted in order to test whether these inventories did actually distinguish between the high school boys and the institutionalized delinquents. Each of the three inventories showed a statistically significant difference between the two samples. These findings tend to substantiate the claim that the inventories measure self factors associated with delinquency.

Only after evaluation of the reliability and validity of the neutralization inventory were the three basic hypotheses subjected to test. The first hypothesis stated that *there will be a significant difference between the neutralization scores of institutionalized delinquents and high school boys.* This hypothesis is supported by the findings which indicate that the institutionalized delinquents score higher on the neutralization inventory, and in each of its four subscales, than did the high school boys.

Further analysis was undertaken to investigate any connection of neutralization with age and race. The results indicate no statistically significant differences between the neutralization scores of high school boys 15 and 16 years old and those 17 and 18 years old. No statistically significant differences appeared between the 15 and 16 year old institutionalized delinquents and those 17 and 18 years old. These findings together indicate no significant connection between neutralization and age.

The findings indicate a significant difference between white and Negro high school boys on two of the four neutralization inventory subscales. Differences on the other two neutralization subscales and the total inventory were not statistically significant. White and Negro institutionalized delinquents obtained significantly different scores on two of the neutralization subscales, but not on the other two subscales or the total inventory. These findings establish no clear connection between neutralization and race, but they do suggest that race should be controlled for in any study of neutralization. Hypothesis #1 was, therefore, tested for white and Negro boys separately.

Hypothesis #1 was supported for both white and Negro boys separately. White institutionalized delinquents scored significantly higher on the neutralization inventory, and each of its four subscales, than did the white high school boys. Negro institutionalized delinquents scored significantly higher on the neutralization inventory, and on each of its four subscales, than did the Negro high school boys. Neutralization thus appears to be more characteristic of the institutionalized delinquents than of the high school boys.

The second hypothesis stated that *neutralization scores will tend to form a gradient from high school boys reporting no juvenile court appearances, to high school boys reporting juvenile court appearances, to institutionalized delinquents reporting few juvenile court appearances, to institutionalized delinquents reporting many court appearances.* The findings support only the first step in the hypothesized gradient. The high school boys reporting juvenile court appearances scored significantly higher on the neutralization inventory, and on each of its four subscales, than did those reporting no court appearances. These results held true within both racial categories. The white high school boys reporting appearances scored significantly higher than did the white high school boys reporting no appearances; The Negro high school boys reporting appearances scored significantly higher than did the Negro boys reporting no appearances. The findings do not, however, support the hypothesized gradient beyond this point. There were statistically no significant differences in neutralization scores, either between the high school boys reporting some juvenile court appearances and the institutionalized delinquents reporting few appearances, or between the institutionalized delinquents reporting few juvenile court appearances and the institutionalized delinquents reporting many appearances. No significant difference appeared for white and Negro boys tested separately.

The third hypothesis stated that *there will be a significant difference between the neutralization scores of seriously delinquent boys (many self-reported violations) and less seriously delinquent boys (few self-reported violations).* The findings support this hypothesis. The boys with many self-reported violations (above the median on the abridged "Nye-Short Scale") scored significantly higher on the neutralization inventory, and on each of its four subscales, than did the boys with few self-reported violations (below the median on the abridged "Nye-Short Scale"). These findings held for both white and Negro boys treated separately. Within each racial category, neutralization was more characteristic of boys with many self-reported delinquent acts.

Supplementary findings indicate no significant connection of neutralization with retardation in school (number of grades behind the age-grade level) or with county of commitment. Although high school boys who were behind in school tended to score higher in neutralization than those who were not behind, the differences were not statistically significant. The same was true of differences between institutionalized delinquents who were behind in school and those who were not behind. Although boys committed to the institution from the urbanized counties tended to score higher in neutralization than those from less urbanized counties, none of the differences was statistically significant.

CONCLUSIONS:

The results of this study indicate that "delinquents" tend to accept more excuses for a variety of offenses than do "nondelinquents." The differences appear for both personal and property offenses, and along a continuum of severity, no matter whether delinquency is defined on the basis of institutionalization, reported court appearances, or self-reported violations. These findings support Sykes and Matza's assertion that delinquents will accept the techniques of neutralization more than nondelinquents. The next logical step would be to investigate the assertion that acceptance of these excuses precedes delinquency and makes it possible.

The support for Sykes and Matza's neutralization theory may also be interpreted as support for Reckless and Shoham's norm erosion thesis. The findings certainly indicate a form of norm "erosion" to be more characteristic among the delinquents. At a more general level, the findings support Reckless' containment theory. Rather than indicating that neutralization is the single factor leading to delinquency, the findings may be interpreted as suggesting that neutralization is one self-factor which, in contributing to norm erosion, weakens inner containment and increases the risk of delinquency. This latter conclusion seems preferable. Delinquency consists of many kinds of different behaviors, and it seems probable that different combinations of self factors, along with outer containment, will be associated with these different forms of deliquency.

This conclusion is supported by the findings, which show that the *M.M.P.I.* items, the *Index of Incipient Alienation*, and the Srole scale also distinguished between the high school boys and the institutionalized delinquents. The indication is that neutralization, incipient alienation, anomia, and certain personality characteristics (*M.M.P.I.*) are all self factors associated with delinquency. Furthermore, the intercorrelations indicate that these self factors do represent different (but related) variables.

Such data cast doubt upon the "single factor" theories. The findings suggest that delinquency is to be explained on the basis of multiple variables.

Sykes and Matza's statement is not only a theory of neutralization; it is also a denial of Cohen's "delinquency subculture" thesis. The neutralization theory maintains that most delinquents do not adhere to a different (subcultural) set of norms, but rather that they basically adhere to the conventional norms while accepting more justifications for deviance. In this sense, the norms have been "eroded," but not substantially replaced. The findings tend to support this position. Possible scores on the neutralization inventory range from 40 to 200, yet the mean score for the institutionalized delinquents was only 110.74. These data do not indicate a "delinquent subculture"; an "Undecided" response (scored as 3) on each item would have resulted in a total score of 120. For the category of the institutionalized delinquents, they suggest that the attitudes of boys in the specific sample are not as far different from those of the high school boys as the "delinquent subculture" thesis indicates.

Each of the conclusions set forth in this study is meant as a suggestion for additional research. The following represents a sample of some questions which must be answered by further research:

1. Are these excuses accepted before (neutralization) or after (rationalization) the commission of the delinquent act?
2. Are different sets of excuses ("techniques of neutralization") associated with different forms of delinquency?
3. How is neutralization distributed by social class? Is neutralization less prominent among the "middle" than among the "working" class?
4. What is the connection of neutralization and sex? Is neutralization more characteristic of males than of females?
5. What, if any, connections exist between neutralization and personality characteristics? Are certain personality "types" more or less likely to accept the techniques of neutralization?
6. Are these techniques of neutralization in addition to the five listed by Sykes and Matza? Might the five techniques be better subsumed under two or three basic factors (as identified empirically by factor analytic methods)?
7. What are the relationships among the techniques? Are certain techniques highly correlated?
8. Does neutralization hold for adult criminals as well as for juvenile delinquents? Does neutralization vary by offense categories or recidivism?
9. Is neutralization more characteristic of troublesome inmates than of model inmates?
10. Is neutralization related to success in post-institutional adaptation (e.g., parole)?
11. Does neutralization lose its force in post-adolescence? Is there a tendency to accept fewer of the excuses as one moves into adulthood? If so, does this explain part of the fact that delinquents do not automatically continue into crime, but rather "settle down" in early adulthood?

12. How are the techniques of neutralization learned? Does treatment by the juvenile court and social agencies tend to reinforce neutralization by, for example, emphasizing home life and neighborhood pressures rather than an individual's responsibility for his actions?

13. Do boys verbalize more excuses among themselves and to the authorities, than they really accept?

14. What self factors other than neutralization are associated with norm erosion?

15. Does some other self factor (such as alienation) precede neutralization and facilitate the erosion process? What is the process by which the erosion develops?

These are only a few of the possibilities for further research. Containment theory appears to offer a comprehensive approach to crime and delinquency, but much more research is required to specify and measure the variables involved. It is hoped that this study has made some contribution by the exploration of neutralization as only one self factor which, as one facet of norm erosion, weakens inner containment and increases the risk of delinquency.

[For questionnaire see Appenix 1–B].

Appendix 3–L

DAVIES' SCALE FOR MEASURING DIFFERENTIAL PERCEPTIONS OF DEVIANT BEHAVIOR

I. THE WAY I LOOK AT THINGS

We want you to tell us which of the following activities *you* think are delinquent and which are not delinquent. This is not a test. There are no right or wrong answers. The right answer for *you* is the way *you* look at things. Circle *D* if you think the activity or the behavior is definitely delinquent. Circle *ND* if you are sure the activity or behavior is *not* delinquent. Circle *NS* if you are *not sure*. Make sure that your answer is *your* idea and is the way you look at things.

D ND NS 1. Fighting with another boy your age.
D ND NS 2. Drinking beer.
D ND NS 3. Taking things from store counters.
D ND NS 4. Breaking into a neighbor's house.
D ND NS 5. Accepting something stolen by someone else.
D ND NS 6. Going into a movie without paying.
D ND NS 7. Cheating on tests in school.
D ND NS 8. Throwing snowballs at cars driving down the street.
D ND NS 9. Lying to your parents.
D ND NS 10. Throwing stones at school windows.
D ND NS 11. Running away from home.
D ND NS 12. Taking a car to go for a ride and returning it.
D ND NS 13. Dressing sloppy in school.
D ND NS 14. Having your hair longer than the school allows.
D ND NS 15. Sniffing glue.
D ND NS 16. Staying out late at night.
D ND NS 17. Breaking into a grocery store.
D ND NS 18. Walking in the middle of the street.
D ND NS 19. Gambling at school.
D ND NS 20. Being in a gang fight.

John F. Davies, *Differential Perceptions of Delinqunt Behavior*, Ph.D. dissertation, The Ohio State University, 1969, pp. 65-76.

D ND NS 21. Smoking.
D ND NS 22. Threatening to beat up another boy.
D ND NS 23. Taking money from someone's locker at school.
D ND NS 24. Removing stop signs from the street.
D ND NS 25. Setting a fire in a vacant lot.
D ND NS 26. Hitch-hiking on a highway.
D ND NS 27. Pulling a switchblade knife on another boy.
D ND NS 28. Skipping school for a week.
D ND NS 29. Setting a fire in a vacant house.
D ND NS 30. Running through a neighbor's flower garden.
D ND NS 31. Breaking another boy's jaw in a fight.
D ND NS 32. Swearing at a teacher.
D ND NS 33. Acting up on a school bus.
D ND NS 34. Drinking beer that was stolen by someone else.
D ND NS 35. Keeping the change when your mother sends you to the store.
D ND NS 36. Breaking into your parents' home.
D ND NS 37. Hanging around a pool room.
D ND NS 38. Talking back to a teacher.
D ND NS 39. Cutting your initials in a tree in the park.
D ND NS 40. Taking tools from the wood shop at school.
D ND NS 41. Hiding in a restroom when you are supposed to be in class.
D ND NS 42. Breaking traffic laws.
D ND NS 43. Sneaking out of your house at night.
D ND NS 44. Cutting a convertible top with a knife.
D ND NS 45. Pulling a false fire alarm.

II.

We want you to tell us how serious you think each of the following activities or behaviors are. Circle *1* if you think the activity is *not* serious. Circle *2* if you think it is a *little bit serious*. Circle *3* if you think it is *sort of in the middle*. Circle *4* if you think it is *pretty serious*. Circle *5* if you think the activity is *very serious*. Remember, there are no right or wrong answers. The right answer for you depends on how serious *you* think each behavior or activity is.

1 2 3 4 5 46. Pulling a false fire alarm.
1 2 3 4 5 90. Fighting with another boy your age.

III.

Here are some more questions you can help us with. Remember, there are no right or wrong answers. The right answer for *you* is the way you think about them. Put an *X* in front of your answer. Use only *one X* for each question.

91. When do *you* think a boy is delinquent?
   a. When his friends say so
   b. When his parents say so
   c. When his teachers say so
   d. When the police say so
   e. When the juvenile court says so

92. Would you go out of your way to meet a new boy in school if you knew he was delinquent?
   a. Always
   b. Often
   c. Sometimes
   d. Seldom
   e. Never

93. How do you think being delinquent hurts a boy the most?
   a. Because of the way his friends treat him
   b. Because of the way other boys treat him
   c. Because of the way neighbors treat him
   d. Because of the way teachers treat him
   e. Because of the way parents treat him

94. When a boy is delinquent he is:
   a. admired by his friends
   b. looked down on by his friends.
   c. I don't know.

95. When a boy is delinquent he is:
   a. admired by other kids in school.
   b. looked down on by other kids in school.
   c. I don't know.

96. When a boy is delinquent he is:
   a. treated differently by his family.
   b. treated the same as before by his family.
   c. I don't know.

97. When a boy becomes a delinquent, he is:
   a. treated the same by his teacher.
   b. treated differently by his teacher.
   c. I don't know.

98. When a boy becomes delinquent:
   a. kids at school change their opinion of him.
   b. kids at school don't change their opinion of him.
   c. I don't know.

99. When a boy is delinquent, he is:
   a. watched closer by the police.
   b. treated the same as before by the police.
   c. I don't know.

IV.

Here are some more questions you can help us with. Remember, there are no right or wrong answers. Put an *X* in front of the answer to each question that *you most agree with*. Use only *one X* for each question.

100. Some say the difference between a delinquent boy and a boy who is not delinquent is in who gets caught.
   a. I agree with this idea.
   b. I disagree with this idea.
   c. I don't know.

101. Some say that boys who become delinquent are "born losers."
   a. I agree with this idea.
   b. I disagree with this idea.
   c. I don't know.

102. Some say that a boy who is bad will always be a bad boy.
   a. I agree with this idea.
   b. I disagree with this idea.
   c. I don't know.

103. Some say that boys become delinquent to get even with adults.
   a. I agree with this idea.
   b. I disagree with this idea.
   c. I don't know.

104. Some say that the neighborhood that a boy lives in has a lot to do with his becoming delinquent.
   a. I agree with this idea.
   b. I disagree with this idea.
   c. I don't know.

105. Some say that once a boy has been arrested, he doesn't have a chance to stay out of trouble.
   a. I agree with this idea.
   b. I disagree with this idea.
   c. I don't know.

106. Some say that delinquency is learned just like learning to play baseball.
   a. I agree with this idea.
   b. I disagree with this idea.
   c. I don't know.

107. Some say that boys who run around with a gang will become delinquent.
   a. I agree with this idea.
   b. I disagree with this idea.
   c. I don't know.

108. Some say that boys who wear clothes and hair to school that school officials don't approve of are on the way to becoming delinquent.
   a. I agree with this idea.
   b. I disagree with this idea.
   c. I don't know.

109. Some say that boys who hang around a pool room will become delinquent.
   a. I agree with this idea.
   b. I disagree with this idea.
   c. I don't know.

110. Some say that coming from a poor family will lead to being delinquent.
   a. I agree with this idea.
   b. I disagree with this idea.
   c. I don't know.

111. Some say that you can tell that a boy is going to be delinquent when he is in the first grade.
   a. I agree with this idea.
   b. I disagree with this idea.
   c. I don't know.

112. Some say that boys who become delinquent have always been different than other boys.
   a. I agree with this idea.
   b. I disagree with this idea.
   c. I don't know.

113. Some say that delinquent boys do the things they do for thrills or kicks.
   a. I agree with this idea.
   b. I disagree with this idea.
   c. I don't know.

114. Some say that boys become delinquent because their parents do not pay enough attention to them when they are young.
   a. I agree with this idea.
   b. I disagree with this idea.
   c. I don't know.

V. [At this point come 46 items from Gough's Socialization Scale—see Appendix 3-F.]

VI. [Background items]

1. What is your birthdate?
2. Where were you born?
3. What is your father's occupation?
4. Where was your father born?
5. Where do you live?
6. What grade school did you attend?
7. What grade are you in now?
8. Have you ever been picked up by the police?
9. Have you ever been to juvenile court?
10. Have you ever done something serious that you have not been caught for? if so, how old were you at the time?

Chapter 4

The victim-object aspect of doer involvement

The study of criminology has overwhelmingly focused upon the "doer" since criminal law is primarily doer oriented. The entire criminal justice system, including police, courts, and correctional agencies, deals with the doer. There is, however, a complementary aspect to the involvement of violators, namely, the objects and victims upon which the violators focus. A very provocative statement concerning the victims of crime is presented in Appendix 4-A. In many instances, the identification of victims is not easy.

It is recognized that there are some crimes "without victims," such as drug abuse in American society (which probably should not be a crime). But in the great majority of instances the delinquent or criminal behavior of the doer affects an object or a person. Very little research has been done on this aspect of the study of doer involvement.

However, the public in several countries of the world has become increasingly concerned with the problem of injury to victims of violent crime. Some countries and a few states of the United States have established victim compensation laws and administrative agencies to handle cases of injured victims. The movement toward state compensation was reviewed by Gilbert Geiss for the President's Commission on Law Enforcement and Administration of Justice and excerpts from his report are given in Appendix 4-B.

The person as victim

Criminology has become increasingly aware of the problem of victimization and is trying to find ways of identifying what kind of persons become victims of what kind of offenses, discovering the role the victim played in the offense, and postulating explanations for victim involvement. Mendelsohn, a former Rumanian barrister, is credited with having first described a victim-doer relationship. He called attention to the victim's role in stimulating the doer into action that, in turn, led to injury or death of the victim (stimulator).[1] Ellenberger maintained that just as there is a process of criminogenesis, so is there a process of victimogenesis—a process that propels individuals to become victims of crime.[2]

Hans von Hentig made the first systematic attempt to identify the problem of victim instigation, the affinity between victim and doer, and the types of individuals who become targets of crime or who generate aggression in the doer. He did not limit the study of victimology to cases of violent crime but extended it through the whole vista of lawbreaking. Von Hentig observes that "most crimes leave us with an unknown lawbreaker and a known victim" and that "the number of victims surpasses that of perpetrators."[3]

Several of his observations are very pertinent at this point. According to von Hentig, the victim (in a very real sense) quite frequently shapes and molds the criminal, since certain crimes require personal contact for both the preparatory moves and the execution. The criminal focuses on the "assailable" qualities of the victim as well as on his "appetites" and "foibles." Confidence men and card cheats look for people who want to make money in a dishonest way.

Von Hentig calls attention to several types of persons who are readily victimized; the young, the female, the feebleminded, the drug addict, the alcoholic, members of minority groups, immigrants, "dull normals" (apart from feebleminded), the greedy (money hungry), the wanton, the lonesome, the heartbroken, etc.[4]

One is readily lead to conclude from these observations that the victim is a person whose visible personal attributes—physical, mental, economic, and social—make him easy prey to lawbreakers. But it is not known to what extent previous offenders are "on the hunt" for easy prey and to what extent persons not on the hunt are seduced by the visible "come-on" signals ("come take what I have" or "come take advantage of me"), consciously or unconsciously emitted by the potential victim. Both these aspects need to be studied, in the attempt to understand the victim-doer relationship. On the other hand, there seems to be a much less frequent victim-doer relationship,

[1] B. Mendelson, "The Origin of Victimology," *Excerpta Criminologica*, 3 (May-June 1963), pp. 239-241.

[2] Henri Ellenberger, "Relations psychologiques entre le criminel et la victime," *Revue Internationale de Criminologie et de Police Technique*, VIII:2 (April-June 1954), p. 121.

[3] Hans von Hentig, *The Criminal and His Victim*, Studies in the Sociobiology of Crime (New Haven: Yale University Press, 1948), p. 387.

[4] *Ibid.*, pp. 406-428.

in which the victim in actual dyadic interaction agitates the doer and stirs him into violent action. The consequence of this infrequent victim-doer escalation is violence: injury to or death of the victim who triggered the violent episode. Aggravated assaults and homicides often follow the pattern of agitation of the doer by the victim.

Instances of victim instigation in escalation of violence should be typified as following a victim-doer-victim model. Likewise, in instances where the victim, consciously or unconsciously, emits "come-take-what-I-have" signals, the model is also victim-doer-victim, since the victim has spurred the doer into action. However, in what seem to be the most frequent instances, where the doer is "on the hunt" and is looking for prey, the model is doer-victim.

But it must be understood that the study of the victim-doer relationship should not be limited to instances of injury, whether physical or sexual, light or severe. Victimogenesis is present in cases of fraud and swindle as well as in theft from the person or robbery of persons.

Variation in victim risks

A national survey of 10,000 households (c. 1965) conducted for the President's Commission on Law Enforcement and Administration of Justice by the National Opinion Research Center discovered that there were definite class, race, sex, and age risks in victimization, which varied somewhat with type of crime.[5]

> The risks of victimization from forcible rape, robbery, and burglary, are clearly concentrated in the lowest income group and decrease steadily at higher income levels. The picture is somewhat more erratic for the offenses of aggravated assault, larceny of $50 and over, and vehicle theft. Victimization for larceny increases sharply in the highest income group.
>
> National figures on rates of victimization also show sharp differences between whites and nonwhites. Nonwhites are victimized disproportionately by all Index crime. These are homicide, forcible rape, robbery, aggravated assault, burglary, larceny of $50 and over, and auto theft.
>
> The rates for victimization shown for Index offenses against men are almost three times as great as those for women, but the higher rates of burglary, larceny and auto theft against men are in large measure an artifact of the survey procedure of assigning offenses against the household to the head of the household.

[5]The President's Commission on Law Enforcement and the Administration of Justice, *Task Force Report: Crime and its Impact—An Assessment* (Washington D.C.: U.S. Government Printing Office, 1967), pp. 80-81.

The victimization rate for women is highest in the 20 to 29 age group. In fact the victimization rates for women for all the index offenses reported, with the exception of larceny, are greatest in this age group. The concentration of offenses against women in this age group is particularly noticeable for forcible rape and robbery and much less apparent in aggravated assault and the property crimes.

For men the highest Index total rate falls in the 30–39 age category, a result heavily influenced by the burglaries assigned to men as heads of households. Actually, all the Index property offenses against men show peak rates in the older age categories. This is probably due not only to their role as household heads but also to the fact that at older ages they are likely to possess more property to be stolen. Crimes against the person, such as aggravated assault and robbery, are committed relatively more often against men who are from 20 to 29 years of age.

Thus, the findings from the national survey show that the risk of victimization is highest among the lower income groups for all Index offenses except homicide, larceny, and vehicle theft; it weighs most heavily on the nonwhites for all Index offenses except larceny; it is borne by men more often than women, except, of course, for forcible rape; and the risk is greatest for the age category 20 to 29, except for larceny against women, and burglary, larceny, and vehicle theft against men.

Demographic variables in victims of violent crimes

In the instance of murder, the 1968 Uniform Crime Reports indicate that males were victims of murder three times as frequently as females, that 54 out of every 100 victims of murder were Negro, that 6 out of every 10 victims fell into the age group of twenty to forty-five years of age, while only 28 percent fell in the age group twenty to twenty-nine. One fourth of the killings in 1968 were within the family and half of these killings were murder of spouse by spouse. Of these spouse incidents, the wife became the victim in 54 percent of the incidents and the husband in 46 percent.

Of the murders on which information about the circumstances was available, the following data give clues as to the victim focus: spouse killing spouse, 13.7 percent; parent killing child, 3.3 percent; other family killings, 8.7 percent; romantic triangle and lovers' quarrels, 7.2 percent; other arguments, 42.2 percent; known felony type (murder incidental to a felony such as robbery and gangland killings), 17.4 percent; suspected felony type, 7.5 percent. If the cases of other arguments (42.2 percent) consist primarily of escalation between persons who know one another, and if the family cases (25.7 percent) are added to the "other arguments" cases, then it looks as if the majority of victims are known to the doer. Hence, the victim of murder in the United States is not often a stranger to the doer.[6]

[6] *Crime in the United States*, Uniform Crime Reports 1968 (Federal Bureau of Investigation, U.S. Department of Justice, Washington, D.C., August 13, 1969).

Relation of victim to doer in crimes of violence

The 1968 Uniform Crime Reports also call attention to the fact that "most aggravated assaults occur within the family unit or among neighbors and acquaintances. The victim and offender relationship, as well as the very nature of the attack, makes this crime similar to murder."[7]

The findings of the President's Commission on Law Enforcement and the Administration of Justice certainly corroborate the fact that crimes of violence are most frequently perpetrated against family members, related persons, and acquaintances rather than against strangers. This was found to be true in their findings on murder, rape, and aggravated assault. Interestingly enough, the information that the Commission obtained from the District of Columbia Crime Commission Report indicates that 20 percent of its sample of aggravated assault cases "involved a victim and an offender who had been in trouble with each other before."[8]

The relations and interactions of victims and offenders prior to and during the criminal act are important facts to know for understanding and controlling crime and assessing personal risks more accurately.

> In 1965 killings within the family made up 31 percent of all murders. Over one-half of these involved spouse killing spouse and 16 percent parents killing children. Murder outside the family unit, usually the result of altercations among acquaintances, made up 48 percent of the willful killings. In the latter category romantic triangles or lovers' quarrels comprised 21 percent and killings resulting from drinking situations 17 percent. Felony murder, which is defined in this program as those killings resulting from robberies, sex motives, gangland slayings, and other felonious activities, made up 16 percent of these offenses. In another 5 percent of the total, police were unable to identify the reasons for the killings; however, the circumstances were such as to suspect felony murder.

Unfortunately, no national statistics are available on relationships between victims and offenders in crimes other than criminal homicide. However, the District of Columbia Crime Commission surveyed a number of other crimes. Its findings on victim-offender relationships in rape and aggravated assault closely resemble those for murder:

> Almost two-thirds of the 151 (rape) victims surveyed were attacked by persons with whom they were at least casually acquainted. Only 36 percent of the 224 assailants about whom some identifying information was obtained were

[7] *Ibid.*, p. 9.

[8] The President's Commission on Law Enforcement and the Administration of Justice, *Task Force Report: Crime and Its Impact—An Assessment* (Washington, D.C.: U.S. Government Printing Office, 1967), p. 81.

> complete strangers to their victims: 16 (7 percent) of the attackers were known to the victim by sight, although there had been no previous contact. Thirty-one (14 percent) of the 224 assailants were relatives, family friends or boy-friends of the victims, and 88 (39 percent) were either acquaintances or neighbors.

And among 131 aggravated assault victims, only 25 (19 percent) were not acquainted with their assailants:

> Fourteen (11 percent) of the victims were attacked by their spouses, 13 (10 percent) were attacked by other relatives, and 79 (60 percent) were assaulted by persons with whom they were at least casually acquainted.

Again, as in murder, a substantial number (20 percent) of the aggravated assaults surveyed by the District of Columbia Crime Commission involved a victim and offender who had had trouble with each other before.

Racial and interracial aspects of violent crimes

The President's Commission also discovered that the Negro, both male and female, was very much more likely to be victimized by crimes against the person than the white man. In addition, the Commission's findings report that only a small percent of murders, rapes, and aggravated assaults were found to be interracial as between doer and victim.[9]

Another source of the concern about crime, in addition to its violence and its frequency, is the extent to which it is assumed to involve interracial attacks. Therefore a key question in any assessment of the crime problem is to what extent men or women of one racial group victimize those of another. For evidence on the way in which the race and sex of victims and offenders might affect the probability of criminal assault, the Commission, with the cooperation of the Chicago Police Department, studied 13,713 cases of assaultive crimes against the person, other than homicide.

It is Negro males and females who are most likely to be victimized in crimes against the person. A Negro man in Chicago runs the risk of being a victim nearly six times as often as a white man, a Negro woman nearly eight times as often as a white woman.

The most striking fact in the data is the extent of the correlation in race between victim and offender. Negroes are most likely to assault Negroes, whites most likely to assault whites. Thus, while Negro males account for two-thirds of all assaults, the offender who victimizes a white person is most likely also to be white.

The President's Commission on Crime in the District of Columbia discovered similar racial relationships in its 1966 survey of a number of serious crimes. Only 12 of

[9] *Ibid.*, pp. 81–82.

the 172 murders were interracial. Eighty-eight percent of rapes involved persons of the same race. Among 121 aggravated assaults for which identification of race was available, only 9 percent were interracial. Auto theft offenders in the District are three-fourths Negroes, their victims two-thirds Negroes. Robbery, the only crime of violence in which whites were victimized more often than Negroes, is also the only one that is predominantly interracial: in 56 percent of the robberies committed by Negroes in the District of Columbia, the victims are white.

The high proportions of both acquaintance between victim and offender and the interracial character of offenses are further borne out by the findings of another study developed for the Commission. Analyzing data obtained from the Seattle Police Department, this study compared the census tract where the crime occurred with the tract (or other place) in which the offender lived. It found that a relatively large percentage of crimes against persons, as contrasted with crimes against property, had been committed in the offender's home tract—an area likely to be racially homogeneous and in which he is most likely to be known at least by sight.

This analysis shows that a failure to collect adequate data on victim-offender relationships may lead to a miscalculation of the source and nature of the risk of victimization. At present the Nation's view of the crime problem is shaped largely by official statistics which in turn are based on offenses known to the police and statistics concerning arrested offenders; they include very little about victims.

Objects, institutions, and property as victims

Undoubtedly, in certain instances objects of theft and destruction have special symbolic meaning for doers—the grocery store conceived of as an exploiter in racial ghettoes, the public school building perceived as a fortress or hatred by school-attending vandals, precious jewels as the epitome of elegance, etc. The objects of fetishism, which must be compulsively touched, fondled, or possessed, probably have the deepest psychological significance to the doer.

However, apart from the symbolic aspect that gives added drawing power to objects, some indications of the victimization of property and business are available, although the information is very limited. Interestingly enough, the President's Commission on Law Enforcement and Administration of Justice made the following observation: "While any business in a high crime area is obviously in danger, it appears that some businesses, like some people, are more likely to be victimized by crime.[10]

a. *Burglarization of Businesses*

In 1968 the Uniform Crime Reports found that 54 percent of the total burglaries were residential; 46 percent, nonresidential. Daytime burglaries

[10] *Ibid.*, p. 83.

of residences rose 21 percent in 1968 (over 1967) and since 1960 there has been a 247 percent increase in daytime burglaries. "Unattended apartments and homes during daytime hours are becoming increasingly easy prey for the burglar."[11] However, residential and nonresidential nighttime burglary still comprised 65 percent of the reported burglaries in 1968.

The President's Commission on Law Enforcement and Administration of Justice found, among other things, that it is not easy to discover the extent to which businesses and organizations are the victims of crime. But from a pilot survey in 1965 of eight precincts, located in three large cities, the Commission found that almost one out of five businesses was burglarized at least once during the one-year period of study. And almost two-thirds of those that were burglarized were burglarized two to seven times during this period. Undoubtedly, these places must have had a special drawing power.[12]

> It is very difficult to discover the exact extent to which businesses and organizations are the victims of crime. Few attempts are made to keep systematic records or report such crimes to any central place. Police agencies do not ordinarily separate the crimes against individuals from those against organizations. It was not possible in the short time available to the Commission to undertake a systematic census of victimization of different types of industrial, business, professional, religious, or civic organizations throughout the Nation. This task ought to be undertaken, and some assessment procedure developed, using reports, special sample surveys or similar devices.
>
> The Commission was able to make a pilot survey, however, of a sample of neighborhood businesses and organizations in eight police precincts in Chicago, Washington, and Boston. The objective was to discover through interviews what types of victimization businesses and organizations had experienced from crimes such as burglary, robbery, shoplifting, passing fraudulent checks, and employee theft.
>
> Reports to the UCR indicate that nationally about half of all burglaries in 1965 were nonresidential, and that the average worth of the property stolen in such burglaries was about $225. In the Commission survey almost one of every five businesses and organizations in the eight neighborhood police precincts surveyed was burglarized at least once during the one-year period covered by the survey. Considering only those that were burglarized, 62 percent had from two to seven burglaries.
>
> In both Chicago and Washington, but for some reason not in Boston, the burglary victimization rates were highest in the districts where the overall crime rates were highest. Precinct 13 in the District of Columbia, for example, had a victimization rate of 51.8 per 100 organizations—nearly twice that of the precinct with the fewest burglaries—and a third of all the businesses and organizations sampled in that area had been victimized.

[11] Uniform Crime Reports 1968, *op. cit.*, p. 17.

[12] The President's Commission on Law Enforcement and the Administration of Justice, *Task Force Report: Crime and Its Impact—An Assessment* (Washington, D.C.: U.S. Government Printing Office, 1967), p. 83.

b. *Robberies of stores and service stations*

Businesses are also the object of robberies, although undoubtedly, a lot less frequently than of burglaries, since robberies in general are very much less frequent than burglaries. The President's Commission presented the following data on robberies of businesses.[13]

> Nationally, reports to the UCR indicate that in 1965 9 percent of all robberies were of service stations or chainstores, almost 1 percent were of banks, and more than 20 percent were of other types of commercial establishments. The average value of the property stolen varies from $109 for service station robberies to $3,789 for bank robberies.
>
> In the Commission survey the picture that emerges for victimization by robbery is similar to that for burglary, which occurs more frequently. Among the organizations that were robbed, 80 percent reported only one robbery but 2 percent had as many as five. While any business in a high crime rate area is obviously in danger, it appears that some businesses, like some people, are more likely than others to be victimized by crime. Clearly, the reasons for the differences need investigation as guides in prevention.

The Uniform Crime Reports disclosed that 58 percent of robberies in 1968 took place in the streets, which indicates that most of them focused on persons. The principal objects of non-street robberies in 1968 were, however, gas stations, chain stores, commercial houses, banks, and residences; of these, less than one percent were bank robberies. Approximately 60 percent were armed robberies (guns or weapons), while 40 percent of them were unarmed.[14]

c. *Objects of larceny*

An indication of the objects of larceny (in this instance, larceny of $50 and over) in 1968 is also supplied by the Uniform Crime Reports in the following percentages of reported occurrences; pocket picking, 1.3; purse snatching, 2.6; shoplifting, 7.6; theft from automobiles (not accessories), 19.4; theft of accessories from automobiles, 20.1; bicycles, 15.0; theft from buildings, 17.2; theft from coin-operated machines, 1.9; all other kinds of grand larceny, 14.9.[15]

The President's Crime Commission found that employee theft in retail and commercial establishments appear to account for a much larger volume of theft from these institutions than shoplifting by customers. Another

[13] *Ibid.*, p. 83.
[14] Uniform Crime Reports 1968, *op. cit.*, pp. 15–16.
[15] *Ibid.*, p. 24.

indication of this very point of comparison will be given later when estimated losses are considered.[16]

Shoplifting usually involves the theft of relatively small and inexpensive articles, although the professional shoplifter may steal expensive furs, clothes, and jewelry. It is heaviest in the chainstores and other larger stores which do the most retail business. However, it is the smaller establishments, particularly those that operate on a low margin of profit, to which shoplifting may make the difference between success and failure.

In the Commission survey, 35 percent of the neighborhood wholesale and retail establishments surprisingly reported no problem with shoplifting, while sizable percentages of other types of businesses, such as construction companies (30 percent), manufacturers of non-durables (33 percent), finance, insurance, and real estate firms (25 percent), which might not be expected to have any problem, reported some shoplifting difficulties. The average amount of shoplifting experienced by the nontrade establishments was considerably less than that for retail establishments.

As one might expect, the highest rates of shoplifting were reported in the high crime rate districts. The most common items carried off by shoplifters were food, liquor or beer, clothing and footwear, and miscellaneous small items worth less than $10. However, it is the total volume, rather than individual acts, that makes shoplifting a serious problem for most commercial enterprises.

Nationally most large retail businesses estimate their overall inventory shrinkage due to shoplifting, employee theft, and accounting errors at between 1 and 2 percent of total inventory. Experts in industrial and commercial security estimate that 75 to 80 percent of the inventory shrinkage is probably attributable to some type of dishonesty. Among the 47 percent of neighborhood businesses found by the Commission survey to have high rates of shoplifting, 60 percent placed their losses at less than 2 percent of total inventory; another 28 percent estimated they had lost between 2 and 6 percent. Surprisingly, 23 percent of all businesses in the survey were unable to give any estimate at all of the amount of their losses that might be due to shoplifting.

Theft of merchandise or equipment by employees is particularly hard to control because detection is so difficult. Employees have opportunities for theft every working day, whereas the shoplifting customer cannot steal merchandise regularly from the same establishment without arousing suspicion.

Employee theft is also a problem in many industrial concerns. A recent survey by the National Industrial Conference Board of 473 companies indicated that 20 percent of all companies and nearly 30 percent of those with more than 1,000 employees had a serious problem with employee theft of tools, equipment, materials or company products. More than half of the companies with a problem of employee theft indicated trouble with both white and blue collar workers.

In neighborhood establishments surveyed by the Commission only 14 percent reported the discovery of any employee dishonesty. Among those, 40 percent estimated

[16] *Task Force: Crime and Its Impact—An Assessment*, *op. cit.*, p. 84.

losses at no more than $50 a year. Most managers or owners surveyed attempted to establish the honesty of employees before hiring them. Nearly one-third made an effort to check references or to clear the employee with the local police department but 74 percent did not report to the police the discovery of theft by their own employees, preferring to discharge the employee or handle the matter in some other way by themselves.

d. *Public institutions as objects of crime*

Public organizations and utilities such as telephone companies, utility companies, hospitals, public schools, libraries, parks, public transportation, public housing projects, *inter alia* are also victims of crime. The President's Commission surveyed 48 such institutions in Boston, Chicago, and Washington and found vandalism to be the most frequent offense committed against them. Breaking and entering as well as theft from coin machines was reported to be frequent, as was theft of loose equipment and personal possessions. However, employee theft from this class of institution, in great contrast to retail stores, was reported as infrequent, although it was found to be the most common reason for discharge of employees in hospitals.[17]

Public organizations and utilities are repeatedly victimized by crime. While some of the crime committed against these organizations is reported to the police, it is not clear just how much goes unreported and how widespread it is.

To obtain some estimation, the Commission surveyed 48 such organizations in Boston, Chicago, and Washington with special attention to the police districts in which other surveys were being conducted.

The most prevalent and persistent problem reported was vandalism of buildings and equipment. Telephone companies, electric companies, schools, libraries, traffic and highway departments, parks, public transportation, and housing all are victims. Estimates of damage ranging up to $200,000 a year were quoted for such facilities as public housing, transportation, public parks, and recreation facilities in schools. The public school system in Washington, D.C., for example, provided data for 1965 showing a total of 26,500 window panes broken and replaced at a cost of $118,000. A similar report was received in Boston.

Larceny was also a frequently mentioned problem, involving such thefts as stealing loose equipment and personal possessions, theft from coin meters, and breaking and entering. Some organizations make a distinction between amateur and professional theft. For example, the telephone companies distinguished between the organized coinbox larceny using forged keys and the amateur forcible entry involving damage to the equipment. Employee theft was not reported as a serious problem except in hospitals where it represents the most common reason for the apprehension and discharge of employees.

[17] *Ibid.*, p. 84.

Many public facilities reported problems with various forms of violence within their boundaries. Assaults and child molestation occur in parks, libraries, and schools. Emergency rooms of hospitals cited disturbances by drunken and disorderly persons.

The President's Commission calls attention to the fact that violence and child molesting occur in parks, schools, and libraries. "The threat of violent behavior or the presence of disorderly persons was reported to affect markedly the patronage of parks, libraries, and after-school activities, especially in areas with high crime rates."[18]

e. *Estimates of loss from property victimization*

Supplementary insights into property victimization are provided by the President's Commission through a presentation of estimated dollar loss from different types of crime. Such findings present victimization of property not so much from the standpoint of frequency of occurence or frequency of crime which is focused on different types of property or business but rather from the standpoint of the dollar volume of the "take" and of the damage.

The NORC survey of 10,000 households (c. 1965) revealed estimates of gross loss in dollars per reporting respondent by various crimes (*see* Table 4-1).[19]

Table 4-1

Offense	*Gross loss in dollars*
Robbery	274
Burglary	191
Larceny ($50 and over)	160
Auto theft	1,141
Larceny (under $50)	21
Malicious mischief	120
Forgery and counterfeiting	323
Consumer fraud	99
Other fraud (bad checks, swindling, etc.)	906

Certainly on the basis of dollar volume loss to the person, it appears that automobiles are the most luring and lucrative object of doer attention, as reported by surveyed individuals. Bad checks and swindling run a close second, whereas forgery and counterfeiting take a very low third place, robbery falls in a low fourth place, and burglary a low fifth place.

[18] *Ibid.*, p. 84.
[19] *Ibid.*, p. 42.

However, from various sources the President's Commission attempted to estimate the overall economic losses from several different types of crime and, in so doing, gives considerable insight into the differential victimization of business and property. One must be prepared for the fact that estimated cost analysis as an indicator of differential involvement of property and business as objects of crime place robbery, burglary, larceny, and auto theft combine in a very minor loss-risk category. Destruction of property by fire, as reported by insurance companies, contains a very minor item for arson ($74 million out of $1.5 billion). An eye should be focused on victimization of retail trade—the inventory shrinkage, wherein theft by employees far outdistances theft by customers, accounting for 75 to 80 percent of the loss. (This point was made earlier in connection with reported frequency of occurrence.)

The excerpts from the President's Commission which are presented in Appendix 4–C indicate differential loss-risks that in turn indicate differential attractiveness and value of property.

Appendix 4–A

WHAT ABOUT THE VICTIMS OF CRIME?

How great is the hazard of crime? Who are its victims? What harm comes to them? How can they be protected from it or recompensed for their loss? Do the victims of crime invite or encourage the harm that befalls them? Are there various levels of victimization? Are some people "victim prone"? Does every criminal offense necessarily involve a victim?

In considering victims of crime it would probably be helpful to recognize different categories of offenses in terms of the relationship of victims and offenders. For example, it might be useful to classify offenses as those that are:

1. Physically aggressive offenses against the person; for instance: murder, forcible rape, aggravated assault.
2. Physically aggressive offenses against public order such as rioting, exceeding the lawful speed limit, disorderly conduct.
3. Physically aggressive property offenses such as robbery, breaking and entering to commit larceny, pocket-picking or shoplifting.
4. Psychologically aggressive offenses against the person such as statutory rape, seduction or indecent exposure.
5. Psychologically aggressive offenses against public order such as inciting to riot or advocating the overthrow of the lawful government by force.
6. Psychologically aggressive property offenses such as crimes of fraud and false pretenses.
7. Passive offenses such as non-support, neglect of children or others due to criminal negligence.
8. Consensual offenses such as criminal abortion, fornication or prostitution.

If it is granted that some crimes—such as speeding, statutory rape, espionage—do not necessarily have recognizable victims, it may nevertheless be assumed that most offenses do—particularly the common offenses of theft in one form or another—and it

Albert Morris, "What about the victims of crime?" reprinted from *Correctional Research*, Bulletin No. 16, (Boston: Massachusetts Correctional Association, November, 1966), pp. 2-11. Reprinted by permission.

may also be assumed that it is obvious who has been victimized. If someone gets into a house and steals the silver or the TV set presumably the owner is the victim of the theft. No doubt he has been, if the silver was a wedding present or has some other sentimental value and, in any event, he has been inconvenienced, though possibly in a very minor way. Perhaps, too, a heightened awareness of the possibility of being touched by crime has been aroused in him together with a vague sense of uneasiness and insecurity that will probably soon fade away. But until one is so affected the victim of theft from a home is more likely to be identified as the householder who has lost something of greater or less monetary value. This interpretation overlooks the considerable use of insurance against loss by theft of property whether it be of household goods, merchandise in stores and warehouses, or autos left unattended by the thousands in parking lots and streets. To a considerable extent the monetary equivalent of the goods stolen may then be recovered from the insurance company and sometimes there may be no loss and only a trifling inconvenience to the owner.

Who, then, is the real victim? The insurance company that is obligated to pay the loss? But companies that sell insurances against theft would not sell any insurance at all for theft unless this offense were committed; indeed it is when thefts are most numerous and the public feels that the likelihood of loss by theft is great that it is easiest to sell theft insurance. Those who sell insurance may try to reduce the hazards against which they insure but they would be out of business if they succeeded in eliminating them entirely. Their concern is to maintain such actuarial records and such a distribution of risks that they may know what premiums to charge in order to pay off anticipated claims and still make a profit. Ultimately the volume of claims determines the selling price of insurance against any sort of loss by criminal action. It seems, therefore, that for insured losses it is those who buy insurance on that type of loss who ultimately become victims through the necessity of paying higher premiums for their protection.

One assumption commonly made about victims of crime is that they are innocent; perhaps with an admitted rare exception. In part, the validity of such a statement depends on what is meant by "innocent." A woman who wears expensive jewelry at a well-publicized party and then leaves her diamonds in the hotel suite where she is staying for a few days may be completely innocent of any wrong doing and her possessions should be secure from theft or any misuse while she is in residence at the hotel. Nevertheless, the realities of life being what they are, she might have been well-advised to keep them in the hotel safe or a bank vault when she was not wearing them and in leaving them in her room she might be considered to behave with less than adequate forethought and responsibility. So too, the driver who leaves his car door unfastened and the key in the ignition lock invites the theft of his car from any unprincipled fellow who is looking for such an opportunity.

At the other end of the spectrum is the type of victim-precipitated crime represented by the not uncommon cases in which the man who provokes a fight by cursing and threatening another ends up by getting killed by the person he has angered.

Forcible rape, in many cases, follows irresponsible behavior on the part of the victim. A woman waiting at a bus stop for a boy friend who had been delayed complained to a stranger standing by that she guessed she had been "stood up." He invited her to a nearby bar to have a drink while she waited. Afterwards she accepted an invitation to take a ride with him in his car and made no objection when he stopped the car in a secluded spot and kissed her but screamed and fought when her companion insisted on coition.

In an unpublished pilot research on 46 consecutive cases of rape in Massachusetts of such seriousness as to result in the sentencing of the defendants to a state correctional institution, Hozid and Spiller found that 20 of the victims had known the offender before the actual day of the crime and five of these reported having had previous sex relations with the defendants. Seven of the victims had been picked up voluntarily on a street corner or while hitch-hiking prior to the day when the offense was committed and 19 were picked up voluntarily in the same way on the occasion of the offense. Thirty two of the 46 victims were met at a public amusement place, street corner or cafe; and in 31 cases the victims had been drinking before the commission of the offense.

The extremes of age are thought of as increasing the risk that one may be victimized; childhood because it is associated with inexperience, lack of mature judgment, impulsiveness, dependency, and incomplete physical development. On the other hand, old age is associated with failing sensory capabilities, increasing frailty, chronic and incurable degenerative illnesses, loneliness and decline in status and authority. The child, in his immaturity may, therefore be more susceptible to kidnapping both because he is less able to understand what is happening or to resist, less likely to be a good witness against an offender and more likely to generate sympathy and a willingness to accede to a kidnapper's demands because of his dependency. But it should be noted that the same immaturity that may permit a child to go along with the stranger who has candy or to permit sexual fondling by a senile or pathological offender also makes him immune to victimization by such offenses as auto theft, embezzlement, confidence swindling and price-fixing. In turn, the aging person may fall easy prey to the quack doctor who promises him a cure for the ills that beset his failing body or to the dance studio operator or happy times club that offers him—more usually her—under false pretences, a renewal of youth and relief from loneliness with new and interesting friends. But this same age, when accompanied by physical limitations, reduces the likelihood of being victimized by the quack abortionist or peddlers of narcotics.

There is, too, a greater risk of being victimized in some places or situations than others. A man in a crowd going through the turnstiles at a fair or an athletic event is more likely to have his pockets picked there than is a suburban commuter walking to the bus stop en route to his office. A seventeen year old girl hitchhiking is in more danger of being victimized than is one walking to a nearby school in a New England village. But to the girls in either case the risk is with reference to a limited range of offenses; probably sexual attack, manslaughter by automobile, or purse snatching might be among the possible offenses to which they would be differentially vulnerable but they would not, in such circumstances, be victimized by auto theft, arson or adulteration of food-stuffs.

The personalities of victims may also be predisposing factors to victimization. Von Hentig makes much of this and, indeed, develops a classification of victim psychological types; the lonely and bereaved, the acquisitive, the tormentors, the wanton.

Probably these might better be called, not psychological types but traits, and certainly not the only traits that might encourage victimization. It is easy to see how the depressed person might fall prey to the quack doctor, the greedy person be "taken" by the confidence man, the tormentor and the wanton be attacked. But the unsophisticated generous person and the masochist may also lend themselves to victimization as may those with other traits such as adventuresomeness, carelessness, impulsiveness and so on.

In a nationwide police survey of car "thefts" carried out in November 1962 it was discovered that in 42% of the cars taken the keys were conveniently left in the ignition lock. It would seem that the precaution of removing ignition lock keys might appreciably reduce this sort of victimization. More basic, however, than this elementary and desirable precaution is the responsibility of the automobile manufacturers to produce a more nearly theft-proof car. Presumably any car can be hoisted on a truck or removed by a tow car and in such instances and those in which the owner connives at the theft there is not much that a car manufacturer can do. But most cars are not taken for resale by professional thieves; they are taken illegally for temporary use as a means of transportation and this type of victimization, involving driving the car away, should not be beyond the inventive capacity of automotive engineers to solve by providing an ignition system that cannot be easily bypassed, or by installing a bolt that locks the steering mechanism in a straight line when the ignition key is removed such as at least one foreign car manufacturer installs as standard equipment.

Very likely not all victim risks can be reduced by methods as specific as those applicable to car theft. Perhaps if the reports and records of law enforcement agencies were developed so that they would be at least as detailed with reference to victims and the circumstances relative to victim responsibility as they are with reference to crimes and the offenders' part in them, the nature and extent of victim responsibility for crime and victimization might become known in greater detail and refinement and so become a contribution to the reduction of crime.

Appendix 4–B

STATE COMPENSATION TO VICTIMS OF VIOLENT CRIME
by
Gilbert Geis

Programs designed to compensate persons injured by crimes of violence represent, in an important sense, an attempt to placate a public opinion often unnerved and resentful of what is viewed as a rising tide of aggressive criminal activity. In this respect, such programs suggest that State authorities concede an inability to ameliorate to any great degree the threat of violent crime, and that they assume as a public burden the consequences of such crime. It is, of course, obvious that there will always be a certain level of violent activity in any human order and that there will always be a number of innocent victims of the depredations of others. But the emergence and the extraordinary recent popularity of schemes to compensate victims of violent crimes can be most readily understood as a response to the ever increasing degrees of anonymity, urban living, juvenile precocity, social change, and other crime-related factors in American society and throughout the world.

Of the two major components of the ethos underlying victim compensation, the first is essentially compassionate; people have been hurt through no fault of their own; therefore, it is a moral obligation of those more fortunate to assist such persons. The second element is the product of an economic rationality which suggests that failure to make adequate provision for incapacitated persons ultimately deprives all members of the society of common benefits. "No man is an island," viewed as a principle of social policy, may be considered to include elements both of charitable impulses and of impulses of self-interest.

Programs calling for compensation to victims of violent crime are a relatively easy social and political goal, much easier than plans to compensate victims of circumstances which might reasonably be related to their own lack of intelligence or care, or even to their inadvertent misfortune at the hands of natural phenomena, such as lightning. Persons are expected to insure and protect themselves by available methods, against various deprivations, however fortuitous, which might be visited upon them, or, failing this, to locate resources in themselves or elsewhere for self-assistance.

The President's Commission on Law Enforcement and the Administration of Justice, *Task Force Report: Crime and Its Impact—An Assessment* (Washington, D.C.: U.S. Government Printing Office, 1967), pp. 157–172.

Lacking such ability or initiative, they are usually expected to fall under the auspices of regular welfare programs established to serve the disabled or deprived. In the event of consequence which a person could be said to have brought upon himself, however ill-equipped he might have been to have avoided such injury, then it is usually deemed that the matter is of no further social concern unless the person comes within the preestablished programs for those patently beyond self-help.

There are also a number of procedural matters requiring careful attention before a blueprint for victim compensation can adequately be drawn and then given proper evaluative consideration. It must be determined, among other things, who will be eligible for compensation. Victims of designated violent crimes may be compensated or compensation eligibility may be determined in terms of the consequences of an offense rather than in terms of the offense itself. Arson, for example, is generally regarded as a crime against property, though it may inflict injuries upon persons more serious than those involved in what normally are considered to be crimes of violence. It is arguable whether arson victims should fall within the bounds of a victim compensation program.

There are also problems concerned with the way in which possible involvement of the victim in the perpetration of an offense may affect his right to be compensated for the consequences of that offense. Such involvement may conceivably disqualify him altogether for assistance, or perhaps it may be viewed as reducing the amount to which he will be entitled. Among many other questions, the following represent a sample of items which must be given attention in victim compensation proposals: Should crimes involving only members of the same family entitle the injured person to aid? Should payments be granted in a lump sum, or should they be awarded over a period of time with provision for regular review? Should there be a special compensation board to rule upon claims, or should this task be assigned to tribunals already in existence? Should individuals who possess adequate financial resources to pay for their own care and support in the event of criminally inflicted injury nonetheless be given compensation? Should appeals from decisions regarding compensation be allowed, or should an administrative decision represent the final determination of the matter?

Finally, and most importantly, plans for the compensation of victims of violent crime have to be regarded in the light of a range of issues, most of them empirical, concerning the impact of such plans upon various social arrangements. It is possible that victim compensation may contribute to an increase in the amount of crime, presumably because offenders, knowing that their victim will likely be cared for, will feel less inhibited about injuring them. Victims too may take fewer precautions to insure their own safety or, more likely than either of these outcomes, the program may have no notable influence on the extent of violent crime. The impact of victim compensation on the rehabilitation of offenders also represents a question concerning which only speculative answers are presently possible. Will an offender feel less guilty about his act if the victim is not unduly deprived by the crime? And will such a diminution of guilt, if it takes place, encourage further criminal activity, or is it essentially irrelevant to the issue of recidivism?

The historical biography of victim compensation can be drawn from a long and impressive list of policies in earlier times, in a story that usually opens with a recital of the provision in the Code of Hammurabi of ancient Babylonia (c. 1775 B.C.) which evoked communal responsibility for certain crimes where it was impossible to place individual blame. According to the code, "If a robber has not been caught, the robbed man shall declare his lost property in the presence of the god, and the city and governor in whose territory and district the robbery was committed, shall replace for him his lost property." In addition, it was ordered that "if it was a life that was lost, the city and Governor shall pay one mina of silver to his heirs."

Quite likely the rule in the Code of Hammurabi was designed to encourage commerce and trade more than it was established to assist victims out of a sense of an injustice done them. Anthropologists believe that a similar interest in placating the offended and deterring the possible offender in order to maintain harmonious social life underlies the almost ubiquitous provision in preliterate societies for payment of monies or goods by the family of an offender to the family of the victim of violent depredation. It is presumed that, absent such payment, a state of social unrest would be created, marked by unremitting vendettas.

Early systems of law in Western civilization contained essentially similar compensation provisions as found in preliterate societies, often with exquisitely detailed scales of indemnification due to individuals with varying social standings and for various kinds of personal injuries. Gradually, such provisions were replaced by a rudimentary system of State-operated prosecution for criminal offenses, with the authorities decreeing penalties and exacting monetary fines which remained in the State treasury. Civil remedies came to be and remain available to persons who suffer losses through crimes of violence, but it is indisputable that such remedies almost always prove inadequate because of the poor financial condition and prospects of the offender.

The idea of victim compensation, following its disappearance in early times, was revived with great intensity during the last decades of the 19th century and the first decade of the present century, and made up a sizable segment of the proceedings of several quinquennial meetings of the International Prison Congress. At the 1878 meeting in Stockholm, for instance, the chief justice of New Zealand and the secretary of the Howard Association in England provided a preview of the later pioneering roles of their respective countries in victim compensation by joint advocacy of "a more general return, in all nations, to the ancient practice of making reparation to the injured—a principle object in dealing with offenders."

The International Prison Congress' Paris meeting in 1895 saw five prepared papers on victim indemnification, and the delegates adopted the following resolution:

> The Congress believes that there is reason to take into serious consideration the propositions which have been submitted to it with regard to allowing the injured party a portion of the earnings realized by the work of the prisoner in the course of his detention, or with regard to constituting a special fund derived from fines from which aid should be granted to the victims of penal offenses; but

thinking it does not possess at present the elements which are necessary for the solution of these questions, the Congress decided to refer them to the more profound study of the next International Prison Congress.

Thirteen papers, which covered 147 pages of the *Proceedings* dealt with victim compensation during the 1900 meeting of the Congress at Brussels. Only the mildest of responses followed their presentation and discussion, however, with the delegates accepting the following position: "The Congress adopts again the resolution of the Congress of Paris to facilitate by reforms in procedure the legal position of the party seeking relief by civil action." Blatantly misstating both the ingredients and the spirit of the earlier resolution, the Brussels conclusion, unadorned and unenthusiastic, effectively managed to bury the subject of victim compensation as a significant agenda topic at international penological gatherings from thenceforth to the present time.

In his comprehensive worldwide survey, conducted for the British Home Office about a decade ago, Schafer found fewer than a handful of victim compensation programs in existence. He pointed to a French law of 1951 providing for the payment of damages to victims of motorcar accidents in cases where the offender is not known or is found to be partly or totally insolvent. In Switzerland, a fund derived from the sale of confiscated articles may be tapped to provide financial surcease for victims of criminal offenses who press their claims through a court proceeding. Moneys which the state may have extracted from an offender as a guarantee that he will henceforth keep the peace may also be employed to indemnify victims. Reports from prerevolutionary Cuba indicated the existence of an indemnification fund, constituted from a portion of prison earning, fines, donations, unclaimed estates of victims of criminal offenses, and similar sources which could be employed to alleviate the fiscal distress of a person injured by criminal behavior. In practice, it was said at the time, the Cuban fund sometimes did not possess sufficient amounts to provide the necessary compensation, and in such instances relief was awarded on a partial basis. The French provision, restricted to automobile injuries, and the limited provisions in Switzerland and Cuba, represented until the last few years the only extant compensation programs.

Interest in victim compensation can thus readily be seen to have lain dormant, though not far beneath the surface of penological thought, over the years. Revival of active concern at the present time may clearly be attributed directly to the work of Margery Fry, an English penal reformer, who set forth her views in a widely attended article printed in The Observer in 1957.

It was largely on the basis of this demand for compensation from state sources by Miss Fry that authorities in New Zealand and England again began to pay attention to the subject, and it was her call which ultimately led to the inauguration of the present programs of victim compensation in those countries.

The New Zealand Criminal Injuries Compensation Bill, as the Minister of Justice indicated when first presenting it to Parliament, is a "cautious" piece of legislation "as befits a pioneering measure." He hoped that it would be enacted and further "enhance the reputation of New Zealand for pioneering humanitarian reforms." Possible awards were made equivalent to ceilings prescribed by the Workers' Compensation Act. The

Minister thought that the amounts were low, though hardly "niggardly." There was a modest limit of NZ £500 collectible for pain and suffering, and NZ £1,000 possible for general damages or for pecuniary loss other than through loss of wages. Primarily, however, awards were tied closely to loss of earnings, and a maximum recovery was established at NZ £10, 17.6s. weekly (with a possible addition of £1 weekly for a dependent wife and 10s. for each dependent child) for a period of 6 years. Payments under the compulsory third-party insurance required for automobile drivers in New Zealand and social security benefits were to be deducted from these awards. Initially, regular insurance payments were also to be subtracted from compensation grants, but this provision was stricken in committee and subsequently the Government aligned itself with the view that "a man should not be penalised for having the forsight to insure himself."

The bill limited compensation rather broadly to injuries sustained from acts of murder, manslaughter, woundings and assaults of various kinds, and sexual offenses involving violence or perpetrated on immature persons. Apprehension of the offender would not be necessary for compensation, nor would an adequate defense by the accused categorically eliminate the possibility of payment to the victim. The Government reserved to itself the right to attempt to collect compensation from the offender, if possible, though the victim too could have recourse to civil suit. Any amounts recovered by the victim would be deducted from his original compensation award.

The New Zealand measure called for the establishment of a three-man tribunal to pass upon claims, with only the chairman necessarily having judicial qualifications. Board members were to be appointed for a period of 5 years.

The March 1964 White Paper outlining the Government plan underwent extensive debate in Parliament before the final, slightly revised version was promulgated later in the year, to take effect on the first of August. As it ultimately emerged, the victim compensation program was to be administered by a Criminal Injuries Compensation Board, consisting of six legally trained members appointed by the Home Secretary and the Secretary of State for Ireland. A single member would be responsible for a decision on the cases assigned to him, which he would review only on the basis of written submissions. His ruling would be appealable to three members of the board, other than himself. No further appeal or ministerial review would be possible.

Compensation could be awarded where the applicant (or his surviving spouse or dependents acting in his name) suffered personal injury which was either directly attributable to an offense or to an arrest or attempted arrest on his part of a suspected offender. Injuries sustained from an attempt to prevent an offense or to assist a constable in the performance of his duty qualified for compensation. No specific list of offenses rating eligibility was provided. "What matters more than the name of the offense," the Home Secretary told the House of Commons, "is the circumstances of the incident." The victim or his dependent would have had to sustain at least 3 weeks' loss of earnings or an injury for which not less than £50 would be awarded. The claim had to be based on offenses occurring after the commencement of the program, and the circumstances of the injury would have to had been reported to the police without delay. Applicants were required, when requested, to submit to medical examination.

The White Paper made it clear, in addition, that all applications growing out of sexual offenses, particularly if there had been a delay in reporting the offense, would be examined closely to determine if there was any responsibility for the act on the part of the victim. Awards would be possible for pain and suffering growing from victimization by rape or by other sexual offenses and for childbirth resulting from such offenses when the woman was not eligible for a maternity grant under the National Insurance Scheme. Compensation would not be awarded, however, for the maintenance of a child born as a result of a sexual offense. Offenses committed against a member of the offender's family living with him at the time, as well as motoring offenses, would also be excluded from compensation.

Payments in general were to be made in a lump sum rather than periodically. For the living victim, payment would be equivalent to loss of earning or of earning capacity, but could not exceed twice the average of industrial earnings at the time when the injury was sustained. Provocation would be considered to reduce the amount of compensation or to serve to reject the claim altogether.

The nature of the cases ran a considerable gamut, though a large majority fell into the general category of injuries suffered which could be "directly attributable"—the words of the White Paper—to a criminal offense. Persons compensated included a prisoner attacked by a fellow prisoner with a knife, a policeman assaulted when arresting an offender, and a man who aggravated a slipped disc when chasing a suspect. Several awards were made even though it was not possible to trace the assailant.

By the end of May 1966, total compensation payments had risen to £570,327. The highest awarded by the board had been made the previous month—£15,580 to a 19-year-old university student who had been attacked by a gang of youths and struck over the head with a brick. The injury produced restricted right arm and leg movement, impaired vision of the left eye, and slurred speech as well as discernible personality changes and impaired intellectual ability.

For the month, 141 cases were resolved, 7 at hearings before 3 members of the board, either on appeal by the applicant or by a single member referring the case for such hearings. Final awards were made in 123 of the cases; in 6 of them the award was reduced because of the applicant's partial responsibility. No awards were made in 15 cases and 3 applications were withdrawn. Total compensation paid for the month was £77,026. Using the sum for this month, the last for which a board resume is presently available, it seems likely that the annual operating cost of the victim compensation program in Britain—when expenses other than those of payments are included—is on the verge of exceeding the estimated yearly total of approximately £1 million cited in various early reports.

Interest in victim compensation in the United States was based in large measure on an awareness that the social and political conditions which proved hospitable to such a program abroad prevailed, often in fact in an aggravated condition, in this country. Arthur J. Goldberg, while a Supreme Court justice, served an important function as catalyst, able to provide legitimated support for importation of the idea of compensation for victims of criminal violence onto the American scene, and his reiterated suggestions that the United States pay attention to victim compensation are almost invariably quoted in discussions of such programs.

The support in public opinion for Goldberg's position was clearly indicated in a Gallup poll survey conducted toward the end of 1965. Though the issue addressed concerned homicide, usually the most extreme form of deprivation, it is not unlikely that the responses can be generalized with some validity to the underlying issue of victim compensation. In the Gallup survey persons were asked: "Suppose an innocent person is killed by a criminal—do you think the state should make financial provisions for the victim's family?" Sixty-two percent of the national sample thought that the state should make such provision, 29 percent disagreed, and 9 percent registered no opinion on the question.

Since the time of the Gallup survey, at least nine States have considered various forms of victim compensation programs during legislative sessions, and in several other jurisdictions different officials have promised the introduction of such legislation. For the moment, California and New York represent the only States which have enacted programs of compensation for victims of criminal violence, with the California program in particular differing sharply in significant aspects from those abroad. In addition, a bill on victim compensation has been introduced in the U.S. Senate and seven measures have been presented to the House of Representatives. The history and content of this legislative effort will be considered below.

The victim compensation legislation effective at the beginning of 1966 in California provides for a program intimately tied to the operation of the State's social welfare system and to principles governing the administration of general relief and aid to dependent children. It is a program, its sponsor has stressed, geared to need and not to loss. The California program has consistently been under attack for this welfare emphasis, from sources both inside and outside the State. The welfare approach was categorically rejected during debates on victim compensation in Great Britain.

The California Department of Social Welfare has twice amended its regulations since they initially became operative on January 1, 1966. The first set of regulations provided that applications for compensation (the program is known as AVCV—Aid to Victims of Crimes of Violence) are to be processed by county welfare departments in the same manner as applications for Aid to Families with Dependent Children. If the family meets eligibility requirements for the latter program, it is handled under its provisions, except when its "total need" exceeds AFDC limits. Under such conditions, the grant may be supplemented by victim compensation funds. If the family is not eligible for AFDC because of its property holdings or for other reasons, but meets AVCV requirements, then it will come under the new law. The combined value of real and personal property is considered as income on a prorated basis in order to determine the need for compensation. Property valued at $10,500, for instance, would be regarded as a personal income of $15 a month. Property valued at more than $15,500 would automatically exclude its holder from compensation. So too, for a family of four, does an income of $239 a month or more preclude compensation. Proceeds from insurance or amounts recovered by court actions are to be regarded as personal property and "considered income available to meet the family's current needs." Medical and hospital bills are expected to be paid from the applicant's insurance benefits or through an appropriate State medical care program. Nonmedical needs are to be based on the department's regular schedule, though extraordinary financial demands imposed by victimization are to be met by AVCV funds. Perpetrators of crimes and members of their families are not eligible for compensation. Eligibility is made retroactive for offenses which took place up to 5 years prior to the filing of an application for assistance and is restricted to crimes committed in California or elsewhere upon California residents.

Unlike their counterparts in California, New York legislators devoted a considerable amount of time and attention to the subject of victim compensation before moving toward enactment of a measure. The case of Arthur Collins was often employed in New York to focus public attention upon the necessity for victim compensation. In October 1965, Collins had attempted to eject a disorderly person annoying two women from a subway car. In the process, he was stabbed to death in front of his wife and 15-month-old daughter. Collins had served 2 years in the Army prior to securing a job as a computer programmer at Pan American World Airways, and was earning about $6,000 a year at the time of his death. Pan American had continued his salary for an additional month, and given Mrs. Collins a job. Its employees had contributed $3,000 for her, but in order to be able to work she had felt it necessary to send her daughter to her mother in West Germany.

The New York legislative measure, introduced soon thereafter, called for the appointment by the Governor of a three-member Crime Victims Compensation Board. Board members were to be lawyers of at least 10 years' standing, and would serve full time for a period of 7 years. Compensation, "a matter of grace," would be limited to crimes causing a personal physical injury or a death which, except for unusual circumstances, had been reported to the police within 48 hours. Out-of-pocket expenses for medical and hospital services as well as loss of earnings or loss of support would constitute the major reimbursable items, with a board member being permitted to make an immediate grant of $500 in a case of hardship which appeared likely to come within the compensation program. The minimum claim would be $100 or 2 weeks' loss of earnings, and the maximum award would be $15,000. Grants would be reduced by amounts received from insurance and from similar sources.

The crime victims compensation board was charged with determination of whether the claimant would suffer "serious financial hardship" as a result of the crime; if not, compensation would be denied. Single members would review claims, with both the board member and the claimant permitted to request a full board hearing. No judicial review was permissible, though the State could obtain court consideration if it believed that any award was improper or excessive. The act would be applicable only to crimes committed in New York, and only to those committed after October 1, 1966. It would be financed by an appropriation of $500,000 for the 1966–67 fiscal year.

The growing national interest in victim compensation is clearly indicated by the widespread legislative attention that has been given to bills calling for State assistance to persons injured or deprived of their support through the commission of crimes of violence. For the moment, California and New York remain the only States that have placed a compensation law on their statute books, but at least eight others, in addition to the Federal Congress, currently have or recently have had compensation provisions before them. In addition, attorney generals in two other States have indicated that they will sponsor compensation legislation.

Appendix 4-C

COST ESTIMATES OF CRIME

Employee theft, embezzlement, and other forms of crime involving business, which appear in relatively small numbers in the police statistics, loom very large in dollar volume. They make up the bulk of the more than $2 billion which business annually loses in crimes for which losses can be estimated. Direct stealing of cash and merchandise, manipulation of accounts and stock records, and other forms of these crimes, along with shoplifting, appear to constitute a tax of 1 to 2 percent on the total sales of retail enterprises, and significant amounts in other parts of business and industry. In the grocery trade, for example, the theft estimates for shoplifting and employee theft almost equal the total amount of profit. Yet Commission and other studies indicate that these crimes are largely dealt with by business itself. Merchants report to the police fewer than one-quarter of the known offenses. Estimates for these crimes are particularly incomplete for nonretail industries.

Fraud is another offense whose impact is not well conveyed by police statistics. Just one conspiracy involving the collapse of a fraudulent salad oil empire in 1964 created losses of $125 to $175 million. Fraud is especially vicious when it attacks, as it so often does, the poor or those who live on the margin of poverty. Expensive nostrums for incurable diseases, home-improvement frauds, frauds involving the sale or repair of cars, and other criminal schemes create losses which are not only sizable in gross but are also significant and possibly devastating for individual victims. Although a very frequent offense, fraud is seldom reported to the police. In consumer and business fraud, as in tax evasion, the line between criminal and civil fraud is often unclear. And just as the amount of civil tax evasion is much greater than the amount of criminal tax fraud, the amount of civil fraud probably far exceeds that of criminal fraud.

Cost analysis also places the crimes that appear so frequently in police statistics—robbery, burglary, larceny, and auto theft—in somewhat different perspective. The number of reported offenses for these crimes accounts for less than one-sixth the estimated total dollar loss for all property crimes and would constitute an even lower percentage if there were any accurate way of estimating the very large sums involved in extortion, blackmail, and other property crimes.

The President's Commission on Law Enforcement and the Administration of Justice, *Task Force Report: Crime and its Impact—An Assessment* (Washington, D.C.: U.S. Government Printing Office, 1967), pp. 43-51.

Single events that occur sporadically such as riots or the sabotage of a commercial airliner sometimes cause sizable losses. The Watts riots, for example, caused property losses of more than $40 million. Antitrust violations reduce competition and unduly raise prices; the price-fixing conspiracy in the electrical industry alone cost the public very large sums of money.

The National Fire Protective Association maintains estimates on all fires other than those for government and forests. It estimates that out of a total property loss of approximately $1.5 billion in 1965 about $74 million was due to arson. No estimate is available for losses by the government. Forest Service figures indicate that in 1965 about one-fourth of all forest fires were incendiary in origin. Apportioning the $92 million in losses caused by all forest fires, those attributable to incendiarism could be estimated at about $23 million.

Willful or malicious destruction to property is a widespread offense for which there are few statistics. Total arrests for 1965 can be estimated at about 121,500, but it is clear that only a small percentage of offenders are apprehended.

Commission surveys indicate that public service institutions, businesses, and individuals all report extensive damage due to vandalism. Significant losses to public schools, street lighting systems, public housing, and public transit systems, and lesser damage to other public service institutions were indicated by one survey in three cities. Public school glass breakage alone has been estimated at $4 to $5 million nationally. No estimates are available for vandalism of businesses, but it is clear that it is extensive, particularly in high crime rate districts, where vandalism is often so severe that windows are often boarded up to prevent breakage. The average loss rate due to vandalism on housing and construction projects in New York is reported to be nearly 30 percent.

Robbery involves the taking of property by force or threat of force. The estimates made here are for property transfer losses incurred as a result of robberies without the added personal costs due to injuries sustained or time lost from work. The UCR estimates the total number robberies to be 118,916 or 61.4 per 100,000 population in 1965. Data on two-thirds of these indicate an average loss of $254 per robbery and a projected national loss of more than $30 million. The UCR also indicates a recovery rate of about 11.6 percent of the losses due to robbery, burglary, and larceny, making the net reported loss about $27 million.

This total is substantially less than the $49.4 million estimated by the national survey of households. And that survey did not cover any business robberies except those in which the individual interviewed was the victim. Since about 40 percent of all robberies appear to be business robberies, and since most of these would not have been covered by the survey, the total may be as much as $60 to $65 million.

Burglary includes unlawful entry to commit a felony or a theft whether or not force was used. In 1965 there were an estimated 1,173,201 burglaries. Cost data on a little over half of these indicate an average loss of $242 per burglary and a projected national total of about $284 million.

The national survey of households indicated a loss of about $313 million for individuals alone, more than twice the net loss indicated by the UCR for residential burglaries. This means that the total may be as much as $450 to $500 million.

Larceny includes any theft, other than auto theft, not involving force, violence, unlawful entry, or fraud. For 1965, the total number of larcenies known to the police of $50 and over is estimated to be about 2,660,000. The average loss per larceny was $84 and the estimated national loss amounted to $222 million. After the estimated 11.6 percent of recoveries are deducted, the national net loss was approximately $196 million.

Embezzlement involves theft of property or money by persons in a position of trust. Estimating the losses from this offense has been likened to guessing the size of an iceberg. The nature of the offense is such that it is usually kept hidden. It is difficult to estimate how much money is involved even in those cases which are discovered. The victim is often more interested in restitution than in prosecution and in many cases wishes to avoid public disclosure for fear that it will harm the reputation of the business. The UCR maintains data on arrests but not on offenses known to the police or the amounts involved. In 1965 total arrests could be estimated roughly as about 11,500.

Data maintained by the American Bankers Association indicates that banks lost about $15.3 million in 1965. Savings and loan associations are estimated to have lost an additional $1 million. These totals compare with deposits of $332.4 billion for banking and $110.3 billion for savings and loan associations. Arrests in these industries account for about one-third of total arrests for embezzlement. If average embezzlement losses for other industries were about the same, the total national loss would be in the $45 to $55 million category.

This figure is almost surely too low. Fidelity insurance covers only 15 to 20 percent of all firms and sustained losses totalling $45 million in 1964. If it were assumed that the same proportion of uninsured firms had embezzlement losses as did insured firms, and if allowances were made for the high rate of insurance in the banking and savings and loan industries, a national total of around $200 million could be estimated.

Existing data indicates that this is very much a white-collar crime. In 1960, the bank embezzlers were 100 bank presidents, 65 vice-presidents, 145 managers, 345 cashiers, and 490 others, principally tellers and clerks.

The amount of larceny and embezzlement suffered by business that is known to the police is clearly only a small part of such losses incurred by businesses.

Retail firms commonly have a sizable amount of stock shortage, or inventory shrinkage, that cannot be accounted for by any known cause. Markdowns, spoilage and other known causes of loss, such as burglary and robbery, are usually accounted for specifically and not included in the inventory shrinkage. The major part of the shrinkage is therefore due to recordkeeping errors, shoplifting, employee theft, and embezzlement through stock-record manipulation. While there is no reliable way to determine what losses are due to crime and what to error and other causes, the industry commonly estimates that as much as 75 to 80 percent of all shrinkage is the result of some kind of dishonesty. This means in effect a crime tariff, totaling more than $1.3 billion annually, or about 1 to 2 percent of the value of all retail sales.

It is difficult to tell how much of this loss is due to shoplifting and how much due to employee dishonesty. Shoplifting is clearly a widespread offense—suffered to some extent by virtually all retail stores. Grocery supermarkets surveyed in an industry study apprehended nearly six customers per million dollars annual sales. In the Commission's survey of neighborhood businesses in three cities, 65 percent of the wholesale and retail businesses and 47 percent of all businesses surveyed experienced some shoplifting losses. Many larger businesses, such as department stores, maintain special security staffs to deal with shoplifting and employee theft.

The few studies that exist and the experts consulted by the Commission are nearly unanimous in asserting that employee theft accounts for a far greater percentage of inventory loss than does shoplifting, with some sources indicating that the percentage might run as high as 75 to 80 percent of the total.

Fraud covers any method of obtaining money or property by cheating or false pretenses, except through forgery or counterfeiting. It includes the intentional passing of bad checks and consumer fraud.

It has sometimes been asserted that this is the most common of all offenses. It seems clear that it is a very widespread offense and that the amounts involved are substantial.

To get some idea of the extent of fraud against individuals, the NORC national survey of households asked whether individuals had been cheated, given a bad check or swindled out of money or property in any way. The responses indicated a rate of over 250 cases per 100,000 as compared with less than 40 cases of arrest for fraud per 100,000 population reported to the police by both individuals and businesses. The average loss was $906, the average recovery $150 and the average net loss $756. Based on the survey, the total estimated national loss for individuals would be around $370 million.

The survey also asked whether individuals had been cheated by anyone misrepresenting what he was selling or charging a higher price than that he first quoted. The responses indicated a rate of about 120 cases per 100,000 population with an average loss of $99, and average recovery of $20 and an average net loss of $78. This would give a national total of about $18 million a year in consumer fraud—a figure that is almost certainly understated.

Special studies also provide a useful source of information regarding fraud. The National Better Business Bureau indicates that fraudulent and deceptive practices in the home repair and improvement field have been its most frequent complaint since 1953 and cause an estimated $500 million to $1 billion in losses to consumers annually.

Studies also indicate sizable losses to the public from fraudulent solicitations for charities (as much as $150 million in some years) and from frauds involving credit cards ($20 million annually). Phony land promotion schemes, defective TV tubes, fraudulent insurance claims, worthless life insurance, fraudulent bankruptcies, improper debt consolidations, home study rackets, and numerous other schemes all cause the public inestimable losses. Losses to businesses and individuals from check frauds and bad checks run into the millions.

Estimates are sometimes given of as much as half a billion dollars for the forgery offense but these appear to be based on limited surveys. The American Bankers Association estimates that total forgery losses on banking instruments probably do not exceed $60 million annually for all individuals and businesses. This averages out to a little less than $1 per year for each of the Nation's 60-million-plus checking accounts.

Banks bear about \$3 to \$4.5 million of this loss while the remainder falls upon other businesses and individuals. The Treasury Department estimates that in fiscal year 1965 public losses from forged U.S. Government checks were about \$4 million and about \$0.6 million from forged bonds.

PART II

THE STUDY OF THE OPERATION OF THE CRIMINAL JUSTICE SYSTEM

Chapter 5

An analysis of the criminal justice system

The criminal justice system of any given country is by no means an integrated system; indeed, in most places, it is likely to be unintegrated. The various procedural steps in the handling of cases that find their way into this system are the main connecting links that tie the system together.

The way stations

Without attempting to give a complete catalogue of the criminal justice system in the United States, it can be said that it consists, sequentially from *alpha* to *omega*, of the following way stations: (1) local, state, and federal police, including county sheriffs and township constables; (2) agencies of detention, including lockups, jails, and detention homes for delinquent adolescents, as well as measures such as bail and personal recognizance that serve as a substitute for detention while awaiting court processing; (3) offices of prosecutors in various courts; (4) lower courts that hold preliminary hearings in felony cases and adjudicate misdemeanors and violations of local ordinances; (5) criminal courts with jurisdiction over felonies, plus appellate and supreme courts, both state and federal; (6) probation procedure and service as an adjunct to court handling; (7) jails and workhouses that receive persons sentenced for ordinance violations and for misdemeanors; (8) correctional institutions, adult and juvenile, male and female, that receive commitments from courts, usually for the more serious felony cases—although, in the instance of juvenile offenders the commitments are likely to include cases that the courts feel need institutional confinement; (9) release from correctional institutions on work furlough arrangements (before expiration of sentence or parole), through expiration of sentence, by the action of a paroling authority in the instance of adult offenders in prisons or of a review committee in juvenile institutions; (10) parole agencies that make pre-parole investigations for parole boards and supervise cases released by the board on parole, as well as the so-called after-care service that handles juveniles released from correctional institutions; (11) use of newly developing "half-way" houses (small local residential centers, city-based and frequently operated by private agencies, for individuals on probation and parole who need a supportive residential anchor); (12) and lastly, the criminal justice system in the United States embraces the pardoning and commutation procedures—the use of the so-called clemency powers, which traditionally go with the offices of governor and President.

Behind the criminal justice system, with its many sequentially related way stations, is a body of administrative law that grants certain functions and powers to various parts of the system and these powers make allowances for extensions and changes. In many instances, it is hard to find the specific law behind a particular operation or procedure falling within the criminal justice system. Such an operation or procedure has come about by extension of the right of the state, county, municipality, township, and federal governments to establish measures of control.

The role of criminal laws

The input of the law enforcement and court processing way stations of the criminal justice system, apart from the decisions of complainants to complain and of police officers and court officials to take action, is controlled preliminarily by the definitions of criminal behavior as given in the criminal laws of the various states and of the federal government, plus local ordinances. Certain special legal provisions have been developed for the determination of juvenile delinquency, including age limits (under eighteen or sixteen years of age), plus certain clauses that apply specifically to juveniles such as waywardness offenses that are additions to violations of various sections of the criminal code.

The criminal laws in the United States have been amassed in the so-called penal codes of the state and federal governments, plus accumulated ordinances of cities and townships, so that any particular offense represents a violation of some specific section of the (published) revised code. As revisions are made and new criminal laws are passed, they become part of the criminal code. There is no doubt that the criminal codes in the United States are accumulative. Crimes are seldom deleted from a code, in spite of the fact that some of the definitions apply to conditions that no longer exist.

After several years of study, the American Law Institute published a report intended to act as a base line for the modernization of the criminal code and its administration in America. The content of the report may be gleaned from the following modified index of the various sections. One should notice particularly the listing under definitions of specific crimes.

The Proposed Model Penal Code[1]

Coverage:

General principles of liability
General principles of justification
Responsibility
Inchoate crimes (attempt, solicitation, incapacity, possessing weapons, etc.)
Authorized disposition of offenders (degrees of felonies, fines, young adult offenders, imprisonment, release on parole, etc.)
Authority of court in sentencing (criteria of court for using probation, imposing fines, extended term of imprisonment, consecutive or concurrent terms in multiple sentences, commitment for observation, remand for psychiatric examination, credit time of detention prior to sentence for the same crime).
Definitions of specific crimes (a. Offenses against the existence or stability of the state. b. Offenses involving danger to the persons: criminal homicide, assault, reckless endangering, threats, kidnapping and criminal coercion, sexual offenses).
Definitions of specific crimes

- a. Offenses against existence or stability of the state
- b. Offenses involving danger to the person
    - criminal homicide
    - murder
    - manslaughter
    - negligent homicide
    - causing or aiding suicide
    - sentence of death for murder
- c. Assault, reckless endangering, threats
- d. Kidnapping and related offenses, coercion
- e. Sexual offenses
    - rape and related offenses
    - deviate sexual intercourse by force or imposition
    - corruption of minors and seduction
    - sexual assault
    - indecent exposure

[1]The American Law Institute, *Model Penal Code* (proposed official draft, submitted by the Council to the Members for Discussion at the Thirty-ninth Annual Meeting on May 23, 24, 25, and 26, 1962, May 4, 1962, the Executive Office, The American Law Institute, 133 S. 36th St. Philadelphia, Pa.), pp. 123–241.

f. Offenses against property
    - arson, criminal mischief and other property destruction
    - burglary and other criminal intrusion
    - robbery
    - theft and related offenses
    - forgery and fraudulent practices

g. Offenses against the family

h. Offenses against public administration
    - bribery and corrupt influence
    - perjury and other falsification in official matters
    - obstructing Governmental operations, escapes
    - abuse of office

i. Offenses against public order and decency
    - riot, disorderly conduct, and related offenses
    - public indecency

j. Additional articles (such as narcotics, alcoholic beverages, gambling, and offenses against tax and trade laws).

Treatment and correction

a. Suspension of sentence, probation
b. Fines
c. Short-term imprisonment
d. Long-term imprisonment
e. Release on parole
f. Loss and restoration of rights incident to conviction or imprisonment

Organization of correction

a. Department of correction
b. Board of Parole
c. Administration of Institutions
d. Division of Parole
e. Alternative: Division of Probation and Parole
f. Division of Probation.

Besides the problem of being outdated in much of its coverage, the criminal law in the United States, as well as in other countries, presents many operational inconsistencies, among them the differential acceptance of laws by individuals and groups and the variant law-abidingness of different persons and various segments of society.

Differential acceptance emerges primarily from the scheme of social values (and/or lack of values) that individuals and groups have developed. However, it is also true that definitions of criminal behavior are in themselves a reflection of the value orientation of people. In modern times, the additions to the criminal code (new laws, covering new conditions) are likely to reflect the values and attitudes of the power elite in any particular state or country.

Nevertheless, the entrance into the criminal justice system is based upon a willingness to take action on violations and violators and bring both of them to the front door of the system.

Shortcomings of the American criminal justice system

The input and output of the criminal justice system are controlled by the manner in which the various parts operate, but the decisions of the staff or personnel who constitute the alpha-to-omega way stations in the system are of primary importance. The decisions to hold or not to hold, to send forward or not, to divert, to commit, to release, etc., are made by the personnel at the various steps in the total process. How far a case goes into the system and at what point it is released from the system are largely matters of decision. Only in a minority of instances is the processing within or through the system of a particular case determined by the type of behavior and/or the type of offender.

In addition to the human factor of erring or making poor judgments, the decisions on how to handle cases are, to a large extent, determined by the quality of the personnel who are assigned to the various steps in the criminal justice system. The decisions as well as the quality of the decisionmakers are in large measure influenced by the many accumulated problems of the system and its various parts. Appendix 5-A reviews some of the problems that the President's Commission on Law Enforcement and the Administration of Justice spotted in its *Task Force Report: The Police*. Appendix 5-B covers some of the problems that this commission called attention to in its *Task Force Report: The Courts*. Appendix 5-C reveals the problems that the President's Commission uncovered in its *Task Force Report: Corrections*.

The major problems that impede more effective functioning of the various parts of the criminal justice system by influencing the decisions of personnel to handle cases in a certain way as well as determining the quality of the handling, may be listed as follows:

1. Heavy load of cases at all way stations in the system.
2. Deficiences in personnel, both in number and quality.
3. Difficulties in attracting good personnel.
4. Mass handling of cases at all levels of the system.
5. Lack of proper information on individual cases to make appropriate decisions.
6. Division of authority and administrative fragmentation.
7. Obstacles to consolidation and coordination of different parts of the system.
8. Lack of standards at all points in the handling of offenders.

9. Great disparity in the way offenders are handled by the same way stations in the system.
10. Discrimination in the operation of various parts of the system due to the race and/or low economic status of offenders.

Attitude of the public

Even in democratic countries such as the United States there seems to be a general resignation to the prevailing functions and functioning of the various way stations in the criminal justice system. In recent years some dramatic, although possibly unfortunate, challenges of two of the way stations, the police and the courts, have been publicized through the mass media, as for example the trial of the famous "Chicago Seven" for confronting the police and the public at the time of the Democratic convention in Chicago, August 1968.[2]

Actually, the legal profession and sociologists and political scientists have given little attention to the way the public views the operation of the criminal justice system. Some expressions of expert opinion are registered in special commissions and hearings of the federal and state governments. Some get registered in news coverage and editorial comment. However, an interest appears to be growing in making soundings of how different segments of the public view the operation of the criminal justice system.

Appendix 5-D presents a schedule prepared by the Criminal Law Education and Research Center of the School of Law, New York University, the director of which is Dr. Gerhard O. W. Mueller. It is to be administered to several samples of respondents in different countries, so as to obtain a comparative perspective of how various segments of the public view police tactics in different types of violations.

Appendix 5-E presents a schedule to discover, by mail or house-to-house survey methods, how tolerant or intolerant white and black adults of the lower and middle classes are toward various juvenile violations, and how tolerant or intolerant they are toward the way juvenile delinquency is handled.

The results of the latter survey have been tabulated. In general, the lower-class adult respondents showed more intolerance of delinquency in youth than middle-class adult respondents; black more than white. The prevailing attitude of all the respondents was toward an intolerance of the

[2] *The Tales of Hoffman from the Trial of the Chicago 7*, a Documentary of Courtroom Confrontations from the Most Incredible Trial in American History, edited from the official transcript by Mark L. Levine, George C. McNamee, and Daniel Greenberg (New York: Bantam Books Inc., 1970).

way delinquents were handled after being caught and of the measures now prevalent for control and prevention of juvenile delinquency. See Appendix 5-E for a summary of the major findings generated in Columbus, Ohio, by Frederick L. Faust.

Appendix 5-A

EXCERPTS FROM TASK FORCE REPORT: THE POLICE

In summary, the Commission has found:

Many departments lack qualified leadership. Police chiefs and personnel in middle management ranks should be required to have sufficient education and training to enable them to administer the complex affairs of a police force, and should receive salaries sufficient to attract and retain top administrators.

Many departments are not organized in accordance with well-established principles of modern business management. They should be reorganized in accordance with such of those principles as best apply to the police, and those principles themselves should be periodically reexamined in the light of the changing nature of the police role.

Many departments resist change, fail to determine shortcomings of existing practice and procedures through research and analysis, and are reluctant to experiment with alternative methods of solving problems. The police service must encourage, indeed put a premium on, innovation, research and analysis, self-criticism and experimentation.

Many departments lack trained personnel in such fields as research and planning, law, business administration and computer analysis. Specialist units, staffed by sufficient personnel trained in a variety of disciplines, should be utilized to plan and project programs, evaluate and streamline procedures, improve management and administration, engage in special operations and establish methods for maximizing the use of personnel. Inhouse legal advice must be made available to medium-sized and large police forces on a full-time basis.

Many departments fail to deploy and utilize personnel efficiently. Police administrators should study such matters as (a) the basis for deploying uniformed personnel; (b) the use of one- or two-man motor patrol; (c) whether or not, and for what purposes, men should be assigned to foot patrol, whether men so assigned should serve alone or in pairs; (d) the feasibility of "team policing"; (e) the extent to which civilians can be used

President's Commission on Law Enforcement and the Administration of Justice, *Task Force Report: The Police* (Washington, D.C.: U.S. Government Printing Office, 1967), pp. 44, 46, 51-52, 57, 63, 71-72, 109, 125-126, 133-134, 144-145, 208-209, 216.

in staff and clerical work; and (f) the extent to which such police activities as jailing, communications, records, and laboratories can be "pooled" with other departments or assumed by other governmental units.

Many departments have not adequately applied technological advances that would be beneficial to law enforcement. Regional information storage and retrieval systems, communications and command-control systems, and radio-frequency-channel sharing concepts must be adapted to the police service.

Finally, States, through their commissions on police standards or other appropriate agencies, should provide financial and technical assistance to departments to conduct surveys and make recommendations to improve police organization, management, and operations. [p. 44].

There is little justification for American police forces not to be well organized. Available for the asking since the turn of the century has been a large and authoritative general body of guidance in public administration. And for some 30 years there have been adaptations of this to police management prepared by such knowledgeable police authorities as O. W. Wilson and V. A. Leonard, and the International City Managers' Association.

The crux of the problem seems to be that relatively few police forces have taken advantage of this valuable compilation of organization and management principles. This is the more regrettable in view of successes achieved by the departments that have utilized them.

Almost all highly regarded police practitioners, public officials, management consultants and university faculty members agree that an essential need in police organization and management is for all police departments, preferably with the assistance of recognized consultants, to examine their internal organizations in order to determine whether:

The force's work is apportioned among the various individuals and units according to a logical plan.

Lines of authority and responsibility arc made as definite and direct as possible.

The number of subordinates who can be effectively supervised by one officer is not exceeded.

There is "unity of command" throughout the organization.

Responsibility, once placed, is accompanied by commensurate authority, and that once delegated, the user is held to account for the use he makes of it.

The efforts of the organizational units and of the component members are coordinated so that all will be directed harmoniously toward the accomplishment of the police purpose. The components thus coordinated will enable the organization to function as a well-integrated unit. [p. 46]

Many American police forces do not utilize their available field personnel effectively. The most significant weakness appears to be the failure of departments to distribute patrol officers in accordance with the actual need for their presence. Other weaknesses, present to varying degrees in various forces, include too great reliance on foot patrol without providing officers with either modern communications or mobility; the extensive use of two-man motor patrol; detectives deployed in pairs; loose and insufficient patrol and detective supervision, and a lack of unity at the field level among investigators; outmoded report preparation systems; and the assignment of too many diverse tasks to police field officers. These weaknesses are outward signs of the failure of many police departments to develop field assignments on the basis of systematic evaluation of street needs. [p. 51]

At least seven steps must be taken to assure that police departments derive maximum utilization from field personnel:

Distributing available field officers according to need for their services.

Improving supervision of the field force.

Improving coordination of effort among field personnel.

Improving patrol techniques by critically analyzing the need for foot patrol and two-man motor patrols. Unless there is found extraordinary personnel hazards of more than an occasional nature, uniformed personnel should be deployed singly.

Deploying investigators singly unless there is an unusual series of cases which demands that two or more men be assigned jointly.

Modernizing report preparation and duplicating techniques.

Relieving police offiers of certain routine menial tasks. [p. 52]

Only token progress has been made in introducing technology into the police world. Some police departments, mainly the largest ones, have taken solid steps alone or in collaboration with nearby forces toward applying advances in science and technology to law enforcement. They have done so in spite of the costliness of equipment. Laudably, those large forces that have installed information storage and retrieval and communications systems have invited smaller forces to draw on the larger departments' facilities once the systems become operative.

The technical development potentially most profoundly affecting criminal justice operations is the advent of computer-based information systems. Some pioneering installations have been or in the immediate future will be established at the city, county, State, and National levels.

A greatly expanded development of computer-based information systems is one concrete step that would make a dramatic impact on the police service. Such systems can aid the police in the following functions:

Police patrol—Enabling a police officer to check the identification of people and property against a central "wanted" file in a few minutes.

Crime investigation—Providing a police officer or investigative agent with supporting information files such as crime patterns, *modus operandi*, criminal associates and personal appearance and, hopefully in the future, matching latent fingerprints from a crime scene against a central fingerprint file. The latter process, when it is developed, would constitute a major breakthrough in the war on crime.

Manpower deployment—Altering police deployment in response to changing patterns of crime on an hourly or daily basis.

Federal, State, and local budgeting—Collecting uniform statistics on agency operations and workloads, providing a basis for estimating personnel needs and for optimum allocation of men and dollars. [p. 57]

A necessary response, now more than ever before, is police departments and policemen that are better trained in the law and more sensitive to current judicial pronouncements. Such sensitivity will mean that the enormous power and responsibility entrusted to the police will be exercised more discriminately and effectively. Cases will be more expertly screened, and those cases which ultimately go forward will have a sounder evidentiary foundation.

A major instrument for insuring this increased effectiveness is the introduction of lawyers into the law enforcement process, particularly in the areas of planning and investigation. Even the best policeman and the best police administrator will, at times, need the advice of a lawyer who is knowledgeable in administrative and criminal law. In fact, the better the officer and the department, the more sensitive they will be to the complexity of the law, and the more likely to test their judgments against those of the legal advisor. [p. 63]

The increased pooling of resources among police jurisdictions is essential to the provision of effective records, communications, and laboratory services. Certain records must be maintained, and certain records services provided, on an areawide basis.

Communications systems must be improved through interjurisdictional contractual arrangements, coordination among radio systems, and through an increased role for the State as a coordinating agency.

Crime laboratory services must be available to every police department. With proper training, the routine gathering of evidence can be performed on the local level, but expensive analytical services must be provided by areas capable of supporting them, preferably by the State. Often the resources of poorly operated laboratory facilities in close proximity can be combined to establish one good facility.

One auxiliary service, detention, is not concerned with the fulfillment of basic police responsibilities and should be handled by a correctional agency whenever possible. If it is necessary for the police in some States to continue to provide detention services, consideration should be given to coordination and consolidation among police departments.

Comprehensive reorganization under a metropolitan-type government offers the best possibilities for fully unifying police services on an areawide basis, but such reorganization is difficult to accomplish.

The provision of police service through use of subordinate service taxing districts offers a viable means of achieving consolidation within the existing framework of local government, especially through a county policing agency operating under a county charter.

At present, consolidation is perhaps most easily achieved through the use of intergovernmental agreements or contracts. The prime advantages are that permissive legislation is already available, and that consolidation can be accomplished without appreciably disturbing existing governmental structures. [pp. 71–72]

Obstacles to the coordination or consolidation of the police services of different jurisdictions are similar to the barriers faced in restructuring and relocating other functions of local government. They tend to be among the most formidable for the police, principally because police service is generally among the most local of governmental services and because even the smallest local governmental jurisdictions like to believe that they can provide at least minimal needed police service. Often, political and social pressures linked to the desire for local self-government, rather than legal restrictions, offer the most significant barriers to the coordination and consolidation of police services. But it is important for all jurisdictions to be aware of any legal obstacles to coordination or consolidation which may exist. [p. 109]

It has often been stated that policing a community is personal service of the highest order, requiring sterling qualities in the individual who performs it. The Commission's evaluation of police work confirms this observation. Few professions are so peculiarly charged with individual responsibility. Officers are compelled to make instantaneous decisions—often without clearcut guidance from a legislature, the judiciary, or from departmental policy—and mistakes on judgment could cause irreparable harm to citizens, or even to the community.

Complexities inherent in the policing function dictate that officers possess a high degree of intelligence, education, tact, sound judgment, physical courage, emotional stability, impartiality, and honesty. While innumerable commissions and expert observers of the police have long recognized and reported this need, communities have not yet demanded that officers possess these qualities, and personnel standards for the police service remain low.

The failure to establish high professional standards for the police service has been a costly one, both for the police and for society. Existing selection requirements and procedures in the majority of departments, do not screen out the unfit. Hence, it is not surprising that far too many of those charged with protecting life and property and rationally enforcing our laws are not respected by their fellow officers and are incompetent, corrupt, or abusive. One incompetent officer can trigger a riot, permanently damage the reputation of a citizen, or alienate a community against a police department. It is essential, therefore, that the requirements to serve in law enforcement reflect the awesome responsibility facing the personnel that is selected. [pp. 125–126]

The Nation's police departments are encountering serious difficulty in maintaining their forces at authorized strength. A survey conducted by the National League of Cities in 1966 disclosed that over 65 percent of the departments surveyed were understaffed; that these departments were 5,840 officers, or 5 percent below authorized strength; and were 11,864 officers, or 10 percent below preferred strength. In 1965, for example, Baltimore was 229 officers below strength; Cleveland, 512; Pittsburgh, 80; Kansas City, 215; and Memphis, 78.

Since, on the average, police departments are currently 5 percent below authorized strength, since the authorized strength of police departments has increased at the rate of approximately 3 percent each year, and since an average of 5.4 percent of existing personnel leave their departments each year (due to resignation, dismissal, retirement, or death) 50,000 new police officers will be needed in 1967 alone. [p. 133]

Although police departments are encountering difficulty in hiring new officers, this is not due to a dearth of applicants, but to a lack of qualified applicants. In 1961, only 22.3 percent of the applicants for positions in 368 police departments were accepted. The applicant success rate in many departments is far lower. For example, in 1965, only 2.8 percent of the candidates for the Los Angeles Police Department were eventually accepted into the force. In 1966, only 29 of 1,033 applicants were hired by the Dallas Police Department.

There is a critical need, therefore, for police departments to attract more acceptable applicants to careers in law enforcement. This is particularly true in light of the recommendation that educational standards be elevated and that candidates be more carefully screened to insure acceptable emotional stability. [p. 134]

The need for strengthening police relationships with the communities they serve is critical today in the Nation's large cities and in many small cities and towns as well. The Negro, Puerto Rican, Mexican-American, and other minority groups are taking action to acquire rights and services which have been historically denied them. As the most visible representative of the society from which these groups are demanding fair treatment and equal opportunity, law enforcement agencies are faced with unprecedented situations on the street which require that they develop policies and practices governing their actions when dealing with minority groups and other citizens.

Even if fairer treatment of minority groups were the sole consideration, police departments would have an obligation to attempt to achieve and maintain good police-community relations. In fact, however, much more is at stake. Police-community relationships have a direct bearing on the character of life in our cities, and on the community's ability to maintain stability and to solve its problems. At the same time, the police department's capacity to deal with crime depends to a large extent upon its relationship with the citizenry. Indeed, no lasting improvement in law enforcement is likely in this country unless police-community relations are substantially improved.

Poor police-community relations adversely affect the ability of the police to prevent crime and apprehend criminals. People hostile to the police are not so likely to report violations of law, even when they are the victims. They are even less likely to report suspicious persons or incidents, to testify as witnesses voluntarily, or to come forward and provide information. For example, a study in St. Louis found that 43 percent of Negroes and 36 percent of whites believed that "most of the city residents seem to be afraid to contact their police." Yet citizen assistance is crucial to law enforcement agencies if the police are to solve an appreciable portion of the crimes that are committed:

> To most Negroes, policemen constitute an outgroup whose members are antagonistic toward them. Consequently, they will do nothing to help the police * * * They are afraid they will be treated as roughly as the criminal.

Public hostility can and does influence police field operations. For example, it may make officers reluctant to act; it may also induce the use of unnecessary force, verbal abuse, or other improper practices. The danger under which the policeman must work may make him "less judicious, indeed less discreet, in the exercise of his authority." When unfriendly crowds begin to gather, officers will necessarily have to call for reinforcements and use greater force to secure the offender and control the onlookers. Even if not excessive, such force will often lead to increased police-public tensions. On the other hand, "the cooperation of the public * * * diminishes, proportionately, the necessity of the use of physical force and compulsion for achieving police objectives." Hostility by racial minorities or others may also provoke police officers and therefore increase the likelihood that they will discriminate in exercising their discretion. Consequently, poor police-community relations tend to perpetuate themselves. [pp. 144-145]

The violations in which police are involved vary widely in character. The most common are improper political influence; acceptance of gratuities or bribes in exchange for nonenforcement of laws, particularly those relating to gambling, prostitution, and liquor offenses, which are often extensively interconnected with organized crime; the "fixing" of traffic tickets; minor thefts; and occasional burglaries. The Commission's work also revealed some instances of police officers in high-crime neighborhoods engaging in such practices as rolling drunks and shakedowns of money and merchandise in the very places where respect for law is so badly needed.

Government corruption in the United States has troubled historians, political reformers, and the general public since the middle of the 19th century. Metropolitan police forces—most of which developed during the late 1800's when government corruption was most prevalent—have often been deeply involved in corruption. The police are particularly susceptible to the forms of corruption that have attracted widest attention—those that involve tolerance or support of organized crime activities. But the police, as one of the largest and most strategic groups in metropolitan government, are also likely targets for political patronage, favoritism, and other kinds of influence that have pervaded local governments dominated by political machines. Against both forms of corruption, responsible police leaders have fought a continuing battle—one that appears to be steadily gaining. [pp. 208-209]

A State Commission on Police Standards can do much to improve local law enforcement. Without removing control of law enforcement from local agencies, a Commission can help to establish adequate personnel selection standards, to strengthen training procedures, to coordinate recruitment, and to improve the organization and operations of local departments.

Commissions on Police Standards and Training now exist in several States. Some of them are more effective than others; all could be significantly improved. In most States, the Commissions do not have the power either to establish mandatory standards or to give financial assistance to local departments. This lack of authority limits their impact. If properly constituted and empowered, however, State Commissions on Police Standards could play a significant role in the process of upgrading police effectiveness. [p. 216]

Appendix 5–B

EXCERPTS FROM TASK FORCE REPORT: THE COURTS

Most cases are disposed of outside the traditional trial process, either by a decision not to charge a suspect with a criminal offense or by a plea of guilty. In many communities between one-third and one-half of the cases begun by arrest are disposed of by some form of dismissal by police, prosecutor, or judge. When a decision is made to prosecute, it is estimated that in many courts as many as 90 percent of all convictions are obtained by guilty pleas.

Many overburdened courts have come to rely upon these informal procedures to deal with overpowering caseloads, and some cases that are dropped might have been prosecuted had sufficient resources been available. But it would be an over-simplification to tie the use of early disposition solely to the problem of volume, for some courts appear to be able to deal with their workloads without recourse to such procedures. Furthermore, the flexibility and informality of these discretionary procedures make them more readily adaptable to efforts to individualize the treatment of offenders than the relatively rigid procedures that now typify trial, conviction, and sentence. It would require radical restructuring of the trial to convert sentencing procedures into a comparable opportunity for the prosecution and the defense to discuss dispositional alternatives. Moreover, by placing less emphasis on the issue of culpability, discretionary procedures may enable the prosecutor to give greater attention to what disposition is most likely to fit the needs of those whose cases he considers. The pressures on the prosecutor to insist on a disposition that fits the popular conception of punishment are less before conviction, when the defendant has not officially and publicly been found guilty.

There are many cases in which trial would be clearly inappropriate. Often it becomes evident that the accused is innocent. Often while he appears to be technically guilty, criminal prosecution would serve no legitimate purpose.

President's Commission on Law Enforcement and the Administration of Justice, *Task Force Report: The Courts* (Washington, D.C.: U.S. Government Printing Office, 1967), pp. 4, 5, 7, 8, 9, 11, 12, 15, 16, 18, 23, 29, 30, 32, 34, 37–38, 41–42, 43, 50, 53, 55, 56, 59, 65, 67–68, 73, 75, 80, 82–83, 88, 90.

In addition, there are obvious practical advantages to disposing of large numbers of cases without trial. The results are relatively prompt and certain compared to trial dispositions and therefore represent a substantial economy of resources. Even when criminal prosecution is appropriate, charges may be dropped or reduced in exchange for a plea of guilty simply to conserve resources for more important cases. [p. 4]

In some cases invocation of the criminal process against marginal offenders seems to do more harm than good. Labeling a person a criminal may set in motion a course of events which will increase the probability of his becoming or remaining one. The attachment of criminal status itself may be so prejudicial and irreversible as to ruin the future of a person who previously had successfully made his way in the community, and it may foreclose legitimate opportunities for offenders already suffering from social, vocational, and educational disadvantages.

Among the types of cases in which thoughtful prosecutors commonly appear disinclined to seek criminal penalties are domestic disturbances; assaults and petty thefts in which victim and offender are in a family or social relationship; statutory rape when both boy and girl are young; first offense car thefts that involve teenagers taking a car for a short joyride; checks that are drawn upon insufficient funds; shoplifting by first offenders, particularly when restitution is made; and criminal acts that involve offenders suffering from emotional disorders short of legal insanity.

In addition, a large proportion of the cases in the criminal courts involve annoying or offensive behavior rather than dangerous crime. Almost half of all arrests are on charges of drunkenness, disorderly conduct, minor assault, petty theft, and vagrancy. Many such offenders are burdened by economic, physical, mental, and educational disadvantages. In many of these cases effective law enforcement does not require prosecution. [p. 5]

A prosecutor should have several kinds of information if he is to make sound charge decisions. He must evaluate the strength of his case. Police reports usually provide him with some facts about the offense, but often he needs more. Before a prosecutor decides whether to charge or dismiss in any case that is not elementary, he should review the case file to determine whether more evidence and witnesses are available than the police have uncovered. In addition, the prosecutor needs to know enough about the offender to determine whether he should be diverted from the criminal track. Greater involvement of court probation departments and the availability of probation officers for consultation with the prosecutor and defense counsel at this stage of the proceedings are clearly advisable. Often the prosecutor needs to know whether there are facilities in the community for treating such medical or behavioral problems as the offender may have and whether those facilities will accept him.

In cases in which there is an indication that intensive treatment or supervision is needed, the prosecutor and defense counsel should be able to obtain a thorough investigation of the accused's background and treatment needs. A special division might be created in the prosecutor's office or in the public defender's office to conduct such an investigation. In some places the parties might call upon the probation office for help; in others a representative from a community agency could be designated. Some communities might choose to create a new agency to coordinate community services for offenders, conduct background investigations, and prepare treatment programs for consideration by prosecutor and defense counsel. . . . What is essential is that the relevant information be gathered so that dispositional decisions can be made on a rational basis.

Defense counsel has an important role to play at this stage, and he should be involved wherever an intrusive disposition or significant penalty is likely. Counsel can assist in gathering information and formulating a treatment program; he can help persuade the prosecutor of the appropriateness of a noncriminal disposition.

It is unusual for either attorney to have sufficient information; it is even more unusual for them to share it. But the early accumulation and sharing of information might well lead to early agreements between the prosecution and the defense about how some cases should be disposed of, thus saving time and futile legal maneuvering. The prosecutor should have the benefit of defense counsel's views and suggestions, as well as an idea of how strong the case for the defense is. By the same token, defense counsel should be familiar with the prosecution's case and the prosecutor's views in order to advise his client whether to seek a noncriminal disposition, to plead guilty, or to insist on a trial.

A conflict often exists between the need for a frank exchange of information and defense counsel's obligation to act only in ways favorable to his client. Defense counsel may possess information adverse to his client, or the prosecutor may have erroneous information which defense counsel knows paints an unjustifiably favorable picture of his client. Obviously all exchanges of information must be explicitily authorized by the defendant, and appropriate provision should be made to ensure that a defendant's statements and information disclosed are not used against him in the event of a trial. But subtle and difficult questions of professional responsibility will remain. Experience may offer guides for some of the problems presented; other norms may be provided by efforts such as the American Bar Association's redefinition of the Canons of Professional Ethics or the consideration of the role of counsel by the ABA Special Project on Minimum Standards for Criminal Justice.

The Precharge Conference. A conference between the prosecutor and defense counsel before formal charges are filed would provide an opportunity for them to discuss the appropriateness of noncriminal disposition of the case.

Prosecutors should establish guidelines for convening such conferences, indicating those classes of cases in which conferences might be held as a matter of course, for example, when the offense involves conduct characteristic of a recognized disorder, such as alcoholism or mental disease; when the offense is a minor crime against property; or when the age of the defendant, his history of family and employment stability, or the absence of any prior criminal record indicate that he is a good risk. Discussions should of course be held when there are indications that the evidence of guilt is insufficient for trial or otherwise raises doubts in the prosecutor's mind whether prosecution of the case is warranted. The object of discussion in such cases would be whether the charges should be dismissed outright. The guidelines should also provide that in cases not specifically covered, conferences may be convened at the discretion of the prosecutor and defense counsel may submit appropriate information showing the desirability of a conference.

When there is a factual basis for the charge, the central concern at the precharge conference should turn to the question of what disposition is most appropriate for the offender and whether prosecution or noncriminal methods are the preferable way to attain that disposition. Among the factors that might be weighed in determining whether to adopt a noncriminal disposition are: (1) the seriousness of the crime and the effect upon the public sense of security and justice if the offender were to be treated without criminal conviction; (2) the place of the case in effective law enforcement policy, particularly for such offenses as tax evasion, white collar crimes, and other instances where deterrent factors may loom large; (3) whether the offender has medical, psychiatric, family, or vocational difficulties; (4) whether there are agencies in the community capable of dealing with his problems; (5) whether there is reason to believe that the offender will benefit from and cooperate with a treatment program; and (6) what the impact of criminal charges would be upon the witness, the offender, and his family. Even if the case is ultimately prosecuted, the conference will have served many useful purposes, including an increase in the discovery and consideration of the facts on both sides, a narrowing of the trial issues, and formulation of a sounder basis for negotiated guilty plea discussions.

Adoption of the proposed precharge conference will no doubt entail some added administrative burden for prosecutors, but that burden should not be exaggerated. In many communities, for example, much of the needed offender information may be gathered from existing sources. Moreover, as some cases which might have been sent forward for prosecution are diverted to noncriminal disposition and others are routed out earlier in the process, prosecution resources would be freed for concentration on serious offenders and disputed cases.

Noncriminal Alternatives. When the prosecutor decides that a case should not be prosecuted criminally, a simple dismissal will often be appropriate: Investigation may reveal that the accused is not guilty of the offense for which he was arrested, or that although he is guilty, the offense is minor and there is no reason to believe he will commit such an offense again. But there are many cases where some followup should be provided: The offender may be an alcoholic or a narcotics addict; he may be mentally ill; he may have been led to crime by his family situation or by his inability to get a job. If he is not helped, he may well return to crime. [pp. 7–8]

The question of guilt or innocence is not contested in the overwhelming majority of criminal cases. A recent estimate is that guilty pleas account for 90 percent of all convictions; and perhaps as high as 95 percent of misdemeanor convictions. But the Commission has found it difficult to calculate with any degree of certainty the percentage of cases disposed of by guilty plea, since reliable statistical information is limited.

A substantial percentage of guilty pleas are the product of negotiations between the prosecutor and defense counsel or the accused, although again precise data are unavailable. Commonly known as "plea bargaining," this is a process very much like the pretrial settlement of civil cases. It involves discussions looking toward an agreement under which the accused will enter a plea of guilty in exchange for a reduced charge or a favorable sentence recommendation by the prosecutor. Even when there have been no explicit negotiations, defendants relying on prevailing practices often act on the justifiable assumption that those who plead guilty will be sentenced more leniently.

Few practices in the system of criminal justice create a greater sense of unease and suspicion that the negotiated plea of guilty. [p. 9]

Other forms of plea bargaining may involve judge shopping. In places where there are wide sentencing disparities, a plea of guilty may be entered in exchange for the prosecutor's agreement that the defendant will appear before a particular judge for sentencing. [p. 11]

The negotiations should be freed from their present irregular status so that the participants can frankly acknowledge the negotiations and their agreement can be reviewed by the judge and made a matter of record. Upon the plea of guilty in open court the terms of the agreement should be fully stated on the record, and, at least in serious or complicated cases, reduced to writing. If there is a written memorandum, it should contain an agreed statement of the facts of the offense, the opening positions of the parties, the terms of the agreement, background information relevant to the correctional disposition, and an explanation of why the negotiated disposition is appropriate. This material should be probed by judicial questioning. Use of a memorandum is preferable to relying entirely upon judicial questioning, because it should encourage more thoughtful negotiations and a more complete consideration of the agreement by the judge. Regardless of which procedure is chosen, the judge's questions at the time of plea should be transcribed and filed. [p. 12]

The penal codes of most jurisdictions are the products of piecemeal construction, as successive legislatures have fixed punishment for new crimes and adjusted penalties for existing offenses through separate sentencing provisions for each offense. As a result the sentencing distinctions among offenses are in excess of those which could rationally be drawn on the basis of relative harmfulness of conduct or the probably dangerousness of the offenders.

Although each offense must be defined in a separate statutory provision, the number and variety of sentencing distinctions which result when legislatures prescribe a separate penalty for each offense are among "the main causes of the anarchy in sentencing that is so widely deplored." Experience indicates that offenses may be grouped into broader categories for purposes of delimiting the permissible sentences. This is the approach taken in the Model Penal Code, which groups all felonies into three categories of relative seriousness. The most serious grade of felony, felonies of the first degree, includes offenses such as murder and rape accompanied by serious bodily injury; second degree felonies include burglary at night, arson, and aggravated assault, and third degree felonies include theft in excess of $500, perjury, forgery of a check, and bribery. The Code provides a single range of prison sentence for all offenses in each grade of felony. For example, the prison term authorized for felonies of the second degree has a maximum of 10 years and a minimum to be set by the court of between 1 and 3 years. [p. 15]

Because of the need to deter potential offenders and to isolate dangerous persons from the community, it is necessary that long prison sentences be available for those who have committed the most serious offenses or for those who are likely to commit further crimes. Mandatory sentences, however, prevent the courts from basing their sentences on the relative importance of these factors in each case. Judges and prosecutors often regard punishment by long mandatory terms as unreasonably harsh, and they are faced with the dilemma of adhering to the statutory requirement or avoiding it to produce results that seem to be just in individual cases. [p. 16]

Two unfortunate characteristics of sentencing practices in many lower courts are the routine imposition of fines on the great majority of misdemeanants and petty offenders and the routine imprisonment of offenders who default in paying fines. These practices result in unequal punishment of offenders and in the needless imprisonment of many persons because of their financial condition.

The consequences of the failure to pay a fine are extremely severe in many States. The New York Court of Appeals only last year ruled unconstitutional a statute which permitted the court to imprison a defendant for one day for each dollar of a fine which he had not paid. However, other jurisdictions still retain comparably harsh sanctions for nonpayment.

It is unlikely that all of the discriminatory consequences of fines will ever be eliminated. There will continue to be many instances in which offenders are deserving of punishment but the judges' realistic alternatives are limited to fines or jail. The fact that our society has not devised suitable alternative punishments gives rise to a vexing dilemma in the use of fines. For so long as jail is the routine alternative to a fine, those unable to pay will be punished more severely than those of greater means. Putting all offenders in jail is a wholly unacceptable alternative, as is relieving those unable to pay a fine of all penalties. [p. 18]

Within certain limits a lack of uniformity in sentences is justifiable. Indeed the reason for giving judges discretion in sentencing is to permit variations based on relevant differences in offenders.

The problem of disparity arises from the imposition of unequal sentences for the same offense, or offenses of comparable seriousness, without any reasonable basis. The existence of unjustified disparity has been amply demonstrated by many studies.

Unjustified disparity adversely affects correctional administration. Prisoners compare their sentences, and a prisoner who is given cause to believe that he is the victim of a judge's prejudices often is a hostile inmate, resistant to correctional treatment as well as discipline. [p. 23]

No findings of this Commission are more disquieting than those relating to the condition of the lower criminal courts. . . . Burgeoning population and increasing urbanization have aggravated rather than ameliorated these problems. These courts still operate with the most meager facilities, with the least trained personnel, and with the most oppressive workload. Practices by judges, prosecutors, and defense counsel which would be condemned in the higher courts may still be found in these courts. [p. 29]

A general description of the lower criminal court system in the United States is complicated by the fact that there is no single system. Within each State courts and procedures vary from city to city and from rural area to urban area. In most States the lower courts are separate entities having different judges, court personnel, and procedures from other criminal courts, but in some places an integrated criminal court handles all phases of all criminal cases, with an administrative subdivision or branch for petty offenses. Generally the lower courts process felony cases up to the point of preliminary hearing and misdemeanor and petty offense cases through trial and ultimate disposition. But the categories of offenses classified as misdemeanors and felonies vary, and an offense which is a felony in one State may be a misdemeanor in another. [p. 30]

It is clear that the lower courts are generally manned by less competent personnel than the courts of general jurisdiction. There are judges, attorneys, and other officers in the lower courts who are as capable in every respect as their counterparts in more prestigious courts, but the lower courts regularly do not attract such persons.

In almost every city judges in courts of general jurisdiction are better paid, are more prominent members of the community, and are better qualified than their lower court counterparts. In some cities lower court judges are not required to be lawyers. The conduct of some judges reveals inaptitude and a lack of familiarity with rules of evidence or developments in case law. [p. 32]

Justice of the peace courts are the rural counterparts of the urban lower criminal courts. These courts developed in an era of slow transportation and communication to provide isolated small communities with a quick means of hearing minor criminal cases and exercising committing authority locally. But the conditions which gave rise to the development of justices' courts largely disappeared with the advent of modern means of travel and almost instantaneous communication. As a result, the lay-manned, fee-paid court is an anachronism.

Use of the fee system in justice courts has been condemned for years. Most authorities have agreed that it distorts the administration of justice. [p. 34]

Bail is a procedure for releasing arrested persons on financial or other condition to ensure their return for trial. Money bail is a prime example of a traditional practice in the criminal law that has not proven adequate to meet the needs of an evolving concept of criminal justice. . . . The system's major fault is exclusive reliance on the posting of money to ensure the defendant's return. Typically an arrested person is brought by the police before a committing magistrate or judge who fixes an amount of money as security for his appearance at trial. In some courts bail schedules set an amount for each offense, and if the defendant can post that amount, the judge seldom considers the case individually. Under either method if the defendant can post the required amount or can pay a bondsman to post it for him, he is released until trial. If he cannot, he remains in jail. If the defendant fails to appear for trial, the bond may be forfeited. [p. 37]

A central fault of the existing system is that it detains too many people, with serious consequences for defendants, the criminal process, and the community. The aim of reform, therefore, must be to reduce pretrial detention to the lowest level without allowing the indiscriminate release of persons who pose substantial risks of flight or of criminal conduct.

Another serious fault of the present bail system is that it fails to promote decisions founded on facts about the accused. Money bail is traditionally set on the basis of the alleged offense rather than on the background of the particular defendant, principally because little information about him is ordinarily available except his prior criminal record. As a result, prohibitively high bail may be set where there is in fact little risk of flight, while at the same time unreliable defendants are released with inadequate assurance that they will appear for trial. [p. 38]

Little attention has been given to procedures for gathering the facts needed for the many decisions which must be made earlier in the process, decisions as to whether to press criminal charges, whether to go to trial, and what the disposition should be if the case does not go to trial. There is a pressing need to develop new fact-finding procedures and to make better use of the ones that now exist in order to ensure that such important decisions are based on fuller exploration of the facts of the case. [pp. 41–42]

In most jurisdictions in the United States the preliminary hearing is not a useful factfinding device. The prosecution rarely introduces more evidence than the minimum required to show probable cause and generally may meet its burden with hearsay testimony. In many places testimony at the hearing is not recorded or otherwise perpetuated. [p. 43]

Justice is most seriously threatened when prejudice distorts its capacity to operate fairly and equally, whether the prejudice that blinds judgment operates purposefully, as in discrimination in jury selection or sentencing based on racial factors, or unintentionally, through substantially disadvantaging the poor. . . . There is evidence that the same segregated system often results in enforcement of a dual standard of justice: Charges and sentences habitually are more severe in cases where Negro defendants are asserted to have committed crimes against the person of white victims than in other cases involving identical crimes.

It is also evident that the treatment of the poor is often disproportionately harsh in the courts, principally because of the litigation disadvantages which they suffer. They lack resources demanded by an adversary procedure, and there is a relatively restricted range of dispositional possibilities available for poor defendants. These problems mirror the disadvantages to which the poor are subject in almost every aspect of social and economic life. Clearly a major effort must be made to make poverty irrelevant as possible in criminal justice as well as other vital areas. [p. 50]

The accused's right to effective assistance of counsel is not satisfied by the appointment of counsel at or shortly before trial. The Supreme Court has held that counsel must be provided at the preliminary examination or arraignment where these are critical stages in the criminal process. Under the Court's recent decision in Miranda v. Arizona, statements obtained as a result of police interrogation of a suspect in custody are inadmissible at trial unless counsel has been made available to him or he has waived his right to counsel.

The lawyer can help his client meet some of the problems directly associated with a pending criminal charge. An attorney can present to the court facts about the accused's family status, employment history, and ties in the community to prove that he should be free pending trial. Counsel often can persuade an employer, landlord, creditors, or others not to act against his client as a result of his arrest. When there is a detainer issued by another jurisdiction, counsel sometimes can arrange for disposition of these charges. Because of the shortage of defense counsel, it would be unrealistic to suggest that an appointed counsel or a defender must himself perform all of these functions, particularly those which call for investigation. Services which do not require the particular expertise of a lawyer can be performed by a non-professional staff, but it is essential that counsel be appointed early in the process so that this assistance can be made available when it is most needed. [p. 53]

Any proposal for expanding the availability of defense counsel invites three fundamental questions: How many lawyers will be required; how much will their services cost; and is the supply of lawyers adequate to meet the increased demand for legal services? [p. 55]

According to Silverstein's estimate approximately 60 percent of all felony defendants and between one-quarter and one-half of all misdemeanor defendants are unable to contribute anything to the cost of their defense, and it is reasonable to assume that at least 50 percent of the defendants in appeals and postconviction proceedings need appointed counsel. [p. 56]

Two basic methods of providing legal services to poor defendants are employed in the United States. The most prevalent, the assigned counsel system, is the only method used in about 2,750 of the 3,100 counties in the country, including many of our largest cities. Under an assigned counsel system lawyers in private practice are appointed on a case-by-case basis by the court to represent defendants who cannot afford to hire an attorney.

Under a defender system salaried lawyers devote all or a substantial part of their time to representing defendants who are unable to retain counsel. Defender systems are presently in operation in about 250 counties having approximately one-third of all felony defendants in the country. Although the defenders represent a majority of indigent defendants in these counties, their efforts are generally supplemented by appointment of individual practitioners. Some defender offices receive all of their financial support from charitable foundations or the local bar association, from individual lawyers, and from other private sources. (p. 59]

The quality of justice depends in large measure on the quality of judges. Good judges are essential for settling all types of legal controversies, whether the issue involves the custody of a child, the interpretation of a private business agreement or a will, or the power of the government to enforce a regulatory statute.

The trial judge is at the center of the criminal process, and he exerts a powerful influence on the stages of the process which precede and follow his formal participation. Many decisions of police, prosecutors, and defense counsel are determined by the trial judge's rulings, by his sentencing practices, and even by the speed with which he disposes of cases. His decisions on sentencing and probation revocation affect the policies and procedures of correctional agencies. And to a great degree the public's impression of justice is shaped by the trial judge's demeanor and the dignity he imparts to the proceedings in his courtroom. [p. 65]

In sum, merit selection plans provide a more rational procedure for selecting judges than popular election alone. The essential elements of merit selection are that the qualifications of prospective judges are screened, and the field is narrowed to a panel of a few nominees whose legal training, character, and temperament mark them as potentially superior judges. Whether the ultimate method of selecting a nominee from this panel is appointment or election by the voters, a good judge is likely to be selected. [pp. 67–68]

The district or county attorney in most States is a locally elected official. In larger communities the prosecutor has a staff of assistants, as many as 216 in Los Angeles County or 153 in Chicago. But the great majority of the county's more than 2,700 prosecutors serve in small offices with at most one or two assistants, and frequently the prosecutor and his assistants are part-time officials. Their official duties are to prosecute all criminal cases and in most jurisdictions to represent the local government in civil cases, but when not engaged on a case they are free to practice law privately. This pattern of outside practice is common in the rural counties and smaller cities, although it may be found in our largest cities.

The high political orientation of the prosecutor's office contributes to the problem of low pay and part-time service. In almost all States local prosecuting attorneys are chosen by the voters of the community. Only four States and the Federal system provide for the appointment of prosecutors, and even in these jurisdictions partisan considerations appear to play a vital part in their selection. While in a few communities highly competent men have made a career in the office, in most places the incumbent moves on after one or two terms. [p. 73]

Although each State has a single code of criminal laws, the State prosecutorial function, like the police and the courts, is fragmented among a number of independent agencies. The States are geographically divided into districts or counties, each of which has a prosecutor's office headed by an elected or appointed official. In many urban areas one prosecutor, typically the district attorney, is responsible for felony cases while another independent officer, perhaps the corporation counsel or city attorney, deals with less serious offenses and sometimes the early stages of felony cases. [p. 75]

There is widespread consciousness of the archaic and inefficient methods used in many courts to process, schedule, and dispose of their business. Judges, attorneys, professional organizations have pointed out ways in which the courts are poorly structured and organized, instances in which their administrative and business methods are inadequate, and their common failure to treat jurors and witnesses decently.

Many authorities have also expressed concern that the criminal law system is not as fair or effective as it should be because it fails to work expeditiously. In those courts in which high volume interferes with the orderly movement of cases and creates tremendous pressure to dispose of business, one may observe concomitant delay in the disposition of cases and hasty consideration when these cases come to be heard. Undue delay is as inconsistent with the goals of the system as a hasty process in which decisions are made without opportunity for deliberation.

The courts' inability to handle their volume of cases has many deleterious effects. Most criminal cases are disposed of by dismissal or by plea of guilty. Dismissals often result from the prosecutor's desire to keep his caseload down to a more manageable size and from the loss of evidence due to the reluctance of witnesses to appear. Defendants often manipulate the system to obtain sentencing concessions in return for guilty pleas. Conversely defendants unable to secure pretrial release on bail are under heavy pressure to plead guilty and begin serving their terms promptly.

As the backlog of cases mounts, delay increases and the pressure to dispose of cases becomes overwhelming. Clearing the dockets comes to be an end in and of itself, and haste rather than intelligent deliberation is the norm of practice. Disposition by dismissal or by guilty plea is often characterized by hasty decision with little attention given to penal and correctional considerations. [p. 80]

Proposals for the unification and simplification of court structures have long been part of programs for court reform. The Model State Judicial Article, which has been endorsed by the American Bar Association embodies the most recent statement of these principles. . . . Other model constitutional provisions have been drafted by the National Municipal League and the American Judicature Society.

Integration of all courts in a State into a single State court system which consolidates courts at the same level is a recurring element of reform. The unseemly and potentially venal institution of the profit-making court, which is seen primarily as a source of local revenue, is eliminated, and all fines and fees are paid to the State treasury. At the same time local inability to finance adequate courts and related facilities is alleviated. [pp. 82-83]

Courts have not developed a system for monitoring their workload to ensure that necessary priorities are established and that routine cases are not unduly delayed. Traditionally court management and scheduling have centered around three types of documents. The first is the case file, in which original documents, warrants, indictments, motions, judgments, and the like are maintained as the permanent and official historical record of the case. The second, the docket, typically a looseleaf volume made up of separate sheets for each case, is an operating document consisting of entries for each important event in a case from beginning to end. The third, which is generally used by the court to determine its future operations, is the calendar, a list of all cases pending in court or those at a particular stage of the process, for example, those awaiting trial. [p. 88]

Citizens who serve as witnesses and jurors are vital to the handling of a criminal case. For many citizens it is almost entirely through this service that their impressions of the system are formed.

In recent years there has been growing concern that the average citizen identifies himself less and less with the criminal process and its officials. In particular, citizens have manifested reluctance to come forward with information, to participate as witnesses in judicial proceedings, and to serve as jurors. The causes of these negative attitudes are many and complex, but some aspects of the problem may be traced directly to the treatment accorded witnesses and jurors. [p. 90]

Appendix 5–C

EXCERPTS FROM TASK FORCE REPORT: CORRECTIONS

There are today about 400 institutions for adult felons in this country, ranging from some of the oldest and largest prisons in the world to forestry camps for 30 or 40 trusted inmates. Some are grossly understaffed and underequipped—conspicuous products of public indifference. Overcrowding and idleness are the salient features of some, brutality and corruption of a few others. Far too few are well organized and adequately funded. Juvenile institutions tend to be better, but also vary greatly. The local jails and workhouses that handle most misdemeanants are generally the most inadequate in every way.

Although most inmates of American correctional institutions come from metropolitan areas, the institutions themselves often are located away from urban areas and even primary transportation routes. The original reasons for such locations were diverse and, to a large extent, now outdated: interest in banishing dangerous persons to a remote locale; belief that a rural setting is salutary for slum-reared delinquents; the desire of rural legislators to create public employment among their constituents. Remoteness interferes with efforts to reintegrate inmates into their communities and makes it hard to recruit correctional staff, particularly professionals. [p. 4]

Corrections is fragmented administratively, with the Federal Government, all 50 States, the District of Columbia, Puerto Rico, most of the country's 3,047 counties, and all except the smallest cities having one or more correctional facilities, if only a primitive jail in which to lock up overnight those who are "drunk and disorderly." Typically, each level of government acts independently of all the others. The Federal Government has no control over State corrections. The States usually have responsibility for prisons and parole programs, but probation is often a county or municipal function. Counties do not have jurisdiction over the jails operated by cities and towns. This situation is in sharp contrast to correctional systems in other urban and industrialized countries, where correctional activity usually is the responsibility of the central government.

President's Commission on Law Enforcement and the Administration of Justice, *Task Force Report: Corrections* (Washington, D.C.: U.S. Government Printing Office, 1967), pp. 4, 5, 6, 11, 14, 15, and 16.

Responsibility for the administration of corrections is divided not only among levels of government but also within single jurisdictions. There has been a strong historic tendency for juvenile and adult corrections to follow separate paths. The development of public support for rehabilitative programs occurred earlier for juveniles than for adults. Today, however, progressive programs for adults resemble those for juveniles, and the separation of adult and juvenile programs sometimes interferes with overall planning and with continuity of program for offenders. The ambiguity and awkwardness resulting from this division are nowhere more apparent than in the handling of older adolescent and young adult offenders, who often defy precise classification and are handled poorly by both the juvenile and the adult correctional system. [p. 5]

Over 121,000 people were employed in corrections on an average day in 1965, 15 percent in community programs, which handled 67 percent of all offenders, the other 85 percent in institutions, where 33 percent of all offenders were confined.

Functionally classified, 63,000, or 52 percent of all staff, were custodial employees —guards, supervisors, and house parents. Another 34,000 or 28 percent, were engaged in service or administrative functions. Thus, only 24,000 workers, or 20 percent, were primarily engaged in activities specifically designated as aimed at treatment. This figure includes all the probation and parole workers, as well as social workers, psychologists, and teachers.

Correctional agencies across the country face acute shortages of qualified manpower, especially in positions charged with responsibility for treatment and rehabilitation. Thousands of additional probation and parole officers are required now to achieve minimum standards for effective treatment and control. Many more thousands will be needed in the next decade. [p. 6]

Traditional prisons, jails, and juvenile institutions are highly impersonal and authoritarian. Mass handling, countless ways of humiliating the inmate in order to make him subservient to rules and orders, special rules of behavior designed to maintain social distance between keepers and inmates, frisking of inmates, regimented movement to work, eat, and play, drab prison clothing, and similar aspects of daily life—all tend to depersonalize the inmate and reinforce his belief that authority is to be opposed, not cooperated with. The phrase much heard in inmate circles—"do your own time"—is a slogan which expresses alienation and indifference to the interests of both staff and other inmates. Such an attitude is, of course, antithetical to successful reintegration. [p. 11]

Correctional decision-making is characteristically handicapped by several deficiencies. First, data essential to the making of sound decisions often are not available. In determining whether to grant parole, for example, decisions usually are based on scanty information collected at the time the offender was committed to the institution. Information on changes that have occurred during confinement is not usually available or is inadequate.

Second, information that is available may be irrelevant to the outcomes which determine whether the decision was sound. It is characteristic of any decision-making process that those involved often are not aware of the particular bits of information they employ in arriving at a judgment. Moreover, the information they use may, by empirical standards, be unrelated to the judgment being made. The question of relevance cannot be answered by argument but only by careful research. [p. 14]

There is a clear need for an improved capability in the information gathering and analysis process and continued experimental development to improve the predictive power of the information gathered. These needs imply increased manpower and the training requisite to the development of sophistication and skill in the investigative-diagnostic process.

Tiny county jails, for example, cannot begin to meet necessary standards or provide effective rehabilitative programs; neighboring jurisdictions need to group together to do this. Indeed the entire split in most jurisdictions between misdemeanant facilities (under local control, usually of law enforcement officials) and those for felons (usually handled by State correctional authorities) has operated generally to hinder advances in misdemeanant systems. To a lesser extent, the administrative separation of the juvenile and adult systems has created anomalies. At another level, specialized services for offender groups such as women, the mentally ill, the dangerous inmate, and long-term prisoners cannot in most States be provided as well as they could be in regional or even Federal facilities. [p. 15]

Changes are also needed in the internal organization of most correctional agencies. Their bureaucratic structure is typically hierarchical, with rigid chains of communication and command. Official directives tend to lose their rationale and justification as they filter down through the system. For every official directive there are likely to be many unofficial interpretations which occur in discussions outside of the official channels of communication. Many subordinate officials have to depend upon unofficial versions of policy in order to gain any sense of what is expected of them.

The most acute shortages in terms of numbers are among professional staff—probation and parole officers, teachers, psychologists, and psychiatrists—who carry on diagnosis, treatment, and research. Improvements in salary, working conditions, and educational opportunities will help to overcome these shortages. The much greater involvement of guards and house parents in treatment functions, discussed above, will also be valuable. Corrections has great potential for the use of volunteers and sub-professional aides, particularly as these people help bring offenders and staff into greater contact with the community.

In many areas, corrections remains in the hands of persons without adequate qualifications or training for their task. Administrators, even in some cases individual wardens or probation supervisors, are, as noted, often appointed largely on the basis of political considerations. Standards for appointment, and education and training programs to meet them, are badly needed.

At present, the meager training which is available is mostly of an inservice variety. There is need for advanced training in universities. Administrators, for example, need training in the fields of law, government, social sciences, and business administration. Specialists need advanced work in mathematics and statistics, social science research, computer sciences, sociology, and psychiatry and psychology. [p. 16]

Appendix 5–D

SCHEDULE FOR OPINION SURVEY OF POLICE TACTICS

[Note: This is an illustration of one of several kinds of situations or happenings which will be presented to the respondents, in order to procure their opinions and attitudes toward police tactics.]

A few minutes after a serious collision of two cars at the Washington Bridge exit of the Hudson River Drive, in which both occupants of a Volkswagen lost their lives, Police Officer Smith finds José Sanchez, a Puerto Rican grocery delivery boy, obviously intoxicated and lightly bleeding from the brow, sitting on the lawn in the immediate vicinity of the collision. Smith is convinced that José is the possible perpetrator.

	Under Presently Applicable Law May the Police Officer			Should the Police Officer be Permitted To			What is the Police Officer Really Going To Do		
	Yes	No	Don't Know	Yes	No	Don't Know	Yes	No	Don't Know
A. At the Scene of the Crime									
1. Stop the person concerned or possibly detain him.									

Prepared by the Criminal Law Education and Research Center, New York University Law School, Dr. Gerhard O. W. Mueller, Director. It is contemplated to administer 6 types of case situations, using the same questions and answer format, to samples of police officers, law students, housewives, undergraduate college students, laborers, and prisoners in Berlin, Rome, Tel Aviv, London, Montreal, and New York.

	Under Presently Applicable Law May the Police Officer			Should the Police Officer be Permitted To			What is the Police Officer Really Going To Do		
	Yes	No	Don't Know	Yes	No	Don't Know	Yes	No	Don't Know
2. Search his persons, belongings (car and briefcase)									
3. Ask him where he comes from and where he is going to and about his involvement									
4. Take him into the squad car, possibly pulling him in									
5. Put handcuffs on him									
6. Hit him with the night-stick if he: a. Resists.									
b. Gives unsolicited false answers									
B. At the Precinct House									
If the suspect does not admit his involvement									
1. To put him under physical pressure									
2. To work on him "psychologically" in order to make a statement									

	Under Presently Applicable Law May the Police Officer			Should the Police Officer be Permitted To			What is the Police Officer Really Going To Do		
	Yes	No	Don't Know	Yes	No	Don't Know	Yes	No	Don't Know
3. To trick him									
4. To hide a microphone in his detention cell									
5. To promise him immunity or help									
6. Not to give him an attorney									
7. To promise to prosecute him only for a minor offense									

C. General	Yes	No	Don't know
1. Do you believe that the police does a good job in the fight against crime in the following			
a. Surveillance and prevention of crime through presence and visibility			
b. Detection and arrest			
2. Should the police receive			
a. Higher salaries			
b. Better training			

Appendix 5–E

THE RESEARCH SCHEDULE AND THE MAJOR FINDINGS IN A STUDY OF THE PUBLIC'S TOLERANCE OF JUVENILE DELINQUENCY

DOS Form
Revised 10/15/69

YOUR FEELINGS ABOUT JUVENILE DELINQUENCY
(CHILDREN IN TROUBLE)

Delinquency Opinion Survey
Columbus, Ohio

This survey is being made to find out peoples' feelings about Juvenile Delinquency. YOUR HELP IS NEEDED! The results will be furnished to the Ohio Youth Commission, the Franklin County Juvenile Court, and other youth serving agencies in Columbus.

Please answer the following questions and return this form in the enclosed stamped envelope. It will only take about 10 to 12 minutes of your time.

There are no right or wrong answers. The right answers for you are the ones that best show how you feel. DO NOT GIVE YOUR NAME.

THANK YOU FOR YOUR HELP.

Taken from Frederick Lewis Faust, "Dimensions of Delinquency Tolerance: Differential Tolerance of Juvenile Delinquent Behavior by Adult Members of Different Socio-Economic Classes and Racial Groups," Ph.D. Dissertation, The Ohio State University, 1970, pp. 111–113 (for the schedule) and pp. 96, 98–101, 107–109 (for conclusions and interpretation).

1. If you saw teenagers from your neighborhood doing the following things, would you feel that they were (A) delinquent?
   (B) not delinquent?

   (Put the *letter* of your choice in front of each of the following)

   ____________ Swearing at a teacher
   ____________ Fighting with another teenager
   ____________ Cutting someone with a knife
   ____________ Riding bicycles across peoples' yards
   ____________ Taking things from store counters
   ____________ Breaking into a house
   ____________ Staying out late at night
   ____________ Turning in a false fire alarm
   ____________ Selling drugs to other kids

2. If you saw teenagers from your neighborhood doing the following things, would you (A) do nothing?
   (B) report it to the kids' parents?
   (C) report it to the police or other authority?
   (D) do something to protect yourself and your family in the future?

   (Put the *letters* of your choice in front of each of the following)

   ____________ Breaking into a house
   ____________ Turning in a false fire alarm
   ____________ Swearing at a teacher
   ____________ Cutting someone with a knife
   ____________ Selling drugs to other kids
   ____________ Riding bicycles across peoples' yards
   ____________ Fighting with another teenager
   ____________ Taking things from store counters
   Staying out late at night

3. Should teenagers who are caught doing the following things be
   (A) turned loose?
   (B) warned and turned over to their parents?
   (C) put under juvenile court supervision?
   (D) sent away to an institution?

   (Put the *letter* of your choice in front of each of the following)

   ____________ Taking things from store counters
   ____________ Selling drugs to other kids

_______ Staying out late at night
_______ Turning in a false fire alarm
_______ Fighting with another teenager
_______ Swearing at a teacher
_______ Cutting someone with a knife
_______ Riding bicycles across peoples' yards
_______ Breaking into a house

4. Would the following things help to cut down the amount of delinquency?

(Put an "X" in the column of your choice for each of the following)

	Yes	*Maybe*	*No*
a. Better housing for families.	___	___	___
b. Closer supervision of children by parents.	___	___	___
c. More things for families to do together.	___	___	___
d. More and better police.	___	___	___
e. Better jobs for parents.	___	___	___
f. Tighter controls by schools.	___	___	___
g. More parks and playgrounds.	___	___	___
h. Stricter controls on violence on T.V.	___	___	___
i. More and better schools.	___	___	___
j. Tougher handling of kids by juvenile courts.	___	___	___
k. More and better job training for teenagers.	___	___	___
l. More and better institutions for delinquents.	___	___	___

In order to compare your feelings about juvenile delinquency with those of others, we would like to have some facts about yourself.

Again, YOU DO NOT NEED TO GIVE YOUR NAME.

---

5. Are you a man or woman?
   _______ Man
   _______ Woman

6. Are you married or single?
   _______ Married
   _______ Single

7. How old are you?
   _______ 18-19
   _______ 20-24
   _______ 25-29
   _______ 30-39
   _______ 40-49
   _______ 50-64
   _______ 65-over

8. What is the last grade you were able to attend school?
   - ______ Elementary (grades 1-6)
   - ______ Junior High (grades 7-9)
   - ______ High School (grades 10-12)
   - ______ College (without degree)
   - ______ College (with degree)

9. How many children do you have?
   - ______ None
   - ______ One
   - ______ Two
   - ______ Three
   - ______ Four or more

10. Were you, or any of your brothers or sisters, ever in trouble with the police when you were children?
    - ______ Yes
    - ______ No

11. Have any of your children ever been in trouble with the police?
    - ______ Yes
    - ______ No

PLEASE RETURN THIS FORM IN THE ENCLOSED STAMPED ENVELOPE.

THANK YOU AGAIN.

The design of the investigation involved a cross-sectional public opinion survey, employing the mailed-questionnaire technique of data collection, from a stratified random sample of 500 adult residents in each of four comparison areas. The four geographic areas selected for comparison represented the lower-class white, lower-class Negro, middle-class white, and middle-class Negro populations of the city of Columbus, Ohio. A control for the variance anticipated in questionnaire returns was accomplished through a follow-up survey, involving the personal delivery of questionnaires to randomly selected samples of residents who failed to respond to the mailed questionnaire. The final sample sizes for the survey were: lower-class white, 182; lower-class Negro, 155; middle-class white, 303; middle-class Negro, 187; total survey sample, 827. From the analysis of data, then, it was found that tolerance of juvenile delinquency varies by socio-economic class and racial group, in such a manner that:

1. White and Negro adults of the middle class are more tolerant of juvenile delinquent behavior, than white and Negro adults of the lower class.

2. White adults of the lower and middle classes are more tolerant of juvenile delinquent behavior, than Negro adults of the lower and middle classes.

3. Adults of the lower and middle classes, and white and Negro racial groups, are more tolerant of juvenile offenses against persons than of either juvenile offenses against property or miscellaneous types of juvenile offenses.

4. Adults of the lower and middle classes, and white and Negro racial groups, tend to be highly intolerant of juvenile offenses which would be felonies if committed by adults, less intolerant of juvenile offenses which would be misdemeanors if committed by adults, and the least intolerant of juvenile offenses which would not be crimes if committed by adults.

5. Middle-class white adults are more tolerant of juvenile delinquent behavior, than are adults of the middle-class Negro, lower-class white, and lower-class Negro groups—except that, middle-class white adults are less tolerant of juvenile offenses which would be felonies if committed by adults, than are adults of any of the other three groups.

6. Lower-class Negro adults are less tolerant of juvenile delinquent behavior, than are adults of the middle-class white, middle-class Negro, and lower-class white groups—except that, lower-class Negro adults are more tolerant of juvenile offenses which would be felonies if committed by adults, than are adults of any of the other three groups.

7. Middle-class white adults are inclined to define, as nondelinquent, those juvenile offenses which would not be crimes if committed by adults, lower-class Negro adults are inclined to define such offenses as delinquent, and lower-class white and middle-class Negro adults are divided in their definitions concerning such offenses with no clear tendency in either direction.

8. Adults of the lower and middle classes, and white and Negro racial groups, are inclined to report juvenile offenses to the juveniles' parents—except that, all groups are inclined to report to the police or other authorities those juvenile offenses which would be felonies if committed by adults, and there is a tendency on the part of middle-class white adults not to take any reporting action concerning juvenile offenses which would not be crimes if committed by adults.

9. Adults of the lower and middle classes, and white and Negro racial groups, feel that juveniles who are caught committing offenses which would not be crimes if committed by adults, and offenses which would be misdemeanors if committed by adults, should be warned and turned over to their parents; and, that juveniles who are caught committing offenses which would be felonies if committed by adults should be placed under juvenile court supervision.

10. Adults of the lower and middle classes, and white and Negro racial groups, do not favor sending juveniles to correctional institutions, even if they are caught committing serious types of offenses which would be felonies if committed by adults.

11. Lower-class Negro adults are highly in favor of greater community efforts to prevent juvenile delinquency, lower-class white and middle-class Negro adults are less in favor of such efforts, and middle-class white adults are the least in favor of greater community efforts toward delinquency prevention.

12. Adults of the lower and middle classes, and white and Negro racial groups, are highly in favor of stronger measures to control the delinquent behavior of juveniles.

In addition to their theoretical implications, it is felt that the results of this investigation have some general implications for the planning of action programs dealing with various facets of delinquency correction, prevention, and control. Below are several examples of the manner in which inferences may be made from the findings of the study that might prove helpful in the planning of specific activities. These are not to be considered as exhaustive of the possible implications of the study results. Also, it should be recognized that these are "implications" and, by no means are they to be taken, alone, as sufficient justification for action.

In view of the finding that lower-class Negro adults tend to be quite intolerant of juvenile delinquent behavior, considerable support for delinquency prevention programs, which are targeted in lower-class Negro neighborhoods, might be expected (and thus encouraged) from adult residents of such areas. Somewhat less community support for such programs might be expected in middle-class white neighborhoods, considering the greater tolerance of delinquency by middle-class white adults. Also, in light of the findings concerning differential tolerance by age group, it might be anticipated that middle-age and older adults may be more receptive to, and supportive of, such programs than younger adults (i.e., 18 through 29 years of age).

The general disinclination of respondents in all four of the subsample groups to favor institutionalization of juvenile offenders, even for the types of offenses which would be felonies if committed by adults, suggests a rather strong skepticism concerning the possible rehabilitative benefits of juvenile correctional institutions. At the same time, there seemed to be considerable support for probation services (which are taken to represent community-based programs). This is consistent with the findings of the Harris Poll, reported in *The Public Looks at Crime and Corrections.*[1] It would appear, then, that much needs to be done in the area of public information and community relations, if administrators of juvenile correctional facilities desire general community support for their programs (e.g., volunteer services, contributions of special supplies and equipment from community groups, etc.). On the other hand, it might be anticipated that proposals for community oriented correctional services would be rather well received by members of the middle and lower-class, white and Negro, communities. This would suggest that local funding for programs of this nature might be more readily obtained, while state and/or Federal resources may have to be tapped in order to get the necessary financial support for residential (institutional) facilities and programs such as juvenile detention and rehabilitation centers.

A comparison of the findings pertaining to the prevention and control dimensions of delinquency tolerance tends to suggest that, while lower-class Negro adults would favor greater community efforts in delinquency prevention (i.e., improved living conditions, better educational and employment opportunities for juveniles, etc.), they would also be supportive of stronger measures of delinquency control (i.e., stronger "law and order" measures). In view of many recent events, it seems likely that such support would be at least somewhat contingent upon certain factors, in addition to delinquency tolerance, which are not reflected in the present investigation (e.g., more and better police, but contingent upon the increase being in "Negro" officers).

Once again, the above inferences are offered as examples of the manner in which

[1] Louis Harris and Associates, *The Public Looks at Crime and Corrections*, Joint Commission on Correctional Manpower and Training, Washington, D.C., 1968.

the results of delinquency tolerance findings may be interpreted, in relation to specific activities, or planned activities, in the areas of delinquency correction, prevention, and control. It is hoped that the results of this investigation, their theoretical implications, and their implications for action will serve to demonstrate the value of, and promote increased interest in, the study of differential tolerance of juvenile delinquent behavior.

Chapter 6

The input into the way stations

Some offenders, both juvenile and adult, are brought into the criminal justice system although undoubtedly they constitute a very small proportion of all offenders. The available insights from self-reported involvement suggest by implication that the number of offenders who enter the system must be infinitesimally small in relation to all offenders. However, criminology does not know the difference, if there is any, between offenders who do get ushered into the system and those who do not. One suspects that the main difference, if any at all, between those who do and those who do not enter the system at the first way station (police) is probably determined by nothing other than the decision of the victim or observer to complain and of the police to arrest. Likewise, as cases are processed at subsequent points in the system, the difference between those who are sent further into the system and those who are not is in very large measure determined by the decisions of the personnel at these various way stations.

On-the-spot arrests and complaints

The two main avenues of entrance into the system at the first way station (the police) are on-the-spot arrests by patrolmen and arrests that follow investigations of complaints coming into the police department from victims and observers. The former are very likely to involve offenses such as drunkeness, disorderly conduct, vagrancy, prostitution, and traffic violations rather than offenses against the person or against property. While patrolmen may happen to be on hand in some instances of personal and property crimes and able to make on-the-spot arrests, the great majority of the few crimes against the person and property that come to the attention of the police are directed to them via complaints. Many of these are not acted upon by the police, while some are investigated but do not lead to arrest.

The phenomenon of nonreporting

In the instance of offenses that come to the attention of the police via the route of complaints, criminologists and law enforcement administrators have, for years, recognized the fact that most criminal occurrences are not reported by victims or observers. More than a generation ago, at the inception of a system of uniform crime reporting in the United States as developed by the International Association of Chiefs of Police, listed the following four reasons for non-reporting:[1]

1. The offense may be known only to the person committing it.
2. Relatives or friends of the offender may not report it.
3. Fear of annoyance or publicity prevents others from reporting it.
4. Some people are too ignorant or indifferent to report.

Sellin, some years later, presented a revised list of reasons for nonreporting.[2]

1. Offense may be of a private nature, such as blackmail, sex, abortion.
2. The injured party may not wish the offense to be discovered.
3. The inconveniences of reporting to the police and possibly testifying in court are too much.
4. Public opinion does not favor the enforcement of certain laws, such as gambling and prohibition.
5. Some offenses are of a nature hardly reportable by offenders themselves, such as carrying concealed weapons, traffic violations, disorderly conduct, vagrancy.
6. In times of crises, changes in public sentiment cause an increased or decreased reportability.

As will be noted from both lists, the principal reasons for nonreporting appear to fall under the general category of unwillingness to report.

The President's Commission on Law Enforcement and Administration of Justice attempted to procure firsthand information from a field study on the extent of and the reasons for nonreporting of crime. A survey of 10,000 households was made for the Commission, which inquired as to "whether the person questioned, or any member of his or her household, had been a victim of crime during the past year, whether the crime had been reported,

[1] Uniform Crime Reporting: *A Complete Manual for Police* (New York: Committee on Uniform Crime Records, International Association of Chiefs of Police, 1929), p. 22.

[2] Thorsten Sellin, *Research Memorandum on Crime in the Depression* (New York: Social Service Research Council, 1937), pp. 69–70.

and, if not, the reasons for not reporting." Other surveys bearing on the problem were also conducted for the Commission.

As would be expected, the amount of criminal occurrences reported by interviewed persons greatly exceeded the amount of crime actually reported to the police. The rate per 100,000 population of crimes against the person was found in the household survey to be twice that actually reported to the police, while the rate of property crimes was still greater than for the crimes known to the police.[3] Even this disparity between the occurrences recorded in the surveys and those actually reported to the police was thought to be an understatement. See reprinted statement in Appendix 2-B.

Surveys made in a limited number of precincts in Washington, Boston, and Chicago, and focused solely on the victimization of the person interviewed, indicated an even greater discrepancy between the reported and unreported volume of crime.[4]

The reasons for not reporting, as given by the interviewed persons in the 10,000 household survey, are presented in Table 6-1 below, broken down by type of crime. Overall, the two main reasons for not reporting are concentrated in: "felt it was a private matter and did not want to harm the offender" and "police could not be effective or would not want to be bothered." The other three reasons listed were much less frequently mentioned: "did not want to take time," "too confused or did not know how to report," and "fear of reprisal."

The reasons for not reporting, as given by the interviewees, vary considerably by type of crime. But an inverse relationship is observable between the first two (principal) reasons for not reporting. If the first reason is highest for a particular offense, the second will be considerably lower; if the second is highest, the first will be much lower.

One should notice that Table 6-1 also indicates that the percentage of criminal happenings in which the event was not reported to the police by the interviewees varied by type of crime from 11 to 90 percent. But there seems to be very little relation between extent of nonreporting and the reasons for not reporting.

Police processing of cases

If and when police investigation leads to the discovery of a suspected wrong-doer or wrong-doers, the question becomes one of a decision of whether or not to arrest. After arrest and further investigation, the police

[3]President's Commission on Law Enforcement and Administration of Justice, *Task Force Report: Crime and its Impact—An Assessment* (Washington, D.C.: U.S. Government Printing Office, 1967), pp. 17-19.

[4]*Ibid.*, pp. 17-18. *Also see* Appendix 2-B.

Table 6-1. Victims' most important reason for not notifying police.[5] (In percentages)

Crimes[a]	*reasons for not notifying police* Felt it was private matter or did not want to harm offender	Police could not be effective or would not want to be bothered	Did not want to take time	Too confused or did not know how to report	Fear of reprisal	Percent of cases in which police not notified
Robbery	27	45	9	18	0	35
Aggravated assault	50	25	4	8	13	35
Simple assault	50	35	4	4	7	54
Burglary	30	63	4	2	2	42
Larceny ($50 and over)	23	62	7	7	0	40
Larceny (under $50)	31	58	7	3	*	63
Auto theft	[b]20	[b]60	[b]0	[b]0	[b]20	11
Malicious mischief	23	68	5	2	2	62
Consumer fraud	50	40	0	10	0	90
Other fraud (bad checks, swindling, etc.)	41	35	16	8	0	74
Sex offenses (other than forcible rape)	40	50	0	5	5	49
Family crimes (desertion, non-support etc.)	65	17	10	0	7	50

*Less than 0.5%.

[a]Willful homicide, forcible rape, and a few other crimes had too few cases to be statistically useful, and they are therefore excluded.

[b]There were only 5 instances in which auto theft was not reported.

SOURCE: NORC survey.

must decide to hold or not to hold—that is, to hold for court action on a definite charge or set of charges. Holding for court action is referred to as "booking." If they decide to hold, then the next question for the police is whether or not to place the suspected or "booked" person into the "lockup" that most central police stations or precinct police stations of medium to large cities operate. In the instance of township police who have no police station (sometimes a cell in the fire hall is made available in small towns) and in the instance of sheriffs who have made arrests outside cities and towns (in unincorporated parts of the county), the cases held and booked are kept in the county jail. According to a specified law and/or local practice, the

[5]The President's Commission on Law Enforcement and Administration of Justice, *Task Force Report: Crime and its Impact—An Assessment* (Washington, D.C.: U.S. Government Printing Office, 1967), p. 18.

arrested and booked person can be placed on bail as a substitute for detention. Even here there is an area of decision—to hold or not, whether or not to place on bail, where bail is presumably a guarantee of the "booked" person's appearance in court at a specified time.

James Q. Wilson[6] addressed himself to the problem of obtaining some first-hand information on how patrolman operates, particularly with reference to the so-called "common offenses" such as drunkenness, disorderly conduct, assault, driving while intoxicated, gambling, and vandalism. His data were collected from field interviews and field observations in eight communities of varying size and complexity. The major findings of Wilson's study are summarized in Appendix 6-A, some of the more important of which are telescoped as follows:

a. there are definite limits to what a front-line police officer can do;
b. front-line officers are particularly sensitive to the behavior of teen-agers, low income persons, and Negroes;
c. officers tend to be "underinterferers" and "underreporters";
d. specialized bureaus for law enforcement within a police department influence active policy toward the problem concerned;
e. police are unlikely to arrest persons in a family quarrel;
f. police departments tend to affect or to develop a "style" which varies with different cities.

Reiss and Black attempted to penetrate the interrogation procedure that uniformed police on field patrol use in questioning "suspects." Of 248 encounters observed by the research team in which the police questioned an adult suspect in the field, 47 percent resulted in arrest. It was found that only 25 percent of the arrests in the high crime rate police precincts studied were made in "on-view" settings, the rest being "dispatched" arrests. But, no matter whether an arrest is a "dispatched" arrest (the majority in the Reiss-Black study) or an "on-view" arrest, the point is established that decision-making on the part of the police is an important factor in determining whether or not a person enters the initial way station of the criminal justice system. Some of the important findings of Reiss and Black on "on-view" arrests are duplicated in Appendix 6-B.[7]

Policy varies considerably between police departments as to the use of fingerprinting. A generation ago only persons arrested for the most serious offenses were fingerprinted. The policy now is to fingerprint a wider assortment of arrested offenders. The prints are usually sent to the F.B.I. in Washington where they are filed and cleared. The returned clearance from

[6]James Q. Wilson, *Varieties of Police Behavior* (Cambridge, Massachusetts: Harvard University Press, 1969).

[7]Albert J. Reiss, Jr. and Donald J. Black, "Interrogation and the Criminal Process," *The Annals of the American Academy of Political and Social Science*, 374 (November 1967), pp. 47-57.

the F.B.I., which is completed in the span of a few days, indicates the arrest and prison record of the offender and whether he is wanted in other jurisdictions. The fingerprint clearances should be looked upon as supplementary input of information on arrested persons. Just what effect fingerprint clearances have on police action or decisions in individual cases is not known exactly. Actually, they are not supposed to affect the prosecuting attorney's processing of cases or to be submitted as information in court hearings.

Use of detention and alternates

There is a point in the arrest input where decisions must be made whether or not to place the arrested person in detention (the police "lockup" or the jail). Law and approved practice enable the arrested offender to make bail or bond, in which instance the offender is diverted from detention while awaiting trial and during court processing. The problem that has faced society for many years at this point of input is that few offenders can "make" bail or bond and that bondsmen charge outlandish fees. In view of this, the Vera Foundation conducted a demonstration in the lower court system of New York, in which certain persons were placed on "personal recognizance" with the understanding that they appear in court the next morning or Monday following the weekend holiday. The experiment indicated that most of the offenders who were placed on personal recognizance did appear in court. Those that did were overwhelmingly persons who had lived at the same address and held the same job for six months or more—an indication of favorable risk. See Appendix 6-C for details of this experiment, called the "Manhattan Bail Project." Such a study points the way to justified use of diversion practices—diversion from the lockup of persons who cannot make bail. (See the subsequent section on the use of bail at the pre-trial phase of felony cases.)

Handling of juvenile cases

There are obvious similarities and differences between the handling of juvenile delinquency and adult crime in the input process up to the point of holding the offender in detention. Complaints against juvenile offenders go mainly to the police, but some go directly to the juvenile courts. In large cities, the complaints on waywardness offenses and incorrigibility are sent mainly directly to the juvenile court. School attendance departments as well as principals' offices also send cases of truants and unmanageable youths directly to the juvenile court. Parents and relatives also complain directly to the juvenile court on wayward and incorrigible children. The closest approximation to this input procedure in adult crime takes place when complaints are sent directly to the prosecutor's office, by-passing the police. Such complaints seldom get processed in the same way as the overwhelming majority that go to the police directly.

The juvenile occurrences routed by the complaining process to the police and/or to the juvenile court are very much closer to the actual involvement of youth in crime than are the complaints that turn out to represent adult involvement. Whether this is due to the fact that juveniles do not cover up as readily as adults, or because a closer watch is kept on juveniles, is a question that cannot be answered at this time. Actually, the juvenile complaints are overwhelmingly referrals of specific children or youths to the police and court. In addition, police take children into custody "on-the-spot" or "on-view" just as they make "on-view" arrests of adults.

Assuming that juveniles come to the attention of the police for delinquency, police policy and/or the decision of individual officers determine whether the youth is held for the juvenile court or not. Usually the police hold the more serious cases. The large city juvenile bureaux of police departments make their decisions on whether or not to hold for the juvenile court after a cursory investigation. Likewise, the intake departments of large city juvenile courts make decisions on whether to hold for further processing on the basis of a cursory investigation.

The next step in the input process of juvenile offenders has to do with holding the youths in detention. Juvenile courts usually have some sort of detention facility available to them. In small counties that do not have a special detention facility, male youths are detained in a separate cell or facility of the county jail. The detained girls may stay with the sheriff's wife. Sometimes detained children are placed in other institutional homes or even with private families.

The selection process in detention input of children is mostly determined by the juvenile court staff, not by the police. Under juvenile procedure, most children are permitted to return to their own homes, while awaiting court hearing. There is no usage in the American juvenile delinquency procedure of bail, or bond, or personal recognizance as in the instance of the handling of adult offenders at the pre-hearing level. Only known runaways, uncontrollables, and children from bad family situations are placed in juvenile detention. A favorable attitude has evolved in the United States toward diverting as many children and youths from detention while awaiting court handling as is justifiable in terms of risk to society. However, no basic research has been done on the typology of cases held in detention compared with those released to their own families, nor have any studies of the outcome of the two sets of cases been made.

Bail and its alternates

The practice of release on bail at the pre-trial level of the felony court as well as at the preliminary hearing phase (in felony cases) of the lower court and at the pre-hearing phase of misdemeanant cases before the lower court is looked upon as a means of overcoming unnecessary hardships that the criminal justice system imposes upon defendants. But it is also considered a practical means of reducing overcrowding in county jails and police lockups. The basic problem concerning bail is that it places the defendant at the mercy of bondsmen who charge high rates to guarantee the client's appearance in court. Even more unfortunate is the fact that bail is beyond the reach of the indigent offender. Appendix 6-D presents findings on the bail problem in the United States by the President's Commission on Law Enforcement and the Administration of Justice.[8] One should note not only the problems connected with the bail system as it now exists but also some of the diversions (without bail) from jail while awaiting trial. But notice should also be taken of the problem created by dangerous offenders being released on bail because of its availability.

An experiment in diversions from court

In a more recent attempt at diversion, the Vera Foundation of New York is demonstrating the feasibility of diverting appropriately selected cases from court hearing. By arrangement with the prosecutor's office of Manhattan's Criminal Court, the Vera project calls for screening of cases by counselors and consequent recommendation of diversion from court hearing and action. The screened cases are supervised by the counselor staff of the project for a period of three months, at the end of which the case is returned to court and, if successful in adjustment, a dismissal of the charge is recommended to the court. This is a diversion that is badly needed in the horribly overcrowded court system. Here again, the decision to divert must be based on appropriate information that allows the counselor to specify the fair-to-good risks. The project goes under the name of the Manhattan Court Employment Project. See Appendix 6-E.

The role of the prosecutor

After the police have decided to "book" an offender and hold him for court action, he is delivered before the lower courts of the United States. If he is

[8]The President's Commission on Law Enforcement and Administration of Justice, *Task Force Report: The Courts* (Washington, D.C.: U.S. Government Printing Office, 1967), pp. 37-40.

booked on a misdemeanor charge or a violation of a local ordinance, his case is adjudicated then and there. There are very few postponed trials before lower courts for such minor cases. The postponed actions usually involve instances where the defendant requests time to procure a defense attorney and/or requests jury trial. The prosecutor's role in misdemeanor cases or ordinance violations is quite minimal—mostly a listing of cases referred from the police and a summary presentation of the case to the court. However, in felony cases, the prosecutor's office has a much more procedural role to play. The prosecutor and/or his assistants confer with defense attorneys and with court-appointed public defenders (in instances of indigent cases).

The President's Commission on Law Enforcement and Administration of Justice found that "the question of guilt or innocence is not contested in the overwhelming majority of criminal cases." It estimated that pleas of guilty take place in about 90 percent of the felony convictions and about 95 percent of the misdemeanor convictions.[9]

At this point in the criminal justice process, there is "bargaining" between the prosecutor's office and the defendant (often through his defense counsel or his appointed legal defender), relative to a plea of guilty (usually to a lesser plea such as unarmed robbery instead of armed robbery). The bargaining between prosecutor and the defendant is called "plea bargaining" which results in "negotiated justice." See Appendix 6-F for a statement on negotiated justice (plea bargaining) by the President's Crime Commission.

If the defendant indicates that he will enter a plea of not guilty, the usual procedure is for the prosecutor in the local jurisdictions of most states to hold grand jury hearings that may either exonerate or lead to an indictment. However, in some states the prosecutor is permitted by law to bring the case to trial on "information," which means that the investigation he has been able to make of the case warrants a trial on the charge brought forward from the police through the lower court. At this point, the defendant may be permitted to make bail, which gives him limited freedom while guaranteeing his appearance at his court trial, or he may be remanded in custody to await his trial (in instances where he cannot make bail or where the situation is too serious to permit the defendant to make bail).

Juvenile procedure

It should be understood that the procedure for handling the cases of juvenile delinquents referred by police or other sources to the juvenile courts is quite different from the process for handling adult cases booked by the

[9] *Task Force Report: The Courts* (Washington, D.C.: U.S. Government Printing Office, 1967), p. 9.

police and held for court action. In the first place, juvenile procedure does not contain a lower court to decide on minor violations and bind felony cases over to the prosecutor. The juvenile cases, no matter whether referred by police or other sources, come to the attention of an intake department in the juvenile courts of large cities. At this point, the court personnel at intake decide whether or not the complainant (police or other) should file an *affidavit*, which swears that the youth committed a particular violation or was truant, incorrigible, or wayward. Under the aegis of the U.S. Supreme Court's Gault decision, the child and his parents or guardians are notified that they should appear in court at a specified time to answer the charges contained in the affidavit and that they may obtain legal counsel. If the intake department of the juvenile courts of large cities does not ask that an affidavit be filed, the case is handled unofficially. If an affidavit is filed at intake, the case is handled officially.

Procedure from this point on varies considerably among the juvenile courts of large urban areas. Usually, a probation officer is assigned to the case and makes a "social" investigation. When the child and his parents appear before the juvenile judge, they have the right to be confronted by the complaining parties and also to cross-examine the complainants through their attorney. For the most part, this part of the court procedure is seldom followed. Usually the presiding judge or referee reads the affidavit and looks at the social history that the probation officer has prepared. He then asks questions and gives an opportunity to the "defendant," his counsel (if any), and his parents to make statements. Then he decides whether to dismiss the case (seldom); to place the case on probation—i.e. to be supervised by a court probation officer and to remain at home under the regulations of court supervision—or to commit the adolescent to a state or private institution for delinquent children.

In the small counties, the juvenile procedure is usually a part of regular court procedure, and whether the criminal court, a probate court, or some other court is given jurisdiction is determined by law. The clerk of the court is likely to route the case to the prosecutor, if the criminal court is designated as the court to handle juvenile cases or to make the decision whether or not to hold, if the probate court is the designated court for juvenile delinquents. The role of the prosecutor and/or his assistants in the juvenile court procedure of separately organized juvenile courts of large urban counties is not well defined. The extent to which he or his assistant is actually present at hearings before the juvenile judge or referee of the separately organized juvenile courts in counties with large cities is not known.

Whether the juvenile procedure takes place before regular courts or before separately organized juvenile courts, one should bear in mind the fact that there is no bail system for juveniles. The intake department or the clerk of the courts or some other authority makes the decision whether to place the child in a detention facility or to allow the child to return home while awaiting his hearing before the judge. Heretofore, the decisions whether or not to place in the detention facility have been guided by (1) whether the child is a bad "runaway" risk, (2) whether home conditions are bad, and (3) whether the adolescent was involved in serious activity or behavior. The first of these considerations corresponds somewhat to those that the police and prosecutors take into account in permitting restricted freedom on bail. The second is purely a child protection matter—to get him out of a very bad and demoralizing home environment—and is not a consideration in bail procedure of adult offenders. The third consideration also applies to adult cases—the behavior is much too serious to allow the person restricted freedom while awaiting court processing.

The court hearing

Returning to the adult criminal justice procedure, the next step after processing by the police and the prosecutor is the court hearing or trial. In the lower courts that have jurisdiction over the misdemeant cases and violations of local ordinances, the court hearing or trial is summary. The prosecutor calls the case, the defendant stands before the magistrate, a policeman may be on hand to testify if requested by the prosecutor or judge, the judge asks whether the defendant has anything to say. If there is a request on the part of the defendant for a jury trial or for a defense counsel, the judge assigns the case to the docket a week or two hence. If no such request is made, the judge then and there pronounces sentence: guilty or not guilty. He also imposes as a part of the finding of guilty a fine, imprisonment, or probation (suspended imprisonment). The lower court, dealing with misdemeanor cases and violations of local ordinances, seldom has a probation service. Only in large cities do some of the lower courts (so-called municipal courts) have a probation service which permits the convicted offender to live in the community under court restrictions.

The adult felony cases that come through the lower courts and through the processing of the prosecutor's office are given a trial, if indicted and if a plea of not guilty is entered. The trial may be by jury or the defendant may waive jury and consent to a trial merely before the judge. But, as indicated earlier, the overwhelming majority of felony cases plead guilty (in negotiated justice with the prosecutor). In this instance, the case is heard by the presiding judge of the felony court, in order to make a decision as to commitment of the guilty pleader to prison (or in rare cases to a mental institution for diagnosis) or to suspend the sentence that the felony calls for and to place the guilty party on probation (under supervision of the court).

Felony courts, especially those in the counties of large cities, are using the suspended sentence (i.e., probation), not only in the pleas of guilty and pleas of *nolo contendere* but also in the very infrequent cases of the finding of guilt after trial on a not guilty plea (with or without jury). Probation was first used in the 1840s by the Boston criminal court as an extension of the judge's common-law prerogative of allowing cases to be "filed" without a conviction procedure. Later, Massachusetts enacted suspension of sentence (probation) into law and the other states in the United States followed suit. Probation laws vary considerably from state to state in limiting the crimes that are made eligible for suspended sentence (after a finding of guilt or a plea of guilty).

Probation procedure

There is a double aspect to probation. The first is the presentence investigation that is ordered by the court, prior to the court's rendering of a sentence. The presentence investigation is made by a court probation officer or one who is assigned to the court. It includes information on the previous criminal involvement as obtainable from police and prison records and juvenile court record; work history; educational level; family background; present family situation; and sometimes medical history, available mental tests, and/or psychiatric examinations. The presentence investigation is really the first point in the criminal justice system at which important background information on the offenders is made available.

The other aspect is supervision of the probationer in his home community by the probation officer, under rules required by the court such as not frequenting bars, staying within the confines of the community unless given permission to circulate more widely or to leave, keeping away from bad associates, working regularly, supporting the family, reporting to the probation office at specified intervals, etc.

Perhaps a third phase of probation procedure should also be mentioned. This involves taking the probationer back into custody for violation of the conditions of probation or for involvement in another offense. According to practice, the probation officer can order the violator's arrest and his detention in jail, or he can, under his assumed police power, make the arrest himself. In either instance, the probationer is delivered before the court for a hearing on the violation of conditions of probation. The court has the power to order that the original sentence to jail or prison be imposed or to permit the violating probationer to remain on probation under admonition.

While very few courts have good probation case records on hand, and most of those in small counties are seldom able to keep probation records (unless the probation service to such courts is supplied by a state agency), what records there are represent the first step in the present criminal justice system to develop individual case records—records that give the personnel involved the basis for making a decision. It should be understood that, up to this point, the American criminal justice system does not generate case history information that would help police, lower courts, and felony prosecutors to make realistic decisions about individuals.

If a slight departure at this point can be tolerated, one should be aware of the fact that the President's Commission on Law Enforcement and the Administration of Justice lamented the absence of appropriate case information all along the line, preventing the police, prosecutors, and judges from making realistic decisions.[10] See Appendix 6–G for details.

Returning to probation as an important stage in the criminal justice system, it should be realised that there is a need to revise the laws that give the courts power to suspend sentences. They should be made less sepecific and less restrictive, not only for the various types of offenses but also for various types of offenders. In addition, there is much to be said for making probation service, not a local court adjunct whereby the judge appoints his own probation officers and the county or the local government pays for the service, but a state service, administered and financed by the state.

In addition, ways must be found to enable lower courts (for misdemeants) to have a probation service as well as to extend probation service in the felony courts of small counties. Such a trend would probably establish a probation service available to all courts, rather than an adjunct to particular local courts and controlled by the judges of such courts. In such an event, undoubtedly juvenile and adult probation services will be fused under the same agency rather than being separated functionally from one another.

Quite apparent is the fact that probation costs on a *per capita* basis are several times less than those of institutional care (the operating expenses of correctional institutions alone—not the overhead of building costs). In addition, it should be noted that probation enables the adult male to earn a living in the community and to support his wife and family, where such exist. This, in turn, surmounts the additional burden of the family's going on relief or public assistance. Many other advantages can be cited in favor of the use of probation. It is even suspected that the settling-down process is greater on probation than in imprisonment and that there is less stigma accruing to a "stint" on probation than to a term of imprisonment. Appendix 6–H should be consulted in reference to an overall view of the probation system in the United States as found by the President's Crime Commission (c. 1966).[11]

However, a very important trend is beginning to be noticed. As the use of

[10] *Task Force Report: The Courts* (Washington, D.C.: U.S. Government Printing Office, 1967), pp. 41–43.

[11] *Task Force Report: Corrections* (Washington, D.C.: U.S. Government Printing Office, 1967), pp. 27–30.

probation (suspended sentence) increases, proportionally fewer offenders are sent to prison and fewer juveniles are committed to schools for delinquents. Probation tends to divert the rehabilitable cases from correctional institutions, leaving the less improvable cases for institutionalization. Many authorities expect that correctional institutions in the future will receive primarily "hard-core" offenders consisting of unimprovable human material; hence, correctional institutions may have to develop programs that can take care of habitual, unimprovable offenders, consisting undoubtedly of anti-social sociopaths.

Correctional institutions

The input of cases at the way station of correctional institutions consists mostly of offenders who have been sentenced or committed by courts. In a few instances, correctional institutions receive individuals who have been removed from probation as a result of court hearing in probation violation cases, and, in a few instances they receive parolees who have failed on parole and are returned.

Most of the correctional institutions in the United States, whether for committed juvenile or adult offenders, have developed a sort of classification procedure at admission. The newly admitted inmate is usually medically examined and given psychological and educational tests. In addition, social history and social background information is accumulated. In adult prisons, fingerprint clearances are obtained from the Federal Bureau of Investigation, to determine previous arrest involvement and incarcerations. The latter procedure is not followed in juvenile institutions. On the basis of the accumulated information on the individual case, a committee makes institutional and program assignments.

Several states with multiple correctional institutions have developed special diagnostic or classification units, to which the newly committed offender is sent initially. Juvenile correctional systems are less likely than adult correctional systems to operate so-called classification or diagnostic centers.

Classification procedure, based on a study of the newly admitted individual case, is seldom found in so-called workhouses that are operated by certain large cities for short-term misdemeanant violators. County jails have almost never been able to develop diagnostic procedures for the cases admitted for short sentences.

The correctional institutions that have been able to develop a diagnostic procedure at admission also use staff committees to reassign inmates to a different institution or a different program within the original assigned institution. Sometimes the reassignment is based on difficulties or discipline problems presented by the inmate; in most instances, it is based on rehabilitative progression.

With the possible exception of the case records in well-developed probation offices, the correctional institutions generate more case history information on individual offenders than do any other way stations in the criminal justice system. Unfortunately, the important case data on incoming and on released inmates are not covered in either the U.S. Bureau of Prisons' enumeration of *National Prisoner Statistics* or the U.S. Children's Bureau *Statistics on Public Institutions for Delinquent Children.*

Release from the institution

The last step in the criminal system is release from the correctional institution. In the instance of adult prisons, the release may be either on parole or on expiration of sentence. In most of the prison systems in the United States, the release is on parole. The less frequent release upon expiration of the sentence signifies that the offenses for which such prisoners were committed are not covered by parole or that the prisoners involved have been retained to their maximum sentence before release, because of security reasons or as disciplinary action. However, release upon expiration of sentence means that the State is finished with the custody of the individual.

On the other hand, release on parole represents a release prior to legal expiration of the sentence. Parole is a release to the community under the rules of a paroling authority and under the supervision of a parole officer. Each state has what is termed a paroling authority, which might consist of a secretary to the governor, an institutional board, or a full-time parole board that controls parole (under law) for all prisons of the state.

Additional information on the individual prisoner is generated by the paroling authority, which not only accumulates a summary of his prison record but also, in many instances, requires a "preparole" investigation by a parole officer, who investigates the work and residence plans of the prospective parolee. The parole authority usually holds short hearings at the time prisoners are eligible under law for parole. Then, on the basis of the institutional report, the preparole investigation, and the hearing, the parole board makes a decision whether or not to place the prisoner on parole.

The parole board also holds revocation hearings, when a parolee has been returned to prison for violation of his parole. It then makes a decision from the available reports and from quizzing the returnee, whether to terminate the parole and order the parolee back to prison or to continue him on parole.

The release of juvenile offenders from juvenile correctional institutions is not as systematized as the release of adult offenders from prison. In the first place, the laws covering juvenile delinquency in the various states do not carry varying lengths of sentences, indeterminate sentences, or reduction of time served for good behavior in the institution, and do not provide for a paroling authority. It is usually an institutional committee of staff personnel that decides that the juvenile inmate is ready for release, although the pressure of large intake, overcrowding, and lack of facilities frequently take precedence over other considerations in releasing juvenile inmates. Juvenile correctional practice frequently calls its release procedure by the name of "placement," a term borrowed from social work. The children released on placement or aftercare[12] are usually supervised by "field counsellors," who have usually made the preliminary investigation and have presented a plan for release, prior to the actual release. They act pretty much as do the parole officers in adult cases, and they also have authority to return the juvenile to the institution for obvious failure to make adjustments to family, school, and neighborhood.

While, at the present time, the correctional institutions and the parole (aftercare) system of release generates the most case information on individuals within the entire criminal justice system, the unfortunate situation arises that the detailed case information applies to only a very small part of the total number of offenders who enter the system from the point of complaint and arrest. If there were some way of developing adequate and useful case information at all points in the criminal justice system, our knowledge of the crime and delinquency problem would be greatly enhanced, and administrators would have data upon which to make revisions and improvements in the various way stations of the system.

[12]Some juvenile correctional systems use the term "aftercare," a term borrowed from English practice.

Appendix 6–A

SUMMARY OF WILSON'S STUDY OF THE VARIETIES OF POLICE BEHAVIOR

In order to discover how the police handle the problem of crime and delinquency, it is necessary to get at the front-line worker. [pp. 2–3] The question for research is how patrolmen behave. [p. 4] In other words, how do they maintain order and enforce the law. The investigation, for the most part, covers the way the so-called "common offenses," specifically drunkeness, disorderly conduct, assault, driving while intoxicated, gambling, and vandalism, are handled by the police in eight communities: Albany, Amsterdam, Brighton, Nassau County, Newberg, Syracuse, Highland Park, and Oakland. Four of these communities represent fair-sized cities with industrial complexes and with a sizable proportion of the low socioeconomic class, including Negro population. Four of them represent small, suburban-type localities, primarily with a middle and upper-class concentration. The information was obtained by field observation and field interviews. [pp. 12–13]

It was discovered that there is a definite limit as to what police can do, because most crimes are property crimes which leave very few clues and practically no witnesses. [p. 25] It was discovered that the social environment of the slum is very apt to be apprehensive about crime and yet at the same time, is likely to be hostile to the police. [p. 30] The police were found to have a much different orientation to the problem of crime than court personnel. It appears as if the police "play it by ear." Patrolmen are alert to signals of danger and signals of impropriety. [p. 39] It was found that they were particularly sensitive to the behavior of teenagers, Negroes, and low income persons [p. 40] These categories of persons represent the high risk categories from the standpoint of police. The study indicated that police "*underenforce*" the law. They tend to mind their own business, to keep their mouths shut, and not to "stick their necks out." The patrolman not only "underenforces" the law, he also "underinterferes." [pp. 49–50] It was found that many patrolmen admit trying to avoid patrol work. [p. 52]

Police administrators were found to have difficulty specifying in advance when a patrolman should interfere. They were able to indicate *how to interfere* much more

James Q. Wilson, *Varieties of Police Behavior* (Cambridge, Mass.: Harvard University Press, 1969), Second printing.

readily than *when to interfere*. [pp. 64-65] The police administrator tends to define the function of his agency much more in terms of law enforcement than in terms of maintenance of order. [p. 67] He is much more concerned with how patrolmen behave in particular cases than how they handle over-all crimes. [p. 69] However, administrators and patrolmen see eye to eye on critical issues such as public criticism of police work, so called leniency of courts, and "hot calls." [p. 78]

The study discovered that police discretion by patrolmen in the eight communities varied enormously. It appeared that there were two major determinants: 1. whether the situation is one of law enforcement or one of maintenance of order, and 2. whether the police response to the situation is police invoked or citizen invoked. When these two major determinants are put together, one finds that four different cells of action against crime ensue.

	Police Invoked	Citizen Invoked
Law Enforcement		
Order Maintenance		

In regard to police-invoked law enforcement, the study discovered that issuing of police tickets for driving offenses varies enormously among the eight communities. For example, Syracuse police issued almost ten times the number of tickets that Albany police issued, in spite of similarity in population [p. 96] Highland Park had about twice as many tickets issued as Brighton and yet both communities are upper class.

It was found that police administration can influence police behavior by creating separate, specialized units for law enforcement. [p. 96] Police policies toward gambling and commercialized vice also vary with political factors. As a matter of fact, police activities in these two areas can produce a sort of de-centralized illegal "industry." [p. 101]

In regard to citizen-invoked law enforcement, it appears that when a victim calls the police department, the police have no discretion as to whether to intervene or not but that the police have considerable discretion on how to interfere. [p. 111] Most of the citizen-invoked law enforcement deals with crimes of theft such as larceny, burglary, and auto stealing.

But even in these areas, the four high crime-rate cities were found to differ very markedly in their rates of arrest for larceny offenses. From the police point of view, a felony arrest is a "good pinch." [p. 113] Arrests for grand larceny and robbery were found to vary with the population characteristics of 41 communities in New York, while juvenile arrests in the communities varied much more with police policy and citizen attitude than with population characteristics. [p. 114]

Police-invoked maintenance of order stems mostly out of instances of disorder and cases of drunkenness. If the drunk and disorderly person has no home, is a "tramp," comes from out of town, and is dressed sloppily, the chances are that the police will take action. However, in spite of this trend in policy, only a minority of arrests for drunkenness in the eight communities studied were made "solely on the initiative of the officer." [p. 121] In other words, even in most drunkenness and misconduct cases, the officer is summoned to the scene.

Yet, within this general frame of reference, the communities varied greatly in the police arrests for drunkenness. For example, Amsterdam, with a sizable working class population, had many more places licensed to sell liquor and beer than the upper class communities such as Brighton and Highland Park. Yet Amsterdam had fewer arrests for drunkenness than did the other places. Hence, there was less tolerance of drunkenness in these upper class localities. [p. 122] Furthermore, the police in Albany and Oakland arrested a much larger proportion of "drunks" than Syracuse. The relation between rates of arrests for drunkenness and the socioeconomic status of the communities is very slight, as we found in examination of intoxication rates in relation to median family income in 41 communities of New York State. [p. 128].

While there is citizen-invoked maintenance of order, police were found to be reluctant to intervene in such calls and were unlikely to arrest persons in a reported quarrel that they had not themselves seen. [p. 130] However, high correlation was found between arrest rates for ordinary assaults and the proportion of the non-white population in 41 New York communities in 1962. [p. 131] Interestingly enough, wives transfer their indignation from their husbands to the police, if the patrolman "does more than take her side verbally." [p. 133] In the eight communities studied, a large variation in the rate of assault arrests was apparent. It looks as if it is not easy for the police to officiate over disputes, especially between private parties. Hence, there appears to be a sort of "privatizing" of citizen disputes. [p. 136]

Apparently there are several "styles" which are identifiable in police work. One of these is the "watchman style," which emphasizes law enforcement. This is to be found namely in the areas of traffic tickets, illicit enterprizes, and surveillance of juvenile delinquency. Another is the "legalistic style" which apparently grows out of the conception that it is the function of the law to punish. Then there is the "service style," which is found primarily in upper-class communities. The "citizen expects the police to display the same qualities as its department store salesmen, local merchants, and public officials—courtesy, neat appearance, and a deferential manner." [p. 201] Politics also affect the police style. Police apparently are sensitive to the political environment and to the "political culture." For example, the arrest rates for drunkenness and larceny were found to be twice as high in the communities which had a professional city council and a professional city manager than in places which had the ordinary partisan-elected mayor and city council, whereas the rate for driving while intoxicated was only found to be 50% higher. (This finding was based on 1960 FBI arrest statistics for a sample of cities which had a population between 25,000 and 100,000, a median family income of between $5,000 and $7,500, and a non-white population that did not exceed 5% of the total. [pp. 272–275]

Appendix 6–B

EXCERPTS FROM THE REISS-BLACK STUDY OF POLICE INTERROGATIONS IN THE FIELD

The data for this paper were gathered through direct observation by thirty-six observers in high-crime-rate police precincts of Boston, Chicago, and Washington, D.C., during the summer of 1966. It should be emphasized that the information pertains only to questioning of suspects by uniformed police officers in encounters of field patrol.

Patrolmen are the first police to enter most crime situations and hence the first to have contact with any suspects available in the immediate setting. Typically, the police are mobilized to handle incidents in one of two major ways. The great majority of incidents handled by patrolmen arise subsequent to a citizen complaint by telephone followed by a "*dispatch*" to the patrol car. The second major way in which the police become involved in incidents is through "*on-view*" work—police intervention in a field situation that occurs at the officer's discretion rather than in response to a radioed command. The "stop-and-frisk" is an example of an on-view incident. The two types of mobilization carry with them differential opportunities for discretionary action and differential limiting conditions on how the officer exercises his discretion.

Patrolmen conduct interrogations in only about one-third of their encounters with suspects. The proportion is roughly the same in dispatched situations and on-view situations. The frequency with which patrol officers interrogate is greater than that with which they conduct personal and property searches, as only one-fifth of the police-suspect transactions included a search. However, in almost one-third of the encounters where an interrogation took place, a search of person, property, or both also was conducted.

One characteristic of field interrogations distinguishing them from those conducted in an interrogation room at a police station is that, not uncommonly, more than one suspect is questioned at the same time. In over one-third of the interrogations observed, two or more persons were questioned, and in about one-fifth, three or more were

Albert J. Reiss, Jr. and Donald J. Black, "Interrogation and the Criminal Process," *The Annals of the American Academy of Political and Social Science*, 374 (November 1967), pp. 51–55. Reprinted by permission.

questioned. That the field interrogation is so often a confrontation between group and group places is somewhat at odds with popular stereotypes of the interrogation as an encounter between one or more officers and a lone suspect. In the absence of other patrol units to lend assistance, the classic technique of separating suspects for interrogation is often unavailable to officers in a field setting. The support and surveillance given by his fellows may well mitigate some of the suspect's vulnerability in such field confrontations.

Most field interrogations—about three-fourths—took place only in a field setting, usually on the street or in a private place such as a dwelling. Nine in ten included interrogation at the field setting, some also involving questioning during transportation to the police station or at the station itself. Less than 5 percent of the suspects were interrogated only at the station.

There were 248 encounters in which an adult suspect was interrogated in a field setting by the police. The type of evidence available to the officer on guilt of the suspect is clearly a function of how the officer entered the setting. Of the 248 encounters where an adult suspect was questioned, 116 (47 percent) eventuated in an arrest; exactly one-fourth of the arrests were made in on-view settings. In 93 percent of the on-view arrests as contrasted with 42 percent of the dispatched arrests the officer would have been able to offer some testimony that a crime event took place in his presence or that he had both evidence and observation that the suspect was definitely linked to the crime, for example, the suspect had a stolen car in his possession. The differences are even greater considering the fact that in 66 percent of all on-view, as compared with 24 percent of all dispatched arrests, the *only* evidence available was the on-view testimony of the officer that the offense occurred in his presence.

On the whole, the kind of interrogation that the officer conducts in field settings is relatively unproductive of admissions. Of the 116 *arrests* (including suspects never booked) that included interrogation by officers, 91 (78 percent) did not eventuate in admission. Of the 132 encounters where persons were interrogated and not arrested, 121 (92 percent) did not involve an admission. About 86 percent of all encounters involving interrogation did not result in an admission. This is substantially below the figure reported for in-station interrogations where about 50 percent of all interrogated suspects are reported to make an admission.

The kind of interrogation conducted in field settings seems remarkably unproductive of admissions of guilt. Of all admissions in field situations, more were made voluntarily prior to questioning than were made after questioning. Among encounters with arrested persons, there were 25 admissions out of 116 interrogations; 68 percent of these were voluntary admissions before questioning, and the questioning served only to provide the officer with additional information or evidence. Among those not arrested, there were only 11 admissions in 132 interrogations. Of these, 45 percent were voluntary. Assuming that *Miranda* admits of voluntary confessions under nearly all circumstances, questioning in field settings is at least modestly productive of admissions that clearly would be allowed as evidence in court.

Appendix 6–C

MANHATTAN BAIL PROJECT

In the fall of 1961, the Vera Foundation's Manhattan Bail Project pioneered the fact-finding process in New York City by launching a program in the Felony Part of Magistrates Court (now Criminal Court). Assisted by a $115,000 grant from Ford Foundation and staffed by New York University Law Students under the supervision of a Vera Foundation director, the project interviews approximately 30 newly arrested felony defendants in the detention pens each morning prior to arraignment. The interviews are conducted in a cell set aside by the Department of Correction, and consume about 10 minutes. The accused for the most part are indigents who will be represented by assigned counsel. Although the project excluded a variety of serious offenses at the outset, only homicide and some narcotics and sex charges are now excluded.

In evaluating whether the defendant is a good parole risk, four key factors are considered: (1) residential stability; (2) employment history; (3) family contacts in New York City; and (4) prior criminal record. Each factor is weighted in points. If the defendant scores sufficient points, and can provide an address at which he can be reached, verification will be attempted. Investigation is confined to references cited in the defendant's signed statement of consent. Verification is generally completed within an hour, obtained either by telephone or from family or friends in the courtroom; occasionally a student is dispatched into the field to track down a reference. The Vera Foundation staff then reviews the case and decides whether to recommend parole. The following factors are weighed:

EMPLOYMENT

Was defendant working at time of arrest?
How long has he had this job, or any other job?
Was he in a position of responsibility?

Daniel J. Freed and Patricia M. Wald, *Bail in the United States: 1964*, a report to the National Conference on Bail and Criminal Justice, May 27–29, 1964, U.S. Department of Justice, Washington, D.C., and New York, The Vera Foundation, 30 East 39th Street, New York, 1965, pp. 59–64.

How does his employer feel about his reliability?
Will his job remain open if he is quickly released?

FAMILY

Does accused live with his family?
Does he support wife, children, parents, or others?
Are there any special circumstances in family such as pregnancy or severe illness?
Does there appear to be a close relationship between accused and his family?

RESIDENCE

How long has defendant resided in the United States, if he is foreign born?
How long has he lived in New York City or its environs?
How long has he lived at his present address and prior residences?

REFERENCES

Will someone vouch for accused's reliability (e.g., his clergyman, employer, probation or parole officer, doctor)?
Will someone agree to see that he gets to court at the proper time?

CURRENT CHARGE

What is the possible penalty if defendant is convicted?
Are there mitigating factors that are relevant to parole? For example, if the charge is felonious assault, has the victim been only slightly injured? In husband-wife assault cases, will the wife permit her husband to return home?

PREVIOUS RECORD

Is the defendant a first offender?
If not, when was he last convicted?
Of what types of crimes has he been convicted?

OTHER FACTORS

Is defendant a recipient of unemployment insurance or other government checks that tie him to a particular locality?
Is he under medical care which ties him to a hospital or doctor?
Has he previously been released on parole or bail and, if so, has he appeared on time?

For each defendant determined by the project to be a good parole risk, a summary of the information is sent to the arraignment court, and copies of the recommendation and supporting data are given to the magistrate, the assistant district attorney and defense counsel. Counsel reads the recommendation into the record.

Since notification is so essential to a successful parole operation, Vera sends a letter to each parolee telling him when and where to appear in court. If he is illiterate, he is telephoned; if he cannot speak or understand English well, he will receive a telephone call or letter in his native tongue. Notification is also sent to any reference who has agreed to help the defendant get to court. The parolee is asked to visit the Vera office in the courthouse on the morning his appearance is due. If his absence was for good cause, they seek to have parole reinstated.

RELEASE ON RECOGNIZANCE

Once the facts about the accused's community roots are known, the court is in a position to individualize the bail decision. Increasing attention has been given in recent years to opportunities for the widespread release of defendants on their own recognizance (r.o.r.), i.e., their promise to appear without any further security. A great many state and federal courts have long employed this device to allow pre-trial freedom for defendants who the court or prosecutor personally know to be reliable or "prominent" citizens. But the past three years have seen the practice extended to many defendants who cannot raise bail. The Manhattan Bail Project and its progeny have demonstrated that a defendant with roots in the community is not likely to flee, irrespective of his lack of prominence or ability to pay a bondsman. To date, these projects have produced remarkable results, with vast numbers of releases, few defaulters and scarcely any commissions of crime by parolees in the interim between release and trial.

Such projects serve two purposes: (1) they free numerous defendants who would otherwise be jailed for the entire period between arraignment and trial, and (2) they provide comprehensive statistical data, never before obtainable, on such vital questions as what criteria are meaningful in deciding to release a defendant, how many defendants paroled on particular criteria will show up for trial, and how much better are a defendant's chances for acquittal or a suspended sentence if he is paroled.

The results of the Vera Foundation's operation in New York show that from October 16, 1961, through April 8, 1964, out of 13,000 total defendants, 3,000 fell into the excluded offense category, 10,000 were interviewed, 4,000 were recommended and 2,195 were paroled. Only 15 of these failed to show up in court, a default rate of less than $\frac{7}{10}$ of 1%. Over the years, Vera's recommendation policy has become increasingly liberal. In the beginning, it urged release for only 28% of defendants interviewed; that figure has gradually increased to 65%. At the same time, the rate of judicial acceptance of recommendations has risen from 55% to 70%. Significantly, the District Attorney's office, which originally concurred in only about half of Vera's recommendations, today agrees with almost 80%. Since October 1963, an average of 65 defendants per week have been granted parole on Vera's recommendation.

In order to study the influence of its own recommendations, Vera initiated the project with the use of an experimental control procedure. Out of all defendants believed by the project to be qualified for release, half were in fact recommended to the court, while the other half were placed in a control group, and their recommendations withheld. In the project's first year, 59% of its parole recommendations were followed by the court, compared to only 16% paroled in the control group. In short, recommendations based on facts nearly quadrupled the rate of releases.

The subsequent case histories of defendants in both groups were thereafter analyzed. They showed that 60% of the recommended parolees had either been acquitted or had their cases dismissed, compared with only 23% of the control group. Moreover, of the 40% who were found guilty out of the parole group, only one out of six was sentenced to prison. In contrast, 96% of those convicted in the control group were sentenced to serve a jail term.

With Vera's assistance a demonstration release program was also carried on in New York City in the Women's House of Detention. Interviews were conducted with women detainees who had not posted bail. In approximately one-fourth of the cases, recommendations to reopen the bail decision and grant parole were made. The response of the court was favorable and the experiment resulted in decreasing the detention population of that overcrowded facility, in a six month period, from 327 to 164.

The interest and confidence generated by the Manhattan Bail Project led Mayor Wagner to announce in 1963 that New York City would take over and run bail fact-finding services on an extended scale through its Office of Probation. In January 1964, the New York City Board of Estimate allocated $181,600 for the operation of these services in the five boroughs. And the 1963 Report of the New York Assembly Judiciary Committee advocated an extension of Vera-type operations into other counties of the state. The same report also proposed a statute to require every arraigning judge, in court or through probation officers, to ascertain prior to bail-setting all data pertinent to the defendant's likelihood to return for trial. In order to encourage such inquiries the statute would provide that, [except] by waiver of the defendant, the failure of the judge to ascertain these facts would result in automatic parole.

Appendix 6–D

THE BAIL PROBLEM IN THE UNITED STATES

The shortcomings of the traditional bail system are now widely known and well documented. The National Conference on Bail and Criminal Justice, held in 1964, focused attention on the wastefulness and unfairness of the system. Numerous studies all over the country also have documented its deficiencies. The system's major fault is exclusive reliance on the posting of money to ensure the defendant's return. Typically an arrested person is brought by the police before a committing magistrate or judge who fixes an amount of money as security for his appearance at trial. In some courts bail schedules set an amount for each offense, and if the defendant can post that amount, the judge seldom considers the case individually. Under either method if the defendant can post the required amount or can pay a bondsman to post it for him, he is released until trial. If he cannot, he remains in jail. If the defendant fails to appear for trial, the bond may be forfeited.

The standard rate of premiums paid to bondsmen is about 10 percent of the face amount of the bond, although rates as high as 20 percent have been reported. When bail is set at more than $500, premiums become more than many defendants can afford. A study of New York bail practices indicates that 25 percent of all defendants failed to make bail at $500, 45 percent failed at $1,500, and 63 percent at $2,500. Although the proportion of persons failing to make bail varies widely from place to place, a recent study of large and small counties shows that it often is substantial.

	Felony defendants unable to make bail (percent)
Large Counties:	
Cook (Chicago)	75
Hennepin (Minneapolis)	71
Jefferson (Louisville)	30
Philadelphia (Philadelphia)	14

The President's Commission on Law Enforcement and Administration of Justice, *Task Force Report: The Courts* (Washington, D.C.: U.S. Government Printing Office, 1967), pp. 37–40.

Small Counties:	
Brown, Kans	93
Rutland, Vt	83
Putnam, Mo	36
Anchorage, Alaska	28
Catoosa, Ga	6

The jails in which persons unable to make bail are kept are often overcrowded. Most lack work and recreational facilities. Some do not have space for the inmates to visit with their families or to confer with counsel. Detainees are often indiscriminately mixed with persons convicted of crime, with a result, as Justice William O. Douglas has observed, "equivalent to giving a young man an M.A. in crime."

Unnecessary detention costs the community more than jail expenses. Many persons who fail to raise bail have jobs and dependants. The consequences of their detention are plain: loss of employment and support for the family, repossession of household goods, and accumulation of debts. If the family is put on relief, community funds must be devoted to its support. Loss of employment also means a drop in tax revenues; for the employer it may mean the additional expense of training a replacement. If the defendant is detained and loses his job, or if he must spend his limited money for a bail bond premium, his ability to pay a lawyer is reduced, and the community may incur the additional expense of providing defense counsel.

Pretrial detention also involves serious costs for the defendant. The most obvious cost is imprisonment itself, which is particularly harsh and unjust for the accused when conviction does not result in imprisonment, as is often the case.

A central fault of the existing system is that it detains too many people, with serious consequences for defendants, the criminal process, and the community. The aim of reform, therefore, must be to reduce pretrial detention to the lowest level without allowing the indiscriminate release of persons who pose substantial risks of flight or of criminal conduct.

Another serious fault of the present bail system is that it fails to promote decisions founded on facts about the accused. Money bail is traditionally set on the basis of the alleged offense rather than on the background of the particular defendant, principally because little information about him is ordinarily available except his prior criminal record. As a result, prohibitively high bail may be set where there is in fact little risk of flight, while at the same time unreliable defendants are released with inadequate assurance that they will appear for trial.

The first step of reform is to introduce factfinding procedures which will furnish immediately after arrest verified information about the accused and his community ties. With this information a rational assessment of the risks can be made, and where there is no significant risk, the defendant can be released without bail.

A second step in bail reform is to develop new methods to reduce the risk of flight where it is significant. Forfeiture of money bail is currently the principal sanction, but forfeiture is rarely enforced. When it is, its efficacy is questionable, since the risk of financial loss usually falls on the bondsman instead of on the accused; many bail bonds are written without collateral, and most defendants are virtually judgment proof.

The judge should therefore have a broader set of alternatives than money bail or outright release: he should be given authority to set certain conditions on release. This is the approach taken by the Federal Bail Reform Act of 1966, the first basic change in Federal bail law since 1789. The Act instructs the judge to release persons charged with other than capital offenses on a promise to appear or upon the execution of an unsecured appearance bond, unless the judge determines that such release would not reasonably assure appearance at trial. Thus the Act diminishes reliance on money bail and allows imposition of conditions commensurate with the risks presented.

In a very short time a growing recognition of the need for reform of the bail system has led to impressive progress. Although the foundations of bail reform are now firmly laid, much remains to be done.

Although the steps described above have the potential for reducing many of the abuses of the present bail system, the problem of releasing the dangerous defendant still presents a major dilemma. The bail system recognizes ensuring appearance at trial as the only valid purpose for imposing bail, but society also has an important interest in securing protection from dangerous offenders who may commit crimes if released before trial. In practice the result has been that judges have frequently gone beyond the sole recognized purpose of bail and have set high money bail to prevent release of an arrested person where danger to the community rather than flight is the principal concern. As reliance upon money bail has been challenged by bail reform, pressures to face the problems posed by pretrial release of potentially dangerous persons have increased.

There would be obvious advantages if a system could be devised which would enable the issue of a defendant's dangerousness to be confronted candidly by a judge. But a number of interrelated obstacles stand in the way of such a system.

First, methods and data for predicting dangerousness have not been adequately developed.

A second major obstacle is that imprisonment of an individual based on a prediction of future crimes raises constitutional questions that have not been passed on by the Supreme Court.

On the other hand, strong arguments have been made for a system of preventive detention in lieu of the present use of money bail. It has been pointed out that the difficulty of predicting future dangerousness would be no more of a problem than under the present system, where a judge detains persons he believes dangerous under the rubric of settling money bail to ensure their appearance at trial. In fact, the present invisibility of the issue of dangerousness, by preventing judicial review of specific cases, undoubtedly impedes the development of standards and data concerning dangerousness.

Appendix 6–E

DIVERSION FROM COURT: THE MANHATTAN COURT EMPLOYMENT PROJECT

The Manhattan Court Employment Project (MCEP) is an experimental attempt to intervene in the usual court process just after a defendant's arrest, to offer him counseling and job opportunities and, if he cooperates and appears to show promise of permanent change, to recommend that the prosecutor (District Attorney) and the judge dismiss the charges against him without ever deciding whether he is guilty. Thus, the MCEP attempts to convert a participant's arrest from a losing to a winning experience. The system stands to benefit from this conversion as much as the defendant. Successful participants leave the project working and earning an honest living, the community gains a taxpayer, and the resources of the overburdened criminal justice system are freed to attend to serious cases.

In brief, the MCEP operates as follows: Shortly after each arrested man is brought to the Manhattan Criminal Court for arraignment (appearance before a judge, setting of bail, and assignment of counsel), our screening unit reviews his papers, checks his prior record, and interviews him to see whether he is eligible to take part in the project under standards drafted by project staff and the prosecutor's office. If he is eligible and he and his lawyer agree to his participation, we ask the prosecutor to request the judge to adjourn his case for 90 days and release him on recognizance, i.e. without bail. The court and District Attorney approve about 70 percent of these requests.

A new participant, frequently coming straight from the court's detention cells, is taken to the MCEP office in the court building and is assigned to a Representative (counselor), who will take prime responsibility for him throughout his time with the project. If he needs money or immediate services of some kind, he is sent to the Social Services Unit, which consists of two employees of the city's Department of Social Services (formerly the Department of Welfare) who have been assigned to work with project participants.

The project offers participants two basic services: counseling with their Representatives, or Reps, and job placement through the Career Development Unit. The

Vera Institute of Justice, *The Manhattan Court Employment Project*, Summary Report on Phase One, November 1, 1967 to October 3, 1969, New York, 1970, pp. 7–9.

Representatives, who are nonprofessionals and ex-convicts, go to participants' neighborhoods regularly to talk over problems, meet their families, and just spend time with them. The Reps also see participants at the project offices and in group counseling sessions one evening a week at the project's clubhouse. A majority of participants also develop a continuing relationship with the project's Career Developers, who help prepare them for interviews and for jobs, set up appointments for them, and follow their progress by keeping in close touch with employers and project Reps.

At the end of 90 days, when the participant must appear for his adjourned date in court, we recommend that the District Attorney make one of three possible requests to the court: (1) dismissal of charges (if the defendant has met the basic requirements of the program); (2) a second adjournment to give us more time to work with him; or (3) in the case of defendants we have been unable to work with successfully, return of the cases to the normal court processes. This last recommendation, by agreement with the District Attorney, carries no implication that will be used to the defendant's disadvantage in the continued prosecution of his case.

The project was designed in 1967 under the auspices of the Vera Institute of Justice, a private organization in New York City formed to test and bring about changes in the criminal justice system of the city, and was funded by the Manpower Administration of the United States Department of Labor under a three-year contract.

The MCEP has been envisaged as working in two stages. The first, which this report covers, was the developmental period, in which the chief questions to be explored were the basic ones: whether the project was feasible at all; whether the court would accept and ultimately cooperate with it; whether it was possible to produce and observe a change in a signficant number of participants in a three-month period; whether it was possible to predict what kinds of people might be most receptive to treatment based on jobs; whether our staff—particularly the nonprofessionals—would perform effectively; whether a data system could be designed for supervision and analysis of results. The project's work in the first phase answered these questions in the affirmative. The second phase, while we continue to take in and work with new participants, will be directed at answering four new questions: First, we will look at defendants who have been out of the project for some time to see if the project has had any apparent effect on their job situations and on their rate of recidivism (repeated commission of crime). Second, we will further define the types of defendants who can benefit from the project's services and try to estimate how many there are in the court population. Our experience during the first phase indicates that substantially more defendants than we accepted were eligible under the existing criteria and that the criteria might be expanded. Third, we will take steps to institutionalize the project in the operation of the criminal court so that our services become a standard part of the criminal justice process. Fourth, by demonstrating the effectiveness of our intervention immediately after arrest, we hope to make the point that other kinds of treatment—for addicts, alcoholics, prostitutes, and others—could be used to great advantage at this point in the court process.

Appendix 6–F

THE NEGOTIATED PLEA OF GUILTY

The question of guilt or innocence is not contested in the overwhelming majority of criminal cases. A recent estimate is that guilty pleas account for 90 percent of all convictions; and perhaps as high as 95 percent of misdemeanor convictions. But the Commission has found it difficult to calculate with any degree of certainty the percentage of cases disposed of by guilty plea, since reliable statistical information is limited. Clearly it is very high. The following statistics indicate the number and percentage of guilty plea convictions in trial courts of general jurisdiction in States in which such information was available.

State (1964 statistics unless otherwise indicated)	*Total convictions*	*Guilty pleas*	
		Number	*Percent of total*
California (1965)	30,840	22,817	74.0
Connecticut	1,596	1,494	93.9
District of Columbia (year ending June 30, 1964)	1,115	817	73.3
Hawaii	393	360	91.5
Illinois	5,591	4,768	85.2
Kansas	3,025	2,727	90.2
Massachusetts (1963)	7,790	6,642	85.2
Minnesota (1965)	1,567	1,437	91.7
New York	17,249	16,464	95.5
Pennsylvania (1960)	25,632	17,108	66.8
U.S. District Courts	29,170	26,273	90.2
Average [excluding Pennsylvania]*			87.0

*The Pennsylvania figures have been excluded from the average because they were from an earlier year, and the types of cases included did not appear fully comparable with the others.

The President's Commission on Law Enforcement and Administration of Justice, *Task Force Report: The Courts* (Washington, D.C.: U.S. Government Printing Office, 1967), pp. 9–10.

A substantial percentage of guilty pleas are the product of negotiations between prosecutor and defense counsel or the accused, although again precise data are unavailable. Commonly known as "plea bargaining," this is a process very much like the pretrial settlement of civil cases. It involves discussions looking toward an agreement under which the accused will enter a plea of guilty in exchange for a reduced charge or a favorable sentence recommendation by the prosecutor. Even when there have been no explicit negotiations, defendants relying on prevailing practices often act on the justifiable assumption that those who plead guilty will be sentenced more leniently.

Few practices in the system of criminal justice create a greater sense of unease and suspicion than the negotiated plea of guilty. The correctional needs of the offender and legislative policies reflected in the criminal law appear to be sacrificed to the need for tactical accommodations between the prosecutor and defense counsel. The offense for which guilt is acknowledged and for which the sentence is imposed often appears almost incidental to keeping the business of the courts moving.

Despite the serious questions raised by a system of negotiated pleas, there are important arguments for preserving it. Our system of criminal justice has come to depend upon a steady flow of guilty pleas. There are simply not enough judges, prosecutors, or defense counsel to operate a system in which mos' defendants go to trial. Many of the Commissions proposals, such as the recommendation to expand appointment of counsel for the indigent, will strain the available resources for many years. If reliance on trial were increased at this time, it would undoubtedly lower the quality of justice throughout the system. Even were the resources available, there is some question whether a just system would require that they be allocated to providing all defendants with a full trial. Trial as we know it is an elaborate mechanism for finding facts. To use this process in cases where the facts are not really in dispute seems wasteful.

Some jurisdictions appear to be able to deal with their caseloads without reliance on negotiated guilty pleas. The discussion in this chapter should not be taken as suggesting that plea bargaining should be introduced in courts that have satisfactory alternatives. Particularly in single judge courts it may not be feasible to introduce the safeguards that would enable a negotiated plea system to operate fairly and effectively.

Appendix 6–G

THE NEED FOR EARLY FACTFINDING AT THE VARIOUS WAY STATIONS OF THE CRIMINAL JUSTICE SYSTEM

Attention to procedures for finding facts in the criminal process has centered upon the trial itself, which is the ultimate procedure for presenting evidence concerning the guilt of the accused. In addition, there has been a rapid although uneven, growth in the use of presentence investigations to provide additional information to the judge after trial. To the extent that such procedures as the preliminary hearing and formal pretrial discovery are available for earlier factfinding, they operate in a context that looks forward to trial. Yet disposition of cases by trial is the distinct exception in our system.

Little attention has been given to procedures for gathering the facts needed for the many decisions which must be made earlier in the process, decisions as to whether to press criminal charges, whether to go to trial, and what the disposition should be if the case does not go to trial. There is a pressing need to develop new factfinding procedures and to make better use of the ones that now exist in order to ensure that such important decisions are based on fuller exploration of the facts of the case.

The prompt identification of those cases which should go to trial enables prosecutors and counsel to concentrate greater attention on pretrial preparation, and it encourages early disposition in the remaining majority of cases. It facilitates the scheduling of cases and substantially reduces the burden on jurors and witnesses. And for the defendant early disposition minimizes the deleterious impact of the period between arrest and disposition.

In addition to providing the information needed for these decisions, early factfinding procedures aid in obtaining much information needed at later stages of the criminal process, both for cases that ultimately go to trial and those that do not. After the charge is filed, the judge must consider motions addressed to the indictment, requests for particulars, severances of counts or defendants, changes of venue, and the like, many of which turn on an appreciation of the facts underlying the formal charge. Such facts as the defendant's employment record and his roots in the community are relevant to such different questions as whether he should be released on recognizance,

The President's Commission on Law Enforcement and Administration of Justice, *Task Force Report: The Courts* (Washington D.C.: U.S. Government Printing Office, 1967), pp. 41–43.

whether probation should be granted and if so what type of probation supervision is required. Substantial economies could result if these facts were obtained at an early stage and recorded for use at subsequent steps in the process. The recorded statement of a witness may be submitted to the court as part of the evidentiary basis for a guilty plea, it may be stipulated as the testimony of the witness if a noncriminal disposition is employed, it may be introduced at trial if the witness becomes unavailable, or it may be used for cross-examination. Early factfinding is not only more efficient, but it also improves the certainty of dispositions. It occurs when memories are fresh and detailed recollection more reliable.

The Bail Decision

Gathering information relating to the defendant's ties to the community, job record, family situation, and personal stability at this stage in the criminal process improves quality of bail decisions, and a record of this information also provides the prosecutor and defense counsel with a factual basis for prompt consideration of the range of possible dispositions. Such a record can also save considerable work for the probation officer conducting a presentence investigation.

Bail projects typically use a printed form to assist in collecting the information used in determining the arrested person's eligibility for pretrial release. These forms should contain as broad a range of relevant information about the defendant as can be quickly gathered. Copies of the completed forms should be made available to the prosecutor and defense counsel for their use. Of course, any statements about the offense made by a defendant should be excluded from this form, and in order to maintain the effectiveness of bail projects, defendants must be assured that any information they provide will not be used against them at trial.

Early Disclosure of Police Reports and Witness Statements

It is recommended that a written statement of the facts of the case be prepared by the arresting officer so that the court may promptly determine whether there is cause to hold the accused without requiring the officer's appearance. This brief statement, prepared for submission to the court at initial appearance, should be furnished to defense counsel to enable him to determine whether to challenge the arrest and to provide him with preliminary factual information about the case.

After the defendant's initial appearance, his counsel should begin immediately to consider whether he will press for a noncriminal disposition, seek to negotiate a plea, or litigate the question of guilt. If he is considering the last course, he must also decide whether to ask for a preliminary hearing. To make these decisions wisely counsel must first learn something about the strength of the prosecution's case and the nature of its proof. The simplest method would be for the prosecutor to furnish him with copies of the police report on the case and of statements by prosecution witnesses.

The proper scope and extent of discovery of police reports and witness statements is a matter of heated controversy, and the defendant's right of discovery will be considered later in this section. This discussion deals not with mandatory disclosure, but rather argues in favor of prosecutors exercising their discretion informally to reveal this information to defense counsel. It would not be desirable to require prosecutors to disclose this information in every case. Certain cases will fairly clearly be headed for trial, and in those involving professional or organized crime, national security, or particularly dangerous offenders, the scope of dicovery should be left to litigation. But for cases not raising these problems prosecutors should make disclosure a regular part of the process at this early point. Such disclosure, when made on an informal basis, appears to operate satisfactorily because it serves not only the interest of fairness to the defendant but also the prosecutor's interest in the prompt disposition of cases.

It should be emphasized that most of the traditional arguments against discovery of the prosecutor's file are irrelevant in those cases that do not go to trial. Proof in most criminal cases tends to fall into a limited number of categories: eyewitness identification, accomplice testimony, possession of contraband or the fruits of crime, incriminating statements, or physical evidence. While it is impossible to predict with certainty immediately after the arrest which cases will go to trial and which will not, an experienced prosecutor should be able to make fairly accurate judgments after examining his case file. And since the key items of evidence clearly are sufficient basis for a finding of probable cause in most cases, defense counsel who has seen the police report or statements of key witnesses may often waive the preliminary hearing.

On the basis of bail information and the prosecutor's file, counsel can rationally decide whether to undertake a broader social investigation with a view toward proposing a noncriminal disposition or negotiating a guilty plea. Various means of gathering additional information at this stage, such as making the court's probation service available to the parties or developing a new community agency to provide such a service, are discussed in chapter 1.

The Preliminary Hearing

In most jurisdictions in the United States the preliminary hearing is not a useful fact-finding device. The prosecution rarely introduces more evidence than the minimum required to show probable cause and generally may meet its burden with hearsay testimony. In many places testimony at the hearing is not recorded or otherwise perpetuated. In some jurisdictions the defense does not have the right to subpoena witnesses, and quite often counsel is not appointed for the accused until the time for the preliminary hearing has passed.

One major reason for these deficiencies is the fact that the preliminary hearing is designed to serve a function that is relevant to a small minority of cases, that is, to test whether there is cause to hold an accused person for trial. Yet this standard is clearly met in almost all contested cases. An overburdened system will not hold a large number of carefully conducted and deliberative hearings when they are meaningful in only a small percentage of the cases.

By deciding at an early stage which cases are likely to proceed to trial and which are not, defense counsel can identify cases in which the preliminary hearing is a useful procedure. This should limit the number of hearings, thereby allowing the system to devote the necessary time to them. The rules governing preliminary hearings should be changed, where necessary, to make the hearing more useful by the perpetuation of testimony, fuller examination of witnesses, and the participation of defense counsel.

Depositions

Another device for discovering and recording evidence which has received limited use in criminal cases is the deposition. In civil cases depositions and other forms of pretrial examination of witnesses have been increasingly and successfully used. A criminal defendant in almost all jurisdictions may take the deposition of a witness who may be unavailable to testify at trial, and the prosecution has the same right in about half the States. But depositions for broader discovery purposes in criminal cases are available only in three States.

It is undesirable to confine the use of depositions only to the preservation of testimony of witnesses who may be unavailable at trial. Depositions may be used to find facts as well as to preserve testimony. A deposition could resolve a factual dispute during the negotiating stage, and it could provide the basis for a stipulation of witnesses' testimony at trial. In cases where it is not necessary to conduct a full preliminary hearing before a judge, depositions may be submitted to the court for determination of probable cause. Finally, the depositions of certain witnesses may be made a part of the record in order to demonstrate in court the basis for a negotiated guilty plea.

Depositions would be valuable in preserving the testimony of witnesses even when a trial is not immediately contemplated. When a consent decree is permitted, for example, the prosecutor might need a means of preserving his case against a defendant in the event that he violates the conditions agreed upon. In such cases key witnesses might be deposed and their testimony filed as part of the decree, with an agreement that the depositions may be used as testimony if trial becomes necessary.

With the exception of a few jurisdictions neither the prosecutor nor defense counsel has legal power to compel the appearance of witnesses for pretrial examination after indictment. Defense counsel often encounter difficulties in getting potential witnesses to discuss a case with them. The prosecutor's official status is such that most witnesses will cooperate with him while he investigates the case, although in some places subpoenas and the grand jury process are used for these purposes without legal authority.

The flexibility and utility of the deposition make it an extremely valuable fact-finding procedure in the criminal process. Jurisdictions should amend their statutes or rules to permit the taking of a deposition whenever the prosecutor and defense counsel agree, and a compulsory process should be made available for this purpose. Even when they cannot agree, it would be desirable to allow prosecutors and defense counsel, with the permission of the court, to take depositions.

Appendix 6–H

FACTS ABOUT THE DEVELOPMENT OF PROBATION IN THE UNITED STATES

Slightly more than half of the offenders sentenced to correctional treatment in 1965 were placed on probation—supervision in the community subject to the authority of the court. Table 1 sets forth data from the National Survey of Corrections and the Federal corrections system on the number of persons under probation on an average day in 1965 and the number in institutions or on parole. Also shown are estimates of what these populations are likely to be in 1975. As the table indicates, probation is the correctional treatment used for most offenders today and is likely to be used increasingly in the future.

Table 6–H–1. Number of Offenders on Probation, and on Parole or in Institutions, 1965; Projections for 1975.

Location of offender	*1965*		*1975*	
	Number	*Percent*	*Number*	*Percent*
Probation	684,008	53	1,071,000	58
Parole or institution	598,298	47	770,000	42
Total	1,282,386	100	1,841,000	100

The estimates for probation shown in the above table project a growth in the number of adults on probation almost $2\frac{1}{2}$ times greater than the growth in institutional and parole populations. The projected growth in juvenile probation is also substantial. There are rapidly developing very promising intensive community supervision and residential programs, which could further shift the number of juveniles destined for institutions to community-based treatment. Thus, the projections for juvenile probation might actually be low.

The best data available indicate that probation offers one of the most significant prospects for effective programs in corrections. It is also clear that at least two com-

The President's Commission on Law Enforcement and Administration of Justice, *Task Force Report: Corrections* (Washington, D.C.: U.S. Government Printing Office, 1967), pp. 27–30.

ponents are needed to make it operate well. The first is a system that facilitates effective decision-making as to who should receive probation; the second is the existence of good community programs to which offenders can be assigned. Probation services now available in most jurisdictions fall far short of meeting either of these needs.

Within States, probation coverage is still often spotty. Services for juveniles, for example, are available in every county in only 31 States. In one State, a National Survey staff observer noted, only two counties have probation services. A child placed on probation in the other counties is presumed to be adjusting satisfactorily until he is brought back to court with a new charge.

Table 2 shows the number of delinquents and adult felons on probation at the end of 1965 and the annual costs of these services. It is quickly apparent in terms of the number of persons served and of total operating costs that the juvenile system has relatively greater resources than the adult. Cost comparisons, however, require qualification. The juvenile total includes the cost of many foster homes and some private and public institutional costs.

Table 6–H–2. Number of Felons and Juveniles on Probation, 1965, and Annual Costs of Services for Each Group

Type of probation	*Number on probation*	*Annual costs* $
Felony	257,755	37,937,808
Juvenile	224,948	75,019,441
Total	482,703	112,957,249

Furthermore, juvenile probation in some jurisdictions has a substantial responsibility for orphaned or other nondelinquent dependent children.

Probation in the United States is administered by hundreds of independent agencies operating under a different law in each State and under widely varying philosophies, often within the same State. They serve juvenile, misdemeanant, and felony offenders. In one city, a single State or local agency might be responsible for handling all three kinds of probation cases; in another, three separate agencies may be operating, each responsible for a different type of probationer. All of these probation programs must contend with similar issues.

There are many offenders for whom incarceration is the appropriate sanction—either because of their dangerousness or the seriousness of their offense, or both. But in the vast majority of cases where such a sanction is not obviously essential, there has been growing disenchantment with relying heavily on institutions to achieve correctional goals. The growing emphasis on community treatment is supported by several kinds of considerations.

Objections might be raised as to the validity of such comparisons, since expenditures for probation services are now much too meager. However, with the 1-to-10 cost ratios prevailing, probation expenditures can clearly be increased several fold and still remain less expensive than institutional programs. This is especially true when construction costs, which now run up to and beyond $20,000 per bed in a correctional institution, are included. The differential becomes even greater if the cost of welfare assistance for the families of the incarcerated and the loss in taxable income are considered.

There is an extremely wide variation among States in both the laws permitting probation and the way in which probation is practiced. Probation agencies range from those that depend on the ingenuity of a single probation officer to large multidivisional programs offering clinical, diagnostic, detention, foster care, and local institutional programs.

Badly undermanned in general by staff who are too often undertrained and almost always poorly paid, probation agencies only occasionally mount the type of imaginative programs that fulfill their potential for rehabilitation. The extent to which probation is used varies widely from jurisdiction to jurisdiction, paralleling to a large extent the adequacy of staffing ratios.

Over the past decade, a number of efforts have been made to improve the effectiveness of probation and parole supervision by simply reducing the size of an officer's caseloads. Caseloads have been reduced under experimental conditions from 75 to 30 and to 15. It appears from these studies that the simple expedient of reducing caseloads will not of itself assure a reduction in recidivism. Those experiments with reduced caseloads have shown that to reduce recidivism requires classification of offenders with differential treatment for each class.

Further work is needed to specify with greater accuracy the levels of service required for various kinds of cases. But enough experience is already available to implement a broad, if somewhat rough, system of differential treatment such as is already being used in various forms by a number of agencies.

Differing caseload sizes are only one aspect of the need for differential treatment adapted to the type and circumstances of the offender. Another major requirement for using a differential treatment system is an adequate case analysis and planning procedure.

Such planning must determine the kind and intensity of supervision needed by the probationer. For some, assignment to relatively high caseloads for nominal supervision may well be indicated. Other probationers will require assignment to specialized caseloads with varying intensity and kinds of supervision. Programs may range from assistance in dealing with important social agencies such as schools, to group counseling or family counseling. Alcoholics, addicts, and those with mental or physical problems may require special treatment. Still other kinds of treatment for probationers are the various community residential programs described in the next chapter.

Another important part of probation planning is determination of the period during which various kinds of probation supervision are required. Studies of both probation and parole outcome reveal consistently that most difficulties with offenders occur within the first 1 to 2 years under supervision. For those who avoid difficulty through this period, the probability is exceedingly good that they will no longer be involved in criminal activity. Some offenders require extended periods of probation; for them, reduced supervision may be feasible during the latter portion of their probation terms. However, for the vast majority of offenders, inflexible and lengthy probation terms result in unnecessary restraints and costs.

More manpower is needed for probation services than is now available. Data as to exact size of the manpower gap based on careful experimentation with differential treatment must await further studies. However, sufficient data are available now to give a fair approximation of the numbers of officers needed.

Using as a desirable caseload average for juveniles and adult felons the level of 35 suggested in chapter 6 an approximate picture of the need for probation officers can be gained. Table 3 shows the size of caseloads in which probationers are currently supervised. With fewer than 4 percent of the probation officers in the Nation carrying caseloads of 40 or less, it is obvious that the gap between optimal and actual levels of staffing is great.

Table 6-H-3. Percentage Distribution of Probationers, by Size of Caseload in Which Supervised, 1965

Caseload size	*Juvenile probation (Percent)*	*Felony probation (Percent)*
Under 40	3.7	0.8
41-60	19.7	5.0
61-80	49.2	14.1
81-100	16.7	13.1
Over 100	10.7	67.0

In 1965 there were 6,336 juvenile probation officers and 2,940 probation officers supervising offenders convicted of felonies. These officers are responsible for both presentence investigations and supervision. Providing enough officers to conduct needed presentence investigations and also reduce average caseloads to 1 officer for each 35 offenders would immediately require an additional 5,300 officers and supervisors for juveniles and 8,500 for felons.

Chapter 7

A review of statistics on input and output

Criminology as a field of study and research is very dependent upon data that are recorded about the persons, both adult and juvenile, who enter and leave the various way stations of the criminal justice system. Such statistics should be able to indicate the volume of officially acted-upon cases at the various steps in the system, as well as the differential input by regions, states, size of communities, and urban tracts. Volume statistics, if adequately enumerated, should also indicate the differential reduction in the flow of cases from one way station to another, so as to reveal how much drop-out takes place at various points. In addition, if the enumeration of crime and delinquency statistics at the main way stations of the criminal justice system were able to give uniform information on the persons being taken into or through the system, criminologists would be able to compute "categoric" risks for those entering the first way station, for those being released from this station, and for those being held for the next station, and so on throughout the entire system. These categoric risks could be computed if uniform information were collected on age, sex, race, occupational status, previous contacts with the system, etc., for each person entering or leaving the various way stations. Categoric risks for entrance and exit could also be computed by area, if this information were available.

Unfortunately, the statistics that are kept at present have many shortcomings in terms of uniform enumeration at the different steps in the criminal justice system (both adult and juvenile). There are way stations in the system that have not as yet developed uniform national statistics; these include detention in jails and workhouses, the use of bail or bond, the processing of cases in the prosecutor's offices, and the sentencing of cases in the courts. The only three enumerations that at present contain fairly uniform statistics on movement into and out of the particular way station are the *Uniform Crime Reports*, collected by the Federal Bureau of Investigation from local police jurisdictions, the *National Prisoner Statistics*, collected by the Federal Bureau of Prisons, and the statistics on the movement of juvenile delinquents into and out of state training schools for juvenile offenders. However, even these three sets of statistics yield more insight into the differential volume of cases than they do into the kinds of persons who enter and who are discharged from these major way stations. Much still needs to be done in order to obtain uniform coverage on personal data.

At any rate, it behooves the student of criminology to review the condition of statistical bookkeeping at the major way stations of the criminal justice system. Undoubtedly, the best set of uniform nationwide statistics has been developed by the Federal Bureau of Investigation; called *Uniform Crime Reports*, it is assembled and published annually. The data are collected in a standardized way from local cooperating police departments, according to a manual of instructions. There are still some small police agencies that do not prepare reports, although in 1970, for instance, 91 percent of the population of the United States was covered by cooperating police departments: 97 percent of the population in standard metropolitan areas; 88 percent in other cities; 71 percent in rural areas.[1]

The index crimes

The data assembled in the annual *Uniform Crime Reports* represent the statistics on input into the initial way station of the criminal justice system, namely the police. First of all, the statistics on the so-called "index" crimes need to be understood. It was the technical opinion of experts from the International Association of Chiefs of Police (an American organization), more than forty years ago, that the following seven offenses had a high probability of being reported in most police departments in a uniform manner:

1. murder and nonnegligent manslaughter
2. forcible rape
3. robbery
4. aggravated assault
5. burglary
6. larceny ($50 and over)
7. auto theft.

[1] *Crime in the United States: Uniform Crime Reports—1970* (Washington, D.C.: Federal Bureau of Investigation, U.S. Department of Justice, August 31, 1971), p. 59.

These offenses have become known as "index" crimes or as "crimes known to the police" and are sometimes referred to as the major seven.

A manual developed by the F.B.I. for the use of cooperating police departments indicates just how reports on the major seven offenses should be handled. If a complaint coming to the attention of a local police agency involves two or more of the major seven offenses, an order of priority must be followed. Offense no. 1 in the above list takes precedence over offense no. 2; 2, over 3; 3, over 4, and so on. Reports that carry multiple offenses are recorded as one offense in this order of priority.

As a matter of fact, it is best to look upon the reporting of the major seven crimes as a compilation of reported "events" in a single order of priority. For example, if a woman is forcibly raped by two men, her jewels forcibly taken, and she dies as a result of the violence, the occurrence is reported as homicide, because homicide occupies a higher order in the priority listing than forcible rape and robbery. The occurrence is reported also as *one* event, although two men were involved and three different crimes were committed. If a person is robbed by one man and at the same time is knocked unconscious by him through use of a blackjack, the occurrence is recorded as one (event) robbery, because robbery occupies number 3 position in the listing of the major seven offenses and aggravated assault occupies number 4 position.

What is still less realised by persons who use the reports on index crimes is that, in the instance of crimes against the person (criminal homicide, forcible rape, robbery, and aggravated assault), one offense is counted for each victim. For example, if a man murders two persons in any given episode, the count is two—for the two victims. Likewise, if one man assaulted a husband and wife with a "blackjack" in their home during the course of burglary, two offenses of aggravated assault are reported. In this situation, the assault takes precedence over the burglary.

On the other hand, in the instance of the index crimes against property (burglary, larceny-theft, and auto theft), one offense is counted for each "distinct operation or attempt." Under the "hotel or lodging house" rule, only one offense is counted if one or more "sneak thieves" enter two or more rooms in one hotel. However, one offense is counted for each hotel in which rooms were entered in the same operation. On the other hand, the "hotel" rule does not apply to apartment houses. In this instance, one offense is counted for each separate apartment entered; the same applies for separate offices or suites, although in the same building. One offense is counted if one or more articles are stolen from one store or place at any one time or if one or more articles are taken from one or more persons at the same time. Finally, one offense is counted for each automobile stolen. The reader here should consult the first part of the excerpts from the *Uniform Crime Reporting Handbook*, duplicated in Appendix 7-A.

One should look upon the reporting of the major offenses as perhaps the most important input of criminal events, taking place as close after the happening as is possible to obtain in the present system of things. It should be noticed that provision is made on monthly reporting sheets of the major seven occurrences for the recording of unfounded (i.e. false or baseless) complaints, which are subtracted from the original complaints.

The major seven or index crimes should be looked upon in criminology as a uniform volume (extent) indicator—at least, a limited volume indicator. Because of their uniformity, they can represent an index of change in volume from year to year. This is one of the major functions of the index crime reports and also explains why they are called "index" crimes. Criminologists and administrators are thus able to say that the volume of reported crime has increased 176 percent in ten years (1960–1970), while population has only increased 13 percent.[2]

In addition to indications of yearly changes, the index crimes give an indication of differential volume by regions of the country, states, standard metropolitan areas, other cities, and rural areas. See for example Table 7–1, which presents the rates of occurrence of the seven index crimes by metropolitan communities, cities, and rural areas. Such statistics enable sociologists and others to say that the volume rate of reported events is much higher in the metropolitan areas than in other cities, and it is lowest in rural areas (except for the infrequent events of murder and forcible rape).

In conclusion, it should be understood that the reported events do not cover demographic information on persons involved, either as "doers" or as victims. In other words, they do not cover variation in sex, age, race, etc. However, by going to local police departments, sociologists, criminologists, and others can obtain the location of the reported events and can plot these locations by census tracts, thus obtaining area variation within cities.

Clearances of the index crimes by arrest

The clearances of the index crimes gives a sequential indication of the input of cases into the law enforcement way station of the criminal justice system and represent police "solutions" of the reported crimes. As noted in the *Uniform Crime Reporting Handbook*'s excerpts in Appendix 7–A, "an offense is 'cleared by arrest' when at least one person (1) is arrested, (2) charged with the commission of the offense, and (3) turned over to the court for prosecution (whether following arrest, court summons or police notice)."

It should be understood that, in the count of clearances of the index crimes, it is the "offenses" that are being counted as cleared and not the arrests. If three persons commit one offense and all three are caught and arrested, charged, and held for court (booked, in other words), the clearance count is just one. If only one or two of the three reported persons are caught

[2] *Ibid.*, p. 2.

Table 7-1. Index of Crime, United States, 1970[3]

Area	Population*	Total crime index	Violent** crime	Property** crime	Murder and non-negligent man-slaughter	Forcible rape	Robbery	Aggravated assault	Burglary	Larceny ($50 and over)	Auto theft
United States Total	203,184,772	5,568,197	731,402	4,836,795	15,812	37,273	348,380	329,937	2,169,322	1,746,107	921,366
Rate per 100,000 inhabitants	—	2,740.5	360.0	2,380.5	7.8	18.3	171.5	162.4	1,067.7	859.4	453.5
Standard Metropolitan Statistical Area	140,226,949	—	—	—	—	—	—	—	—	—	—
Area actually reporting***	97.2%	4,691,725	634,446	4,057,279	12,093	30,847	331,819	259,687	1,797,699	1,420,012	839,568
Estimated total	100.0%	4,762,638	641,078	4,121,560	12,265	31,302	333,810	263,701	1,825,851	1,446,224	849,485
Rate per 100,000 inhabitants	—	3,396.4	457.2	2,939.2	8.7	22.3	238.0	188.1	1,302.1	1,031.3	605.8
Other Cities	24,092,789	—	—	—	—	—	—	—	—	—	—
Area actually reporting	87.8%	396,450	37,895	358,555	906	1,877	8,149	26,963	155,296	163,380	39,879
Estimated total	100.0%	445,129	43,695	401,434	1,070	2,124	9,098	31,403	174,775	182,246	44,413
Rate per 100,000 inhabitants	—	1,847.6	181.4	1,666.2	4.4	8.8	37.8	130.3	725.4	756.4	184.3
Rural	38,865,034	—	—	—	—	—	—	—	—	—	—
Area actually reporting	71.3%	267,388	28,735	238,653	1,534	2,614	3,639	20,948	129,021	88,702	20,930
Estimated total	100.0%	360,430	46,629	313,801	2,477	3,847	5,472	34,833	168,696	117,637	27,468
Rate per 100,000 inhabitants	—	927.4	120.0	807.4	6.4	9.9	14.1	89.6	434.1	302.7	70.7

*Population is Bureau of the Census

**Violent Crime is offenses of murder, forcible rape, robbery and aggravated assault; property crime is offenses of burglary, larceny $50 and over and auto theft.

***The percentage representing area actually reporting will not coincide with the ratio between reported and estimated crime totals since these data represent the sum of the calculations for individual states which have varying populations, portions reporting and crime rates.

[3] *Uniform Crime Reports—1970*, *ibid.*, p. 64.

Table 7-2. Clearances by arrest of index crimes, by cities and rural areas, 1970[4]

Population group	*Crime index total*	*Murder and non-negligent manslaughter*	*Forcible rape*	*Robbery*	*Aggravated assault*	*Burglary breaking or entering*	*Theft ($50 and over)*	*Auto theft*
*TOTAL CITIES								
4,068 cities; total population 102,316,000								
Offenses known	3,310,390	8,898	21,038	201,897	186,560	1,247,541	1,045,234	599,222
Percent cleared by arrest	20.1	86.5	56.4	29.1	64.9	19.4	11.7	16.9
**RURAL AREA								
1,350 agencies; total population 21,136,000								
Offenses known	211,490	1,049	1,916	2,619	14,447	105,023	70,317	16,119
Percent cleared by arrest	25.7	87.7	70.2	47.6	75.2	21.1	16.5	38.2

*These cities range from 2,500 population to cities of over 250,000 population.
**Rural areas are defined as places of a population under 2,500.

[4] *Uniform Crime Reports—1970, op. cit.*, pp. 108–109.

and booked, even though one of the reported three managed to escape arrest at the time, the clearance also counts as one. If the third person is later caught and booked, no clearance is counted. On the other hand, if the police catch a person who is suspected of breaking and entering three different stores and he is booked for all these offenses, the clearance count is three.

Table 7-2 gives the clearance count in 1970 for index crimes by police agencies serving cities with populations of 2,500 and over and by police agencies (usually sheriff's offices) serving rural areas (under 2,500 population). One notices that the percentage of clearances is higher in the rural than in the urban jurisdictions (with one exception, namely the clearances for murder and nonnegligent manslaughter). If the complete breakdown by size of cities had been duplicated in Table 7-2, a slight but fairly regular decline in the percentage of clearances would have been noticeable, moving from the cities between 2,500 and 10,000 population up through the largest cities. Such a trend might be expected in view of the greater possibility for offenders to escape police action in the larger centers than in the smaller and rural places, in spite of increasing availability of technical equipment and technical police services in the larger jurisdictions, while the risk of getting caught in rural areas, in spite of fewer technical facilities, is probably greater. Perhaps the greater risk is due to less mobility and less anonymity in the smaller towns and rural areas; maybe there is slightly more willingness to help law enforcement in smaller places.

It is apparent also from the statistics in Table 7-2 that the percentage of clearances by arrest varies greatly by type of offense among the seven index crimes. The percentage of clearance is greatest for murder and nonnegligent manslaughter, next highest for aggravated assault, next for forcible rape, and next for robbery. In the cities over 2,500 population, a decreasing sequential order in percentage of clearance continues for burglary, auto theft, and larceny over $50, while in the rural areas, the order is auto theft, burglary, and larceny over $50. It appears that clearance by arrest is quite low for larceny over $50, auto theft, burglary, and robbery in the cities, whereas clearance is very low in rural areas for larceny over $50 and burglary. On the other hand, in both urban and rural areas the clearance rate is highest (in descending order) for murder and nonnegligent manslaughter, aggravated assault, and forcible rape. In rural areas, the clearance rate is also relatively high for robbery and auto theft, although the reasons for this are not at all apparent.

Arrest reports

It should be realized by students of criminology as well as by researchers that arrest reports, while not the first input into the criminal justice system at the police way station, are the first input of recorded data on a personal basis. While the count is of arrests according to defined limits, it is at the same time a count of persons—that is, persons arrested. The arrest count is not a count of "charges" but of persons taken into custody (arrested). If later in the investigation a person is released without a charge, the case still is recorded as an arrest, just as are the cases held for court on charges.

If the police take into custody a person who is subsequently charged with two or more offenses, this instance is counted as only one arrest. On the other hand, if two or more persons are taken into custody for committing one offense, each person taken into custody is counted as an arrest. If the police discover that a man taken into custody committed an offense prior to the present one, he is counted as just one arrestee. If a person is taken into custody, is released on bond, and commits another offense while under bond, the arrest count is two.

However, in the instance of juveniles, if they are warned by the police but not held for the juvenile court, this does not count as arrests. Likewise, juveniles coming to the attention of the police for problems of neglect or waywardness are not recorded as arrests. Only juveniles taken into custody for violating the regular sections of the criminal code and who are turned over to the juvenile court are counted in the arrests.

Reference to the excerpts from the *Uniform Crime Reporting Handbook* as given in Appendix 7-A will help clarify the reporting system of arrests. See the sections dealing with "Age, sex, and race of persons arrested"; "How to prepare the age, sex, and race of persons arrested return"; and "Juveniles."

Because reported arrest data represent the first recorded input of persons into the criminal justice system, arrests are of great value to the study of criminology. The arrest data enable the criminologist to study demographic differentials ("categoric risks") of persons who become officially involved at the way station of arrest. Just what "being taken into custody by the police" means in terms of "total" involvement of the individual concerned or of all arrested persons concerned is a question—it probably represents an infinitesimally small and highly selected sample of offenses and offenders. As noted in the previous chapter, much depends upon the decisions whether or not to hold the person after the offense comes to the attention of the police through complaint or on-the-spot surveillance.

Nevertheless, arrest data enable the criminologist to study certain demographic chances of being taken into custody, namely variation by sex, age, and race, for the different types of offenses. It is from arrest data that the criminologist discovers that disproportionately more males are arrested than females; Negroes, more than whites; persons in the younger age categories, more than those in the older age categories.

To what extent is the sex differential due to behavioral differences of males and females, the roles they play in society, or the greater willingness of the public to report males and the greater willingness of police to arrest males than females? Likewise, how much of the age differential in arrests is due to behavioral differences of young persons as compared with more mature persons, their roles in society, or the willingness of the public to complain and the readiness of the police to arrest? The same sort of questions can be asked with reference to the race differentials in arrests. There are strong suspicions, voiced especially in the material which the President's Commission on Law Observance and the Administration of Justice was able to assemble, that the Negro, like persons of low economic status or minority status, are relatively "over-complained-upon" by the public and "over-acted-upon" by the police in American society.

Some criminological researchers, usually of the sociological variety, have found their way to the arrest records of urban police departments and have been able to plot on the maps of the cities the differential distribution of the locations where the crimes are reported to have taken place and the locations of the residences of the arrested persons.[5] Such data from local police departments have supplied the basis for the so-called "ecological" studies of crime and delinquency, which attempt to discover the variation in the reported offense rates by various tracts and zones in cities. The tract or zone differences are obviously related to the socioeconomic structure of the city. They are also related to the willingness of victims to complain and to the decisions of the police to take action.

Persons charged

The next way station in law enforcement that is reported uniformly and annually by police departments to the F.B.I. is the so-called "return on persons charged." Here again, reference should be made to the appropriate excerpts from the *Uniform Crime Reporting Handbook* as given in Appendix 7-A. In this set of reports, the count is made of arrested persons who are turned over to the prosecutor's office for prosecution as well as of persons who are summoned, notified, or cited to appear in court. Persons who are arrested but are released without charge are not counted in the statistics on charges (although counted in the statistics on arrest). The count is one for each person arrested and held for prosecution. If several persons are arrested for one crime and held for prosecution, each person is counted in the "charge" return.

This set of statistics includes follow-up data that have application to a succeeding way station of the criminal justice system. In the instance of adult offenders, the police report adults found guilty of the offense charged

[5] *See* Walter C. Reckless, *The Crime Problem*, 4th ed. (New York: Appleton-Century-Crofts 1967), pp. 119–127.

or of a lesser plea, as well as the cases acquitted or dismissed. In the instance of juveniles, the reports on persons charged merely count the number of juveniles referred to the juvenile court (not their outcome).

It should be understood that the "charge feed-in" to the criminal justice system by the police is smaller than the preceding "feed-in" of arrests. As has been indicated above, the reason for this is that there are cases that the police release after arrest. Evidently, the police sometimes decide during their investigative or screening procedure that there is no basis for charging, the persons taken into custody were not involved, or the evidence for their involvement is dubious. Due to the way the statistics are reported by the F.B.I., it is not possible to tell the exact percentage of dropouts from arrest to charge (held for prosecution), nor is it possible to tell the age, sex, and race difference of the dropouts. In addition, it is not possible to analyze the sex, age, and race differences of persons found guilty of the offense charged, compared with those found guilty of a lesser plea or with those acquitted or dismissed. However, it should be possible to obtain such differential data in a local police department by tracking down the case information on a consecutive sample of arrests and tracing these cases through the court procedure.

Prosecution statistics

Persons charged by the police are turned over to the prosecutor's office of lower courts. If cases are bound over later to the felony court by the lower court, the felony charges enter the prosecutor's office of this court of general jurisdiction (felony court). Hence, there are two prosecutor's way stations, and both of these should produce uniform statistics on charges processed, as well as the detention, bail, or personal recognizance handling of persons while awaiting processing by the prosecutor. Dr. Peter P. Lejins made the following statement on the need for a uniform, integrated set of prosecution statistics, in order for administrators and researchers to be able to gauge what is taking place within the criminal justice system.[6]

> There is an area of law-enforcement activities with reference to a suspect, or, if in the end result he is found to be guilty of the offense, with reference to the offender, which begins with his arrest by the police and ends with his appearance in the court for the definitive hearing of the case. In the course of this segment of criminal procedure, decisions are made and actions taken by the prosecuting attorney, by the judge of the inferior court, who may hold preliminary hearings for various purposes, by the grand

[6] Peter P. Lejins, "National Crime Data Reporting System: Proposal for a Model," Appendix C, *Task Force Report: Crime and its Impact—An Assessment* (Washington, D.C.: The President's Commission on Law Enforcement and Administration of Justice, 1962), pp. 191–192.

jury, and by the sheriff or other official who operates the jail or other detention facility, in the result of which actions the suspect may be released on his own recognizance, released on bail, detained in jail, indicted or not indicted by the grand jury, or have his case simply dismissed by the prosecuting attorney, who may reach the conclusion that no offense was committed or that there is not enough evidence to prosecute. Although most of the decisions reached are legal decisions and a record of these is made, statistics pertaining to this area of law enforcement activities are not available not only on a national scale, but by and large, also not on a State or local level. At least these statistics are not available in tabulations that would provide a clear picture of the varying fate of this population made up of the persons arrested by the police, which is so to say the input into this segment of law-enforcement procedure. If one remembers that there are also no national judicial criminal statistics and that on a State or local basis, too, such statistics are either nonexistent or contain too little information, one can well understand the frequent comment that after the police report the arrests, a total statistical blackout sets in until, very much later in the criminal procedure, the National Prisoners Statistics pick up the thread and give the number of prisoners in State and Federal institutions as a clear and reliable datum.

It is true that we know the type of things that happen, but we do not know the numerical distribution at all and hence the relative frequency with which various measures are being used with regard to offenders: we do not know how many were indicted by the grand jury or, for that matter, how many went to the grand jury; we do not know how many were acquitted by the courts or were fined or placed on probation; we do not know how many went to the local jails to serve short-term sentences nor how many were in the process released on bail or kept in detention while awaiting trial.

One can hardly expect a broad-scale evaluation of this entire segment of law enforcement activities and rational planning for the future with this little information as to what is actually going on. Even if this lack of information can be explained and understood historically, in the contemporary society it stands as a case of weakness or neglect and must be remedied. If the national judicial criminal statistics, when renewed and developed, would clear up one part of this uncharted territory, the segment following the arrest but prior to the case's reaching the court would still not be taken care of statistically. Therefore, it is recommended here that this complex of law enforcement procedures and actions be structured as a unit for statistical purposes and referred to as prosecution statistics. The National Crime Data Agency should consider the development of a statistical program for this area as one of its early and most important assignments.

Since the component elements of prosecution statistics which tentatively comprise prosecuting attorney's statistics, recognizance, bail statistics, and detention statistics, involve—although interrelated—separate agencies, personnel staffs and types of activities, studies must be made and plans developed for each of these separately, but then, of course, integrated. The procedures outlined in the respective sections of this proposal should be followed in developing uniform reporting categories and initiating appropriate promotional activities to secure the cooperation of the agencies and staffs involved.

As to the role of detention in the prosecution statistics, it should be noted that presently most detention takes place in jails which are also the institutions for serving short-term sentences. Although prosecution statistics should of course contain the data on detention, this data may have to be basically reported in the jail statistics when such are, hopefully, developed (see the respective section of the proposal). Since the thought is often expressed that the detention facilities in the future should be separate from the short-term incarceration facilities and several specialized detention facilities have already been developed, this whole area organizationally may be in a state of flux for a considerable period to come. The planning for the statistics will have to take this into consideration and the necessary adjustments in the reporting categories and standard reporting procedures will have to be made.

Jail and workhouse statistics

Some county jails keep a set of records on the turnover of cases, whether these are detention cases (awaiting court processing, where bail or bond has not been granted) or short-sentence cases (committed for a minor crime or misdemeanor). There is no question that the input and output of jail cases, whether for detention or commitment, constitute one of the most crucial and important way stations in the criminal justice system. Unfortunately, a uniform set of jail statistics has not been developed and little interest has been generated in such a nationwide development. The experts on matters such as jail administration and crime reporting would probably say that at the present time there would be very few sheriffs' offices, which operate the county jails, that would cooperate in filling in the standard schedules and sending them to the designated federal office that in turn collects uniform jail statistics.

The U.S. Census has taken jail censuses decenially of the number of persons contained therein (on a certain day), by age, sex, race, marital status, educational level, occupation, etc., just as it takes a census of persons contained in other institutions decennially (on a certain day). It has conducted also some special censuses of inmates. These censuses are able to give a demographic cross section of inmate population on hand at a certain time but are not helpful for analysis of input or output at this particular way station.

Under recent federal law, the national jail census has become the responsibility of National Criminal Justice Information and Statistics Service of the Law Enforcement Assistance Administration, U.S. Department of Justice. The National Criminal Justice Information and Statistics Service, however, entered into an agreement with the U.S. Bureau of Prisons to conduct the national jail census of 1970, which was done as of March 15, 1970. It should be noted that this census was limited to local facilities that hold persons for 48 hours or more and excluded jails operated by state governments as well as by so-called "drunk tanks" and city lockups that usually hold persons for less than 48 hours.

According to these specifications, there were 4,037 jails in the United States at the time and 160,863 inmates on hand.[7] The 1970 jail census included several important items for the study of jails as a functioning agency in the criminal justice system, but the census did not contain information on the input and output of the jails—that is, the number of persons admitted and released during 1970; it only gave the number of persons on hand as of March 15, 1970.

Students and researchers in criminology should take special notice of the need in the future to separate the detention (while awaiting trial) function of the jail from the short-sentence function. They represent two different way stations in the criminal justice system and separate facilities are necessary to take care of each function adequately. The city workhouses, since they are short-sentence institutions, should be included in the statistics covering the short-sentence input and outgo of prisoners but should not be included in state and federal prison statistics (which cover the longer term sentences of felony offenders).

Court statistics

There are at present no uniform court statistics for the country as a whole. The Bureau of the Census, following an act of Congress in 1931, began the collection of judicial statistics in 1932 and continued its effort until 1946 with the publication of the court statistics for 1945, when the task was abandoned According to Lejins:[8]

> The main reason for the failure and discontinuance was the inability to secure the cooperation of the courts in reporting their data to the Census. . . . Also not all of the courts of general jurisdiction which were supposed to be covered by the program took part in it in those States that were supposed to be participating. . . . This dismal picture of noncooperation by the courts, however, must be viewed together with the fact that extremely limited staff support was made available to the program by the Bureau of the Census.

The Bureau of the Census, however, contended that "the demand for these statistics is considered insufficient to justify the funds and personnel required for their collection." Actually, during the fourteen years of collection of

[7] National Criminal Justice Information and Statistics Service, *1970 National Jail Census*, (Washington, D.C.: Law Enforcement Assistance Administration, U.S. Department of Justice, February 1971), p. 1.

[8] *Ibid.*, p. 185.

Judicial Criminal Statistics, the coverage on volume of dispositions dropped very markedly: from approximately 131,000, 140,000, and 158,000 in the years of 1933, 1934, and 1935 to 49,000, 48,000, and 57,000 in the years of 1943, 1944, and 1945.[9]

In the last report by the Bureau of the Census on Judicial Criminal Statistics (for the year 1945), only some of the courts in 25 states reported to the census. In 1932, when the system was introduced, 16 states reported data from some of their courts. The number of states cooperating never exceeded 30 (the level reached in 1935 and 1936).

The reports dealt with defendants disposed of by courts of general jurisdiction in the cooperating states. This meant that the coverage was primarily on serious felony cases plus certain misdemeanors that did not fall under the jurisdiction of inferior courts of country, municipal, and township government. If certain felonies happened to be disposed of in the minor courts that mostly handle misdemeanants, these cases were not covered in the judicial court statistics. It appears that the 1932–1945 series of judicial statistics as collected by the Bureau of the Census represented coverage primarily on the more serious felony cases (defendants).

In 1945, the cooperating courts in 25 states reported 57,426 defendants disposed of, of whom 75 percent were convicted and sentenced, and 25 percent were disposed without conviction.[10] Of the defendants who were convicted and sentenced, 39 percent were given a prison or reformatory sentence; 32 percent, probation or suspended sentence; 21 percent, a jail or workhouse sentence; 8 percent, other sentences.[11] The variation among the various states in the percentage convicted ranged all the way from 58 to 90 percent, while the percentage of those sentenced to prison or reformatory, given probation, committed to a local jail or workhouse also had a great range: prison and reformatory sentences from 29 to 71 percent, probation from 16 to 65 percent, jail or workhouse 2 to 41 percent. The wide variation in sentencing procedure is due to the development and use of probation services in the local courts throughout the individual states, to the availability of local jails and workhouses for commitments, and to prevailing sentencing practices of the judges.

The procedural outcome for the defendants disposed in the reporting courts as of 1945 was broken down by type of offense and, as would be expected, the range of variation was considerable. The variation in the percentage of types of sentences by types of offenses is extremely large, again reflecting differential policy and facilities.[12]

[9] *Judicial Criminal Statistics, 1945* (Washington, D.C.: United States Department of Commerce, Bureau of the Census, 1947), p. 1.

[10] *Ibid.*, Table 1, p. 2.

[11] *Ibid.*, Table 4, p. 5.

[12] *Ibid.*, Table 5, p. 6; Table 8, p. 7.

There is no doubt that efforts must be made to revive the reporting of dispositions by local courts and to find ways and means to obtain cooperation from the officers and/or clerks of these courts. It may be that a permanent crime-data collecting agency within the U.S. Department of Justice will eventually assume the task of collecting and reporting dispositions by local, state, and federal courts.

Some states have been able to establish a reporting system of the input of court cases. However, it is the United States District Courts who have developed a uniform set of statistics for the federal district courts. One notices in the five sample tables duplicated in Appendix 7-B that the reports on "defendants" apply to those who have been brought before the courts. There are statistical breakdowns on type of disposition such as dismissed without trial, disposed of by plea of guilty or *nolo contendere*, disposed of by court trial, and disposed of by jury trial; these categories are further broken down into cases that were and were not convicted. The dispositions by plea of guilty and *nolo contendere* in the federal districts courts constitute the overwhelming majority of dispositions, which dispositions represent an enormous time-saver in court procedure. The U.S. Courts' statistics also give data on dispositions according to various classes of federal offenses. In addition, they supply uniform information on the convicted defendants according to imprisonment sentences and suspended sentences (probation), by the various uniform classes of federal offenses.

In 1969, 85 percent of the cases appearing before 89 federal district courts of the United States (not including the District of Columbia, the Canal Zone, Guam, and the Virgin Islands) were disposed of without trial; 5 percent, by court trial; 10 percent, by jury trial. See Table 7-B-1 in Appendix 7-B for details. Table 7-B-4 of the selected tables duplicated in Appendix 7-B indicates that, among federal offenses reported by the district courts, Class VI offenses (counterfeiting, burglary, interstate transportation of stolen property, marijuana, Selective Service Act, etc.) were the most frequent while Class IV offenses (theft, postal fraud, forgery) were second in case-load volume. Of individual offenses, apart from offense classes, auto theft was the most frequently dealt with offense in the federal courts in 1969; ordinary theft, second; liquor law and internal revenue charges, third; marijuana violations, fourth. See Table 7-B-4 in Appendix 7-B.

The handling of cases by types of federal violations in 1969 is given in Table 7-B-6. The conviction rate of particular offenses ranges mostly from 60 to 90 percent, the obvious exceptions being "wagering tax violations" (13.5%).

In 1969, 44 percent of the cases in federal district courts were imprisoned, 43 percent also were given probation (suspended sentence), 6 percent received a fine only, while all other sentences constituted 8 percent. See Table 7-B-9. The prior criminal record of the convicted defendants is also reported according to type of sentences received in "this trip" before the court. Of the cases on which prior record was available or discoverable, 64 percent had a prior criminal record. See Table 7–B–14.

Demographic information on sex, age, and race of the defendants is usually not presented in the court statistics, and consequently it is impossible for criminologists to spot variation in procedure according to these parameters. In some of the published tables the federal court statistics provide data on dispositions according to commitment under the federal Youth Correction Act and the Federal Juvenile Delinquency Act; these dispositions give some indication of differences in the handling of juvenile and adult cases. In the federal courts, there are very few female defendants. Hence, the criminologist can assume that the sex differential in dispositions of defendants is of very little consequence. However, it would be important to have the breakdown of defendants by race, in order to discover current judicial policy in sentencing practices.

Reference to the F.B.I. system of reporting of persons charged and to the excerpts from the *Uniform Crime Reporting Handbook* in Appendix 7–A will indicate that the available returns on "persons charged" contain follow-through information on what happened to the cases in court. In the absence of uniform court reports for the whole country, the F.B.I. annual return of persons charged gives limited insight. In Table 7–3 the disposition of persons charged in 1970 is presented by type of disposition and by type of offense. One notices that in the limited number of cities on which data are given (3,025), the percentage of cases reported by the police agency as found guilty of the offense charged varies greatly by type of offense. It appears that the percentage found guilty is very high (considerably above average) for the less serious offenses and is much below average for the serious charges such as homicide, forcible rape, robbery, and aggravated assault. In the charges for burglary, vandalism, auto theft, and arson, the percentage reported as found guilty is very small. The acquitals and dismissals appear to be considerably above average for the serious offenses. Notice should also be made of the high percentage of referrals to juvenile courts in the instances of charges for robbery, burglary, larceny, auto theft, arson, buying and receiving stolen property, and vandalism.

In the F.B.I.'s statistics on dispositions (in the cases charged), it is not readily discernible whether the cases classified under "guilty of offense charged," particularly in the felony offenses, represent the original charge as brought to the court by the police or whether they represent changes in the charge due to the process of "negotiated pleas of guilty" which were estimated, by the President's Crime Commission, to take place in 90 to 95 percent of the instances.

Juvenile court statistics

Starting in the late forties, the U.S. Children's Bureau began to collect and publish annual statistics on the number of cases disposed of in juvenile courts in the selected sampling units (areas) that are used by the U.S. Census.

Table 7-3. Disposition of persons formally charged by the police, 1970[13]

[3,025 cities; 1970 population 68,897,000]

Offense	*Charged (held for prosecution)*	*Guilty*		*Acquitted or dismissed*	*Referred to juvenile court*
		Offense charged	*Lesser offense*		
Total	**2,602,511**	**63.3** [%]	**3.5** [%]	**15.2** [%]	**18.0** [%]
Criminal homicide:					
(*a*) Murder and nonnegligent manslaughter	3,585	35.2	20.1	34.3	10.4
(*b*) Manslaughter by negligence	961	38.4	10.8	42.2	8.3
Forcible rape	4,915	27.7	15.6	34.8	21.9
Robbery	23,320	25.2	11.1	23.6	40.1
Aggravated assault	38,466	36.3	14.5	31.1	18.1
Burglary—breaking or entering	97,282	23.1	8.6	12.9	55.3
Larceny—theft	236,495	45.6	3.9	14.5	36.0
Auto theft	47,519	18.7	5.3	13.9	62.1
Violent crime[1]	70,286	31.9	13.7	29.0	25.3
Property crime[2]	381,296	36.5	5.3	14.0	44.2
Subtotal for above offenses	452,543	35.8	6.6	16.4	41.2
Other assaults	123,729	46.4	4.0	36.0	13.7
Arson	3,163	17.8	4.6	15.4	62.2
Forgery and counterfeiting	13,903	55.9	10.3	21.2	12.6
Fraud	28,133	65.4	4.3	26.8	3.5
Embezzlement	2,884	51.1	6.2	32.3	10.3
Stolen property; buying, receiving, possessing	20,043	36.6	6.7	21.3	35.4
Vandalism	35,320	24.8	1.4	19.9	53.8
Weapons; carrying, possessing, etc.	37,164	58.3	6.2	22.0	13.5
Prostitution and commercialized vice	11,818	67.5	2.7	27.2	2.6
Sex offenses (except forcible rape and prostitution)	19,278	51.9	7.9	21.2	18.9
Narcotic drug laws	93,583	40.6	5.9	25.1	28.4
Gambling	27,877	69.0	3.7	26.0	1.3
Offenses against family and children	22,919	55.1	2.9	29.1	12.9
Driving under the influence	177,846	75.8	15.4	7.9	.8
Liquor laws	105,005	65.1	1.5	12.3	21.1
Drunkenness	803,823	91.5	.3	6.7	1.5
Disorderly conduct	217,237	60.5	1.0	23.0	15.4
Vagrancy	29,606	68.2	.9	23.9	7.1
All other offenses	376,637	48.4	1.5	16.8	33.2

[1] Violent crime is offenses of murder, forcible rape, robbery and aggravated assault.
[2] Property crime is offenses of burglary, larceny and auto theft.

[13] *Crime in the United States: Uniform Crime Reports—1970* (Washington, D.C.: Federal Bureau of Investigation, U.S. Department of Justice, August 31, 1971), Table 15, p. 114.

The enumeration of the delinquency cases disposed of in these sample courts was separated from the dependency and neglect cases also disposed of by these courts. At this time, the delinquency cases also included traffic violations of juveniles, if and when brought to the juvenile courts. The first report on juvenile court statistics appeared in 1951 and covered the fiscal years 1946 to 1949.[14] But the principal coverage in this first report was for the fiscal year 1949.

In the fiscal year 1949, 413 juvenile courts reported 70,616 delinquency cases disposed of. The dispositions were classified according to official and unofficial—in later reports these are called judicial and nonjudicial. Official or judicial refers to a disposition in which the court acted upon a formal petition or motion, while unofficial or nonjudicial refers to a disposition in which the case was adjusted by a court officer (not necessarily or usually the judge) without invoking a formal petition or motion.

The dispositions were classified by the particular locality served by the court, by age, and by sex while the two main dispositions, official and unofficial, were in turn broken down into specific categories of handling. However, as the annual reports continued, the coverage of the enumeration narrowed down to type of disposition, by sex and locality. It appears that (c. 1956) the Children's Bureau shifted from using actual cases reported to estimated dispositions for the entire United States, as calculated from the actual return for the sample juvenile courts covered.[15]

One other important change occurred at about this time (in the 1957 and 1958 reporting). Traffic cases were separated in the enumeration from delinquency cases and were accorded separate tabulation. Likewise, at this time (the 1957 coverage), the dispositions were classified by cases coming to the attention of juvenile courts in "urban" areas, "semi-urban" areas, and "rural" areas, these classifications being based upon the court's service area in which 70 percent or more, 30 to 69 percent, and less than 30 percent respectively of any jurisdiction served communities of 10,000 population and over.

In the most recent report available at the time of this analysis, namely the dispositions for 1969,[16] the estimated dispositions for the entire United States were classified by sex of the delinquent youth and also by urban, semi-urban, and rural areas. The estimates were made from data collected from 491 juvenile courts, within 230 of the 2,000 sampling units used by the U.S. Bureau of the Census.

[14] "Juvenile Court Statistics 1946–1949," *U.S. Children's Bureau Statistical Series*, No. 8 (Washington, 1951).

[15] "Juvenile Court Statistics 1956," *U.S. Children's Bureau Statistical Series*, No. 47 (Washington, 1958).

[16] *Juvenile Court Statistics 1969*, Statistical Series 95 (Washington, D.C.: U.S. Department of Health, Education, and Welfare, Social and Rehabilitation Service, Office of Juvenile Delinquency and Youth Development), © 1971.

The 1969 juvenile court statistics presented yearly estimates of delinquency cases disposed of by juvenile courts, including traffic offenses, from 1940 to 1969. The 1940 estimate was 200,000; the 1969, 1,599,900 cases.[17] The 1969 report presented the number and percent of dispositions, exclusive of traffic cases, from 1958 to 1969 according to urban, semi-urban, and rural districts. It also presented the estimated number and percentage of boys and girls, exclusive of traffic offenses, disposed of by juvenile courts from 1958 to 1969.

It is interesting to note that the total number of estimated dispositions exclusive of traffic cases more than doubled in the 12-year span in urban and semi-urban areas but only increased slightly in the rural areas.[18] Boys' cases comprised 81 percent of the estimated dispositions in the juvenile courts during 1958 and 77 percent during 1969, indicating a slight proportional decrease, whereas girls, cases increased from 19 to 23 percent in the same 12-year time span.[19] Mention should also be made of the fact that the 1969 report also broke down the estimated dispositions, exclusive of traffic offenses, into the judicial and nonjudicial manner of handling the cases coming to the attention of the juvenile courts. In 1958 the judicial and nonjudicial cases were estimated to amount to 50 percent each, while in 1969 the judicial estimates had dropped to 44 and the nonjudicial estimates had increased to 56 percent of the cases.[20]

One notices from the above review that there is only one personal datum (sex of the juvenile) that is reported in the annual collection of juvenile court dispositions. Consequently, this set of data cannot be used for the study of "categoric" risks for being handled differentially by age (say under 15 versus over 15 years of age), by race, by family composition, by social class, etc. The main value of the juvenile court dispositions is to indicate differential volume by urban/rural areas and differential handling according to the two types of dispositions. The value of the juvenile court disposition statistics is thus very limited. Hopefully, better coverage may eventually come about.

Probation statistics

There is a lack of unified probation statistics. Some states make an attempt at probation accounting at the level of adult felony courts. Probation at the juvenile level is often subsumed under state reports on the intake and dispositions of juvenile courts. For the most part, very few probation

[17] *Ibid.*, Table 5, p. 10.
[18] *Ibid.*, Table 6, p. 11.
[19] *Ibid.*, Table 8, p. 12.
[20] *Ibid.*, Table 7, p. 11.

departments keep adequate reports on their intake and output. And it is not easy to compare probation data in one jurisdiction with another jurisdiction, whether adult or juvenile. Statistical accounting of probation operations in the so-called lower courts of various jurisdictions is seldom made. As a matter of fact, probation in the lower courts (for misdemeanants) is not well developed.

A statement on the need for standard probation reporting on a nationwide basis as well as on the difficulties which must be overcome in getting nationwide reporting was prepared for the President's Crime Commission by Dr. Peter P. Lejins.[21]

There are no national probation statistics in this country, although many efforts have been made in the course of the past 10 years or so to explore the possibilities of developing such a series. The National Council on Crime and Delinquency and the Administrative Office of the U.S. Courts have been especially active in this respect. Some individual States have been rather successful in developing probation statistics. Probation, contrary to parole, offers a special difficulty in developing national or even statewide compilations, because the probation departments are frequently attached to individual courts and thus are not subject to statewide administration. Thus, if the National Agency were to initiate a national probation statistics series, it would have to deal with several different types of contributing agencies which control access to the information.

It should be noted that the differences between the juvenile and the adult fields have perhaps more repercussions on collection of statistical data in the area of probation than in any other phase of the law enforcement and correctional processes. The overlap area, generally between the ages of 16 and 21, in which various jurisdictions have differing upper age limits for juveniles, is an especially complicated situation to handle in terms of uniformity and comparisons. Many jurisdictions have concurrent adult and juvenile court jurisdictions within these age brackets and the local policies differ beyond the text of the legal provisions. Since the decision-making with regard to placement on probation rather than institutionalization of the offender is obviously strongly affected by the differences in the attitudinal climate characteristic of the juvenile and adult fields, as was pointed out in the section of the proposal just cited, the differential handling of the same age brackets as juveniles or as adults in different areas of the country injects factors which severely endanger the surface meaning and the comparability of the data.

Confusion haunts the field of probation because of the probation officer's function as an investigator of the social and personal background of the offender for the purposes of a pretrial or presentence report to the judge and his function as a treatment officer for the offender whose "sentence" is to be placed on probation. These are in essence two entirely different functions, which in practice often intertwine. Both services are often

[21] Peter P. Lejins, "National Crime Data Reporting System: Proposal for a Model," Appendix C, *Task Force Report: Crime and its Impact—An Assessment* (Washington, D.C.: The President's Commission on Law Enforcement and Administration of Justice, 1962), pp. 195-196.

performed by the personnel of one and the same probation department. The data with reference to both are extremely important for the proper understanding, evaluation and management of the two functions, and the national reporting models should provide for the collection of both types of data. As was already suggested, probation activities as presentence investigations belong more properly into the judicial statistics, but from the point of view of access to the data the issue may have to be reconsidered on the basis of a more detailed feasibility study.

Again it should be pointed out that the general models suggested in this proposal for the development of the uniform reporting categories and the promotion of a national statistical program should be applied. It must also be repeated that the location of the juvenile probation agency-statistics series within the general program of the National Agency will depend on the policy decision whether to handle the juvenile area data as a unified system, whether to have the specific juvenile agency-statistics series operated as independent agency-statistics series, or whether to include them together with the corresponding adult statistics into the program of one unit-probation statistics.

Statistics pertaining to the probationary system as a method of treatment of adjudicated offenders must reflect the number of persons placed on probation, the number violating probation by committing new offenses or by technical violations, and the number of persons successfully completing probation. With regard to the last item, the juvenile field offers special difficulties in view of the frequent vagueness of the length of the probationary sentence, which is often formulated as "maturity" but in reality often falls short of that.

In the last few years, under the leadership of the National Council on Crime and Delinquency and specifically its Research Center at Davis, California, the possibility of developing and using a standard set of probation statistics has been explored. Probation Management Institutes were conducted at which the feasibility of uniform data collection and data reporting on probation cases was discussed and an exploratory effort was made by the Research Center with the help and cooperation of twenty-two probation agencies throughout the country, to discover the feasibility of reporting standard information and to evaluate the worth of standard statistical data in estimating the outcome of probation cases.[22]

This study demonstrated the capability of several probation agencies to collect standardized data with a reasonable investment of time and effort. Shown too, is the usefulness of the collected data—the information derived is of practical value and can be accepted with reasonable confidence. In short, the system worked for those agencies that participated and for the group of probationers studied. However, it must be remembered that three of the original twenty five agencies terminated paritipation in the study due to either personnel or records insufficiencies. In addition, at least fifteen

[22]Peter S. Venezia and Alvin W. Cohn, *Probation Information: a Tentative Model* (Davis, California: Research Center, National Council on Crime and Delinquency, December 1968), (mimeographed), pp. 50–54.

of the agencies represented at the Probation Management Institutes were unable to participate for the same reasons. There were some indications, too, that a few of the agencies that took part in the study would have difficulty with participation in an on-going program. Thus, the issue of agency resources comes to the fore. At this time, it appears that a majority of the nation's probation agencies would need some form of help with augmenting their personnel and/or record-keeping in order to achieve the capability of full-scale participation in an on-going reporting system.

Several issues related to feasibility evolve from the large number and variety of probation agencies which would be, of necessity, in the program. Probation in the United States is administered by hundreds of independent agencies operating under different laws in each state and under widely varying philosophies, often within a given state. In order to build a comprehensive system of nationwide data reporting, a majority of these agencies would have to be involved in the planning, development, and implementation of the system. This, along with the needs for coder training and the processing of data on more than a quarter of a million probationers annually, presents a staggering problem in logistics. With regard to the differences among agencies, a single state or local agency might be responsible for handling three types of probation cases: juvenile, misdemeanant, and adult felony. In another jurisdiction, three separate agencies may be operating, each responsible for a different type of probationer. All of these probation programs must contend with situations of varying diversity, with the misdemeanant probation system subject to its own unique problems. The need, then, would seem to be for three distinct reporting systems rather than for one all-inclusive program as is the case in the parole field.

Allied to the above considerations is the requirement that the program provide for continuous feedback from agencies as to their information needs. The information pumped out of the system must first of all be of use to the participating agencies. They, in turn, must maintain a level of data-collection accuracy which permits the information to be used with confidence. To these ends, a field staff would have to be maintained in addition to research personnel. On-going field consultation with individual agencies, along with tailor-made analyses of agency data would be the key features which would differentiate a uniform probation reporting program from a national head-count system.

The above discussion underscores the obvious—a definitive answer as to the feasibility of uniform probation reporting has not yet been obtained. The first tentative step has yielded promising results, but much more exploration remains. Prior to committing personnel and funds to the implementation of a reporting system, the needs and capabilities of probation agencies across the country must be determined. This might best be done by a series of regional seminars and field consultations with individual agencies. It may well be that such an exploration might indicate the most fruitful approach to building a reporting program to be a substantial investment in improving the data collection-retrieval systems of individual agencies. Should this prove necessary, once it was accomplished the national program could be a natural outgrowth of the effort. A uniform probation reporting system then would rest upon a broad and solid foundation.

Prisoner statistics

Statistics on prisoners in the United States were the first criminal statistics to be collected systematically on a nationwide basis. The Bureau of the Census made a collection of prisoners "on hand" in penal institutions on a certain day in each decennial census from 1850 to 1890. It made special enumerations of prisoners in 1904, 1910, and 1023, Beginning with 1926 and lasting until 1946, the Bureau of the Census took an *annual* census of prisoners in state and federal prisons and reformatories.[23]

The reported information on prisoners received from courts during the year was most comprehensive: sex, race, age, country of birth, offense for which committed, type of sentence, number of times previously imprisoned, month of admission, state, and region of the country (in which the institutions were located). The information on prisoners discharged during the year from the prisons and reformatories was classified according to sex, method of discharge, length of time in prison, type of offense for which committed, type of sentence, and number of times imprisoned previously. Both sets of data (admissions and discharges) were tabulated according to states and regions of the United States.

In addition to the statistics on admission from courts and discharges from the institution, the Census Bureau's enumeration of 1926 included the count on prisoners in prisons and reformatories at the beginning and end of the year, classified only by sex. And the 1926 statistics enumerated the admissions to prisons and reformatories during the year from sources other than commitments from courts, namely prisoners returned from parole, escapees returned to prison, and transfers from other penal institutions. The 1926 Census Bureau coverage did not include prisoners held for trial.

In calling attention to the value of the "new" set of statistics on prisoners as collected in 1926, the Bureau of the Census at the time contended that such statistics indicate "the application of penal policies for various classes of offenders and in different parts of the country." The Bureau also claimed that the newly developed set of statistics show the "prevailing characteristics of those offenders who are punished by imprisonment."[24]

By the time of its last published volume on prisoner statistics, namely for the year 1946, the Bureau of the Census claimed that in the interim years (1926–1946), it had achieved the goal of developing uniform, comparable statistics on prisoners. It had developed a standard schedule for recording the information and a uniform system of coding the data from the schedules

[23] *Prisoners in State and Federal Prisons and Reformatories 1926* (Washington, D.C.: 1929); *see* the report under the same title for 1946, published in 1948.

[24] *Ibid.*, p. 2.

In addition, the Bureau of the Census had this to say in its 1946 report:[25]

Statistics on prisoners provided the basic information needed for an intelligent consideration of the problems of penology and make it possible for administrators and students of penology in each State to compare the treatment of prisoners within their State with that shown for other States.

However, in the 1946 enumeration, the Bureau of the Census used the designation "felony prisoners" received from courts and "felony prisoners" discharged. Pretty much the same sort of "breakdowns" in the enumeration were used in 1946 as in 1926.

The 1946 statistics represented the last set of prisoner statistics that the Bureau of the Census published. Supposedly, the Bureau collected the statistics for one, two, or three years after 1946 but did not publish a report. A bulletin sheet (Series P-80, No. 15), issued in 1949 by the Bureau as one of its Current Population Reports, printed the count on the *Movement of Prisoners in State and Federal Prisons and Reformatories 1947*. A similar sort of bulletin sheet was printed under the sponsorship of the Federal Bureau of Prisons for the prisoner data of 1948 and 1949 in bulletin sheets that appeared in 1950 and 1951.

The annual reports on prisoners published from 1950 on by the Federal Bureau of Prisons did not include the personal data on individual prisoners that had been reported by the U.S. Bureau of the Census (with the exception of tabular classifications by sex). The major focus of the new series of annual reports was upon movement of prisoners into and out of institutions (see Table 7–4). The Bureau of Prisons collection is, therefore, mainly useful to indicate volume of intake and outgo, by regions and states. Trends of intake are frequently computed by rates per 100,000 population of the various states and regions. In the reports which compute rates of admissions of prisoners to state institutions from courts per 100,000 population, comparisons of importance to criminology can be made by regions and states. Such comparisons reflect, for the most part, differential penal policy of the various states and regions and only in small part differential involvement in crime. But the actual relative values cannot be indicated at the present state of knowledge. However, in view of the fact that there were only slightly more than 66,000 prisoners committed to state institutions by courts in 1967 and that, in urban jurisdictions comprising only slightly more than one third of the population of the United States, 2,310,722 persons in 1967 were charged by the police (63.5% found guilty of offense charged, 2.4% found guilty of a lesser plea, 16.2% dismissed, and 17.9% referred to the juvenile court),[26] one suspects that much has gone over the dam in differential

[25] *Prisoners In State and Federal Prisons and Reformatories 1946* (Washington, D.C.: U.S. Bureau of the Census, 1948), p. 2.

[26] *Crime in the United States, Uniform Crime Reports—1967* (Washington, D.C.: Federal Bureau of Investigation, U.S. Department of Justice, 1968), Table 15, p. 109.

Table 7-4. Movement of sentenced prisoners in state and federal institutions, by sex, for the United States: Calendar year 1967[27]

Movement of sentenced prisoners	All institutions			Federal institutions			State institutions (a)		
	Total	Male	Female	Total	Male	Female	Total	Male	Female
Prisoners present: January 1, 1967	199,654	192,704	6.950	19,245	18,598	647	180,409	174,106	6,303
December 31, 1967	194,896	188,661	6,235	19,579	18,942	637	175,317	169,719	5,598
Percent change	−2.4	−2.1	−10.3	1.7	1.8	−1.5	−2.8	−2.5	−11.2
Admissions, total	220,932	213,985	6,947	23,376	22,631	745	197,556	191,354	6,202
Admitted except transfers	132,437	126,567	5,870	16,014	15,320	694	116,423	111,247	5,176
Court commitments	77,850	74,400	3,450	11,447	10,962	485	66,403	63,438	2,965
Returned as violators of conditional release (b)	17,583	16,821	762	1,774	1,718	56	15,809	15,103	706
Other admissions (c)	37,004	35,346	1,658	2,793	2,640	153	34,211	32,706	1,505
Transferred from other institutions	88,495	87,418	1,077	7,362	7,311	51	81,133	80,107	1,026
Departures, total	225,690	218,028	7,662	23,042	22,287	755	202,648	195,741	6,907
Discharged, except transfers	137,865	131,298	6,567	15,617	14,941	676	122,248	116,357	5,891
Releases, total	96,377	91,675	4,702	12,361	11,840	521	84,016	79,835	4,181
Conditional releases, total	64,830	61,341	3,489	8,037	7,677	360	56,793	53,664	3,129
Paroles	57,721	54,486	3,235	5,297	5,021	276	52,424	49,465	2,959
Other Conditional releases (d)	7,109	6,855	254	2,740	2,656	84	4,369	4,199	170
Unconditional releases, total (e)	31,547	30,334	1,213	4,324	4,163	161	27,223	26,171	1,052
Deaths, except executions	652	639	13	57	57	—	595	582	13
Executions	2	2	—	—	—	—	2	2	—
Other departures (f)	40,834	38,982	1,852	3,199	3,044	155	37,635	35,938	1,697
Transferred to other institutions	87,825	86,730	1,095	7,425	7,346	79	80,400	79,384	1,016

(a) Excludes Alaska. (b) Figures shown do not include some violators who were returned with new or additional sentences and were included as "court commitments." (c) Includes escapees returned, returns from court and authorized temporary absences, and "other" admissions. (d) Includes 45 conditional pardons (44 male, 1 female). (e) Includes 12 full pardons (all male). (f) Includes escapes, court orders, authorized temporary absences, and "other" departures.

[27] *National Prisoner Statistics: Prisoners in State and Federal Institutions for Adult Felons 1967*, 44 (Washington, D.C.: Bureau of Prisons, U.S. Department of Justice, July 1969), Table 3, p. 10.

handling at the various way stations prior to court commitment. It is undoubtedly a good guess to say that differences in commitment rates by states reflect differential handling policies much more than differentials in criminal involvement.

The more recent annual reports on prisoners also contain statistics on trends for prisoners on hand at the end of the year and prisoners received from courts during the year. Such figures enable criminologists to analyze changes in the processing of felony offenders (as reflected in prisoner statistics). Certainly, the trend in the past generation or so has been toward diverting more and more offenders from institutions, especially through the increased use of probation. The steady decline in recent years of the number of prisoners committed by courts to prisons and reformatories certainly in no way reflects a decline in criminal involvement.

It appears that the Federal Bureau of Prisons' enumeration of prisoners only classified admissions from courts by type of offense in its 1963 report. Beginning with the 1954 report and continuing through the 1962 report, the enumerations of prisoners included data on the individual federal and state institutions. This phase of reporting seems to have been abandoned in 1964.

From time to time, the Federal Bureau of Prisons made special analyses of prisoner data.[28] The last one available at this writing was *State Prisoners Admissions and Releases, 1964*, which contained data on age, sex, race, type of offense and length of sentence for prisoners committed to state institutions and which also on length of time served for the first releasees by type of offense and by race.

At the beginning of 1971, the National Criminal Justice Information and Statistics Service of the Law enforcement Assistance Administration took over from the Federal Bureau of Prisons the responsibility of publishing the National Prisoner Statistics. (At the time of this writing—February 1972—the author has not seen the new report and cannot comment on the value of its coverage for the study of criminology.)

Delinquent children in public institutions

The U.S. Children's Bureau some years ago initiated a statistical series with regard to the care of children in various welfare and institutional

[28]National Prisoner Statistics, *State Prisoners: Admissions and Releases, 1964* (Washington, D.C.: Federal Bureau of Prisons, 1967). The other special reports issued on prisoners by the Federal Bureau of Prisons were: *Prisoners in State and Federal Institutions, 1950*, which contains much more personal data on prisoners than subsequent special publication, approximately the wealth of data to be found in the 1926–1946 collection by the Bureau of the Census; *Prisoners Released from State and Federal Institutions, 1951; Prisoners Released from State and Federal Institutions, 1952 and 1953; Prisoners Released from State and Federal Institutions, 1960; Characteristics of State Prisoners, 1960.* The last (1960) included enumerations by sex, age, race, and type of offense but does not equal the coverage of the special report of 1950 and still less the Census reports of 1926–1946.

programs. The Bureau made an enumeration of children residing in public training schools for delinquents on a certain day of 1953. The juvenile inmates were classified by sex, race, region, and length of resident care.[29] This statistical enumeration was continued under the title of *Statistics on Public Institutions for Delinquent Children* for the years 1956, 1958, 1962, 1963, 1964, 1966, and 1967. The pattern of enumeration changed in the 1956 coverage to include the number of children on hand on December 31, 1956 by sex, race, and region; a count on the returnees by size of institution, by region, and by sex; the percentage of runaways by sex and size of institution; and the length of stay by size of the institution and by sex.

The statistics on delinquent children in public institutions were taken over in 1969 by the National Center of Social Statistics of the U.S. Department of Health, Education, and Welfare. The report for the fiscal year 1969–1970 generally follows the coverage developed by the Children's Bureau in the latter years of its existence.[30] At the time, 343 public institutions for delinquent children were known to exist in the United States and reports on movement were received from 325 of them. During the fiscal year (July 1 to June 30), 85,304 youths were admitted to state-operated institutions for delinquents, while 10,437 were admitted to city/county operated institutions. The movement out of the public institutions for delinquents in the fiscal year 1969–1970 comprised 81,549 from the state and 10,373 from the city/county institutions.[31] The number of youths on hand as of June 30, 1970 was approximately 50,000.

In subsequent enumerations, the Children's Bureau adopted a reporting model somewhat similar to the coverage on prisoners in state and federal institutions, namely, the movement of the population into and out of the training schools for the fiscal year ending June 30. The 1967 coverage of "movement into" included delinquents committed by court, returned from aftercare or parole, transferred from other institutions for delinquents, and other admissions according to states. The coverage of "movement out of" included the children discharged with no other agency supervision, those placed on aftercare or parole, those transferred to another institution for delinquents, and other discharges, also according to the several states. The 1967 enumeration also gave the average length of stay (in months) by states. Other items reported were not immediately concerned with input or output.

While there are many important items covered in the 1969–1970 report on public institutions for delinquent children, yet there is no reported

[29] *Some Facts about Public State Training Schools for Juvenile Delinquents, 1953*, 33 (Washington, D.C.: U.S. Children's Bureau Statistical Series, 1956).

[30] See *Statistics on Public Institutions for Delinquent Children 1970* (Washington, D.C.: National Center for Social Statistics, U.S. Department of Health, Education, and Welfare, June 30, 1971).

[31] *Ibid.*, Table 3A, p. 11 and Table 3B, p. 12.

coverage on age, sex, and race. As is true of adult prisoner statistics, the criminologist is not able to obtain insights into the "who factor" in the movement of cases in and out of these public institutions. However, differential risks for commitment, per 100,000 respective population, could be computed from available data by states and regions, the conclusions from which would indicate variation in policies in handling juvenile as well as adult offenders.

Parole statistics

Release of adult prisoners from prison on parole and on expiration of sentence is one of the last way stations in the criminal justice system. With regard to adult prisoners, one should be mindful of the fact that, while parole is used quite extensively in most state and federal institutions, varying proportions of releases of prisoners on expiration of the sentence also take place, in which instances the conditional release on parole does not apply.

However, it is very difficult to obtain statistical data on the types of cases leaving prison on expiration and those leaving prison on conditional release (parole). The researcher would have to go to the files of the individual prison, in order to make meaningful studies of the differences between the two samples of releasees. As for knowledge of outcome, it is virtually impossible to obtain such information on the expiration cases, unless their fingerprints were cleared through the F.B.I., while it is often possible to obtain outcome information on parole cases from the various paroling authorities.

Technically, the successful termination of parole, frequently accompanied by restoration of civil rights, is the last way station in the criminal justice system, although the successful termination of aftercare or parole supervision of juvenile cases may only be, in a large proportion of instances, a preliminary waiting period before the youths are knocking at the doors of the first way station in the adult criminal justice system.

In recent years, many states in the United States have greatly improved their parole system and, in consequence, have published very revealing annual reports. By way of illustration, Table 5 is taken from the published *Annual Report 1969* of the Ohio Adult Parole Authority.[32] One notes that the coverage includes cases on hand as of July 1, 1968, cases received during the year, the returnees and new sentences of returned parolees, and the count on final releases from parole during the fiscal year.

For the past several years, the experts and administrators in the parole field have felt the need to have a nationwide uniform set of parole statistics and have given effective expression to this very important idea. The Research

[32] See p. 25. Note that the compilation of data is for the fiscal year 1969, ending June 30, 1969.

Table 7–5. Parole data by institution, fiscal 1969[a], for the State of Ohio

INSTITUTION	Cases July 1, 1968	Cases received during year	Total cases on parole in year	Returns and new sentences	Percent of total	ratio*	Final releases	Percent of total	ratio*
Ohio Penitentiary	712	423	1,135	145	12.8	34.3	377	33.2	89.1
London Correctional	914	705	1,619	155	9.6	22.0	593	36.6	84.1
Marion Correctional	677	553	1,230	101	8.2	18.2	461	37.5	83.4
Chillicothe Correctional	217	344	561	30	5.3	8.7	126	22.4	36.6
Ohio State Reformatory	818	989	1,807	215	11.9	21.7	595	32.9	60.2
Lebanon Correctional	673	634	1,307	139	10.6	21.9	487	37.2	76.8
Ohio Reformatory for Women	191	163	354	24	6.8	14.7	135	38.1	82.8
TOTAL OHIO CASES	4,202	3,811	8,013	809	10.1	21.2	2,774	34.6	72.8
COMPACT CASES IN OHIO	732	643	1,375	52	3.8	8.1	356	25.9	55.4
GRAND TOTAL	4,934	4,454	9,388	861	9.2	19.3	3,130	33.3	70.3

*Ratio of the number in this category to the number released on parole.

[a]This table is numbered Table 4 in the Ohio report.

Center of the National Council on Crime and Delinquency, in conjunction with the parole agencies of the United States, established a system for the collection and use of Uniform Parole Statistics (c. 1964). While the pilot project of the Center started with only a limited number of parole agencies cooperating, the present project includes a membership of 55 parole agencies in 50 states, the Federal Government, the Commonwealth of Puerto Rico, and has the collaboration of the National Parole Board and Dominion Bureau of Statistics in Canada.

Appendix 7–C presents a statement on information collection and computerized "feedback" of the Uniform Parole Statistics project. One notices that the "feed-in" includes important data on the individual parolee, while the overall coverage includes also basic data on parole outcome. The system of retrieval of data, general or specific within the limits of data coverage, is called DIALOG. The retrieval codes within the DIALOG system of the Uniform Parole Reports are also presented in Appendix 7–C.

There is no question that this new development in uniform reporting will set the model for police reporting, jail reporting, court reporting, probation reporting, and institutional reporting. And if there can be an agreed-upon uniformity of case information at all points, administrators and researchers will have appropriate information by which to ascertain the operation of differential handling and outcome of persons at various way stations of the criminal justice system. Criminologists then would have comparative data on which to base their research.

A national center for criminal justice statistics

It is hoped that the National Center for Criminal Justice Statistics, which has been developed within the National Institute on Law Enforcement and Criminal Justice as part of the total program of Law Enforcement Assistance Administration (federal), will be able to develop a meaningful, useful system of uniform nationwide statistics that will collect, store, and feedback (through retrieval) pertinent information on the input and output of the total system of handling offenders, both adult and juvenile.

Dr. Peter P. Lejins recommended to the President's Crime Commission the establishment of a National Crime Data Agency, to be located in the U.S. Department of Justice. Whether or not the newly-established National Center for Criminal Justice Statistics will be able to follow the comprehensive model proposed by Dr. Lejins is not discernible at this time. But certainly the model proposed by him, plus a system of information input and retrieval comparable to that generated by the Uniform Parole Statistics, would go far toward giving the United States complete statistical coverage at all way stations in the handling of juvenile and adult offenders. Dr. Lejin's proposal is replicated in part in Appendix 7–D. One should take special note of the fact that he specifies that the National Crime Data Agency should not only collect information of value to the operation of all phases of the criminal justice system but also criminal record data on individuals who enter and leave the criminal justice system.

Appendix 7–A

THE F.B.I.'s SYSTEM OF UNIFORM CRIME REPORTING

Not all crimes come readily to the attention of the police—embezzlement for example. Some important crimes happen infrequently, such as kidnapping (often this is for the purpose of robbery or other crime and not for ransom). So, the International Association of Chiefs of Police, for practical purposes, limited the reporting of "offenses known" to the following crime classifications because they are crimes which are most likely to be reported to police and they occur with sufficient frequency to provide an adequate basis for comparison:

(1) Criminal homicide (subdivided as to 1a, murder and non-negligent manslaughter and 1b, manslaughter by negligence); (2) forcible rape; (3) robbery; (4) assault (subdivided as to aggravated and simple); (5) burglary (breaking and unlawful entering); (6) larceny—theft (except auto theft) (subdivided as to \$50 and over in value and under \$50 in value); and (7) auto theft.

These are the Part I classes of the uniform crime classification. All other crimes and violations are reported under the Part II crime classes. No "offenses known" data is collected for the Part II classes, only arrest information.

Persons arrested for all violations except traffic in the reporting jurisdictions are represented in the annual report on arrests, Age, Sex and Race of Persons Arrested. This return deals only with persons arrested and all arrests are included even though the person is later released without being formally charged. It provides a wide range of information on crime and some characteristics of persons arrested for crimes.

The annual Return C provides police with a form wherein they can report the number of persons they formally charge for criminal acts (turn over for prosecution) and how these persons are disposed of by the courts, including both adults and juveniles.

To insure that you have the needed information, your record system should meet the following standards:

1. A permanent written record is made of each crime as soon as the complaint is received. All reports of crimes and attempted crimes are included, regardless of the value of property involved.

Reprinted from *Uniform Crime Reporting Handbook*, Federal Bureau of Investigation, United States Department of Justice (Washington, D.C.: U.S. Government Printing Office, 1965), pp. 2-4, 8, 39-44, 47-48, 56-60, 67-71.

2. Staff, or headquarters, control exists over the receipt of complaints. This is to insure that each is promptly recorded, properly classified and subsequently counted.

3. An investigative report is made in each case. It shows fully the details of the offense as alleged and as disclosed by the police investigation. Each case is closely followed to see that reports are made promptly.

4. All reports are checked to see that the crime class conforms to the uniform classification of offenses.

5. The offense reports on crimes cleared by arrest or by exceptional means are so noted.

6. Arrest records are complete, special care being taken to show the final results of the charge.

7. Records are centralized; records and statistical reports are closely supervised by the chief administrative officer; periodic inspections are made to see that the rules and regulations of the local agency on records and reports are strictly followed.

8. Statistical reports meet the Uniform Crime Reporting standards and regulations.

The monthly form used to collect "Offenses Known" data is the Return A. It is important that you count on your report all Part I crimes, "Offenses Known," that occur in your jurisdiction. Reports are collected for urban places (cities or towns) and rural areas. Police count crimes that happen within the city (urban) limits. Sheriffs, county and state police count crimes that happen in the county (rural area) outside urban places of 2,500 or more inhabitants.

For crime reporting, cities are places that have 2,500 or more people according to the latest U.S. census. There are a few places that are designated as urban under a special rule.

Offenses (crimes) come to the attention of a law enforcement agency in a number of ways. Check over your record system to be sure that all possible sources are covered by the records to be used in preparing crime reports:

(1) The telephone brings most of them to your attention.

(2) Also, a citizen may walk into your office and report that a theft or other crime has occurred.

(3) An officer on duty sees or hears of a crime. A record should be made even though there is no arrest.

(4) An officer on duty makes an arrest during, or shortly after, the commission of a crime. He makes the arrest before any complaint or report is received at headquarters. For example, a shop-keeper calls to a policeman on the street and reports a shoplifting. The policeman sees the thief and makes an arrest. This is referred to variously as an "on view," "pickup," or "original" arrest. Include such incidents in the records used in compiling crime reports.

(5) Sometimes crimes are reported by citizens to the prosecuting attorney or judge. Generally, you can arrange to have these officials notify you of the crime that has occurred in your jurisdiction. Also, urban police can arrange to be notified if a sheriff's office, county police, county detectives, or state police receive the first notice of a crime that has happened in a city (urban place).

(6) If you receive a warrant of arrest and it is your first notice of a Part I offense in your jurisdiction, the offense should be counted.

One of the primary objectives of the Uniform Crime Reporting Program is to provide reliable and meaningful data for administrative and operational use of law enforcement agencies. One of the means utilized to attain this goal is the use of the "crime index." Seven selected offenses are used in an attempt to measure the extent, fluctuation and distribution of crime in the United States. The count is based on the number of these selected offenses being reported to police or coming to their attention (offenses known). The following offenses are used in compiling the crime index:

(1) Murder and non-negligent manslaughter, (2) forcible rape, (3) robbery, (4) aggravated assault, (5) burglary, (6) larceny $50 and over, and (7) auto theft.

(Note: Manslaughter by negligence, simple or minor assaults and larceny under $50 are not included in the crime index.)

As noted above, police count those crimes that occur within the city limits; a sheriff counts only those crimes that occur in the county outside the cities. This avoids duplication.

If the crime occurs in another city or another county, do not count it. This is true even though you may arrest the offender. Examples: (1) The Maple City Police arrest an auto thief in an auto stolen in Oak City. Oak City counts the crime. (2) The Locust County Sheriff arrests the murderer of a woman killed in Locust City, the county seat and an urban place. The sheriff does not count the murder on his report because it occurred in Locust City and the Locust City Police Department will report it.

The FBI mails supplies each month to contributors. If your agency is on our mailing list of contributors, you will receive these basic supplies:

(1) Tally Sheet for Return A—this is a handy worksheet that you keep in your office;

(2) Return A—for mailing to the FBI after you have filled it out;

(3) Self-addressed return envelope requiring no postage.

SCORING

This means the number of offenses to be counted in any criminal event. Only two general rules are needed for scoring if we group our Part I crimes as to (1) crimes against the person and (2) crimes against property.

OFFENSES AGAINST THE PERSON (criminal homicide, forcible rape, and assault.) Count one offense for each victim. This means that the number of offenses scored equals the number of persons unlawfully killed, raped, maimed, wounded or assaulted, plus attempts.

Example: An unknown man murders three persons. There are 3 victims, so count 3 offenses.

Assault is sometimes troublesome. If the facts are in dispute and you can't tell the aggressors from the victims, count the number of persons assaulted as the number of offenses.

Example: Answering a "riot" call, police find that seven persons were in a fight. A variety of weapons are strewn about. None of the participants is particularly co-operative. Each one claims innocence but is vague as to who is responsible for the assault. Three of the seven are severely wounded and receive emergency medical treatment. All seven are arrested. While all the facts of the fight are not known, we do know that three persons are severely wounded. Count three offenses of aggravated assault, 4d, cleared. Also count four offenses in 4e, other assaults, cleared.

OFFENSES AGAINST PROPERTY (robbery, burglary, larceny-theft, and auto theft.) Count one offense for each distinct operation or attempt.

Robbery examples:

Forty patrons are present in a nighclub when it and the 40 patrons are held up by armed bandits. This is 1 distinct operation, count 1 offense. (The number of people held up makes no difference if it is one distinct operation in an offense against property.)

Three men "strong-arm" and rob a man on the street. One operation, one offense.

Burglary—Forcible or Unlawful Entry Examples: Special "Hotel" rule—consider hotels and lodging houses as single units without regard to the number of rooms entered at one time.

Example: Six rooms in a hotel are broken into by 2 "sneak thieves" on 1 occasion. Under the "Hotel" rule count just one offense.

Apartment houses—count one offense for each apartment entered ("Hotel" rule does not apply to apartments).

Offices—Count one offense for each suite of offices entered in a building.

Example: One night a building is broken into. In all, 21 offices (rooms or partitioned spaces) are ransacked. These offices are occupied by (1) a lawyer, (2) a doctor, (3) Apex Co., and (4) Elite Co., who do not share their space and are not related in a business way (four separate units or "distinct operations," four offenses).

Larceny-theft: One article or several articles stolen from one place on the same occasion is a distinct operation. Count one offense. This is true even if several articles belonging to different persons are stolen at the same time from one place.

Attempts: Count opposite "under $50" in value. The article may be worth more, but no value is obtained.

Auto theft: Count one for each vehicle stolen. Also count each attempt. You may recover a car very soon. This does not change the rule: A car stolen by a person not having lawful access to it must be counted as an actual offense (car taken for temporary use and actually returned by the taker to the owner is not counted).

UNFOUNDED COMPLAINTS

"Unfounded" means that the investigation proves that the crime did not happen or was not attempted.

Example: You receive a report of a burglary. Investigation shows that a man climbed through the window of his own home. He locked himself out by mistake. A neighbor thought it was a burglar and called the police.

OFFENSES CLEARED BY ARREST

An offense is "cleared by arrest" when at least one person is (1) arrested, (2) charged with the commission of the offense, and (3) turned over to the court for prosecution (whether following arrest, court summons or police notice).

A clearance by arrest can be taken when the offender is a person under 18 and he is cited to appear in Juvenile Court or before other juvenile authorities. This clearance can be taken even though no actual physical arrest was made.

Keep clearly in mind that offenses and not arrests are being counted. It makes no difference how many are arrested. There can be no more offenses cleared than offenses that occurred.

If several persons commit 1 crime and only 1 is arrested and charged, list the crime in column 5 of Return A as cleared by arrest. When the other offenders are arrested (say, in the next month) do not list a clearance by arrest a second time for the one offense.

Several crimes may be cleared by the arrest of one person.

Examples:

1. A man commits murder. He is arrested, charged, and turned over to the court. You score 1 offense of murder and 1 offense of murder cleared.

2. Five thieves break into a warehouse. You arrest and charge one of them. Score 1 offense of burglary—forcible entry, and 1 such offense cleared by arrest. Later the other four thieves are arrested and charged. No entry is made on Return A. The one offense has already been listed as cleared by arrest.

3. You identify a suspect with five forcible entry burglaries. You arrest him and charge him with the five offenses. These 5 offenses are cleared by the arrest of 1 person.

In compiling data for the annual returns which are discussed in the following sections of this Handbook, both Part I and Part II of the Uniform Classification are used for compiling facts about persons arrested and persons charged. It is just as essential to have maximum uniformity in collecting these figures as it is in getting statistics for the monthly returns.

Definition of Part II Classes. In November, 1932, the FBI adopted a Standard Classification of Offenses for the compilation of criminal statistics. This classification was devised and adopted in order that police, judicial, and penal statistics might be uniformly compiled in terms of a single classification of offenses. The Standard Classification is substantially the same as the Uniform Classification with the exception of certain changes in the Part II classes of offenses. The brief list of offenses under each of the following classes of Part II indicates the general content and scope of the class. Although the offenses listed here may not be identical in name with those in local jurisdictions, they are sufficiently descriptive to serve as a guide in determining what offenses should be included in or excluded from each class. The offense classes which follow are numbered in accordance with the listing shown under the Part II classes of offenses included on the annual returns.

8. Other Assaults
9. Arson

10. Forgery and Counterfeiting
11. Fraud
12. Embezzlement
13. Stolen Property; Buying, Receiving, Possessing
14. Vandalism
15. Weapons, Carrying, Possessing, etc.
16. Prostitution and Commercialized Vice
17. Sex Offenses
18. Narcotic Drug Laws
19. Gambling
20. Offenses Against the Family and Children
21. Driving under the Influence
22. Liquor Laws
23. Drunkenness
24. Disorderly Conduct
25. Vagrancy
26. All Other Offenses
27. Suspicion
28. Curfew and Loitering Laws—(Juveniles)
29. Run-away—(Juveniles)

Annual reports under this program are:

(1) Return B—Offenses Known.
(2) Age, Sex and Race of Persons Arrested.
(3) Return C—Persons Charged.
(4) Police Employee Data.

The FBI mails these and tally sheets annually at the end of the calender year to all contributing law enforcement agencies.

RETURN B—ANNUAL RETURN OF OFFENSES KNOWN

The purpose of Return B is to summarize the figures submitted on the 12 monthly Return A's and to provide an opportunity to make any necessary adjustments in the monthly figures submitted previously.

AGE, SEX, AND RACE OF PERSONS ARRESTED

This is the basic report for the collection of arrest data. The purpose of this return is to provide police with a record of their total arrest activity for criminal acts in all the crime classes and to furnish basic data concerning personal characteristics of persons arrested during the year.

Figures tallied on the form represent *persons arrested, and are a count of arrests, not charges*. You may arrest the same person several times during the year for similar or several different violations. Each separate arrest should be counted. You may arrest a person on several charges at one time; however, only one arrest is scored.

The form provides for a compilation of arrest totals broken down by specific age groups, by sex and by race for all Part I and Part II offense classifications, except traffic violations.

Data for persons 18 years of age and over is tabulated on the white Age, Sex and Race of Persons Arrested form while arrests of persons under 18 are scored on the pink portion of the form. Arrests are tallied by sex within certain age groups.

Arrests are tallied also by race. The race designations are: White, Negro, Indian, Chinese, Japanese, and All Other. Persons of Mexican birth or ancestry who are not definitely Indian or of another nonwhite race should be counted as members of the white race.

HOW TO PREPARE THE AGE, SEX, AND RACE OF PERSONS ARRESTED RETURN

Show in this report all persons taken into custody during the past calendar year for committing an offense of the indicated types in your local jurisdiction. This includes:

(1) Those persons you arrest and release without any formal charge being placed against them.

(2) Juveniles taken into custody or arrested but who are warned and released without being charged.

Enter opposite each offense the number of persons taken into custody listing them according to age and sex of the persons arrested and according to race without regard to sex.

Persons whom you arrest for other jurisdictions are not counted on the return. This is to avoid duplication. The agency for whom you make the arrest will report it on their return.

With respect to arrests for Federal offenses in those cases where the arrest is for a Federal crime occurring in your jurisdiction and the offense is also a crime under your state penal code, when you make the arrest independent of a Federal agency or assist in making the arrest, it should be counted on your Age, Sex and Race of Persons Arrested form.

JUVENILES

For purposes of Uniform Crime Reporting, a juvenile should be counted as "arrested" when the circumstances are such that if he or she were an adult, an arrest would be tallied. Juveniles taken into custody should be listed opposite the classification of the offense for which they were taken into custody. For example, if a juvenile is arrested for committing an offense of larceny he should be listed opposite the larceny-theft classification on this report, even though the technical charge placed against him is "Juvenile delinquency." Police "contacts" with juveniles where no offense has been committed should not be scored as arrests. Instances where a juvenile is taken into custody for his own protection, such as "neglect," and no crime committed, should not be listed as an arrest.

Violations growing out of local juvenile acts other than runaway and curfew and loitering law violations should be included in the "all other" classification. This would include "arrests" in the usual sense and also any situation where the young person, in lieu of an actual arrest, is summoned, cited, or notified to appear before the juvenile or youth court or similar official for a violation of the law. Provision is made on the pink section of the form to enter arrests for runaway and curfew and loitering law violations.

SCORING

The unit of scoring is the person arrested or summoned and not the number of charges placed against the person. One is counted for each person as follows:

(1) Count one for each person on each separate occasion (day) he is arrested or charged. (Note the difference between this and a case where a person is charged with several crimes after one arrest.)

Example: Adam Adamson is arrested and charged with burglary on May 5. One month later he is arrested and charged with drunkenness. He is counted as *one person arrested for each incident.*

(2) If 2 or more persons are arrested for committing 1 offense, each is counted as a separate arrest or charge.

Example: Two thieves are arrested and charged with burglary of a tire shop. Count two persons arrested opposite burglary—breaking or entering.

(3) If a person is arrested for committing a burglary and while in custody you determine he has committed another local burglary, do not score an additional arrest. Score one arrest only for the offense on which he was originally arrested.

(4) If the person who was arrested is released on bond and then you discover he has committed another local burglary and you arrest him again, this would constitute two persons arrested.

RETURN C—ANNUAL RETURN OF PERSONS CHARGED

The object of the annual Return C is to show the total number of persons who are formally charged by the police and turned over to the courts. The return gives a complete picture of the number of persons dealt with by the courts. This return provides information relating to the final step in the handling of an offender by police. It is a record of what happened to those individuals held and turned over to the courts for prosecutive action.

The figures collected on the Return C will not be the same as those reported on the Age, Sex and Race of Persons Arrested return because many of the persons you arrest or "book" (and tally on the Age, Sex, and Race of Persons Arrested) will be released without prosecution. By the same token, the figures on the Return C will not balance out with those on the Return B since the Return B deals with offenses known or criminal acts while the Return C has to do with persons arrested and charged—those who commit the criminal acts or violations.

Figures for persons charged are collected for all offenses contained in both the Part I and Part II crime classes.

Count on Return C all persons charged by you for committing offences (Part I and Part II) within your jurisdiction who are turned over to the courts for prosecution. Do not include persons arrested and released by police. Do include those persons charged and released at any prosecutive level. For purposes of this Program a person is considered charged when he is held for prosecution before any court of jurisdiction for any criminal offense. This includes persons whose cases will be heard by justices of the peace, magistrates, or other judicial officers who have authority to impose punishment for the offense committed. A person also is considered charged when he pays a fine or forfeits bail on any citation or summons.

Count persons actually physically arrested and *persons summoned, cited, or notified to appear.*

Scoring—All persons you arrest are not held for prosecution or charged. On Return C count only those individuals who are (1) arrested and turned over for prosecution, and (2) those who are summoned, notified, or cited. Do not count on Return C persons arrested and later released without any formal charge being placed against them. Do not count arrests you made for other authorities (Federal, other states, cities, towns, counties, etc.). Score one person charged for each arrested and held for prosecution. The unit of count is each person. Several persons may be arrested and formally charged for one crime. Each is counted as a person charged. One person may be arrested and formally charged more than once in a year. Each separate occasion is counted.

Column 2.—Persons arrested and held for prosecution are tallied in this column.

Column 3.—Persons responding to court summonses and police notices are counted in this column (persons who waive trial, plead guilty and pay a fine are included).

Column 4.—Enter opposite the proper class the total number of persons charged who are turned over to the courts for prosecution. This is the sum of columns 2 and 3.

Juveniles are included on the Return C only when they are turned over or referred to juvenile court jurisdiction (including probation to department, etc.) or when they are waived to criminal court jurisdiction. Juveniles who are arrested, summoned or notified should be included in Columns 2 or 3 and 4. Juveniles who are handled by the police through warning and release are not considered as being formally charged by police.

DISPOSITION

Columns 5, 6, 7, 8, and 9 are provided to show what happened to the persons who were charged (column 4). If cases of persons charged last year were disposed of this year, those dispositions may be included in the appropriate disposition column but they are not entered as charged again in column 4. Show the disposition only in such cases.

ADULTS GUILTY (columns 5 and 6)

You will notice "Adults Guilty" dispositions are separated into two columns: "Of offense charged" and "Of lesser offense." Adults charged by the police who are found guilty by the courts during the calendar year are entered in one of these two columns.

Guilty of offense charged (column 5) means the person was found guilty in court of:

(1) The same charge as was placed against him by the police (if there was more than one charge or count, he must be found guilty of the most serious); or,

(2) A different charge *with the same penalty as the original or with a greater penalty.*

Guilty of lesser offense (column 6) means the person was found guilty of (1) a lesser offense than the one charged by the police, or (2) an offense less than the most serious if there was more than one charge (or count).

Disposition of cases involving juveniles which are waived to adult court should be handled the same as adults, with the disposition scored in columns 5, 6, 7, or 9. Disposition of juvenile cases handled by the juvenile court are not entered in columns 5, 6, or 7, but are entered in column 8 only.

There is no provision on the Return C to show persons arrested and released.

ACQUITTED OR OTHERWISE DISMISSED (column 7)

In column 7 count all adults whose cases were disposed of through dismissal of the charges *at any prosecutive step*. This includes subsequent dismissal of a case by the local prosecutor when prosecution has been previously authorized by him and legal process obtained. Include *nolle prosequi*, dismissed due to death of defendant, etc. Score in this column all defendants who were acquitted by a judge, jury, magistrate or in any other legal proceeding after having been charged, notified or summoned.

When juveniles whose cases are waived to criminal court are acquitted, enter the acquittal in column 7.

REFERRED TO JUVENILE COURT JURISDICTION (column 8)

This column pertains only to juveniles and shows *police disposition* of juvenile cases. Once the juvenile is turned over by police to the juvenile court, probation department or officer within the jurisdiction of the juvenile court, the case is considered disposed of by the police for purposes of Return C.

Juvenile dispositions should not be tallied in columns 5 or 6 when they are considered as guilty. For purposes of this return all juveniles turned over to juvenile court jurisdiction are included in column 8 only. It is not necessary, therefore, to determine the final disposition of the case by juvenile authorities in order to complete the Return C although this information would be valuable for your own administrative and investigative purposes.

Juvenile dispositions shown in column 8 will be only those juveniles previously entered in column 4 as arrested and charged. Dispositions of juveniles whose cases are waived to criminal court are treated the same as adults and entered in columns 5, 6, 7 or 9.

When you arrest a juvenile for a crime committed in your jurisdiction but turn him over to another jurisdiction for handling, enter the disposition in column 9.

Juveniles you arrest and release to parents with a warning are not considered to be charged and would not be entered on Return C. (Juvenile arrests of this type are counted on the Age, Sex, and Race of Persons Arrested return.)

OTHER (column 9)

This is a residual column where you will enter dispositions of cases included in column 4 but which cannot be entered in columns 5, 6, 7 or 8. The following types of cases would be some of those most frequently entered in column 9: (1) Persons arrested and charged by police whose cases remain pending or undecided at the year's end. (2) Persons charged by police for a local crime but who were tried elsewhere.

Appendix 7–B

SELECTED TABLES FROM THE 1969 REPORT ON FEDERAL OFFENDERS IN THE UNITED STATES DISTRICT COURTS

Table 7–B–1
United States District Courts
Defendants disposed of by type of disposition
fiscal year 1969

Type of disposition	*Total*	*Not convicted*	*Convicted*
TOTAL	32,796	5,993	26,803
Disposed of without trial:			
Dismissed	4,867	4,867	—
Plea of guilty or *nolo contendere*	23,138	—	23,138
By court trial	1,635	483	1,152
By jury trial	3,156	643	2,513
PERCENT DISTRIBUTION	100.0	100.0	100.0
Disposed of without trial	85.4	81.2	86.3
By court trial	5.0	8.1	4.3
By jury trial	9.6	10.7	9.4

Federal Offenders in the United States District Courts 1969, Administrative Office of U.S. Courts, Rowland F. Kirks, Director, Washington, D.C., March 1, 1971. The tables in Appendix 7-B exclude the United States District Courts for the District of Columbia, Canal Zone, Guam and the Virgin Islands. The table numbers used here, namely, 1, 4, 6, 10 and 14 are the table numbers used in the 1969 report, as found on pp. 29, 32, 34, 47, and 59.

Table [7-B-4]
89 United States District Courts
Offense Class and Type of Trial of Defendants, Fiscal Year 1969

Offense class	*Total defendants disposed of*	*Defendants tried*		*Tried by court*		*Tried by jury*	
		Number	*Percent*	*Number*	*Percent*	*Number*	*Percent*
TOTAL	**32,796***	**4,791**	**14.6**	**1,635**	**5.0**	**3,156**	**9.6**
Special Offenses	7,407	475	6.4	225	3.0	250	3.4
Immigration laws	4,045	75	1.9	22	0.5	53	1.3
Wagering tax violations	96	2	2.1	—	—	2	2.1
Federal regulatory statutes	3,266	398	12.2	203	6.2	195	6.0
TOTAL LESS ABOVE	25,389	4,316	17.0	1,410	5.6	2,906	11.4
CLASS I	1,950	156	8.0	51	2.6	105	5.4
Fraud—Group A	370	49	13.2	13	3.5	36	9.7
Embezzlement	1,524	96	6.3	31	2.0	65	4.3
Obscene mail	56	11	19.6	7	12.5	4	7.1
CLASS II	1,036	170	16.4	39	3.8	131	12.6
Income tax fraud	597	95	15.9	22	3.7	73	12.2
Other fraud	439	75	17.1	17	3.9	58	13.2
CLASS III—Liquor, Internal Revenue	2,261	449	19.9	155	6.9	294	13.0
CLASS IV	5,058	726	14.4	225	4.4	501	9.9
Theft	2,792	405	14.5	142	5.1	263	9.4
Postal fraud	594	113	19.0	24	4.0	89	15.0
Forgery	1,672	208	12.4	59	3.5	149	8.9
CLASS V	2,046	485	23.7	149	7.3	336	16.4
Border registration, addicts	63	4	6.4	4	6.4	—	—
Assault and homicide	469	172	36.7	53	11.3	119	25.4
Miscellaneous general offenses	1,514	309	20.4	92	6.1	217	14.3
CLASS VI	6,196	1,176	19.0	527	8.5	649	10.5
Counterfeiting	622	140	22.5	36	5.8	104	16.7
Burglary	328	47	14.3	10	3.0	37	11.3
Interstate transportation of stolen property	1,121	165	14.7	35	3.1	130	11.6
Marihuana	2,189	288	13.2	90	4.1	198	9.0
Selective Service Act	1,744	486	27.9	340	19.5	146	8.4
Other National defense laws	82	14	17.1	7	8.5	7	8.5
Sex offenses	110	36	32.7	9	8.2	27	24.5
CLASS VII—Auto theft	4,420	545	12.3	153	3.5	392	8.9
CLASS VIII	2,422	609	25.1	111	4.6	498	20.6
Narcotics	1,293	298	23.0	79	6.1	219	16.9
Robbery	1,129	311	27.5	32	2.8	279	24.7

*Includes 61 defendants disposed of whose cases were remanded to State or local courts.

NOTE: Percents may not add to total due to rounding.

Table [7–B–6]
89 United States District Courts
Offense Class and For those Convicted, How Convicted, Fiscal Year 1969

Offense class	Defendants disposed of			Initial plea unchanged		Initial plea not guilty, changed to		Convicted by		Percentage distribution of convicted defendants[1]		
	Total	Convicted										
		Number	Percent	Guilty	Nolo contendere	Guilty	Nolo contendere	Court	Jury	Initial plea unchanged	Changed plea	Court or jury
TOTAL	**32,796**	**26,803**	**81.7**	**16,407**	**543**	**5,621**	**567**	**1,152**	**2,513**	**.2**	**23.1**	**13.7**
SPECIAL OFFENSES	7,407	6,639	89.6	5,193	246	642	202	170	186	81.9	12.7	5.4
Immigration laws	4,045	3,959	97.9	3,723	10	158	4	20	44	94.3	4.1	1.6
Wagering tax violations	96	13	13.5	5	4	2	—	—	2	—	—	—
Federal regulatory statutes	3,266	2,667	81.7	1,465	232	482	198	150	140	63.6	25.5	10.9
TOTAL LESS ABOVE	25,389	20,164	79.4	11,214	297	4,979	365	982	2,327	57.1	26.5	16.4
CLASS I	1,950	1,718	88.1	1,121	46	384	56	32	79	67.9	25.6	6.5
Fraud—Group A	370	257	69.5	106	10	81	26	5	29	45.1	41.6	13.2
Embezzlement	1,524	1,421	93.2	996	35	292	29	23	46	72.6	22.6	4.9
Obscene mail	56	40	71.4	19	1	11	1	4	4	50.0	30.0	20.0
CLASS II	1,036	773	74.6	249	63	248	99	23	91	40.4	44.9	14.7
Income tax fraud	597	502	84.1	114	52	184	75	17	60	33.1	51.6	15.3
Other fraud	439	271	61.7	135	11	64	24	6	31	53.9	32.5	13.7
CLASS III—Liquor, Internal Revenue	2,261	1,934	85.5	1,080	19	488	22	105	220	56.8	26.4	16.8
CLASS IV	5,058	4,127	81.6	2,309	55	1,146	84	142	391	57.3	29.8	12.9
Theft	2,792	2,281	81.7	1,328	31	598	35	94	195	59.6	27.8	12.7
Postal fraud	594	405	68.2	134	16	134	32	11	78	37.0	41.0	22.0
Forgery	1,672	1,441	86.2	847	8	414	17	37	118	59.3	29.9	10.8

Table [7-B-6] *(continued)*

Offense class	Defendants disposed of			Initial plea unchanged		Initial plea not guilty, changed to		Convicted by		Percentage distribution of convicted defendants[1]		
	Total	Convicted										
		Number	Percent	Guilty	Nolo-contendere	Guilty	Nolo-contendere	Court	Jury	Initial plea unchanged	Changed plea	Court or jury
CLASS V	2,046	1,470	71.8	690	28	373	31	106	242	48.8	27.5	23.7
Border registration, addicts	63	30	47.6	22	—	6	—	2	—	73.3	20.0	6.7
Assault and homicide	469	354	75.5	139	4	75	9	39	88	40.4	23.7	35.9
Miscellaneous general Offenses	1,514	1,086	71.7	529	24	292	22	65	154	50.9	28.9	20.2
CLASS VI	6,196	4,383	70.1	2,316	38	1.066	44	377	542	53.7	25.3	21.0
Counterfeiting	622	494	79.4	184	3	188	8	26	85	37.9	39.7	22.5
Burglary	328	254	77.4	147	—	69	2	9	27	57.9	28.0	14.2
Interstate transportation of stolen property	1,121	932	83.1	535	8	245	10	18	115	58.3	27.5	14.3
Marihuana	2,189	1,672	76.4	1.076	5	371	11	58	151	64.7	22.8	12.5
Selective Service Act	1,744	900	51.6	314	20	165	12	252	137	37.1	19.7	43.2
Other National defense laws	82	64	78.1	38	2	11	1	6	6	62.5	18.8	18.8
Sex offenses	110	67	60.9	22	—	16	—	8	21	32.8	23.9	43.3
CLASS VII—Auto theft	4,420	3,791	85.8	2,670	40	631	21	110	319	71.5	17.2	11.3
CLASS VIII	2,422	1,968	81.3	779	8	643	8	87	443	40.0	33.1	26.9
Narcotics	1,293	1,007	77.9	394	2	348	4	63	196	39.3	35.0	25.7
Robbery	1,129	961	85.1	385	6	295	4	24	247	40.7	31.1	28.2

[1] Percents may not add to 100.0 percent due to rounding.

Table 7-B-9
89 United States District Courts
Alternatives Used in the Sentencing of Convicted Defendants, by Offense Class, Fiscal Year 1969

		Imprisonment					
			Adults only				
Offensive class	*Total convicted defendants*	*Total*	*Regular sentence*	*Indeterminate sentence*	*Mixed sentence*	*YCA*	*FJDA*
TOTAL	**26,803**	**11,535**	**7,082**	**2,594**	**221**	**1,296**	**342**
SPECIAL OFFENCES	6,639	1,735	1,541	103	18	60	13
Immigration laws	3,959	1,401	1,324	68	2	6	1
Wagering tax violations	13	—	—	—	—	—	—
Federal regulatory statutes	2,667	334	217	35	16	54	12
TOTAL LESS ABOVE	20,164	9,800	5,541	2,491	203	1,236	329
CLASS I	1,718	177	94	51	9	20	3
Fraud—Group A	257	33	24	7	2	—	—
Embezzlement	1,421	128	60	43	7	18	—
Obscene mail	40	16	10	1	—	2	3
CLASS II	773	160	129	28	3	—	—
Income tax fraud	502	95	80	14	1	—	—
Other fraud	271	65	49	14	2	—	—
CLASS III—Liquor, Internal Revenue	1,934	546	402	66	62	13	3
CLASS IV	4,127	1,675	993	429	63	144	46
Theft	2,28	843	508	191	18	89	37
Postal fraud	405	142	85	37	17	2	1
Forgery	1,441	690	400	201	28	53	8
CLASS V	1,470	853	598	158	14	47	36
Border registration, addicts	30	9	5	2	1	1	1
Assault and homicide	354	199	111	50	1	21	16
Miscellaneous general offenses	1,086	645	482	106	12	25	20
CLASS VI	4,383	2,329	1,330	533	34	383	49
Counterfeiting	494	297	157	99	14	25	2
Burglary	254	161	81	36	2	24	18
Interstate transportation of stolen property	932	599	343	201	15	37	3
Marihuana	1,672	692	360	71	3	240	18
Selective Service Act	900	518	345	121	—	51	1
Other national defense laws	64	21	21	—	—	—	—
Sex offenses	67	41	23	5	—	6	7
CLASS VII—Auto theft	3,791	2,373	1,099	583	13	506	172
CLASS VIII	1,968	1,687	896	643	5	123	20
Narcotics	1,007	800	559	200	4	33	4
Robbery	961	887	443	443	1	90	16

[1] Percents may not add to 100.0 percent due to rounding. Percent not computed where base is 25 or less.
[2] Includes deportation and all sentences where period of imprisonment or probation is four days or less, or fine only which is remitted or suspended.

Table [7–B–9] *(continued)*

Probation											
	Adults only							*Percent*[1]			
Total	*Imme-diate*	*Delay*	*Split*	*FJDA*	*No Super-vision*	*All other*[2]	*Fine only*	*Im-prison-ment*	*Pro-bation*	*All other*[2]	*Fine only*
11,383	**8,630**	**430**	**1,312**	**353**	**658**	**2,203**	**1,682**	**43.0**	**42.5**	**8.2**	**6.3**
1,475	855	96	130	21	373	2,098	1,331	26.1	22.2	31.6	20.0
418	144	76	47	4	147	2,040	100	35.4	10.6	51.5	2.5
7	6	—	—	—	1	3	3	—	—	—	—
1,050	705	20	83	17	225	55	1,228	12.5	39.4	2.1	46.0
9,908	7,775	334	1,182	332	285	105	351	48.6	49.1	0.5	1.7
1,494	1,326	3	121	13	31	12	35	10.3	87.0	0.7	2.0
208	185	1	9	—	13	2	14	12.8	80.9	0.8	5.4
1,268	1,128	2	107	13	18	10	15	9.0	89.2	0.7	1.1
18	13	—	5	—	—	—	6	40.0	45.0	—	15.0
501	357	6	106	—	32	3	109	20.7	64.8	0.4	14.1
335	232	—	91	—	12	2	70	18.9	66.7	0.4	13.9
166	125	6	15	—	20	1	39	24.0	61.3	0.4	14.4
1,346	1,008	14	299	16	9	—	42	28.2	69.6	—	2.2
2,375	1,936	58	270	84	27	17	60	40.6	57.5	0.4	1.5
1,395	1,133	36	153	63	10	8	35	37.0	61.2	0.4	1.5
238	186	3	45	1	3	2	23	35.1	58.8	0.5	5.7
742	617	19	72	20	14	7	2	47.9	51.5	0.5	0.1
517	391	23	43	28	32	19	81	58.0	35.2	1.3	5.5
17	11	1	—	—	5	—	4	30.0	56.7	—	13.3
129	94	3	10	15	7	8	18	56.2	36.4	2.3	5.1
371	286	19	33	13	20	11	59	59.4	34.2	1.0	5.4
2,019	1,604	59	177	74	105	23	12	53.1	46.1	0.5	0.3
194	151	4	36	2	1	3	—	60.1	39.3	0.6	—
93	44	3	12	34	—	—	—	63.4	36.6	—	—
329	266	12	42	4	5	4	—	64.3	35.3	0.4	—
969	759	33	58	26	93	7	4	41.4	58.0	0.4	0.2
376	342	5	26	—	3	4	2	57.6	41.8	0.4	0.2
32	25	1	—	3	3	5	6	32.8	50.0	7.8	9.4
26	17	1	3	5	—	—	—	61.2	38.8	—	—
1,379	942	159	135	112	31	27	12	62.6	36.4	0.7	0.3
277	211	12	31	5	18	4	—	85.7	14.1	0.2	—
204	155	9	22	2	16	3	—	79.4	20.3	0.3	—
73	56	3	9	3	2	1	—	92.3	7.6	0.1	—

[1]Percents may not add to 100.0 percent due to rounding. Percent not computed where base is 25 or less.
[2]Includes deportation and all sentences where period of imprisonment or probation is four days or less, or fine only which is remitted or suspended.

Table [7-B-14]
89 United States District Courts
Prior Criminal Record and Type of Sentence of Convicted Defendants, Fiscal Year 1969

			Prior Criminal Record Reported								
					Total with prior record					Prior prison record	
Type of Sentence	*Total*	*Prior record not reported*	*Total*	*No prior record*	*Number*	*Percent*	*Juvenile record*	*Pro-bation record*	*Other record*	*Number*	*Percent*
TOTAL	**26,803**	**6,744**	**20,059**	**7,294**	**12,765**	**63.6**	**935**	**4,285**	**2,812**	**4,732**	**23.6**
Percent	100.0	100.0	100.0	100.0	100.0	—	100.0	100.0	100.0	100.0	—
Imprisonment	43.0	36.2	453	21.9	58.7	—	65.8	37.5	53.1	79.8	—
Probation	48.2	40.7	50.8	70.8	39.3	—	33.0	59.1	45.1	19.2	—
Fine and other	8.7	23.1	3.9	7.2	2.0	—	1.2	3.4	1.8	1.0	—
Number											
Imprisonment—Total	11,535	2,442	9,093	1,600	7,493	82.4	615	1,607	1,493	3,778	41.5
Adult regular	7,082	1,947	5,135	911	4,224	82.3	197	826	801	2,400	46.7
Adult indeterminate	2,594	286	2,308	314	1,994	86.4	109	354	408	1,123	48.7
Adult mixed	221	47	174	20	154	88.5	3	35	39	77	44.3
Youth Corrections Act	1,296	119	1,177	273	904	76.8	193	317	230	164	13.9
Federal Juvenile Delinquency Act	342	43	299	82	217	72.6	113	75	15	14	4.7
Probation—Total	12,928	2,745	10,183	5,167	5,016	49.3	309	2,533	1,267	907	8.9
Adult—Direct from court	8,630	380	8,250	4,371	3,879	47.0	215	2,059	967	638	7.7
Adult—Delayed probation	430	107	323	119	204	63.2	22	59	41	82	25.4
Adult—Split sentence	1,312	146	1,166	407	759	65.1	30	336	225	168	14.4
FJDA	353	23	330	212	118	35.8	37	61	19	1	0.3
No supervision	2,203	2,089	114	58	56	49.1	5	18	15	18	15.8
Fine only	1,682	1,271	411	299	112	27.3	1	79	24	8	1.9
All other	658	286	372	228	144	38.7	10	67	28	39	10.5

Appendix 7–C

NEW DEVELOPMENTS IN ON-LINE INFORMATION RETRIEVAL TECHNIQUES IN THE UNITED STATES AS APPLIED TO THE UNIFORM PAROLE REPORTS

ERNST A. WENK
MARK S. RADWIN
ROGER K. SUMMIT
CONAL MCHUGH

Two major developments in the field of information sciences have taken place during recent years that will have an impact on criminal justice information systems design. The design of large integrated information systems permitting decision-making based on studied and conceptualized information elements is one, and the development of on-line information retrieval techniques supplying the tools for linking these information elements in a rational fashion to the human decision maker is another.

Following a brief general discussion of the status of information collection in Criminal Justice, the UNIFORM PAROLE REPORTS system will be described. This system is maintained by the parole agencies of the United States and the Research Center of the National Council on Crime and Delinquency and reports on parole outcome of individuals.

One hundred years ago, the 41st Congress of the United States passed a statute which made it the duty of the Attorney General to collect statistics of crime. The program failed for lack of support by police departments and lack of uniformity in collection and processing of the data. The International Association of Chiefs of Police adopted the cause, but it was not until 1930 that Uniform Crime Reports were established.

Judicial statistics have had more success due to their limitation to the United States Courts. The hazards associated with voluntary participation and independent legal and procedural bases were avoided. The first report published by the Attorney General was for 1871, and was based on summary data from each court. In 1935 an individual case card system brought uniformity to the data, which is now computerized.

In corrections, the approach has been somewhat different, perhaps because the

Reprinted by permission from *Abstracts on Criminology and Penology*, Vol. 10, No. 1, January-February 1970, pp. 8–17.

Bureau of the Census initiated the national program—an annual series since 1926. The original data were counts of all prisoners in Federal and State institutions for felons. There was difficulty in the addition of each further item as the intake and release data are, in many correctional agencies, in a form which makes it difficult to tabulate items, and the laborious clerical work involved is often beyond an institution's resources.

The history of failures and partial successes warns that work has to be done soon to develop programs for data collection from all areas of the field and to create an integrated system capable of responding to many kinds of information requests across sub-system boundaries.

Legislation passed in the United States Congress in 1968 made it possible to develop a National Center for Criminal Justice Statistics within the National Institute on Law Enforcement and Criminal Justice. This contributes significantly to the integration and further development of the statistical and informational programs in operation and provides needed leadership in the field. In pursuing these objectives, the Law Enforcement Assistance Administration is funding the development and testing of a model information system comprising several state agencies. The Federal Bureau of Investigation is expanding and updating its National Crime Information Center. The U.S. Bureau of Prisons plans to improve the National Prisoner Statistics program. The Bureau of the Census has studied and published a report describing the information needs in Criminal Justice. The Social Indicators group of the Department of Health, Education and Welfare is exploring possibilities for victimization statistics.

The program (Uniform Parole Reports) was initiated four years ago by parole officials from several states during a meeting under the sponsorship of the National Parole Institutes. Parole Board members, parole administrators, staff of the National Parole Institutes, and research specialists discussed issues involved in creating a national parole data collection system. This group formulated a proposal for action which led to the selection and definition of the items to be reported, to a feasibility study, and to the pilot study aimed at designing a uniform national reporting system in the field of parole.

Originally designed with an expected membership of twenty paroling agencies, the pilot study grew during the four years of its development to a formidable system. The membership includes 55 agencies in fifty States, the Federal Government, the Commonwealth of Puerto Rico, and collaboration of the National Parole Board and Dominion Bureau of Statistics in Canada. The UNIFORM PAROLE REPORTS provides information on parolees and their experience during the first twelve months following parole. The computerized UPR data files contain close to 100,000 individual records. The ongoing monthly contributions by the members are in excess of 2,000 records.

The following are reported:

Identification Data:

- Name
- Identification number
- Birth data

Agency releasing
Sex
Agency supervising

Historical Data:

Effective date of sentence
Date of admission to confinement from which paroled
Type of admission (new commitment; probation violation or parole violation)

Offense
Prior prison sentences
Prior sentences other than prison
Age at admission
Age at time of release on parole
Time served in prison
History of drug use
History of alcohol misuse

Parole Outcome Data:

Date of release to parole supervision
Length ot time under parole supervision
Outcome of first year on parole:

a. no difficulties and no discharge or death during this period
b. if applicable: types of difficulty and date of earliest difficulty

New offense
Data of discharge or death

It is important to note that the items, definitions, and reporting procedures were developed in co-operation with representatives of the states' paroling authorities, with the present data-reporting capabilities of the various state agencies in mind. The requirements for data recording are within the reach of all states, thus making it possible for most states to report on all persons released to parole supervision.

A systematic information feedback program has been established for the participants in the UNIFORM PAROLE REPORTS system, providing regular reports on parole outcomes as related to various offender attributes. A set of seven standard tabulations was made for those persons paroled during the prior year. Separate tables were compiled for men and women for each of the participating agencies and for the combined data. The set of information distributed to the users includes approximately 2,000 different tables containing the information on 56,882 persons released on parole during 1965, 1966, and 1967.

The creation of hundreds of tables compiled from many thousands of individual records appears by a computer of the first generation, a type characterized by low speed, low capacity, and a lack of sophisticated operating system programs. This standard reporting program was the ideal program for a computer installation of the second generation type which are specifically designed for bulk processing and can easily handle a number of pre-specified requests simultaneously in group or batch processing.

The objective of information retrieval in UNIFORM PAROLE REPORTS is to identify and retrieve the records, from within a file or collection of records, which are relevant to a particular information need. The information retrieval system called DIALOG, developed by members of the Information Sciences group of the Lockheed Palo Alto Research Laboratory and applied to the data of the UNIFORM PAROLE REPORTS will be described. In preparation for the support of on-line retrieval, indexes to the records are developed by extracting data elements from the records and then associating the record identification number with them. Retrieval is then accomplished by scanning the indexes in response to a query and to identify those records containing the desired data.

When performed by a computer this index scanning can be accomplished much more rapidly than sequentially examining each record—an important factor if an immediate response is desired. By examining the indexes created for information retrieval, it is also possible to perform preliminary analysis of the data file under consideration. DIALOG provides the user ten commands such as BEGIN, EXPAND, SELECT, COMBINE, DISPLAY, PRINT, etc., with which he can manipulate and examine desired files of data. When a command is sent to the computer, a reply is sent back on the TV-like display screen in response to the command. Based on this feedback from the computer, the user is able to browse through files containing thousands of records in a matter of minutes.

DIALOG is a general-purpose system for on-line interactive information retrieval and data analysis developed by members of the Information Sciences Laboratory of the Lockheed Palo Alto Research Laboratory. DIALOG has been programmed in assembly language for the IBM 360 Series computer systems.

The user input to DIALOG consists of a series of one of several succinctly defined commands and associated operands that each call for the performance of one of the basic data processing operations. Extensive use is made of the full hierarchies of storage available to the system so as to take best advantage of their relative speeds and capacities. DIALOG output may be directed by the user to display, typewriter, line-printer, magnetic tape, or photocomposition devices. Formats may be prespecified and called by number or user specified at the time of use.

DIALOG Retrieval Codes for UNIFORM PAROLE REPORT File

RETRIEVAL CODE	DESCRIPTION	RETRIEVAL CODE	DESCRIPTION
PS	NUMBER OF PRIOR PRISON SENTENCES	BD	BIRTH DATE
		BY	BIRTH YEAR
PN	NUMBER OF PRIOR NON-PRISON SENTENCES	BM	BIRTH MONTH
		SD	SENTENCE DATE
TA	TYPE ADMISSION	SY	SENTENCE YEAR
OF	ORIGINAL OFFENSE	SM	SENTENCE MONTH

RETRIEVAL CODE	DESCRIPTION	RETRIEVAL CODE	DESCRIPTION
NO	NEW OFFENSE	AD	ADMISSION DATE
AG	AGE WHEN ADMITTED	AY	ADMISSION YEAR
DU	DRUG USAGE	AM	ADMISSION MONTH
AU	ALCOHOL USAGE	RD	RELEASE DATE
SX	SEX	RY	RELEASE YEAR
PA	PAROLING AGENCY	RM	RELEASE MONTH
AP	PAROLING AGENCY AREA	DD	DIFFICULTY DATE
RA	RECEIVING AGENCY	DY	DIFFICULTY YEAR
AR	RECEIVING AGENCY AREA	DM	DIFFICULTY MONTH
YP	YEARS IN PRISON	DT	DISCHARGE/DEATH DATE
PP	PAROLE PERFORMANCE	DY	DISCHARGE/DEATH DATE
MS	MONTHS SUPERVISED ON PAROLE	DM	DISCHARGE/DEATH MONTH
DE	DEATH	TS	TYPE SENTENCE
ID	IDENTIFICATION NUMBER		

RETRIEVAL CODE	DESCRIPTION
ON	ORIGINAL OFFENSE/NEW OFFENSE
OP	ORIGINAL OFFENSE/PAROLE PERFORMANCE
OY	ORIGINAL OFFENSE/YEARS IN PRISON
OS	ORIGINAL OFFENSE/MONTHS SUPERVISED
NS	NEW OFFENSE/MONTHS SUPERVISED
PT	PAROLE PERFORMANCE/TYPE ADMISSION
SP	PAROLE PERFORMANCE/PRIOR NON-PRISON SENTENCES
TP	PAROLE PERFORMANCE/PRIOR PRISON SENTENCES
SI	PAROLING AGENCY/STATE INSTITUTION

OFFENSE CODE	DESCRIPTION
00	NO NEW MAJOR CONVICTIONS AND NO MAJOR OFFENSE ALLEGED WITH GUILT ADMITTED
01	WILLFUL HOMICIDE
02	NEGLIGENT MANSLAUGHTER
10	ARMED ROBBERY
11	UNARMED ROBBERY
20	AGGRAVATED ASSAULT
30	BURGLARY
40	THEFT OR LARCENY, EXCEPT VEHICLE
50	VEHICLE THEFT

OFFENSE CODE	DESCRIPTION
60	FORGERY, FRAUD, OR LARCENY BY CHECK
61	OTHER FRAUD
70	RAPE, FORCIBLE
71	RAPE, STATUTORY
72	SEX OFFENSES AGAINST JUVENILES (EXCLUDING RAPE)
73	PROSTITUTION AND PANDERING
74	ALL OTHER SEX OFFENSES NOT AGAINST JUVENILES
80	VIOLATIONS OF NARCOTIC DRUG LAWS
81	VIOLATIONS OF ALCOHOL LAWS
90	ALL OTHERS

Appendix 7–D

A NATIONAL CRIME DATA REPORTING SYSTEM
by
Peter P. Lejins

For the purpose of developing a national crime and delinquency data reporting program, the establishment of a special national agency is recommended. In this proposal, this agency will be referred to as the National Crime Data Agency; for the purpose of brevity, it is occasionally cited simply as the National Agency.

While one may assume that geographically such an agency should be located in the Nation's Capital, from the administrative standpoint, several possibilities exist and should be studied further. Location in the Department of Justice or the Bureau of the Census, and status as an independent agency have been suggested. At this point of the deliberations, it appears to be most advantageous, and this proposal so recommends, that the Agency be located in the Department of Justice. While this location would convey as much prestige and authority as any, an additional factor in its favor is the fact that most of the Federal, State, and local agencies whose cooperation in the program must be secured are in one way or another connected with the administration of justice.

The purpose and primary objective of the National Crime Data Agency is the operation of a national crime data reporting system. It should be recognized that the information which is by and large available with regard to crime, its control and prevention, falls into two major categories:

1. First, there is what is generally and popularly known as criminal statistics and what actually consists of reported actions of the law enforcement and correctional agencies with regard to offenders, and data collected by the respective agencies about these offenders. Thus, police statistics report either the fact that an offense has been registered by the police as a "crime known to the police," or they report the arrests. The criminal court statistics report the cases filed

"National Crime Data Reporting System: Proposal for a Model," in the President's Commission on Law Enforcement and Administration of Justice *Task Force Report: Crime and Its Impact—An Assessment* (Washington, D.C.: U.S. Government Printing Office, 1967), pp. 182–184.

with the court and the court dispositions in these cases. The parole statistics report the offenders released on parole and placed with the parole system, violations of parole, successful termination of parole, etc. This type of crime data is referred to in this proposal as "agency statistics." These statistics report the volume of actions by the various law enforcement and correctional agencies and data about offenders in terms of certain characteristics and in the form of tabulations. These statistics do not as a rule identify agency action with an individual and thus it is impossible to connect the actions of two or more agencies with reference to one and the same individual offender.

2. Secondly, there is another type of information about offenders, which consists in a listing of law enforcement and correctional involvements of a particular offender, usually supplemented by identifying information and possibly some background data. This is properly referred to as a criminal career record, and in police circles is popularly known as the rap sheet. An orderly collection of such criminal career records or files on individual offenders that is kept up to date is considered by many an especially valuable source of information both for understanding the career of a criminal offender and for evaluating the effectiveness of the law enforcement and correctional measures which were applied to him—more valuable than the impersonal tabulations of the agency statistics.

In view of the above, it is here being proposed that the program of the national reporting system should consist of two parts: The operation of an all-inclusive national system of agency statistics in the area of crime and delinquency, which will be referred to in this proposal as System A, or agency statistics system; and the operation of a national criminal-career records system, which could be described as a national registry of criminals but from the point of view of constitutional law and civil rights might better be called a national law enforcement and correctional registry, a title which would emphasize not so much the identification of a person as a criminal, but the fact that certain law-enforcement and correctional actions have been taken with regard to an individual. In this proposal, the latter system will be referred to as System B.

It can be speculated that the agency statistics and criminal-career records, although outwardly very different, basically are linked together and in the case of perfect reporting actually contain the same information. The tabulations of the agency statistics are after all made on the basis of individual reports, punch-cards or "line items" pertaining to individual offenders. Likewise, the criminal-career records are made up of items which represent the actions of law-enforcement and correctional agencies and are reported also in the statistical tabulations of these agencies. One can further speculate that, given perfect reporting and modern electronic equipment, both agency statistics and criminal-career records may be stored as a single repository of data, subject to recall for different purposes. A request for all the actions taken by law enforcement and correctional agencies with regard to a certain individual will produce his criminal-career record; a request for all violations of probation by commission of a new offense in a certain year by an offender population of a certain jurisdiction will produce an agency statistical tabulation.

It should be noted that while System A as such is to be interpreted as an information system serving all the consumers of such information identified earlier in this proposal, System B is envisaged as a combined operational and information system in the sense that, on the one hand, it will perform the functions of the present criminal identification sections or bureaus of the police departments, supplying law-enforcement agencies with identification and criminal-record data and expand this service to correctional agencies, and, on the other hand, it will serve as a national source of data on criminal careers and life histories of criminals and juvenile delinquents for research purposes, thus providing the presently lacking material for broad-scope studies of the effects of law enforcement and correctional measures on the criminal as related to his background, thereby making possible the evaluation of the law-enforcement and correctional programs.

It is further recommended that besides the administrative setting for the operation of the national crime data reporting system, the National Agency should have as a second major component an Office of Analysis and Development. The traditional title of "research and development" is deliberately avoided here, because the term research would give an undue emphasis to a function which is not envisaged as a major function of the Agency (see in this connection the reference made above to an agency of the type of a "national academy of criminology"). The Office of Analysis and Development would be charged with the performance of three major tasks:

1. Development of national statistical and criminal-record programs, this development to be handled by the Program Development Section. When these programs are ready for routine operation, they are to be handled by the Office of National Crime Data Reporting. The program-development task can be further analyzed into two types of activities:

    a. Development of uniform categories for the data to be reported by the law enforcement and correctional agencies as well as the setting of standard reporting procedures to be followed by the cooperating agencies. The wide variation in the legal and administrative provisions as well as in the practices of law-enforcement and correctional agencies, which are for the most part matters of State and local rather than national government, makes this task of developing uniform categories and standard reporting procedures one of the most crucial, if not the most crucial element in the development of the national reporting program. The experience of the "Uniform Crime Reports" in developing uniform crime categories and reporting procedures in the area of police statistics should serve as an example and as a starting point for similar developments for all the other types of crime data reporting.

b. Promotion of the new statistical programs by exploring and developing the best methods for securing the cooperation and compliance with the set procedures by the law-enforcement and correctional agencies.

2. Interpretation of the statistical data at the time of publication is to be handled by the Analysis and Interpretation Section. The experience of the several last decades has shown that one of the major problems with the publication of statistical data in the area of crime in this country is the interpretation or rather misinterpretation thereof especially by the mass media and the general public, and hence by the electorate. Therefore, it is recommended that a competent unit be developed for the basic analysis and interpretation of the data—even if minimal and limited to the indispensable and noncontroversial—simultaneously with their release. Especially since this is not a proper task and area of competence for the operating agencies, the availability of a National Agency as a location for such an interpreting function is very important. This proposal recommends that no raw statistical data on crime of national scope ever be published without being accompanied by a competent basic interpretation. This basic interpretation does not, of course, preclude—and hopefully will invite—further analysis, interpretation, criticism, etc., by individual students of criminology and private organizations.

3. In addition to administering the basic crime data reporting system, the National Agency must have facilities for conducting studies which would aid in the interpretation of the data supplied by the basic systems or would add to this information. A Special Studies Section should be in charge of this assignment. These studies can be sample and/or control group studies; they can be done once, from time to time, or periodically. An example of such a study might be a series of sample studies done from time to time to ascertain the relationship between reported and unreported crimes, or a study to ascertain the role of price markup to cover up losses from theft in the retail trade as a factor in under-reporting this type of larceny.

Chapter 8

The study of output in the criminal justice system

An overview of recorded output

It is at the correctional way stations in the criminal justice system that a limited amount of information on output has been generated. Output data are not readily available at the earlier way stations, such as police, lock-ups, jails, bail-bond procedures, prosecutors' handling of cases, and court sentencing. How do the cases not booked by the police compare with those that are charged? What are the differences in outcome or future behavior between those released and those held for the next step? What happens to the cases not charged?

A series of similar questions can be raised at the succeeding way stations up to the point of probation, commitment to a correctional institution, and release from correctional institutions. What is the outcome difference between offenders held in a lock-up or jail awaiting hearing and those freed on bond? and what is the impact of the lock-up or jail on detainees? The same sort of questions regarding juvenile offenders can also be asked but not answered: what is the likely future behavior or outcome of those held for the juvenile court by the police *versus* those not held, of those placed in detention by the court officers *versus* those allowed to go home while awaiting hearing, etc.

Very little is known as to the difference between cases handled one way or another by the prosecutor, particularly with reference to personal characteristics of the individuals concerned. Employment outcome and involvement in further criminal activity are almost impossible to follow up in the prosecutor's case load, in view of the fact that punitive and/or correctional measures intervene.

It is a well-established fact that at the prosecutor's way station in American criminal courts more than 90 percent of the cases are handled by plea bargaining although is it not known what impact this has. What are the differences in the cases pleading in one way as opposed to another, with regard to previous and subsequent criminal involvement according to personal characteristics? Likewise, what are the differences between the juvenile offenders referred to the juvenile court who are held for court action (official hearing) and those handled unofficially by a court officer? And what is the outcome of those cases handled unofficially without a hearing compared with those disposed by a juvenile judge or referee?

Personal data in output statistics

As noted in the previous chapter it is asking too much at present for the way stations of the criminal justice system to collect personal data on their total input of cases. And even more so, they cannot be expected to collect outcome data on cases with which they have dealt, as a part of routine operations. It certainly became clear looking at the statistics on input (previous chapter) that even personal data on cases were lacking after police arrest and up to probation supervision. Some courts keep statistics on the processing of cases in general without keeping individual case information. Prosecutors' offices keep practically no statistics. Very few lock-ups and jails make annual reports on admission and release according to personal information. The same can be said for most municipal workhouses.

An integrated set of national statistics for adult and juvenile offenders might overcome the unavoidable shortages of case information all along the line. Since at the police level and at the prison level of handling adult offenders fingerprints are taken and cleared through the F.B.I., here is a potential but limited source of follow-up data—how much recorded involvement and for what offenses. But these finger-print clearances are not ordinarily available to researchers, while the police and prisons themselves usually do not make statistical compilations of such clearance data. Although not complete in coverage, finger-print clearances could certainly report recidivism as a form of outcome since, in recent years, the annual reports of the F.B.I. have been presenting data on criminal careers, based upon finger-print clearances of persons who are multiple recidivists.

Reporting data on outcome is quite feasible for two-way stations, namely probation and parole, since many probation and parole offices have been tabulating such information for more than a generation. By the very nature of their work, probation and parole offices must investigate and supervise individual cases and must make reports relative to recommendation for termination of the supervision or to return to court or prison clients who have violated the rules and must also make reports relative to closing cases because of arrest on a new criminal charge.

The labeling process as output

It has been suspected that the "labeling process" (i.e. stigmatization because of contact with the law) increases in impact as cases go further and further into the criminal justice system. In other words, a person arrested but released by the police is supposedly less stigmatized than one held for court, while a person given a suspended sentence (probation) by the court is not stigmatized as much as one sentenced to prison. The extent to which such a proposition is true is not really known and to obtain insight into labeling, researchers would not only need to sample public attitudes toward offenders who have or have not passed through the various way stations but also to obtain information on how offenders themselves differentially perceive themselves in their passage through the criminal justice way stations.

An initial effort, to detect how the male juvenile delinquent perceives future social liability as he passes through the hands of the police and juvenile court in Mahoning County, Ohio (Youngstown being the principal city) was made by Jack D. Foster.[1] Interviews, based on a structured schedule, were held with a consecutive sample of 196 male subjects who were processed by the juvenile bureau of the Youngstown police department and the juvenile court of Mahoning County.

The various way stations in the process of handling delinquent boys in Youngstown consist of: (1) advise and release at the police bureau, (2) police probation (the boys come to report to the bureau, usually on a weekly basis, for a period of several weeks), (3) advise and release at the juvenile court (which means that the intake worker felt that it was not necessary to retain the boy for further court processing), (4) probation at the juvenile court (which means that the boy's case was considered serious enough to require supervision by a court officer, although the boy was allowed to return to his home), and (5) commitment by the juvenile judge or referee to an institution for juvenile delinquents (the most serious cases). At station no. 1, the sample of boys interviewed consecutively totalled 37; at station no. 2, 43; at no. 3, 57; at no. 4, 26; at no. 5, 25; other, 8, totalling 196 boys. The schedule that Foster used for interviewing each boy individually is duplicated in Appendix 8-A. The immediate concern is with

[1] Jack D. Foster, "Social Intervention following Delinquent Behavior: The Complainant, the Police and the Delinquent Boy" (Ph. D. dissertation, The Ohio State University, 1971).

responses to items covered in Part III of the schedule, dealing with perceptions of social liability which result from the intervention.

Some of the high points in Foster's findings, relative to perceived social liability resulting from contact with police and court, are summarized as follows:

a. From approximately two-thirds to four-fifths of the Youngstown respondents at the five way stations did not feel that their mothers or their fathers will think worse of them for having got into trouble with the law.

b. Even a larger percentage of the boys at the various points in the juvenile justice system said that neither their mothers nor their fathers would hold this brush with the law against them in the future.

c. The boys' perceptions of whether their teachers will think worse of them varied at the five way stations somewhat more than the perceptions given above: for those released by the police (1), 92 percent said their teachers would not think worse of them; for those placed on police probation (2), 62 percent; released by juvenile court (3), 71 percent; placed on probation by the juvenile courts (4), 59 percent; those committed to an institution (5), 32 percent.

d. Somewhat higher proportions of the respondents at the five way stations in Youngstown felt that the employers "will hold this against you" and a still higher percentage felt that the police will hold the contact against them as compared with the boys' expectations from mother, father, and teachers. Or to state the finding in terms of the conclusions in statements a, b, and c above, a smaller proportion of the respondents at the various way stations felt that employers and police would not hold the encounter against them as compared with what they expected from mother, father, and teachers.

On the basis of such findings, Foster concluded that "it would seem that the sociologists who advocated the labeling hypothesis have overestimated the degree to which juveniles subjected to public intervention for law-violating behavior perceive that they have incurred social liability (i.e. been labeled), or that the event has substantially affected their lives either now or in the future."

Certainly, if and when researchers are able to obtain insight into the differential impact of the labeling process at various way stations, not only in the juvenile but also in the adult criminal justice system, American criminology would have an important indicator of what input into the system does to a person in terms of stigmatization, apart from any positive efforts of the correctional phases of the system.

As mentioned earlier, the public's attitudes toward juvenile and adult offenders who have been processed by the various way stations of the criminal justice system is the complimentary aspect to the offender's own perceptions of the "Mark of Cain." However, further research needs to be done on the public aspect of labeling of juvenile and adult offenders. Certainly, there is considerable support for the trend toward greater acceptance of offenders "back into society" than in previous decades of American history. One can cite the growing willingness of employers in the United States to hire ex-prisoners as employees.

Nevertheless, it is supected that willingness to overlook and willingness to accept persons who have been officially involved in delinquency and crime has developed in certain sectors of the public more than in other sectors. In other words, differential stigmatization or labeling undoubtedly exists among the various socio-economic classes, religious denominations, and racial and nationality groups. Research of the future will have to indicate how much and how varied is stigmatization.

It is also imperative to discover in future research the comparative dimensions of labeling and stigmatization on the part of the various sectors of the public. Is labeling of insane persons, especially those committed to and subsequently released from state institutions, as great or as varied as labeling of adults committed to and released from prisons? How badly is the prostitute labeled these days? The unmarried girl with an illegitimate child? The homosexual male? The alcoholic? The drug addict? The chronic unemployed? The school dropout?

Whatever stigma or liability the officially processed offender may face from society in general or certain groups in particular, impact of the criminal justice way stations must fit into the system of public labeling, apart from any possible reconstruction of life and attitudes the offender may develop as a result of the way he was handled and treated by the police, courts, and correctional institutions.

Prediction of outcome

a. *The Warner-Hart pioneer study*

Interestingly enough, one of the first major efforts of criminological research in the United States dealt with prediction of outcome of cases placed on probation and parole. The prediction effort began in the early twenties with the pioneer study of the parole outcome of Massachusetts Reformatory cases by Sam B. Warner.[2] His contention was that "no information should be considered by the Board of Parole unless it differs as to parole successes and parole violators."[3]

But actually it was Hornell Hart[4] who created the first predictive model, using Warner's data. He discovered that, among 64 variables that Warner collected in his sample of parole successes and failures, there were 15 that

[2] "Factors Determining Parole from the Massachusetts Reformatory," *Journal of the American Institute of Criminal Law and Criminology*, XIV:2 (August 1923), pp. 172–207.

[3] *Ibid.*, p. 187.

[4] "Predicting Parole Success," *Journal of the American Institute of Criminal Law and Criminology*, XIV:3 (November 1923), pp. 405–413.

stood the test of predicting parole failure in 99 out of 100 instances. He found 20 items that predicted outcome of paroles at a lesser but still significant level of chance. For example, parole violators more than nonviolators *inter alia* had bad associates, had brothers who had served jail sentences, and had fathers who had also been sent to jail. See Table 8–1 for a duplication of Hart's re-working of Warner's data.

Of considerable interest for this period in the history of research in criminology is the fact that Hart projected the idea of computing a prognostic score for each man appearing before the parole board, which would reveal his statistical chances of making a go of parole or failing on parole.

On the basis of such scores it would be possible to make reports to the Board in a form somewhat like the following:

> Jim Jones has a prognostic score of 93 points. In the past experience of the Board among men with prognostic scores in the neighborhood of 93 points, only 19 percent have violated their paroles.
>
> Will Smith has a prognostic score of 21 points. In the past experience of the Board among men with diagnostic scores close to 21 points, 80 percent have violated their paroles.[5]

Table 8–1. Classification of paroled prisoners from the Massachusetts Reformatory, showing the percentages of successful paroles and of parole violations falling into each group, and showing what percentages of the prisoners paroled in each group succeeded.[6]

*Warner's No**	*Characteristics for which observed contrasts are quite unlikely to be due to chance*	*Percent distributions* Successful paroles	*Parole violations*	*Percent successful*
	All paroles studied	100	100	49.75
38	Men guilty of "other" crimes	11	2	85
37	Partly support unnamed persons	14	2	88
38	Men guilty of assault and battery	10	3	77
34	Occupation "none"	6	2	75
49	No criminal record	19	7	73
58	Accidental offenders	26	10	72
12	Religion of prisoner "other answers"	14	7	67
34	Extent of occupation "regular"	22	14	61
58	"Responsible" and "normal" offenders	30	22	58
41	Means of committing crime: fraud	46	59	44
22	Men using cigarettes	59	77	43
31	Character of associates "bad"	43	56	43

[5] *Ibid.*, p. 411.
[6] *Ibid.*, p. 410.

*Numbers in this column refer to the numbers of the corresponding sections in Warner's tables.

*Warner's No**	*Characteristics for which observed contrasts are quite unlikely to be due to chance*	*Percent distributions* Successful paroles	Parole violations	*Percent successful*
38	Men guilty of larceny	28	37	43
49	Men with three or more criminal records	51	68	43
37	Claim to be contributing to parents	40	55	42
66	Six or more times guilty misconduct in the reformatory	26	38	41
48	Served one or more jail sentences	43	65	40
10	Claim parents own property	22	35	39
38	Guilty of breaking and entering	24	37	39
33	Claim to attend church regularly	14	23	38
52	Evidence of disease "not answered"	10	17	37
49	Men with reformatory records	12	21	36
7	Marital relations of parents "fair," "unpleasant," or "questionable"	7	15	32
53	Serious illness, "not answered"	6	15	29
54	Surgical operations "not answered"	6	16	27
23	Uses drugs	2	7	22
29	Character of home "bad"	2	8	20
6	Mother drank	1	4	20
14	Father served jail sentence	1	15	6
14	Mother arrested or jailed	0	4	0

Table 8-2. Expectancy rates of parole violation and non-violation[7]

Points for number of factors above the average	*Number of men in each group*	*Expectancy rate for success or failure*			
		Percent violators of parole			*Percent non-violators of parole*
		minor	*major*	*total*	
16–21	68	1.5	—	1.5	98.5
14–15	140	.7	1.5	2.2	97.8
13	91	5.5	3.3	8.8	91.2
12	106	7.0	8.1	15.1	84.9
11	110	13.6	9.1	22.7	77.3
10	88	19.3	14.8	34.1	65.9
7–9	287	15.0	28.9	43.9	56.1
5–6	85	23.4	43.7	67.1	32.9
2–4	25	12.0	64.0	76.0	24.0

[7] Ernest W. Burgess, "Factors Determining Success or Failure on Parole," Part IV, in *the Workings of the Indeterminate-Sentence Law and the Parole System in Illinois* (A report to the Honorable G. Clabaugh, Chairman, Parole Board of Illinois, submitted by Andrew A. Bruce, Ernest W. Burgess, and Albert J. Harno, Chicago, Illinois, August 18, 1928), p. 248, Table XXVII.

b. *Burgess' parole prediction*

By the end of the twenties (1928), Ernest W. Burgess had completed his monumental study of parole prediction in the State of Illinois, using a sample of 3,000 cases (1,000 from each of three prisons). The parolees had been on parole for at least two and one half years, and some for as long as four to five years. Burgess was able to compute an expected success or failure rate based on the chances that a parolee with a particular combination of factors (case-history items that statistically distinguished successes or failures) would succeed or fail on parole.

In the same vein of thought as Hart, Burgess suggested that a summary sheet should be developed on each prisoner appearing before the parole board, so that its members could tell at a glance the violation rate on each case-history factor covered in the summarized report. Table 8-3 gives Burgess' illustration of a summary sheet on two cases; the violations rate in each case is computed for 12 significant case-history factors.

Table 8-3. Proposed summary sheet based on expectancy rates for twelve significant case-history factors.[8]

Significant factors	*Violation rate*	
	case A	*case B*
General type of offense		
Robbery	—	12.6
Burglary	26.3	—
Parental and marital status		
Both parents living	—	15.2
Married at time of commitment	23.6	—
Criminal type		
First offender	—	15.8
Professional offender	52.4	—
Social type		
Farm boy	—	1.0
Gangster	22.7	—
Community factors		
Resident in community where arrested	14.1	14.1
Residence in open country	—	12.5
Residence in underworld	42.3	—
Statement of trial judge and prosecuting attorney		
Recommended leniency	—	16.9
Protests against leniency	46.7	—
Previous criminal record		
No criminal record	—	16.3
Reformatory record	34.1	—

[8] *Ibid.*, p. 247, Table XXVI.

Significant factors	*Violation rate* case A	*Violation rate* case B
Work record previous to commitment		
No work record	28.0	—
Regular work	—	8.8
Punishment record in institution		
No punishment	17.0	17.0
Intelligency rating		
Average	—	17.1
Superior	26.8	—
Psychiatric type		
Egocentric	24.3	—
Psychiatric prognosis		
Favorable	—	14.8
Unfavorable	30.5	—

Several years later, after the Illinois system had established the position of sociologist-actuary to make predictive estimates of each prisoner coming before the board of parole for a parole hearing, a set of 27 case-history items was devised for use in making the assessment. In a typical set of predictive analyses by sociologist-actuary Sam Daykin (c. 1939), the following assessments were made for the parole board:[9]

Case A. 16 favorable and 11 unfavorable items. This inmate is in a class in which 29 percent may be expected to violate the parole agreement. 15 percent may be expected to be minor violators. 14 percent may be expected to be major violators.

Case C. 8 favorable and 19 unfavorable items. This inmate is in a class in which 70 percent may be expected to violate the parole agreement. 35 percent may be expected to be minor violators. 35 percent may be expected to be major violators.

At a later date, the Illinois system reduced its actuarial evaluations of prospective parolees to 12 factors.

c. *Subsequent prediction studies*

A series of important contributions to outcome prediction followed closely on the heels of Burgess' contribution, the most notable of which were the studies by Sheldon and Eleanor Glueck,[10] George B. Vold,[11] and Elio D.

[9] Walter C. Reckless, *Criminal Behavior* (New York: McGraw-Hill, 1940), pp. 491, 498.

[10] Sheldon and Eleanor T. Glueck, *Five Hundred Criminal Careers* (New York: Alfred A. Knopf, 1930).

[11] George B. Vold, *Prediction Methods and Parole; a Study of Factors Involved in the Violation and Non-violation of Parole in a Group of Minnesota Adult Males* (Hanover, N. H.: The Sociological Press, 1931).

Monachesi. The following lengthy excerpt from Monachesi's study of probation prediction (adult and juvenile cases in Ramsey County, Minnesota—St. Paul) will supply certain technical details regarding the methodology available at the time.[12]

> The case-records of 1515 probationers (896 juvenile delinquent probation cases, and 619 adult District Court probation cases), handled by the Ramsey County, Minnesota, Probation Office in 1923, 1924, and 1925 were utilized. These cases were studied and the information bearing on them was classified in accordance with a list of major categories and appropriate sub-categories. The cases were grouped as non-violators and violators of probation, and the proportion of offenders in each sub-category for each major category was computed separately for juveniles and adults. The resulting proportions, or percentages, were designated as violation rates for each sub-category and were compared with the average violation rate of the total number of juvenile and adult cases separately. On the basis of this comparison it was possible to ascertain the amount by which the violation rate of any one particular sub-category deviated from the average violation rate of the group as a whole. However, the results indicate that the differences between violation rates of different sub-categories are in general larger than could be ascribed to chance alone.
>
> Four methods were employed in the construction of prediction tables for juveniles. The first table was based upon all pre-probation categories, and each individual was scored by the Burgess method. The second table was based upon pre-probation categories which did not deal with factors pertaining to the father and the mothers of probationers, and the Burgess scoring method was again used. The similarity in distributions obtained by these two tables was measured by a Pearsonian r of $+.924$. The third table was based upon pre-probation factors, eliminating those concerned with the fathers and the mothers of probationers. The remaining factors involved in the life of each individual were weighed by assigning arbitrary values to the amount by which the violation rate of each sub-category differed from the average violation rate. This table was found to correlate with the second table with an r of $+.885$. The fourth table was based on those categories used in the second and third tables, but the Glueck scoring method was used. The distribution obtained for this table was found to correlate with the distribution obtained in the second table by an r of $+.865$. Because of the high value of the coefficients of correlation, the only method used in scoring the adults was the Burgess method and only those pre-probation categories which did not deal with the mothers and fathers of probationers were utilized in the construction of the adult prediction table.
>
> Experimenting with the scoring technique indicated that the most satisfactory results were obtained by using the Burgess method of scoring on those categories not concerned with the fathers and the mothers of probationers.

[12]Elio D. Monachesi, *Prediction Factors in Probation* (Hanover, N.H.: The Sociological Press, 1932), pp. 111–113.

In order to check the reliability of the material a total of 252 cases (151 juvenile cases and 101 adult cases) was re-read and re-classified. The methods employed to measure the degree of consistency between the first and second classifications were the Pearsonian coefficient of correlation, the coefficient of mean square contingency, and an analysis of the scatter diagram. The most satisfactory of these three measures was found to be an analysis of the scatter diagram. The results indicate that the material contained in the Ramsey County Office files is such in character as to make possible some degree of accuracy in re-classification.

If the predictions made at the time of granting probation materialized within reasonable time limits then, and then only, would it be possible to say that prediction of outcome of probation worked in actual practice.

Unfortunately, administrators of probation and parole systems, both juvenile and adult, have seldom used prediction charts as a guide to decision-making in individual cases. And yet the character of the available data needed to make predictions of outcome is not much different from the character of data on which actuarial tables are based in life insurance.

Nevertheless, the prediction model has had rather wide use in criminological research in the United States, after the pioneer demonstrations of the twenties and thirties. As a matter of fact, the prediction model has often been extended to forecast those who are likely and those who are not likely to get involved in delinquency. One should refer back to Chapter 3—*The "Who" Factor in Involvement.* Appendix 8–B presents selected references from a very extensive bibliography on prediction studies as prepared by Don M. Gottfredson and Kelley B. Ballard. One will notice the extension of the prediction model of research to problems other than those of probation and parole outcome.

Research on outcome

At the same time that prediction studies were being developed (beginning in the twenties and extending into the thirties), follow-up studies, attempting to gauge outcome in terms of recidivism or relapse into delinquency and crime, were being generated in the three main correctional way stations (probation, correctional institution, and parole). Appendix 8–C lists in chronological order the pioneer outcome studies published in the twenties and thirties.

A minority of these reports and follow-up studies attempted to use criteria for outcome that supplemented sheer reported involvement in crime and delinquency, including school performance, employment stability, social adjustment, etc. However, even when restricting outcome to involvement or noninvolvement in further offenses, the outcome studies were not able to develop a standard time-period coverage for recording the extent of recidivism. The time periods used varied in the number of years after supervision on probation or parole or after release from the institution.

Several obvious observations can be made about these genuine efforts to discover whether correctional output was gravitating toward success or failure. Although modern countries have attempted to improve the quality of probation and parole service and the quality of program in correctional institutions (in the latter instance, to overcome negative and deleterious impact), it appears that outcome as measured by recidivism is much more related to selection policy than to the possible impact of the various correctional programs. By selection policy, in this instance, is meant the administrative determination of who is and is not placed on probation by the courts, who is and who is not sentenced to a correctional institution, and who is and who is not granted parole.

In view of the fact that courts place the more favorable cases on probation and tend to sentence the more serious offender and the "hard core" offender to institutions while the releasing authorities (parole boards or institutional committees) tend to give early release to the cases who have not had an unfavorable adjustment in the institution and do not display too many unfavorable factors for post-institutional adjustment, there seems to be no question that in the United States probation cases should be expected to dispaly the least recidivism (which follow-up studies indicate) and that institutionalized cases will show the greatest amount of relapse into crime and delinquency.

One should also expect that the rate of relapse of cases on probation and on parole will be somewhat lower during the period of supervision by the so-called caretaking agents than subsequently, that is, when the probationer or parolee is granted his final release.

In addition, there is some likelihood that follow-up reports that are made over a long time span, say 10 years, will show improvement with the passage of time, during which period an aging, "settling down," or maturation process has begun to operate, independent of the possible impact (good or bad) the correctional way stations may have had on its clients.

Unfortunately, correctional programs for the handling and treatment of juvenile and adult offenders are not injections of vaccines or chemicals that generate an immunity against involvement in crime. Whether the clients of correctional programs will ever be able to obtain more than a partial immunity from recidivism is dubious. The sociologists who are increasingly emphasizing the impact of the so-called "labeling process," whereby persons can be worsened by stigmatization of entrance into the criminal justice system, infer that there is this extra liability with which offenders must contend, although there is a glimmer from actual field research that labeling may have been overstated by our theoretical scholars.

Procedure and results of two outcome studies

a. *The Gluecks' study*

One of the most important of the early outcome studies is that made by Sheldon and Eleanor T. Glueck and published in 1930[13] of 510 young adult male prisoners from the Massachusetts Reformatory. These prisoners were released on parole from the institution during the years 1911 to 1922 and their combined postinstitutional and postparole periods ranged from 5 to 15 years. The recorded criminal involvement of 422 of the original sample of 510 was traceable. The records show that 89 of the 422 (21.1 percent) had no traceable record, that 26 (6.2 percent) committed crimes for which they were not arrested (why or how is not clear), and that the remainder, 307 (72.7 percent), committed crimes that were officially recorded. Hence, almost 80 percent of the sample were failures according to the Gluecks' method of counting.

The Gluecks classified the failures into partial failures (16.8%) and total failures (62.1%). The former included the cases that had received two convictions on minor charges, arrests for not more than three minor offenses, five arrests for automobile traffic violations and/or drunkenness (although no single case in the partial failure category depended for its categorization on just the drunkenness and traffic violations). The total failures included the cases that had been arrested three or more times for serious offenses, arrested more than three times for minor offenses, convicted one or more times for a serious offense, and more than five times for drunkenness. In addition, total failures also included cases of desertion or dishonorable discharge from the armed services, cases wanted for escape or for being a fugitive from justice, and cases known to have committed serious offenses or continous minor offenses, "for which they were not arrested or prosecuted." Hence, the total failures on this sort of categorization were found by the Gluecks to be almost four times more numerous than the partial failures.[14]

The Gluecks also discovered that the distribution of 489 of the 510 cases according to the same definitions of success, partial failure, and total failure indicated the following percentage counts respectively: 6.6, 5.7 and 87.7. In still another comparison, the Gluecks concluded that there was some indication for the operation of a settling-down process with aging, since the percentage of successes greatly increased in the *post period* of 5 to 15 years and the percentage of total failures measurably declined.[15]

[13]Glueck, *Five Hundred Criminal Careers.*

[14]*Ibid.*, pp. 188–189.

[15]*Ibid.*, pp. 190, 359–360.

In the instance of 356 of the 510 reformatory parole cases, the investigators were of the opinion that they possessed sufficient information to indicate whether the reformatory itself had had an impact on their post-release outcomes. Of the 356 cases, 128 had committed serious offenses prior to commitment as well as during and after parole; hence, it was concluded that the reformatory "had no effect in curbing their criminality." But in 129 cases (36.3% of the 356), it was presumed that the reformatory had a favorable impact, since they had committed serious offenses in the pre-reformatory period, showed some improvement during the parole period, and still some improvement in the postparole period. There were 55 cases of the 356 (15.4%) that were adjudged by the Gluecks as not having been helped by their reformatory stay or by their supervision on parole, since they committed serious offenses not only prior to incarceration but also during their parole period, and yet these cases showed some improvement after termination of parole supervision. In addition, there were 44 cases in which the reformatory had a temporary influence or in which parole had influenced them, since these men committed serious offense prior to institutionalization and after parole supervision but showed improvement during the parole period.[16]

When the Gluecks followed the reformatory cases for an additional five-year postrelease period after the first follow-up, they found that 32.1 percent of the cases with available information were nondelinquent (had settled down), in contrast to 21.1 percent in the first follow-up period. By the time the fifth year of the second postrelease period had been reached, the percentage of nondelinquents had reached 42.7. Here again, the Gluecks felt that there was continued evidence of a settling-down process with age.[17]

Other soundings of outcome, supplementary to recidivism, were made by the Gluecks in their first follow-up study. For example, they obtained comments from interviews with a large proportion (301) of the original sample (510) of ex-prisoners. Almost two-thirds of those given follow-up interviews indicated that incarceration in the reformatory had had a deterrent effect and that the reformatory stay had had a good influence as a result of teaching trades and of affording regularity in life. Of the 301 cases interviewd, 68 percent acknowledged benefits from their institutional stay, while 32% said they had received no benefit.[18] The latter comments by the ex-prisoners contained some of the following negative replies: schooling in crime, acquisition of bad habits and bad associates, difficulties in achieving a social or industrial rehabilitation on the outside, because of the "police tactics" of their parole officers; embitterment because of incarceration, and other various harmful influences.[19]

[16] *Ibid.*, pp. 225–226.

[17] Sheldon and Eleanor T. Glueck, *Later Criminal Careers* (New York: 1937), pp. 75–76.

[18] Glueck, *Five Hundred Criminal Careers*, p. 297.

[19] *Ibid.*, pp. 299–300.

The interviewed ex-prisoners also lodged other criticisms against the reformatory: lack of intelligent classification of inmates, the homosexual practices within the prison, the abundance of petty prison rules, the poor level of industrial training, and a poor school program.[20]

In 291 of the 510 original cases, the Gluecks were able to assess information on the character of the releasee's home and neighborhood: of the home environments 24.7% were found to be favorable; 41.6% fair, 33.7% unfavorable; of the neighborhood, 20.2% favorable, 40.1% fair, and 39.7% unfavorable.[21]

The judgments of the staff of the follow-up study with reference to the postparole family and social adjustments may be summarized as follows: almost one half of the cases available for such judgment displayed poor family relations in the postparole period; there was an increase in church attendance during the period over the amount of attendance during the prereformatory period; the negative employment of leisure time increased in the postparole over the preparole period; those who used leisure time harmfully drank to excess and associated with bad companions; about half of the contacted sample ran around with bad associates.[22]

Consequently, this first gigantic effort toward assessing the outcome of released prisoners included the tabulation of recorded reinvolvement of the ex-prisoners in crime and also an attempt to assess their postrelease social adjustments and their perceptions of the impact of their institutional stay.

b. *Glaser's study*

It seems appropriate to call attention to another monumental outcome study, conducted by Daniel Glaser more than a generation after the one conducted by the Gluecks. Glaser dealt not only with follow-up information on failures and releases from federal correctional institutions, but he also attempted to penetrate the "black box," namely to get insights into the impact of institutional stay as seen through the eyes of prisoners and successful releases. The impact part of the study will be dealt with subsequently but at this juncture, the main consideration is Glaser's approach to the study of outcome.

Following up, in 1960, the available recorded information on a sample of prisoners released from federal prisons in 1956 (a sample of every tenth releasee, totalling 1,015 cases), the Glaser investigation discovered that approximately 31 percent had been re-imprisoned at some point during the four-year time span. The breakdown was as follows: 26.6 percent were re-imprisoned for a new felony; 1.1 percent for violation of parole or of

[20] *Ibid.*, p. 313.
[21] *Ibid.*, p. 215.
[22] *Ibid.*, p. 215.

conditional release, when suspected of a new felony; and 2.8 percent for parole violation, when no violations were alleged. In addition, 3.9 percent of the sample of 1965 federal prison releasees received nonprison sentences for "felony-like" offenses. Hence, the total failure percentage approximated 35.[23]

On the other hand, 65% of the 1956 federal prisoner sample were successes, of which 52.2% had no further criminal record and 12.8% had minor involvements (but no felony convictions).[24]

Apparently, the aim of this preliminary sounding on postrelease violators from federal prisons was to reenforce the fact, emanating from several contemporary investigations, that the majority of released prisoners do not return to prison, in spite of a prevailing "legend" that two-thirds do return as recidivists.

However, the principal contribution of the Glaser report to the study of outcome was a detailed analysis of recorded case data and interview information obtained from a sample of failure cases, i.e. released prisoners returned to federal prisons as violators, and a sample of postrelease successes, namely those who came through the postrelease period without being returned to prison. Hence, the Glaser study involved two separate samples—both failure cases and success cases—while the prevailing model for outcome studies, as established by the Gluecks, usually involved only one sample, namely releases from one correctional institution (such as the Massachusetts Reformatory) and traced the successes and failures within this sample of releases.

Glaser's failure study collected case information and interview material from 308 prisoners returned to four federal prisons (Leavenworth, Terre Haute, Milan, and Chillicothe) in 1958–1959. Glaser classified these returnees (failure cases) according to case information, a categorization unique in outcome studies to date. Of the 308 returnees, 30 percent were classified as marginal failures, which included "defective-communication" cases and "other nonfelony" violators. The former represented, in the investigator's opinion, rather dubious revocations of parole, based on dubious information relative to alleged violations. The latter grouping (nonfelony) of marginal failures consisted of a noncriminal violation of parole rules, such as absconding, drinking, not seeking work, etc.

Two hundred and fifteen of the 308 failure cases (70 percent) were categorized as "clear recidivism" cases and they included 178 instances (58%) who did not recidivate until some time after release from prison and 37 cases (12%) labeled as "immediate" recidivists who relapsed into crime very soon after release. The "sometime after release" is not spelled out but it appears that it refers to relapse after 3.6 months, which was the median time

[23]Daniel Glaser, *The Effectiveness of a Prison and Parole Program* (Indianapolis: Bobbs-Merrill, 1964), p. 20.

[24]*Ibid.*, p. 20.

between release and violation for the total sample of failure cases.[25]

The success cases in Glaser's investigation consisted of 250 ex-prisoners who had been released from five federal correctional institutions (Leavenworth, Terre Haute, Milan, Chillicothe, and Ashland)[26] and who had been committed to prison by the federal courts in the 15 jurisdictions from which the failure cases originally came. The interviews were held with the successful cases in 1960–1961 and case data from the files of the local probation offices were collected. (Remember that in the federal system, the probation officers in the federal district courts act as parole officers for the ex-prisoners released on parole or on conditional release). Hence, there is some correspondence between the failure and the success cases, certainly with regard to site of origin, prison from which released, and time of contact, which approximates a matching procedure.

The investigation also categorized the successes. Of the sample of 250, 210 (84%) were classified as "clear reformation" cases, which in turn were broken down into the following sub-categories: 80 (32%), "late reformation after criminal career"; 37 (15%), "early reformation after criminal career"; 3 (1%), "crime-facilitated reformation"; 48 (19%), "reformation after crime interval"; 26 (10%), "reformation after only one felony"; 16 (%), "crime-interrupted noncriminal career."

The cases that had three or more felony convictions or who had depended on crime for a livelihood for five years or more were categorized as having had a criminal career; those with two felony convictions but less than five years' "dependence" on crime were classified as having a crime interval; those who had committed only one felony were labeled as "one-crime cases". Those criminal career cases released from prison after they attained 30 years of age were considered "later-reformation" cases; those released from prison before 30 years of age were characterized "early reformation" cases; those whose settling down was helped by experience gained in crime involvement were designated as "crime facilitated" cases; and those who had disengaged themselves from crime at least a year before last commitment to a federal prison were looked upon as "crime interval" cases.[27]

Forty (16%) of the 250 were categorized as "marginal reformation" cases, of which 12 were classified as "economic retreatism"; 9, as "juvenile retreatism"; 4, as "addictive retreatism"; 13, as "crime-contacting noncriminals"; 2, as "nonimprisoned criminals."[28] The economic retreatists

[25] *Ibid.*, p. 78.

[26] Since the institution at Ashland, Kentucky is a Federal Youth Center for males sixteen to twenty-one, failure cases who originally had been released from this correctional institution were not returned to it but were returned to one of the four other federal prisons.

[27] *Ibid* pp. 55–56.

[28] *Ibid.*, p. 84.

apparently abandoned striving for "economic self-sufficiency." The juvenile retreatists were those who continued to associate with juveniles and seemed unable to achieve adult independence. The addictive retreatists fell back on heavy dosages of legal drugs, avoiding the complications accompanying heroin usage. The crime-contacting noncriminals in the Glaser scheme of classification represented those who on the surface maintain legitimate occupations but who, at the same time, maintain contacts with known criminals. The nonimprisoned criminals, comprising the last subclassification in Glaser's categories of "marginal reformation" success cases, drew support from criminal activity while on parole but did not receive prison sentences. The criminal involvement of these marginal reformation cases appeared to fall in the field of illegal service rather than in actual predatory offenses.[29]

California's application of prediction to parole

While there have been scattered efforts by paroling authorities to use predictive knowledge for making judgments about releasing offenders, there has been very little systematic application of prediction to the selection of inmates of correctional institutions for release on parole and for differential handling of offenders on parole. The State of California is perhaps the prime mover in applying the predictive model to the screening and supervision of parolees. Evidently, the state administrators were convinced of the validity of several research efforts that had studied the outcome or performance of different groups of offenders on parole. These researches pointed the way to the development of base expectancy rates and to the application of expected performance to the amount of supervision necessary for various groups of parolees on parole.

The following summary of California's application of "base expectancies" to differential handling of parolees was made by Don M. Gottfredson. One should note that, among other important points, the use of base expectancies (prediction of outcome for various groups of offenders) has a potential for reduction of institutional overcrowding and a consequent reduction of institutional costs. The application of base expectancy rates also has potential for determining the amount of supervision which individuals need on parole. In this connection one should note that cases given minimal supervision show no increase in parole violation rate.[30]

[29] *Ibid.*, pp. 64–72.

[30] Excerpts from Don M. Gottfredson, "Research Significance for Parole Operations" (Paper delivered before the Centennial Congress of the American Correctional Association, Cincinnati, Ohio, October 13, 1970).

Previous studies provided the background for development of parole prediction methods in California beginning in 1958. The methods developed and tested for adult male and female prisoners and for confined juveniles have demonstrated validity for test samples released in different years, in samples released to different geographical areas in different seasons of the year, and in samples released from different institutions.

These prediction measures were called "base expectancies" because they were thought to provide a base for further research by quantifying expectations concerning parole outcomes. They do this by summarizing experience with parolees having different characteristics, on the basis of their parole performance. The base expectancies devised were intended primarily as a tool for studing effectiveness of treatment. They were believed also to have a potential practical application of assistance in programs intended to reduce confinement costs and increase utilization of parole management resources.

An assumption basic to one application of prediction methods to problems of prison overcrowding and increased confinement costs was that some presently confined inmates could be released earlier if appropriate procedures for their identification were formulated. The overall expectation, based on experience, was that about half the total parolee group would experience major difficulties before two years after their release (with major difficulties including any prison return, absconding, or sentence to jail for 90 days or more). But 30 percent of offenders, which could be identified by base expectancy scores, could be expected to complete a two-year period with only 30 percent experiencing major difficulties. Another identifiable one-third could be expected to have such difficulties in two-thirds of the cases. It was then possible to screen the entire confined population of California's prisons, first by base expectancy scores, then by further clinical criteria. The result was a group of men referred for parole consideration at a date earlier than originally scheduled; some were paroled.

A second application of base expectancy measures was the establishment of minimal supervision caseloads of both male and female parolees. Persons classed as having a high probability of successful parole completion received minimal supervision. Experience demonstrated that these cases may be given less supervision with no increase in the parole violation rate. This enabled parole workers to deploy their forces from areas where help was less needed to concentrate efforts to where it might be more helpful

In the case of women parolee case management, using base expectancy measures as a starting point, a new classification and supervisory system was established. The best risks received only minimal attention. The parole agent time thus saved was redeployed in treatment oriented supervision of judged amenable parolees and in surveillance of judged nonamenable cases.

In supervision of men parolees, the saved time was used for more intensive supervision of "middle risk" parolees. This was an application of a research result reporting no difference with reduced caseloads in the case of good and poor risks but a favorable gain (fewer violations) with parolees in the middle risk group.

These efforts had resulted in substantial monetary savings by 1961, with no increase in parole violations. In the case of the relatively minor effort regarding female parolee case management, the institution population was reduced, and it was the opinion of correctional administrators that this program avoided the necessity for building a new women's prison.

In 1961, the California legislature approved a Department of Corrections program intended to increase correctional effectiveness. This program was based on a screening of inmates by base expectancy scores, combined with programs for more intensive institution and parole case services. The goal was reduction of institutional costs for non-violent cases by release slightly ahead of the expected time. That is, the program called for: (1) screening by base expectancy scores; (2) earlier parole of a group of inmates for whom base expectancy scores are predictive of successful parole and no danger is judged to be present; and (3) establishment of small institutional treatment units and low caseload parole programs for closer attention to inmates in the base expectancy groups with average parole success predicted. Nine such units were established, each treating 60 to 125 inmates.

Thirty-eight parole caseloads were established with 30 rather than the usual up to 70 parolees per agent. Seventeen were established as part of the new program, 14 were part of a previously established experimental program, and the other seven resulted in redeployment of agents after establishment of minimal supervision caseloads for base expectancy predicted "good risks."

By 1963 the Department of Corrections was able to report to the legislature that the program had reduced the institutional population by more than 840 men and women. It asserted that support savings were at least $840,000 and that eight and a half million dollars in capital outlay were deferred. These savings were attributed to the new program and to initial efforts by the paroling authorities to base decisions partly on base expectancy measures.

By 1968, the Department of Corrections reported the further development called the Work Unit program. Its aim was a classification system for parolees that balances the amount of time the parole officer has available for direct case activity with the amount of time each parolee requires for appropriate supervision. To permit such an arrangement, three classes of parole supervision were established: (1) special supervision for parolees who require more than average parole agent time; (2) regular supervision for parolees requiring moderate time; and (3) conditional supervision for parolees requiring a minimal amount of time. The program objectives were to increase community protection, improve performance of parolees, and save institutional costs. The base expectancy measure provides a basis for the parolee classification system. In its 1968 report, the Department asserts that the major program results up to that time had been a reduction by 17 percent of the prison return rate for new crimes and violation of parole, an improved performance despite caseloads of more vulnerable people, and savings estimated at one and a half million dollars for institutional operating expenses yearly and construction savings of ten million dollars.

In 1969 the Department reported to the legislature that total prison returns for new crimes and violation of parole rules were reduced by 25 percent since the 1965 start of the parole Work Unit program. They concluded (on the basis of base expectancy scores) that 1,543 additional men have succeeded on parole who, on the basis of past experience, would have failed. Again, considerable savings were reported in both per capita costs and ultimate need for major capital outlay. The saving from men kept in the community rather than back in prison was estimated as the equivalent of the entire population of an average sized major prison. Savings on operating expenses were estimated at four and a half million dollars yearly and in construction savings at twenty million dollars.

Relation of decisions, stigma, and time-lapse to outcome

Since studies of outcome have come into vogue, there has been a growing realization that the overall outcome of any sample of offenders depends in large part upon the decision-making process of persons in control of the destiny of the probationers, parolees, or ex-inmates. Officials, such as police, probation officers, and parole officers, are the ones who primarily make the decision to return the ex-offender to the court or to the institution. It is their decision which affects the record of outcome—namely failure. In some instances, however, the decision might rest with persons who complain to the authorities, whether or not victims of aggression. In the past there has been no way to standardize the readiness of victims or authorities to take action on a probationer, parolee or ex-inmate. Some authorities might even argue that the stigmatizing "halo" that an officially acted-upon offender wears is a big factor in increasing the risk of being acted upon for recidivism, since the ex-offender is under watchful suspicion.

Just how much the failure rates, as judged by relapse or recidivism, would decline if ex-offenders could be accorded special concessions and special privileges is a very realistic issue. Undoubtedly the failure rates would decline precipitously. Perhaps, research in the future can be conducted to see how much failure rates of adult probationers, parolees, and ex-prisoners would differ between a sample placed in communities that had no knowledge of their previous experiences and a sample placed in their communities of origin with all the impact of police, probation, parole, and neighborhood alertness. Sweden has been approaching the former sort of arrangement by placing some ex-prisoners in communities different from those of origin and attempting to curtail completely local knowledge of the previous penal experience of the relocated offender.

In the numerous attempts to gauge outcome during and after probation or parole as well as during a period of release from correctional institutions (juvenile and adult), whether on parole or not, the time factor has always been an unstandardized variable, thus making comparisons with various samples practically impossible. Some outcome studies might gauge success or failure a few years after release from supervision or else several years after release from an institution, including a long post-release period following termination of parole or aftercare supervision. Certainly, in the instance of adult releases, the period is related to a settling-down process that accompanies aging.

There is reason to believe that most ex-incarcerated offenders who are going to recidivate will do so within a few months of release, no matter whether under parole (aftercare) supervision or not. In view of this, a standard period of one year after release from the correctional institution appears to be a realistic time period for future outcome studies for gauging recidivism or relapse into delinquency and crime. The one year time period can certainly be applied to probation supervision cases (those which were not committed to correctional institutions) as well as to the postinstitutional release cases.

In the instance of the cases supervised by probation and/or parole officers, it should be possible to measure the outcome (new arrest *versus* no arrest record) of cases one year after termination of probation or parole supervision. Such an indication would obviate the suspected positive effect of actual supervision on the client's steering clear of involvement during supervision.

Perceived impact as a possible gauge

A measure of outcome needs to be developed that is not dependent upon the decisions of the caretakers of society who undoubtedly increase the failure rates by their prejudicial decisions. One possible alternative is to find a measure of impact of probation experience, of institutional stay, and of parole supervision as seen through the eyes of the so-called "client" (the offender) as well as through the eyes of his caretakers. Studies of impact as perceived by the client himself and by persons in whose care he has been placed are probably most feasible for those offenders who have been committed to correctional institutions, although they should be feasible for offenders on probation as well as under parole supervision.

a. *Unfavorable biographical views of prisoners*

Before embarking upon a series of research efforts to measure the impact that the inmate feels the correctional institution had upon him, one should be mindful of the fact that the revelations of prisoners from the very inception of the prison one hundred and fifty years ago have been very unfavorable with regard to the overall impact upon them. The published accounts of prisoners' reactions to their prison experience, even as early as the 1820's, were scathing including comments such as: fails to reform, prison officers immoral, convicts treated inhumanely, use of pardons is abused, corruption exists in the handling of accounts.[31] An English convict two generations later claimed that the English prisons at the time were "breeding dens for the procreation of professional thieves."[32] Yet a generation later a burglar called prison a school for crime and indicated how he was influenced in prison by his cellmates and how he associated with his former cellmates in criminal activity after release.[33] Another prisoner, also writing in the twenties, contended that prisons steeped the inmates in crime, that they were full of horrors, that corporal punishment was terrible, and that ex-prisoners developed criminal ventures with their former cellmates. Regarding corporal punishment, he says, "the flogging just hardened me, that's all. I found myself somewhat more determined, more confident, and with a feeling that I would play this game of violence to the finish."[34] A prisoner, writing about his thirty-five years of prison experiences, claimed that prisons crush and terrify, increase the prisoner's hatred toward society, and make him determined to even the score when released.[35] "Prison stupor—mental deterioration—was claimed to be one of the serious by-products of prison experience.[36] A young offender, who spent the greater part of his adolescent life in schools for delinquent boys, reveals the same deleterious impact of correctional institutions: an antisocial reaction to rigid and brutal discipline resulting in the development of antisocial grudges, as well as the acquisition of criminal techniques, a criminal code, and a criminal set of attitudes.[37]

b. *The pioneer study of Galway*

Beginning in the middle forties, the author was able to interest several of his graduate students in making studies of institutional impact as perceived by the inmates themselves, particularly at the point of release. The first of these studies was conducted by Edward J. Galway at the Federal Reformatory, Chillicothe, Ohio (c. 1946–47).[38] He interviewed 275 consecutively released inmates, privately and individually, just prior to their departure from the institution.

[31] By One Who Knows, *Inside Out; An Interior View of the New State Prison*, (New York: 1823), pp. x-xl.

[32] By a Ticket-of-Leave Man, *Convict Life; Revelations Concerning Convicts and Convict Prisons* (London: 1880), p. 27.

[33] By a Burglar, *In the Clutch of Circumstance; My Own Story* (New York: 1922), p. 54 ff.

[34] Jack Black, *You Can't Win* (New York: 1926), pp. 267, 278.

[35] Charles L. Clark and Earle Edward Eubank, *Lockstep and Corridor; Thirty-five Years of Prison Life* (Cincinnati: 1927), pp. 162–163.

[36] Victor Nelson, *Prison Days and Nights* (Boston: 1933).

[37] Clifford R. Shaw, *The Jack-Roller* (Chicago: 1930), pp. 47–163.

[38] Edward J. Galway, "A Measurement of the Effectiveness of a Reformatory Program" (Ph.D. dissertation, The Ohio State University, 1948).

The initial question asked in these interviews was: "Have you got anything out of being here?" Seventy-two percent of the departing inmates gave a positive reaction, namely that the institutional stay had been of benefit to them. The positive impact responses fell into four groups: the socializing and maturing value of institutional stay, the deterrent effect of being institutionalized, the acquisition of skills during commitment (educational and vocational), and miscellaneous improvements (such as curing alcoholic habits and increase in health). The minority of negative responses from departing inmates included such perceptions as no changes in their habits and attitudes, only "pulled time" during institutional stay, and actually worsened by the imprisonment (very few instances).

Galway discovered that 38 percent of the inmates who, on entrance to the reformatory, were placed in "close" custody gave negative replies, while only 17 percent of those who had initially been classified as "medium outside" custody gave negative replies. He found also that the distribution of positive and negative were not obviously related to recorded disciplinary actions during commitment, although only 60 percent of those who had received three or more disciplinary actions for rule violations during their stay gave favorable replies. Nor were negative replies more frequent from those departing inmates who had been previously institutionalised in a correctional institution prior to this "trip." However, the inmates released on expiration of sentence (evidently the poorer risks who had been denied early release on parole) gave only 50 percent positive replies to the question. The departing inmates who represented the lowest educational level among the 275 interviewed subjects reacted more favorably than their better-educated fellow inmates to their institutional stay. The departing Negro inmates also gave a higher percentage of positive replies than the departing white inmates (89 versus 68 percent).

Galway made an analysis of the staff members that the departing inmates had indicated as knowing them best during their institutional stay. The 275 subjects between them nominated 125 specific staff members of the institution, comprising about 40 percent of the total staff. On the basis of the 275 nominations, independent of how many different staff members were listed, the distribution according to branch of service was as follows: custody (guards or officers), 108; trade training (vocational programs), 39; farming operations, 32; prison industries, 18; maintenance work, 18; culinary (food service), 17; classification and institutional parole workers, 14; clerical, 13; education, 9; medical, 5; chaplain, 2. Obviously, it was not the so-called professional person in the institution with whom the inmate built up a relationship but rather the nonprofessional.

When Galway contacted each nominated staff person and asked for his opinion on what the departing inmate had got out of his stay, he found that their responses did not correlated with the inmates' perceptions. He surmised that the officers of the correctional institution, although they were supposed to know the departing inmate better than any other officer of the reformatory, did not have the understanding to enable them to sense positive or negative changes in the prisoners during their institutional stay.

The departing inmates were also asked to nominate a fellow inmate who knew them best. When Galway interviewed these nominees, he discovered that the nominated fellow inmates made impact evaluations similar to those that their released "brothers" had made about themselves. This finding raises the question as to whether the remaining nominated inmates actually knew their departing brothers better and had better insights than staff or whether they were slanted in their perceptions of institutional impact, for whatever reason, in the same direction as the releasees.

c. *A replication study by Moran*

Approximately six years after the original Galway study, the author had occasion to interest another graduate student, Mark R. Moran, in interviewing individually each departing inmate at the very point of release from the U.S. Reformatory at Chillicothe, Ohio. From the tabulation of the responses of 250 consecutively departing inmates from Chillicothe in 1953,[39] it was found that 68 percent professed to have obtained a great deal from their stay; 23 percent, something; 9 percent, not much.

Another question in these terminal interviews was put as follows: "Do you think you have changed at all during your stay?" The replies to three structured answers to this question were as follows: a lot, 73.2 percent; some 20.4 percent; very little, 6.4 percent. This question was followed by a related inquiry: "In what way do you think you have changed?" The answers obtained from the 250 departing inmates were classified as follows: learned a lesson, 69; more settled, 43; attitude improved, 35; grown up, 24; matured, 23; think befored acting, 21; assume responsibility, 13; control temper, 9; work habits improved, 8; no answer, 4. Actually most of these responses could be classified under "improved maturation."

The 1953 Chillicothe (Moran) inquiry also attempted to penetrate the problem, so often mentioned in negative aspects, as to whether fellow inmates in a correctional institution had detrimental effects on an inmate. The question was put as follows: "Do you think the fellows here make a fellow worse?" The responses were as follows: no, 34 percent; some, 21.6 percent; depends upon the person, 28.4 percent; yes, 15.1; no answer, less than 1 percent.

The Moran interview schedule asked the departing inmate to "Name the staff member that helped you the most," and to indicate "What was his

[39] Mark R. Moran, "Inmate Concept of Self" (Ph.D. dissertation, The Ohio State University, 1954).

branch of service?" The distribution of replies (nominations) was as follows: custodial (housing, maintenance, supervisory), 37.6 percent; non-custodial maintenance, 19.2; industry foremen, 12.8; trade training supervisors, 11.6; professional workers (social workers, teachers, doctors), 17.6; no answer, 1.2. The distribution of nominated staff who helped the departing inmates most is fairly close to the nomination of staff who knew them best in the Galway interviews at the same institution six years earlier, although the percentage of nomination of professional workers rose somewhat in the intervening period.

Another impact question that will be mentioned at this point was stated as follows in the 1953 (Moran) terminal interviews with 250 departing inmates at Chillicothe: "What part of the program did you get the most out of?" The first choice listings were as follows: work assignment, 112; trade training, 45; recreation and athletics, 28; school, 20; religious program, 16; library, 15; cell-house or dormitory life, 8; health, 4; food, 1; no answer, 1.

Moran also attempted to penetrate the departing inmate's perception of himself as an inmate. It appears that this line of investigation likewise brought to the fore favorable responses from departing inmates, as can be judged from their answers to the following questions.[40]

"Is a fellow able to keep his self-respect in this institution?" Answers: all of the time, 71 percent (of the 250 inmates); some of the time, 26 percent; not much of the time, 3 percent. "Do the inmates here think they are better off than the inmates in a state prison?" A lot, 48 percent; quite a bit, 21; some better, 30; no answer, less than 1 percent. "Do inmates here think they are lower than a G.I.?" (Remember that 60 percent of them had had armed service experience.) Yes, 50 percent; no, 49 percent; no answer, less than 1 percent. "After you got used to the place here, which one of the following best describes how you thought of yourself during your stay here?" Student, 58 instances; trainee, 64; patient, 9; about like I always felt, 35; pulling time, 81; criminal, 3. The first three are considered favorable concepts and give a cumulative total of 52 percent of the 250 answers. "Pulling time," a sort of convict concept, comprised one-third of the answers. "Did you think of yourself as a convict during your stay here?" Not much of the time, 70 percent; some of the time, 23; all the time, 7. "Do the personnel here try to make the fellows think they are convicts?" None do, 43 percent; one or two do, 38; more than two do, 19. "Do the personnel here throw their weight around?" None do, 30 percent; one or two do, 53; more than two do, 17. "Are there 'sweet boys' and their 'daddies' around here?" Very few, 60 percent; some, 32; a lot, 8. "Does strong-arming happen here among the inmates?" Not at all, 44 percent; very little, 35; some, 21. "Is the inmate council here any good for helping a fellow get adjusted?" A lot of good, 57 percent; some good, 34; not much good, 9.

[40]This summary of Moran's findings is presented in Walter C. Reckless, "The Impact of Correctional Programmes on Inmates," *British Journal of Delinquency*, VI:2 (September 1955), pp. 144–145.

d. *Bright's study*

Another pioneer study of impact, made under the direction of the author in 1950, is the one by David Eugene Bright who studied a sample of 250 prisoners at the Ohio Penitentiary in Columbus, Ohio (a maximum security prison for the older and more involved adult male offenders). Bright administered his impact schedule, not at the point of release but rather on a certain day (May 1, 1950), to five selected groups comprising fifty prisoners each: (1) those who had been in the penitentiary three months, (2) those who had been in 15 months, (3) those who had been in three years, (4) those who had been selected to be transferred to an honor farm, and (5) those who were living in the honor dormitory of the penitentiary, thus sharing the greatest privileges.

Bright found evidence in the responses to the schedule, which was mass administered at one sitting (with the administrator making an introductory statement to elicit cooperation and with the administrator reading out the questions and the answer format), to support the following three propositions: (a) the longer the stay in the prison, the more adverse the inmate attitudes as revealed by answers to questions regarding the prison staff, the prison programs, and the physical facilities of the prison; (b) the lower-paid, nonprofessional staff members were perceived by the inmates as having more impact than the higher-paid more professional staff, as judged by nominations of staff members who had done something for the inmate and of those whom the inmate liked the best; and (c) the better the programs and facilities to which the inmates were exposed in this prison, the more favorable the attitude of the responding prisoners toward their prison stay.[41]

e. *Sabnis' study*

Still another pioneer impact study carried out by M. S. Sabnis, completed in 1951 under the author's direction, generally confirmed the main findings in the Galway, Moran, and Bright studies. This is of considerable importance, since Sabnis' sample of inmates was taken from the incarcerated delinquent boys in the National Training School for Boys in Washington, D.C., whereas the Chillicothe sample represented a slightly older group of young offenders and the Ohio Penitentiary sample consisted of still older and still more difficult prisoners. In other words, it is possible that impact does not vary as much with age and type of institution as it does with the staff,

[41] David Eugene Bright, "A Study of Institutional Impact upon Adult Male Prisoners" (Ph.D. dissertation, The Ohio State University, 1951), pp. 84–85.

programs, facilities, and atmosphere of the correctional institution (still a conjecture at this point of knowledge). Among other findings from the responses of the incarcerated youths, Sabnis had evidence to show that impact tends to vary inversely with the length of incarceration (the shorter the more favorable, the longer the more unfavorable), that the nonprofessional staff were nominated by the inmates as being closest to them and as helping them the most during their institutional stay, and that certain programs within the institution have more perceived impact than other programs.[42]

f. *Studies by Eynon and Simpson*

In 1960 a large-scale study of institutional impact, as seen through the eyes of the "clients" of a large training school for committed delinquent boys in the State of Ohio, was undertaken by the author and his colleague, Dr. Thomas G. Eynon. One of the important features of the design of this study was the administration of a schedule to "clients" at the point of admission (approximately one week after entrance) and to others at the point of release (usually the day before). A schedule was administered to the accumulated group of subjects just recently admitted and another was administered to the boys who were ready for release (this institution usually released its boys on a certain day each week). From several sets of items in both the admission and the release schedules, it was possible to obtain "before" and "after" indications of attitudes and perceptions and make appropriate comparisons to show change during institutional stay.

Jon E. Simpson made the study of the before and after responses wherever possible and, in addition, analyzed certain sets of perceptions that only applied to the youths who had completed their institutional stay and were being released.[43] More particularly, Simpson's study was able to focus (1) on the way the inmate of a training school for committed delinquent boys views himself in a so-called residential bureaucracy and the degree to which he claims to have integrated himself during his stay, (2) the extent to which the inmates felt they had been subjected to negative inmate pressures, (3) the direction of perceived changes in themselves during institutional stay, and (4) inmate perceptions of improvement in

[42]M. S. Sabnis, "A Measurement of Impact of Institutional Experience on Inmates of a Training School" (Ph.D. dissertation, The Ohio State University, 1951), pp. 149–150.

[43]Jon Eaton Simpson, "Selected Aspects of Institutionalization as Perceived by the Juvenile Offender" (Ph.D. dissertation, The Ohio State University, 1961). For a condensed summary, see Jon E. Simpson, Thomas G. Eynon, and Walter C. Reckless, "Institutionalization as Perceived by the Juvenile Offender," *Sociology and Social Research*, 48:1 (October 1963), pp. 13–23.

themselves during the period of commitment.[44] See Appendix 8–D for the impact items in the schedule.

The sample in the Simpson (Eynon and Reckless) research project consisted of 372 out of 485 boys who had been committed to the Boys Industrial School of Ohio, at Lancaster, Ohio (BIS) *for the first time* (so-called first timers) during the period January 15 to June 30, 1960. One hundred and thirteen of the original first admissions during the period of admission could not be included in the "before-and-after" analysis for a variety of reasons, the main one being that they had been transferred to other institutions. It should be noted that only first admissions to BIS were taken as subjects, because of the necessity to exclude bias from previous commitments. The intake at BIS in 1960 consisted principally of boys under eighteen years of age who were mainly violators of probation from the juvenile courts of the large urban communities of Ohio. The daily population of the school at the time of the study averaged 887 boys, thus making BIS one of the largest schools for delinquent boys in the country. The median length of stay at the time was six months, the median age at the point of release was sixteen years; two thirds of the sample of 372 boys were white; one third, Negro. On self reporting items, the median age at which the sample had first contact with the police was thirteen and one-half years. The self reports revealed that the sample had an average (median) of 3.5 contacts with the police and/or juvenile courts before coming to BIS. The most commonly reported offenses on the self reports were auto theft, burglary, truancy from school, incorrigibility, and stealing, in this order of self-reported frequency.[45]

The items on the admission and release schedule were checked for a sixth-grade reading comprehension level, according to the word lists developed by Dr. Edgar Dale.[46] The items were also pretested on the basis of distribution of favorable or unfavorable answers. All items were eliminated in which the responses were distributed more than 75 percent or less than 25 percent in either direction. This was done in order to avoid non-discriminating items (stereotyped items).

Simpson's findings from the admission–release study of perceived impact of institutional stay in a large bureaucratic school for delinquent boys are summarized as follows:[47]

1. Contrary to expectations, the boys in the total sample tended to reply in a favorable direction to the series of seventeen questions developed to elicit the boys'

[44] *Ibid.*, p. 9.

[45] *Ibid.*, pp. 23–27.

[46] Edgar Dale and Gerhard Eichholz, *Children's Knowledge of Words*, an Interim Report (Columbus, Ohio: Bureau of Educational Research and Service, The Ohio State University, 1960). Dr. Dale is in process of publishing a final report, under title of *The Words We Know: A National Inventory*.

[47] *Op. cit.*, pp. 108–111.

feelings concerning their integration in the institutional structure of the Boys' Industrial School.

2. Very few statistically significant differences in the perceptions of the subjects concerning their integration in this residential institution were found in comparisons between subgroups based on ten independent variables selected for this investigation. Although the direction of the significant variations supported the second hypothesis, the magnitude of these subgroup differences was negligible.

3. As predicted in the third hypothesis, the views of the boys pertaining to their integration in the institutional structure were more favorable at the point of release than were their expectations at the point of admission; but the variations on the indices which were used to measure the stability of the inmates' perceptions were small and in some cases not statistically significant.

4. The answers of the total sample to the items concerning inmate pressures provided support for the expectation that the respondents would not express the belief that they had been exposed to adverse inmate pressures. Nevertheless, the negative inmate pressures were apparently more extensive than would be desired in terms of the achievement of treatment and rehabilitation goals.

5. The findings explicitly refuted the fifth hypothesis which anticipated that there would be significant subgroup variations in reporting exposure to negative pressures from the other inmates. Furthermore, the directional forecasts included in this hypothesis were contradicted by the direction of the subgroup differences. There was a tendency for the more sophisticated rather than the less sophisticated offenders to state that they had been exposed to adverse inmate pressures.

6. Although it was hypothesized that there would be no change during confinement in the subjects' self-concepts, value orientations, and willingness to participate with others in an agreeable manner, the replies of the total sample at the point of release were consistently and significantly (with the exception of the self-labeling items) more favorable than their views at the point of intake. A majority of the variations were slight in magnitude, but the pattern of favorable change was consistent.

7. Many of the inter-subgroup variations at the point of intake and/or release on the three self-concept instruments were not statistically significant. In general, the release responses of the individual subgroups were more favorable than their intake replies, but the variations were small in magnitude and they tended to be nonsignificant. The answers of the more mature offenders exhibited greater favorable change than the replies of the less sophisticated offenders. The pattern of the subgroup differences associated with the value orientation and agreeableness instruments was quite similar except that most of the variations between the intake and release scores for individual subgroups were significant at the .05 level.

8. The eighth hypothesis was supported on the basis of the responses of the total sample which indicated that the boys perceived no basic improvement in themselves as a result of their incarceration. The subjects' answers at the point of release, though not preponderantly unfavorable, were less positive than their expectations at intake.

9. Almost all of the subgroups responded more unfavorably at the point of release to the improvement indices than they did at the point of admission, but the

differences tended to be nonsignificant. Moreover, the magnitude of the negative variation in the replies furnished by the less mature subgroups was often greater than the difference between the intake and release perceptions of the more sophisticated subgroups.

g. *The TICO study*

Following up the impact study at the Boys Industrial School, the author and his colleague, Dr. Thomas G. Eynon, undertook, during 1964 and the four years following, to make an impact study of a small, secure, self-enclosed institution for very difficult juvenile delinquent boys, fifteen years of age and over, called Training Institution, Central Ohio, and located in Columbus, Ohio. This institution at the time had a capacity of approximately 200 youths. Considerable emphasis was placed upon the atmosphere and relationships developed in the small dormitory units by the so-called youth leaders and educational and training programs were also pitched at a good level. The institution prided itself in the availability of full-time professional counsellors (social workers and psychologists) to help the boys with problems of adjustment. At the time of the study, the period of stay in the institution was approximately two years.

Drawing upon experience in previous impact studies, especially the one done at the Boys Industrial School in Ohio (mentioned immediately above) and also upon a series of conferences with staff members at TICO, Drs. Eynon and Reckless decided to develop two schedules to show: (1) the inmate's perception of impact as seen at the point of release and (2) the staff member's assessment of what the departing inmate got out of his institutional stay as seen through the staff member's eyes. It is the second schedule that distinguishes this study from the previous studies of impact. It was filled out by the staff member who was requested to do so, because he knew the released subject best during his stay.

Inspection of the instrument used to obtain the staff member's assessment of the departing inmate, as reproduced in Appendix 8–E, will indicate that the instrument is really a rating scale (on a ten point scale), containing 15 items. The instrument also includes two questions (items 15 and 16 in the staff member's assessment schedule) that represent projections into the future. However, the statistical analysis in the TICO study was primarily concerned with item 16 (projection of the boy's "eventual outcome.")

The schedule used to assess impact as perceived by the inmate at the point of release (see Appendix 8–E) consisted of 60 items, which were selected from a pre-test schedule of 320 items according to computer factor analysis. The researchers then instructed the computer to return six clusters of "impact" items. Convenient labels were placed on each of the six clusters: interpersonal approach, consisting of 17 items; inmate code of acting, 8 items; rejection of the institution, 8 items; inmate pressure, 5 items; rejection of positive impact, 15 items; and self labeling, 7 items. Most of the items on the inmate's schedule of perceived impact followed a five-point Likert type response: strongly agree, agree, undecided, disagree, and strongly disagree. Some followed a four-point response pattern.

The responses of a sample of 443 consecutively released inmates were scored in the unfavorable direction (high score was unfavorable and low score favorable on any item or cluster of items) and the average score on each of the six clusters was divided by the maximum score in that cluster, to give a ratio, wherein .500 would be halfway toward the most unfavorable or the most favorable direction.[48]

CONCLUSIONS

The impact of the long-term, secure, treatment-oriented institution of TICO was perceived by the departing inmates in a sort of middle range of favorable to unfavorable direction—not overly unfavorable and not markedly favorable. Since only moderate to low positive correlations existed between the scores on the six factors of impact, it can safely be said that the boys' clustered perceptions of impact showed very little concomitance in directions.

On the other hand, staff ratings of the boys according to 15 behavioral (impact) items were found to be quite favorable, much more favorable than the boys' perceptions. There was practically no directional concomitance between the scores on the boys' perceptions and the ratings on the 15 separate assessments by the staff but there was a very, very slight directional concomitance between the boys' perceptions of impact and the staff's total assessment score (i.e., a summated score on the 15 items combined).

Staff's projection of outcome of the released boys was also quite favorable. [See question 16 in the staff member's assessment of Appendix 8-E.] Less than 7 percent were predicted as likely to get into serious trouble, although the reason for being admitted to TICO was based on seriousness of behavior. The projecion of outcome by staff and the staff assessment of impact followed one another in directional concomitance, which means that if a staff member rated the impact of the institution on the boy quite favorably, he was also likely to project favorable outcome for him after release or *vice versa*.

However, there appears to be only a very slight, if any, concomitant relation between the average scores on the six factors of the boys' perceptions of impact and the four categories of outcome (from most unfavorable to most favorable). On the other hand, staff projection of outcome and staff assessment of impact followed one another

[48]Thomas G. Eynon, Harry E. Allen, and Walter C. Reckless, "Measuring Impact of a Juvenile Correctional Institution by Perceptions of Inmates and Staff" (Funded by the Office of Research, The Ohio State University, Columbus, Ohio, September 1968, unpublished). A revised statement of this research report was published in the *Journal of Research in Crime and Delinquency*, 8:1 (January 1971), pp. 93–107.

in concomitant direction, which fact might ordinarily be expected—favorable assessment of impact with favorable projection of outcome and vice versa.

One seems forced to conclude that, in this study of one secure but treatment-oriented institution for older delinquent boys (long term stay), the departing inmates' perceptions of impact (in the middle range of favorability) do not move in a concomitant direction with staff assessments of impact and with staff projections of outcome (both of which were quite favorable). It could be that the departing boys are a bit apathetic in their backward view on two-years of institutionalization, while the staff's backward and forward view is more optimistic. Perhaps, the counselor staff, which made the assessments and the outcome projections, is overly hopeful, because of its professional commitments. Perhaps, the boys are unfavorable in their backward view, because society "did them wrong."

If future research, which used a similar instrument for the boys' view of impact and the staff assessment of the impact of the institution on the individual boy, still finds that there is a discrepancy in the impact view of the boys and the impact view of the staff, then one is faced with the task of deciding which impact rating is the more appropriate to use—inmate or staff. The authors are inclined to choose inmate over staff, because he is the one whose self we wish to re-build or strengthen.[48]

Glaser's research on impact

As a part of his follow-up study of male offenders, principally inmates sentenced to and released from federal correctional institutions, Glaser was able to obtain selective insights into the impact of institutional stay on successful and unsuccessful outcome. At the conclusion of interviews with 250 "successful" federal releasees, Glaser's interviewers asked the following question: "When would you say you changed most permanently from being interested in committing crime?" The distribution of answers were as follows" 4 percent of the respondents reported that they had changed before sentencing; 13 percent, at the time of sentencing or between sentencing and imprisonment; 52 percent, during imprisonment; 16 percent, after release; 10 percent denied any change; and 4 percent reported that they "did not know when they changed."[49] Consequently, these responses from successful cases imply that considerable reformation takes place during institutionalization.

a. *Relationship of prison inmates*

For years sociological criminologists and correctional administrators have been concerned with the effect that relationships between inmates in an

[49]Glaser, *op. cit.*, p. 89.

institution have on the development of negative attitudes and on failure after release. In interviews with 1,137 prisoners (c. 1959) representing various stages in their institutional stay, Glaser's investigators obtained structured answers to the question: "Which of these (four statements) tells best what you try to do with other inmates?" The percentage distribution of the selected responses were as follows: 20 percent, "try to stay to myself as much as possible"; 17 percent, "try to know many inmates but not be very friendly with any of them"; 38 percent (the most preferred response), "try to make a few inmate friends"; 24 percent, "try to make as many friends as I can among the other inmates."[50] The distribution of the responses was interpreted by Glaser as indicating in general the maintenance of "voluntary isolation" of prisoners from other prisoners and this isolation increased with the age of the inmate and with the amount of previous incarceration. It appeared to have a high point at the beginning of the inmate's sentence, to reduce itself at the middle point in institutional stay, and to increase once again near the point of release from the institution.[51]

The interview schedule for the prison panel of 1,137 inmates included the following two questions: (1) "At what assignment in this institution do you think you could get along best with other inmates? Why?"; (2) "At what assignment in this prison do you think you would have the most trouble with other inmates? What kind of trouble?" The general conclusions from the responses (perceptions) of the interviewees were as follows: the prisoners get along best with inmates on jobs that have a small number of assignees, where contact is low with the rest of the population, in trade-training programs, at points of limited access to contraband supplies and services, and at points in the total program where inmates are carefully selected and assigned.[52]

Perceptions of "what an inmate might try to get or do in prison and why" were also obtained from the prison panel of 1,137 federal prisoners. Out of nine different responses, the four most frequent responses were the following: "try to learn a trade or get more school credit to help you get a better job on the outside"; "try to improve yourself psychologically by getting counselling or by study"; "try to understand yourself better," and "try to get a pay job to make some money while in prison"[53] (and this was before "work release" on paid jobs was introduced in the federal prison system).

b. *Relationship with staff*

Following the earlier studies of Galway, Bright, and Moran, the Glaser inquiry also attempted to gauge the impact of the correctional institution

[50] *Ibid.*, p. 91.
[51] *Ibid.*, p. 98.
[52] *Ibid.*, pp. 101, 105.
[53] *Ibid.*, Table 5.9, p. 112.

by studying the inmates' perceptions of which staff member they liked the best. This question was posed in interviews with federal prisoners who had been institutionalized for approximately six months and those who were approaching the end of their stay (near release). Twenty-four percent of the interviewees in the overall sample at five federal institutions said they did not like any officer better than any other, while 43 percent claimed there was no specific officer whom they disliked more than any other. The replies on these items did not vary appreciably between the six-months and the near-release cases.[54]

However, the percentage of the interviewees who said they liked a specific staff member best varied considerably by type of federal institution: Milan, 56; Terre Haute, 67; Leavenworth, 68; Chillicothe, 92; Ashland, 96.[55] Interestingly, the latter two institutions were those for young offenders and, comparatively speaking at the time, had more freedom of movement for inmates, fostered closer staff relations with inmates, generated a more relaxed atmosphere, etc. (Note that this interpretation is the writer's, based on his knowledge of the five institutions at the time of the Glaser interviews.) From a review of the reasons given by interviewed federal inmates (six-months and near-release cases combined), Glaser concluded that (a) "inmates are most influenced by staff who act toward them in a friendly and considerate—rather than hostile—tone and manner" and (b) "inmates are most influenced by staff who treat them with fairness and predictability."[56]

It will be recalled that in the interviews with the 250 successful releasees, the researchers on the Glaser study found that 131 of the interviewees reported change in themselves coming about during imprisonment. Of these 131 cases (successful releasees) 65 (almost half) claimed that a staff member of the prison helped to bring about the favorable change, while only 11 (8 percent) attributed the favorable change to the influence of a fellow inmate.[57] From the testimonials of these interviewees, Glaser formulated the following two propositions: (1) "The prison employee who has the greatest reformative influence on an offender is the one who is able to demonstrate sincere and sustained concern for and confidence in the offender's rehabilitation"; (2) "The prison employee's concern is most effectively manifested by gestures of interest and acts of assistance for the offender which exceed the minimal requirements of the employee's job in the prison."[58]

Without leads from answers to pertinent interview questions, Glaser made an overall interpretation of two trends in progressive prison administration current at the time of his study. It was his opinion that promotion of

[54] *Ibid.*, p. 125.
[55] *Ibid.*, p. 126, Table 6.1.
[56] *Ibid.*, p. 133.
[57] *Ibid.*, p. 141.
[58] *Ibid.*, p. 146.

group responsibility among the inmate population, whether in matters of inmate participation in disciplinary committees or in matters of promoting group responsibility via rewards to certain units of inmates, or by integration of inmates at certain points of prison management such as inmate councils and membership on operating committees with staff members, was quite likely to have a positive impact on prisoners.[59]

c. *Participation in prison educational programs*

Glaser's interviewers were able to contact 449 prisoners at five federal prisons both at the six-months interval and at the point of "near release." Among other information gathered, they found that 292 (65 percent) of the respondents had been "enrolled in one or more courses in the prison school." Of these 292 enrollees, 58 percent said they had learned as much in the prison school as they would have on the outside, 33 percent said they learned less than they would have learned in programs on the outside, and 9 percent said they did not know whether they learned more or less.[60] After examining several sources of outcome data related to participation in educational programs in prison before release, Glaser concluded that enrollment in prison education programs is related to an above-average successful outcome at postrelease when "the education is extensive and occurs in the course of prolonged confinement."[61] But the connection between participation in education in prison and outcome at postrelease is the opposite in instances of released offenders who had extensive felony records. Glaser was also of the opinion that a small amount of participation in prison education programs seems to be related to an unfavorable postrelease outcome.[62]

d. *Expectations in the world outside*

In the interviews with 1,137 inmates of five federal correctional institutions, Glaser's inquiry attempted to tap the expectations of the prisoners with regard to which persons or agencies on the outside were likely to help or to make it difficult for them after release. Seventy-six percent of the first choices of persons or agencies likely to be of help fell in the area of close relatives, while 81 percent of first choices of those likely to make it hard fell in the area of nonrelatives, especially law-enforcement personnel and criminal friends.[63] In a still large investigation of expectations from a specified assortment of 14

[59] *Ibid.*, pp. 214–223.
[60] *Ibid.*, p. 267.
[61] *Ibid.*, p. 282.
[62] *Ibid.*, pp. 282–283.
[63] *Ibid.*, p. 367, Table 15.2.

correctional institutions, state as well as federal, the inmates were asked whether they expected that "people in your neighborhood will try and make trouble for you when you get out, if you go back there." Only a minority of respondents expressed such fear.[64]

As a result of interviews with various samples of federal prison inmates at various stages of their confinement as well as with releasees, Glaser came to the following conclusions *inter alia* regarding the impact of the ex-prisoner's world to which he had been released, especially as the offenders viewed the matter themselves: (a) hostility toward others in the outside world as well as expectation of harm declines as the date of release draws near, (b) the overwhelming majority of prisoners return to neighborhoods in which they previously resided and in which their involvement with crime is known, (c) postrelease failure rates are somewhat higher for prisoners released to a neighborhood different from the one in which they resided at the time of commitment, (d) the ex-prisoners who live alone have a higher failure rate than those who live with family or relatives, (e) discord—usually family discord—within the place of residence of the releasee is related to failure, (f) prisoners soon after release come across former friends, (g) former prison acquaintances are met quite early by releasees, (h) the reestablishment of contact with former inmate acquaintances is "highly associated with reimprisonment," (i) new friends acquired after release come to know about the ex-prisoner's record, (j) the acquisition of new friends who do not know about the prisoner's record is related to successful outcome, (k) fears of police harassment during the postrelease period are rather widespread among prisoners, but (l) harrassment is actually encountered only by a small percentage of ex-prisoners.[65]

e. *Inmate attitudes and perceptions*

In the summer of 1962, the Glaser investigation was extended to include interviews with inmates in 14 assorted correctional institutions, both state and federal, at various stages of imprisonment (at entrance, at the middle point of institutional stay, and at the terminal point). The questionnaire that was used concentrated primarily on the perceptions of the inmates as they viewed themselves as prisoners. The 14 correctional institutions consisted of the following: 2 federal prison camps and 1 state prison camp, 3 federal and 2 state reformatories and institutions for youthful offenders, 2 federal and 3 state penitentiaries (maximum security), and 1 federal correctional institution. The number of interviewees approximated 2,500.[66] However,

[64] *Ibid.*, p. 371.
[65] *Ibid.*, pp. 400–401.
[66] *Ibid.*, pp. 552–555.

Glaser's investigators were not able to obtain the cooperation of this large sample of inmate respondents in filling out much of the administered questionnaire.

In attempting to tap inmate attitudes and perceptions, a four-item "inmate loyalty" scale, a three-item criminal identification scale, and a four-item criminality direction scale were developed and administered at 13 of the 14 federal and state prisons (excepting Ashland, the Federal Youth Center). Perceived loyalty to inmates appeared to increase somewhat with previous convictions as did perceived criminal identification and perceived criminal direction. The trend of the responses to these three scales was not consistent according to stage in prison stay (entrance versus terminal), although visible differences in responses were apparent in the sub-groups of respondents categorized by number of previous commitments to prison.[67]

An instrument was also developed by Glaser's researchers to measure perceptual rating of self and others, including closest friend in prison, inmates in general, various staff officers, mother, father, wife or girl friend, and "ex-cons" in general. The ratings or "esteem" of self and others were structured for scoring purposes along a six-point continuum (scale), ranging from friendly to unfriendly, hardworking to lazy, fair to unfair, dependable to undependable, etc. Hence the "esteem" rating was a veritable adjective checklist comprising 22 pairs of adjectives. The published study reported the findings of the inmate "esteem" scores for the Ashland institution (young federal offenders) according to a sample of prisoners at admission, at a post-admission period, and at the point of release. There was a slight decline in the esteem score of the prisoner's own self, a large decline in esteem for inmates in general, a sizable increase in esteem for caseworkers, a slight pickup in esteem for the mother, and a sizable decline in esteem for the wife or girl friend during institutional stay.[68]

When the Ashland inmate respondents were grouped by degrees of custody within the institution (from close to minimum), the average esteem scores for work supervisor and caseworker were found to be higher among the minimum security than among the medium and close custody inmates. But the average esteem scores that focused on the unit officer (who is in charge of the sleeping quarters and supervises the free time in and around the sleeping quarters) are much higher for the maximum and medium custody inmates than for the minimum custody inmates. Inmates who evaluated their sentences as "very fair" had better esteem scores toward work supervisor, caseworker, and unit officer than those who rated their sentences as fair, unfair, or very unfair.[69]

[67] *Ibid.*, pp. 564–565, including Table E.3.
[68] *Ibid.*, p. 569, Table E.4.
[69] *Ibid.*, p. 572, Table E.6.

In a limited number of respondents from the 13 federal and state correctional institutions, not including Ashland, the average esteem scores (on fifteen pairs of adjectives, also rated from 1 to 6) did not vary between inmates at the entrance and those at the terminal point of their institutional stay, and the average esteem scores were quite homogenous for self, closest inmate friend, work supervisor, caseworker, and unit officer.[70] Under proper conditions of rapport, Glaser believed that social perception measures (such as esteem scores which indicate how inmates view themselves and others) can provide fairly sensitive indications of changes in prisoner outlook during institutional stay. In addition, he inferred that such indicators can be of help to correctional staff in dealing constructively with individual prisoners.[71]

An attempt was made to get the cooperating inmate respondents in 13 federal and state prisons to answer questions that would enable the researchers to classify the inmates according to the extent to which they conceived of themselves in prison as a "Square John," an "Outlaw," a "Right Guy," and a "Politician," using labels of inmate types which had been identified by Clarence Schrag. (The Square John has loyalty to the prison administration, although he is not a squealer or stool pigeon. The Outlaw has few loyalties, is daring, ruthless, and shows very little heed for ordinary social pressures. The Right Guy is loyal to inmate society and refuses to cooperate with the prison administration. The Politician has loyalty to the inmate community but he uses his knowledge of inmate society to bargain for the goodwill of the prison administration.)

In order to get at so-called "pure" type cases in this study, Glaser made a cutting point in the upper range of the responses of the inmates to the "prisoner type" questions. He selected for special study those inmates who scored in the high range of one type only—the upper 34 percent. The four "pure type" respondents were then classified by high, medium, and low scores on the inmate loyalty, the criminality direction, and the criminal identification scales (mentioned earlier). The "Square Johns," as expected, were lower than the other three "pure types" in their inmate loyalty, criminality direction, and criminal identification scores, whereas the "pure Outlaw type" scored higher on inmate loyalty, criminality direction, and criminal identification than the other three types.[72] It is possible that such insights, if carried forward with greater finesse, might also give predictive indications to correctional administrators of what differential impact the prison staff and program is likely to have on various types of inmates, varying from acceptance to resistance.

[70] *Ibid.*, p. 574, Table E.8.

[71] *Ibid.*, p. 575. [The author is making a very liberal interpretation of Glaser's conclusion on this matter.]

[72] *Ibid.*, p. 582, Table E.11.

Obiter dicta

Clearly, criminological research must become actively concerned with the outcome of cases handled by the various way stations of the criminal justice system, and the researchers in the field must discover feasible and uniform ways of judging outcome, which is the output of the way stations. Up to the present, statistics on outcome have been primarily developed in the area of probation, institutionalization, and parole. The need for more uniform and more meaningful follow-up statistics in these areas of concern is certainly apparent.

In addition to statistics on outcome, there is also a great need to develop measures that can gauge the impact of various measures of handling offenders on the individual offender. At present, the few attempts that have been made to penetrate this "black box" have concentrated primarily on the so-called "client's" own perceptions of what happened to him during institutional stay; similar attempts could be made to gauge the impact of probation and parole experience.

The rating by the inmate himself of perceived changes in attitude and outlook on life during his institutional stay might be analyzed by criminological research. Likewise, the probationer's and parolee's own rating of what changes—if any—took place during his supervision on probation or parole is certainly another feasible lead for the study of impact.

Coupled with the inmate's or client's own perception of extent and direction of change could be the "involved" staff member's or the probation and parole officer's rating of observed changes in his client. It is quite possible that such ratings of observed changes by correctional personnel could be objectified and widely used to supplement the recorded statistics of outcome. Such ratings, if validated, would have much more value than outcome statistics, which depend so largely on factors that follow (post hoc) correctional treatment but that have not contributed to it.

The ratings of change in the institutionalized "client" as seen by a fellow inmate also need to be explored, to determine whether such ratings have good validity and to see to what extent and in what direction they supplement the perceptions of the departing inmate himself and those of the staff.

Finally, it may be necessary to develop valid "pencil and paper" tests that can be administered on admission to the institution and at release, at the beginning and termination of probation and parole and that are found to be valid for measuring the direction of change in the "client" during his period of institutionalization or supervision outside an institution.

Appendix 8–A

SCHEDULE FOR INTERVIEWING MALE JUVENILE DELINQUENTS RELATIVE TO THEIR PERCEPTIONS OF SOCIAL LIABILITY RESULTING FROM CONTACT WITH POLICE AND COURT

No.________

INTERVIEW SCHEDULE

PART I. *Background Information*

Name of Subject________________________ Age_____ School__________

Address________________________ Ethnicity__________

________________________ Offense__________

________________________ Disposition__________

* * * * * * * * * * * *

Father's Occupation________________________ Education Level__________

Mother's Occupation________________________ Education Level__________

School History:____

____

____

____

____

____

____

Jack D. Foster, "Social Intervention following Delinquent Behavior: The Complainant, the Police and the Delinquent Boy" (Ph.D. dissertation, The Ohio State University, 1971).

Previous Intervention: ______________________________

____

____

Date of Interview: ______________ Remarks: ______________________________

PART II. *General Information*

1. Who are your two very best friends? (a) ______________________

   (b) ______________________

2. How do you like school? ☐ Very Much ☐ Some ☐ Neutral ☐ Not Much ☐ Very Bad

3. Do you want to complete High School? ☐ Yes ☐ Maybe ☐ No

4. Would you like to go to college? ☐ Yes ☐ Maybe ☐ No

5. What kind of job would you like to get when you get out of school?

   ____

6. How do you get along with your teachers? ______________________

   ____

   Would you say you get along ☐ Very Well ☐ "OK" ☐ So So ☐ Poorly ☐ Very Badly

7. How do you get along with your parents? ______________________

   ____

   Would you say you get along ☐ Very Well ☐ "OK" ☐ So So ☐ Poorly ☐ Very Badly

   How about your father? ☐ Very Well ☐ "OK" ☐ So So ☐ Poorly ☐ Very Badly

   How about your mother? ☐ Very Well ☐ "OK" ☐ So So ☐ Poorly ☐ Very Badly

8. Do you think your father expected you to get into trouble? ☐ Yes ☐ Maybe ☐ No

9. Do you think your mother expected you to get into trouble? ☐ Yes ☐ Maybe ☐ No

10. Have your best friends (mentioned above) been in trouble too? If so, in what way? ______________________

    ____

    Are they in the same trouble you are now? ______________________

PART III. *Perceptions of Social Liability*

1. Do you feel that people will think worse of you as a result of your getting into trouble like this? ☐ No ☐ Maybe ☐ Yes

2. How about your mother; will she think worse of you? ☐ No ☐ Maybe ☐ Yes

   How about your father; will he think worse of you? ☐ No ☐ Maybe ☐ Yes

   How about your teachers; will they think worse of you? ☐ No ☐ Maybe ☐ Yes

   How about your friends; will they think worse of you? ☐ No ☐ Maybe ☐ Yes

3. As far as you can see, will this create any special difficulty in completing school now? ☐ None ☐ Some ☐ Much

   If none, why not? (If yes, in what way?) ______________________________

   ____

   ____

4. As far as you can see, will this create any special difficulty in getting the job you want? ☐ None ☐ Some ☐ Much

   If none, why not? (If yes, in what way?) ______________________________

   ____

   ____

5. Do you think people will continue to hold this trouble against you? ☐ No ☐ Maybe ☐ Yes

   How about your mother; will she hold this against you? ☐ No ☐ Maybe ☐ Yes

   How about your father; will he hold this against you? ☐ No ☐ Maybe ☐ Yes

   How about your teachers; will they hold this against you? ☐ No ☐ Maybe ☐ Yes

   How about the police; will they hold this against you? ☐ No ☐ Maybe ☐ Yes

   How about future employers; will they hold this against you? ☐ No ☐ Maybe ☐ Yes

How about your friends; will they hold this against you? ☐ No ☐ Maybe ☐ Yes

PART IV. *Perceptions of the Administration of Justice*

1. What did you think would happen to you because you got into this trouble?

____

____

Was this ☐ less serious than you expected?
☐ about what you expected?
☐ more serious than you expected?

2. How do you feel about what happened? Do you think the police treated you right? ☐ Yes ☐ Maybe ☐ No

If not, what do you think they should have done? ______________________

____

____

How about the judge (or referee); did he treat you right? ☐ Yes ☐ Maybe ☐ No.

If not, what do you think they should have done? ______________________

____

____

3. Do you think kids like yourself are picked on by the police? ☐ Yes ☐ Maybe ☐ No

If yes, why do you think they would want to pick on you? ________________

____

____

4. Do you think other kids have gotten more breaks from the police than you have? ☐ Yes ☐ Maybe ☐ No

If yes, why do you think this happens? ____________________________

____

____

5. If you were a policeman, what would you have done in this situation? ________

____

____

Appendix 8–B

SELECTED BIBLIOGRAPHY ON PREDICTION OF OUTCOME

Adams, S., and Margaret Thompson, "Probation Characteristics and Probation Performance: A Prototype of a Prediction Instrument for Adult Probation," *Research Report Number 10*. California: Los Angeles County Probation Department, October, 1963.

Allen, R. L., "A Review of Parole Prediction Literature," *Journal of Criminal Law*, 32, 548–554, January, 1942.

Anonymous, "Relationship Between Causation and the Prediction of Juvenile Delinquency," *International Review of Criminal Policy*, 7–8, 29–30, January–July, 1952.

Anonymous, "The Detection of Pre-Delinquency," *International Review of Criminal Policy*, 7–8, 81–82, January–July, 1952.

Anonymous, "The Selection of the 'Pre-Delinquent' Juvenile," *International Review of Criminal Policy*, 9, 74–79, January, 1956.

Araki, F., "The Possibility of Predicting Delinquency," *Investigation Study, 61*, 44, 1956.

Argow, W. W. "A Criminal-Liability Index for Predicting Possibility of Rehabilitation," *Journal of Criminal Law and Criminology, 26*, 561–577, 1935.

Arkoff, A., "Prison Adjustment is an Index of Ability to Adjust on the Outside," *Journal of Correction Education, 9,* 1–2, January, 1957.

Ashmore, D. L., *Predicting Delinquency with the California Psychological Inventory and Social Data: A Comparison of Recidivists and Non-Recidivists.* Oregon: Masters Thesis, University of Oregon, Eugene, 1960.

Attorney-General's Survey of Release Procedures, *Parole, 4,* Chapter 11, Appendix A. Washington: Department of Justice, 1939.

Attorney-General's Survey of Release Procedures, *Probation, 2,* Chapter 10. Washington: Department of Justice, 1939.

Axelrad, S., and Selma J. Glick, "Application of the Glueck Social Prediction Tables to 100 Jewish Delinquent Boys," *Jewish Social Service Quarterly,* 30, 127–136, 1953.

Taken from an extensive bibliography on *Prediction of Delinquency and Crime*, prepared by Don M. Gottfredson and Kelley B. Ballard, Research Center, National Council on Crime and Delinquency, Davis, California, mimeograph draft as of May 25, 1970. This list of selected references purposely does not include studies mentioned in the text.

Ball, J. C., *Social Deviancy and Adolescent Personality: An Analytic Study with the MMPI.* Louisville: University of Kentucky Press, 1962.

Ballard, K. B., and D. M. Gottfredson, *Predictive Attribute Analysis and Prediction of Parole Performance.* Vacaville: Institute for the Study of Crime and Delinquency, December, 1963.

Balogh, J. K., "A Validation of the Kvaraceus K.D. Verbal Proneness Scale with Matched White Male Subjects," *Journal of Criminal Law, Criminology, and Police Science, 52,* Number 3, 305–307, 1961.

——, and P. Finn, "A Methodological Study of Juvenile Delinquency Proneness Among Negroes," *Exceptional Children, 27,* 397–399, March, 1961.

Barbash, J. T., *An Investigation of the Predictability of Prison Adjustment,* Doctoral Dissertation, Temple University, 1956.

Barron, A. J., "An Experiment with Ohlin's Prediction Report," *Crime and Delinquency, 3,* Number 8, 276–281, 1962.

Beall, H. S., and J. H. Panton, "The Use of the MMPI as an Index to Escapism," *Journal of Clinical Psychology, 12,* 392–39 , October, 1956.

Bennett, C. C., and C. R. Rogers, "The Predicting of the Outcome of Treatment," *American Journal of Orthopsychiatry, 11,* 210–222, 1941.

Benson, G., "Classification, Allocation, and Prediction Tables," *British Journal of Delinquency, 1, 4,* 271–275, April, 1951.

——, "Prediction Methods and Young Prisoners," *British Journal of Delinquency, 9, 3,* 192–199, 1959.

Betts, G. L., "The Selection of Incipient Army Criminals," *Science, 106,* 93–96, 1947.

Beverly, R. F., "Base Expectancies and the Initial Home Visit Research Schedule," *Research Report Number 37,* Youth and Adult Corrections Agency, 34. Sacramento, California, January, 1964.

Black, B. J., and Selma J. Glick, *Recidivisms at the Hawthorne-Cedar Knolls School: Predicted Versus Actual Outcome for Delinquent Boys,* Research Monograph Number 2. New York: Jewish Board Guardians, 1952.

Blair, W. R. N., "A Comparative Study of Disciplinary Offenders and Non-Offenders in the Canadian Army, 1949," *Canadian Journal of Psychology, 4,* 40–62, 1950.

Blaser, A., *Recidivism and Good Behavior of Juvenile Delinquents of the Canton of Lucerne.* Berne: Paul Haupt, 1963.

Blum, R. H. "Predicting Criminal Behavior: An Annotated Bibliography," *Journal of Correctional Psychology,* Monograph Number 1, 1957.

Briggs, P. F., R. D. Wirt, and R. Johnson, "Application of Prediction Tables to the Study of Delinquency," *Journal of Consulting Psychology, 25,* 46–50, 1961.

Burgess, E. W., "Factors Determining Success on Parole," *Journal of Criminal Law,* 19, 241–306, May, 1928.

Caldwell, M., "A Review of a New Type of Probation Study Made in Alabama," *Federal Probation, 15,* 3–11, June, 1951.

Capwell, Dora F., "Personality Patterns of Adolescent Girls: Delinquents and Non-Delinquents," *Analyzing and Predicting Juvenile Delinquency with the MMPI.* Minneapolis, Minnesota: University of Minnesota Press, 29–37, 1953.

Cassell, R. N., "Validation of Psychological Instruments for Predictions of Delinquency Proneness," Research in Progress: Air Force Personnel and Training

Research Center, Lackland Air Force Base, Our Lady of the Lake College, San Antonio, Texas.

——, and R. Van Vorst, "Level of Aspiration as a Means for Discerning Between 'In-Prison' and 'Out-Prison' Groups of Individuals," *Journal of Social Psychology, 40,* 121–135, August, 1954.

Cavanaugh, J. R., S. Gerstein, E. R. Peters, and J. Mathieu, "Profile of a Probation Violator," *United States Armed Forces Medical Journal, 1,* 1051–1064, 1950.

Clark, J. H., "Additional Applications of the AWOL Recidivists Scale," *Journal of Clinical Psychology, 9,* 62–64, 1953.

Clayton, Mae Belle, *The Construction of a Home Adjustment Questionnaire Which May Be Used as an Aid in the Detection of Symptoms of Juvenile Delinquency,* Doctoral Dissertation, Microfilm, Ann Arbor, Michigan: University of Michigan.

Clements, S. D., *The Predictive Utility of Three Delinquency Proneness Measures,* Doctoral Dissertation, University of Houston, 1960.

Conner, J. E. "Predicting Parole in Post War Kentucky," *A Statistical Study of Parolees from the Kentucky State Reformatory with Factors for Predicting Success or Failure,* Kentucky Division of Probation, Frankfort, Kentucky, 1951.

Conrutt, R. J., and L. V. Corotto, "The Use of Bender-Gestalt Cut-Off Scores in Identifying Juvenile Delinquent," *Journal of Projective Techniques, 24,* 353–354, December, 1960.

Coombs, W., I. Farr, W. Ilnyckyz, and M. Miyazoe, "Characteristics and Methods of Disposition Related to Successful Outcome in Cases of Juvenile Delinquency," Report Prepared for Research Committee. Winnipeg: University of Manitoba, School of Social Work, 1960.

Coulter, W. M., "The Szondi Test and the Prediction of Antisocial Behavior," *Journal of Projective Techniques,* 24–29, March, 1959.

Cowden, J. E., "Predicting Institutional Adjustment and Recidivism in Delinquent Boys," *Journal of Criminal Law, Criminal and Police Science, 57,* 1, 39–44, 1966.

Craig, Maude M., "An Experiment in the Prediction of Delinquency: An Application of the Glueck Prediction Scale," *Crime in America,* 299–311, 1961.

Curtis, H. A., F. J. King, and R. P. Kropp, "Validity Studies of Scores from a Delinquency Proneness Scale," *Psychological Reports, 12,* 271–278, 1963.

Davids, A., Catherine Kidder, and M. Reich, "Time Orientation in Male and Female Delinquents," *Journal of Abnormal Social Psychology, 64,* 239–240.

Dinitz, S., W. C. Reckless, and Barbara Kay, "A Self Gradient Among Potential Delinquents," *Journal of Criminal Law, Criminology and Police Science, 49,* 230–233, 1958.

Duncan, O. D., L. E. Ohlin, A. J. Reiss, and H. R. Stanton, "Formal Devices for Making Selection Decision," *American Journal of Sociology, 58,* 573-584, 1953.

Dunham, R. E., "Factors Related to Recidivism in Adults," *Journal of Social Psychology, 39,* 77–79, February, 1954.

Durea, M. A., "The Differential Diagnosis of Potential Delinquency," *American Journal of Orthopsychiatry, 9,* 394–399, 1939.

Elliot, A. E., "Parole Readiness: An Institutional Dilemma," *Federal Probation, 28,* 1, 26–30, 1964.

England, R. W., *Post-Probation Recidivism Among 500 Federal Offenders,* Doctoral Dissertation, University of Pennsylvania, 1954.

Evjen, V. H., "Current Thinking on Parole Prediction Tables," *Crime and Delinquency,* 8, 3, 215–238, 1962.

Farber, B., *An Evaluation and Revision of the Burgess and Wallin Rating Scale as a Prediction Instrument*, Doctoral Dissertation, University of Chicago, 1953.

Feldman, H., and A. A. Maleski, "Factors Differentiating AWOL from Non-AWOL Trainees," *Journal of Abnormal Social Psychology, 43*, 70–77, 1948.

Fisher, W. E., J. H. Ward, F. E. Holdreged, and H. G. Lawrence, "Prediction of Unsuitability Discharges," Research, USAF, Lackland AFB, Texas, WABB-96-60-260, October, 1960.

Force, R. C., and J. K. Meyers, "Prediction of Separation of Air Force Trainees," *Journal of Psychological Studies, 11*, 28–31, 1959.

Fordua, D. J., "Predicting and Selection of Delinquents," *Juvenile Delinquency: Facts and Facets*, Washington, D.C., United States Department of Health, Education, and Welfare, Children's Bureau, 1961.

Fradkin, H. E., *Criminal Background and Self-Conception in Prognostic Factors in the Life of Prisoners,* Doctoral Thesis, Ohio State University, 1958.

Freeman, H. E., *The Prediction of Recidivism Among Youthful Offenders in the Highfield Treatment Program*, Doctoral Thesis, New York University, 1956.

Freeman, R. A., and H. M. Mason, "Construction of a Key to Determine Recidivists from Non-Recidivists, Using the MMPI," *Journal of Clinical Psychology, 8*, 207–208, 1952.

Gair, E. L., and Marilyn C. Lee. "Pattern Analysis: The Configural Approach to Predictive Measurement," *Psychological Bulletin, 50*, Number 2, 140–148, 1953.

Gardner, G. E., and N. Goldman, "Childhood and Adolescent Adjustment of Naval Successes and Failures," *American Journal of Orthopsychiatry, 15*, 584–596, 1945.

Gibbens, T. C. N., "Prediction in Criminology," *Howard Journal, 8*, 202–205, 1952.

Gillin, J. L., *Predicting Criminal Behavior*. Madison: University of Wisconsin Press, 10 Micro Cards, 1952.

Glaser, D., "A Reconsideration of Some Parole Prediction Factors," *American Sociological Review, 19*, 335–341, June, 1954.

——, "Parole Follow-Up Studies in the Federal Correctional System," *Research and Potential Application of Research in Probation, Parole, and Delinquency Prediction*, Research Center, New York School of Social Work, July, 1961.

——, "Prediction Tables as Accounting Devices for Judges and Parole Boards," *Crime and Delinquency, 8*, Number 3, 239–258, 1962.

——, "Testing Correctional Decisions," *Journal of Criminal Law, Criminology, and Police Science, 45*, 679–684, March, 1955.

Glick, Selma J., "Spotting Potential Delinquents in the School," *Exceptional Children, 20*, 342–346, 1954.

Glueck, Eleanor T., "Efforts to Identify Delinquents," *Federal Probation, 24*, 49–56, June, 1960.

——, "Toward Improving the Identification of Delinquents," *Journal of Criminal Law, Criminology, and Police Science, 53*, 164–170, 1962.

Glueck, S., and Eleanor T. Glueck, *Family Environment and Delinquency*. London: Routledge and Kegan Paul, 1962.

——, *Predicting Delinquency and Crime*. Boston: Harvard University Press, 293, 1959.

Goodman, L. A., "The Use and Validity of a Prediction Instrument II, The Validity of Prediction," *American Journal of Sociology, 58*, 510–512, March, 1953.

Gottfredson, D. M., "A Shorthand Formula for Base Expectancies," *Research Report Number 5*. Sacramento: California Department of Corrections, December, 1961.

——, "Assessment and Prediction Methods in Crime and Delinquency," *Task Force Report: Juvenile Delinquency and Youth Crime*, President's Commission on Law Enforcement and Administration of Justice, 1967.

——, K. B. Ballard, and J. A. Bonds, *Base Expectancy (Form CDC-BE 62-A) California Institution for Women*. Sacramento: Institute for the Study of Crime and Delinquency and Research Division, California Department of Corrections, California, September, 1962.

——, and J. A. Bonds, *A Manual for Intake Base Expectancy Scoring*. Sacramento: Research Division, California Department of Corrections, April, 1961.

——, J. A. Bonds, and J. D. Grant, "Combining Clinical and Statistical Prediction for Correctional Decisions." Sacramento: Research Division, California Department of Corrections, California, June, 1961.

Gough, H., "Clinical Versus Statistical Prediction in Psychology," *Psychology in the Making*. New York: Knopf, 1962.

——, "Systematic Validation of a Test for Delinquency," *American Psychologist, 9*, 8, 381, 1954.

——, and D. R. Peterson, "The Identification and Measurement of Predispositional Factors in Crime and Delinquency," *Journal of Consulting Psychology, 16*, 207-222, 1952.

——, E. A. Wenk, and V. V. Rozynko, "Parole Outcome as Predicted from the CPI, the MMPI, and a Base Expectancy Table," *Journal of Abnormal Psychology*, Vol. 70, No. 6, December, 1965.

Gould, L. C., and C. Schrag, "Theory Construction and Prediction in Juvenile Delinquency," *Proceedings of the Social Statistics Section*, American Statistical Association, Washington, 1962.

Grant, J. D., "It's Time to Start Counting," *Journal of Crime and Delinquency, 8*, 3, July, 1962.

——, "The Navy's Attack on the Problems of Delinquency," Rehabilitation Research, United States Naval Retraining Command, Camp Elliot, San Diego, California, April, 1955.

Gunderson, E. K., K. B. Ballard, and P. S. Hugh, "The Relationship of Delinquency Potential Scale Scores of Naval Recruits to Later Military Performance," *9th Technical Report*, United States Naval Retraining Center, Camp Elliot, San Diego, California, July, 1959.

Hakeem, M., *Forecasting Parole Outcome by Parole Officers and Laymen*, Doctoral Dissertation, Ohio State University, 1950.

——, "Prediction of Parole Outcome from Summaries of Case Histories," *Journal of Criminal Law, Criminology, and Police Science, 52*, 145-155, 1961.

Hand, J., and D. Lebo, "Predicting the Institutional Adjustment of Delinquent Boys," *Journal of Criminal Law, Criminology, and Police Science, 45*, 694-696, March, 1955.

Hathaway, S. R., and E. Monachesi, "A New Approach to Identifying and Helping Delinquent Children," Minnesota, University of Minnesota Press, 71-79, 1954.

——, *Analyzing and Predicting Delinquency with the MMPI*, Minneapolis: University of Minnesota Press, 1953.

——, and L. A. Young, "Delinquency Rates and Personality," *Journal of Criminal Law, Criminology, and Police Science, 50*, 433-440, January-February, 1960.

Hawkins, N. G., and J. K. Jackson, "Scale Analysis and the Prediction of Life Processes," *American Sociological Review, 22*, 579-581, October, 1957.

Hayner, N. S., "Why Do Parole Boards Lag in the Use of Prediction Scores?" *The Pacific Sociological Review, 1*, 73–76, 1958.

Herzog, E., "Identifying Potential Delinquents," *Juvenile Delinquency, Facts and Facets Number 5*, Washington, D.C.: United States Department of Health, Education, and Welfare, Social Security Administration, Children's Bureau, 1960.

Holt, R. R., "Clinical and Statistical Prediction: Reformulation and Some New Data," *Journal of Abnormal and Social Psychology*, 56, 1–12, January, 1958.

Jacques, O. M., "Predicting Juvenile Delinquency Proneness by Group Tests," *Personnel and Guidance Journal, 36*, 489–492, March, 1958.

Jarvis, D., "Prediction Tables and the Probation Officer," *Probation, 8*, 153–154, June, 1958.

Jenkins, R. L., and Eva Blodgett, "Prediction of Success or Failure of Delinquent Boys from Sentence Completion," *American Journal of Orthopsychiatry, 30*, 741–756.

Kanun, C., and E. D. Monachesi, "Delinquency and the Validating Scales of the MMPI," *Journal of Criminal Law, Criminology, and Police Science, 50*, 525–530, 1960.

Keys, N., and N. S. Guilford, "The Validity of Certain Adjustment Inventories in Predicting Behavior Problems," *Journal of Educational Psychology, 28*, 641–655.

Kibrick, M. R., *Predicting Success or Failure on Probation of the White Delinquent Girls*, Masters Thesis, Ohio State University Library, 1943.

Kirby, B. C., "Parole Prediction Using Multiple Correlation," *American Journal of Sociology, 59*, 539–550, May, 1954.

Knapp, R. R., "Personality Correlates of Delinquency Rate in a Navy Sample, *Journal of Applied Psychology, 47*, 68–71, 1963.

Kvaraceus, W. C., "Forecasting Juvenile Delinquency: A Three Year Experiment," *Exceptional Children, 27*, 429–435, April, 1961.

——, "Prediction Studies of Delinquent Behavior," *Personnel and Guidance Journal, 34*, 146–149, November, 1955.

LaGrone, and Schnieder, "Prediction of Behavior of Civilian Delinquents in the Armed Forces," *Mental Hygiene, 28*, 456–475, 1944.

Lively, E. L., S. Dinitz, and W. C. Reckless, "Self Concept as Predictor of Juvenile Delinquency," *American Journal of Orthopsychiatry, 32*, Number 1, 159–168.

Long, H. L., "A Proposed Rating System for Measuring Parolee Adjustment," *Journal of Criminal Law, 31*, 693–695, March-April, 1941.

Lottier, S., *Adjustment During Rating: A Scale for Predicting Adjustment During Probation or Parole*, Psychopathic Clinic. Detroit: Recorders Court.

——, "Predicting Criminal Behavior," *Federal Probation, 7*, 8–12, October-December, 1943.

Lykken, D. T., and R. Rose, "Psychological Prediction Actuarial Tables," *Journal of Clinical Psychology, 19*, 139–151, 1963.

McCormick, T. C., "Note on the Validity of Mathematical Probability in Social Research," *American Journal of Sociology, 10*, 626–631, 1945.

MacNaughton-Smith, P., "The Classification of Individuals by the Possession of Attributes Associated with a Criterion," *Biometrics*, June, 1963.

Mannering, J. W., and D. Babst, *Wisconsin Base Expectancies for Adult Male Probationers*, Progress Report Number 1, June, 1962.

Mannheim, H. and L. T. Wilkins, *Prediction Methods in Relation to Borstal Training*, London: Her Majesty's Stationery Office, 1955.

Meehl, P. E., and A. Rosen, "Antecedent Probability and the Efficiency of Psychometric Signs, Patterns, or Cutting Scores," *Psychological Bulletin, 52*, 194–215, 1955.

Monachesi, E. D, "A Comparison of Prediction with Actual Results of Probation," *American Sociological Review, 10*, 26–31, February, 1945.

——, "Personality Characteristics and Socio-Economic Status of Delinquents and Non-Delinquents," *Journal of Criminal Law, 40*, 570–583, 1950.

——, "Personality Characteristics of Institutionalized and Non-Institutionalized Male Delinquents," *Journal of Criminal Law, 41*, 167–179.

Morlock, J. E., *Predicting Delinquency in a Homogenous Group of Pre-Adolescent Boys in Ohio State University*, Doctoral Dissertation, Ohio University, 1947.

Morrison, R. L., "Predictive Research: A Critical Assessment of Its Practical Application," *British Journal of Delinquency, 6*, 99–115, 1955.

Mueller, P. F. C., "Outcome Prediction for Women Parolees Through CDC-BE-CIW-62A," *Research Report Number 6*, California Department of Corrections, Sacramento, California, 1960.

New York City Youth Board, *A Study in Variance from Predicted Delinquency*. New York: The Board, January, 1962.

New York City Youth Board, Research Department, *An Experiment in the Validation of the Glueck Prediction Scale*, Progress Report from November 1952 to December 1956, New York, July, 1957.

New York City Youth Board, Research Department, *Delinquency Predictions, 1952–1960, A Report of Progress*, New York, October, 1961.

Ohlin, L. E., *Selection for Parole: A Manual of Parole Prediction*. New York: Russell Sage Foundation, 1951.

——, and O. Duncan, "The Efficiency of Prediction in Criminology," *American Journal of Sociology, 54*, 441–451, March, 1949.

——, and R. A. Lawrence, "A Comparison of Alternative Methods of Parole Prediction," *American Journal of Sociological Review, 17*, 268–274, June, 1953.

Peterson, H., "Prediction Studies and the Struggle Against Juvenile Criminality as a Means of Crime Prevention," *Excepta Criminologica, 3*, Number 2, 132–134, 1963.

Prigmore, C. S., "An Analysis of Rater Reliability on the Glueck Scale for the Prediction of Juvenile Delinquency," *Journal of Criminal Law, Criminology, and Police Science, 54*, Number 1, 30–41.

Reckless, W. C., S. Dinitz, and Barbara Kay, "The Self Component in Potential Delinquency and Potential Non-Delinquency," *American Sociological Review, 22*, 556–557, 1957.

Reiss, A. J. Jr., "The Accuracy Efficiency and Validity of a Prediction Instrument," *American Journal of Sociology, 56*, 552–561, May, 1951.

Robison, S. M., *Can Delinquency Be Measured?* New York: Columbia University Press, 1936.

Rogers, C. R., B. L. Kell, and Helen McNeil, "The Role of Self-Understanding in the Prediction of Behavior," *Journal of Consulting Psychology, 12*, 174–186, 1948.

Rose, A., and G. H. Weber, "Predicting the Population in Institutions for Delinquent Children and Youths," *Journal of Criminal Law, Criminology, and Police Science, 50*, 124–131, July, 1959.

Rose, G., "Research and Methodology: Follow-Up and/or Prediction," *British Journal of Delinquency, 7*, 309–317, April, 1957.

Rumney, J., and J. P. Murphy, *Probation and Social Adjustment*, New Brunswick, New Jersey, Rutgers University Press, Chapter 14, 1952.

Sadler, W., "Pre-Institutional Recognition and Management of the Potential

Delinquent," *Handbook of Correctional Psychology*. New York: Philosophical Library, 130–147, 1947.

Sampson, L. W., "After Careers of 424 Paroled Wisconsin Criminals," *Journal of Criminal Law, 25*, 607–620, November-December, 1934.

Sandhu, H. S., "An Instrument for Measuring Delinquency Potential: Validation of Socialization Scale or Delinquency Scale in India," *Journal of Correctional Work, 7*, 92–101, 1960.

Sarbin, T. R., E. A. Wenk, and D. W. Sherwood, "An Effort to Identify Assault-Prone Offenders," *Journal of Research in Crime and Delinquency*, January, 1968.

——, "Contribution to the Study of Actural and Individual Methods of Prediction," Bibliography *American Journal of Sociological Review, 48*, 593–602, March, 1963.

Scarpitti, F. R., "Delinquent and Non-Delinquent Perceptions of Self, Value and Opportunity," *Social Problems, 13*, 1, 60–65, 1965.

——, Ellen Murray, S. Dinitz, and W. C. Reckless, "The Good Boy in High Delinquency Area: Four Years Later," *American Sociological Review, 25*, 555–558, 1960.

Schachtel, E. G., "Notes on Rorschach Tests of 500 Juvenile Delinquents and a Control Group of 500 Non-Delinquent Adolescents," *Journal of Projective Techniques, 15*, 144–172, 1951.

Schneider, A., C. W. LaGrone, S. Glueck, and Eleanor T. Glueck, "Prediction of Behavior of Civilian Delinquents in the Armed Forces," *Mental Hygiene, 28*, 456–475, July, 1944.

Schnur, A. C., "Prison Conduct and Recidivism," *Journal of Criminal Law, 40*, 36–42, 1949.

——, "Predicting Institutional and Post-Institutional Behavior," *Journal of Correctional Education, 5*, 28–30, April, 1953.

——, "The Valididity of Parole Prediction in Wisconsin," *Social Forces, 29*, 322–328, March, 1951.

Schuessler, K. F., "Parole Prediction: Its History and Status," *Journal of Criminal Law and Criminology*, November, 1954.

Shelley, E. V., and H. H. Toch, "The Perception of Violence as an Indicator of Adjustment in Institutionalized Youthful Offenders," *Journal of Criminal Law, Criminology, and Police Science, 53*, 463–469.

Silver, R. W., and J. Derr, "A Comparison of Selected Personality Variables Between Parents of Delinquent and Non-Delinquent Adolescents," *Journal of Clinical Psychology, 22*, 1, 49–50, 1966.

Simpson, J. E., S. Dinitz, B. Kay, and W. C. Reckless, "Delinquency Potential of Pre-Adolescents in High Delinquency Areas," *British Journal of Delinquency, 10*, 211–215, January, 1960.

Snygg, D., "Predicting the Behavior of Individuals," *Canadian Journal of Psychology, 3*, 19–29.

Stott, D. H., "A New Delinquency Prediction Instrument Using Behavioral Indications," *International Journal of Social Psychology*, 6, 195–205, Autumn, 1960.

——, "The Prediction of Delinquency from Non-Delinquency Behavior," *British Journal of Delinquency, 10*, 195–210, 1960.

Stouffer, S. A., L. Guttman, E. Z. Suchman, P. F. Lazarfield, and S. A. Star, *Measurement and Prediction*, IV, Princeton University Press, 1950.

Stuckert, R. P., "A Configuration Approach to Social Prediction," *Sociometry*, 21, 225–237, September, 1958.

Thorne, G., "Discriminations Within the Delinquency Continuum Using Gough's Socialization Scale," *Journal of Consulting Psychology, 5*, 6, 314–318, 1958.

Tibbits, C., "Reliability of Factors Used in Predicting Success or Failure on Parole," *Journal of Criminal Law, 22*, 844–853, March, 1932.

Tolman, R., "Some Differences in Attitudes Between Groups of Repeating Criminals and of First Offenders," *Journal of the American Institute of Criminal Law and Criminology, 30*, 196–203, July, 1939.

Tuteur, W., "Can Violent Behavior Be Predicted?" *Correlative Psychiatry and Journal of Social Therapy, 9*, Number 1, 39–43, 1963.

Van Vechten, C. C., *A Study of Success and Failure of One Thousand Delinquents Committed to a Boy's Republic*, Doctoral Thesis, University of Chicago, 1935.

Vold, G. B., "Comments on the Efficiency of Prediction in Criminology," *American Journal of Sociology, 54*, 451–452, May, 1949.

——, "Do Parole Prediction Tables Work in Practice?" *Publication of the American Sociological Society, 25*, 136–138, 1931.

——, *Prediction Methods and Parole*. Hanover, New Hampshire: The Sociological Press, 1931.

Walters, A. A., "Research Note: A Note on Statistical Methods of Predicting Delinquency," *British Journal of Delinquency, 6*, 297–301, 1956.

Wattenberg, W. W., "A Comparison of Repeaters and Non-Repeaters Among Boys in Trouble with the Police in Detroit in 1946–1947," *Michigan Academy of Science, Arts, and Letters, 35*, 395–405, 1951.

Weinberg, S. K., "Theories of Criminality and Problems of Predictions," *Journal of Criminal Law, Criminology, and Police Science, 45*, 412–424, November, 1954.

Werner, E., and E. Gallistel, "Prediction of Outstanding Performance, Delinquency and Emotional Disturbance from Childhood Evaluations," *Child Development, 32*, 225–260, June, 1960.

Wilkins, L. T., "Some Developments in Prediction's Methodology in Applied Social Research," *British Journal of Sociology, 6*, 348–363, December, 1955.

——, G. P. Hill, and T. C. N. Gibbons, "Symposium on Predictive Methods in the Treatment of Delinquency," *British Journal of Delinquency, 6*, 82–98, 1955.

——, and P. MacNaughton-Smith, "New Predictions and Classification Methods in Criminology," *Journal of Research in Crime and Delinquency, 1*, 19–32, 1964.

Wirt, R. D., and P. F. Briggs, "Personality and Environmental Factors in the Development of Delinquency," *Psychological Monographs: General and Applied, 73*, Number 15, 485, 1959.

——, "The Efficiency of Ten of the Gluecks' Predictors," *Journal of Criminal Law, Criminology, and Police Science, 50*, 478–479, January-February, 1960.

Witmer, H., "Some Factors in Success or Failure on Parole," *Journal of Criminal Law*, 18, 384–403, 1927.

Zololski, F. C., "Studies in Delinquency: II. Prediction of Delinquency in Boys," *Journal of Genetic Psychology, 74*, 119–123, March, 1949.

Appendix 8–C

IMPORTANT AMERICAN STUDIES OF OUTCOME IN CHRONOLOGICAL ORDER, 1920–1940

1. Charles H. Chute, "Probation and Suspended Sentence," *Journal of Criminal Law and Criminology*, Vol. 12, 1921–1922, pp. 561–562.
2. New York State Probation Commission, *Probation in New York State*, Albany, N.Y. no date (c. 1922).
3. *Twelth Annual Report of the Adult Probation Department of Cook County, Illinois,* October 1, 1922 to September 30, 1923.
4. Francis H. Hiller, *Probation in Wisconsin,* National Probation Association, New York, 1926.
5. Edwin J. Cooley, *New Goals in Probation,* Albany, N.Y., 1926.
6. William Healy and Augusta F. Bronner, *Delinquents and Criminals; Their Making and Unmaking*, New York, 1926.
7. Clair Wilcox, *The Report of the Pennsylvania State Parole Commission to the Legislature* 1927, Part II, Philadelphia, 1927.
8. State of New York, *Twentieth Annual Report of the New Yort State Probation Commission for the year 1926*, Albany, N.Y., 1927.
9. Mabel A. Elliott, *Correctional Education and the Delinquent Girl*, Harrisburg, 1928.
10. New York State Crime Commission, *From Truancy to Crime: A Study of 251 Adolescents*, Albany, N.Y., 1928.
11. The New York Crime Commission, *A Study of Problem Boys and their Brothers; Case Studies of Delinquents and Non-delinquents in the Same Family,* Albany, 1929. Subsequent to probation, 20 of 25 cases still in difficulties.
12. William Healy, *et al, Reconstructing Behavior in Youth,* New York, 1929.
13. Sheldon and Eleanor T. Glueck, *Five Hundred Criminal Careers,* New York, 1930.
14. George B. Vold, *Prediction Methods and Parole,* Minneapolis, 1931.
15. Clark Tibbitts, "Success or Failure on Parole Can be Predicted," *Journal of Criminal Law and Criminology*, Vol. 22, 1931–1932, pp. 11–50.
16. Elio D. Monachesi, *Prediction Factors in Probation*, Hanover, N.H., 1932.
17. Sheldon and Eleanor T. Glueck, *Five Hundred Delinquent Women*, New York, 1934.

A selective list that originally appeared in footnotes of Walter C. Reckless, *Criminal Behavior*, New York, 1940, pp. 364–393.

18. Sheldon and Eleanor T. Glueck, *One Thousand Juvenile Delinquents; Their Treatment by Court and Clinic*, Cambridge, Mass., 1934.

19. Charlotte Ruth Klein, *Success and Failure on Parole: A Study of 160 Girls Paroled from the State Training School at Geneva, Ill.*, M.A. thesis, University of Chicago, 1935.

20. Courtland C. Van Vechten, Jr., *A Study of Success and Failure of One Thousand Delinquents Committed to a Boy's Republic*, Ph.D. dissertation, University of Chicago, 1935.

21. Ferris F. Laune, *Predicting Criminality*, Northwestern University, Evanston, Ill., 1936.

22. William Healy and Augusta F. Bronner, *New Light on Delinquency and its Treatment*, New Haven, 1936.

23. Alida C. Bowler and Ruth S. Bloodgood, *Institutional Treatment of Delinquent Boys, Part 2: A Study of 751 Boys*, U.S. Department of Labor, Children's Bureau, Publication 230, Washington, D.C., 1936.

24. The Commonwealth of Massachusetts, *Annual Report of the Board of Probation for the Year ending December 31, 1936*, Boston, 1937.

25. State of New York, *Seventh Annual Report of the Division of Parole of the Executive Department* for the year January 1, 1936 to December 31, 1936, Albany, N.Y., 1937.

26. Sheldon and Eleanor T. Glueck, *Later Criminal Careers*, New York, 1937.

27. Ernest W. Burgess, "Parole and the Indeterminate Sentence," in the State of Illinois, *Twentieth Annual Report of the Department of Public Welfare*, A. L. Bowen, Director, June 30, 1937.

Appendix 8–D

SCHEDULE OF ITEMS TO GAUGE IMPACT OF A JUVENILE CORRECTIONAL INSTITUTION AS PERCEIVED BY ITS INMATES

The schedule used in the Simpson study contained *inter alia* 146 items dealing with impact of institutional stay as perceived by the boy at the point of his release. The remainder of the total of 264 items in the administered release schedule consisted of a scale to gauge value orientation, developed by Simon Dinitz and Walter C. Reckless, the Guilford-Martin Personnel Inventory, which measures the respondent's objectivity, agreeableness, and cooperativeness; self-reporting inventories (following the Nye-Short pattern), getting at the extent of involvement in predelinquent and deliquent behavior, the age of first involvement in such behavior, and the number of companions in each act.

The total schedule was administered to the youths a day prior to their release from the institution. Usually, it was group administered, since several boys were scheduled for release on a certain day each week. After obtaining the boys' cooperation and dispelling fears of self revelation, the administrator (who was Simpson, in this project) distributed the schedules and read out each item and the answer format. Most items in the schedule, in fact all of the so-called "impact items," were "pitched" at a sixth-grade word-level of comprehension (according to Dr. Edgar Dale's word comprehension list).

The 146 impact items in the schedule had been "pre-tested" on 75 youths at the Boys Industrial School, in order to spot ambiguous questions and in order to eliminate questions which failed to discriminate on a 75–25 percent dichotomous basis. In other words, if responses to the pre-tested items were more than 75 and less than 25 percent in the dichotomous direction, such items were eliminated.

Out of the 146 impact items, Eynon, Reckless, and Simpson developed certain small clusters of items which obviously had to do with perceptions of a specific phase of

These "impact" items were designed by Thomas G. Eynon and Walter C. Reckless as a means of measuring what the boys in a large state training school for committed delinquents obtained from their institutional stay according to their perceptions. They were used in Jon E. Simpson's study, "Selected Aspects of Institutionalization as Perceived by the Juvenile Offender" (Ph.D. dissertation, The Ohio State University, 1961).

institutional life. Eight such clusters or inventories were identified which were products of judgment of the researchers rather than Guttman scaling or factor analysis. These 8 inventories are as follows:

1. The Rules of the Game, consisting of six items from among the 146 impact items. This cluster dealt with the perceived way an individual should behave if he was going "to get along successfully during his confinement."

2. A Helplessness Inventory, which also comprised six items. It was designed to "elicit the respondent's feelings of futility, frustration, powerlessness, etc., in coping with the bureaucratic structure of the institution."

3. An Impersonality inventory focused on "the personal, intimate qualities of the inmate-staff relationships as well as the boy's views concerning his integration in the institution." The items in the first two inventories were included in the schedule which had been administered to the boys at admission and, hence, it was possible to compare the boys' "expectations at the point of admission with their observations (perceptions) at the point of release."

The next three inventories attempted to gauge whether the boy inmates perceived any changes themselves during their institutional stay. The items for these three inventories were included in the schedule which was used at admission as well as the one used at release. Hence, changes could be scored. In this series, Inventory 4, called the Outlook Inventory, consisted of seven items "pertaining to the subject's feelings of bitterness, tension, anxiousness, and so forth." Inventory 5, the Self-Feelings Inventory, contained four items which dealt with the extent of the subject's problems and "the ways in which he would attempt to resolve these problems." Inventory 6 was entitled the Self-Labeling Inventory and consisted of 5 items, by which the subject could indicate whether he "viewed himself as a person who had been delinquent, a pupil at a boarding school, a private at a military school, an inmate of an institution, or a criminal."

Two additional inventories were "constructed in order to assess the boys' views concerning the extent to which they had benefited from their stay at this school." Inventory 7 was designated Self-Improvement Inventory and Inventory 8, General Improvement Inventory. Response to the items in no. 7 indicated whether the inmate "perceived improvement in himself as a result of his institutional experience, while the responses to the items in no. 8 indicated whether the inmate "felt he profited from his experience" and whether he felt "that other boys would also be helped by such an experience." While these two inventories were somewhat similar, they were kept separate and dealt with separately because the items in no. 7 were not included in the schedule administered at admission. Hence, items in no. 8 (not in no. 7) could be used to get a measure of change from admission to release.[1]

It should be noted that in the "impact" items that follow, their listing represents the number they occupied in the release schedule administered by Simpson at the Boys

[1] See Simpson, *op. cit.*, pp. 35-37.

Industrial School of Ohio (Lancaster, Ohio, now called Fairfield School) in the first six months of 1960.

NOW THAT YOU HAVE BEEN AT BIS

CIRCLE "Y" FOR YES AND "N" FOR NO

Y N 26. Do you think you got a "bum rap" by being sent to BIS?

Y N 27. If you keep out of trouble on the outside will it be because of what you learned here at BIS?

Y N 28. While you were here did you find out why you got into trouble?

Y N 29. Do you worry about things as much as you did when you first came to BIS?

Y N 30. While you were here, did you have the feeling that only a few officers know you?

Y N 31. Do you like yourself better now than when you first came to BIS?

Y N 32. Would you agree to stay at BIS an extra month in order to take trade training?

Y N 33. Do you think that the cottages at BIS are too large?

Y N 34. If you had known what it is like at BIS, do you think it would have stopped you from "messing off" at home?

Y N 35. When you get home, are you going to run around with the same gang you did before you came to BIS?

Y N 36. Do you think you have learned more bad things during your time at BIS than you would have in the same time outside?

Y N 37. Have you volunteered for jobs while here?

Y N 38. Do you think it really helps a guy to be at BIS?

Y N 39. Did any of the officers ever "forget the rules" to make things easier for you?

Y N 40. Did any of the other boys pick on you while you were here?

Y N 41. If you were the superintendent of BIS, would you make any changes in the way this place is run?

Y N 42. Do you think that the officers here give the boys a square deal?

Y N 43. Did the other guys ever accuse you of "getting up your pounds" because you wouldn't "mess up" with them?

Y N 44. Have you ever committed a crime?

Y N 45. Do you think that sending you to BIS was a good deal for you?

Y N 46. Were the officers at BIS too busy to help you with your problems?

Y N 47. If a guy can get along here, he can get along on the outside?

Y N 48. Will you have a tough time getting a good job after you get home because you have been at BIS?

Y N 49. While you were here did you get to know Mr. Snodgrass?

Y N 50. Do you feel your health has improved since you came to BIS?

Y N 51. Were you given a real chance to make good before being sent here?

Y N 52. Have you ever broken a rule here at BIS?

Y N 53. Did you get a chance to learn the trade you were really interested in?

Y N 54. Would you say that the officers at BIS really tried to help you?

Y N 55. Has any group of boys put the "nut" on you or your friends at BIS?

Y N 56. Do the people in your neighborhood back home think that BIS helps boys?

Y N 57. Do you feel that the cards will be stacked against you because you have been at BIS?

Y N 58. Do the other guys consider you to be a "slick"?

Y N 59. Do you think you are a "cool cat"?

Y N 60. Will you try to keep secret the fact that you have been at BIS?

Y N 61. Do you think you are a better guy because you have been here?

Y N 62. If you felt you were going to get into real trouble would you ask to be sent back to BIS before it happened?

Y N 63. Did you like all the officers with whom you came in contact here at BIS?

Y N 64. Was it more trouble than it was worth to get help from officers at BIS?

Y N 65. If a friend of yours got into trouble, would you want him to be sent here?

Y N 66. Most guys are interested in just getting by while they are here?

Y N 67. Do you think the food at BIS is clean?

Y N 68. Were you "tight" with any of the officers here at BIS?

Y N 69. Do you believe that you have learned to get along better with other people?

Y N 70. Do the monitors give orders to the boys?

Y N 71. Do you think that being at BIS is paying for the things that you did wrong?

Y N 72. Was the nightman in your cottage a helpful guy?

Y N 73. Are you able to control your temper better than before you came here?

Y N 74. Did any officer give you or your friends physical punishment while you were here?

Y N 75. Do you feel that judges are law officers?

Y N 76. Did you ever steal back anything that was taken from you here at BIS?

Y N 77. Do you think that your stay here has helped you?

NOW THAT YOU ARE LEAVING BIS, *DO YOU SEE YOURSELF AS A PERSON WHO HAS BEEN A:*

Y N 78. delinquent

Y N 79. pupil at a boarding school

Y N 80. private at a military school

Y N 81. criminal

Y N 82. inmate of an institution

Y N 83. patient in a hospital

Y N 84. boy at a correctional school

NOW THAT YOU ARE LEAVING BIS, *DO YOU FEEL:*

Y N 85. bitter

Y N 86. about the same as always

Y N 87. friendly

Y N 88. caught

Y N 89. hopeful for the future

Y N 90. relaxed

Y N 91. untroubled

Y N 92. outcast

Y N 93. ready to make a fresh start

Y N 94. happy

DID ANY OF THE FOLLOWING THINGS HELP YOU WHILE YOU WERE HERE:

Y N 95. being left alone

Y N 96. being told what to do

Y N 97. some adult took an interest in you

Y N 98. watched your step

REGARDLESS OF WHAT THEY SAY, THE BEST WAY TO GET ALONG HERE IS TO:

Y N 99. play it cool

Y N 100. stay out of the way of adults

Y N 101. show that you are really sorry for what you did

Y N 102. try to figure yourself out

Y N 103. keep your mouth shut

Y N 104. make friends with adults

Y N 105. talk about yourself to some adult

Y N 106. run errands for the adults and monitors

Y N 107. play it straight

AT THE PRESENT TIME DO YOU THINK OF YOURSELF AS:

Y N 108. someone who has a lot of problems

Y N 109. someone who has made a mistake

Y N 110. someone who knows how to play it cool

Y N 111. someone who won't let anybody push him around

Y N 112. someone who wishes he hadn't done it

Y N 113. someone who will straighten out

Y N 114. someone who had got a raw deal

DID BIS SEEM TO BE A PLACE WHERE:

Y N 115. a guy waits around for others to tell him what to do

Y N 116. a guy must obey a lot of phony rules

Y N 117. a guy feels guilty most of the time

Y N 118. a guy can't figure out what is going to happen next

Y N 119. a guy is just another number

Y N 120. a guy can lose his temper easy

Y N 121. a guy will never get a break

Y N 122. a guy feels lost most of the time

SOME MORE ABOUT MY EXPERIENCES AT BIS

210. How many members of the staff (officers) at BIS knew you:
______All of them
______Most of them
______About half of them
______Only a few of them
______None of them

211. What is the name of the Adult at BIS who knew you the best:
NAME:______________________ JOB:______________________

212. Do you think that most of the members of the staff (officers) here did what they could to help you:
______All of them did
______Most of them did

______About half of them did
______Only a few of them did
______None of them did

213. Pick the one who helped you the most while at BIS:
______Superintendent
______Assistant Superintendent
______Psychologist
______Social Worker
______Counselor
______Cottage Parent
______Teacher
______School Principal
______Trade Instructor
______Work Supervisor
______Chaplain
______Doctor or Nurse
______Cook
______Other (Give his or her job)______________
______Nobody

214. What is the name of the adult at BIS who has helped you the most:
Name:______________________Job:______________________

215. With what officer at BIS did you share good news:
______Superintendent
______Assistant Superintendent
______Psychologist
______Social Worker
______Counselor
______Cottage Parent
______Teacher
______School Principal
______Trade Instructor
______Work Supervisor
______Chaplain
______Doctor or Nurse
______Cook
______Other (Give his or her job)______________
______Nobody

216. With what adult could you best talk about personal problems:
______Superintendent
______Assistant Superintendent

______Psychologist
______Social Worker
______Counselor
______Cottage Parent
______Teacher
______School Principal
______Trade Instructor
______Work Supervisor
______Chaplain
______Doctor or Nurse
______Cook
______Other (Give his or her job)____________________
______Nobody

217. Pick one of the following programs which did you the *most good* at BIS:
______Work Assignments
______Trade Training
______Recreation and Athletics
______School
______Cottage life
______Medical care
______Religious services
______Military training

218. What was your last assignment:
______Was in a training job
______Went to school
______Went to school and was in a training job
______Cottage assignment and school
______Cottage assignment and training job
______Other (write in)____________________

219. How did you like your school classes
______I liked all of them
______I liked most of them
______I liked about half of them
______I liked a few of them
______I didn't like any of them
______I didn't go to school

220. Do you think all the boys here should go to school:

PART TIME (Pick one)	*FULL TIME* (Pick one)
______Everyone should go	______Everyone should go
______Most should go	______Most should go

______Half should go
______Only a few should go
______Nobody should go

______Half should go
______Only a few should go
______Nobody should go

221. Do you think the religious program at BIS has helped you:
______It has helped a lot
______It has helped some
______It has helped a little
______It has not helped at all

222. Do the guys at BIS make it hard on the guys who take religion seriously:
______All of them do
______Most of them do
______About half of them do
______Only a few do
______None of them do

223. Did you go to church (Mass) or Sunday school before you came to BIS:
______Yes—How often__________
______No

224. Do you think that the main training job you had here will help you when you leave:
______Yes—Why____________________
______No —Why____________________
______Didn't have a training job

225. How did you like your supervisor in your main training job:
______Liked him a lot
______Liked him some
______Did not like him very much
______Did not like him at all
______I didn't have a training job
______I didn't have a training supervisor

226. Would you have changed cottages if you could have:
______I didn't want to change cottages
______I didn't care where I lived
______I would have liked to move from my cottage—
Why____________________

227. What about the guys in your cottage:
(Pick one)
______I liked most of them

(Pick one)
______I disliked most of them

______I liked some of them ______I disliked some of them
______I liked one or two of them ______I disliked one or two of them

228. Do you think that your cottage supervisor did what he (or she) could to help you:
______Most of the time
______Some of the time
______Very little of the time
______None of the time

229. Do the officers here try to make the guys think they are criminals:
______None of them do
______One or two of them do
______Most of them do

230. When you did a good job here at BIS, did you get praised for it by an officer:
______Always
______Usually
______Sometimes
______Seldom
______Never

231. Who do you blame for being sent to BIS:
______Parents
______Brothers or Sisters
______Yourself
______Police
______Judge
______Friends
______Other (write in)____________________

232. Is something wrong:
______Because you do it
______Because you get caught

TO BE ANSWERED ONLY BY THOSE WHO WERE IN A TRADE PROGRAM
(Others go to next page)

233. How would you rate the shop training program at BIS:
______good
______fair
______poor

234. Do you expect to use the shop skill you have learned:

(Pick one)	(Pick one)
To make a living	As a hobby or for odd jobs
______Yes	______Yes
______No	______No

235. Were you assigned to the shop you wanted:
______Yes
______No

236. Do you believe that you were assigned to the shop that was best for you:
______Yes
______No

237. Do you believe that the aptitude and interest tests are helpful:
______Yes
______No
______Didn't take the tests

238. Do you intend to tell a prospective employer that you got your trade training at BIS?
______Yes
______No
______Not sure

239. Do you feel that you should have been given a transfer to some other assignment:
______Yes
______No

EVERYBODY ANSWER FROM HERE ON

240. Who makes life easier for the average boy at BIS:
(Pick only one)
______Officers
______Other boys
______Nobody

241. Is a guy able to keep his self-respect at BIS:
______All of the time
______Most of the time
______Some of the time
______Not much of the time
______None of the time

242. Do you believe that BIS should have *more:* (Pick only one)
 ______Academic schooling
 ______Military training
 ______Trade training
 ______Other (write in)____________________

243. Here at BIS, who did you talk to about your troubles:
 ______Officers
 ______Other boys
 ______Both officers and other boys
 ______Nobody

244. What do the officers think is the most important thing here: (Pick only one)
 ______Care of buildings and grounds
 ______Welfare of the boys
 ______Following the rules
 ______Making things easy for the officers

245. Now that you are leaving BIS, who do you think will help you the most on the outside:
 ______Father or Stepfather
 ______Mother or Stepmother
 ______Friends
 ______Brothers or Sisters
 ______Minister
 ______Police
 ______Field Counselor
 ______Other (write in)____________________

246. Do you think that the other guys here helped you or made you worse:
 ______They helped me a lot
 ______They helped me some
 ______They didn't change me
 ______They made me a little worse
 ______They made me much worse

247. Did you have trouble getting along with the officers here at BIS:
 ______A lot of trouble
 ______Some trouble
 ______A little trouble
 ______No trouble

248. Did you have trouble getting along with the other boys here at BIS:
 ______A lot of trouble

______Some trouble
______A little trouble
______No trouble

249. What do you plan to do when you get home:
______Get a job
______Go to school
______Get a job and go to school
______Other (write in)____________________

250. When I get home, I expect people will:
______Give me a fair break
______Not care one way or another
______Give me a rough time

251. As I see it, my biggest problem when I get home will be:

____

252. What kind of guy do you expect your field counselor to be when you get home:
______A guy who will be on my back most of the time
______Just another cop
______A guy with whom you can talk over personal problems
______A law officer only interested in "watching me"
______A good guy whose job it is to help me stay out of trouble

253. What are your chances of staying out of trouble after leaving here:
______Good
______Fifty-fifty (50-50)
______Poor
Why:____

254. Did coming to BIS make your chances of staying out of trouble on the outside:
______Much better
______A little better
______No different
______A little worse
______Much worse

255. In your opinion, how serious (bad) was the thing you did that got you sent to BIS:
______Yery bad
______Rather bad
______Not so bad
______Not bad at all

256. How much do you think you got out of your stay here:

______A great deal
______A fair amount
______Very little
______Nothing

257. Who were your two best friends among the boys while you were here at BIS: (Please write their names on the lines below)

1.______________________________
2.______________________________

258. Who were the two boys you didn't like at all while you were here: (Please write their names on the lines below)

1.______________________________
2.______________________________

Appendix 8–E

SCHEDULE USED IN IMPACT STUDY AT TRAINING INSTITUTION- CENTRAL OHIO

INMATE PERCEPTION OF IMPACT

DO NOT SIGN YOUR NAME DO NOT SIGN YOUR NAME

THE WAY I LOOK AT THINGS

This is not a test. There are no right or wrong answers. The right answer for you is the way you look at things. Make sure you answer each question the way you really think. CIRCLE the answer which best expresses *how you look at things.*

1. The best way to make it at TICO is to be a slick.
   Strongly agree Agree Undecided Disagree Strongly disagree

2. At the present time, do you think of yourself as someone who had a raw deal?
   Strongly agree Agree Undecided Disagree Strongly disagree

3. Now that you are leaving TICO, do you feel ready to make a fresh start?
   Strongly agree Agree Undecided Disagree Strongly disagree

4. The best way to make it at TICO is to act tough.
   Strongly agree Agree Undecided Disagree Strongly disagree

5. Do the other boys make it hard or easy on a guy for following the rules at TICO?
   Very hard Hard Not sure Easy Very easy

Developed by Thomas G. Eynon and Walter C. Reckless and administered individually and privately to all released boys during the last part of 1963 until the first half of 1968, as the terminal step in the "going-home" procedure before the door was opened for them. This schedule is duplicated in Eynon and Reckless, "Measuring Impact of a Juvenile Correctional Institution by Perception of Inmates and Staff," *Journal of Research in Crime and Delinquency*, 8:1 (January 1971), pp. 102–107.

6. Regardless of what they say, the best way to get along here is to make friends with adults?
   Strongly agree Agree Undecided Disagree Strongly disagree

7. TICO seems to be a place where a guy waits around for others to tell him what to do?
   Strongly agree Agree Undecided Disagree Strongly disagree

8. Now that you are leaving TICO, do you see yourself as a person who has been a private at a military school?
   Strongly agree Agree Undecided Disagree Strongly disagree

9. Did any of the other boys pick on you while you were here?
   Most of the time Some of the time Very little of the time None of the time

10. Most of what you learn at TICO is learned from the other boys.
    Strongly agree Agree Undecided Disagree Strongly disagree

11. At the present time do you think of yourself as someone who will straighten out?
    Strongly agree Agree Undecided Disagree Strongly disagree

12. If I keep out of trouble on the outside, it will be because of what I have learned here at TICO.
    Strongly agree Agree Undecided Disagree Strongly disagree

13. I think I am a better guy because I have been here?
    Strongly agree Agree Undecided Disagree Strongly disagree

14. Now that you are leaving TICO, do you feel happy?
    Strongly agree Agree Undecided Disagree Strongly disagree

15. Did some adult take an interest in you and help you while you were here?
    Helped me a lot Helped me some Helped me a little Didn't help me

16. Have you ever broken rules here at TICO?
    Quite a few A few One or two None

17. Have you ever been "punched out?"*
    Lots of times Several times Once or twice Never

18. Now that you are leaving TICO, do you see yourself as a guy who has paid his debt to society?
    Strongly agree Agree Undecided Disagree Strongly disagree

*In the vernacular of the boys at TICO, "punched out" means hit with fists or slapped with hands by a staff member.

19. At the present time, do you think of yourself as someone who won't let anybody push him around?
Strongly agree Agree Undecided Disagree Strongly disagree

20. Now that you are leaving TICO, do you feel hopeful for the future?
Strongly agree Agree Undecided Disagree Strongly disagree

21. Now that you are leaving TICO, do you feel untroubled?
Strongly agree Agree Undecided Disagree Strongly disagree

22. At the present time, do you think of yourself as someone who has made a mistake?
Strongly agree Agree Undecided Disagree Strongly disagree

23. Did the other guys ever accuse you of "getting up on your pounds" because you wouldn't "mess up" with them?**
Most of the time Some of the time Very little of the time None of the time

24. I would agree to stay at TICO an extra month.
Sure would Maybe Don't know Probably not Sure wouldn't

25. TICO seems to be a place where a guy can lose his temper easy?
Strongly agree Agree Undecided Disagree Strongly disagree

26. At the present time, do you think of yourself as someome who wishes he hadn't done it?
Strongly agree Agree Undecided Disagree Strongly disagree

27. TICO seems to be a place where a guy will never get a break?
Strongly agree Agree Undecided Disagree Strongly disagree

28. Did you like the officers with whom you came in contact here at TICO?
Most of them Some of them One or two of them None of them

29. Did watching your step help you while you were here?
Helped me a lot Helped me some Helped me a little Didn't help me

30. Now that you are leaving TICO, do you see yourself as a person who has been a patient in a hospital?
Strongly agree Agree Undecided Disagree Strongly disagree

31. Regardless of what they say, the best way to get along here is to talk about yourself to some adult.
Strongly agree Agree Undecided Disagree Strongly disagree

**In TICO inmate language, "getting up your pounds" signifies that a boy has found ways of getting in well with persons in authority, so as to receive small privileges.

32. Did the officers at TICO really try to help you?
    Most of the time Some of the time Very little of the time None of the time

33. The best way to make it at TICO is not to rat?
    Strongly agree Agree Undecided Disagree Strongly disagree

34. If a guy can get along here, he can get along on the outside?
    Strongly agree Agree Undecided Disagree Strongly disagree

35. I learned more bad things during my time at TICO than I would have in the same time outside?
    Strongly agree Agree Undecided Disagree Strongly disagree

36. I like myself better now than when I first came to TICO?
    Strongly agree Agree Undecided Disagree Strongly disagree

37. Regardless of what they say, the best way to get along here is to run errands for the officers?
    Strongly agree Agree Undecided Disagree Strongly disagree

38. I am able to control my temper better than before I came here?
    Strongly agree Agree Undecided Disagree Strongly disagree

39. If a friend of mine got into trouble, I would want him to be sent here?
    Sure would Maybe Don't know Probably not Sure wouldn't

40. If I felt I were going to get into real trouble, I would ask to be sent back to TICO before it happened?
    Strongly agree Agree Undecided Disagree Strongly disagree

41. While at TICO, the average guy learns how to get along better with other people?
    Strongly agree Agree Undecided Disagree Strongly disagree

42. It really helps a guy to be at TICO?
    Strongly agree Agree Undecided Disagree Strongly disagree

43. The average guy gets a chance to improve himself at TICO?
    Strongly agree Agree Undecided Disagree Strongly disagree

44. Now that you are leaving TICO, do you feel friendly?
    Strongly agree Agree Undecided Disagree Strongly disagree

45. If I felt I were going to get into real trouble, I would ask to be sent back to TICO before it happened?
    Strongly agree Agree Undecided Disagree Strongly disagree

46. Now that you are leaving TICO, do you see yourself as a delinquent?
Strongly agree Agree Undecided Disagree Strongly disagree

47. Now that you are leaving TICO, do you see yourself as a person who has been a pupil at a boarding school?
Strongly agree Agree Undecided Disagree Strongly disagree

48. While he's here, the average guy finds out why he got into trouble?
Strongly agree Agree Undecided Disagree Strongly disagree

49. I got a bum rap by being sent to TICO?
Strongly agree Agree Undecided Disagree Strongly disagree

50. Regardless of what they say, the best way to get along here is to play it straight?
Strongly agree Agree Undecided Disagree Strongly disagree

51. The food at TICO is clean?
Strongly agree Agree Undecided Disagree Strongly disagree

52. The program at TICO is:
Very good Good 50/50 Poor Very poor

53. My stay at TICO has helped me?
Strongly agree Agree Undecided Disagree Strongly disagree

54. If you were the superintendent at TICO, would you make any changes in the way this place is run?
Quite a few A few One or two None

55. The best way to make it at TICO is to outsmart the cottage leader?
Strongly agree Agree Undecided Disagree Strongly disagree

56. TICO seems to be a place where a guy must obey a lot of phony rules?
Strongly agree Agree Undecided Disagree Strongly disagree

57. Regardless of what they say, the best way to get along here is to try to figure yourself out?
Strongly agree Agree Undecided Disagree Strongly disagree

58. Sending me to TICO was a good deal for me?
Strongly agree Agree Undecided Disagree Strongly disagree

59. Now that you are leaving TICO, do you see yourself as a criminal?
Strongly agree Agree Undecided Disagree Strongly disagree

60. Guys try to put the "nut" on you at TICO?***
    Most of the time Some of the time Very little of the time None of the time

CLASSIFICATION OF SCHEDULE ITEMS INTO 6 FACTORS

Interpersonal Approach Score (17 items) Sum of columns 3, 6, 11, 14, 15, 18, 20, 21, 22, 26, 28, 29, 31, 37, 44, 50, 57 (High score indicates unfavorable direction)

Inmate Code Score (8 items) Sum of columns 1, 4, 7, 10, 27, 33, 55, 56. (High score indicates unfavorable direction)

Rejection of Institution Score (8 items) Sum of columns 16, 19, 24, 25, 35, 40, 52, 54. (High score indicates unfavorable direction)

Inmate Pressure Score (5 items) Sum of columns 5, 9, 17, 23, 60. (High score indicates unfavorable direction)

Rejection of Positive Impact Score (15 items) Sum of columns 12, 13, 32, 34, 36, 38, 39, 41, 42, 43, 45, 48, 51, 53, 58 (High score indicates unfavorable direction)

Self-Labeling Score (7 items) Sum of columns 2, 8, 30, 46, 47, 49, 59 (High score indicates unfavorable direction)

STAFF MEMBER ASSESSMENT

DIRECTIONS: Circle the number corresponding to the amount of the characteristic exhibited by the boy.

1. He is honest in his relationships with others:
   1 2 3 4 5 6 7 8 9 10
   Never Always

2. His interpersonal approach to others is:
   1 2 3 4 5 6 7 8 9 10
   Very poor Very good

3. He is at ease with himself:
   1 2 3 4 5 6 7 8 9 10
   Never Always

***In TICO language putting the "nut" on you means that inmates put pressure on you to behave in accordance with their ideas and demands.

4. He identifies with the staff:

1	2	3	4	5	6	7	8	9	10
Never									Always

5. He thinks like a hood:

1	2	3	4	5	6	7	8	9	10
Always									Never

6. He plays the inmate game:

1	2	3	4	5	6	7	8	9	10
Always									Never

7. He rejects the institution:

1	2	3	4	5	6	7	8	9	10
Very much									Very little

8. His attitudes seemed to have changed for the:

1	2	3	4	5	6	7	8	9	10
Worse									Better

9. The other boys influenced him:

1	2	3	4	5	6	7	8	9	10
Very Much									Very little

10. The other boys picked on him:

1	2	3	4	5	6	7	8	9	10
A lot									Very little

11. He thinks the institution has been to him:

1	2	3	4	5	6	7	8	9	10
Very harmful									Very helpful

12. He feels that what happened to him here was:

1	2	3	4	5	6	7	8	9	10
Very bad									Very good

13. His self-concept is:

1	2	3	4	5	6	7	8	9	10
Very poor									Very good

14. He feels that being sent to the institution was:

1	2	3	4	5	6	7	8	9	10
Very bad									Very good

15. He defines himself as a:

1	2	3	4	5	6	7	8	9	10
Bad person									Good person

16. What do you think will be the boy's eventual outcome?
______Headed for more serious trouble Why? ______________
______Will barely get along within the law ______________
______Will make a pretty good adjustment ______________
______Will become a solid citizen ______________

17. What do you think will be the biggest problem for this boy when he gets home?
____
____

Signed: ______________
Date: ______________

PART III

CONCLUSION

Chapter 9

Reflections on prevention, control, and treatment of crime and delinquency

Unfortunately, the recipes for effective prevention, control, and treatment of so-called criminals and delinquents have not as yet been found, in spite of the fact that the United States has often tried over the last one hundred years to develop programs and make changes that were thought to have some potentiality in this direction.

Prevention in the United States

Welfare-minded citizens, administrators of agencies, and public officials must be given credit for attempting to develop programs that were regarded as having possibilities for prevention of juvenile delinquency. Most of these programs focused on youth in the so-called slums (now called the inner city). Settlement houses attempted to reach the wayward youth as did the YMCA and the Boys' Clubs of America. Public parks and playgrounds were established also with the purpose of preventing delinquency among other related purposes. The public schools in the United States established truancy departments whose attendance officers or visiting teachers *inter alia* attempted to reduce delinquency incidental to nonattendance.

By the 1920's, it was becoming clear to specialists in the field as well as to the interested academicians that these well-intended programs were not reaching the youths who were gravitating toward delinquency, especially the ones who were involved with gangs and bad companions. Some attempts were made by the agencies themselves to overcome obvious shortages in their reaching and holding power.

A new approach was evolved by Clifford R. Shaw and Henry D. McKay of the Institute for Juvenile Research in Chicago. The project was called the Chicago Area Project and it focused on citizen participation in various neighborhood committees and cooperative self-help units, in order to encourage interest in improving neighborhood life as well as in the prevention of delinquency. As of the mid-fifties, eleven local citizen units had been developed since the inception of the program in 1934. *Inter alia* the projects in the various areas of Chicago attempted to reach the "unreached" youths, particularly the boys in street-corner gangs, by using locally designated youth leaders. In the preliminary stages of the development of the Chicago Area Project, which took place in the steelmill area of Chicago's south side (a high delinquency area), Shaw and McKay found the ways and means to place youth leaders who were products and residents of the area, over several neighborhood gangs (one to each gang), with the intended purpose of diverting the group from delinquent activities and shunting their activities and interests into visibly acceptable channels. As a matter of fact, Shaw and McKay held daily conferences with these initial youth leaders, so as to help them in their approaches to the re-direction of group behavior.[1]

Solomon Krobin, twenty-five years after the development of the Chicago Area Project, made the following evaluation:[2]

> In all probability these achievements have reduced delinquency in the program areas, as any substantial improvement in the social climate of a community must. However, the extent of the reduction is not subject to precise measurement. The effects of improvement in the environment of children are diffuse, cumulative, and intertwined with trends and forces which have their origin outside of programs of this character. In the final analysis, therefore, the Area Project program must rest its case on logical and analytic grounds.

This statement is of importance because it stresses the difficulty of developing criteria with which to evaluate the effectiveness of such programs as preventive agents.

Soon after World War II, in 1947, the New York City Youth Board developed a program to reach children, young people, and their families with incipient problems in high delinquency areas, as well as those who heretofore had resisted services and help from social agencies. Referral units were established for the public and parochial schools in each high

[1] See Walter C. Reckless, *The Crime Problem*, 4th ed. (New York: Appleton-Century-Crofts, 1967), pp. 778–782.

[2] Solomon Krobin, "The Chicago Area Project—A 25-Year Assessment," *The Annals of the American Academy of Political and Social Science*, 322 (March 1959), pp. 22–28.

delinquency area of the city. Then contracts were made with social agencies to treat or assist the referrals from the Board's referral units.

The New York City Youth Board project was looked upon as a demonstration of a "reaching out" approach. The social workers of the referral units went to the "clients," instead of having the clients come to the agency and request help (which was the standard practice at the time). Likewise, workers of the Youth Board program also "reached out" to street gangs in their natural habitat—street corner, pool room, candy store, etc. Such workers developed or already had the capacity to relate to the youths in these gangs and to work "around the clock" with them. This aspect of the program was somewhat similar to reaching the "unreached" gang youths in the Chicago Area Project. The group workers of NYCYB were "detached" workers, working with youths in their "hangouts" rather than in the settlement house, the YMCA, or the Boys Club. The "reaching out" approach to delinquent youth was used in prevention projects in several cities, not only the reaching out to problem families with potentially delinquent children but also to streetcorner gangs who will not go near a settlement, a boys club, or a playground.[3]

Seven specialized prevention projects were developed and supported as a result of financial assistance from the President's Committee on Juvenile Delinquency and Youth Crime, established by President Kennedy in 1961. The largest of these was centered in the Lower East Side of Manhattan and was known as Mobilization for Youth. This project was established in 1958 by local agencies and organizations in the area and received help initially from the Research Center of the Columbia University School of Social Work and from the National Institute of Mental Health.

The program was organized into four sections: the world of work; the world of education; community organization; and services to individuals and families; attempting to reach delinquent youth, nondelinquent youth, parents, and other adults in a low-income area. For example, an Urban Youth Service Corps attempted to provide employment for out-of-school, unemployed young people and an On-the-Job Training Project to upgrade skills of young people was established. Neighborhood councils and neighborhood service centers were developed, the latter operating in storefront buildings. The social workers of these centers intervened for family members in getting the necessary help required.[4]

While the above-mentioned programs *inter alia* attempted to reach the boy in high delinquency areas who was ordinarily "unreached" by existing agencies, certain programs developed a sort of experimental model. In such programs, an attempt was made to identify potential delinquents and to expose a part of the sample of youths to the special services, while exposing

[3]See Walter C. Reckless, *op. cit.*, pp. 783–785.
[4]*Ibid.*, pp. 789–791.

the other part of the sample to less service or not exposing them at all to the program.

Perhaps the first such semi-experimental prevention project was developed in 1935 in two outlying areas of Boston and became known as the Cambridge-Sommerville Youth Project. Some of the details of case selection were described in Chapter 3. It should be remembered that the project began with an initial screening process at the school level, to identify the pre-adolescent boys who were gravitating toward delinquency. In fact, "matched pairs" of boys were identified, according to case history data. Then a split half was made: half of the sample was given intensive counseling and follow-up services while the other half of each matched pair was not given such services, (merely follow-up contacts). Hence half of the potentials were exposed to intensive guidance (the "treatment" group) and half were not exposed (the "control" group).[5]

In 1948, Powers and Witmer, who studied the outcome results of this project, concluded that "the special work of the counselors was no more effective than the usual forces in the community in preventing boys from committing delinquent acts."[6] In 1956, Joan and William McCord traced the outcome of approximately 75 percent of the subjects in the original project and discovered that there was practically no difference in the amount of committed offenses in childhood and adulthood between the treated and the untreated cases. The McCords were of the opinion that if the program of guidance-counseling could have been started earlier in the lives of the boys (prior to twelve years of age) and if the counselors could have contacted the boys more often (at least once a week), the prevention impact would have been more successful.[7]

Almost a generation after the initiation of the Cambridge-Sommerville Youth Project, a demonstration project, known as the Boston Delinquency Project was activated between 1954 and 1957. It operated on the principle that "during the ages twelve to nineteen, the dominant set of influences on the behavior of lower-class adolescent groups derive from the group's conception of prestige-conferring behavior and valued objectives." Therefore, the project's task was to induce changes in the value system of boys' groups in the lower classes. To activate a semi-experimental model, the staff assigned to the project worked intensively with seven groups of street-corner boys and less intensively with seven other corner groups. Some evidence was generated to the effect that the workers induced a modest amount of positive

[5] *Ibid.*, pp. 782–783.

[6] Edwin Powers and Helen Witmer, *An Experiment in Prevention of Delinquency*, New York, 1951, pp. 324–326.

[7] Joan and William McCord, "A Follow-up Report on the Cambridge-Sommerville Youth Study," *The Annals of the American Academy of Political and Social Science*, 322 (March 1959), p. 96.

change in the behavior of the groups while they were in contact but that reported law violations increased during the period of the worker's "announced departure."[8]

A more recent prevention project, which also followed a sort of experimental model, was developed by the Seattle Atlantic Street Center (Seattle, Washington) in 1962. The project attempted to study the "Effectiveness of Social Work with Acting-Out Youth." From the seventh grades of two inner-city high schools, 127 boys were selected as being potentially high risks for delinquency, and out of this number, 54 were randomly chosen as subjects for an intensive casework program—the "experimental" boys. Forty-four of the 127 high-risk boys who were selected became the control group (not subject to intensive casework of the project). The experimental subjects (reduced slightly in number to 51) were assigned to three trained male social workers. They volunteered to participate in weekly group sessions at the Center. The social workers kept close contact with the experimental subjects at home, in the neighborhood, and at school.

The intensive contact of the social worker with a small case load was supposed to implement five goals that were presumed to have preventive potential if achieved: 1. confrontation (forcing the experimental boy and his family to come to grips with their problems), 2. support (such as bolstering the ego of the client, intervention on his behalf, etc.), 3. reality orientation (unwinding denial and defense mechanisms), 4. social-psychological development (better understanding of relationships with others and of motivations of behavior), and 5. ego identity (the development of a positive identity).[9]

Here again, the available evidence does not support the conclusion that the program was able to direct the experimental boys away from delinquency involvement.

One final experimentally-designed prevention project should be mentioned. This is a research project that the author and his colleague, Dr. Simon Dinitz, undertook in the seventh grades of inner-city junior high schools in Columbus, Ohio, beginning in 1963.[10] As a result of their research on the sixth-grade inner-city white boys, it was discovered that those who managed to avoid delinquency involvement tended to be boys who had a "good" self concept, while those who gravitated toward delinquency tended to have a "poor" self concept. Incidentally, the sixth-grade teachers' estimate of boys headed for trouble with the law and those not headed for

[8] Walter C. Reckless, *op. cit.*, pp. 785 787.

[9] James R. Seaberg, "An Example of Social Work Intervention with Acting-Out Youth" (Seattle Atlantic Street Center, 2103 S. Atlantic Street, Seattle, Washington).

[10] Walter C. Reckless and Simon Dinitz, *Youth Development Project: An Experimental Program for Prevention of Delinquency in Vulnerable Seventh-Grade Boys of the Inner City, Columbus, Ohio* (Columbus, Ohio: The Ohio State University Research Foundation, May 31, 1970).

trouble correlated with interview-schedule evidence of a projection of a poor self concept and a good self concept by the boys themselves and also with the mothers' estimate (by interview) of the direction in which their sons were headed.

After three years of preliminary study to discover what in the way of content might be effective with sixth-grade boys in three schools situated in high delinquency areas, the author and his colleague decided to initiate their prevention program in the seventh-grade of those junior high schools in Columbus that serviced the high delinquency areas.

At the time, and during the program, the seventh grades of the Columbus junior high schools operated so-called self-contained classes, in which the teacher retained the pupils for three consecutive class periods (120 minutes). The self-contained classes concentrated upon world geography, social studies, and Ohio history (required by law). Permission was obtained to establish one all-male self-contained class in each of seven junior high schools that were situated in the inner city. In addition, the project received permission to infuse into the all-male self-contained classes "lesson plans" that represented a presentation of "role models" as a supplement to the three standard subjects. The presentation and discussion of role models—such as how a blind boy gets along, what are the characteristics of the best adult male worker on "your" city block, what kind of a person do you have to be to hold down a skilled worker's job—represented the principal part of the prevention "supplement." It was based on the theory that if a better image or concept of self could be developed, *via* internalizing better role models, a vaccination against delinquency might be expected to take place.

In addition to presentation of role models, the specially selected male teachers of the experimental self-contained classes were given special daily training sessions (after school and paid overtime). In order to improve the classroom climate a special form of discipline was established, entitled "respecting the rights of others," in which a misbehaving boy was asked to sit in front of the classroom door until he felt he was ready to join the class again and "respect the rights of others." The special male teachers were also trained to play the role of a most significant adult in the lives of the experimental subjects.

The boys in the self-contained classes in the seventh-grades represented a split half of boys nominated by their sixth-grade teachers (in May of the preceding school year) as likely to get into trouble with the law. The other half were placed in the regular self-contained classes of the seventh-grade, along with the girls.

Unfortunately, on several counts the project could not show that the potentially delinquent boys in the experimental group fared any better than the untreated potentially delinquent boys, as judged by a four-year clearance with the police files and the school files. Either the "role model medicine" plus classroom climate plus the role of the significant adult were not strong or effective enough to make a difference, or the ordinary data by which to judge outcome, such as grades, attendance, and conduct reports in the school records and the referral to the police department for delinquency involvement were not adequate criteria by which to judge differential outcome between a "treated" and an "untreated" group. It could also be the case that one school-year's exposure to a "significant other" teacher, to a feasible classroom climate, and to role model lesson plans is not sufficient for impact on thirteen-year-old inner-city boys. Perhaps two or three years exposure might be required to vaccinate against ordinary deviance.

Attention in the United States has been focused primarily upon juvenile delinquency, the general assumption being that if the recipe for preventing delinquency can be found, this will also prevent adult crime. Undoubtedly, this line of thinking is largely correct. However, it must also be admitted that a sizable proportion of adult offenders are reasonably free of official and unofficial delinquency as adolescents and begin gravitating toward deviant and criminal activity as adults. Particularly is this likely to be true of the adult offenders who are not products of biophysical defects and mental problems that may be traced to birth or early childhood.

Should adult prevention focus upon problems of personal adjustment such as family relations, work habits and opportunities, free-time activities, driving habits, social contacts, use of alcohol and frequency of saloon participation, etc.? Or should adult prevention direct its efforts toward overcoming the fluidity of modern life and alienation from social groups, as well as the breakdown of neighborhood and family life?

One readily surmises that such suggestions for preventing adults from gravitating toward crime overlap with suggestions for basic changes in American society that might have the effect of containing crime, or reducing the ease with which persons get involved. Is it possible to decrease the rate of change in American society all the way from the spread of fashions and fads to habits of daily living? Is it possible to reduce mobility of the population and encourage attachment to a locality? Is it possible to encourage identity of persons with and strong attachments to local groups, especially the family? Is it possible to create a law-abiding attitude and a law-abiding tradition, including genuine respect for law and order and particularly respect for police and courts? Is it possible to re-structure society, communities, and group life in the United States, so as to increase control over behavior of persons?

The realistic answer to the last question is: probably NO, at the present time; but YES, in the future. Undoubtedly, the first requirement for inducing fundamental change in the basic living habits of Americans is a preponderant willingness on the part of citizens to recognize the need for containment and the development of a controlling social structure. The author's projection into the future is that the crime and delinquency problem will become so bad that the overwhelming majority of citizens will welcome restrictive changes in the structure of American society that have potential for containment.

Measures of control

Most authorities would agree that in the United States the major functions of control over crime and delinquency have been delegated to the criminal law, the police, and the courts. This does not contradict the claim that in a democracy public opinion can play a major role in control and that the news media have power for generating and focusing public opinion not only on critical issues in the on-going criminal happenings but also on the breakdown and inefficiency of the American criminal justice system.

It is certainly not going too far beyond the realm of reality to claim that the United States has a very weak system of police and courts, a very weak public opinion supportive of measures of control, and a very disorganizing news media. An outside observer—the man from Mars—might easily gain the impression that the American public becomes stirred more readily about problems such as polution, health, working conditions, housing, rights of women, accidents, roads, than about the problem of crime and delinquency, which has had a rather low priority over the years. One merely needs to cite the recommendations of the Wickersham Crime Commission in the thirties to indicate that practically no follow-up measures resulted from the important work of this commission.

Likewise, one is almost tempted to predict the same thing with reference to the President's Commission on Law Observance and the Administration of Justice (c. 1967) as well as the subsequent commissions on violence in the United States (the so-called Kerner and Eisenhower commissions). Certainly, willingness to accept and to follow through with recommendations of important crime commissions is most important. The lack of it indicates low priority or even unwillingness. Can the crime problem become a major problem in the United States and a problem of first-order priority for action? Can public interest in appropriate action for the control of crime and delinquency be sustained? Hopefully, YES in the future but realistically, NO in the present.

One wonders whether the basic reluctance to come to grips with measures of control is a fear of infringement on individual rights. This is so ingrained in the traditions of the United States that one could very readily contend that the protection of freedom of the individual is more important to Americans than the control of crime, especially when the latter infringes on the former. Here again, the prediction is that the American public reluctantly will have to place crime control above individual freedom, if it is willing to take a stance of high priority for the containment of crime.

Is it possible to discover the impact of the press and the news media on the problem of crime as well as on public willingness to take appropriate action for improved measures of control? In America, crime is a happening of prime interest to the press and news media, primarily because of its attention value. Our news media still operate on the paramount importance of attention-getting events since is the "gee-whiz" emphasis of new stories that sells papers and TV time in the United States. Important cases must be tried in the press, statements from witnesses gathered even before the trial, interviews with and graphic "snap-shots" of the offender taken, etc. In cases that catch front-page attention or prominence in news broadcasts, it is almost impossible to have police and court procedure function in an effective uniform manner. Could newspapers and news media discipline themselves with reference to the spectacular events of crime and contain reporting to objective facts on the case? Or are laws necessary to bring this about, including a requirement to banish crime news to back-page listing of factual statements of events and happenings, without headlines or flare, muck-raking pictures, and stirring interviews?

Much more documented by surveys and commission studies are the shortcomings of the police and court system in the United States. In practically all large cities and counties the court system and the police are "swamped" with the terrific loads of cases whilst in the small jurisdictions, police and courts appear to be qualitatively unequal to the task of handling cases. The recommendations of crime commissions point toward more personnel (police as well as court), better pay, better selection of and higher qualifications for such personnel, more adequate "before-job" training, and adequate "on-the-job" training.

One or two of these recommended means of improving police and court systems will be commented upon. Police work in the United States must acquire greater status and police must be given a better public image; the public must have as much confidence in the police as they do in school teachers and nurses. Hence, police work must be professionalized and the public must subscribe to its professionalization. It is possible that the many police science and police administration courses that have developed in junior colleges as well as in four-year universities and in graduate departments of universities, will help fulfill this need for professional acceptance.

The staff of the prosecutor's office needs to be studied from the standpoint of what techniques are necessary to do a good job in screening cases and preparing them for trial or hearing. The prosecutor needs to be a specially-trained person, certainly with a law degree supplemented by university courses in criminology, corrections, and public administration. The prosecutors need to be appointed by governors or supreme courts on the basis of recommendations from the local bar associations rather than elected.

Judges of criminal courts likewise need to have relevant legal training with appropriate supplementation from the study of criminology, corrections, and public administration. They also should be appointed officials rather than elected and should be appointed on recommendation from the local bar association.

However, there is a basic need to make changes in the city-county system of criminal justice. The overwhelming majority of towns, cities, and counties have not been able financially (by tax support) to establish adequate police and courts. The county, the township, the city, and the state have been sacred administrative units in the United States, but the demands for basic services such as education, health facilities, roads, transportation, and law enforcement have far outdistanced the ability of the units of local (nonfederal) government to handle these needs. Yet the resistance to any change in the system of local administration is overwhelming in the United States.

In spite of the sacred place that local government occupies in the American democratic traditions, it is only a question of time until police and court systems will have to be placed on a district basis: a unified district police system (not municipal police, constables, and sheriffs but an integrated, well-trained, district-wide police), supported by state and federal appropriations. The same must be said for courts. No longer can the dimensions of the crime problem be handled by justice-of-the-peace courts, municipal courts, felony courts in the townships, cities, and counties.

One item is of particular importance to a revised district-wide court system, and this is the integration of court functions under a unified court rather than the separation of functions according to lower courts that act as courts of preliminary hearing as well as courts for adjudication of misdemeanant cases and violations of city ordinances and felony courts that handle cases of the more serious offenses and cases usually carrying sentences to state prisons.

The district police system should probably develop substations in districts with extensive territorial coverage, in order to economize on time and transportation. Likewise, subdistrict courthouses may also need to be developed in an integrated district court system, where the district is very extensive geographically. District police lockups might need to be organized to conserve time and transportation, but there should be one jail that takes care of short-sentence cases on the lesser charges.

District jails, supported by state and federal taxes rather than county funds are almost a necessity. There is not a handful out of the 3,000 counties in the United States that are capable, financially or administratively, of operating an adequate jail program. In the changeover to district police and district courts, the district jail would primarily be concerned with the short-sentence cases and not with cases awaiting trial or police processing, because of failure to be placed on bail or personal recognizance. Such cases should primarily be housed in district lockups (detention centers) in or close to the police station so as to expedite police processing.

The experts in criminal law are becoming increasingly sensitive to basic changes that are necessary in the criminal or penal laws of the various states. The recommended changes by various commissions appear to emphasize *inter alia* the need for greater uniformity in the criminal laws of the various states and the greater need to have indeterminate sentences applying to most crimes and to make provisions for long-term retention of dangerous offenders as a special protective device. In other words, the allotting of specific sentences for specific offenses appears to be on the way out of the revised penal codes. Likewise, greater leeway in penal codes is being given to courts in order to facilitate the placement of the non-dangerous offenders on probation and the early release from the prison or correctional institution where consistent with the protection of society.

Whether the United States will ever be able to completely unify its criminal code, so that all states and the federal government have the same is questionable. Many experts would say that this is impossible, especially with the necessity of administering federal laws in district federal courts. They would also indicate that a uniform code for all the states and the federal government is particularly impractical, in view of the large number of administrative agencies of the federal government, each of which has special laws, machinery, and police or investigators. However, apart from the provisions of the many federal agencies such as customs and immigration, pure food and drug, federal trade commission, federal narcotics bureau, etc., it is still possible to have an integrated criminal code for all the states and the federal government and unified police and court systems, supported financially by state governments and the federal government.

Crime control is certainly not easy in a large fluid country with ready access to transportation and escape. State and county lines also make police coverage and court jurisdiction especially difficult. Resistance to means of identification also interferes with law enforcement in a modern mobile world. An integrated criminal law for the entire country (state and federal), an integrated set of police units in appropriate districts, an integrated district court system, an increase in the public priority rating of the crime problem, the support of the public for better courts, better laws, better police, the revision of the news media's coverage of crime and delinquency, all these measures would aid in the control of crime—at least in keeping it within bounds. Control in this sense means containing the problem and holding it within limits. Control does not signify prevention.

Treatment of offenders

By treatment of offenders is meant the manner in which they are handled at the various way stations of the criminal justice: police, detention, prosecutors, courts, jails, workhouses, probation, prisons and correctional institutions, parole and aftercare. The range of treatment runs all the way from summary handling to attempted therapy although one should realize that treatment of offenders at the law-enforcement and correctional levels is seldom able to follow the medical model. The best that can be expected of police work is appropriate decisions at the point of arrest, detention, and booking for court action. In the contacts with offenders under investigation, the approach should be individualized as much as possible within the limits of protection of society. An overnight stay in police lockups or short stays in jails awaiting trials should be as humane and as non-punitive as possible.

Likewise, appropriately liberal decisions must be made in juvenile cases as to which youths require detention or home care while awaiting juvenile court processing. These decisions are sometimes made by police and other times by juvenile court officers. In spite of the terrific load of cases coming before lower courts for preliminary hearing and for trial on a misdemeanor, the prosecutors and judges have the responsibility of individualizing the handling of offenders as much as possible as well as making appropriate decisions. The prosecutors and judges of the felony courts have a similar responsibility, bearing in mind the protection of society in instances of dangerous cases. This is not easy to do in view of American society's insistence on due process of law and the full rights of the confronted individuals as against the protection of society.

The short-sentence institutions, which include county jails and city workhouses, have responsibility for appropriate care as well as appropriate custody but the custody does not have to be brutal or impersonal; constructive programs can be developed in these institutions. It is not too much to expect that properly screened inmates should be allowed to hold jobs during the day and return to the institution in the evening. Nor is it impossible to expect that supervised groups of jail and workhouse inmates can be used for care and improvement of city and county property during the working day. Certainly appropriate medical services can be provided in jails and workhouses as well as time-occupying programs with a vocational, recreational, and educational emphasis.

Probation in juvenile as well as in adult criminal courts is on the increase and its use must be based on proper screening of cases plus appropriate supervision. In view of the fact that courts will never be able to have a sufficient number of probation officers in order to insure small case loads, probation officers must decide which cases require close supervision and which can be entrusted to minimal supervision. Hopefully in the future, probation officers will be able to find agencies as well as volunteer citizens with whom probationers can identify and from which they can profit by being vitally attached to a group or a person. Great advances in the knowledge of how to perform probation services have been made. The question at present is how to procure persons for probation work who have the "know how" as well as the interest in rehabilitation of probationers. Unfortunately, the range in the quality of probation service runs all the way from poor to excellent. The author would guess that the majority of probation offices are still operating at a fair to poor rehabilitation level. The working conditions, the pay scale, and the public image of probation service must be elevated to a level just as high as school teaching, in order to attract dedicated persons.

All that has been said about probation work can generally also be applied to parole. However, the selection of good to fair risks for parole among prison inmates and/or correctional institutions inmates (adult as well as juvenile) is more difficult than the selection of good and fair risks for probation at the court level. In most instances the persons selected for probation are so-called "first timers" who have not been in court previously. The cases in correctional institutions and prisons that are released on parole or aftercare are likely to have been involved in the more serious episodes of crime and delinquency or are likely to be repeaters.

Penal and correctional institutions for adult and juvenile offenders, mostly state operated, have tried valiantly to overcome punitive, mass handling and to develop programs of education, vocational training, industry, recreation, health, and religion that aim at the rehabilitation of the offender. There are a handful of institutions that have been able to develop some forms of individual and group therapy, the latter form usually taking the pattern of "guided" group interaction, which is thought to have the potential of inculcating a new outlook on life and a new image of self as a result of participation in small discussion groups with other inmates.

The more advanced penal and correctional institutions in the United States during the last generation have developed special programs and facilities for newly admitted inmates, which serve as an orientation period but also as a period for study and classification of individual cases. The classification procedures are based upon accumulated clinical and case history reports—medical, psychological, and social. As a result of the individualized clinical appraisal, the inmate is assigned to the appropriate, available institutional facility befitting his security risk and to appropriate, available vocational and educational programs. Such a procedure in a gross sort of way approximates the medical hospital model. Likewise, advanced correctional institutions sometimes have procedures for reclassification and reassignment of cases.

As a special adjunct to the correctional institution as well as to probation and parole, pre-release guidance centers (so-called "halfway houses") have developed in recent years under local, state, and federal auspices in several cities of the United States. These pre-release guidance centers are small residential units, occupying a renovated small office building, an apartment building, or a large house in the inner city. In a few instances, the centers have been established in a part of a large central YMCA.

The pre-release guidance centers represent a sort of residential base, primarily for male offenders, adult and juvenile, who need a backlog of support, help, and control for a period of a few months, so that they can be assisted in their adjustments to community life. Perhaps, the most important emphasis has been placed on adult offenders' procuring a job and making an adjustment to the demands of employment. Most of the counseling assistance in the pre-release guidance centers takes place in the area of employment. However, the counselors at the "half-way houses" also attempt to help the residents with their personal problems. Sometimes, group discussions approximating therapy sessions are also held two or three times a week, usually in the evenings. Outside contacts and recreation, at night and on weekends, are encouraged. After a certain period, home visits, especially on weekends, are permitted. The "halfway houses" for juvenile offenders route their residents to school or to work during the day and also permit, at the appropriate time, home visits. The counseling services and the group sessions are essentially the same for juveniles as for adult residents.

If it can be demonstrated by appropriate research that pre-release guidance centers have a positive impact on their residents, this impact must be generated in a comparatively short length of time, say approximately three months. It could very well be that an atmosphere of trust, counseling, and mutual support in a small residential center for 15 to 20 residents fosters important changes in outlook on life and in selfcontrol, although the "half-way" houses also have their misfits, difficult cases, and actual failures (which lead to return to the correctional institution in the instance of parole cases or sentence to a correctional institution in the instance of probation cases).[11]

It is not known exactly what positive impact the more advanced correctional institutions or the more backward ones have upon inmates. It has been suspected for years that fellow inmates (through inmate society) are quite apt to affect other inmates adversely and often interfere with the inmate population's deriving positive benefit from institutional stay. The suspicion has also been widespread for many years that untrained custodial staff are quite apt to make inmates worse in their attitudes toward life and society, interfering with positive gains from available institutional programs.

Perhaps one of the most important limitations in the positive impact of the institution on the inmate is the limited attractiveness of staff positions in correctional institutions. It is hard to get state appropriations that can pay salaries comparable to those that can be obtained elsewhere. This is true of the "untrained" custodial staff, such as custodial officers in institutions for

[11] *One should consult* Oliver J. Keller, Jr. and Benedict S. Alper, *Halfway Houses: Community-Centered Correction and Treatment* (Lexington, Massachusetts: D.C. Heath, 1970); *also see* John J. Galvin (ed.), *Treating Youth Offenders in the Community*, (Washington, D.C.: Correctional Research Associates, June, 1966).

adult offender and cottage officers in institutions for juvenile offenders and is also true for educational, medical, psychological, and case-worker staff. Apart from the relatively poor pay scale, the work image is also poor. Very few physicians, psychiatrists, psychologists, social workers, and teachers want to work in prisons and schools for delinquent youth, for this does not give a good professional image.

Nevertheless, prisons and correctional institutions for adult and juvenile offenders, both males and female, have made great progress in overcoming punitive methods of handling inmates. Whether these humane gains are registered in more a positive impact of institutional stay is unfortunately not known. How much the older punitive measures made offenders worse and how much the newer methods and programs make inmates better can only be surmised. The author thinks the recent developments in correctional institutions are able to reduce the negative and increase the positive impact.

However, if one is mindful of the fact that the growth of probation in the next generation will skim off the "cream of the crop" of juvenile and adult offenders passing through the court system, then the institutions for juvenile and adult offenders will increasingly receive the "hard core" cases from the courts, which may necessitate the development of program and staff that can cope appropriately with such a selected group of offenders. Programs of rehabilitation may need to shift emphasis in order to handle the new intake adequately. Hence, positive impact may not be the major concern as much as protective custody within humane limits. Finally, such a trend toward committing to institutions primarily difficult and dangerous offenders will also force a revision in parole selection and in parole supervision on the outside, to conform with the demands of protection of society.

Index